Writings on Standing Armies

Writings on Standing Armies

Selected, Edited, and with
an Introduction by
David Womersley, General Editor

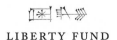

LIBERTY FUND

This book is published by Liberty Fund, Inc., a foundation established to encourage study of the ideal of a society of free and responsible individuals.

The cuneiform inscription that serves as our logo and as a design element in Liberty Fund books is the earliest-known written appearance of the word "freedom" (*amagi*), or "liberty." It is taken from a clay document written about 2300 B.C. in the Sumerian city-state of Lagash.

Library of Congress Cataloging-in-Publication Data

Names: Womersley, David, author.
Title: Writings on standing armies / selected, edited, and with an introduction by David Womersley, general editor.
Description: Carmel, Indiana: Liberty Fund, Inc., [2020] | Series: The Thomas Hollis library | Includes index. | Summary: "An authoritative edition of the most important late seventeenth and early eighteenth century pamphlets on the "Standing Armies" controversy"—Provided by publisher.
Identifiers: LCCN 2019036537 (print) | LCCN 2019036538 (ebook) | ISBN 9780865979116 (hardcover) | ISBN 9780865979123 (paperback) | ISBN 9781614872863 (epub) | ISBN 9781614876625 (kindle) | ISBN 9781614879329 (pdf)
Subjects: LCSH: Standing army—Early works to 1800. | Militia—Early works to 1800. | Great Britain—History, Military—17th century. | Great Britain—History—1660-1714—Pamphlets
Classification: LCC DA66 .W66 2020 (print) | LCC DA66 (ebook) | DDC 355/.02130941—dc23
LC record available at https://lccn.loc.gov/2019036537
LC ebook record available at https://lccn.loc.gov/2019036538

LIBERTY FUND, INC.
11301 North Meridian Street
Carmel, Indiana 46032

CONTENTS

Appendixes

THE THOMAS HOLLIS LIBRARY

Thomas Hollis (1720–74) was an eighteenth-century Englishman who devoted his energies, his fortune, and his life to the cause of liberty. Hollis was trained for a business career, but a series of inheritances allowed him to pursue instead a career of public service. He believed that citizenship demanded activity and that it was incumbent on citizens to put themselves in a position, by reflection and reading, in which they could hold their governments to account. To that end for many years Hollis distributed books that he believed explained the nature of liberty and revealed how liberty might best be defended and promoted.

A particular beneficiary of Hollis's generosity was Harvard College. In the years preceding the Declaration of Independence, Hollis was assiduous in sending to America boxes of books, many of which he had had specially printed and bound, to encourage the colonists in their struggle against Great Britain. At the same time he took pains to explain the colonists' grievances and concerns to his fellow Englishmen.

The Thomas Hollis Library makes freshly available a selection of titles that, because of their intellectual power, or the influence they exerted on the public life of their own time, or the distinctiveness of their approach to the topic of liberty, comprise the cream of the books distributed by Hollis. Many of these works have been either out of print since the eighteenth century or available only in very expensive and scarce editions. The highest standards of scholarship and production ensure that these classic texts can be as salutary and influential today as they were two hundred and fifty years ago.

David Womersley

INTRODUCTION

On 9 December 1767 Thomas Hollis presented Harvard College with a volume of tracts which he had assembled for his own personal use, made up of pamphlets on the related subjects of a standing army and a militia.[1] It contains the following five items, all of which (together with the most important pamphlets written in favor of the creation and retention of a standing army) have been included in the present Liberty Fund edition:

1. John Trenchard, *An History of Standing Armies in England*. London, 1739.

2. Anonymous, *Reasons Against a Standing Army*. London, 1717.

3. "Cato" [Thomas Gordon], *A Discourse of Standing Armies*. London, 1722.

4. [John Toland], *The Militia Reform'd*. London, 1698.

5. "C. S." [Charles Sackville, second Duke of Dorset], *A Treatise Concerning the Militia*. London, 1752.

Hollis's purpose in sending books to Harvard as well as to Switzerland and elsewhere in Europe was to promote the public understanding of liberty.

1. Houghton Library, Harvard University, press mark HOU GEN *ED75. H7267.Zz753t. The date of the donation is recorded on a Harvard College library bookplate pasted into the volume.

Why did Hollis think these tracts had a role to play in that project of political education? To understand the thinking which lay behind Hollis's decision to donate this very personal book to Harvard we must begin by reviewing the circumstances that led up to the composition of the earliest of the tracts included in the volume, John Trenchard's *A Short History of Standing Armies in England*, first published in 1697 in the course of a controversy which had begun earlier the same year.

The "Standing Army" Crisis of 1697–1698

Together with his wife Mary, William III had been crowned on 11 April 1689. Only a few weeks later, on 5 May, England declared war on France, thus initiating a conflict that would be known by a variety of names: the War of the League of Augsburg, or the War of the Grand Alliance, or the Nine Years War. Over the coming months William put together a coalition of nations (Scotland, Austria, Spain, Savoy, and some German states) to frustrate what he saw as the ambitions of Louis XIV toward European hegemony and universal monarchy.

The ensuing war was contested principally in the Low Countries and proved to be "a prolonged, bloody, and frequently discouraging struggle."[2] Early French successes by sea and land only began to be reversed by William as late as 1694 with the capture of Huy. But by 1696 France, England, and the Low Countries were all exhausted by the financial strain of such a protracted conflict.[3] Secret negotiations for a peace had begun as

---

2. Claydon, *William III*, p. 1.

3. "The Nine Years War is estimated to have cost £49,320,000, about £5,500,000 per annum, that is, over three times the average level of government expenditure during James's reign. All forms of taxation were sharply increased, including poll taxes and a new regular direct tax, the aid or land tax (which brought in over £19 million during the war). But total revenue from all sources during the war years amounted to only £32,766,000, leaving a gap of over £16 million that had to be borrowed" (J. R. Jones, *Country and Court: England 1658–1714* [London: Edward Arnold, 1978], p. 65). See, for a corroborating contemporary perception, Blackmore, *History*, pp. 9–10. Michael Braddick provides a helpful longer perspective: "During the Nine Years War there were on average nearly 117,000 men in military service each year (more than 40,000 in the navy and over 76,000 in the army). This necessitated annual average spending of nearly £5.5m. Thus, even though

early as 1692, but by the middle years of the decade they had been given added urgency by economic pressures. Formal negotiations for peace began in May 1697, and were concluded in September. The principal terms of the resulting Treaty of Ryswick—all territories captured by any side since 1688 were to be handed back; the Dutch were to be allowed to garrison eight "barrier" fortresses in the Spanish Netherlands; Louis promised not to aid William's enemies and finally recognized him as the rightful king of England; and the town of Orange was to be handed back to the House of Nassau—made it clear that this was a truce, not a genuine peace. It offered a pause in which all protagonists could draw breath. But it placed on the table no durable resolution of the underlying problem of mastery in Europe that had precipitated hostilities.[4] In the event, it was a truce that lasted for less than five years before it was interrupted by the outbreak of the War of the Spanish Succession in May 1702.

Nevertheless, the signing of the Treaty of Ryswick was popular with William's new subjects. In England there was little public appetite for war, and only the most sharp-sighted could have glimpsed in the nation's new-found ability to launch and pursue military operations on the Continent the harbinger of an imperial future. So when in the winter of 1697 William returned to England from the negotiations in the Low Countries, he was met with acclamation:

> He returned to *England*, and upon the 16th of *November*, at the Citizens request, made His Publick Entry thro' *London*, being attended by all the Men of Quality in very great State, and never, (I am sure,) in one Day saw so many People (and all of them His own Subjects) in all His Lifetime; and in whose Affections He Triumphed as much as ever he had done at any time over His Enemies; and may He always

---

taxes produced £3.64m per annum, the government quickly ran into debt. The War of Spanish Succession saw over 135,000 men in arms (about 43,000 in the navy and 93,000 in the army), at a cost of £7.06m per annum. Tax revenues now reached £5.36m per annum but even this could not save the government from accumulating still larger debts. By the end of the Nine Years War the debt was £16.7m. It was reduced to £14.1m by the outbreak of the War of Spanish Succession, but by 1713 had climbed again, reaching a dizzying £36.2m" (Braddick, *State Formation*, p. 265). See also Claydon, *William III*, pp. 13, 233.

4. *ODNB*, s.v. "William III."

do the first, and never have occasion for the second, but may we long live under the Benign Influence of His Reign, who hath Rescued our Religion and Liberties out of the Jaws of Hell, and Destruction, so intrepidly Fought our Battles for us, and now at length restored unto us the Comforts, and Blessing of a Firm and Honourable Peace.[5]

However, no one knew better than William that the present peace was anything but firm. Therefore he was privately determined to retain his army of at least 87,000 experienced soldiers in preparation for the next—and imminent—round of his unconcluded struggle with Louis XIV.[6] But a coalition of Tories and radical Whigs—the New Country Party—which had come into embryonic existence as early as 1693, and which had on occasion already successfully resisted the measures of the ruling Whig Junto, was preparing at the same time to reactivate a long-standing topic of anti-Stuart resentment by agitating both within and without doors for the disbanding of the army.[7]

The leaders of the New Country Party were the dissident Whigs Paul Foley and Robert Harley.[8] Their achievement had been to exploit their extensive personal connections in the House of Commons to open up channels of communication and cooperation not only with disaffected Tories such as Sir Thomas Clarges and Sir Christopher Musgrave but also with "Old" or radical Whigs displeased by the compromises of stance and principle that had been inevitable in the evolution of the Whigs from a party of protest and revolution to a party of government.[9] As Toland would

5. Jones, *History of Europe*, sig. Xxiʳ⁻ᵛ; see also Jones, *Theatre of Wars*, p. 98.

6. The estimate is Macaulay's (*History*, 6:2731). It is broadly in line with more recent assessments: see above, pp. x–xi, n. 3.

7. On 28 September 1697 James Vernon, one of the secretaries of state, had warned that Parliamentary pressure for the disbanding of the army was to be expected (Schwoerer, *Armies*, p. 163). On the New Country Party, see J. P. Kenyon, *Robert Spencer, Earl of Sunderland 1641–1702* (London: Longmans, Green, 1958), pp. 247–48; Claydon, *William III*, pp. 195–96, 202–3; and Hill, *Harley*, pp. 25–28.

8. Paul Foley (1644/45–99), commonwealth Whig; Exclusionist; Speaker of the House of Commons, 1695–99. Robert Harley (1661–1724), first Earl of Oxford and Mortimer; initially a Shaftesburian Whig, later an idiosyncratic Tory; statesman. See Macaulay, *History*, 6:2743. For the broad moment of the attack on the army, see Claydon, *William III*, pp. 216–17.

9. The classic account of this transformation remains John Kenyon's Ford Lectures, published as *Revolution Principles: The Politics of Party 1689–1720*

in a few years gloatingly put it (referring to William III's eventual rejection of the Junto Whigs in 1700): "see the Instability of human Councils; some of those surly Whigs grew by degrees the most pliant Gentlemen imaginable, they could think no Revenue too great for the King, nor would suffer his Prerogative to be lessened; they were on frivolous Pretences for keeping up a Standing Army to our further Peril and Charge . . . so these Apostates were abandoned by their former Friends, and left to the Support of their own Interest, which appeared to be so very little with any Party, that the King did wisely cashier them."[10]

The current crisis over the size of the land force was well chosen for the assembly of this checkered coalition of divergent interests and discordant sentiments, for (as Macaulay would remark) resistance to standing armies was a banner under which even the most unlikely allies could unite: "One class of politicians was never weary of repeating that an Apostolic Church, a loyal gentry, an ancient nobility, a sainted King, had been foully outraged by the Joyces and the Prides: another class recounted the atrocities committed by the Lambs of Kirke, and by the Beelzebubs and Lucifers of Dundee; and both classes, agreeing in scarcely anything else, were disposed to agree in aversion to the red coats."[11]

The first blow in their campaign, John Trenchard and Walter Moyle's *An Argument Shewing that a Standing Army Is Inconsistent with a Free Government, and Absolutely Destructive to the Constitution of the English Monarchy*, was published in October 1697, some two months before the debate proper began in Parliament.[12] J. A. Downie has described the behind-the-scenes collaborations that produced the first wave of anti–standing army pamphlets:

> John Trenchard was the opposition *chef de propagande* during the standing army controversy. His role can be documented. He coordinated the writing, printing and publishing of all the important contributions. Harley was the opposition leader in parliament. But their

---

(Cambridge: Cambridge University Press, 1977). For a contemporary response, see, e.g., Charles Davenant, *The True Picture of a Modern Whig* (1701).

10. John Toland, *The Art of Governing by Parties* (1701), pp. 31–32.

11. Macaulay, *History*, 6:2732.

12. Below, pp. 1–50.

roles merged from time to time. . . . Contact between the two men was extensive and prolonged.[13]

An Argument was swiftly answered by writers supportive of the position of the king and advocates of the retention of at least a fraction of the army, and two of these immediate replies—John Somers's *A Letter, Ballancing the Necessity of Keeping a Land-Force in Times of Peace: with the Dangers that May Follow On It* and Daniel Defoe's *Some Reflections on a Pamphlet Lately Published*—are reprinted in this volume.[14]

So the ground of the subsequent quarrel was to some extent already staked out and the lines of engagement already defined when, on 3 December 1697, William opened Parliament and in the course of the speech from the throne remarked that England's safety would be endangered "without a land force." When it transpired that the majority in Parliament against a standing army was not to be moved and that accordingly at least some of William's forces would have to be stood down—including the elite "Blue Guards" that William had brought with him in 1688 from the United Provinces—the king's dignity was undoubtedly damaged. Swift would list among those "who have made a mean contemptible Figure in some Action or Circumstance of their Life" "King Wm 3rd of England, when he sent to beg the House of Commons to continue his Dutch Guards, and was refused."[15]

The course taken by the ensuing debates in Parliament was summarized by Abel Boyer in his *History of William III*, so there is no need here to rehearse the mere circumstances of 1697–98.[16] We can turn instead to the intellectual background to the quarrel, and consider how the

13. Downie, *Harley*, pp. 32–33. Harley, however, had not been one of the first movers in the controversy, although he did provide advice to Trenchard as the controversy developed (pp. 29 and 32).

14. Below, pp. 51–67 and 69–109. For a bibliography of the controversy, see Schwoerer, "Chronology" 382–90; supplemented by J. A. Downie, "Chronology and Authorship of the Standing Army Tracts: A Supplement," *Notes and Queries* 221 (1976): 342–46.

15. Swift, *Prose Writings*, 5:85. William's Blue and Dutch Guards had to be either disbanded or sent overseas because the Parliamentary resolution stipulated that only natural born Englishmen could serve in the retained land force (Downie, *Harley*, p. 35).

16. See Appendix E.

arguments mounted for and against a standing army in late seventeenth-century England compare on the one hand with apparently similar arguments in antiquity and early modern Europe, and on the other with apparently similar arguments which periodically flared up in England throughout the eighteenth century. In the case of both we will find that a superficial similarity of language and sentiment disguises important underlying discontinuities.

The Classical and Early Modern Intellectual Background

The questions of where to locate, of in whose hands to place, and of how to exercise the state's powers of military force lie behind a perennial topic in political theory, and coalesce into a recurrent problem in political practice.

The political thinkers and historians of antiquity had been acutely aware of the dangers that might arise should an army become attached more deeply to its general than to the state. Such transference would be very natural—nothing more, after all, than a reversion to a point of departure. For these thinkers suspected that civil society itself had begun in the personal loyalty felt by soldiers toward a successful commander.[17] Yet they also knew that, for a city to endure, the duty of obligation, although it may have originated in the personal ascendancy enjoyed by a charismatic *imperator* as a result of his immediate contact with the men he led, had to be institutionalized and transferred to the *urbs*—hence the strong component of city-worship in classical paganism. Were that transference ever to falter, the threat to the state would be grave. Yet such an eventuality was always to be feared. For the qualities of a good general, the Roman thinkers of the later empire well knew, were also naturally imperial qualities: *experto crede*.[18]

For historians such as Sallust and poets such as Lucan, the resurgence of the personal attachment of an army to its general, to the point where it might overwhelm their patriotism, was the herald and companion of civil

17. Polybius, VI.4–6.
18. "Ducis boni imperatoriam virtutem esse" (Tacitus, *Agricola*, XXXIX.2).

wars: those paradoxical conflicts which could not really be called *bella*, first because they were by definition unjust, and second because they were not waged against an external *hostis*.[19] It had been so in the struggles between Marius and Sulla,[20] and it would be so again in the civil wars precipitated by Caesar's crossing of the Rubicon.[21] In such terrible conflicts even the armies of the Republic might be tainted by the political heresy of a merely personal loyalty that had sprung up first among their adversaries. In book 9 of the *Pharsalia*, Lucan relates an encounter between Cato and some of the remnants of Pompey's forces after their defeated leader's assassination in Egypt. One of the Pompeians explains why they are now abandoning the cause of the Republic:

> Nos, Cato,—da veniam—Pompei duxit in arma,
> Non belli civilis amor, partesque favore
> Fecimus. Ille iacet, quem paci praetulit orbis,
> Causaque nostra perit; patrios permitte penates
> Desertamque domum dulcesque revisere natos.[22]

To which Cato replies with biting irony:

> Ergo pari voto gessisti bella, iuventus,
> Tu quoque pro dominis, et Pompeiana fuisti,
> Non Romana manus?[23]

Yet the armies—the *manus*—of antiquity, whether they remained under the control of the state or reserved their allegiance for their general, were in important ways different from the standing armies which would loom so large in the political imagination of late seventeenth- and

---

19. David Armitage, "What's the Big Idea? Intellectual History and the *Longue Durée*," *History of European Ideas* 38 (December 2012): 502.

20. Sallust, *Catiline*, XI.5.

21. Lucan, *Pharsalia*, I.373–88; IV.185; IV.501–2, 572–73; VII.285–87.

22. "Pardon us, Cato—it was love of Pompey, not of civil war, that roused us to arms, and we took sides out of favor for him. But he lies low, whom the world preferred to peace, and our cause has ceased to exist; allow us to return to our native homes, our deserted households, and the children of our love" (IX.227–31).

23. "It seems then, soldiers, that you too fought with the same desire as others, in defense of tyranny—that you were the troops of Pompey, and not of Rome" (IX.256–58).

early eighteenth-century England. While the *manus* of Republican Rome posed in some sense the same essential threat (namely, that deadly force designed to be directed against an external *hostis* might be redirected inward to coerce or intimidate the native population), they were however not permanently supported by the resources of the state. They might—indeed, they occasionally did—plunder the nation's treasure.[24] They might pillage their fellow citizens. But typically they did not seek to perpetuate their existence as an army. Like the nameless Pompeian soldier rebuked by Cato, their desire was to be paid, disbanded, and then given leave to return home ("patrios permitte penates / Desertamque domum dulcesque revisere natos"). The soldiery of antiquity—until at least the establishment of a permanent military force under the principate of Augustus—was thus still essentially in some respects a militia, albeit one with the potential to cause great domestic harm.

During the late republic and the early principate Roman military culture changed. Caesar's *Bellum Civile* shows how in the first century B.C. "the phenomenon of continuous military service created unprecedented bonds between generals and soldiers."[25] But in one respect Caesar's depiction of the soldiery is ambiguous. Although his legions are shown to be remarkably loyal to their supreme commander, nevertheless "they still have the capacity to disobey or to behave violently. In the hands of a lesser general, we must conclude, the military hierarchy might well have deteriorated."[26] In the surviving books of his *Historiae* Tacitus showed this process of military degeneration happening during the chaotic events of A.D. 69, the year of the four emperors:

> Tacitus complicates, and in part reverses, the familiar picture of fickle soldiers who gradually assimilate themselves to the character of their commander, whether he is honourable or defective. . . . we see soldiers on all sides gradually develop a mistrust of their immediate commanding officers, which prolongs the war by fragmenting the armies and making them less efficient fighting machines.[27]

24. Lucan, *Pharsalia*, III.84–168 (Caesar's looting of the Roman treasury).
25. Ash, *Ordering Anarchy*, p. 5.
26. Ash, *Ordering Anarchy*, p. 7.
27. Ash, *Ordering Anarchy*, p. 168.

These successive developments in the classical past perhaps go some way toward explaining how it happened that, in the standing army debates in England at the end of the seventeenth century, apparently contradictory qualities were attributed to standing armies. They could be both terrifyingly effective instruments in the controlling hands of ambitious generals, but also alarmingly ungovernable hordes let loose on a defenseless society.

It was Niccolò Machiavelli who developed the Western discussion of the political problem of force beyond the formulations of antiquity. Machiavelli's interest in this question had been aroused and focused by the disturbances of the *quattrocento*, in which the Italian city-states had experimented with the use of mercenaries, generally with disastrous results. In *The Prince*, the *Discourses*, and *The Art of War*, Machiavelli repeatedly contrasted recent Italian experience with Roman history.[28] Guided by what he saw in that contrast, Machiavelli had argued that the marvelous expansion of the Roman Republic had been due to the willingness of its male population to take up arms on behalf of the state. He went on to generalize this observation about early Roman history into a political principle, insisting that a militia was always and necessarily superior to a mercenary army, and (furthermore) was an infallible symptom of free government.[29] What was the train of thought which led to this uncompromising conclusion? Those who were content to subcontract their defense to paid professional soldiers had placed their ease above their liberty, and had thereby laid themselves open to tyranny. The decline and fall of Roman power, in this civic humanist analysis, could be

28. *The Prince*, chaps. 12–14; the *Discourses*, bk. 2; *The Art of War*, bk. 1, chaps. 2–9; bk. 7, chap. 17.

29. In so arguing Machiavelli was going against some influential earlier Italian political thinkers and jurists. For instance, Bartolus of Sassoferrato (1313–57) had insisted that a true king "does not form his bodyguard of citizens" ("On the Tyrant"). On the composition of the Florentine militia, and why it is mistaken to see Machiavelli arguing narrowly for a citizen militia (an error into which I myself have fallen), see the following: Carlo Dionisotti, *Machiavellerie* (Turin: G. Einaudi, 1980), pp. 3–59; Paul Anthony Rahe, *Against Throne and Altar: Machiavelli and Political Theory under the English Republic* (New York: Cambridge University Press, 2008), p. 9; and Robert Black, "Machiavelli and the Militia: New Thoughts," *Italian Studies* 69 (2014): 41–50.

traced to the replacement of the militia of the Republic by the professional, and increasingly mercenary, standing armies of the Empire.[30]

Machiavelli's preference for militias over mercenaries was elaborated and fleshed out with historical detail by the thinkers who followed him. The over-running of the provinces of the western Empire in the fifth century by the northern barbarians had destroyed Roman military and political power in Europe. The constitutions of the Gothic states which replaced that empire had embraced a different principle of military establishment. The general of the conquering army was made king, and he divided the conquered lands among his principal officers, or barons. They in their turn parcelled out their lands among their tenants. Both the barons and their tenants held their lands from the king in return for the duty of military service. There was no standing army, and when military forces were required, the king summoned his barons, who repaired to his standard accompanied by their vassals.

Andrew Fletcher would describe the virtue of these feudal governments in terms of the way their military institutions secured important political benefits:

> this constitution of government put the sword into the hands of the Subject, because the Vassals depended more immediately on the Barons, than on the King; which effectually secured the freedom of those Governments. For the Barons could not make use of their Power to destroy those limited Monarchies, without destroying their own Grandeur; nor could the King invade their privileges, having no other Forces than the Vassals of his own Demeasnes to rely upon for his Support in such an Attempt.[31]

However, it was a matter of historical fact that feudal governments had expired in Europe around 1500, to be replaced by increasingly absolutist

---

30. It is important to bear in mind that there is no necessary equivalence between a standing army and a mercenary army, although both share the characteristic of fighting for money. A mercenary army will fight for whoever can pay them, but may not be permanent. A standing army is permanent but is not generally for hire to the highest bidder. Nevertheless, the terms might still be used as synonyms: see *Gulliver's Travels*, p. 186.

31. *A Discourse Concerning Militia's and Standing Armies* (1697); below, p. 153.

monarchies which went on during the following century to acquire the command of permanent military forces as one of the principal instruments of their power:

> One of the hallmarks of European government in the latter half of the seventeenth century was the development and political employment of the standing army. Between the conclusion of the Thirty Years' War and the end of the wars of Louis XIV most major and minor continental states created regular armed forces for the defence of the homeland, offence against an international opponent, to repress internal political and social opposition, and in slavish imitation of the fashionable French. . . . During this period standing armies became the storm troops of the absolute monarchs who were wrestling with the problems of centralising their authority in order to make their governments more effective.[32]

How and why had this occurred? Opinions differed.

The English neo-Machiavellian James Harrington had traced the extinguishing of feudalism in England to the absolutist ambitions of the Tudors, who had undermined the power of the barons in order to secure the position of the crown. Andrew Fletcher, on the other hand, ascribed the demise of feudalism to the effects of the luxurious living which had become possible thanks to the three cardinal inventions of modernity: printing, gunpowder, and the compass.[33] According to Fletcher, the pursuit of luxury had induced the barons to emancipate their vassals in return for payment, and so effectively to convert their feudal establishments into ready cash.[34] At the same time, the pursuit of luxury had induced the common people to prefer the payment of taxes to military service. But whether you went with Harrington or with Fletcher, the result was that, in the modern world, the power of the sword had passed from the hand of the subject to the hand of the monarch, who now had at his disposal a professional, permanent standing army which was as

32. Childs, *Army*, p. 83; see also p. 203.
33. Below, pp. 154–55.
34. An argument that would be adopted and deepened by Fletcher's compatriot, Adam Smith (Smith, *Wealth of Nations*, III.iv, pp. 418–19).

convenient for the control of his own subjects as for the defense of the realm against external enemies—always provided, of course, that he could find the wherewithal to pay for it.[35]

Seventeenth-Century English Experience and the Idea of a Standing Army

The debate over standing armies that arose in England at the end of the seventeenth century can be seen as a particular and acute instance of the political problem of military force. However, the seventeenth-century English debate did not merely go over old ground. It possessed some distinctive and innovative aspects. But these new and distinctive features have been to some degree camouflaged by a linguistic anomaly.

We first encounter the English phrase "standing army" in 1603, when Richard Knolles used it to refer to the domestic policy of Tamerlane: "He kept alwaies a standing armie of fortie thousand horse, and three-score thousand foot readie at all assaies."[36] For the next forty years or so the *OED* lists no more than a handful of further occurrences of the phrase, until we reach the outbreak of hostilities between Charles I and Parliament in 1642, when unsurprisingly it became much more common. However, although a fondness for a standing army is swiftly included in the list of despotic inclinations characteristic of the Stuarts, Cromwell too had seen its attractions. Clause XXVII of the Instrument of Government of 1653 had been particularly alarming: "The Instrument had . . . provided for a 'constant yearly Revenue' for the maintenance of '10,000 Horse and Dragoons, and 20,000 Foot, in England Scotland, and Ireland, for the Defence and Security thereof, and also for a convenient

---

35. For a textbook example of the stages whereby this might be brought about, see adv. 29 in Trajano Boccalini, *Advices from Parnassus* (1706), p. 45. In his essay "Upon Universal Monarchy" Charles Davenant had explained how Louis XIV had weakened the French nobility as a prelude to acquiring a standing army (Charles Davenant, *Essays* [1701], p. 269). "Provided that he could raise sufficient cash for their pay and upkeep, Charles [II] could recruit troops when he chose and employ them as he wished" (Childs, *Army*, pp. xvii–xviii).

36. Knolles, *Turkes*, p. 235. Cf. Schwoerer, *Armies*, p. 2.

number of Ships for guarding the Seas.' . . . For Cromwell's critics these soldiers resembled the hired 'Janizaries' of the 'grand Senieur,' who aided in the enslavement of the people."[37] However, this pattern of usage across the seventeenth century disguises the fact that the phrase "standing army" is at first used broadly to refer to an army which is kept together in peacetime (no matter how it is funded or sustained). But then at the end of the century it is used much more narrowly to refer to an army that is kept together during peacetime *and paid for out of taxation.*

The intellectual roots of the seventeenth-century English standing army debate extended deep into the European past. But that late seventeenth-century debate derived its particular energy from much more recent developments. Its participants were guided by the long-standing Western anxiety about the possibility that an unscrupulous general might use his troops against his personal internal enemies, rather than against the external enemies of the nation. At the same time, that traditional anxiety had acquired a new edge for the subjects of William III because of the enhanced fiscal powers of the Williamite state.

These new fiscal powers had been created to allow England to shoulder the unaccustomed burden of a Continental war waged without respite over many years: namely, the War of the Grand Alliance.[38] The Williamite apologist Sir Richard Blackmore would refer to these developments with deceptive mildness, calling them "Ways and Means as were least Burdensom and uneasy to the People."[39] Nevertheless, Blackmore clearly understood how the new system of deficit finance worked:

> The former Parliaments chose rather to Establish Funds for Publick Supplys, than to use any Methods of raising them within the year; divers Branches of the King's Revenue were by His Majestys own consent, subjected to great Anticipations, and the most easy and obvious Funds were already setled, and sufficiently loaded; . . . [40]

---

37. Gaby Mahlberg, *Henry Neville and English Republican Culture in the Seventeenth Century: Dreaming of Another Game* (Manchester: Manchester University Press, 2009), p. 143. Cf. *Stuart Constitution*, pp. 342–48.

38. See Dickson, *Financial Revolution*, chaps. 1–4, pp. 3–89.

39. Blackmore, *History*, p. 6.

40. Blackmore, *History*, pp. 20–21; see also pp. 44–51.

Therefore after the accession of William III "an effective and predictable tax regime was the asset against which, ultimately, the government was securing its credit."[41]

However, these new fiscal instruments, and the innovative powers which accompanied them, meant that for the first time in English experience a peacetime army might be supported out of regular taxation rather than sustaining itself by the less regular and reliable, but hitherto inevitable, expedients of parliamentary grants, marauding, pillaging, and billeting.

The political situation created by these new instruments and powers was disturbing and unprecedented. Until the 1690s the financial sinews of the English state had been comparatively weak.[42] During the Civil War both Parliamentarians and Royalists had encountered extraordinary problems of supply. Both sides had been reduced to expedients such as sequestrating money and valuables, and pawning jewels.[43] Loans were to be had only at ruinous rates of interest.[44] Therefore, as recently as 1656, and reflecting in Machiavellian style on English experience in the Civil War, James Harrington had dismissed the notion of a standing army supported by taxation as

> a mere fancy, as void of all reason and experience as if a man should
> think to maintain such an one by robbing of orchards; for a mere tax
> is but pulling of plumtrees, the roots whereof are in other men's
> grounds, who, suffering perpetual violence, come to hate the author
> of it. And it is a maxim that no prince that is hated by his people can

41. Braddick, *State Formation*, p. 267.

42. See Braddick, *State Formation*, part 3, "The Fiscal-Military State," pp. 177–286.

43. Charles had pawned the crown jewels in Holland (May, *History*, lib. 2, pp. 41–42, 84) and had requested gifts of plate from his supporters (May, *History*, lib. 2, p. 87). Parliament had also called in plate and other valuables (May, *History*, lib. 2, pp. 83–84, 97). Problems in funding the war even when it was under way persisted on the side of both Charles (May, *History*, lib. 3, pp. 12–13) and the Parliament (May, *History*, lib. 3, pp. 38–39). However, the most recent research suggests that the Parliamentarians coped better than did the Royalists with these financial pressures of waging war (Braddick, *State Formation*, pp. 215–16).

44. E.g., the 8 percent that Parliament paid the City for a loan to fund the suppression of the Irish rebellion in 1641 (May, *History*, lib. 2, p. 11).

be safe. Arms planted upon dominion extirpate enemies and make friends, but, maintained by a mere tax, have enemies that have roots and friends that have none.[45]

Harrington's perceptions were perhaps slightly in arrears of reality. It seems that the taxation-gathering abilities of the state had been strengthened by the pressures of the Civil War: "The increase in the military capacity of the English state between 1642 and 1646 was a more dramatic change than anything achieved in the preceding three generations. It rested on reform of taxation, mainly undertaken between 1640 and 1643, which produced sums of money vastly greater than those available to earlier regimes. Reliable flows of money supported more effective borrowing, further increasing the military potential of the state."[46] Nevertheless, Harrington's dismissal of the notion of a standing army paid for out of taxation is a valuable indication of contemporary perceptions, even if the underlying realities were already beginning to shift.

Peacetime armies had always been thought to pose a threat to the liberty of the subject, as their prohibition in the Bill of Rights of 1689 had made clear. However, that in 1689 the danger such armies posed was conceived principally to be one against liberty rather than property is suggested by the fact that the Bill of Rights prohibits them only in "this kingdom" (i.e., England) but not (for instance) in Ireland. Until the 1690s the threat posed by standing armies to the subject's property (as opposed to his liberty) had been more spasmodic. Before the financial innovations introduced under William III the threat to property had been more a question of the bad luck of being pillaged or billeted on,[47] rather than of the imposition of the regular and inescapable burden of taxation. This

---

45. Harrington, *Oceana*, p. 60.

46. Braddick, *State Formation*, p. 221. Cf. "[In the 1640s] the share of national wealth successfully taxed by government roughly doubled, and the proportion of income raised through parliament rose from around 25 per cent to 90 per cent or more" (ibid., pp. 233–34).

47. This might create real inconveniences, as Thomas Coningsby explained in the House of Commons on 16 November 1685: "[Soldiers] debauched the manners of all the people, their wives, daughters, and servants. Men do not go to church where they quarter for fear mischief should be done in their absence" (Childs, *Army*, p. 13).

was why no legislation against a standing army was passed between 1660 and 1685: "There was no necessity for such radical action, as parliament could always emasculate any plans to enlarge the army by refusing to vote additional revenues."[48] But by the late 1690s, the situation had changed dramatically:

> After 1690 massive military commitment was reflected in the size of the armed forces, numbering well over 100,000. The significance of such numbers is not always clear, but one way of appreciating this commitment is that the combined population of England's seven biggest cities (aside from London) was probably smaller than the number of men in arms around 1700. This was a substantial burden on an agrarian economy and, by Tudor and early Stuart standards, a miraculous governmental achievement.[49]

At the same time, in the aftermath of the Glorious Revolution ownership of the army had subtly changed:

> Although the army [of the reign of Charles II] was basically apolitical it was very much the king's force and was bound to be employed according to royal rather than parliamentary policies. This emphasis remained uncorrected until the Mutiny Act of 1689 gave parliament control over military discipline and the huge cost of the War of the Grand Alliance ensured that parliament assumed the dominant interest in England's national finances.[50]

So in the autumn and winter of 1697 standing armies—now properly so called because they had become a permanent part of the resources of the state and were paid for out of taxation—might for the first time be resisted on the grounds of both liberty and frugality. For "there can be little doubt that the real burden of taxation per capita increased considerably in this period [the later seventeenth century]."[51]

---

48. Childs, *Army*, p. xviii.
49. Braddick, *State Formation*, p. 214.
50. Childs, *Army*, p. xvii.
51. Braddick, *State Formation*, p. 214.

The Pamphlets of 1697–1698: Styles, Sources, and Arguments

The unfamiliar literary conditions under which the debate on standing armies of 1697–98 took place were explained by Macaulay:

> The press was now free. An exciting and momentous political question could be fairly discussed. Those who held uncourtly opinions could express those opinions without resorting to illegal expedients and employing the agency of desperate men. The consequence was that the dispute was carried on, though with sufficient keenness, yet, on the whole, with a decency which would have been thought extraordinary in the days of the censorship.[52]

Macaulay is referring to the lapse of the Licensing Act of 1685, which Parliament had refused to renew in 1694. However, to follow Macaulay in saying that the press was now free would be to fall into exaggeration. The Licensing Act had not been renewed, not because it was suddenly recognized to be offensive, but rather—as John Locke, the man who prepared the case for its discontinuance, pointed out—because it had proved to be ineffective. It had neither prevented the publication of seditious matter nor prescribed penalties for offences. Therefore, the argument ran, it should be allowed to lapse. But we should not therefore leap to the unwarranted conclusion that members of Parliament had suddenly realized that state control of the press was morally repulsive. The nonrenewal of the Licensing Act signalled no change of heart in Parliament concerning freedom of expression. Rather, it pointed in precisely the opposite direction. It indicated a desire on the part of government either to find or to create more effective ways of policing the press. One such means lay ready to hand in the common law. The law of seditious libel was a powerful instrument for the intimidation of authors considered disaffected and for the suppression of publications deemed obnoxious, and it would be used effectively by successive administrations until the early nineteenth century.[53] But the coincidence of the lapse of the Licensing Act and the

---

52. Macaulay, *History*, 6:2736.

53. On which subject see the forthcoming study by Tom Keymer, *The Poetics of the Pillory: English Literature and Seditious Libel 1660–1820* (Oxford: Oxford University Press).

passage of the Triennial Act in December 1694 did have implications for the production of political literature. Political pamphlets increased greatly in number as general elections necessarily became more frequent as a result of the Triennial Act.[54]

Macaulay came closer to the truth when he drew attention to the overall decency and politeness of the debate on standing armies. In comparison with the lampoons and personal attacks which both animate and disfigure the controversies of the reign of Charles II, the standing army pamphlets of 1697–98 taken as a group display a new moderation of tone. Bantering irony (on which Defoe remarked in his replies to Trenchard and Moyle) is the closest they came to the exuberant stridencies of Carolean polemic.[55] Their style, however, is far from bland. Strikingly modern and colloquial turns of phrase, even on occasion what appear to be neologisms, recur to enliven pamphlets that might otherwise have dwindled into mere lists of historical examples—what Macaulay loftily dismissed as "claptraps and historical commonplaces without number, the authority of a crowd of illustrious names, all the prejudices, all the traditions, of both the parties in the state."[56] A further interesting point of style is Defoe's frequent use of biblical language, which to some extent ran against the trend in political discourse since the Restoration.[57] No doubt this in part simply reflected his upbringing as a Trinitarian dissenter. But it also served to separate the two sides in the debate along religious lines, as Defoe was keen to draw attention to the Socinian—and perhaps more than Socinian—inclinations of those who had set their faces against the maintenance of a standing army.[58]

54. Downie, *Harley*, p. 1.

55. See below, pp. 73, 88, 365, and 374.

56. Macaulay, *History*, 6:2736. For examples of colloquialisms, see below, p. 121, n. 14. For neologisms, see below, p. 317, nn. 155 and 156; p. 326, n. 186; and p. 356, n. 256.

57. "Political language does seem to have become more sober in the late seventeenth century, with less overtly apocalyptic rhetoric; and new discourses did arise to challenge the early protestant interpretation of history. In particular, it has been claimed that political actors and writers began to analyse their times through classical analogies with Greece and Rome, rather than constantly reaching for the book of Revelation and the examples of Old Testament kings" (Claydon, *William III*, pp. 43–44).

58. Below, pp. 380 and 386.

The matrix of examples and sources for the debate had been established from the outset by Trenchard and Moyle in *An Argument Shewing that a Standing Army Is Inconsistent with a Free Government* (1697). To begin with we find a series of lurid instances of the miseries of military despotism drawn from ancient history. Here the principal guide was Machiavelli, whose bitter comparisons of mercenaries and militias seems to have provided an initial point of entry into the historical record, although the later participants in the debate added further examples. Even so, the pamphleteers were far from scholarly. Often no particular source is cited for an example (although the flamboyantly detailed referencing in Toland's *The Militia Reform'd* is a remarkable contrast with the general insouciance over precision of reference). There are some surprising inclusions among the classical sources (for instance, Aulus Gellius), as well as some surprising absences. One might have expected more use to be made of Tacitus. It may be, however, that the writers of these pamphlets were reluctant to stray too far from the classical authors they had studied at school: hence, perhaps, their fondness for epigraphs and tags drawn from Horace and from books 2 and 3 of the *Aeneid*, over which as pupils they must have spent long and painful hours.

The lessons of antiquity were reinforced by further examples, necessarily non-Machiavellian, taken from later sixteenth- and seventeenth-century European and Levantine history (the inclusion of references to the very recent history of the Near East and the Ottoman Empire is a point of particular interest, stimulated as it no doubt had been by the recent publications on that subject by Sir Paul Rycaut).[59] But especially telling for the first readers of these pamphlets, one imagines, were the examples drawn from recent English experience; that is to say, the examples supplied by Cromwell's rule, and by the "late reigns" of Charles II and

---

59. Sir Paul Rycaut, *The Present State of the Ottoman Empire* (1667) and *The History of the Turkish Empire* (1680). Both these texts had been included in the list of "Political Discourses and Histories worth reading" which Henry Neville had placed before the three political dialogues in the second edition of his *Plato Redivivus* (1681). There is a recent edition of *The Present State of the Ottoman Empire*, edited by John Anthony Butler (Tempe, Ariz.: Arizona Center for Medieval and Renaissance Studies, 2017). On this subject, see now Noel Malcolm, *Useful Enemies: Islam and the Ottoman Empire in Western Political Thought, 1450–1750* (Oxford: Oxford University Press, 2019).

James II. Here the opponents of standing armies drew heavily on the constitutional library of vulgar Whiggism: on the various printings of Rushworth's *Collections*; on Nathaniel Bacon's *An Historicall Discourse of the Uniformity of the Government of England* (1647), *The Continuation of an Historicall Discourse of the Government of England* (1651), and *An Historical and Political Discourse of the Laws and Government of England* (1689); on very recently published works, such as Roger Coke's *A Detection of the Court and State of England* (1697); and possibly even on soon-to-be-published works such as Edmund Ludlow's *Memoirs* (1698–99), the original manuscript of which had been artfully massaged for publication by one of the participants in the standing army debate, John Toland, so as to temper a text saturated in the millenarianism characteristic of at least some Parliamentarians in the middle decades of the century to the cooler religious disposition of the Whigs of the late 1690s.[60]

The arguments constructed on both sides of the debate out of these varied materials were not conspicuous for either finesse or power (although a partial exemption from this charge might be made for John Somers). Macaulay exposed the contradictions in the different assertions of those opposed to standing armies (as Defoe had done before him):

> If an army composed of regular troops really was far more efficient than an army composed of husbandmen taken from the plough and burghers taken from the counter, how could the country be safe with no defenders but husbandmen and burghers, when a great prince, who was our nearest neighbour, who had a few months before been our enemy, and who might, in a few months, be our enemy again, kept up not less than a hundred and fifty thousand regular troops? If, on the other hand, the spirit of the English people was such that they would, with little or no training, encounter and defeat the most formidable array of veterans from the continent, was it not absurd to apprehend that such a people could be reduced to slavery by a few regiments of their own countrymen?[61]

60. For which see the introduction to Ludlow, *Voyce*, pp. 1–80. Trenchard's comments in the *Short History* about the Irish Massacre and Charles I's implication in it suggest that he may have had prepublication knowledge of Ludlow's *Memoirs*. Tony Claydon has analyzed the enduring, but only tepidly or partially millenarian, public piety of the 1690s (Claydon, *William III*, pp. 229–30).

61. Macaulay, *History*, 6:2738. Cf. below, pp. 91 and 241.

These strictures may have been accurate. Nevertheless, they were beside the point. Trenchard, Moyle, Toland, and the other writers against standing armies were appealing to prejudice rather than to reason, and they found their account more in a disorderly profusion of examples than in fine-drawn ratiocination. In the next century Samuel Johnson, composing the life of his friend the poet Richard Savage, would specify the topic of a standing army as one of those on which it seemed impossible for men not to exhibit "that partiality which almost every man indulges with regard to himself":

> the liberty of the press is a blessing when we are inclined to write against others, and a calamity when we find ourselves overborne by the multitude of our assailants; as the power of the crown is always thought too great by those who suffer by its influence, and too little by those in whose favour it is exerted; and a standing army is generally accounted necessary by those who command, and dangerous and oppressive by those who support it.[62]

This meant that the defenders of standing armies were in a sense always arguing uphill and trying to introduce rationality and dispassion into a debate which, notwithstanding its historical and constitutional scenery, was really about the creation and enforcement of a bugbear (a word which crops up repeatedly in the pamphlets themselves).[63] For the moment of the debate interacted tellingly with broader political circumstances:

> Trenchard's propaganda demonstrated that public opinion could be influenced by the press. In 1697 and 1698 it was not only opinion inside parliament which mattered, but extra-parliamentary viewpoints. The disbandment issue was one which could actually be used to change the face of parliament. By the terms of the triennial act, there had to be a general election in 1698. The anti-army pamphleteers, therefore, were aiming not merely at persuading their representatives in parliament to vote for disbandment, they were also attempting to pander to the desires of the electorate to secure an electoral victory. It was clearly to the advantage of country gentlemen not to maintain an

---

62. Johnson, *Lives*, 3:142.
63. For examples, see below, pp. 36, 81, 90, 349, 356, 394, 427, 453, and 468.

army. No army, less taxation. The equation was not a complex one, and the country propagandists hammered out the solution in their pamphlets.[64]

As we have seen, the link between a standing army and the burden of taxation had only recently been forged. A traditional topic of grievance (standing armies) had been made to lend itself to a campaign against what was in fact a new evil, created by the fiscal innovations of the early 1690s (increasing taxation).

The outcome of the Parliamentary debates of 1697–98 would show how little headway can be made against entrenched prejudices, even when they are mobilized against unfamiliar objects. In 1698 the Commons passed a vote to disband all troops raised since 1680, when Charles II had no more than 7,000 men on foot in England.[65]

The Eighteenth-Century Afterlife

The standing army controversy, properly so called, ended in 1698 with what looked like a victory for the opponents of military modernization. But the language of anti-army suspicion which the protagonists in that controversy had found in earlier seventeenth-century documents of resistance and correction to Stuart monarchy—documents such as the Petition of Right (1628) and the Grand Remonstrance (1641)[66]—and which they had then revived, intensified, and reapplied to new political issues, survived beyond that moment of revival and remained available for subsequent deployment, albeit in ideological campaigns which had objects very different from those that had engaged the energies of Trenchard, Moyle, and Toland.

When, in the wake of the Jacobite rebellion of 1715, George I kept his troops in arms, the unconstitutional nature of the measure was denounced by disaffected Tories and Jacobites, who had no scruples about letting fall

64. Downie, *Harley*, p. 33. Cf. Blackmore, *History*, pp. 13–15.

65. Downie, *Harley*, p. 30. Note the studied blandness of Blackmore's account of this transaction (Blackmore, *History*, pp. 57–58).

66. For the texts of these documents, see Appendixes A and B, below, pp. 577–608.

from their lips a political language originally forged to attack the exiled royal dynasty which lay close to their hearts.[67] These protests revived with particular intensity in 1718 and 1721, when the House of Commons again debated the question of a standing army.[68] An index to the level of suspicion on this score during these years is to be found in the fact that the barracks constructed as a consequence of the Quarantine Act of 1721 were feared to be intended for a standing army (the inclusion of "the Plague, a standing Army" in the political ciphers of the Academy of Lagado in Swift's *Gulliver's Travels* reflects this suspicion).[69]

While these concerns still vibrated on the public ear, Thomas Gordon, writing as "Cato," published one of the central texts on the subject, *A Discourse of Standing Armies; Shewing the Folly, Uselessness, and Danger of Standing Armies in Great Britain* (1722). The publication in 1724 of an alarmist work such as *A Discourse Upon the Present Number of Forces in Great-Britain and Ireland* demonstrates that the subject remained vivid in the public imagination during this period. As the anonymous author of a slightly earlier pamphlet had justifiably remarked, "the People of the British Nation, are most Apprehensive of a *Standing Army*."[70] The fears of

67. The Whiggish and pro-Hanoverian journal *The Briton* remarked that "STANDING ARMIES have furnish'd the *Jacobite Malecontents* with a Topick for declamatory Ribaldry, from the Revolution to these Times" (*The Briton*, 27 [5 February 1724] [1724], p. 117). See also Ambrose Philips, *The Freethinker*, nos. 19 and 20 (26 May 1718 and 30 May 1718).

68. See, for an example of the tone in which much of the debate was conducted, the sardonic comments on the "mild Administration of a Standing Army" in *The Necessity of a Plot: Or, Reasons for a Standing Army. By a Friend to K. G.* (1720?), below, p. 486.

69. *A Compleat History of the Late Septennial Parliament*, 4th ed. (1722), p. 62; *Gulliver's Travels*, p. 283. *Gulliver's Travels* was first published in 1726, but composition had begun in earnest in 1722, and some elements of the final text (principally some of Parts 1 and 3) went back to the reign of Queen Anne. On the topical connection between plague and standing armies in the early 1720s, see "Cato" [Thomas Gordon], *A Discourse of Standing Armies; Shewing the Folly, Uselessness, and Danger of Standing Armies in Great Britain* (1722), below, p. 526; and George Granville, Baron Lansdowne, *A Letter from a Noble-Man Abroad, to his Friend in England* (1722), p. 5.

70. *An Equal Capacity in the Subjects of Great Britain for Civil Employment, the Best Security to the Government* (1717), p. 26; cf. Charles Hornby, *A Second Part of the Caveat against the Whiggs* (1712), p. 26, and William Thomas, *A Letter to Robert*

Englishmen were kept vivid by ideological suspicion, but also by a collective memory of the "disorders resulting from martial law, billeting and extra-parliamentary taxation" during the seventeenth century.[71] The prominence of the public dislike for a standing army meant that the language associated with it could be applied metaphorically to quite unmilitary activities. In 1730 while pursuing a literary quarrel with Alexander Pope, Leonard Welsted expressed his regret at the involvement of "Voluntiers" in the squabble through a figure of speech: "A Militia, in Case of publick Invasion, may perhaps be thought necessary, but yet one could always wish for an Army of regular Troops."[72]

It was, however, the middle decades of the century which saw the most interesting revival of anti–standing army and pro-militia language—interesting because, when taken together with the crisis of 1697–98, they form a fine example of that classic snare of intellectual history, namely when a familiar language is used to engage with new and unfamiliar objects, and is deployed in pursuit of subtly altered objectives.

In the 1730s the hiring of 12,000 Hessian mercenaries led to a flare-up of standing army language and sentiment.[73] In the following decade the early phases of the War of the Austrian Succession (1740–48), in which 16,000 Hanoverians were taken into English pay, saw another localized eruption. Chesterfield deplored how in these episodes (as he put it) the Hanoverian rudder was steering the English ship, and he advanced the general principle of British foreign policy that "except when the *Dutch* are in Danger, it can never be the Interest of this Nation to embark in the Troubles of the Continent."[74] The language of the standing army debate

---

Walpole Esqr. (1716?), p. 4. See also William Shippen's opposition to the continuance of a standing army in a series of Parliamentary speeches delivered between 1724 and 1731, and collected as *Four Speeches* (1732).

71. Manning, *Apprenticeship*, p. 266; cf. Schwoerer, *Armies*, p. 3. For speculation concerning the reasons for the eventual acceptance of a standing army by the British, see Manning, *Apprenticeship*, p. 429.

72. Leonard Welsted, *Epistle to Pope* (1730), p. viii.

73. See the appendix to *The Craftsman*, vol. 6 (1731); and cf. Horatio Walpole, *Considerations on the Present State of Affairs in Europe* (1730) and Anonymous, *The Case of the Hessian Forces in the Pay of Great-Britain Impartially and Freely Examin'd* (1731).

74. Chesterfield, *The Case of the Hanover Forces in the Pay of Great-Britain* (1742), pp. 30, 45; see also Chesterfield, *A Vindication of a Late Pamphlet* (1743), p. 26.

(for instance, when the Hanoverian mercenaries were referred to as "Janizaries"),[75] and some of its general flavor of suspicion of the measures of kings and courts, were reapplied to this new question, which was at bottom about the Continental commitments which had entered English politics with the accession of the House of Hanover, and the associated resentment of the influence exerted by the "little, low Interest of *Hanover*" and "the narrow Views and petty Concerns of a *German* Electorate."[76] "The Interests and Influence of Hanover are no longer to be disguised or concealed, but openly avowed, as the Rule of our Conduct, and the Spring of our Actions," fulminated Chesterfield.[77] However, although his language seemed to echo the insularity of Trenchard and Moyle, Chesterfield was no enemy of an imperial policy *tout court*. Rather, he deplored Britain's links with Hanover because they inhibited the nation's diplomatic movement, and thus threatened to hamper its freedom to pursue its now evident imperial destiny.

In 1745 the advance of the Jacobite army as far south as Derby without meeting any opposition raised a panic, and this turned men's minds once more to the desirability of a militia.[78] The pro-militia pamphlets composed over the following few years seem to revive the vocabulary and to adopt the argumentative postures of Trenchard, Moyle, and Toland. Yet once again this is deceptive. After 1745 it is clear that a militia is being advocated

75. Chesterfield, *The Case of the Hanover Forces in the Pay of Great-Britain* (1742), p. 75; cf. below, p. 28, n. 71.

76. Chesterfield, *The Case of the Hanover Forces in the Pay of Great-Britain* (1742), p. 83; Chesterfield, *A Vindication of a Late Pamphlet* (1743), p. 22.

77. Chesterfield, *A Vindication of a Late Pamphlet* (1743), p. 55.

78. "Two disgraceful events, the progress in the year forty-five of some naked highlanders, the invitation of the Hessians and Hanoverians in fifty-six, had betrayed and insulted the weakness of an unarmed people. The country Gentlemen of England unanimously demanded the establishment of a militia; . . ." (Gibbon, *Autobiographies*, p. 180). See, e.g.: Anonymous, *A Proposal for a Regular and Useful Militia* (Edinburgh, 1745); Anonymous, *A Plan for Establishing and Disciplining a National Militia* (1745); Anonymous, *An Examination of the Several Schemes for Suppressing the Rebellion* (1746); Anonymous, *A Scheme for Establishing a Militia* (Eton, 1747); Anonymous, *Thoughts Occasioned by the Bill for the Better Regulating of the Militia* (1747); *A Bill for the Better Ordering of the Militia forces in that part of Great-Britain called Scotland* (1750); Anonymous, *The Counterpoise* (1752): "C. S." [Charles Sackville, second Duke of Dorset], *A Treatise Concerning the Militia* (1752).

in addition to, not (as was the case in 1697–98) *instead of* a standing army. By mid-century the existence of a standing army was increasingly accepted and uncontested, although still attacked by diehards such as the Jacobite William Shippen (who made a point each year of voting against the Army Estimates). An empire needs a standing army, and because regular imperial troops must often serve overseas, the consequent weakness in homeland defense had to be supplied by a militia. Post-1745, pro-militia arguments implicitly assume the continuance of a standing army; they are not written in the hope of disbanding it. The anonymous author of *The Counterpoise* (1752) acknowledged as much:

> *The design of this Discourse is to shew a good Militia may be obtained in this Country at little or no expence; and to point out the imminent dangers which may arise to any Country by keeping up a Standing Army, without having, at the same time, a sufficient Power to controul and ballance it. A good Militia is here proved to be such Power* [sic].[79]

But even though the main point contended for in 1697–98 had thus been conceded, the late seventeenth-century language in which the standing army had been attacked endured as a kind of ghostly survival.

It is therefore not surprising that by mid-century the political heat had seeped away from the issue of standing armies. The fact that in 1754 Chesterfield could recommend the topic to his son as a suitable subject on which to practice his parliamentary oratory suggests how far it had receded from the front line of political warfare. As recently as 1738 Chesterfield had himself spoken vehemently in the House of Lords against a standing army, and had deployed with relish all the paranoid tropes so beloved by the opponents of standing armies since 1697:

> Slavery and arbitrary power are the certain consequences of keeping up a standing army; if it be kept up for any number of years. It is the machine by which the chains of slavery are rivetted upon a free people,

---

79. Anonymous, *The Counterpoise* (1752), p. 2. Cf. also the wording of one of Adam Ferguson's stipulations about the dignity attaching to militia rank in his project for the establishment of a militia: "That Rank in the Militia shall be equal, in all respects, to that which is acquired in the Standing Army" (Adam Ferguson, *Reflections Previous to the Establishment of a Militia* [1756], pp. 38–39).

and wants only a skilful and proper hand to set it a going. . . . It is the only machine by which the chains of slavery can be rivetted upon us.[80]

Writing to his son sixteen years later, however, Chesterfield's tone of casualness and jaded familiarity shows that now the whole subject was decidedly *vieux jeu*:

Take some political subject, turn it in your thoughts, consider what may be said, both for and against it, then put those arguments into writing, in the most correct and elegant English you can. For instance, a Standing Army, a Place Bill, etc.; as to the former, consider, on one side, the dangers arising to a free country from a great standing military force; on the other, consider the necessity of a force to repel force with. Examine whether a standing army, though in itself an evil, may not, from circumstances, become a necessary evil, and preventive of great dangers.[81]

In 1754 the question of standing armies is an exhausted topic, nothing more than a picked bone on which parliamentary tyros could cut their oratorical teeth.

If the War of the Austrian Succession had marked the beginning of the end for the issue of standing armies as a matter of practical politics, the Seven Years War (1756–63) further confirmed its essential moribundity, while at the same time providing further examples of how the pungent rhetoric it had generated lent itself to being employed for quite different—even contrary—purposes. Edward Wortley Montagu's *Reflections on the Rise and Fall of the Ancient Republicks. Adapted to the Present State of Great Britain* (1759), a jeremiad on Britain's dismal performance in the early part of the Seven Years War disguised as a work of ancient history, illustrates well the reapplication of this political language.

---

80. *The Life of the Late Earl of Chesterfield* (Philadelphia, 1775), pp. 32–35; quotation on p. 34. Chesterfield's opinions on this subject were far from constant. In 1732 he had spoken *against* the proposed reduction in the armed land force from 18,000 to 12,000 (Chesterfield, *Miscellaneous Works*, 4 vols. [London, 1779], 1:122).

81. To his son, 26 March 1754, in *The Letters of Philip Dormer Stanhope, 4th Earl of Chesterfield*, ed. Bonamy Dobrée, 6 vols. (London: Eyre & Spottiswoode, 1932), 5:2102.

The Peace of Aix-la-Chapelle which had concluded the War of the Austrian Succession proved (like the Treaty of Ryswick) to be nothing more than a brief armed truce. In the early 1750s tensions between the French and English in India began once more to rise as the English East India Company resisted French attempts to establish control over the Carnatic and the Deccan. In the West Indies, England and France squabbled over the "neutral" islands. Most gravely, in America the ambitious French strategy to link their settlements in Canada with Louisiana by means of a series of forts along the Ohio and the Mississippi had led to skirmishes with the English colonists, who were themselves now seeking to break out from the eastern seaboard and acquire additional territory west of the Allegheny Mountains.

The British response to these French provocations was muffled and slow. But eventually, in October 1754, British regiments under the command of General Braddock set sail for the colonies, and measures for raising troops in America were put in motion. The outcome was, to begin with, disastrous. In July 1755 Braddock led his troops into a French ambush on the Monongahela and suffered dreadful casualties. Public sentiment in Britain was further depressed by the apparent fruitlessness of the naval blockade of Brest which from July to December had been entrusted to Hawke, and which had somehow failed to engage the French fleet under the command of de la Motte. The new year brought fresh reasons for alarm, in the form of well-founded fears of a French invasion. The resulting public panic over the state of the nation's defenses prompted Pitt and Townshend to propose a Militia Bill that cleared the Commons in May 1756, but was rejected by the Lords.[82] To fill the gap, mercenary troops were once more imported from Hanover and Hesse. The final provocation arrived that same month, with news that French forces had landed in Minorca.

A formal declaration of war with France followed. A squadron of ten ships under the command of Admiral Byng had been sent to relieve

---

82. This crisis also produced a flurry of pamphlet activity: Adam Ferguson, *Reflections Previous to the Establishment of a Militia* (1756); Anonymous, *Reflections on the Present State of Affairs* (1756); Anonymous, *A Seventh Letter to the People of England* (1756); Anonymous, *Some Short Observations on the Late Militia Bill* (1756).

Minorca. But Byng was slow to reach the theater of operations, and once there failed to engage the enemy with resolution, instead returning to Gibraltar and leaving the Minorcan garrison to struggle on until it finally surrendered after a gallant defense on 28 June 1756. British public opinion was outraged, and a scapegoat was required. Byng was the sole and inevitable candidate. After a court-martial in February 1757 he was shot the following month on his own quarterdeck.

But now the tide of war was beginning to turn in Britain's favor. In the summer of 1756 the collapse of Newcastle's Continental diplomacy and his inadequacy as a war leader had led him to make overtures to William Pitt, then the most effective speaker in the Commons, and a man whose Patriot platform was proving popular in the country at large and devastating in the House. Eventually, after several months of maneuvering and false starts, by the summer of 1757 Pitt and Newcastle were working in harness, the latter as First Lord of the Treasury, but the former as the truly dominant figure in both the Cabinet and the Commons.[83]

The change in the direction of policy and the tone of administration was immediate. The Militia Bill was reintroduced; it finally passed the Lords in June 1757. The German mercenaries were sent home and two new regiments were raised from the same Highland clans that, a mere twelve years before, had seemed to threaten the very existence of the Hanoverian regime. The American colonists were by turns flattered, encouraged, and cajoled into making greater efforts for their own defense and for the security and extension of the empire. Frederick the Great, Britain's ally on the Continent, was generously supported with money and men; considerable French forces which might otherwise have made a nuisance of themselves in America were thus tied up in central Europe. In less than three years the strength of the British navy was increased by 55,000 men and seventy ships, and with that reinforcement the operational reach of British arms was transformed.

---

83. On the workings of this ministry, see Richard Middleton, *The Bells of Victory: The Pitt-Newcastle Ministry and the Conduct of the Seven Years War* (Cambridge: Cambridge University Press, 1985).

Montagu's *Reflections* was written as a response to these developments. It was replete with pro-militia and anti-mercenary sentiment. In the preface Montagu announced one of his major themes:

> The points which have lately exercised so many pens, turn upon the present expediency, or absolute insignificancy, of a *Militia*, or, what principles conduce most to the power, the happiness, and the duration of a free people.[84]

And in his final chapter, "Of the British Constitution," in which he applied the lessons of antiquity to contemporary Britain, Montagu returned to the importance of establishing a militia:

> Nothing but an extensive Militia can revive the once martial spirit of this nation, and we had even better once more be a nation of soldiers, like our renowned ancestors, than a nation of abject crouching slaves to the most rapacious, and most insolent people in the universe [i.e., the French].[85]

Montagu's support for a militia naturally entailed an opposition to the use of mercenaries, which was a ruinous practice, as ancient history everywhere taught, but particularly the history of Carthage:

> For the number of native Carthaginians, which we read of, in any of their armies, was so extremely small, as to bear no proportion to that of their foreign mercenaries. This kind of policy, which prevails so generally in all mercantile States, does, I confess, at first sight appear extremely plausible. . . . But a short detail of the calamities which they [the Carthaginians] drew upon themselves by this mistaken policy, will better shew the dangers which attend the admission of foreign mercenaries into any country, where the natives are unaccustomed to the use of arms. A practice which is too apt to prevail in commercial nations.[86]

---

84. Montagu, *Reflections*, p. 3.

85. Montagu, *Reflections*, p. 260. For other passages in which Montagu makes plain his support for the institution of a militia, see pp. 40, 43, 44, 45, 86, 90, 106, 107, 130, 133, 146, 149, 212, 229, 237, 238, 256–57, 258, 259, 261, 262, and 263.

86. Montagu, *Reflections*, p. 124. For other passages attacking the use of mercenaries, see pp. 25, 34, 35, 38, 71, 88, 114, 121, 122–23, 125, 127, 128, 130, 135, 228, 238, 254, 257, and 261.

And, drawing on Sallust, Montagu generalized from Roman history the role played by "that instrument of tyranny and oppression," a standing army, in the undermining of civil liberty:

> For when once the idea of respect and homage is annexed to the possession of wealth alone, honour, probity, every virtue, and every amiable quality will be held cheap in comparison, and looked upon as aukward and quite unfashionable. But as the spirit of liberty will yet exist in some degree in a state which retains the name of Freedom, even though the manners of that state should be generally depraved, an opposition will arise from those virtuous citizens, who know the value of their birth-right, *Liberty*, and will never submit tamely to the chains of faction. Force then will be called in to the aid of corruption, and a standing-army will be introduced. A military government will be established upon the ruins of the civil, and all commands and employments will be disposed of at the arbitrary will of lawless power. The people will be fleeced to pay for their own fetters, and doomed, like the cattle, to unremitting toil and drudgery for the support of their tyrannical masters.[87]

At the levels of language, sentiment, and argument, there is nothing here that could not have been found in the pages of Trenchard and Moyle sixty years before. But the political causes in which Montagu was deploying these linguistic and intellectual materials were very different from theirs. His family had formed an alliance with William Pitt, whose imperial strategy they supported.[88] An important element in that strategy had been the Militia Bill of 1756. As had been the case with the advocates of a militia in the years immediately following the Jacobite rebellion of 1745, therefore, Montagu's support for a militia and his opposition to the use of mercenaries in 1759 entailed no opposition to the maintenance of a Hanoverian standing army, no matter how harmful such permanent forces had been in antiquity. Indeed, the purpose of a militia in 1759 was precisely to reduce the burdens on, and to give greater effectiveness to,

87. Montagu, *Reflections*, pp. 99, 180–81. For other passages expressing disapproval of a standing army, see pp. 172 and 256–57.

88. For evidence of Montagu's support for Pitt, see Montagu, *Reflections*, pp. 261–63. For his family's connections with Pitt, see Montagu, *Reflections*, pp. xix–xx and n. 27.

Britain's regular professional army in the discharge of its imperial responsibilities. Although the language of hostility to a standing army still endured, by the end of the Seven Years War no one seriously expected it to be disbanded. As John Butler's satirical *A Consultation On the Subject of a Standing Army* (1763) shows clearly enough, this topic now preoccupied only a motley crew of superannuated, ill-assorted, and irrelevant politicians, and even then at only a formal level.

The militia which was eventually embodied in 1759 included an important writer among its officer corps, albeit one whose greatness lay some years in the future. Edward Gibbon, newly returned from a period of residence in Switzerland following his rash conversion to Roman Catholicism, served as a captain in the South battalion of the Hampshire militia from 12 June 1759 until 23 December 1762.[89] In draft B of his *Memoirs* (composed in 1789) Gibbon amused himself "with the recollection of an active scene which bears no affinity to any other period of my studious and social life."[90] Gibbon's account is a convenient lens with which to bring into focus how the whole subject of militias and standing armies looked in the final third of the eighteenth century, and to review the very important treatment of those subjects by Adam Smith in *The Wealth of Nations*. Gibbon began with the general idea of a militia:

> The defence of the state may be imposed on the body of the people, or it may be delegated to a select number of mercenaries; the exercise of arms may be an occasional duty or a separate trade, and it is this difference which forms the distinction between a militia and a standing army.[91]

In the earlier seventeenth century the militia had decayed into "less the object of confidence than of ridicule."[92] But the next century had shown how a necessary change of policy could reconfigure public opinion (the skills of narrative compression Gibbon had learned composing *The Decline and Fall* are impressively on display in this passage):

89. Gibbon, *Autobiographies*, pp. 183, 188.
90. Gibbon, *Autobiographies*, pp. 177–78.
91. Gibbon, *Autobiographies*, p. 178.
92. Gibbon, *Autobiographies*, p. 178.

The impotence of such unworthy soldiers was supplied from the aera of the restoration by the establishment of a body of mercenaries: the conclusion of each war encreased the numbers that were kept on foot, and although their progress was checked by the jealousy of opposition, time and necessity reconciled, or at least accustomed, a free country to the annual perpetuity of a standing army.[93]

This gradual growth in the public acceptance of a standing army nevertheless created a rhetorical opportunity for those who saw themselves as "patriots" (a word which Gibbon employs in the disdainful Johnsonian sense of factious agitators on behalf of "liberty" who in reality seek only their own advantage):

> The zeal of our patriots, both in and out of Parliament (I cannot add, both in and out of office) complained that the sword had been stolen from the hands of the people. They appealed to the victorious example of the Greeks and Romans, among whom every citizen was a soldier; and they applauded the happiness and independence of Switzerland, which, in the midst of the great monarchies of Europe, is sufficiently defended by a constitutional and effective militia.[94]

But Gibbon the historian of the Roman Empire and resident of the Pays de Vaud insisted that both the Roman and Swiss examples were poorly adapted to the circumstances of late seventeenth- and early eighteenth-century England. The "patriots" had ignored "the modern changes in the art of war, and the insuperable difference of government and manners," to both of which Gibbon's literary and military experience had sensitized him.[95] Furthermore, to focus on the Swiss militia without at the same time understanding the very different political circumstances of the cantons (and in particular the lightness of their taxation) was to mislead, and perhaps also to be misled. As for the Romans, in the later stages of the republic although their *manus* was technically a militia, the duration of the campaigns on which it was employed and the resulting improvements

---

93. Gibbon, *Autobiographies*, p. 179.

94. Gibbon, *Autobiographies*, p. 179.

95. Gibbon, *Autobiographies*, p. 179. Note as well the famous comment: "The Captain of the Hampshire grenadiers (the reader may smile) has not been useless to the historian of the Roman Empire" (p. 190).

in discipline and technique meant that it was "transformed into a standing army."[96]

Gibbon's assertion that the Roman militia had mutated into a standing army is a striking formulation. It was a metamorphosis repeated, although imperfectly, in eighteenth-century England, as the militia was continued in existence once any real threat of a French invasion had been destroyed by Hawke's victory in Quiberon Bay (20 November 1759). This prolongation of embodiment required the militia to serve at a distance from their native counties, to subject themselves to a regular martial discipline, and in return to receive payment. The result was a change in character:

> At a distance from their respective counties these provincial corps were stationed, and removed, and encamped by the command of the Secretary at War: the officers and men were trained in the habits of subordination, nor is it surprizing that some regiments should have assumed the discipline and appearance of veteran troops. With the skill they soon imbibed the spirit of mercenaries, the character of a militia was lost; and, under that specious name, the crown had acquired a second army more costly and less useful than the first.[97]

Nevertheless, this corruption of a militia into the semblance of a standing army had produced at least one positive, if unintended, consequence:

> The most beneficial effect of this institution was to eradicate among the Country gentlemen the relicks of Tory, or rather of Jacobite prejudice. The accession of a British king reconciled them to the government, and even to the court; but they have been since accused of transferring their passive loyalty from the Stuarts to the family of Brunswick; and I have heard Mr. Burke exclaim in the house of Commons, "They have changed the Idol, but they have preserved the Idolatry."[98]

Gibbon's analysis of the social consequences of the militia—namely, that it had converted the Tory country gentry into adherents of the Hanoverian dynasty—contrasts vividly with the suspicions of the Crown which had

---

96. Gibbon, *Autobiographies*, p. 180.
97. Gibbon, *Autobiographies*, p. 182.
98. Gibbon, *Autobiographies*, p. 182.

motivated the advocates of a militia in 1697–98. This was a paradoxical outcome which might indeed deserve the reflections of a philosophic mind.

Gibbon's insight concerning how a militia might become a standing army is arresting when we recall how those two institutions had been discussed by both sides in the Williamite controversy. In that Machiavellian moment, it had seemed as if militias and standing armies were so different in kind that there was no possibility of converting one into the other. Indeed, the whole argument against standing armies was premised on the assumption that militias were by definition proof against the political temptations which standing armies, by contrast, were constitutionally unable to resist. But if militias and standing armies were in fact mutually convertible, as a later generation could observe as a visible matter of fact, where did that leave the arguments of both sides in the dispute of 1697–98?

In putting forward the mutual convertibility of militias and standing armies Gibbon was following the speculative and historical argument of his friend Adam Smith. In *The Wealth of Nations*, book 5, chapter 1, "Of the Expence of Defence," Smith had repeatedly asserted the necessary and natural superiority of a standing army over a militia:

> A militia, however, in whatever manner it may be either disciplined or exercised, must always be much inferior to a well disciplined and well exercised standing army.
>
> . . . the history of all ages, it will be found, bears testimony to the irresistible superiority which a well-regulated standing army has over a militia.
>
> A well-regulated standing army is superior to every militia. . . . It is only by means of a standing army, therefore, that the civilization of any country can be perpetuated, or even preserved for any considerable time.[99]

99. Smith, *Wealth of Nations*, V.i.a.23; V.i.a.28; V.i.a.39; pp. 699–700, 701, 705–6. However, in correspondence Smith would deny that his analysis amounted to an outright dismissal of militias. In April 1760, writing to Strahan, he had expressed concern that a recent publication (Hooke's *Memoirs*) might "throw a damp upon

However, Smith also went out of his way at several points in *The Wealth of Nations* V.i.a to show how a long-embodied militia could rival the professional competence of a standing army:

> A militia of any kind, it must be observed, however, which has served for several successive campaigns in the field, becomes in every respect a standing army. The soldiers are every day exercised in the use of their arms, and, being constantly under the command of their officers, are habituated to the same prompt obedience which takes place in standing armies. What they were before they took the field, is of little importance. They necessarily become in every respect a standing army, after they have passed a few campaigns in it. Should the war in America drag out through another campaign, the American militia may become in every respect a match for that standing army, of which the valour appeared, in the last war [i.e., the Seven Years War], at least not inferior to that of the hardiest veterans of France and Spain.[100]

The implication was clear. *Pace* Trenchard and Moyle, Smith contended that there was no essential and immutable distinction between militias and standing armies. Each could mutate into the other under the pressure of changing circumstances; and this was the true lesson inculcated by the history of militarism in the heyday of the Roman republic. Machiavelli had seized on those years as illustrating the invincibility of a citizen militia. But Smith saw the history of this period very differently, and his more penetrating analysis is worth quoting at length:

> From the end of the first to the beginning of the second Carthaginian war, the armies of Carthage were continually in the field, and employed under three great generals, who succeeded one another in the command; . . . The army which Annibal led from Spain into

---

our militia." In October 1780, writing to Andreas Holt, he defends himself against the allegation of denigrating militias: "A Gentleman of the name of Douglas, has Written against Me. . . . He fancies that because I insist that a Militia is in all cases inferior to a well regulated and well disciplined standing Army, that I disapprove of Militias altogether. With regard to that subject, he and I happened to be precisely of the same opinion" (Smith, *Correspondence*, pp. 68 and 251).

100. Smith, *Wealth of Nations*, V.i.a.27; p. 701.

Italy must necessarily, in those different wars, have been gradually formed to the exact discipline of a standing army. The Romans, in the mean time, though they had not been altogether at peace, yet they had not, during this period, been engaged in any war of very great consequence; and their military discipline, it is generally said, was a good deal relaxed. The Roman armies which Annibal encountered at Trebia, Thrasymenus, and Cannae, were militia opposed to a standing army. This circumstance, it is probable, contributed more than any other to determine the fate of those battles. . . .

Annibal was ill supplied from home. The Roman militia, being continually in the field, became in the progress of the war a well disciplined and well exercised standing army; and the superiority of Annibal grew every day less and less. Asdrubal judged it necessary to lead the whole, or almost the whole of the standing army which he commanded in Spain to the assistance of his brother in Italy. In his march he is said to have been misled by his guides; and in a country which he did not know, was surprized and attacked by another standing army, in every respect equal or superior to his own, and was entirely defeated.

When Asdrubal had left Spain, the great Scipio found nothing to oppose him but a militia inferior to his own. He conquered and subdued that militia, and, in the course of the war, his own militia necessarily became a well-disciplined and well-exercised standing army. That standing army was afterwards carried to Africa, where it found nothing but a militia to oppose it. In order to defend Carthage it became necessary to recall the standing army of Annibal. The disheartened and frequently defeated African militia joined it, and, at the battle of Zama, composed the greater part of the troops of Annibal. The event of that day determined the fate of the two rival republicks.[101]

Smith's anti-Machiavellian conclusion was inescapable: "From the end of the second Carthaginian war till the fall of the Roman republick, the armies of Rome were in every respect standing armies."[102] Under the later empire, however, the metamorphosis had been reversed as military

101. Smith, *Wealth of Nations*, V.i.a.31–34; pp. 702–3.
102. Smith, *Wealth of Nations*, V.i.a.35; p. 703.

discipline had been relaxed: "The civil came to predominate over the military character; and the standing armies of Rome gradually degenerated into a corrupt, neglected, and undisciplined militia, incapable of resisting the attack of the German and Scythian militias, which soon afterwards invaded the western empire."[103]

Not only did Smith reject the conviction of the seventeenth-century country Whigs that militias and standing armies were utterly different in kind. He also challenged their faith that militias were inseparably found in the company of liberty, while standing armies inevitably brought servitude in their wake:

> Men of republican principles have been jealous of a standing army as dangerous to liberty. It certainly is so, wherever the interest of the general and that of the principal officers are not necessarily connected with the support of the constitution of the state. The standing army of Caesar destroyed the Roman republick. The standing army of Cromwell turned the long parliament out of doors. But where the sovereign is himself the general, and the principal nobility and gentry of the country the chief officers of the army; where the military force is placed under the command of those who have the greatest interest in the support of the civil authority, because they have themselves the greatest share of that authority, a standing army can never be dangerous to liberty. On the contrary, it may in some cases be favourable to liberty. The security which it gives to the sovereign renders unnecessary that troublesome jealousy, which, in some modern republicks, seems to watch over the minutest actions, and to be at all times ready to disturb the peace of every citizen. Where the security of the magistrate, though supported by the principal people of the country, is endangered by every popular discontent; where a small tumult is capable of bringing about in a few hours a great revolution, the whole authority of government must be employed to suppress and punish every murmur and complaint against it. To a sovereign, on the contrary, who feels himself supported, not only by the natural aristocracy of the country, but by a well-regulated standing army, the rudest, the most groundless, and the most licentious remonstrances can give

103. Smith, *Wealth of Nations*, V.i.a.36; p. 704.

little disturbance. He can safely pardon or neglect them, and his consciousness of his own superiority naturally disposes him to do so. That degree of liberty which approaches to licentiousness can be tolerated only in countries where the sovereign is secured by a well-regulated standing army. It is in such countries only, that the publick safety does not require, that the sovereign should be trusted with any discretionary power, for suppressing even the impertinent wantonness of this licentious liberty.[104]

It was a devastating conclusion which sounded, to those who had ears to hear it, the death knell for the old country Whig prejudice against standing armies.

Conclusion

When, from the security of the reign of Victoria, Macaulay reviewed the debate on standing armies which had followed the Treaty of Ryswick, it had seemed to him a purely historical controversy, so thoroughly had men's opinions on this subject been remodeled and improved:

> No man of sense has, in our days, or in the days of our fathers, seriously maintained that our island could be safe without an army. And, even if our island were perfectly secure from attack, an army would still be indispensably necessary to us. The growth of the empire has left us no choice. The regions which we have colonized or conquered since the accession of the House of Hanover contain a population exceeding twenty-fold that which the House of Stuart governed. There are now more English soldiers on the other side of the tropic of Cancer in time of peace than Cromwell had under his command in time of war. All the troops of Charles II. would not have been sufficient to garrison the posts we now occupy in the Mediterranean Sea alone. The regiments which defend the remote dependencies of the Crown cannot be duly recruited and relieved, unless a force far larger

104. Smith, *Wealth of Nations*, V.i.a.41; pp. 706–7. Another jousting engagement with the prejudices of the late seventeenth-century Whigs comes when Smith argues (contra Andrew Fletcher; see above, p. xx, and below, p. 154) that the invention of gunpowder, "which at first sight appears to be so pernicious," in fact favors the permanency of civilization (Smith, *Wealth of Nations*, V.i.a.44; p. 708).

than that which James collected in the camp at Hounslow for the purpose of overawing this capital be constantly kept up within the kingdom. The old national antipathy to permanent military establishments, an antipathy which was once reasonable and salutary, but which lasted some time after it had become unreasonable and noxious, has gradually yielded to the irresistible force of circumstances. We have made the discovery, that an army may be so constituted as to be in the highest degree efficient against an enemy, and yet obsequious to the civil magistrate. We have long ceased to apprehend danger to law and to freedom from the licence of troops, and from the ambition of victorious generals. An alarmist who should now talk such language as was common five generations ago, who should call for the entire disbanding of the land force of the realm, and who should gravely predict that the warriors of Inkerman and Delhi would depose the Queen, dissolve the Parliament, and plunder the Bank, would be regarded as fit only for a cell in Saint Luke's.[105]

Today, it is perhaps Macaulay's absolute confidence that the problem of how to reconcile the possession of deadly force with liberty and civil society had been solved once and for all that looks dated.

The forms that problem has assumed in more recent decades—for instance, the threat of "Caesarism" so feared by Gore Vidal in America after the Second World War, or more recently the dismaying durability of military regimes in the Middle East—look very different from the standing army controversy which animated Parliament and the coffee-houses of London in 1697–98. Yet there is an underlying affinity between these apparently discrepant things, and it is that affinity which gives the pamphlets brought together in this volume an enduring interest and importance.

David Womersley

105. Macaulay, *History*, 6:2731–32.

ABBREVIATIONS

Aesop, *Fables*	*Aesop's Fables, with their Morals* (1706)
Anonymous, *Secret History*	Anonymous, *Secret History of the Reigns of K. Charles II. and K. James II.* (1690)
Ash, *Ordering Anarchy*	Rhiannon Ash, *Ordering Anarchy: Armies and Leaders in Tacitus' Histories* (London: Duckworth, 1999)
Backscheider, *Defoe*	Paula Backscheider, *Daniel Defoe* (Baltimore and London: Johns Hopkins University Press, 1989)
Bacon, *Essayes*	Sir Francis Bacon, *The Essayes or Counsels, Civill and Morall* (Oxford: Clarendon Press, 1985)
Bentivoglio, *Relations*	Guido Bentivoglio, *Historicall relations of the United Provinces & of Flanders written originally in Italian by Cardinall Bentivoglio; and now rendred into English by the Right Honourable Henry, Earle of Monmouth* (1652)
Blackmore, *History*	Sir Richard Blackmore, *A Short History of the Last Parliament* (1699)

Blackstone, *Commentaries*

Sir William Blackstone, *Commentaries on the Laws of England*, 4 vols. (Oxford: Clarendon Press, 1765–69)

Boccalini, *Advices*

Trajano Boccalini, *Advices from Parnassus* (1706)

Bolingbroke

Bolingbroke, *Political Writings*, ed. David Armitage (Cambridge: Cambridge University Press, 1997)

Boyer, *William III*

Abel Boyer, *The History of King William the Third. In III Parts*, 3 vols. (1702–3)

Braddick, *State Formation*

Michael J. Braddick, *State Formation in Early Modern England, c. 1550–1700* (Cambridge: Cambridge University Press, 2000)

Buckingham, *Plays*

Plays, Poems, and Miscellaneous Writings Associated with George Villiers Second Duke of Buckingham, ed. Robert D. Hume and Harold Love, 2 vols. (Oxford: Oxford University Press, 2007)

Burnet, *History*

Gilbert Burnet, *Bishop Burnet's History of His Own Time*, 2 vols. (1724–34)

Burnet, *Tracts*

Gilbert Burnet, *A Second Collection of Several Tracts and Discourses* (1689)

Childs, *Army*

John Childs, *The Army, James II and the Glorious Revolution* (Manchester: Manchester University Press, 1980)

Clarendon, *History*

Edward Hyde, Earl of Clarendon, *The History of the Rebellion and Civil Wars in England*, ed. W. Dunn Macray, 6 vols. (Oxford: Clarendon Press, 1888)

Claydon, *William III*

Tony Claydon, *William III and the Godly Revolution* (Cambridge: Cambridge University Press, 1996)

Coke, *Detection*

Roger Coke, *A Detection of the Court and State of England* (1697)

Coke, *Writings*	*The Selected Writings of Sir Edward Coke*, ed. Steve Sheppard, 3 vols. (Indianapolis: Liberty Fund, 2003)
Connolly, *Religion*	S. J. Connolly, *Religion, Law and Power: The Making of Protestant Ireland 1660–1760* (Oxford: Clarendon Press, 1992)
Cromwell, *Speeches*	*The Writings and Speeches of Oliver Cromwell*, ed. W. C. Abbott, 4 vols. (Oxford: Clarendon Press, 1988)
Defoe, *Cavalier*	Daniel Defoe, *Memoirs of a Cavalier*, ed. James T. Boulton (London: Oxford University Press, 1972)
Defoe, *Moll Flanders*	Daniel Defoe, *The Fortunes and Misfortunes of the Famous Moll Flanders*, ed. G. A. Starr and Linda Bree (Oxford: Oxford University Press, 2011)
Defoe, *Robinson Crusoe*	Daniel Defoe, *The Life and Strange Surprizing Adventures of Robinson Crusoe, of York, Mariner*, ed. J. D. Crowley (London: Oxford University Press, 1972)
Dickson, *Financial Revolution*	P. G. M. Dickson, *The Financial Revolution in England: A Study in the Development of Public Credit 1688–1756* (London: Macmillan, 1967)
Downie, *Harley*	J. A. Downie, *Robert Harley and the Press: Propaganda and Public Opinion in the Age of Swift and Defoe* (Cambridge: Cambridge University Press, 1979)
Ellis, *Coffee-House*	Markman Ellis, *The Coffee-House: A Cultural History* (London: Weidenfeld and Nicolson, 2004)
ESTC	*English Short Title Catalog*
Evelyn, *Diary*	*The Diary of John Evelyn*, ed. E. S. de Beer, 6 vols. (Oxford: Clarendon Press, 1955)

Fink, *Classical Republicans*   Zera S. Fink, *The Classical Republicans: An Essay in the Recovery of a Pattern of Thought in Seventeenth-Century England*, 2nd ed. (Evanston, Ill.: Northwestern University Press, 1962)

Fletcher, *Political Works*   Andrew Fletcher, *Political Works*, ed. John Robertson, Cambridge Texts in the History of Political Thought (Cambridge: Cambridge University Press, 1997)

Franklin, *Constitutionalism*   Julian H. Franklin, ed. and trans., *Constitutionalism and Resistance in the Sixteenth Century: Three Treatises by Hotman, Beza, & Mornay* (New York: Pegasus, 1969)

Gibbon, *Autobiographies*   *The Autobiographies of Edward Gibbon*, ed. John Murray (London: John Murray, 1896)

Gibbon, *Decline and Fall*   Edward Gibbon, *The History of the Decline and Fall of the Roman Empire*, ed. David Womersley, 3 vols. (London: Allen Lane, 2004)

Grey, *Debates*   Anchitell Grey, *Debates of the House of Commons, from the Year 1667 to the Year 1694*, 10 vols. (1763)

Gulliver's Travels   Jonathan Swift, *Gulliver's Travels*, ed. David Womersley (Cambridge: Cambridge University Press, 2012)

Harrington, *Oceana*   James Harrington, *The Commonwealth of Oceana and A System of Politics*, ed. J. G. A. Pocock, Cambridge Texts in the History of Political Thought (Cambridge: Cambridge University Press, 1992)

Hill, *Harley*   Brian W. Hill, *Robert Harley: Speaker, Secretary of State and Premier Minister* (New Haven: Yale University Press, 1988)

History of Oxford	*The History of the University of Oxford*, ed. T. H. Aston, 8 vols. (Oxford: Clarendon Press, 1984–94)
Hobbes, *Behemoth*	Thomas Hobbes, *Behemoth, or The Long Parliament*, ed. Stephen Holmes (Chicago and London: University of Chicago Press, 1990)
Hobbes, *Leviathan*	Thomas Hobbes, *Leviathan*, ed. Richard Tuck, Cambridge Texts in the History of Political Thought (Cambridge: Cambridge University Press, 1996)
Hume, *Essays*	David Hume, *Essays Moral, Political, and Literary*, ed. Eugene F. Miller, rev. ed. (Indianapolis: Liberty Fund, 1985)
Johnson, *Lives*	Samuel Johnson, *The Lives of the Poets*, ed. Roger Lonsdale, 4 vols. (Oxford: Clarendon Press, 2006)
Johnson, *Works*	*The Works of the Late Reverend Mr. Samuel Johnson* (1710)
Jones, *Continuation*	David Jones, *A Continuation of the Secret History of White-Hall* (1697)
Jones, *First Whigs*	J. R. Jones, *The First Whigs: The Politics of the Exclusion Crisis 1678–1683* (London: Oxford University Press, 1961)
Jones, *History of Europe*	David Jones, *A Compleat History of Europe* (1698)
Jones, *Secret History*	David Jones, *The Secret History of White-Hall* (1697)
Jones, *Theatre of Wars*	David Jones, *A Theatre of Wars between England and France* (1698)
Jones, *Tragical History*	David Jones, *The Tragical History of the Stuarts* (1697)
Kenyon, *Stuart England*	J. P. Kenyon, *Stuart England* (Harmondsworth: Allen Lane, 1978)

Knolles, *Turkes*	Richard Knolles, *The Generall Historie of the Turkes* (1603)
Life of Chesterfield	*The Life of the Late Earl of Chesterfield* (Philadelphia, 1775)
Locke, *Treatises*	John Locke, *Two Treatises of Government*, ed. Peter Laslett, Cambridge Texts in the History of Political Thought (Cambridge: Cambridge University Press, 1960)
Ludlow, *Memoirs*	Edmund Ludlow, *Memoirs*, 3 vols. ("Vevey" [i.e., London], 1698–99)
Ludlow, *Voyce*	Edmund Ludlow, *A Voyce from the Watch Tower, Part Five: 1660–1662*, ed. A. B. Worden, Camden Fourth Series, vol. 21 (London: Royal Historical Society, 1978)
Macaulay, *History*	Thomas Macaulay, *The History of England from the Accession of James the Second*, ed. C. H. Firth, 6 vols. (London: Macmillan, 1915)
Machiavelli, *Chief Works*	Niccolò Machiavelli, *The Chief Works and Others*, trans. Allan Gilbert, 3 vols. (Durham, N.C.: Duke University Press, 1965)
Machiavelli, *Opere*	Niccolò Machiavelli, *Opere*, ed. Mario Bonfantini, La letteratura italiana: Storia e testi, vol. 29 (Milano e Napoli: Riccardo Ricciardi, 1954)
Machiavelli, *The Prince*	Niccolò Machiavelli, *The Prince*, trans. Peter Bondanella (Oxford: Oxford University Press, 2005)
Machiavelli, *Tutte l'opere*	*Tutte l'opere di Niccolò Machiavelli segretario e cittadino Fiorentino*, 3 vols. ("Londra," 1772)
Machiavelli, *Works*	*The Works of the Famous Nicholas Machiavel*, 3rd ed. (1720)

Malcolm, *Reason of State*	Noel Malcolm, *Reason of State, Propaganda, and the Thirty Years' War: An Unknown Translation by Thomas Hobbes* (Oxford: Clarendon Press, 2007)
Manning, *Apprenticeship*	Roger B. Manning, *An Apprenticeship in Arms: The Origins of the British Army 1585–1702* (Oxford: Oxford University Press, 2006)
Marvell, *Poems and Letters*	*The Poems and Letters of Andrew Marvell*, ed. H. M. Margoliouth, 2nd ed., 2 vols. (Oxford: Clarendon Press, 1952)
Marvell, *Prose Works*	*The Prose Works of Andrew Marvell*, ed. M. Dzelzainis, Annabel Patterson, Nicholas von Maltzahn, and N. H. Keeble, 2 vols. (New Haven: Yale University Press, 2003)
May, *History*	Thomas May, *The History of the Parliament of England* (1647)
Miller, *James II*	John Miller, *James II* (New Haven: Yale University Press, 2000)
Molesworth, *Denmark*	Robert Molesworth, *An Account of Denmark*, ed. Justin Champion (Indianapolis: Liberty Fund, 2011)
Montagu, *Reflections*	Edward Wortley Montagu, *Reflections on the Rise and Fall of the Ancient Republicks*, ed. David Womersley (Indianapolis: Liberty Fund, 2015)
More, *Utopia*	Sir Thomas More, *Utopia*, ed. George M. Logan and Robert M. Adams, rev. ed., Cambridge Texts in the History of Political Thought (Cambridge: Cambridge University Press, 2002)
Neville, *Plato Redivivus*	Henry Neville, *Plato Redivivus*, in Caroline Robbins (ed.), *Two English Republican Tracts* (Cambridge: Cambridge University Press, 1969)

Novak, *Defoe*   Maximillian E. Novak, *Daniel Defoe: Master of Fictions* (Oxford: Oxford University Press, 2001)

ODNB   *Oxford Dictionary of National Biography*

OED   *Oxford English Dictionary*

Oeuvres complètes   Montesquieu, *Oeuvres complètes*, ed. Daniel Oster (Paris: du Seuil, 1964)

POAS   *Poems on Affairs of State: Augustan Satirical Verse, 1660–1714*, ed. G. de F. Lord et al., 7 vols. (New Haven: Yale University Press, 1963–75)

Pocock, *Harrington*   *The Political Works of James Harrington*, ed. J. G. A. Pocock (Cambridge: Cambridge University Press, 1977)

Pocock, *Moment*   J. G. A. Pocock, *The Machiavellian Moment: Florentine Political Thought and the Atlantic Republican Tradition* (Princeton, N.J.: Princeton University Press, 1975)

Richetti, *Defoe*   John Richetti, *The Life of Daniel Defoe* (Oxford: Blackwell Publishing, 2005)

Robbins, *Commonwealthman*   Caroline Robbins, *The Eighteenth-Century Commonwealthman: Studies in the Transmission, Development and Circumstance of English Liberal Thought from the Restoration of Charles II until the War with the Thirteen Colonies* (Cambridge, Mass.: Harvard University Press, 1961)

Rushworth, *Collections*   John Rushworth, *Historical Collections* (1659)

Rycaut, *Present State*   Paul Rycaut, *The Present State of the Ottoman Empire*, 3rd ed. (1670)

Sanderson, *History*   Sir William Sanderson, *A Compleat History of the Life and Raigne of King Charles* (1658)

Schwoerer, *Armies*	Lois G. Schwoerer, *"No Standing Armies!":* *The Antiarmy Ideology in Seventeenth-Century England* (Baltimore: Johns Hopkins University Press, 1974)
Schwoerer, "Chronology"	Lois G. Schwoerer, "Chronology and Authorship of the Standing Army Tracts, 1697–1699," *Notes and Queries* 211 (1966): 382–90
Sharpe, *Personal Rule*	Kevin Sharpe, *The Personal Rule of Charles I* (New Haven: Yale University Press, 1992)
Sidney, *Discourses*	Algernon Sidney, *Discourses Concerning Government*, ed. Thomas G. West (Indianapolis: Liberty Fund, 1990)
Skinner, *Foundations*	Quentin Skinner, *The Foundations of Modern Political Thought*, 2 vols. (Cambridge: Cambridge University Press, 1978)
Smith, *Correspondence*	*Correspondence of Adam Smith*, ed. E. C. Mossner and J. S. Ross (Oxford: Clarendon Press, 1977)
Smith, *Wealth of Nations*	Adam Smith, *An Inquiry into the Nature and Causes of the Wealth of Nations*, ed. R. H. Campbell and A. S. Skinner, 2 vols. (Oxford: Clarendon Press, 1976; Indianapolis: Liberty Fund, 1982)
Speck, *Revolutionaries*	W. A. Speck, *Reluctant Revolutionaries: Englishmen and the Revolution of 1688* (Oxford: Oxford University Press, 1988)
Stuart Constitution	J. P. Kenyon (ed.), *The Stuart Constitution 1603–1688: Documents and Commentary* (Cambridge: Cambridge University Press, 1966)
Swift, *Correspondence*	*The Correspondence of Jonathan Swift, D.D.*, ed. David Woolley, 4 vols. (Frankfurt: Peter Lang, 1999–2007)

Swift, *Prose Writings*	*The Prose Writings of Jonathan Swift*, ed. Herbert Davis et al., 14 vols. (Oxford: Basil Blackwell, 1939–68)
Temple, *Memoirs*	William Temple, *Memoirs of What Past in Christendom, From the War Begun in 1672. To the Peace Concluded 1679* (1692)
Temple, *Works*	*The Works of Sir William Temple*, 2 vols. (1720)
Toland, *Restoring*	John Toland, *The Art of Restoring* (1714)
Twysden, *Scriptores*	Sir Roger Twysden, *Historiae Anglicanae Scriptores X* (1652)
Vertot, *Sweden*	Abbé Vertot, *The History of the Revolutions in Sweden, Occasioned by the Change of Religion, and Alteration of the Government in that Kingdom*, trans. J. Mitchel (1696)
Vindiciae	"Stephanus Junius Brutus, the Celt," *Vindiciae, Contra Tyrannos*, ed. and trans. George Garnett (Cambridge: Cambridge University Press, 1994)
Whole Kingdoms	[John, Lord Somers?], *The Judgment of Whole Kingdoms and Nations* (1710)
William, *Declaration*	*The Declaration of His Highnes William Henry, By the Grace of God Prince of Orange, &c* (1688)

John Trenchard and Walter Moyle

An Argument Shewing that a
Standing Army Is Inconsistent with
a Free Government

1697

1. "The stag could get the better of the horse in fighting, and used to expel him from their common pasture, until the loser in their long struggle implored the help of man and took the bit. But when afterward, glorying in his triumph, he parted from his foe, he could dislodge neither the rider from his back, nor the bit from his mouth" (Horace, *Epistles*, I.x.34–38). See also Aesop, *Fables*, fab. 45, "Of the Horse and the Stag," pp. 70–72, and Phaedrus, *Fabulae Aesopiae*, IV.4 (where, however, the horse contends with a boar, not a stag). This fable was commonly cited in early modern resistance theory (e.g., *Vindiciae*, p. 92) as a reminder that the roots of monarchical power lay in fraud and coercion, rather than in that "general consent" which is the foundation of just governments (Sidney, *Discourses*, pp. 30–31). In 1698 this Horatian epistle would be paraphrased by Walter Pope, who explained its moral as "*May they, who t'enslave England are inclind, / No better Usage, from their Rider, find*" (Walter Pope, *Moral and Political Fables, Ancient and Modern* [1698], pp. 110–13). It would be alluded to by Chesterfield in 1738 when he spoke in the House of Lords against a standing army:

> The young fiery courser is never brought at once to submit to the curb, and patiently to take his rider upon his back. If you put the bit into his mouth, without any previous preparation, or put a weak and unskilful rider upon his back, he will probably break the neck of his rider: but by degrees you may make him tamely submit to both. A free people must be treated in the same manner: by degrees they must be accustomed to be governed by an army; by degrees that army must be made strong enough to hold them in subjection. (*Life of Chesterfield*, pp. 34–35)

AN
ARGUMENT,
Shewing, that a
STANDING ARMY
Is inconsistent with
A Free Government, and absolutely destructive
to the Constitution of the English Monarchy.

Cervus Equum pugna melior communibus herbis
Pellebat, donec minor in certamine longo
Imploravit opes hominis fraenumq; recepit.
Sed postquam victor violens discessit ab hoste,
Non Equitem dorso, non fraenum depulit ore.
                              Horat. Epist. 10.[1]

LONDON;
Printed in the Year 1697.

Dedication,

To all those whom it may concern.
Qui capit ille facit.[2]

When I consider your great Zeal to your Country, how much you have expos'd your selves for its Service, and how little you have improved your own Fortunes, I think it is but Justice to your Merits to make your Encomiums the Preface to the following Discourse. 'Tis you that have abated the Pride, and reduced the Luxury of the Kingdom: You have been the Physicians and Divines of the Commonwealth, by purging it of that Dross and Dung, which corrupts the Minds, and destroys the Souls of Men. You have convinced us that there is no Safety in Counsellors, nor Trust to be put in Ships under your Conduct.

You have clear'd the Seas, not of Pyrats,[3] *but of our own Merchants, and by that means have made our Prisons as so many Store-houses to replenish your Troops. In fine, to use the Expression of the Psalmist,* Your Hearts are unsearchable for Wisdom, and there is no finding out your Understanding.[4]

---

2. A Latin tag meaning literally "he who takes it, makes it"; i.e., those who take offense at a remark thereby demonstrate that it applies to them. The English saying "If the cap fits, wear it" is an approximate equivalent. For a similar usage in a political work, see William Sancroft (?), *Modern Policies, Taken from Machiavel, Borgia, and Other Choice Authors* (1657), "To the Reader," sigs. A6ᵛ–A7ʳ: "*This Book is like a Garment in a Brokers Shop, not designed to any one person, but made for any that it fits.*"

3. The later seventeenth century was the golden age of piracy. For a contemporary account of the reasons for its recent growth, see Anonymous, *Piracy Destroy'd* (1701).

4. A conflation of Proverbs 25:3 ("the heart of kings is unsearchable") and Isaiah 40:28 ("Hast thou not known? hast thou not heard, that the everlasting God, the

5

When I consider all this, and [iv] *compare your Merits with your Preferments,
how you came by them, and your behaviour in them, I cannot but think a
Standing Army a Collateral Security to your Title to them, and therefore must
commend your Policy in promoting it.* For by these Kings reign, and Princes
decree Justice.[5] *These will be our Magistrates, who will not bear the Sword in
vain. These, like the Sons of* Aaron,[6] *will wear their* Urim *and* Thummim[7] *on
their Backs and Breasts, and will be our Priests, who will hew the Sinners to
pieces, as* Samuel *did* Agag *before the Lord in* Gilgal.[8] *By these you will be
able to teach us Passive Obedience,*[9] *as Men having Authority, and not as the*

Lord, the Creator of the ends of the earth, fainteth not, neither is weary? there is
no searching of his understanding").

5. Proverbs 8:15.

6. The Book of Exodus describes how Aaron and his sons were anointed and
consecrated as a perpetual caste of priests at the hands of Moses and by the express
command of God. However, it was also Aaron who made the Golden Calf that
was idolatrously worshipped by the Jews (Exodus 32:1–6).

7. Divinatory devices that formed part of the vestments of the early Jewish
priests. In the late seventeenth century, however, the phrase might also bear a taint
of freethinking or religious skepticism. In 1669 John Spencer, in his *Dissertatio de
Urim et Thummim,* had argued that elements of Jewish religion had been borrowed
from the Egyptians, an argument which clearly possessed explosive implications
for Christianity.

8. "Then said Samuel, Bring ye hither to me Agag the king of the Amalekites.
And Agag came unto him delicately. And Agag said, Surely the bitterness of
death is past. And Samuel said, As thy sword hath made women childless, so shall
thy mother be childless among women. And Samuel hewed Agag in pieces before
the LORD in Gilgal" (1 Samuel 15:32–33).

9. "Passive obedience" was originally the submission of Christ to the will of his
Father, leading to his suffering and death upon the Cross. It was applied by extension to the duty of the subject not to resist the supreme power in the state (*OED,*
s.v. "obedience"). Though it was claimed by the Stuarts and their apologists to be
a perpetual, divine, and natural law of obligation, the idea of passive obedience
had recently been subjected to a withering Whig critique, which had exposed both
its conceptual deformity and its relative novelty as a political doctrine. Locke had
eloquently mocked the ethical monstrosity buried within it:

Who would not think it an admirable Peace betwixt the Mighty and the
Mean, when the Lamb, without resistance, yielded his Throat to be torn by
the imperious Wolf? *Polyphemus*'s Den gives us a perfect Pattern of such a
Peace, and such a Government, wherein *Ulysses* and his Companions had
nothing to do, but quietly to suffer themselves to be devour'd. And no doubt
Ulysses, who was a prudent Man, preach'd up *Passive Obedience,* and

Scribes. You will have your Reasons in your Hands against resisting the higher Powers, and will prove your Jus Divinum[10] *by the Sword of the Lord and of* Gideon.[11]

Your Honours most obedient Slave and Vassal,[12]
A. B. C. D. E. F. G.

---

exhorted them to a quiet Submission, by representing to them of what concernment Peace was to Mankind; and by shewing the inconveniencies might happen, if they should offer to resist *Polyphemus*, who had now the power over them. (Locke, *Treatises*, p. 417)

Writing of the middle ages, Roger Coke had observed that the "Doctrines of Passive Obedience, and submitting to the Absolute Will and Pleasure of the King, were Strangers to those Days," and he traced the inception of this, to his eyes, incoherent political doctrine to no earlier than 1678:

The *Tories* had got a new invented Doctrine of inconsistible Terms, called, *Passive Obedience:* I would willingly be informed in the Grammatical Construction of these two Words, how a Noun Adjective or Participle, can alter the Signification of a Noun Substantive; for if any one be subject to another, and be commanded or forbidden by this other, it is Disobedience if he does not the Command of this other: How therefore Passive joined to Disobedience, can make it Obedience, had need of a better Interpretation than what the *Tories* give; which is, if you cannot obey, you must suffer: But this is another Proposition; and so Disobedience here is Disobedience still; and the true Construction of *Passive Obedience*, is Disobedience, and be hang'd for it. (Coke, *Detection*, pp. 206, 531–32)

See also Sidney, *Discourses*, p. 15, and *Whole Kingdoms*, pp. 44–67.

10. "Divine right," the principle on which Stuart kings had rested their kingly authority. See. J. N. Figgis, *The Divine Right of Kings* (Cambridge: Cambridge University Press, 1914).

11. The battle cry of the Jews against the "host of Midian" (Judges 7:18, 20).

12. Deliberately provocative terms here used with mordant sarcasm.

An Argument, *shewing that a* Standing Army *Is Inconsistent with a free Government, and absolutely destructive to the Constitution of the English Monarchy*

When I consider what a dismal Scene of Blood and Desolation hath appeared upon the Theatre of *Europe* during the Growth and Progress of the *French* Power,[13] I cannot sufficiently applaud and admire our thrice happy Situation, by which we have long enjoy'd an uninterrupted course of Peace and Prosperity, whilst our Neighbouring Nations have been miserably harassed by perpetual War: For lying open to continual Invasion, they can never enjoy Quiet and Security, nor take a sound Sleep, but, *Hercules* like, with Clubs in their hands:[14] So that these Halcyon Days[15] which we enjoy amidst such an universal Hurricane, must be solely attributed to our Tutelar God *Neptune*, who with a Guard of winged Coursers so strongly intrenches us, that we may be said to be *mediâ*

13. The militaristic and expansionist policy of France under Louis XIV had alarmed Europe, and its frustration was the long-standing ambition of William of Orange, later William III of England. At the moment of publication, English forces had very recently been in action on the Continent against the French in the War of the League of Augsburg (1689–97), which had been concluded by the Treaty of Ryswick in October 1697.

14. The son of Zeus and Alcmene, Heracles or Hercules was one of the legendary Greco-Roman heroes. He is often depicted with a club, which was said to be his favorite weapon.

15. Fourteen days of calm weather, anciently believed to occur about the winter solstice when the halcyon was brooding (*OED*, s.v. "halcyon," B1). Hence, a period of temporary but precious peace. For contemporary usage, see, e.g., Jones, *Secret History*, p. 14.

9

insuperabiles undâ,[16] and not unfitly compar'd to the Earth, which stands fix'd and immoveable, and never to be shaken but by an internal Convulsion. And as Nature has been thus liberal to us in our Situation, so the Luxuriancy of our Soil makes it productive of numerous Commodities [2] fit for Trade and Commerce: And as this Trade renders us Masters of the Silver and Gold of the East and West without our toiling in the Mine, so it breeds us multitudes of able-bodied and skilful Seamen to defend the Treasures they bring home, that even Luxury it self,[17] which has been the Bane and Destruction of most Countries where it has been predominant, may in some measure be esteemed our Preservation, by breeding up a Race of Men amongst us, whose manner of Life will never suffer them to be debauched, or enervated with Ease or Idleness. But we have one thing more to boast of besides all these Felicities, and that is, of being Free-men and not Slaves in this unhappy Age, when an universal Deluge of Tyranny[18] has overspread the face of the whole Earth; so that this is the Ark out of which if the Dove[19] be sent forth, she will find no resting place till her Return.

Our Constitution is a limited mix'd Monarchy, where the King enjoys all the Prerogatives necessary to the support of his Dignity, and

16. "Unconquerable in the midst of the waves"; a reworking of Virgil, *Aeneid*, III.202 ("nec meminisse viae media Palinurus in unda"; "Palinurus did not remember the way amid the waves," part of Aeneas's description of the Trojans' voyage from the sack of Troy).

17. Ancient historians such as Sallust had identified the taste for luxury and the consequent avidity for money as a source of Roman decline (e.g., *Bellum Jugurthinum*, XXXV.10). In the early modern period the association between luxury and political corruption had strengthened into a cardinal element in civic humanist republicanism (see Pocock, *Moment*, pp. 135–37 and 430–31). A suspicion of luxury was also common among vulgar Whig thinkers, although later in the eighteenth century scientific or philosophical Whigs such as David Hume would construct subtle arguments against the prejudice that luxury was "the source of all the corruptions, disorders, and factions, incident to civil government" ("Of Refinement in the Arts," in Hume, *Essays*, p. 269).

18. Trenchard and Moyle have in mind not only the growth of monarchical absolutism in France since the accession of Louis XIV in 1643 but also the recent subversion of a number of originally "free" governments (such as that of Denmark: see below, p. 21, n. 50).

19. Genesis 8:6–12.

Protection of his People, and is only abridged from the Power of injuring his own Subjects: In short, the Man is loose, and the Beast only bound; and our Government may truly be called an Empire of Laws, and not of Men;[20] for every Man has the same right to what he can acquire by his Labour and Industry, as the King hath to his Crown, and the meanest Subject hath his Remedy against him in his Courts at *Westminster:* No Man can be imprisoned, unless he has transgressed a Law of his own making, nor be try'd but by his own Neighbours; so that we enjoy a Liberty scarce known to the antient *Greeks* and *Romans.*

And lest the extraordinary Power intrusted in the Crown should lean towards Arbitrary Government, or the tumultuary Licentiousness of the People should encline towards a Democracy, the Wisdom of our Ancestors hath instituted a middle State, *viz.* of Nobility, whose Interest it is to trim [3] this Boat of our Commonwealth, and to skreen the People against the Insults of the Prince, and the Prince against the Popularity of the Commons, since if either Extream prevail so far as to oppress the other, they are sure to be overwhelmed in their Ruin. And the meeting of these three States in Parliament is what we call our Government: for without all their Consents no Law can be made, nor a Penny of Money levied upon the Subjects; so that the King's Necessities do often oblige him to summon this Court, which is the Grand Inquest of the Kingdom, where the People speak boldly their Grievances, and call to account overgrown Criminals, who are above the reach of ordinary Justice: so that the Excellence of this Government consists in the due ballance of the several constituent Parts of it, for if either one of them should be too hard for the other two, there is an actual Dissolution of the Constitution; but whilst

---

20. An allusion to Livy's praise of the early Roman Republic following the expulsion of the Tarquins: "The new liberty enjoyed by the Roman people, their achievements in peace and war, annual magistracies, and laws superior in authority to men will henceforth be my subject"; "liberi iam hinc populi Romani res pace belloque gestas, annuos magistratus imperiaque legum potentiora quam hominum peragam" (*Ab Urbe Condita*, II.i.1: cf. Aristotle, *Politics*, III.xvi). For significant earlier seventeenth-century English discussion, see Harrington, *Oceana*, p. 20. The tag was popular among commonwealth Whigs: see, e.g., Sidney, *Discourses*, pp. 17, 472.

we can continue in our present Condition, we may without Vanity reckon our selves the happiest People in the World.

But as there is no degree of Human Happiness but is accompanied with some Defects, and the strongest Constitutions are most liable to certain Diseases; so the very Excellence of our Government betrays it to some Inconveniences, the Wheels and Motions of it being so curious and delicate that it is often out of order, and therefore we ought to apply our utmost Endeavours to rectify and preserve it: and I am afraid it is more owing to the accident of our Situation, than to our own Wisdom, Integrity or Courage, that it has yet a Being; when we see most Nations in *Europe* over-run with Oppression and Slavery, where the Lives, Estates and Liberties of the People are subject to the lawless Fancy and Ambition of the Prince, and the Rapine and Insolence of his Officers; where the Nobility, that were formerly the bold Assertors of their Countries Liberty, are now only the Ensigns and Ornaments of the Tyranny, and the People Beasts [4] of Burden, and barely kept alive to support the Luxury and Prodigality of their Masters.

And if we enquire how these unhappy Nations have lost that precious Jewel *Liberty*, and we as yet preserved it, we shall find their Miseries and our Happiness proceed from this, That their Necessities or Indiscretion have permitted a standing Army to be kept amongst them, and our Situation rather than our Prudence, hath as yet defended us from it, otherwise we had long since lost what is the most valuable thing under Heaven: For, as I said before, our Constitution depending upon a due ballance between King, Lords and Commons, and that Ballance depending upon their mutual Occasions and Necessities they have of one another; if this Cement be once broke, there is an actual Dissolution of the Government. Now this Ballance can never be preserved but by an Union of the natural and artificial Strength of the Kingdom, that is, by making the Militia to consist of the same Persons as have the Property; or otherwise the Government is violent and against Nature, and cannot possibly continue, but the Constitution must either break the Army, or the Army will destroy the Constitution: for it is universally true, that where-ever the Militia is, there is or will be the Government in a short time; and therefore the

Institutors of this Gothick Balance[21] (which was established in all Parts of *Europe*) made the Militia to consist of the same Parts as the Government, where the King was General, the Lords by virtue of their Castles and Honours, the great Commanders, and the Freeholders by their Tenures the Body of the Army; so that it was next to impossible for an Army thus constituted to act to the disadvantage of the Constitution, unless we could suppose them to be Felons *de se*.[22] And here I will venture to assert that upon no other Foundation than this, can any Nation long preserve its Freedom, unless some very particular Accidents contribute to it; and I hope I shall make it [5] appear, that no Nation ever preserved its Liberty, that maintained an Army otherwise constituted within the Seat of their Government: and let us flatter our selves as much as we please, what happened yesterday, will come to pass again; and the same Causes will produce like Effects in all Ages.

And here I can't avoid taking notice of some Gentlemen[23] who a few Years since were the pretended Patriots of their Country, who had nothing in their Mouths but the sacred Name of *Liberty*, who in the late Reigns could hardly afford the King the Prerogative that was due to him,[24] and

21. An allusion to the widespread belief that the political institutions of the primitive Germans (or Goths) contained elements which were protective of individual liberty, such as elective monarchy, trial by jury, militias rather than professional armed forces, and regular consultative assemblies. In the wake of the collapse of the Roman Empire in the West in the fifth century A.D. and the consequent descent of the northern barbarians into southern Europe, these political institutions had spread throughout the continent. For a typical account of this process, see Fletcher, *Political Works*, p. 3, and below, p. 152–53. Cf. also Sidney, *Discourses*, p. 167.

22. I.e., suicides. In the late seventeenth and early eighteenth centuries the phrase was often used in a political context to refer to a people's or a parliament's suicidal blindness to its natural self-interest: see, e.g., Marvell, *Prose Works*, 2: 297–98; Neville, *Plato Redivivus*, p. 174; Jones, *History of Europe*, p. 233; Toland, *Restoring*, p. 6; and Blackmore, *History*, p. 5.

23. I.e., the Court Whigs.

24. The royal prerogative is the special right or privilege exercised by the British monarch over all other persons; in particular, the special privileges of action they enjoy under the common law (*OED*, s.v. "prerogative," 2a). The phrase "the late reigns" refers to the reigns of Charles II and James II, when attempts by the king to enlarge the scope and operation of the royal prerogative were a source of

which was absolutely necessary to put in motion this Machine of our Government, and to make the Springs and Wheels of it act naturally, and perform their Function: I say, these Gentlemen that could not with Patience hear of the King's ordinary Guards, can now discourse familiarly of twenty thousand Men to be maintained in times of Peace; and the odious Excuse they give for this infamous Apostacy is, that if they should not gratify the Court in this modest Request, another Party may be caressed who will grant this, or any thing else which is asked, and then they say matters will be much worse; as if Arbitrary Government was a different thing in their hands, from what it is in others, or that the Lineaments and Features of Tyranny would become graceful and lovely when they are its *Valet de Chambres*.[25] But let them not deceive themselves, for if they think to make their Court this way, they will quickly find themselves outflattered by the Party they fear,[26] who have been long the Darlings of Arbitrary Power, and whose Principles as well as Practices teach them to be Enemies to all the legal Rights, and just Liberties of their Native Country; and so these wretched Bunglers will be made use of only to bring together the Materials of Tyranny, and then must give place to more expert Architects to finish the Building.

[6] And tho we are secure from any Attempts of this kind during the Reign of a Prince[27] who hath rescued us from a Captivity equal to what *Moses* redeemed the People of *Israel* from:[28] A Prince whose Life is so

---

grievance and ultimately of political instability. The "late reigns" loomed large in the "country" political imagination during the 1690s:

> The back-benchers' historical sense was also revealed in the assumption that any shortcoming in William's government must be, in some sense, a survival from Charles and James's days. The Restoration court had become such a paradigm of corruption, that it seems to have been difficult for Clarges and his allies to imagine abuses unconnected with it. The corrupt methods of contemporary courtiers were usually traced back to the 1670s and 1680s, so that the charge against William's executive became the perpetuation of old evils rather than the invention of new. (Claydon, *William III*, p. 200; and cf. p. 203, where Claydon discusses the use of the trope of "the late reigns" in the standing army pamphlets)

25. Manservants.
26. I.e., the Tories.
27. I.e., William III.
28. Exodus 2–15.

necessary to the Preservation of *Europe*, that both Protestant and Popish Princes have forgot their antient Maxims, and laid aside their innate Animosities, and made it their common Interest to chuse him their Patron and Protector: A Prince in whom we know no Vices but what have been esteemed Vertues in others, *viz.* his undeserved Clemency to his Enemies,[29] and his exposing too much that Life upon which depends not only our Safety, but the Liberties of all *Europe*, and the Protestant Religion through the World: I say, was this most excellent Prince to be immortal (as his Great and Glorious Actions) we ought in common Prudence to abandon all thoughts of Self-preservation, and wholly to rely on his Care and Conduct. But since no Vertue nor pitch of Glory will exempt him from paying the common Debt to Nature,[30] but Death hath a Scythe which cuts off the most noble Lives; we ought not to intrust any Power with him, which we don't think proper to be continued to his Successors: and doubtless our great Benefactor will not regret this, or any thing else that can reasonably be demanded in order to compleat that Deliverance so far advanced by his invincible Courage and Conduct; for to set us, like *Moses*, within view of the promised Land,[31] with a *ne plus ultra*,[32] is the greatest of all Human Infelicities, and such I shall always

29. Clemency was one of the virtues attributed to Julius Caesar (Suetonius, "Divus Iulius," LXXIII–LXXV).

30. A periphrasis for dying; cf. Titus Oates, *Eikon basilike, or, The picture of the late King James* (1696), p. 91.

31. And Moses went up from the plains of Moab unto the mountain of Nebo, to the top of Pisgah, that is over against Jericho. And the LORD shewed him all the land of Gilead, unto Dan, and all Naphtali, and the land of Ephraim, and Manasseh, and all the land of Judah, unto the utmost sea, and the south, and the plain of the valley of Jericho, the city of palm trees, unto Zoar. And the LORD said unto him, This is the land which I sware unto Abraham, unto Isaac, and unto Jacob, saying, I will give it unto thy seed: I have caused thee to see it with thine eyes, but thou shalt not go over thither. (Deuteronomy 34:1–4)

32. I.e. [go] no further (*OED*, s.v. "ne plus ultra," 2). According to ancient mythology this phrase (or, in some accounts, "nec plus ultra" or "non plus ultra") was engraved on the Pillars of Hercules which guarded the western mouth of the Mediterranean. Charles V had taken the phrase "plus ultra" for his motto, the deletion of the negative signifying his imperial ambitions in the New World.

take our Case to be, whilst a standing Army must be kept up to prey upon our Entrails, and which must in the hands of an ill Prince (which we have the misfortune frequently to meet with) infallibly destroy our Constitution. And this is so evident and important a Truth, that no Legislator ever founded a free Government, but avoided this *Caribdis*,[33] as a Rock against which his Commonwealth must certainly be shipwrack'd, as the *Israelites, Athenians, Corin[7]thians, Achaians, Lacedemonians, Thebans, Samnites,* and *Romans;* none of which Nations whilst they kept their Liberty were ever known to maintain any Souldiers in constant Pay within their Cities, or ever suffered any of their Subjects to make War their Profession; well knowing that the Sword and Sovereignty always march hand in hand, and therefore they trained their own Citizens and the Territories about them perpetually in Arms, and their whole Commonwealths by this means became so many several formed Militias: A general Exercise of the best of their People in the use of Arms, was the only Bulwark of their Liberties; this was reckon'd the surest way to preserve them both at home and abroad, the People being secured thereby as well against the Domestick Affronts of any of their own Citizens, as against the Foreign Invasions of ambitious and unruly Neighbours. Their Arms were never lodg'd in the hands of any who had not an Interest in preserving the publick Peace, who fought *pro aris & focis,*[34] and thought themselves sufficiently paid by repelling Invaders, that they might with freedom return to their own Affairs. In those days there was no difference between the Citizen, the Souldier, and the Husbandman, for all promiscuously took Arms when the publick Safety required it, and afterwards laid them down with more Alacrity than they took them up:[35] So

33. In Greek legend, a dangerous whirlpool off the coast of Sicily, opposite the cave of the sea monster Scylla. For Odysseus's passage between these twin perils, see *Odyssey* XII. For contemporary usage in the context of recent political history, see Jones, *Secret History,* p. 55. The following paragraphs show a general debt to a passage in Marchamont Nedham's *The Excellencie of a Free-State* (1656); see the edition of that text by Blair Worden in the Thomas Hollis Library (Indianapolis: Liberty Fund, 2011), pp. lviii, n. 98, and 90–92.

34. I.e., for their religion (*aris,* "altars") and their homes and families (*focis,* "hearths"). Cf. Marvell, *Prose Works,* 2:272 and n. 268.

35. "The danger of luxury . . . is not that it produces effeminacy of taste or even mutability of fashion, so much as that it leads to choice and consequently to specialization" (Pocock, *Moment,* p. 430).

that we find amongst the *Romans* the best and bravest of their Generals came from the Plough, contentedly returning when the Work was over,[36] and never demanded their Triumphs[37] till they had laid down their Commands, and reduced themselves to the state of private Men. Nor do we find that this famous Commonwealth ever permitted a Deposition of their Arms in any other hands, till their Empire increasing, Necessity constrained them to erect a constant stipendiary Souldiery abroad in Foreign Parts, either for the holding or winning of Provinces: Then Luxury increasing with Dominion, the strict Rule and Discipline [8] of Freedom soon abated, and Forces were kept up at home, which soon prov'd of such dangerous Consequence, that the People were forced to make a Law to employ them at a convenient distance; which was, that if any General marched over the River *Rubicon*,[38] he should be declar'd a publick Enemy: and in the Passage of that River this following Inscription was erected; *Imperator sive miles, sive Tyrannus armatus quisquis sistito, vexillumq; armaq; deponito, nec citra hunc amnem trajicito:*[39] and this made *Cesar* when he

36. The most famous example of such austere rectitude was Lucius Quinctius Cincinnatus. In 458 B.C. Cincinnatus was called from his plough and made dictator to lead an army charged with rescuing Roman forces besieged by the Aequi on Mount Algidus. Having defeated the Aequi and rescued his fellow citizens, Cincinnatus laid aside his office and returned to his farm (Livy, *Ab Urbe Condita*, III. xxvi–xxix). Livy points out that the story of Cincinnatus is a rebuke to those "who despise all human qualities in comparison with riches, and think there is no room for great honors or for worth but amid a profusion of wealth"; "qui omnia prae divitiis humana spernunt neque honori magno locum neque virtuti putant esse, nisi ubi effuse afluant opes" (III.xxvi.7), and he goes on to remark with admiration that "on the sixteenth day Quinctius surrendered the dictatorship which he had received for six months"; "Quinctius sexto decimo die dictatura in sex menses accepta se abdicavit" (III.xxix.7). See also Machiavelli, *Discourses*, bk. 3, chap. 25.

37. The Roman triumph consisted of a procession incorporating religious elements, which was granted by the Senate to a victorious general in celebration of a successful and important campaign against a foreign enemy. For commentary, see most recently Mary Beard, *The Roman Triumph* (Cambridge, Mass.: Belknap, 2007).

38. A small river falling into the Adriatic a little to the north of modern-day Rimini (known in antiquity as Ariminum). It marked the boundary between republican Italy and the province of Cisalpine Gaul.

39. "General, whether you are a soldier or a tyrant in arms, pause here; lay aside your standard and your weapons, and do not pass beyond this stream."

had presumed to pass this River, to think of nothing but pressing on to the total Oppression of the Empire, which he shortly after obtained.[40]

Nor, as I said before, did any Nation deviate from these Rules but they lost their Liberty; and of this kind there are infinite Examples, out of which I shall give a few in several Ages, which are most known, and occur to every ones reading.

The first Example I shall give is of *Pisistratus*, who artificially prevailing with the *Athenians* to allow him fifty Guards for the Defence of his Person, he so improv'd that Number, that he seiz'd upon the Castle and Government, destroy'd the Commonwealth, and made himself Tyrant of *Athens*.[41]

The *Corinthians* being in apprehension of their Enemies, made a Decree for four hundred Men to be kept to defend their City, and gave

40. A compressed version of Lucan's account of Caesar's crossing of the Rubicon: "When Caesar had crossed the stream and reached the Italian bank on the further side, he halted on the forbidden territory: 'Here,' he cried, 'here I leave peace behind me and legality which has been scorned already; henceforth I follow Fortune. Hereafter let me hear no more of agreements. In them I have put my trust long enough; now I must seek the arbitrament of war.' Thus spoke the leader and quickly urged his army on through the darkness of night"; "Caesar, ut adversam superato gurgite ripam / Attigit, Hesperiae vetitis et constitit arvis, / 'Hic,' ait, 'hic pacem temerataque iura relinquo; / Te, Fortuna, sequor. Procul hinc iam foedera sunto; / Credidimus satis his, utendum est iudice bello.' / Sic fatus noctis tenebris rapit agmina ductor / Inpiger, . . ." (*Pharsalia*, I.223–29).

41. Pisistratus (fl. 561–527 B.C.), Athenian tyrant. Herodotus relates how he seized power:

> Pisistratus then, having an eye to the sovereign power, raised up a third faction. He collected partisans and pretended to champion the hillmen; and this was his plan. Wounding himself and his mules, he drove his carriage into the marketplace with a tale that he had escaped from his enemies, who would have slain him (so he said) as he was driving into the country. So he besought the people that he might have a guard from them: and indeed he had won himself reputation in his command of the army against the Megarians, when he had taken Nisaea and performed other great exploits. Thus deceived, the Athenian people gave him a chosen guard of citizens, of whom Pisistratus made not spearmen but clubmen: for the retinue that followed him bore wooden clubs. These with Pisistratus rose and took the Acropolis; and Pisistratus ruled the Athenians, disturbing in no way the order of offices nor changing the laws, but governing the city according to its established constitution and ordering all things fairly and well. (I.59)

Tymophanes the Command over them, who overturned their Government, cut off all the principal Citizens, and proclaim'd himself King of *Corinth.*[42]

Agathocles being the Captain-General of the *Syracusians*, got such an Interest in the Army, that he cut all the Senators to pieces, and the richest of the People, and made himself their King.[43]

The *Romans* for fear of the *Teutones* and *Cimbri*, who like vast Inundations threatned their Empire, chose *Marius* their General, and, contrary to the Constitution of their Govern[9]ment, continued him five Years in his Command, which gave him such opportunity to insinuate, and gain an Interest in their Army, that he oppressed their Liberty: and to this were owing all the Miseries, Massacres, and Ruins which that City suffered under him and *Scylla*, who made the best Blood in the World run like Water in the Streets of *Rome*, and turn'd the whole City into a Shambles of the Nobility, Gentry and People.[44]

---

42. Timophanes (fl. 360 B.C.) was the brother of the statesman and general Timoleon. He was granted a force of four hundred mercenaries by the city of Corinth for the purpose of holding the city's rivals in check. However, Timophanes used his own great wealth to corrupt these mercenaries into his own private retinue. He was assassinated by Timoleon after putting to death a number of leading citizens. See Xenophon, *Hellenica*, VII.iv.6; Diodorus Siculus, XVI.lxv.3; and Plutarch, "Timoleon," IV.v.

43. Agathocles (361–289 B.C.) had been banished for twice attempting to overthrow the oligarchical party in the Sicilian city of Syracuse. Returning in 317 B.C. with an army of mercenaries, and notwithstanding an undertaking to observe the city's democratic constitution, he established himself as a tyrant and either banished or murdered some 10,000 citizens. In chap. 8 of *The Prince* Machiavelli had cited Agathocles as an example of "those who have become princes through wickedness" ("De his qui per scelera ad principatum pervenere"; Machiavelli, *The Prince*, pp. 30–32). Trenchard and Moyle seem to be loosely translating the following passage from chap. 8 of *The Prince* in what they say about Agathocles: "Ad uno cenno ordinato, fece da' sua soldati uccidere tutti e senatori e gli più ricchi del populo; li quali morti, occupò e tenne el principato di quella città sanza alcuna controversia civile." See also Harrington's comments: "Agathocles . . . being captain general of the Syracusans, upon a day assembled the senate and the people, as if he had something to communicate with them, when at a sign given he cut the senators in pieces to a man, and all the richest of the people, by which means he came to be king" (Harrington, *Oceana*, p. 57).

44. A severely compressed but largely accurate account of the civil conflict of 88 B.C. in Rome between Gaius Marius (157–86 B.C.), successful general, reorganizer

The same thing enabled *Cesar* totally to overthrow that famous Commonwealth; for the Prolongation of his Commission in *Gaul* gave him an opportunity to debauch his Army, and then upon a pretended Disgust he marched to *Rome*, drove out the Senators, seiz'd the Treasury, fought their Forces, and made himself perpetual Dictator.[45]

Olivaretto de Fermo desired leave of his fellow-Citizens, that he might be admitted into their Town with a hundred Horse of his Companions; which being granted, he put to the Sword all the principal Citizens, and proclaim'd himself their Prince.[46]

Francis Sforza being General of the *Milanese*, usurped upon them, and made himself Duke of *Millain*.[47]

---

of the Roman army, and seven times consul, and his former lieutenant Lucius Cornelius Sulla (or Sylla) (138–78 B.C.), the leader of the *optimates* or aristocratic party. Following the death of Marius and his own appointment as dictator in 82 or 81 B.C., Sulla purged the city of those he deemed undesirable by means of proscription. Although only 1,500 individuals were actually proscribed, it is estimated that some 9,000 were in fact killed.

45. Gaius Julius Caesar (102–44 B.C.) was proconsul in Gaul and Illyricum from 58 to 49 B.C., fighting the celebrated campaigns which extended Roman power to the shores of the northern Atlantic and established his own reputation as a military genius. Fearing prosecution from his enemies in the Senate once he was obliged to demit office, Caesar crossed the Rubicon (cf. above, p. 17, n. 38, and p. 18, n. 40) early in 49 B.C. at the head of the 13th Legion, thereby initiating the first Civil War. Once he had defeated the Republican party, Caesar returned to Rome in triumph and was made perpetual dictator, thus provoking the resentment which led to his assassination in 44 B.C. In chap. 16 of *The Prince* Machiavelli discusses Caesar as an example of a prince who indulged in unsustainable extravagance (Machiavelli, *The Prince*, p. 56).

46. Oliverotto of Fermo (1475–1502), a mercenary hailing from the Marche, seized power in Fermo in 1501, and then joined in a conspiracy against Cesare Borgia. Arrested at Senigallia, Oliverotto was strangled on Borgia's orders at the end of 1502. Machiavelli gives a very detailed account of Oliverotto's coup d'état in chap. 8 of *The Prince* (pp. 32–33). It is likely that this is the source that Trenchard and Moyle have summarized, but see also Harrington, *Oceana*, p. 57.

47. Francesco Sforza (1401–66) commanded a troop of mercenary soldiers in the pay of Duke Filippo Visconti of Milan (1412–47) and in 1441 married the duke's daughter Bianca Maria. After Visconti's death Sforza gradually assumed control of Milan, becoming duke in 1450. Machiavelli discusses Sforza in chap. 7 of *The Prince* as an example of "new principalities acquired with the arms of others and by Fortune" (Machiavelli, *The Prince*, p. 24; see also chap. 14, pp. 50–51). See also bk.

After *Christiern* the Second King of *Denmark* had conquer'd *Sweden*, he invited all the Senators and Nobility to a magnificent Entertainment, where after he had treated them highly for two days, he most barbarously butcher'd them: None escaped this Massacre but the brave *Gustavus Ericson*, who was then a Prisoner; but he afterwards escaping through a thousand Difficulties, by his good Fortune, Courage and Conduct, drove the *Danes* out of *Sweden*, and restor'd the *Swedes* to their ancient Kingdom. Nothing then was thought too great for their Generous Deliverer, every Mouth was full of his Praises, and by the Universal Voice of the People he was chosen their King; and to consummate the last Testimony of their Gratitude, they trusted him with an Army: [10] but they soon found their Mistake, for it cost them their Liberty; and having granted that *unum magnum*,[48] it was too late to dispute any thing else: His Successors having been pleased to take all the rest, and now they remain the miserable Examples of too credulous Generosity.[49]

The Story of *Denmark* is so generally known, and so well related by a late excellent Author, that it would be Impertinence in me to repeat it; only this I will observe, that if the King had not had an Army at his Command, the Nobles had never deliver'd up their Government.[50]

---

1 of *The Art of War* (Machiavelli, *Chief Works*, 2:574) and Neville, *Plato Redivivus*, p. 181.

48. That one great thing.

49. Christian (or Christiern) II (1481–1559), king of Denmark and Norway, 1513–23, and king of Sweden, 1520–23. Gustav Eriksson Vasa (1496?–1560), king of Sweden, 1523–60. The Stockholm Bloodbath (8–9 November 1520), a mass execution of Swedish nobles by Christian II, provoked resentment among the Swedish population at Danish rule. Gustav Vasa was able to capitalize upon this and become king. Although Vasa was considered a great king, his rule was harsh, and he kept a standing army. Swedish history was topical in England at this time. A translation of the detailed history by the Abbé Vertot of the events to which Trenchard and Moyle refer had been published the year before the appearance of their pamphlet (Vertot, *Sweden;* see pp. 109–13).

50. In 1694 Robert Molesworth had published *An Account of Denmark as it was in the Year 1692*, a pungently Whiggish history of the events which had led to Denmark's becoming an hereditary and absolute monarchy. Molesworth's version does not entirely corroborate Trenchard and Moyle's allegation that the threat of violence was crucial to the success of that coup d'état. Although Molesworth reports that the public oath-taking whereby the Danish aristocracy gave away their customary liberties took place in the presence of the soldiery and armed burghers, he

Our Countryman *Oliver Cromwell* turn'd out that Parliament under which he serv'd, and who had got Immortal Honour through the whole World by their great Actions; and this he effected by the Assistance of an Army, which must be allowed to have had as much Vertue, Sobriety, and publick Spirit, as hath been known in the World since amongst that sort of Men.[51]

The last Instance I shall give, is of a French Colony, as I remember in the *West Indies*, who having War with the neighbouring *Indians*, and being tired in their March with the extremity of Heat, made their Slaves carry their Arms, who taking that opportunity fell upon them, and cut them to pieces; a just Punishment for their Folly.[52] And this will always be the fate of those that trust their Arms out of their own hands: for it is a ridiculous Imagination to conceive Men will be Servants, when they can be Masters. And as Mr. *Harrington* judiciously observes, Whatever

---

suggests that the Danish aristocrats were not so much intimidated as dazed and overcome with an inexplicable loss of nerve:

> It is observable, that among so many Great Men, who a few days before seemed to have Spirits suitable to their Birth and Qualities, none had the Courage during those three last days, either by Remonstrance, or any other way, to oppose in any manner what was doing. And I have heard very intelligent Persons, who were at that time near the King, affirm, That had the Nobles shewed ever so little Courage in asserting their Privileges, the King would not have pursued his Point so far as to desire an Arbitrary Dominion. (Molesworth, *Denmark*, pp. 63–64)

See also Neville, *Plato Redivivus*, p. 136. The Danish coup d'état resonated strongly in the minds of commonwealth Whigs; see, e.g., Sidney, *Discourses*, p. 420.

51. On 20 April 1653 Oliver Cromwell (1599–1658) dissolved the Rump Parliament, clearing the chamber with the help of a troop of musketeers, seizing the papers which were then upon the table, and also taking possession of the mace (the symbol of the authority of the House of Commons). In so doing he was acting not only out of his own exasperation with the Rump Parliament, but also in response to the exasperation of the Parliamentarian army, which Cromwell had led and modeled into an effective fighting force. Cromwell and Gustav Vasa (see above, p. 21, n. 49) had been associated in English popular political writing of the early Restoration as types of the unscrupulous, Machiavellian ruler: see Anonymous, *A Parly Between the Ghosts of the late Protector, and the King of Sweden, at their Meeting in Hell* (1660) and Anonymous, *Hell's Higher Court of Justice* (1661).

52. Unidentified.

Nation suffers their Servants to carry their Arms, their Servants will make them hold their Trenchers.[53]

Some People object, That the Republicks of *Venice* and *Holland* are Instances to disprove my Assertion, who both keep great Armies, and yet have not lost their Liberty. I answer, that neither keep any standing Forces within the Seats of their Government, that is, within the City of [11] *Venice*, or the great Towns of the United Provinces; but they defend these by their own Burghers, and quarter their Mercenaries in their conquered Countries, *viz.* the *Venetians* in *Greece*, and the Continent of *Italy*, and the *Dutch* in *Brabant* and *Flanders*; and the Situation of these States make their Armies, so posted, not dangerous to them: for the *Venetians* cannot be attack'd without a Fleet, nor the *Dutch* be ever conquer'd by their own Forces, their Country being so full of strong Towns, fortified both by Art and Nature, and defended by their own Citizens, that it would be a fruitless Attempt for their own Armies to invade them; for if they should march against any of their Cities, 'tis but shutting up their Gates, and the Design is spoiled.

But if we admit that an Army might be consistent with Freedom in a Commonwealth, yet it is otherwise in a free Monarchy; for in the former 'tis wholly in the disposal of the People, who nominate, appoint, discard, and punish the Generals and Officers as they think fit, and 'tis certain Death to make any Attempt upon their Liberties; whereas in the latter,

---

53. James Harrington (1611–77), political theorist. Harrington's *The Commonwealth of Oceana* (1656) describes a constitution drawn up on Machiavellian republican lines. Oceana therefore has a militia, not a standing army, and Trenchard and Moyle allude to a passage from a speech which Harrington imagines being delivered before the embodied militia by "Hermes de Caduceo, lord orator of the tribe of Nubia": "There be (such is the world nowadays) that think it ridiculous to see a nation exercising her civil functions in military discipline, while they, committing their buff unto their servants, come themselves to hold trenchers" (Harrington, *Oceana*, p. 97). "Buff" here means military uniform (*OED*, s.v. "buff," n. 2, 2b) and so is used as a metonym for military service. Cf. Machiavelli's observation in chap. 14 of *The Prince*: "Between an armed and an unarmed man there is no comparison whatsoever, and it is not reasonable for an armed man to obey an unarmed man willingly, nor for an unarmed man to be safe among armed servants" (Machiavelli, *The Prince*, p. 51).

the King is perpetual General, may model the Army as he pleases, and it will be called High-Treason to oppose him.

And tho some Princes, as the Family of the *Medices*, *Lewis* the XIth, and others laid the Foundation of their Tyrannies without the immediate Assistance of an Army,[54] yet they all found an Army necessary to establish them; or otherwise a little Experience in the People of the change of their Condition, would have made them disgorge in a day that ill-gotten Power they had been acquiring for an Age.

This Subject is so self-evident, that I am almost asham'd to prove it: for if we look through the World, we shall find in no Country, Liberty and an Army stand together; so that to know whether a People are Free or Slaves, it is necessary only to ask, Whether there is an Army kept amongst [12] them? and the Solution of that Preliminary Question resolves the Doubt: as we see in *China*, *India*, *Tartary*, *Persia*, *Ethiopia*, *Turkey*, *Morocco*, *Muscovy*, *Austria*, *France*, *Portugal*, *Denmark*, *Sweden*, *Tuscany*, and all the little Principalities of *Germany* and *Italy*, where the People live in the most abandoned Slavery; and in Countries where no Armies are kept within the Seat of their Government, the People are free, as *Poland*, *Biscay*, *Switzerland*, the *Grisons*,[55] *Venice*, *Holland*, *Genoa*, *Geneva*, *Ragusa*, *Algiers*, *Tunis*, *Hamborough*,[56] *Lubeck*, all the free Towns in *Germany*, and *England* and

---

54. The Medici ruled Florence, and later Tuscany, for most of the period 1434–1737. Their political power was based on wealth acquired through trade and banking rather than on military force. Louis XI (1423–83) was king of France from 1461. He strengthened and expanded the French monarchy, and although he maintained a standing army, he preferred to achieve his goals through diplomacy and statecraft.

55. Grisons (or Graubünden, "gray leagues") is the largest and most easterly canton of Switzerland. The name derives from the drab homespun gray cloth worn by the inhabitants, who were celebrated for their rugged independence. They were commonly cited in the seventeenth century as embodiments of sturdy liberty (e.g., Sidney, *Discourses*, pp. 17, 20, 208, 371; and *Newes from Pernassus* ["Helicon," 1622], pp. 32, 49).

56. I.e., Hamburg. By the end of the seventeenth century Hamburg had a population of 70,000 and was an important center of trade and finance in northern Europe. Although it had long enjoyed the title of "Free and Hanseatic City" and had a strong tradition of robust self-defense and self-government, in fact it was only with the Treaty of Gottorp (1768) that Hamburg was released from theoretical subjection to the king of Denmark, and it was only in 1770 that it was recognized as an "immediate" imperial city of Germany (i.e., a city with no overlord

Scotland before the late Reigns.[57] This Truth is so obvious, that the most barefac'd Advocates for an Army do not directly deny it, but qualify the matter by telling us, that a Number not exceeding fifteen or twenty thousand Men are a handful to so populous a Nation as this: Now I think that Number will bring as certain Ruin upon us, as if they were as many Millions, and I will give my Reasons for it.

It's the misfortune of all Countries, that they sometimes lie under an unhappy necessity to defend themselves by Arms against the Ambition of their Governours, and to fight for what's their own: for if a Prince will rule us with a Rod of Iron, and invade our Laws and Liberties, and neither be prevailed upon by our Miseries, Supplications, or Tears, we have no Power upon Earth to appeal to, and therefore must patiently submit to our Bondage, or stand upon our own Defence, which if we are enabled to do, we shall never be put upon it, but our Swords may grow rusty in our hands: for that Nation is surest to live in Peace, that is most capable of making War; and a Man that hath a Sword by his side, shall have least occasion to make use of it. Now I say, if the King hath twenty thousand Men before hand with us, or much less than half that Number, the People can make no Effort to defend their Liberties without the Assistance of a Foreign Power, which is a Remedy most commonly as bad [13] as the Disease; and if we have not a Power within our selves to defend our Laws, we are no Government.

For *England* being a small Country, few strong Towns in it, and those in the King's Hands, the Nobility disarmed by the destruction of Tenures,[58] and the Militia not to be raised but by the King's Command,[59]

---

other than the emperor). Machiavelli had admired the sturdy independence and military self-reliance of German cities in chap. 10 of *The Prince* (Machiavelli, *The Prince*, pp. 38–39; see also *Discourses*, book 2, chap. 19).

57. I.e., the reigns of Charles II (1660–85) and James II (1685–88): see above, p. 13, n. 24.

58. I.e., the destruction of the institutions of feudalism, whereby the military force of a nation was in the hands of the tenants of the barons, under whose command they entered the field.

59. 13 Car. II, c. 6, An Act declaring the sole right of the militia to be in the King (1661) had stipulated that the "command and disposition of the militia and of all forces by sea and land . . . ever was the undoubted right of his Majesty and his royal predecessors, Kings and Queens of England, and that both or either of the Houses of Parliament cannot nor ought to pretend to the same, nor can nor lawfully

there can be no Force levied in any part of *England*, but must be destroy'd in its Infancy by a few Regiments: For what will three or four thousand naked and unarm'd Men signify against as many Troops of Mercenary Souldiers?[60] What if they should come into the Field and say, You must choose these and these Men your Representatives; Where is your Choice? What if they should say, Parliaments are seditious and factious Assemblies, and therefore ought to be abolished; What is become of your Freedom? Or, if they should encompass the Parliament-House, and threaten if they do not surrender up their Government, they will put them to the Sword; What is become of the old English Constitution? These things may be, and have been done in several parts of the World. What is it that causeth the Tyranny of the *Turks* at this day, but Servants in Arms?[61] What is it that preserved the glorious Commonwealth of *Rome*, but Swords in the hands of its Citizens?

And if besides this, we consider the great Prerogatives of the Crown, and the vast Interest the King has and may acquire by the Distribution of so many profitable Offices of the Houshold, of the Revenue, of State, of Law, of Religion, and the Navy, together with the Assistance of a powerful Party,[62] who have been always the fast and constant Friends to Arbitrary Power, whose only Quarrel to his Present Majesty is, that he has knock'd off the Chains and Fetters they thought they had lock'd fast upon us; a Party who hath once engag'd us in an unhappy Quarrel amongst ourselves[63] (the Consequence of which I dread to name) and [14] since in a tedious and chargeable War,[64] at the vast expence of Blood and Treasure, to avoid that Captivity they had prepar'd for us: I say, if any one considers this, he will be convinced that we have enough to do to

---

may raise or levy any war" (*Stuart Constitution*, p. 374). Control of the militia had been a point of tension between Charles I and Parliament in the early 1640s (May, *History*, lib. 2, pp. 39–43, 99–100).

60. Perhaps a memory of the fate of the Duke of Monmouth's militia troops when faced by James II's less numerous but professional army at the Battle of Sedgemoor on 6 July 1685; cf. below, p. 28, n. 68.

61. I.e., the Janizaries; see below, p. 28, n. 71.

62. I.e., the Tories.

63. Presumably a glance at the Civil War (1642–49), which terminated with the execution of Charles I (the "Consequence" that Trenchard and Moyle "dread to name").

64. The War of the League of Augsburg (1689–97).

guard our selves against the Power of the Court, without having an Army thrown into the Scale against us: and we have found oftner than once by too fatal Experience the truth of this; for if we look back to the late Reigns,[65] we shall see this Nation brought to the brink of Destruction, and breathing out the last Gasp of their Liberty; and it is more owing to our good Fortune, than to any Effort we were able to make, that we escaped the fatal Blow.

And I believe no Man will deny, but if *Charles* the First had had five thousand Men before-hand with us, the People had never struck a stroke for their Liberties; or if the late King *James* would have been contented with Arbitrary Power without bringing in Popery, but he and his black Guard[66] would have bound us hand and foot before this time: But when their ill-contriv'd Oppression came home to their own Doors, they quickly shew'd the World how different a thing it was to suffer themselves, and to make other People suffer, and so we came by our Deliverance; and tho the late King had the Nobility, Gentry, Clergy, People, and his own Army against him, and we had a very wise and courageous Prince[67] nearly related to the Crown, and back'd by a powerful State for our Protector, yet we account this Revolution next to a Miracle.

65. The reigns of Charles II (1660–85) and James II (1685–88); see above, p. 13, n. 24.

66. A phrase often associated with James II in polemical writing of this period: "Notwithstanding King *James* saw himself Deserted by the best Men of all Parties, and abandoned to the Black-Guard of *Popish Priests* and *Treacherous Deserters*, yet he went on with such Fury, as he thought himself secure in the Support of this Tatterdemallion Crew" (Anonymous, *A True Account of the Constitution, Principles and Practice of the English Flying Squadron* [1702], p. 13); "The *Clergy* who now seem to be in a state of *Reprobation*, were *smil'd upon* as long as the *Court* had any *hopes* of them, and offer'd this great *grace* of *ruining* their *own Church:* and to *encourage* them to this *pious Work, Preferments* were promised; and because none of any *Reputation* could be gain'd, the *Black-Guard* of the *Church* is call'd *up Stairs,* and *admitted* to the *Closet,* and *Dung-hills* are raked for *Vermin* to *stink* Men out of the *Church*" (Henry Maurice, *The Project for Repealing the Penal Laws and Tests, with the Honorable Means used to effect it. Being a Preface to a Treatise concerning the Penal Laws and Tests* [1688], p. 1); see also Samuel Johnson, *Remarks upon Dr. Sherlock's book intituled The case of resistance of the supreme powers stated and resolved, according to the doctrine of the Holy Scriptures* (1689), p. xvii; and Titus Oates, *EIKΩN BAΣIΛIKH TETAPTH, or, The Picture of the Late King James Further drawn to the Life* (1697), p. 20.

67. I.e., William of Orange, subsequently William III. William was "nearly related to the Crown" by virtue of being married to James II's daughter, Mary.

I will add here, that most of the Nations I instanced before were in-slaved by small Armies: *Oliver Cromwell* left behind him but 17000 Men; and the Duke of *Monmouth*,[68] who was the Darling of the People, was suppress'd with two thousand; nay, *Cesar* seiz'd *Rome* it self with five thousand, and fought the Battel of *Pharsalia*, where the Fate of the World was decided, with twenty two thousand;[69] and most of the [15] Revolutions of the Roman and Ottoman Empires since were caused by the Pretorian Bands,[70] and the Court-Janizaries;[71] the former of which never

68. James Scott (1649–85), Duke of Monmouth and first Duke of Buccleuch; illegitimate son of Charles II and Lucy Walter. Monmouth led an armed rising against James II in 1685, which ended disastrously on 6 July at the Battle of Sedgemoor, where his levies were routed by the smaller, but professional, army of James. For a discussion of his claim to the throne, see Neville, *Plato Redivivus*, pp. 153–72.

69. See above, p. 20, n. 45 for Caesar's march on Rome at the head of the 13th Legion in 49 B.C. In Caesar's day the nominal strength of a Roman legion was 6,000 men, although in practice it was often as little as half this number.

70. The Praetorians were the personal bodyguard of the Roman emperors, and consisted of picked veterans who enjoyed better pay and conditions than ordinary legionaries. The Praetorians were created by Augustus, and originally comprised nine cohorts each of 1,000 men. At first stationed in different parts of Italy, the Praetorians were eventually concentrated by Sejanus into a single camp on the north side of Rome, which increased their effectiveness as an instrument of internal intimidation. In bk. 1 of *The Art of War* Machiavelli had identified the creation of the Praetorian corps as a turning point in the trajectory of Roman decline:

> Because Octavian first and then Tiberius, thinking more about their own power than about the public advantage, began to disarm the Roman people in order to command them more easily and to keep those same armies continually on the frontiers of the Empire. And because they still did not judge that they would be enough to hold in check the Roman people and Senate, they set up an army called Praetorian, which remained near the walls of Rome and was like a castle over that city. Because they then freely began to allow men chosen for those armies to practice soldiering as their profession, these men soon became arrogant, so that they were dangerous to the Senate and harmful to the Emperor. The result was that many emperors were killed through the arrogance of the soldiers, who gave the Empire to whom they chose, and took it away; sometimes it happened that at the same time there were many emperors, established by various armies. From these things resulted, first, division of the Empire, and finally its ruin. (Machiavelli, *Chief Works*, 2:578)

Cf. Harrington, *Oceana*, p. 45, and Sidney, *Discourses*, p. 155, and pp. 455 and 508 (on the sufferings of the Romans under the sway of a "mad corrupted soldiery").

71. The Janissaries were an elite corps in the army of the Ottoman Empire from the late fourteenth to the early nineteenth century:

exceeded eight, nor the latter twelve thousand Men: And if no greater Numbers could make such Disturbances in those vast Empires, what will double the Force do with us? And they themselves confess it, when they argue for an Army; for they tell us we may be surprised with ten or fifteen thousand Men from *France*, and having no regular Force to oppose them, they will over-run the Kingdom. Now if so small a Force can

---

About this time [1360] . . . *Zinderlu Chelil*, then Cadilesher or chiefe Iustice amongst the Turks, but afterwards better knowne by the name of *Cairadin Bassa*; by the commaundement of *Amurath*, tooke order that euerie fifth captiue of the Christians, being aboue fifteen yeeres old, should bee taken vp for the king, as by law due vnto him: and if the number were vnder fiue, then to pay vnto the king for euerie head 25 aspers, by way of tribute: appointing officers for collecting both of such captiues and tribute mony, of whom the aforesaid *Cara Rustemes* himselfe was chiefe, as first deuiser of the matter. By which meanes great numbers of Christian youths were brought to the court as the kings captiues, which by the counsel of the same *Zinderlu Chelil*, were distributed amongst the Turkish husbandmen in ASIA, there to learne the Turkish language, religion, and manners: where after they had been brought vp in all painefull labour and trauaile by the space of two or three yeeres, they were called vnto the court, and choice made of the better sort of them to attend vpon the person of the prince, or to serue him in his warres: where they dayly practising all feats of actiuitie, are called by the name of Ianizars (that is to say, new souldiers.) This was the first beginning of the Ianizars vnder this Sultan *Amurath* the first, . . . so that in processe of time they be grown to that greatnes as that they are oftentimes right dreadfull vnto the great Turke himselfe: after whose death, they haue sometimes preferred to the empire such of the emperours sonnes as they best liked, without respect of prerogatiue of age, contrarie to the will of the great Sultan himself. (Knolles, *Turkes*, p. 191; see also Rycaut, *Present State*, pp. 190–99)

In the seventeenth century the Janissaries were notorious for frequently taking a lead in palace coups (see, e.g., Harrington, *Oceana*, p. 31; see also pp. 98 and 278; and Sidney, *Discourses*, p. 155). In 1628, in debates preceding the Petition of Right, deputy-lieutenants were compared to "janizaries" (Schwoerer, *Armies*, p. 26). "Janisary" (as it was commonly spelled) was a frequent term of abuse for the army during the Civil Wars, from both Royalists and more radical fringes of the Parliamentarians themselves: William Thompson, *Englands Freedome, Souldiers Rights* (1647), p. 6; Anonymous, *Westminster Projects* (1648), p. 4: "their Grandee Janisaries, to wit Sultan *Cromwell*, Bashaw *Ireton*, &c"; John Lilburne, *A Whip* (1648), p. 25; Charles Collins, *An Outcry of the Young Men and Apprentices of London* (1649), p. 3; Anonymous, *A Parliamenters Petition to the Army* (1659), p. 6; Anonymous, *The Dignity of Kingship Asserted* (1660), p. 148: "This God brought upon us for our great *sins*, one while giving up the whole *Nation*, the *Lords* and *majority* of the *Commons*, to the *odious servitude* of a *perjur'd Rump*, under whom, besides *monstrous Taxes*,

oppose the King, the Militia, with the united Power of the Nobility, Gentry and Commons, what will an equal Power do against the People, when supported by the Royal Authority, and a never-failing Interest that will attend it, except when it acts for the Publick Good?

But we are told this Army is not design'd to be made a part of our Constitution, but to be kept only for a little time, till the Circumstances of *Europe* will better permit us to be without them. But I would know of these Gentlemen, when they think that time will be? Will it be during the Life of King *James*,[72] or after his Death? Shall we have less to fear from the Youth and Vigor of the pretended Prince of *Wales*,[73] than now from an unhappy Man sinking under the load of Age and Misfortunes? Or, will *France* be more capable of offending us just after this tedious and consumptive War, than hereafter when it has had a breathing time to repair the Calamities it has suffer'd by it? No: we can never disband our Army with so much safety as at this time; and this is well known by these Conspirators against their Country, who are satisfied that a Continuation of them now, is an Establishment of them for ever: for whilst the Circumstances of *Europe* stand in the present Posture, the Argument will be equal to continue them; if the State of *Europe* should alter to the advantage

---

(which they extorted to maintain their *Janisaries* the *Apostate Souldiers*, by whose *mutiny* and *rebellion*, they were first *constituted*, and by their *assistance* kept up (in *name* and *notion*) as the *Supreme Authority* of *England*)"; John Gauden, *A Sermon* (1660), p. 23; Francis Gregory, *The Last Counsel* (1660), p. 1; Samuel Butler, *Another Ballad Called the Libertines Lampoone* (1674), p. 1: "Cromwel *and his* Janisaries"; cf. Pocock, *Harrington*, p. 10. This midcentury language of abuse had been revived in the late 1680s and thereafter: see Gilbert Burnet, *The Ill Effects of Animosities Among Protestants* (1688), p. 11; Anonymous, *The Mystery of Iniquity* (1689), p. 18; Sir Roger Manley, *The History of the Rebellions* (1691), p. 155; John Tutchin, *A New Martyrology* (1693). At the same time, recent events on the eastern borders of Europe had made the military prowess of the Janissaries freshly topical: John Savage, *An Ancient and Present State of Poland* (1697), p. 10, and Jones, *History of Europe*, pp. 504–5, 601. The various resonances of the term, therefore, constitute a particularly vivid example of the general strategy of the anti–standing army pamphlets, which is to link present realities to the recent and infamous past at the levels of both example and diction.

72. James II would die in exile on 5 September 1701.

73. James Francis Edward Stuart (1688–1766), Jacobite claimant to the thrones of England, Scotland, and Ireland; also known as the Old Pretender.

of *France*, the Reason [16] will grow stronger, and we shall be told we must increase our Number: but if there should be such a turn of Affairs in the World, that we were no longer in apprehension of the French Power, they may be kept up without our Assistance; nay, the very Discontents they may create shall be made an Argument for the continuing of them. But if they should be kept from oppressing the People, in a little time they will grow habitual to us, and almost become a part of our Constitution, and by degrees we shall be brought to believe them not only not dangerous, but necessary; for every body sees, but few understand, and those few will never be able to perswade the Multitude that there is any danger in those Men they have lived quietly with for some Years, especially when the disbanding them will (as they will be made believe) cost them more Money out of their own Pockets to maintain a Militia: and of this we have had already an unhappy Experience. For *Charles* the Second being conniv'd at in keeping a few Guards (which were the first ever known to an English King besides his Pensioners, and his Beef-eaters) he insensibly increased their Number, till he left a body of Men to his Successor great enough to tell the Parliament, he would be no longer bound by the Laws he had sworn to;[74] and under the Shelter and Protection of these he raised an Army that had put a Period to our Government, if a Complication of Causes (which may never happen again) had not presented the Prince of *Orange* with a Conjuncture to assert his own and the Nation's Rights. And tho we have so lately escaped this Precipice, yet Habit has made Souldiers so familiar to us, that some who pretend to be zealous for Liberty, speak of it as a Hardship to his present Majesty, to refuse him as many Men as his Predecessors; not considering that the raising them then was a Violation of our Laws, and that his Government is built upon the Destruction of theirs, and can no more [17] stand upon the same Rubbish, than the Kingdom of Heaven be founded in Unrighteousness.[75]

74. Unlike his father, Charles II had two permanent crack regiments at his command: Monck's Coldstream Guards and Lord Oxford's regiment of horse ("The Blues").

75. Not an allusion to a specific biblical passage, but for a similar sentiment, see Romans 9:14.

But the Conspirators say, we need be in no apprehensions of Slavery whilst we keep the power of the Purse in our own hands, which is very true; but they do not tell us that he has the power of raising Money, to whom no one dares refuse it.

Arma tenenti
Omnia dat qui justa negat.[76]

For 'tis as certain that an Army will raise Money, as that Money will raise an Army; but if this course be too desperate, 'tis but shutting up the *Exchequer*,[77] and disobliging a few Tally-Jobbers[78] (who have bought them for fifty *per Cent.* discount) and there will be near three Millions a Year ready cut and dry'd for them; and whoever doubts whether such a Method as this is practicable, let him look back to the Reign of *Charles* the Second: And I am afraid the Officers of the *Exchequer* have not much reason to value themselves for their Payments in this Reign; at least the Purchasers of the Annuities are of that opinion, and would be apt to entertain some unseasonable Suspicions; if they had not greater Security from his Majesty's Vertue, than the Justice of such Ministers. But if we could suppose (whatever is the fate of other Countries) that our Courtiers design nothing but the Publick Good, yet we ought not to hazard such unusual Vertue, by leading it into Temptation,[79] which is part of our daily Duty to pray against. But I am afraid we don't live in an Age of Miracles, especially of that sort; our Heroes are made of a coarser Allay, and have too much Dross mix'd with their Constitutions for such refin'd Principles; for in the little Experience I have had in the World, I have observed most

76. "He who denies justice to a man bearing arms gives him everything" (because the armed man will then take it by force): Lucan, *Pharsalia*, I.348–49. The lines come from the speech Lucan places in the mouth of Caesar when, having crossed the Rubicon and thereby implicitly declared war on Rome, he is encouraging his fearful soldiers to march on the city. Cf. the observation in chap. 14 of Machiavelli's *The Prince*, quoted above, p. 23, n. 53. Cf. Sidney, *Discourses*, p. 235.

77. I.e., stop paying the interest on the public debt (as Charles II had done on 5 January 1672). Cf. Coke, *Detection*, p. 478, and Jones, *Secret History*, pp. "32–34" (sigs. Bb8ᵛ–Cc1ᵛ).

78. Dealers in government debt (*OED*, s.v. "tally," C1a).

79. Cf. Matthew 6:13; Luke 11:4.

Men to do as much Mischief as lay in their Power, and therefore am for dealing with them as we do [18] with Children and mad Men, that is, take away all Weapons by which they may do either themselves or others an Injury: As I think the Sheep in *Boccaline* made a prudent Address to *Apollo*, when they desired, that for the future Wolves might have no Teeth.[80]

When all other Arguments fail, they call to their Assistance the old Tyrant Necessity, and tell us the Power of *France* is so great, that let the Consequence of an Army be what it will, we cannot be without one; and if we must be Slaves, we had better be so to a Protestant Prince than a Popish one, and the worst of all Popish ones the F—— King. Now I am of Mr. *Johnson*'s Opinion, that the putting an Epithet upon Tyranny is false Heraldry;[81] for Protestant and Popish are both alike; and if I must be a Slave, it is very indifferent to me who is my Master, and therefore I shall never consent to be ruled by an Army, which is the worst that the

80. A slight misremembering of "Advice 88" of Trajano Boccalini's *Advices from Parnassus*, in which the sheep petition Apollo that they too might be given long teeth and sharp horns (Boccalini, *Advices*, pp. 162–63). In the political literature of the seventeenth century, the sheep is a common image of the subject, for men are the "Herds and Flocks of Princes, as Oxen and Sheep are of private Men" (Boccalini, *Advices*, p. 387). Toward the end of the century Locke would challenge the political implications of this image when he argued that men should not "be looked on as an Herd of inferiour Creatures, under the Dominion of a Master, who keeps them, and works them for his own Pleasure or Profit" (Locke, *Treatises*, p. 377); see below, p. 130, n. 38.

81. One of the things, which he says we ought to fear and tremble at, is *Popish Tyranny*. I would fain know whether the word Popish added to Tyranny makes it better or worse? One would think by this Phrase of *Popish Tyranny*, that several of our Prayers in this Reign had been Pastoral. Why, Tyranny is such a word, that nothing added to it can Blacken it. To put a bad Name upon Tyranny is false Heraldry. Popish and Protestant Tyranny are alike, their Effects are the same; and there is no difference betwixt them but only in this, that Protestant Tyranny stole in upon this Nation, and Popish Tyranny cried "*ware Horns*." (Samuel Johnson, *Notes Upon the Phoenix Edition of the Pastoral Letter Part I* [1694], p. 4)

Samuel Johnson (1649–1703), Church of England clergyman and Whig political pamphleteer; domestic chaplain to the Whig martyr William, Lord Russell; imprisoned for his Exclusionist tract *Julian the Apostate* (1682); highly praised by John Hampden, who said that he "never knew a Man of better Sense, of a more innocent Life, nor of greater Virtue, which was proof against all Temptation" (Johnson, *Works*, p. xix).

most barbarous Conquest can impose upon me; which notwithstanding we have little reason to fear whilst we keep the Seas well guarded.

It is certain there is no Country so situated for Naval Power as *England*. The Sea is our Element, our Seamen have as much hardy Bravery, and our Ships are as numerous, and built of as good Materials as any in the World: Such a Force well applied and managed is able to give Laws to the Universe; and if we keep a competent part of it well arm'd in times of Peace, it is the most ridiculous thing in nature to believe any Prince will have thoughts of invading us, unless he proposes to be superiour to us in Naval Power: For the Preparations necessary for such an Undertaking will alarm all *Europe*, give both to us and our Confederates time to arm, and put our selves in a posture of Defence. And whoever considers that the Prince of *Orange* with six hundred Ships brought but fourteen thousand Men,[82] and the mighty Spanish Armado (then the Terror of the World) [19] imbark'd but eighteen thousand,[83] he will be assured that no Invasion can be so sudden upon us, but we shall have time to get ready our whole Fleet, bring some Forces from *Scotland* and *Ireland*, and prepare our own Militia if there shall be occasion for it; especially in times of Peace, when we shall have the liberty of all the Ports of *France*, and shall or may have Intelligence from every one of them.

But they tell us such a Wind[84] may happen as may be favourable to our Enemy, and keep us within our own Ports; which I say, as *France* lies to

82. A reference to the Dutch invasion of England in 1688. "On the Twentieth Day of *October*, the *Dutch* Fleet, consisting of 52 Men of War, 25 Frigats, as many Fireships, with near four Hundred Victuallers, and other Vessels, for the Transportation of 3660 Horse, and 10692 Foot, sail'd from the *Flatts* near the *Briel*, with a Wind at South-West and by South" (Boyer, *William III*, 1:227).

83. The Armada is the name given to the great fleet assembled by Philip II of Spain in 1588 to invade England in a combined operation with Spanish forces stationed in Flanders. The Armada consisted of about 130 vessels containing 8,000 seamen and 19,000 soldiers. Dispersed by bad weather and effective English naval action, only 60 Spanish ships eventually returned to Spain. The total loss of life on the Spanish side was estimated at 15,000.

84. It had been a memorable circumstance in 1688 that the same easterly "Protestant wind" which had wafted William of Orange's fleet down the Channel had confined James II's navy to port (Boyer, *William III*, 1:235–36). Somers also draws attention to this, below, p. 59.

England, is almost impossible: for if we lie about *Falmouth*, or the Land's end, no Fleet from *Brest* or the Ocean can escape us without a Miracle; and if the design be to invade us from any Port in the Channel, a very few Ships (which may safely lie at Anchor) will certainly prevent it: nor is it to be conceived that that cautious Prince[85] will be at a vast Expence for the Contingency of such a Critical Wind, or will send an Army into a Country where their Retreat is certainly cut off, when the failing in any part of his Design will bring a new War upon him, which lately cost a third part of his People, a great many large Countries and strong Towns, with all the Honour he had heaped up by his former Victories, to get rid of.[86]

And here I must confess, that the misapplication of our Naval Force (which is our known Strength) for these last eight Years, is the strongest, as it is the most usual Argument against me: which unriddles a Mystery I did not understand before, tho I never was so foolish as to believe all the Errors of that kind were the Effects of Chance or Ignorance, or that losing so many Opportunities of destroying the French Fleet had not some extraordinary, tho occult Cause; and yet, notwithstanding the restless Attempts of our Enemies, and the paltry Politicks of our own wretched St———n,[87] this Fleet triumphantly defended us, so that our [20] Enemies in eight Years War could not get one opportunity of invading our Country.

It's objected, that the Officers of our Fleet may be corrupted, or that a Storm may arise which may destroy it all at once, and therefore we ought to have two Strings to our Bow. By which I perceive all their Fears lie one way, and that they do not care if they precipitate us into inevitable Ruin at home, to prevent a distant Possibility of it from *France*. But I think this Phantom too may be laid by a well-train'd Militia, and then

85. Louis XIV.

86. A reference to the provisions of the Treaty of Ryswick (1697), which required the French to surrender all territory seized since the Treaties of Nijmegen in 1678–79.

87. I.e., statesmen (a term which at this time could bear the pejorative sense of one who merely meddled in politics).

all their Bugbears[88] will vanish. This Word can be no sooner out, but there's a Volly of small Shot let fly at me: What! must we trust our Safety to an undisciplin'd Mob, who never dream'd of fighting when they undertook the Service; who are not inured to the Fatigue of a Camp, or ever saw the Face of an Enemy?[89] And then they magnify Mercenary Troops, as if there was an intrinsick Virtue in a Red Coat, or that a Raggamuffin from robbing of Henroosts in two Campagns could be cudgel'd into a Hero. Tho I must confess the Conduct of the Court in industriously enervating this Force, does in some measure justify their Objections: For the detestable Policies of the last Reigns[90] were with the utmost Art and Application to disarm the People, and make the Militia useless, to countenance a standing Army in order to bring in Popery and Slavery; and if any Methods were proposed to make it more serviceable, the Court would never suffer them to be debated; and such Officers as were more zealous in exercising their Companies than others were reprimanded, as if they design'd to raise a Rebellion. And now the worthy Patriots of this Reign are taking Advantage of the traitorous Neglect and infamous Policies of the last. But why may not a Militia be made useful? Why may not the Nobility, Gentry, and Free-holders of *England* be trusted with the Defence of their own Lives, Estates and Liberties, without having Guardians [21] and Keepers assign'd them? And why may they not defend them with as much Vigour and Courage as Mercenaries who have nothing to lose, nor any other Tie to engage their Fidelity, than the inconsiderable Pay of Six-pence a day, which they may have from the Conqueror?

Why may not the Laws for shooting in Crossbows be changed into Firelocks, and a competent Number of them be kept in every Parish for the young Men to exercise with on Holidays, and Rewards offered to the most expert, to stir up their Emulation?

88. A fiction designed to frighten children; by extension, an object of needless dread (*OED*, s.v. "bugbear," 1, 2a).

89. All disparaging remarks traditionally leveled at the militia. See Dryden, "Cymon and Iphigenia" (1700), ll. 399–408 for a caricature of the militia as "In peace a charge, in war a weak defence" (l. 402); see below, p. 306, n. 121.

90. Cf. above, p. 27, n. 65, and p. 13, n. 24.

Why may not the whole Militia of *England* be reduced to sixty thousand, and a third part of those kept by turns in constant Exercise?

Why may not a Man be listed in the Militia till he be discharged by his Master, as well as in the Army till he be discharged by his Captain? And why may not the same Horse be always sent forth, unless it can be made appear he is dead or maimed?

Why may not the private Souldiers of the Army, when they are dispersed in the several parts of the Kingdom, be sent to the Militia? And why may not the inferiour Officers of the Army in some proportion command them?

I say, these and other like things may be done, and some of them are done in our own Plantations, and the Islands of *Jersey* and *Guernsey*, as also in *Poland*, *Switzerland*, and the Country of the *Grisons*;[91] which are Nations much less considerable than *England*, have as formidable Neighbours, no Sea nor Fleet to defend them, nothing but a Militia to depend upon, and yet no one dares attack them: And we have seen as great Performances done formerly by the Apprentices of *London*,[92] and in the late

---

91. Cf. above, p. 24, n. 55.

92. During the reign of Edward IV in 1471, the London apprentices (or "trained bands") had repulsed an army of rebels under Thomas Neville, the Bastard of Fauconberg. More recently, in November 1642, Parliament had enticed London's apprentices to enlist in support of the parliamentary cause:

> [Parliament] solemnly declared, that, in such times of common danger and necessity, the interest of private persons ought to give way to the public; and therefore they ordained that such apprentices as would be listed to serve as soldiers for the defence of the kingdom, the Parliament, and the city, (with their other usual expressions of religion and the King's person,) their sureties, and such as stood engaged for them, should be secured against their masters; and that the masters should receive them again at the end of their service, without imputing any loss of time to them, but the same should be reckoned as well spent, according to their indentures, as if they had been still in their shops. And by this means many children were engaged in that service not only against the consent, but against the persons, of their fathers. . . . (Clarendon, *History*, 2:380)

On 26 July 1647 the London apprentices had confirmed their turbulent and military character by petitioning Parliament about the transfer of command of the militia to a group of Presbyterian commissioners (Clarendon, *History*, 4:242).

War[93] by the *Vaudois* in *Savoy*,[94] the *Miquelets* in *Catalonia*,[95] and the Militia in *Ireland*,[96] as can be parallel'd in History: [22] And so it would be with us, if the Court would give their hearty Assistance in promoting this Design; if the King would appear in Person at the Head of them, and give Rewards and Honour to such as deserve them, we should quickly see the young Nobility and Gentry appear magnificent in Arms and Equipage, shew a generous Emulation in outvying one another in Military Exercises, and place a noble Ambition in making themselves serviceable to their Country: as antiently the *Achaians* and *Thebans* from being the most contemptible Nations in *Greece*, by the Conduct of *Pelopidas*,

---

Andrew Fletcher would praise their conduct on the Parliamentary side at the Battle of Naseby (below, p. 167).

93. Cf. above, p. 26, n. 64.

94. The Vaudois had been involved in the War of the League of Augsburg on the side of the Grand Alliance, of which the Austrian Hapsburgs (and hence Prince Eugene of Savoy) were part. For the notable service of the Vaudois militia in that war, see Boyer, *William III*, 2:276, 283; Jones, *History of Europe*, p. 397; and Sidney, *Discourses*, p. 562. Vaudois refugees were an object of the charity of Queen Mary (Boyer, *William III*, 2:403–4).

95. The Miquelets were an irregular Catalonian militia which engaged in military operations against the Castilian and French armies (*OED*, s.v. "Miquelet," 1a). They had enjoyed particular success against the forces of Louis XIV in the autumn of 1695:

> Four Squadrons of *Miquelets* receiving Advice that a Detachment of the Enemy were marching from *Bagnoles* to *Gironne* they encountred them in the way, and gave them a total Defeat. Flush'd with this Success, upon Information that Monsieur St. *Sylvestre* was upon his March with 8000 Men, and between three and four Hundred Mules laden with all sorts of Provisions to revictual *Castle-Folet*, they joined themselves to a Body of *Spaniards*; advanced towards the *French*, and attack'd them so vigorously, that they killed about 2000 of them upon the spot. . . . This good Success was soon after attended with the *Catalans* and *Miquelets* Routing another Body of about 2000 *French*, who were marking to join the 8000 that were defeated before. . . . (Boyer, *William III*, 3:98–99)

More recently, in the summer of 1697, they had served effectively and with distinction at the siege of Barcelona (ibid., pp. 254–55).

96. The Irish campaign fought by William III which culminated in the Battle of the Boyne (1690) was remarkable for the number of occasions when James II's armies were defeated by irregular forces. The deeds of the "Inniskillin Men" were particularly noteworthy (Boyer, *William III*, 2:69–70; and see below, p. 93, n. 64, and p. 323, n. 178).

Epaminondas, and *Philopemen*, came to have the best disciplin'd Troops and most excellent Souldiers in the World.[97]

They object, that such a Militia as this is a standing Army, and will be as dangerous, and much more chargable. I answer;

That there can be no danger from an Army where the Nobility and chief Gentry of *England* are the Commanders, and the Body of it made up of the Freeholders, their Sons and Servants; unless we can conceive that the Nobility and Gentry will join in an unnatural Design to make void their own Titles to their Estates and Liberties: and if they could entertain so ridiculous a Proposition, they would never be obeyed by the Souldiers, who will have a respect to those that send them forth and pay them, and to whom they must return again when their time is expired. For if I send a Man, I will as surely choose one who shall fight for me, as a Mercenary Officer will choose one that shall fight against me; and the late Governments are Witnesses to the truth of this, who debauched the Militia more than ever I hope to see it again, and yet durst never rely upon them to assist their Arbitrary Designs; as we may remember in the Duke of *Monmouth*'s Invasion,[98] their Officers durst not bring them near his Army

97. Pelopidas, a great Theban commander and the restorer of democratic government at Thebes in the winter of 379–378 B.C.; one of the commanders at the Theban victory over the Spartans at Leuctra in 371 B.C. Epaminondas (ca. 420–362 B.C.), another great Theban commander, friend of Pelopidas, with whom he shared the Theban command at the Battle of Leuctra; killed at the Battle of Mantinea (362 B.C.); praised by Machiavelli in the *Discourses*, bk. 1, chaps. 17 and 21, as the preserver of the virtue of the Thebans by means of military discipline; see also bk. 3, chap. 18. Philopoemen (ca. 250–183 B.C.), general of the Achaean League, which he led to repeated victories over the Spartans; praised by Machiavelli in chap. 14 of *The Prince* as exemplifying the duty of a ruler to devote himself to the cultivation of military prowess (Machiavelli, *The Prince*, pp. 51–52). All these ancient worthies were also extolled by Sidney as examples of those men of virtue who "would neither do villainies, nor suffer more than the laws did permit, or the consideration of the publick peace did require" (Sidney, *Discourses*, p. 15).

98. Cf. the comments of Gilbert Burnet concerning the poor performance of the Devonshire militia against the forces of the Duke of Monmouth:

Upon the Duke of *Monmouth*'s landing [in 1685], many of the country people came in to join him, but very few of the Gentry. He had quickly men enough about him to use all his arms. The Duke of *Albermale* [*sic*], as Lord Lieutenant of *Devonshire*, was sent down to raise the Militia, and with them to make head against him. But their ill affection appeared very evidently:

for fear of a Revolt. [23] Nay, the Pensioner-Parliament[99] themselves turn'd short upon the Court, when they expected them to give the finishing stroke to our Ruin.

To the last part of the Objection, That this Militia will be more chargable than an Army; I answer, That since (as I suppose) no Man

---

> Many deserted, and all were cold in the service.... Soon after their landing, Lord *Grey* was sent out with a small party. He saw a few of the Militia, and he ran for it: But his men stood, and the Militia ran from them. (Burnet, *History*, 1:641, 642)

For Monmouth, see above, p. 28, n. 68.

99. The contemptuous name given to the Long Parliament of Charles II (1661–79), so called because of the large number of officeholders under the Crown who sat in it, and who were, at least at the outset, docile to the wishes of the King, before eventually turning "short upon the Court":

> For it is too notorious to be concealed, that near a third part of the House have beneficial Offices under his Majesty, in the Privy Councill, the Army, the Navy, the Law, the Household, the Revenue both in England and Ireland, or in attendance on his Majesties person. These are all of them indeed to be esteemed Gentlemen of Honor, but more or less according to the quality of their several imployments under his Majesty, and it is to be presumed that they brought along with them some Honour of their own into his service, at first to set up with. (Marvell, *Prose Works*, 2:299; cf. Robbins, *Commonwealthman*, p. 53, and Sidney, *Discourses*, pp. 571–72)

That language of royal criticism had been revived against William III during the 1690s (Claydon, *William III*, pp. 199–200). The Act of Settlement (1701) originally provided that such officeholders should be ineligible for the House of Commons, but this clause was quickly repealed. In § 222 of his *Second Treatise*, Locke had specified such corruption of representatives as one of the actions on the part of a "supreme executor" which could legitimately provoke the dissolution of the government:

> He *acts* also *contrary to his Trust*, when he either imploys the Force, Treasure, and Offices of the Society, to corrupt the *Representatives*, and gain them to his purposes: or openly pre-ingages the *Electors*, and prescribes to their choice, such, whom he has by Sollicitations, Threats, Promises, or otherwise won to his designs; and imploys them to bring in such, who have promised before-hand, what to Vote, and what to Enact. Thus to regulate Candidates and *Electors*, and new model the ways of *Election*, what is it but to cut up the Government by the Roots, and poison the very Fountain of publick Security? (Locke, *Treatises*, p. 413; see also Henry Care, *English Liberties* [1680], pp. 98–99, on the choice of MPs and whom to avoid, and Downie, *Harley*, pp. 24–25)

proposes wholly to lay them aside, if we add the extraordinary Expence of maintaining twenty thousand Men to the ordinary Charge of the Militia, it is much more than sufficient to make the latter useful. But if this Objection were true, it ought not to enter into Competition with the Preservation of our Laws and Liberties; for it is better to give a third part of my Estate, if it were necessary, than to have all taken from me.

And tho it should be granted, that a Militia is not as serviceable as an Army kept to constant Discipline, yet I believe these Gentlemen themselves will confess, that sixty thousand of them trained as before, are as good as twenty thousand of their standing Troops, which is the Question; for it's impossible to have them both useful at the same time, they being as incompatible as broad and clipt Money, never current together;[100] and therefore the Court must depend wholly upon a Militia, or else they will not depend upon them at all. And this by the way may silence that Objection, that we must keep our Army till the Militia be disciplin'd; for

100. "Broad money" refers to the broad-piece, a name applied after the introduction of the guinea in 1663 to the "Unite" or 20-shilling piece ("Jacobus" and "Carolus") of the preceding reigns, which was much broader and thinner than the new milled coinage (*OED*, s.v. "unite"). "Clipt money" refers to the crime of clipping the edges of coins made from precious metal, thus reducing their intrinsic value. Gresham's Law, which states that bad money drives good money out of circulation (because in those circumstances people tend to hoard good money whenever they come across it) explains why broad and clipped money would never be "current together," and this indeed happened in the mid-1690s (Blackmore, *History*, pp. 32–33). However, the comparison also has a topical force. In May 1695 Parliament had passed An Act to prevent Counterfeiting and Clipping of the Coin of this Kingdom (Boyer, *William III*, 3:47). In 1696 all clipped money had been called in and recoined:

About five Millions of clipt money was brought into the Exchequer; And the loss that the Nation suffered, by the recoining of the money, amounted to two Millions, and two Hundred Thousand pounds. The Coinage was carried on with all possible haste; About eighty Thousand pounds was coined every Week: Yet still this was slow, and the new money was generally kept up; so that, for several months, little of it appeared. This stop in the free Circulation of money, put the Nation into great disorder: Those who, according to the Act of Parliament, were to have the first Payments in Milled money [a measure to frustrate clipping], for the Loans they had made, kept their Specie up, and would not let it go, but at an unreasonable advantage. (Burnet, *History*, 2:175–76; cf. Jones, *History of Europe*, p. 609, and Blackmore, *History*, pp. 16–20, 23–32)

that will never be done whilst the Court has an Army: and the same Objection will be made seven Years hence as now; so that a small Army can be of no use to us, but to make our Fleet neglected, to hinder the Militia from being trained, and enslave us at home; for they are too few to defend us against an Invasion, and too many for the People to oppose.

I dare speak with the greater assurance upon this Subject, having the Authority of as great Men as the World hath produced for my Justification. *Machiavel* spends [24] several Chapters to prove, that no Prince or State ought to suffer any of their Subjects to make War their Profession, and that no Nation can be secure with any other Forces than a setled Militia.[101] My Lord *Bacon* in several places bears his Testimony against a Standing Army, and particularly he tells us, that a Mercenary Army is fittest to invade a Country, but a Militia to defend it; because the first have Estates to get, and the latter to protect.[102] Mr. *Harrington* hath founded his whole *Oceana* upon a trained Militia;[103] and I have lately read a French Book, called a History of the Politicks of *France*, which says, *Enfin si on veut ruiner Les Anglois il suffit de les obliger a tenir des Troupes sur pied.*[104] Nay, I believe no Author ever treated of a Free Government, that did not express his Abhorrence of an Army; for (as my Lord *Bacon* says)

101. Cf. *The Prince*, chaps. 12 and 13, where Machiavelli states that "Mercenaries and auxiliaries are useless and dangerous" and that a "republic armed with its own citizens is less likely to come under the rule of one of its citizens than a city armed with foreign soldiers" (Machiavelli, *The Prince*, pp. 43, 44). Other relevant passages occur in *The Discourses*, I.43, II.20, and II.30.

102. Principally a reference to a passage in "Of the True Greatnesse of Kingdomes and Estates": "Therfore let any Prince or State, thinke soberly of his Forces, except his *Militia* of Natives, be of good and valiant Soldiers. And let Princes, on the other side, that have Subjects of Martiall disposition, know their owne Strength; unlesse they be otherwise wanting unto Themselves. As for *Mercenary Forces*, (which is the Helpe in this Case) all Examples shew; That whatsoever Estate or Prince doth rest upon them; *Hee may spread his Feathers for a time, but he will mew them soone after*" (Bacon, *Essayes*, pp. 91–92).

103. Cf. above, p. 23, n. 53. The military force of Harrington's Oceana consists of the armed citizens of the republic (Harrington, *Oceana*, pp. xix–xx).

104. The *Traitté de la politique de France* had been published in 1677, and an English translation had soon followed: "In fine, if we had a mind to ruine the *English*, we need but oblige them to keep an Army on foot" (Paul Hay, marquis du Chastelet, *The Politicks of France* [1680], p. 190). A second edition of this work had been published in 1691. For contemporary commentary, see Jones, *Secret History*, pp. 40–46.

whoever does use them, tho he may spread his Feathers for a time, he will mew them soon after;[105] and raise them with what Design you please, yet, like the *West India* Dogs in *Boccaline*, in a little time they will certainly turn Sheep-biters.[106]

Perhaps it will be said, that the Artillery of the World is changed since some of these wrote, and War is become more a Mystery, and therefore more Experience is necessary to make good Souldiers.[107] But wherein does this Mystery consist? not in exercising a Company, and obeying a few words of Command; these are Mysteries that the dullest Noddle will comprehend in a few Weeks. Nay, I have heard that the Modern Exercise is much shorter and easier than the Antient. But the great Improvements in War are in Regular Encampments, Fortification, Gunnery, skilful Ingineering, &c. These are Arts not to be learned without much Labour,

---

105. Cf. above, p. 42, n. 102.

106. In *The Political Touchstone*, Boccalini (in whose fables sheep stand for the populace: see above, p. 33, n. 80) relates the following fable of how to deal with an oppressive soldiery:

> From the Royal Palace issu'd a second Voice, which said, that the Dogs which the Spaniards had transported into the Indys, to guard the Flocks from Wolves, were themselves become Wolves so ravenous, that in devouring the Sheep they surpass'd the voracious Cruelty of Tygers. Upon this all the Virtuosi gave an universal Groan, and each lamented this mighty Affliction. To what Guardians for the future shall Shepherds trust their Flocks and Herds, since they can no longer rely on the Dogs who were wont to be so faithful? And how is it possible, that the World shou'd preserve the Species of Sheep, the most unhappy of all Animals, now they're exposed a Prey not only to the Wolves their Enemys, but even to the Dogs their Friends? . . . [However] the Flemings gave all men to know, that the Dogs, which the Spanish Shepherds had sent into their Country to guard the Flemish Sheep, grew likewise such ravenous Wolves, that they wou'd have destroy'd the whole Flock, had they not prevented 'em by a noble Resentment, and that brave Resolution which was known to the whole Earth. If therefore the old World shou'd fall into the same Calamitys, which are now said to have happen'd in the New, all Men ought to know, that the true Remedy to chastise Dogs, who have got the vicious quality of Sheep-biting, is to give 'em a Dose of Flemish *Nux Vomica*, and dispatch 'em out of the way as they deserve. (Boccalini, *Advices*, p. 372)

107. As Defoe, for instance, would indeed argue: see below, pp. 94, 99–100, 377–78.

and Experience, and are as much gained in the Closet as in the Field; and I suppose no Man will say, that [25] the keeping standing Forces is necessary to make a good Ingineer.

As to actual Experience in War, that is not essential either to a Standing Army or a Militia, as such; but the former may be without it, and the latter gain it according as they have opportunities of Action. 'Tis true, at present the Army hath been trained up in a long War, and hath gained great Knowledge: but these Men will not be lost when they are disbanded, they will be still in *England;* and if the Parliament does give them a Gratuity suitable to the Service they have done their Country, they will be ready to resume their Arms whenever occasion offers.

But I desire to know of these Patriots how comes an Army necessary to our Preservation now, and never since the Conquest before? Did ever the prevailing Party in the Wars of *York* and *Lancaster* attempt to keep up a Standing Army to support themselves?[108] No: they had more Sense than to sacrifice their own Liberty, and more Honour than to enslave their Country, the more easily to carry on their own Faction. Were not the *Spaniards* as powerful, as good Souldiers, and as much our Enemies, as the *French* are now? Was not *Flanders* as near us as *France?* and the Popish Interest in Queen *Elizabeth*'s time as strong as the Jacobite is now? and yet that most excellent Princess never dream'd of a Standing Army, but thought her surest Empire was to reign in the Hearts of her Subjects, which the following Story sufficiently testifies. When the Duke of *Alanson*[109] came over to *England,* and for some time had admired the Riches of the City, the Conduct of her Government, and the Magnificence of her Court, he asked her amidst so much Splendor where were her Guards? which Question she resolved a few days after as she took

108. A reference to the Wars of the Roses (1455–85), a dynastic conflict between the rival houses of York and Lancaster, in which both sides raised forces by arming their tenants. However, although Trenchard and Moyle attribute their not keeping standing armies to honor and sense, it is more likely that they lacked the financial means to maintain such an army.

109. François, duc d'Anjou (1554–84), known also as duc d'Alençon, 1566–76; suitor to Elizabeth I of England, with whom he concluded a contract of marriage (1579), which however was never exercised.

him in her Coach through the City, when pointing to the [26] People (who received her in Crowds with repeated Acclamations) These, said she, my Lord, are my Guards; These have their Hands, their Hearts, and their Purses always ready at my Command: and these were Guards indeed, who defended her through a long and successful Reign of forty four Years against all the Machinations of *Rome*, the Power of *Spain*, a disputed Title, and the perpetual Conspiracies of her own Popish Subjects; a Security the Roman Emperors could not boast of with their Pretorian Bands,[110] and their Eastern and Western Armies.

Were not the *French* as powerful in *Charles* the Second and King *James* his time, as they are after this long and destructive War, and a less Alliance to oppose them? and yet we then thought a much less Army than is now contended for, a most insupportable Grievance; insomuch that in *Charles* the Second's Reign the Grand-Jury presented them,[111] and the Pensioner Parliament[112] voted them to be a Nusance, sent Sir *Jos.*

110. Cf. above, p. 28, n. 70.

111. A grand jury is a jury of inquiry, accusation, or presentment (as distinguished from a petty jury or jury of trial), consisting of from twelve to twenty-three "good and lawful men of a county," who were returned by the sheriff to every session of the peace, and of the assizes, to receive and inquire into indictments, before these were submitted to a trial jury, and to perform such other duties as were committed to them (*OED*, s.v. "jury," 2b; cf. Henry Care, *English Liberties* [1680], pp. 212–20, on the duties and composition of a grand jury). During the reign of Charles II the House of Commons was wary of allowing soldiers to remain in arms, particularly in 1678 during the period of heightened tension arising from the Popish plot. The language of the preamble to 30 Car. II, c. 1, An Act for granting a Supply to his Majesty . . . for disbanding the army and other uses therein mentioned, is eloquent about these parliamentary suspicions, and also displays the courtly idiom in which they found expression:

> We your Majesty's most loyal and obedient subjects the Commons now in Parliament assembled, perceiving that there is no further occasion for the Forces raised since 29 September last, and being sensible that the continuance of them must be a great burden and unnecessary charge to your Majesty, to the intent therefore that the said charge may not continue, and to enable your Majesty completely to pay and to disband all the said Forces as hereafter is mentioned and expressed, we . . . have given and granted . . . for the aims and purposes aforesaid . . . the sum of £206, 462. 17s. 3d. (*Stuart Constitution*, p. 396)

112. Cf. above, p. 40, n. 99.

W——*son*[113] to the Tower for saying, the King might keep Guards for the Defence of his Person, and addressed to have them disbanded. And now our Apostates would make their Court by doing what the worst Parliament ever *England* saw could not think of without Horror and Confusion. They say the King of *France* was in League with our late Kings,[114] so he is with us; and he would have broke it then, if he had thought it safe, and for his Interest as much as now. But they say we have more disaffected Persons to join with him; which I must deny, for I believe no King of *England* in any Age had deservedly more Interest than the present; and if during such an expensive War, in which we have consumed so much Blood and Treasure, paid such vast and unequal Taxes, lost so many thousand Ships, and bore a Shock by recoining our Money,[115] which would have torn up another Nation from its Foundation, and reduced it to its [27] antient Chaos, when most Countries would have sunk under the misfortune, and repined at their Deliverance (as Men in Sickness commonly quarrel with their dearest Friends) I say, if at that time he had so great and universal an Interest, there can be no doubt but in times of Peace, when the People reap the Fruits of that Courage and Conduct he hath shewn in their Defence, he will be the most Beloved and Glorious Prince that ever filled the English Throne.

113. Sir Joseph Williamson (1633–1701), government official, diplomat, and bureaucrat. In 1678 at the height of the Popish plot it was revealed that Williamson, as Secretary of State, had signed documents exempting certain Irish Catholic officers from taking the oaths of allegiance and supremacy, notwithstanding the contrary provisions of the Test Act. On 18 November the Commons confined Williamson to the Tower for this misdemeanor, only for him to be released some hours later by the personal intervention of the king. He was replaced as Secretary of State on 20 February 1679.

114. Principally a reference to the secret clauses of the Treaty of Dover (1670), by which Charles II accepted payments from Louis XIV in return for an undertaking eventually to convert to Roman Catholicism and for assisting the French in their imminent aggression against the Dutch Republic: see Toland, *Restoring*, p. vi. James II's admiration for Louis XIV was notorious. The French king had welcomed James to Paris as a king in exile in 1688 and had furnished him with troops and money to pursue his ill-fated Irish campaign in 1689. For a popular account of the extent of the support Louis was supposed to be prepared to extend to the exiled James to help him regain his throne, see Jones, *Continuation*, pp. 18–20.

115. Cf. above, p. 41, n. 100.

I will make one Assertion more, and then conclude this Discourse, *viz.* That the most likely way of restoring King *James*, is maintaining a Standing Army to keep him out.

For the King's Safety stands upon a Rock whilst it depends upon the solid Foundation of the Affections of the People, which is never to be shaken till 'tis as evident as the Sun in the Firmament, that there is a formed Design to overthrow our Laws and Liberties; but if we keep a Standing Army, all depends upon the uncertain and capricious Humours of the Souldiery, which in all Ages have produced more violent and sudden Revolutions, than ever have been known in unarmed Governments: For there is such a Chain of Dependence amongst them, that if two or three of the chief Officers should be disobliged, or have Intrigues with Jacobite Mistresses; or if the King of *France* could once again buy his Pensioners into the Court or Army, or offer a better Market to some that are in already, we shall have another Rehearsal Revolution,[116] and the People be only idle Spectators of their own Ruin. And whosoever considers the Composition of an Army, and doubts this, let him look back to the Roman Empire, where he will find out of twenty six Emperors, sixteen deposed and murdered by their own Armies;[117] nay, half the History of the World is made up [28] of Examples of this kind: but we need not

116. I.e., a repeat revolution, duplicating and inverting that of 1688 (*OED*, s.v. "rehearsal," 1a), but also an allusion to Buckingham's very popular burlesque play, *The Rehearsal* (1672), thereby implying that a Jacobite restoration would be a ludicrous absurdity. See also below, p. 144, n. 73.

117. Of the twenty-six Roman emperors who reigned from Augustus (63–14 B.C.) to Alexander Severus (208–235), only ten died from natural causes: Augustus, Vespasian, Titus, Nerva, Trajan, Hadrian, Antoninus Pius, Lucius Verus, Marcus Aurelius, and Septimius Severus. However, the remaining sixteen were not all assassinated by their own Praetorians: that was a fate reserved for Caligula, Galba, Domitian, Commodus, Pertinax, Caracalla, and Elagabalus. In chap. 19 of *The Prince* Machiavelli gave extended consideration to the deaths of the Roman emperors, noting that it was their particular misfortune to be obliged to "endure the cruelty and avarice of the soldiers," and that "some of them always lived nobly and demonstrated great strength of character, yet nevertheless lost their empire or were killed by their own soldiers who plotted against them" (Machiavelli, *The Prince*, pp. 65–71; quotations on pp. 66 and 65). See also Juvenal, X.112; Machiavelli, *Discourses*, I.x, and *The Art of War*, bk. 1 (Machiavelli, *Chief Works*, 2:578); Neville, *Plato Redivivus*, p. 110; and Sidney, *Discourses*, p. 50.

go any farther than our own Country, where we have but twice kept Armies in time of Peace, and both times they turn'd out their own Masters. The first under *Cromwell*, expell'd that Parliament under which they had fought successfully for many Years;[118] afterwards under General *Monk* they destroy'd the Government they before set up, and brought back *Charles* the Second, and he afterwards disbanded them lest they might have turned him out again.[119] The other Instance is fresh in every one's memory, how King *James's* Army join'd with the Prince of *Orange*, now our Rightful and Lawful King.[120] And what could have been expected otherwise from Men of dissolute and debauched Principles, who call themselves Souldiers of Fortune? who make Murder their Profession, and enquire no farther into the Justice of the Cause, than how they shall be paid; who must be false, rapacious and cruel in their own Defence. For having no other Profession or Subsistence to depend upon,

118. A reference to the New Model Army led by Cromwell which had fought on the Parliamentarian side in the Civil War before turning against their political masters.

> In composition, size, self-image, and political role the New Model Army was unique in English military history. The effect of the Self-Denying Ordinance by which the army was established was to create a non-aristocratic officer corps, including men from the middle and lower middle classes. Promotion from the ranks on the basis of ability was a radical and innovative policy which had never been practiced before and was not to be followed after the Restoration. The social origins of the officers was one of the reasons for the apprehension over the army. (Schwoerer, *Armies*, p. 52)

119. A reference to the forces stationed in Scotland and commanded by General George Monck (1608–70), later first Duke of Albemarle. Having purged his troops and made them an instrument docile to his own wishes, Monck led them over the border between Scotland and England on 2 January 1660, thus setting in train the events that led to the Restoration of the Stuarts in the summer of the same year. In so doing, he became an object of Whig resentment: see, e.g., Toland, *Restoring*.

120. After landing at Torbay, William of Orange's forces were strengthened by a series of prominent defections from James's side. Lord Cornbury defected to William at once and took with him his regiment. He was followed quickly by Lord Churchill, the colonels of the Tangier regiments, Kirke and Trelawney, and the Duke of Grafton. However, it is misleading to suggest that James was thereby stripped of all military force. The rank and file of the army remained broadly loyal, as did the Catholic officers. See Jones, *Tragical History*, pp. 387–88, and Jones, *History of Europe*, pp. 316–17.

they are forced to stir up the Ambition of Princes, and engage them in perpetual Quarrels, that they may share of the Spoils they make. Such Men, like some sort of ravenous Fish, fare best in a Storm; and therefore we may reasonably suppose they will be better pleased with the Tyrannical Government of the late King,[121] than the mild and gracious Administration of his Present Majesty, who came over to *England* to rescue us from Oppression, and he has done it, and triumphs in it in spight of his Enemies.

In this Discourse I have purposely omitted speaking of the lesser Inconveniences attending a Standing Army, such as frequent Quarrels, Murders and Robberies; the destruction of all the Game in the Country; the quartering upon publick, and sometimes private Houses; the influencing of Elections of Parliament[122] by an artificial distribution of [29] Quarters; the rendring so many Men useless to Labour, and almost Propagation, together with a much greater Destruction of them, by taking them from a laborious way of living to a loose idle Life; and besides this, the Insolence of the Officers, and the Debaucheries that are committed both by them and their Souldiers in all the Towns they come in, to the ruin of multitudes of Women, Dishonour of their Families, and ill Example to others; and a numerous train of Mischiefs besides, almost endless to enumerate. These are trivial as well as particular Grievances in respect of those I have treated about, which strike at the Heart's blood of our Constitution, and therefore I thought these not considerable enough to bear a part in a Discourse of this nature: Besides, they often procure their own Remedy, working Miracles, and making some Men see that were born blind, and impregnable against all the Artillery of Reason; for Experience is the only Mistress of Fools: A wise Man will know a Pike will bite when he sees his Teeth, which another will not make discovery of but by the loss of a Finger.

What I have said here against Standing Armies, I would be understood of such as are the Instruments of Tyranny and their Country's Ruin, and

121. I.e., James II.
122. Trenchard and Moyle allude to the gerrymandering practice whereby the electoral rolls in crucial constituencies could be packed with the names of officers quartered in the locality.

therefore I need make no Apology to our own which was raised by the Consent of the Parliament[123] in this just and necessary War, and next under God and our Great and Glorious Deliverer, have by their Bravery and Conduct preserved our Liberties, and the Protestant Religion through *Europe*. For if in future Reigns any Designs should be levelled against our Laws, we may be assured these Men would be discarded, and others promoted in their rooms who are fit for such Arbitrary Purposes.

Nor do I think it reasonable that our Army should be ruined by that Peace, which by their Courage and Fidelity [30] they have procured for their Country; and I doubt not but the Generosity and Gratitude of the Parliament will give them a Donative equal to their Commissions, which, when the Foreigners are paid and sent home, will amount to no extraordinary Sum; at most 'tis but supposing the War to have six Months longer continuance, which is an easy Composition for the Charge of keeping them. But if there are any Gentlemen amongst them who think we can no otherwise express our Gratitude, but by signing and sealing our own Ruin, I hope we shall disappoint their Expectations, and not give the World occasion to tell so foolish a Story of us, as that we turn'd to grass one of the most powerful Monarchs in the World[124] for breaking our Laws, that we have maintain'd an eight Years War at the Expence of forty Millions of Money, and the Blood of three hundred thousand Men, to justify the glorious Action we have done; that by it we preserv'd all *Europe* besides, and lost our own Liberties; at least I hope it shall not be said we consented to it.

FINIS.

123. A resonant phrase, since the Bill of Rights (1689) had stipulated that no standing army should be kept in this kingdom (i.e., England) during time of peace without the consent of Parliament (see Appendix D, below, p. 629).

124. I.e., James II.

John Somers

A Letter, Ballancing the Necessity of
Keeping a Land-Force in Times of Peace:
with the Dangers that May Follow On It

1697

A

LETTER,

BALLANCING THE

NECESSITY

OF KEEPING

A Land-Force

In Times of

PEACE:

WITH

The DANGERS that

may follow on it

Printed in the Year 1697.

A Letter, Ballancing the Necessity of Keeping
a Land-Force in Times of Peace

SIR,

We have at last an Honourable Peace,[1] which was much Longed for by us all, but Despaired of by many. *England* is now the Wonder of the World; nothing can hurt us, but Animosities and Jealousies [2] among our selves. If we maintain the Peace with as much Prudence and Judgment, as we have shewed Spirit and Courage in carrying on the War, we shall give Laws to all about us; and secure that Quiet, which we have procured to the rest of *Europe*.

The Means of doing this, is now the common Subject of Discourse. All agree in one Thing, That we ought to maintain our Empire on the Sea with powerful Fleets, strong Summer and Winter Guards; and that our Stores ought to be well filled, and our great Ships kept in such a State, that we may be in a condition upon short Warning to set out Royal Fleets. This is so necessary, that I suppose it is needless to spend more time upon it. The only Point in which our Opinions may perhaps differ, is, whether we ought to maintain so considerable a Force at Land, as will be sufficient to make a Stand against an Invasion; or whether the Militia can be made so considerable, that we may trust to it at home, as well as to our Fleets abroad, and be safe in this.

I will not suggest so unbecoming a Thought, as to imagine that any of our Neighbours will seek to take Advantages against us, or break the Peace, and invade us contrary to the Honour and Faith of Treaties. No,

1. The Treaty of Ryswick (30 October 1697) had just concluded the War of the League of Augsburg (or the War of the Grand Alliance); cf. above, p. 9, n. 13.

I will not suspect it. But the best Guaranty of a Peace, is a good Force to maintain it: And the surest way to keep [3] all our Neighbours to an exact Performance of Articles, is to be upon our Guard. They will be then faithful to Agreements; when they see no Opportunities of Surprizing us, and that our Peace does not lay us asleep, and make us forget the Art of War. I mean, it is no Reflection on any of the Neighbouring Princes, when I conclude that their Faith is not so absolute a Security, but that we must help them to be true to their Word, by shewing them that they are not like to gain much by breaking it.

But mistake me not:

When I seem to prepare you to consider the Necessity of keeping a Land Force, I am far from the Thought of a *Standing Army*. Any Man who would pretend to give a Jealousy of the Nation to the King, and suggest that he could not be safe among them without he were environ'd with Guards and Troops, as it was in the late Reigns,[2] ought to be abhorred by every true *English man*, by every Man who loves Liberty, and his Country. The Case at present is, Whether considering the Circumstances that we and our Neighbours are now in, it may not be both prudent and necessary for us to keep up a reasonable Force from Year to Year. The State of Affairs both at Home and Abroad being every Year to be considered in Parliament,[3] that so any such Force may be either encreased, lessened, or quite laid aside, as they shall see cause. I will not Argue with you so unfairly, as to urge much the Rea[4]sons that we have of Trusting the King; for how much soever may be said on this Head, either from his Temper, his Circumstances, his Interest, and the Course of his past Life, either with Relation to the United Provinces, or to us here in *England*, and with how much Reason soever this might be prosecuted, yet I will not lay much Weight on it; for it is not just to press an Argument that puts another Man in Pain, when he goes to answer it: I know it may be said, That Men are but Men; so that we make a dangerous Experiment of their Virtue, when we put too much in their Power: And that what is done to one King, who deserves it, and will manage it faithfully, will be made

2. Cf. above, p. 13, n. 24.

3. Another reminder of the wording of the Bill of Rights; cf. above, p. 50, n. 123.

an Argument to do the same for another King, that has neither Merit nor Capacity to entitle him to so entire a Confidence.[4]

To say all in one Word, if we were in the same Condition in which we and our Neighbours were an Age ago, I should reject the Proposition with Horrour. But the Case is altered; the whole World, more particularly our Neighbours, have now got into the mistaken Notion of keeping up a mighty Force; and the powerfullest of all there happens to be our next Neighbour,[5] who will very probably keep up great Armies: And we may appear too Inviting, if we are in such an open and unguarded Condition, that the Success of the Attempt may seem to be not only probable, but certain. *England* is an open Country, full of Plenty, every where able to Subsist an [5] Army: Our Towns and Cities are all open;[6] our Rivers are all fordable; no Passes nor strong Places can stop an Enemy, that should Land upon us. So that the whole Nation lies open to any Army that should once come into it. To this you may reply, Can an Army be brought together, with a Fleet to bring it over, and we know nothing of it? These Things require time, and we cannot be supposed so destitute of Intelligence as not to know of such Preparations. In such a case, our Fleet will cover us, while our Militia may be exercised, and marched where the Danger is apprehended. This may seem plausible, and will no doubt work on such as do not consider Things with the Attention that is necessary.

4. The problem of the degenerate successor recurs in the literature concerning standing armies. Molesworth reports that Frederick III of Denmark, on the threshold of the coup which would make him an absolute monarch, had qualms on precisely this point:

> He declared that indeed he should be pleased the Sovereignty were entailed on his Family, provided it were done by Universal Consent; but to become Absolute and Arbitrary, was neither his desire, nor did he think it for the benefit of the Kingdom; that he was satisfied he should not make ill use of such an unlimited Authority; but no body knew what Successors he might have; that it was therefore dangerous both for them to give, and for him to receive such a Power as might be abused in future times to the utter ruin of the Nation. (Molesworth, *Denmark*, pp. 56–57)

See also Sidney, *Discourses*, p. 398: "I know not how nations can be assured their princes will always be so good."

5. I.e., France.

6. I.e., unfortified (*OED*, s.v. "open," 8a).

But do not we remember, that we were lately twice almost surprized; once from *La Hogue*,[7] and again from *Calais*.[8] We must not expect that God will always work Miracles for us, if we are wanting to our selves. If in a time of War and Jealousy we were so near the being fatally overrun, without either Warning or Intelligence; it is much more possible to see such Designs laid in a time of Sloth and Quiet, when we are under no Fears nor Apprehensions: And this may be so managed, that the Notice we may have of it, may come too late for us to be able to prevent or resist it. And what will our Intelligence signify, if we are in no condition either to hinder the Descent, or to withstand the Force that may be sent against us. Absolute Governments, where [6] all depends on the Will of the Prince, and where Men are ruined, who fail either in performing what is expected from them, or in keeping the Secresy that is enjoyned them, can both contrive and execute Things in another manner, than can be conceived by those who have the Happiness to live in free Governments. Troops may have such Orders for Marches and Counter-marches, that those who are on the Place shall not be able to judge what is intended, till it is not possible to hinder it. Cross Winds may make this come yet later, to those who have a Sea between them. Orders may be given to many different Persons in many different Places, who shall know nothing of one another, till they meet in a General Rendezvous.

---

7. William of Orange had set sail to invade England from Brielle, just south of the Hague, on 29 October 1688 (see above, p. 34, n. 82).

8. A reference to the attempt made during the previous year, 1696, both to assassinate William III and to restore James II by means of an invasion launched from Calais:

> New Levies were made in *France* that Winter, and a great number of Forces order'd to file off towards *Dunkirk* and *Calais*, . . . But the Design was quickly unravell'd: For towards the beginning of *February* it was a publick Discourse in *France*, that his most Christian Majesty was now fully resolv'd to re-establish King *James*, and had concerted Measures so well, that nothing more remain'd, but the Winds and the Waves to do their Part. . . . On the 18th of *February* (O.S.) King *James* went in a Post Calash to *Calais*, and immediately upon his Arrival, the Troops, Artillery and Stores were order'd to be put on Board with the utmost diligence; whilst the Signal was impatiently expected from the *Jacobites* in *England*, to set Sail. . . . (Boyer, *William III*, 3:145–53; quotation on p. 145; see also Toland, *Restoring*, p. v)

It is true, we must suppose that we shall have good Fleets abroad, but one would not put so great a thing, as the Safety of the Nation, to such a Hazard, nor depend upon a single Security when that is liable to Accidents. The same Wind that may bring over a Fleet, and Army, to invade us, may keep our Ships in Port;[9] so that it shall not be possible for them to look out, or if they should have a favourable Minute to get out, it may so shatter them that they shall not be able to defend either our Seas or our Ports. This may well be supposed, for it really happened when the King landed first in *England*. The late King had then a powerful Fleet, which, if it could have engaged the *Dutch*, would have been probably too hard [7] for them, especially considering the Transport Fleet that they guarded; but the East Wind, that brought over the King, kept them in the River till the *Dutch* had past them; and when they got out, a Storm stop'd and shattered them, so that without being able to come to any Action, they were laid up. And would any Man hazard the Nation upon such a Contingency.

But the last thing in reserve is our *Militia*. Great Bodies may be brought together; The Men are brave, capable of Discipline, and they naturally love their Countrey: Their Officers being Men of Estates, may be well trusted with the Concerns of the Nation, in which they have so good a Stake.

I will never enter upon so invidious an Argument, as to disparage our *Militia*, or derogate from them: I do not doubt but they are much the best in the World, and if they had a Militia to deal with, I should doubt little of the Decision. But you and I have seen Armies too much not to know the difference that is between Troops that have been long trained, who have learned the Art and are accustomed to the Discipline of War, and the best Bodies of raw and undisciplined Multitudes. The whole Method of War is now such, that disciplined Troops must prove a very unequal Match, to much greater Numbers of Men, who yet perhaps, upon half their Practice, might prove too hard for them. I know it will be urged, that our Militia may be so trained and mo[8]delled, as to be made more capable of Service then perhaps they are at present: This is a Work of

9. As had happened in 1688; cf. above, p. 34, n. 84.

Time: a Project that depends upon so many Particulars, and may be subject to so many Slips in the Execution, that it must be confess'd a Nation is much exposed, if its Safety and Preservation must depend upon such Uncertainties. We have Troops that have pass'd through a long Apprentiship, and to our cost have learned that unhappy Trade, which is now become so universal, that it is thereby made necessary; we must either be preserved by it, or we must perish by it. Many gallant Gentlemen have broke the course of their Studies, and the other Methods of Life they were in: It will not only be a hardship put upon them, but it will be the rendring our selves naked and defenceless, if, after all the Reputation that we have risen to in War, we should sink into an unbecoming Remissness in Peace, and upon the remote and uncertain Fears of Dangers that will probably never happen, expose our selves to those which we may certainly look for, as soon as we have put our selves out of a Capacity of resisting them. To tell you Truth, I cannot see some Men grow all of the sudden such wonderful Patriots, so jealous of the Prerogative, and such Zealots for publick Liberty, without remembring what their Behaviour was, some years ago, in the late Reigns;[10] when we had not only all the justest Causes of Jealousie, but all the Certainties of Evidence: The Designs were bare-faced, and the Attempts [9] were bold; and yet some were then silent, and others went into them, with as hearty a Zeal for Arbitrariness as they seem now to put on for Liberty. The Methods they have taken during the War have been so ill disguised, that few will believe they are in earnest, when they talk of Liberty and Law, who seemed to have laboured hard to lay us open to Invasion and Conquest. What they could not compass during the War, they hope now to bring about by laying us asleep in Peace; for if we let go a real Security, and trust to an imaginary one, we may pay too dear for the Experiment, and be convinced of our Error when it will be no more in our Power to correct it.

But I know some will urge the *Roman* and *Lacedemonian* States for our Militia. It is a wrong way of arguing, to apply the Precedent of any one Time to another, unless all Things in both Times did agree. Every Thing is safe in any State, when it is equal, if not superior to those about it.

10. Cf. above, p. 13, n. 24.

Lacedemon and *Rome* were at least upon the same foot with their Neighbours. They were indeed far superior to them: At *Lacedemon* they bred their Youth to nothing but War, or to other Exercises that render them fit for it, and to a short and pointed way of Talking. They had neither Arts nor Learning among them: So that their whole Republick was like a Standing Army, that threatned the rest of *Greece*. The *Romans*, in the Times of their Liberty, were but a little distinguished from them. They allowed indeed [10] of Agriculture, and put their own Hands to it, which the *Lacedemonians* left to their Slaves: But they were all trained to War; and no Man among them could pretend to Imployments, 'till he could reckon up so many Campaigns, and shew the Wounds he had received in them: So that here was a Military Republick. It was not only equal but superior to all about them, for this very thing, and so no wonder if it conquered them. These Precedents can never suit our Times, unless we could change our whole Constitution at home, as well as the State of Affairs abroad, and banish from us not only Luxury but both Wealth and Trade.[11] The accounts that we have of the Militia in *Sweden* are not very encouraging: The new modelling it there has signified little to preserve their Liberty.[12]

Others will perhaps ask, How did our Ancestors not only defend our Countrey, but render it terrible to all about it, particularly to those from whom we seem now to be most in danger? This is a Topick that may furnish a great deal of popular Eloquence, and may impose upon such as

11. Somers's contrasting of the austere virtues of the military republics of antiquity with the different manners of modern European commercial monarchies is an interesting anticipation of Mandeville's *Fable of the Bees*, the first version of which would be published in 1705 as *The Grumbling Hive*.

12. The strength and nature of Sweden's armed forces had recently been described in John Robinson's *An Account of Sueden* (1694), esp. chap. 13, pp. 126–41. Robinson notes that since the Swedish crown had become hereditary the "Standing Forces of the Kingdom have been augmented, yet not so effectually established as its necessities required" (p. 128). Therefore "the present King, on whom the States had conferr'd an *Absolute Power*, to put the *Militia* into such a Method as he should think fit, has made such Regulations in all the Particulars relating to this Matter; as were requisite to bring it to Perfection" (p. 129). Somers is referring to this remodeling of the Swedish militia into an extension of the standing forces of the kingdom.

are proud of the Valour of their Countrey, and have read only so much History as to remember the Names of some Battels, and the Numbers of the Armies. But all were then alike as to this Matter, while all Nations were equally ignorant of War, and were only set on the Arts of Peace; then, no doubt, in those short Wars that broke out, the braver Nation had always the better. But it [11] is evident from the first Beginnings of History down to this day, that Regular Troops were always too hard for a Militia. *Lacedemon, Athens*, and *Thebes*, in their Turns had the better of one another, as their Armies were better trained, and had more Experience in War. At last the King of *Macedon*,[13] who had been much despised by them, subdued them all. *Cyrus*, by training the *Persians*, conquered the *Babylonians*;[14] and *Alexander* by the Army which his Father had trained, thô he had numerous Armies, or rather a great Militia brought against him, yet he made an easy as well as a speedy Conquest of the *Persian* Empire.[15] While the *Romans* were but a Militia, thô they were the best that ever was, they made War on their Neighbours, who were weaker than they, with great Advantage; but when *Hanniball* came against them with a trained Army, they fell before him upon every Occasion, till a long War had taught them that Art, and then they not only beat him out of *Italy*, but forced *Carthage* to a Submission.[16] Nothing

13. Philip of Macedon (ca. 382–336 B.C.), king of Macedon and father of Alexander the Great. Philip's victory at the Battle of Chaeronea (338 B.C.) over the combined armies of Thebes and Athens established Macedonian hegemony over Greece.

14. Cyrus the Great (d. 529 B.C.), founder of the Persian empire. Cyrus expelled Astyages from the throne of Media, defeated and made prisoner Croesus, king of Lydia, subdued the Greek cities of Asia Minor, and finally conquered the Babylonians and took Babylon itself.

15. Alexander the Great (356–323 B.C.), king of Macedon. Inheriting the hegemony of Greece from his father Philip II (see above, p. 62, n. 13), in 334 B.C. Alexander invaded Asia and began his conquest of the Persian empire, which he substantially accomplished in 331 with his victory over the army of the Persian king Darius at Arbela (or Gaugamela).

16. Hannibal (247–182 B.C.), son of Hamilcar Barca and the leader of the Carthaginians against Rome in the Second Punic War (218–202 B.C.). After Hannibal had audaciously led his army over the Alps and invaded Italy from the north, he enjoyed a series of brilliant victories over Roman armies (Ticinus and the Trebia, 218 B.C.; Lake Trasimene, 217 B.C.; Cannae, 216 B.C.). But he was

stood before the *Roman* Armies, as long as they were kept under Discipline, but when all the order of War was broke, and they became a Militia, the Northern Nations in *Europe*, as well as the Saracens in the *East*, overrun the *Roman* Empire.[17] As the Saracens slackened their Discipline, the *Turks* carried it from them: And if they had depended on their *Timariots*, and had not trusted more to their *Janisaries* and *Spahi's*, they had not been the Terror [12] of *Christendom* for so many Ages.[18] So certain it is,

---

unable to convert this military dominance into outright victory. Eventually the difficulties of maintaining an army in enemy territory and a lack of support from Carthage meant that the tide of war turned in favor of Rome. The theater of conflict shifted to North Africa, where Hannibal was finally defeated by P. Cornelius Scipio at the Battle of Zama (202 B.C.).

17. The Roman Empire in the West endured until its final overthrow in either 476 or 479, although its provinces had suffered significant penetration at the hands of the northern barbarians for approximately a century before its final extinction, following on from the initial Gothic crossing of the Danube in 376. After the death of Mahomet in 632, the Saracens or Arabs, invigorated and united by their new religion, spread west and north, laying siege to Constantinople between 668 and 675, and conquering Spain in 713.

18. The Turks originated in the area surrounding the Caspian Sea. Moving south and west, they invaded and subdued Persia in 1038, invaded the eastern provinces of the Roman Empire in 1050, and conquered Jerusalem in 1096. Constantinople was finally taken by the Turks in 1453. *Timariot:* in the Ottoman empire, soldiers who held a *timar*, or portion of land, and who offered in return military service to their overlord:

> The other vse of them (and no lesse profitable than the former) is for that out of them he [the sultan] is alwaies able at his pleasure to draw into the field an hundred and fiftie thousand horsemen well furnished, readie to goe whether soeuer he shall commaund them: with all whom he is not at one farthing charge. Which so great a power of horsemen cannot be continually maintained for lesse than fourteene millions of duckats yearely. Wherefore it is to be maruelled, that some comparing the Turkes reuenewes with the Christians, make no mention of this so great a part of the *Othoman* emperours wealth and strength, seruing him first for the suppressing of all such tumults as might arise in his empire, and then as a most principall strength of his continuall warres, alwaies readie to serue him in his greatest expeditions. (Knolles, *Turkes*, pp. 597–99, 603; quotation on p. 598; see also Rycaut, *Present State*, pp. 172–82)

Cf. Harrington, *Oceana*, pp. 13, 58–59, 278; Neville, *Plato Redivivus*, p. 110. *Janisaries*: see above, p. 28, n. 71. *Spahis*: an elite body of Ottoman cavalry, who like the Timariots were retained on a quasi-feudal basis: "the best horsemen of the

from the Histories of all Nations, that regular and disciplined Troops will be far superior to the best and strongest Militia in the World.

To all this it may be said, How did we do in Queen *Elisabeth*'s Time? Our Militia was then our only Army; to it we trusted, and we were preserved by it. But I must crave leave to put you in mind of some Particulars in this part of our History: We were then in such imminent Danger, that we were given for gone by the wisest Men of the Age: It was the Storms and Winds, the disproportioned Bulk of their Ships, the Stiffness of the Orders, and the Distaste given to the Prince of *Parma*; all which concurred at that time to save *England*:[19] Neither our Militia, nor our Fleet had share in it. There was an extraordinary Concurrence of many Things in that juncture that preserved us: But it were to presume too much on Providence to lay our selves as open as we were then, because we were at that time so wonderfully delivered. But I must tell you our Danger is now much greater: *Spain*, it is true, had then a great Armada, vast Treasures, and well disciplined Armies; But tho' their Army lay near us in *Flanders*, the Scene of their Councils, their Fleet and Treasures were at a great distance from us: And yet all the wise Men of that time thought we must have perished then. The Danger is now both nearer and greater; a mighty Power, well united, and practised in War, and a [13] great Naval Force is in view of us.[20] It will be therefore no Argument, because we run a great risk in *Q. Elisabeth*'s time, but were wonderfully saved, that therefore now, when we may be in greater hazard, and have a more formidable Neighbour at our very Doors, we ought to take no care of our selves, but neglect the Only probable means of our Preservation; we have had Two wonderful Eighty Eights,[21] but we presume too much if we look for a Third, without taking any further Care how, or by what means, we shall be saved.

Turkish empire" (Knolles, *Turkes*, p. 1104; cf. Rycaut, *Present State*, pp. 184–89). Cf. Harrington, *Oceana*, pp. 45, 57, 278.

19. A reference to the Armada; cf. above, p. 34, n. 83. Alessandro Farnese (1545–92), Duke of Parma and Piacenza; regent of the Netherlands for Philip II of Spain, 1578–92.

20. I.e., France.

21. I.e., 1588, the year of the Spanish Armada, and 1688, the year of the Glorious Revolution.

I will add no more on this head, but will only tell you a *Saying of one of the Vere's*,[22] which is still remembred in the Family. The Queen sent to the States for those two famous Generals, to command her Army. It seemed full of Zeal and Courage: The Queen rid up and down through it, to animate the Soldiers, and was every where answered with shouts and Acclamations: She asked one of the Brothers, what he thought of the Army; he answered, It was a brave Army: But she saw by his manner that he was in some doubt about it, so she charged him to explain himself; he said, He had not the Name of a Coward in the World, but he was the only Coward there. They were all wishing to have the *Spaniards* land, and every Man was telling what Feats he would then do; he was the only Man that was trembling for fear of it.

[14] The last and strongest Objection against all this is, That this Force will grow upon us, and continue among us. It will have such an Influence within Doors,[23] that it will maintain it self in the H. of Commons; or, if that should fail, it will turn them out of Doors, and quickly find ways to subsist, to grow upon the Ruins of Liberty and Property. This is a large Field; and History is so full of Instances this way, that it will be easie to open copiously on the subject. From the *Pretorian* Cohorts[24] down to our modern Armies, enough can be gathered to give a very frightful Representation of a Standing Army. Who doubts it? But all the Rhetorick that this head will afford is wrong applied in this case. It is not to be supposed, but that once a year a Parliament must have this matter a fresh under their Consideration.[25] They will see how the State of Affairs varies, either at Home or Abroad; and whether the Forces are brought under such a Management, that there is just cause of Jealousy.

22. Geoffrey Vere (1525–72) had four sons, all of whom were trained as soldiers: John, Francis, Robert, and Horace. The two most accomplished of the four were Francis (later Sir Francis) Vere (1550–1604) and Horace Vere (1565–1635) (later Baron Vere of Tilbury), who both distinguished themselves on the Continent, chiefly in the Low Countries. Somers's anecdote probably refers to Sir Francis Vere, who spent the winter of 1588 in England and was received by Elizabeth. For Macaulay's admiration for Somers's deployment of this anecdote, see Macaulay, *History*, 6:2741–42.

23. I.e., within Parliament.
24. See above, p. 28, n. 70.
25. Cf. above, p. 50, n. 123.

And I leave it to you to judge, whether it is possible in so short a time, so to model and influence it, as to prepare them to invade their Country, and to destroy our Constitution. What *Cesar*, with all his Genius, could not work his Army to, but after Ten Years Conduct and Success,[26] can give small Encouragement to others to attempt to bring it about, in one Year. Perhaps you are more afraid of a Secret Influence, than of Open Violence from them. The short [15] of this is, You are afraid the House will be corrupted: I confess it is hard to answer this, Jealousy is stubborn and incurable; Melancholy when it grows to be a Disease, raises many imaginary Fears; they who are haunted with that sullen Humour, neither know what they are Afraid of, nor why. Possible Accidents are ever before them; and the thinking of these perpetually, ruines their Health, sours their Humour, and makes them neglect all their present and certain Concerns, while they are ever dreaming of what will probably never happen. We must consider our present Danger, and the likeliest Ways of securing our selves from it, without amusing our selves with what may possibly be brought about at some distance of time. Our Representatives do well to secure our Constitution, by the most effectual Means they can think on: But after all, we must trust *England* to a *House of Commons*, that is to it self. When ever the fatal Time comes, that this Nation grows weary of Liberty, and has neither the Virtue, the Wisdom, nor the Force to preserve its Constitution, it will deliver all up; let all the Laws possible, and all the Bars imaginable, be put in the way to it. It is no more possible to make a Government immortal, than it is to make a Man immortal. I do not deny but several Inconveniences may be apprehended from a Standing Force, and therefore I should not go about to perswade you to it, if the Thing did not seem indispensibly necessary [16] to our Preservation. I would not have us venture upon present and certain Ruine, because that which must preserve us now from it, may at some time hereafter have ill Effects on our Liberty. They cannot be Considerable as long as *England* is true to it self;[27] and whensoever the Nation has lost that Noble Sense of Liberty, by which it has been so long preserved it

26. See above, p. 20, n. 45.
27. Possibly an allusion to the final lines of Shakespeare's *King John*: "Naught shall make us rue, / If England to itself do rest but true" (V.vii.117–18).

will soon make Fetters for it self, tho it should find none at hand ready made.

To conclude, This Matter is of so nice, and yet of so important a Nature, that it ought to be severely examined, without false Colours,[28] or popular Rhetorick; you know me to be so jealous[29] of Liberty, to have been always so true to it, to have ventured so much for it,[30] and to have such a Stake in it, that you cannot suspect me. You know that I neither have, nor can have any Views in this Matter, but at our present Safety, as well as the Continuance of our Constitution and Liberty for the future.

28. I.e., misleading metaphors or figures of speech.

29. Here used in its true sense of being protective of, or solicitous for, something or someone (*OED*, s.v. "jealous," 3).

30. A well-placed reminder of Somers's committed activity on the Whig side during the reigns of Charles II and James II. His anonymous *A Brief History of the Succession* (1681) was a defense of the Exclusion Bill. In 1683 he had been one of the lawyers who served in the defense of several prominent Whigs charged with riot in the shrieval elections of 1682. In 1688 he had served successfully as the counsel for the seven bishops who had refused to comply with James II's religious policy.

Daniel Defoe

Some Reflections on a Pamphlet
Lately Published

1697

1. Taken and slightly misquoted from the opening lines of *Hudibras* (1663–78), a poem by Samuel Butler (1613–80) loosely modeled on *Don Quixote*, set in the English Civil War, and burlesquing religious nonconformity and enthusiasm: "When *civil* Fury first grew high, / And men fell out they knew not why; / When hard words, *Jealousies* and *Fears*, / Set Folks together by the ears, / And made them fight, like mad or drunk, / For Dame *Religion* as for Punk, / Whose honesty they all durst swear for, / Though not a man of them knew wherefore: / When *Gospel-trumpeter*, surrounded / With long-ear'd rout, to Battel sounded, / And Pulpit, Drum Ecclesiastick, / Was beat with fist, instead of a stick: / Then did Sir *Knight* abandon dwelling, / And out he rode a Colonelling" (I.i.1–14). On the fact of misquotation, note Defoe's claim that he has "not look'd in a Book during the Composure" of the pamphlet (below, p. 74).

SOME

REFLECTIONS

On a Pamphlet lately Publish'd,

Entituled, AN

ARGUMENT

Shewing that

A Standing Army

Is inconsistent with

A Free Government,

AND

Absolutely Destructive to the

Constitution of the *English*

MONARCHY.

Hard words, Jealousies and Fears,
Sets Folks together by the Ears.
Hudibras Lib. 1.[1]

LONDON:
Printed for E. Whitlock near Stationers-Hall. 1697.

The Preface

Mr. ABCDEFG,[2]

SIR,

Since I am to Address to you Incognito, *I must be excus'd if I mistake your Quality; and if I treat you with more or less Civility than is your due, with respect to the Names or Titles, by which you may be Dignified or Distinguish'd; but as you are in Print, you give your self a just Title to the scandalous Name of a Pamphleteer, a Scribler, a seditious broacher of Notions and Opinions, and what not, for as is the Book such is the Author.*

I confess you are something difficult to be known, for your Note is so often chang'd, and your Trumpet gives such an uncertain sound,[3] that no man can prepare himself to the Battle; sometimes you talk like a Common Wealths Man,[4] sometimes you applaud our present Constitution, sometimes you give high Encomiums *of the King; and then under the Covert of what Kings may be, you sufficiently* Banter[5] *him; sometimes the Army are* Ragamuffins, *sometimes Men of Conduct and Bravery; sometimes our Militia are brave Fellows, and able enough to Guard us, and sometimes so inconsiderable, that a small Army may Ruine us, so that no Man alive knows where to have you.*

Possibly I may not have made a particular Reply to a long Rapsody of Exclamatory Heads; for indeed, Sir, *Railing is not my Talent: Had I more time to consult History, possibly I might have illustrated my Discourse with more*

---

2. The pseudonym used by Trenchard and Moyle: see above, p. 7.

3. An astute reflection on the tonal and textual discontinuities in Trenchard and Moyle's pamphlet.

4. I.e., a radical or republican Whig.

5. Mock (*OED*, s.v. "banter," 1, 2).

lively instances; but I assure you I have not look'd in a Book during the Composure, for which reason I desire to be excus'd if I have committed any Errors, as to the Dates of any of my Quotations.

If I were a Member of the Army, I wou'd thank you mightily for the fine sweet words you give them at the end of your Book: you have a pretty way with you of talking of Kings, and then you don't mean this King; and then of Armies, but you don't mean this Army; no, by no means, and yet 'tis this King that must not be trusted with Men nor Arms, and 'tis this Army that must be Disbanded; and his Majesty is exceedingly obliged to you, Sir, *for your usage of him as a Soldier; for 'tis plain you are for Disbanding him as well as the Army.*

But of all things I magnifie you, Dear Sir, *for that fine turn of Argument, that not to Disband the Army is the way to bring in King* James; *but to Disband them is the most effectual way to hinder them. You have read, no doubt, of the Fable, how the Sheep were persuaded to dismiss the Dogs who they had hired to defend them against the Wolves;*[6] *the Application,* Sir, *is too plain; and this is the Clause makes me suspect you for a Jacobite.*[7]

6. A fable often attributed to Aesop relates that the wolves and the sheep formed a treaty and exchanged hostages. The sheep handed over their guard dogs, the wolves handed over their cubs. When the cubs began to howl for their mothers, the wolves descended on the now defenseless sheep and ate them. The moral customarily drawn from the fable was that it was folly to lower your defenses, even in time of peace.

7. I.e., a supporter of the exiled House of Stuart. This looks like a deliberate provocation on Defoe's part, since Trenchard and Moyle were both commonwealth Whigs, and so ostensibly at the opposite end of the political spectrum from the Jacobites. But in the confused and volatile politics of the late seventeenth and early eighteenth centuries, some feared a paradoxical conjunction of Whiggism and Jacobitism. Either the commonwealth Whigs and the Jacobites might form a tactical alliance to restore the Stuarts, or the corruption of the Junto Whigs might provoke the people to do so (Ludlow, *Voyce*, p. 49). In *Examiner*, 40 (10 May 1711), Jonathan Swift explored the former possibility in a manner half bantering, half paranoid:

> It is likewise very observable of late, that the *Whigs* upon all Occasions, profess their Belief of the *Pretender*'s being no *Impostor*, but a real *Prince*, born of the late QUEEN's Body: Which, whether it be true or false, is very unseasonably advanced, considering the Weight such an Opinion must have with the Vulgar, if they once thoroughly believe it. Neither is it at all improbable, that the *Pretender* himself puts his chief Hopes in the Friendship he expects from the *Dissenters* and *Whigs*; by his Choice to invade the

Well you have driven furiously, and like Jehu *called all the World to see your Zeal for the Lord;*[8] *but like him too you have not Demolished the high Places; you have Demolish'd the Army, but you have not provided against* Jacobitism; *you take care to leave the King naked to the Villany of Assassines,*[9] *for you are not for leaving him so much as his Guards; and you take care to leave the Nation naked to the insults of an Enemy, and the King and the People must defend themselves as well as they can. This is the way indeed to teach us Obedience with a Rod of Iron, and to make us pass under the Axes and Harrows*[10] *of a barbarous Enemy.*

All your Plea is Liberty, an alluring word; and I must tell you, Liberty or Religion has been the Mask for almost all the Publick Commotions of the World: but if Freedom be the English *Man's Right, you ought to have given the King and his Parliament the Freedom of Debating this matter by themselves, without putting your self upon them to raise a Controversie, where for aught you know there may be no occasion.*

What is there no way but an entire Disbanding the whole Army? Can no Expedient be found out to secure us from Enemies abroad, and from Oppression

---

Kingdom when the latter were most in Credit: And had he Reason to count upon the former, from the gracious Treatment they received from his supposed Father, and their joyful Acceptance of it. But further; what could be more consistent with the *Whiggish* Notion of a *Revolution-Principle*, than to bring in the *Pretender*? A *Revolution-Principle*, as their Writings and Discourses have taught us to define it, is a Principle perpetually disposing Men to *Revolutions*: this is suitable to the famous Saying of a great *Whig, That the more Revolutions the better*; which how odd a Maxim soever in Appearance, I take to be the true Characteristick of the Party. (Swift, *Prose Writings*, 3:146–47)

Swift's *Letter from the Pretender, to a Whig-Lord* (1712) is a troubled and mischievous fantasy of this fear of a Jacobite-Whig alliance (Swift, *Prose Writings*, 6:143–46). The behavior of men such as Robert Ferguson (d. 1714), who reeled from extreme and violent Whiggism to conspiring with Jacobites, lent a measure of probability to the apprehension; cf. below, p. 78, n. 16.

8. Cf. 2 Kings 10:16.

9. A reference to the recent failed Jacobite attempt to assassinate William III; cf. above, p. 58, n. 8.

10. A reference to the ritual humiliation of a defeated enemy, whom the Romans obliged to pass under a yoke (normally constructed out of three spears, however).

at home, &c. *no way but this,* Sir, *How do you know what a Parliament may do?*

Parliaments are Magnipotent, tho' they are not Omnipotent, and I must tell you, Sir, *the Commons of* England *are not a Body that can be Enslaved with* 20000 *Men; and all that have ever attempted it, formed their own Ruine in it, and I hope ever will do so; but* the Wicked fear where no fear is, and fly when none pursues.[11]

I wish he wou'd let us know his Character, that we might judge of the Manners by the Man, for I am sure we cannot judge well of the Man by the Manners.

Your most Humble Servant,
D.T.

---

11. Cf. Proverbs 28:1: "The wicked flee when no man pursueth: / But the righteous are bold as a lion."

Reflections on a late Scandalous[12] *Pamphlet,*
Entituled, An Argument against
a standing Army

Some Men are so fond of their own Notions, and so impatient in the Pride of their own Opinions, that they cannot leave Business of Consequence to them to whom it specially and peculiarly belongs, but must, with as much Brass[13] as Impertinence, meddle with a Cause before it comes before them, tho' it be only to show they have more Wit than Manners.

I observe this by the way, before I enter the List of Argument with a Nameless Author of a most Scandalous Pamphlet, call'd, *An Argument against a standing Army.*

If the Author of that Pamphlet be, as he wou'd be thought, a true honest spirited English-man, who out of his meer Zeal for the Safety, Liberty, and Honour of his Country, has made this false Step, he is the more to be consider'd: But if so, why shou'd he fear his Name? The days are over, *God be thank'd,* when speaking Truth was speaking Treason: Every Man may now be heard. What has any Man suffer'd in this Reign for speaking boldly, when Right and Truth has been on his side? Nay, how often has more Liberty been taken that way than consisted with good

12. Here used both in its colloquial sense of "grossly disgraceful" (*OED*, s.v. "Scandalous," 2) and in its more technical sense of "an inducement to sin or err," derived metaphorically from the Greek word σκανδαλον, meaning a stumbling block or a snare, and so used (in its Latin form, *scandalum*) by early Church Fathers such as Tertullian. Cf. Vulgate, Psalm. 118:165 and I Johan. 2:10.

13. I.e., brazenness, shamelessness (*OED*, s.v. "brass," 4a).

77

Manners, and yet the King himself never restrain'd it, or reprov'd it; witness Mr. *Stephen's* unmannerly Books,[14] written to the King himself.

[2] But since the Author Conceals himself from all the World, how can we guess him any thing but a Malecontent, a Grumbletonian, [15] *to use a foolish term*, a Person dissatisfied with his not being Rewarded according to his wonderful Merit, a *Ferg*——,[16] a *Man*——,[17] or the like. Or a down-right *Jacobite*, who finding a French War won't do, wou'd fain bring in Fears and Jealousies to try if a Civil War will. I confess I cannot affirm which of these; but I am of the Opinion he is the latter of the

---

14. Edward Stephens (d. 1706), priest and pamphleteer, had been initially an enthusiastic supporter of the Glorious Revolution, which he thought would bring about a reformation of public manners. When his expectations were disappointed, he instead published critiques of the Williamite monarchy.

15. A contemptuous designation applied in the latter part of the seventeenth century to the members of the so-called Country Party in English politics, who were accused by the Court party of being actuated by dissatisfied personal ambition; hence in later times applied to supporters of the Opposition (*OED*, s.v. "grumbletonian," 1). Cf. Blackmore's account of this grouping in English politics: "These Men were very Zealous to deliver us from our Laws and Libertys, and to restore us to the Privileges of our *Egyptian* Burdens. The ungrateful Murmurers spoke of Stoning the *Moses* that rescu'd them; and unable to bear their happy Deliverance, with Threats and Violence demanded their heavy Tasks, and their old Oppressors. These Men, according to their different Posts and Tempers, in different ways, assisted the Foreign Enemy" (Blackmore, *History*, pp. 11–12).

16. Robert Ferguson (d. 1714); radical, agitator, conspirator, and pamphleteer. Initially active in extreme Whig and dissenting circles, Ferguson associated himself with the first Earl of Shaftesbury, and was scurrilously active during the Exclusion Crisis (1680–81). He was involved in the Rye House plot to assassinate Charles II and served as principal adviser to the Duke of Monmouth's ill-fated insurrection against James II in 1685 (cf. above, p. 28, n. 68). Making good his escape to the Netherlands, in 1688 Ferguson sailed with the Prince of Orange, and in return for his service was made housekeeper of the Excise Office. But within a few months he had become disenchanted with the new regime and turned his hand to Jacobite conspiracy and propaganda, such as the skillful *A Brief Account of Some of the Late Encroachments and Depredations of the Dutch upon the English* (1695). "A radical like Robert Ferguson, the 'Plotter,' like Lilburne before him, worked against every administration because he believed that all ministers were and must, under the existing system, be always oppressive, corrupt, and parasitic" (Jones, *First Whigs*, p. 15).

17. John Manley (ca. 1622–99), republican agitator; an officeholder under the Commonwealth; active in the Rye House plot and the Duke of Monmouth's insurrection; sailed with William of Orange in 1688, but nevertheless was not rewarded by William with any office or preferment.

two,[18] because his insinuations are so like the Common Places of that Party, and his Sawcy Reflections on the King's Person, bear so exact a Resemblance to their usual Treatment of him, that it seems to be the very stile of a Malignant.[19]

I may be readily answer'd to this (I confess) *Let me be what I will, what's that to you, Answer my Argument; If the Doctrine be true, let the Devil be the Parson; Speak to the Point.*

In good time I shall: And to begin with him, I agree with him in all he says, or most part at least of his Preamble, saving some trifling Matters of Stile and of Notion, and we won't stand with him[20] for small things. And thus I bring him to his Fourth Page without any trouble; for indeed he might have spar'd all the Three Pages for any great signification they have, or relation to what comes after.

The Fifth Paragraph in his Fourth Page, and indeed the Substance of the whole Book brings the Dispute to this short Point; *That an Army in* England *is inconsistent with the Safety of the Kingdom; That Liberty and an Army are incompatible; That the King is not to be trusted with either Men, Arms, nor Money, for the last will be the Consequence of the former; lest he that has ventur'd his Life in the Extreamest Dangers for us, shou'd turn our* [3] *Devourer and destroy us.* A great deal of very handsome Language he bestows upon the King on this account, calling him, with a tacit sort of necessary Consequence, *Wolf, Beast, Tyrant,* and the like.

He tells us, *Page 3. All the Nations round us have lost their Liberty by their permitting standing Armies; and that they permitted them from Necessity or Indiscretion.* If from Necessity, 'twas their Misfortune not their Fault. If from Indiscretion, that was their Fault indeed.

But he is not pleas'd to give us one Instance of any People who were brought under that Necessity, and lost their Liberty by it; and yet if he had, 'twas no Argument, but that if we were reduc'd to the same Necessity, we must run the risque of it: Of which more by and by.

In the same Page he lays down the Draught of our Constitution, *Depending on a due Ballance between King, Lords and Commons;* and affirms from thence, *That this Constitution must break the Army, or the Army*

18. Cf. above, p. 74, n. 7.
19. I.e., someone disaffected to the current administration or government.
20. Contend with him (*OED,* s.v. "stand," 10).

destroy this Constitution: and affirms absolutely, with a Confidence Peculiar to himself, *That no Nation can preserve its freedom, which maintains any other Army than such as is composed of a Militia of its own Gentry and Freeholders.* And being gotten into a Positive vein, he says, *What happen'd yesterday, will come to pass again; and the same Causes will produce like Effects in all Ages.* And indeed all is alike true, since nothing is more frequent, than for the same Causes to produce different Effects; and what happened yesterday may never happen again while the World stands, of which King *James*[21] is a visible instance. But to descend to Particulars.

I shall give you only this remarkable Instance; King *Henry* VIII made as vigorous and irregular Efforts to destroy the Religion of the Kingdom (as then 'twas establish'd) [4] as ever King *James* did, and perhaps his Methods were more than ordinarily parallel; he Govern'd this Nation with as absolute a despotical Power, though the Constitution was then the same it is now, as ever King *Charles* II. or King *James* II. attempted to have done, and yet the Effects were not Abdication, or calling in a Foreign Aid. I could go back to other Kings of this Nation, whose Stories might illustrate this; but the Gentleman is Historian good enough, I perceive, to know it; and by the way, 'tis to be observed also, that he did this without the help of a Standing Army: From whence I only observe, as all the present use I shall make of this Instance, that there are ways for a King to tyrannize without a standing Army, if he be so resolv'd: *è contra,*[22] there may be ways to prevent it with an Army, and also that I think this proves, that *the same Causes does not always produce the same Effects;* and a little further, *if the same Causes will produce the like Effects in all Ages,* why then, Sir, pray lay by your Fears, for if ever King *William* (which we are sure he won't) or any King else, goes about to destroy our Constitution, and overturn our Liberties, as King *James* did, the People will call in a Foreign Aid, and cause him to run away, as they did then; *for what happened Yesterday will come to pass again, and the same Causes will produce the like Effects in all Ages.*

21. I.e., James II.
22. Vice versa.

Page the Sixth he begins very honestly, with a Recognition of our Security under the present King, and softens his Reader into a belief of his Honesty, by his Encomiums on his Majesty's Person, which would be well compar'd with his Seventeenth Page, to shew how he can frame his Stile to his Occasion; but in short, concludes, that when he is dead, we know not who will come next; nay, the Army may come and make who [5] they please King, and turn the Parliament out of Doors and therefore in short, we ought not to trust any thing to him, that we wou'd not trust to the greatest Tyrant that may succeed him. So that our Condition is very hard, that the Person of a King is no part of the Consideration, but *a King, be he Angel or Devil, 'tis all one, is a Bugbear,*[23] *and not to be trusted.* A fine Story indeed, and our great Deliverer (as he calls the King) must not regret this, but be contented: that *now he has cleared the World of all our Enemies, but himself,* he should be esteem'd the great *Charibdis*[24] which the Nation was to be split upon, and we must entirely disarm him, *as a Wolf who ought not to be trusted with Teeth*; for these are his own Words.

Then he tells us, *No Legislators ever establisht a Free Government, but avoided this, as the Israelites, Athenians, Corinthians, Accaians, Lacedemonians, Thebanes, Samnites, Romans.* Now 'tis notoriously known, that all these were first establish'd Commonwealths, not Monarchies: and if this Gentleman wou'd have us return to that Estate, then I have done with him; but I appeal to himself, if all these Governments, when they became Regal, did not maintain a Military Power more or less: Nay, God himself, when the *Israelites* would have a King, told them this would be a Consequence:[25] as if it might be inferr'd as of absolute necessity, that a Military Power must be made use of with a Regal Power; and as it may

23. See above, p. 36, n. 88.

24. A whirlpool on the coast of Sicily at present-day Torre Faro, opposite the rock of Scylla (with which Defoe seems to have confused Charybdis, when he speaks of the nation being "split" upon it).

25. See 1 Samuel 8:1–22. When the Israelite elders ask for a king, God tells Samuel to "shew them the manner of the king that shall reign over them" (8:9). Samuel describes an oppressive monarch, and places at the head of the list the creation of a military establishment: "This will be the manner of the king that shall reign over you: He will take your sons, and appoint them for himself, for his chariots, and to be his horsemen; and some shall run before his chariots. And he will appoint him captains over thousands, and captains over fifties; and will set

follow *no King, no Army*, so it may as well follow, *no Army no King*. Not that I think an Army necessary to maintain the King in his Throne, with regard to his Subjects, for I believe no Man in the World was ever *the Peoples King* more than his present Majesty. But I shall endeavour a little to examine by and by, what the King and Nation, so as [6] Matters now stand in the World, wou'd be without an Army.

But our Adversary rests not here, but Page 7, he proceeds; truly he *wou'd not have the King trusted with an Army; no, nor so much as with Arms, all the Magazines too must be taken from him.* And referring to the Estates, mentioned before, he says, *They knew that the Sword and the Sovereignty marcht Hand in Hand, and therefore a general exercise of the People in Arms, was the Bulwark of their Liberties, and their Arms,* that is, Magazines of Ammunition, &c. for the Term is now changed, *were never lodg'd in the Hands of any but the People:* for so the following Words directly imply. *The best and bravest of their Generals came from the Plough, and contentedly return'd to it again when the War was over.* We shou'd have made a fine War against *France* indeed, if it had been so here. And then he goes on with Instances of Nations who left their Liberties when ever they devi- ated from these Rules. At the end of these Examples, our Author tells all the World in short what he would be at: For there he has, like God Almighty, divided the World, and he has set the *Sheep on his right hand, and the Goats on his left*;[26] for he has reckon'd up all the Monarchal Governments in the World, with a *Go ye cursed into the most abandon'd Slavery*,[27] as he calls it; and all the Commonwealths in the World, on the other side, with a *Come ye blessed into freedom from Kings standing Armies,* &c.[28]

Nay he has brought *Algiers* and *Tunis* in for People who enjoy their Liberty, and are free. I suppose he has never been there: and truly, I be- lieve the Freedom he mentions here, wou'd be very like that, or like the

---

them to ear his ground, and to reap his harvest, and to make his instruments of war, and instruments of his chariots" (8:11–12).

26. Matthew 25:33. This quotation and the following two allusions are taken from the Sermon on the Mount.

27. See Matthew 25:41.

28. See Matthew 25:34.

Days when there was no King in Israel, *but every Man, did what was right in his own Eyes.*[29]

[7] Thus far I have follow'd him only with Remarks in general to Page 13. he proceeds then to tell us the Danger of an Army, and the Misfortune of all Countries to be forc'd sometimes to take up Arms against their Governours. A Man ought to be an universal Historian to affirm that, and I have not time to examine it. Now from hence he draws this Assertion, *That 'tis therefore necessary to put us into a Capacity always to be able to Correct our Kings, that we may have no occasion for it; for when we are enabled to do it, we shall never be put upon it.* The English is this, Keep your King so weak that he may always be afraid of you, and he will never provoke you to hurt him. *For,* says he, *the Nation shall be sure to live in Peace which is most capable of making War: But if the King has* 20000 *Men before-hand with us,* observe it [*with us*] *in totidem verbis*[30] I leave his meaning to be construed, *the People can make no Efforts without the Assistance of a Foreign Power.*

Another Consequence of an Army is, *They may come and force the People to choose what Members they please, to sit in Parliament, or they may besiege the Parliament-House, and the like.* Now it happened that both these things have been done in *England,* and yet the People preserved their Liberties, which is a Demonstration beyond the Power of Words, from his old Maxim, *What happen'd Yesterday, will come to pass again,* and *like Causes will have like Effects:* The choice of Members of Parliament were obstructed, and the House of Parliament was besieged and insulted by the Soldiers, and yet the People were not depriv'd of their Liberties; therefore it may be so again, *for what happen'd Yesterday will come to pass again.*

[8] Page 14. He descends to a particular, which reverst, I think, is a lively Instance what a vigorous Opposition may do against a far greater Force than 20000 Men: *If King* Charles *the First,* says he, *had had but* 5000 *Men, the People cou'd never have struck a Stroak for their Liberties.*

---

29. Judges 17:6, 21:25; cf. Judges 18:1.
30. In so many words.

Turn this Story, and let us but recollect what Force the Parliament had, and what the King had, and yet how many Stroaks he struck for his Crown.

The Parliament had the Navy, all the Forts, Magazines and Men in their Hands: The King, when he erected his Standard at *Nottingham*,[31] had neither Ships, Men, Arms, Ammunition or Money, but seem'd to be turn'd loose into the Field, to fight with the Commons of *England*, and all the Militia was in the Hands of the Parliament by the Commission of Array,[32] and yet the King was ready in *Keynton Field*, and at the Head of an Army, sooner than the Parliament were ready to fight him, nor do the Writers of that Side pretend to call that a Victory.[33]

31. Charles I raised his standard at Nottingham on 22 August 1642 and again on the three successive days, thereby declaring his intention to wage war. Clarendon describes the discouraging scene:

> When the King set up his standard at Nottingham . . . he found the place much emptier than he thought the fame of his standard would have suffered it to be; and received intelligence the next day that the rebels' army, (for such now he had declared them,) was, horse, foot, and cannon, at Northampton, . . . whereas his few cannon and ammunition were still at York, being neither yet in an equipage to march, . . . neither were there foot enough levied to guard it: and at Nottingham . . . there were not of foot levied for the service yet three hundred men. (Clarendon, *History*, 2:292–93; cf. Coke, *Detection*, p. 279)

Cf. Defoe, *Cavalier*, p. 145: "I confess, I had very melancholy Apprehensions of the King's Affairs; for the Appearance to the Royal Standard was but small. . . . the King had not got together a Thousand Foot, and had no Arms for them neither."

32. I.e., the public servants who were charged with the responsibility to muster the militia (*OED*, s.v. "array," 3).

33. Normally referred to as the Battle of Edgehill (May, *History*, lib. 3, pp. 15–16), fought between the Royalist and Parliamentarian forces near Banbury on 23 October 1642. The outcome of the battle was inconclusive, as Clarendon recorded: "Indeed the loss of both sides was so great, and so little of triumph appeared in either, that the victory could scarce be imputed to the one or the other" (Clarendon, *History*, 2:366; cf. May, *History*, lib. 3, p. 22: "the King, no lesse then the Parliament, pretended to be victorious in that Battell"). Cf. Defoe, *Cavalier*, pp. 164–65: "If the Parliament had the Honour of the Field, the King reaped the Fruits of the Victory; for all this Part of the Country submitted to him: . . . I thought the King had now in his Hands an Opportunity to make an honourable Peace; for this Battle at Edgehill, as much as they boasted of the Victory to hearten

Then he comes to King *James*, and says he, *If he had not attempted Religion, but been contented with Arbitrary Power, we shou'd ha' let him bound us Hand and Foot*; and tho' King James *had all the Nation, and his own Army against him, yet we account the Revolution next to a Miracle.* To this I reply, No, Sir; no Miracle at all on that Score; for the Nobility, Gentry and People of *England* did not question but they shou'd reduce him to reason, else they had never call'd in the present King, for they did not expect him to work Miracles, but to procure a Free Parliament, *&c.* as is at large express'd in his Majesties Declaration.[34] But here lay the Miracle of the Revolution:

[9] The Providential Removal of the *French* Kings Forces to the Siege of *Philipsburgh*,[35] against all manner of Policy, when if he had made but a

---

up their Friends, had sorely weakened their Army, and discouraged their Party too, which in effect was worse as to their Army."

34. In his Declaration, William claimed that "his Expedition was intended for no other Design, but to have a free and lawful Parliament assembled, as soon as it was possible" (Boyer, *William III*, 1:224; see Appendix C, below, p. 620). Burnet lays heavy emphasis upon this point: "He [William] resolved . . . to see for proper and effectual remedies for redressing such growing evils in a Parliament that should be lawfully chosen, and should sit in full freedom, according to the ancient custom and constitution of *England*, with which he would concur in all things that might tend to the peace and happiness of the Nation." (Burnet, *History*, 1:775)

35. *Philipsburg*, is a very important Fortress near the *Rhine*, called formerly *Udenheim*; it took its Modern Name, from *Philip Christopher de Saleren*, Bishop of *Spire*, and Archbishop of *Trier*. . . . The *French* King caused it to be regularly Fortified, and made it a very important Place. The *Germans* and their Allies, who had blocked it up for a long time, Besieged it, May 16. 1676. and it was surrendred to them upon Articles, *Sept.* the 17th. following. In 1688 *Sept.* the 27th. It was invested by the *French*. The 6th. of *October* the *Dauphin* of *France* came thither, and here made his first Campaign; the first of *November* it was surrendred, when it might have holden out much longer. However this Siege gave liberty to the Prince of *Orange*, now our King, to come over into *England*. *Philipsburg* stands seven Miles S. of *Spire*, and 18 S. W. of *Hiedelberg*. (Abel Boyer, *A Description Historical and Geographical of Flanders, etc.* [1702], p. 93)

The French move against Philipsburg in the autumn of 1688 was decisive in reconciling William of Orange to launching his invasion of England later that same year, since the commitment of French troops to the southeast reassured him that the Low Countries would not be subject to a French invasion. Philipsburg was

feint on the Frontiers of the *Dutch*, they could neither have spar'd their Troops nor their Stadtholder.[36]

The wonderful Disposition of the Wind and Weather which lockt up King *James*'s Fleet, so as to make the Descent easie and safe.[37]

And at last the Flight of King *James*, and the Re-settlement of the whole Kingdom without a Civil War, which was contrary to the Expectations of all the World; this was that which was next to Miraculous.

Now we must come to examine his Quotations, by which I must be excus'd to guess at the rest of his Instances, which indeed, generally speaking, are chosen very remote; he tells us, a very small Army is capable to make a Revolution; *Oliver Cromwel* left behind him but 17000, *Oportet Mendacem esse Memoriam;*[38] *Oliver Cromwel* did not work the Revolution which he brought to pass on the Parliament with less than 35000 Men, and if he left but 17000 behind him, which nevertheless I do not grant, there must be reckoned the Army left in *Scotland*, with General *Monk*,[39] which was at least 12000, and the Settlement in *Ireland*, which at least also took off from the old Army above 10000 Men more, besides those which had chang'd Parties and laid down their Arms: As to the *Pretorian* Soldiers, I don't read that they by themselves made any Revolution in the *Roman* Empire. *Julius Caesar* had a much greater Force when he March'd out of *Gaul;* and they were great Armies who Declared *Domitian, Titus* and *Tiberius* Emperors.[40] Then as to the *Ottoman*

---

one of the fortresses Louis XIV was obliged to hand over under the terms of the Treaty of Ryswick (1697).

36. I.e., William of Orange.

37. See above, p. 34, n. 84.

38. A grammatically incorrect recollection of a common Roman saying, corresponding to our own proverb that "a liar needs a good memory." Cf. Quintilian, *Institutio Oratoria*, IV.ii.91: "Verumque est illud, quod vulgo dicitur, mendacem memorem esse oportere"; "It is true, as the people say, that a liar needs to have a good memory." The proverb would have been familiar to those educated in England, since it was included in a school textbook illustrating points of Latin grammar, the *Sententiae Pueriles* (many editions, from the early sixteenth to the early eighteenth centuries). For an instance of the use of this saying in the context of late seventeenth-century political polemic, see Sidney, *Discourses*, p. 163.

39. See above, p. 48, n. 119.

40. Evidence of Defoe's shaky historical knowledge. Julius Caesar crossed the Rubicon in 49 B.C. at the head of the 13th Legion. Following the reforms of Marius

Empire, of which this Author, I suppose, knows very little; the *Janisaries*[41] have not been less in that Empire till this [10] War, than 70000 Men; what he calls the *Court Janisaries* I know not, but when *Selimus* Depos'd and Murther'd his Father *Amurath,*[42] you will find above 50000 *Janisaries* and *Spahis*[43] in the Action; but if an Army of 17000 Men can enslave this Nation, as he foolishly supposes, our Militia are good for much at the same time.

As to his Paragraph, *p.* 15. wherein he says, we are told, this Army is to be but for a time, and not to be part of our Constitution. I must say to him, I never have been told so, but I am of the Opinion, and shall acquiesce in it, that such an Army and no other, as the King and Parliament shall think needful for our Preservation shall be kept on Foot, so and so long as the said King and Parliament shall think fit; and from them I dare say no Danger can befal our Liberty. We have a blessed happy Union between the King and the Parliament; the King offers not to invade the Peoples Liberties, nor they his Prerogative; he will desire no Army but for their safety, nor they will deny none that is: But here is an Author, who in the beginning of his Pamphlet says, the Safety of the Kingdoms depends upon a due Balance; and at the same time tells us, our Armies, no nor our Magazines, are not to be trusted with the King; is that a due Ballance?

Then he tells you, that saying the Purse is in the Hands of the People, is no Argument at all, and that an Army will raise Money, as well as

---

the nominal strength of the Roman legion was 6,000 men, although in practice it could fall to as low as half that. Domitian, Titus, and Tiberius were all proclaimed emperor without the exertion of armed force. In the second edition of this text, published the same year, Defoe changed this list of emperors to the better one, for his purposes, of Galba, Otho, and Vespasian, who were indeed all made emperor by the armies they commanded.

41. See above, p. 28, n. 71.

42. More historical confusion on Defoe's part. Murad III succeeded his father Selim II in 1574, although he did not depose him in battle. During his reign the Janissary corps degenerated into a predatory band of ruffians. Relations between Europe and the Ottoman Empire were topical in the 1690s. Since 1683 the Turks had been involved in a war with the so-called Holy League (Austria, Poland, Venice, and Russia), which would be concluded in 1699 with the Treaty of Carlowitz (26 January). In the late summer of 1697 the Ottoman sultan Mustafa II had been defeated by Eugene of Savoy at the Battle of Zenta (11 September).

43. See above, p. 63, n. 18.

Money raise an Army; he suggests indeed, that 'tis *too desperate a Course,* as well he may; for I wou'd only ask him, if he thinks an Army of 20000 Men could suppress this whole Kingdom, and live upon Free Quarter on the Inhabitants by Force. I wou'd put him in mind of the Alarum *Ship Money*[44] made in *England,* and yet King *Charles* had then an Army and no Parliament Sitting. Then he supposes a shutting [11] up the *Exchequer,*[45] for indeed he is upon the Point of *Supposing* every thing that has but a *Possibility* in it, and what if the *Exchequer* should be shut up? why this Gentleman wants to be told that the Money is not in *Specie*[46] in the *Exchequer,* and it must be raised and brought thither by the Help of the Army; so that all that amounts to the same thing as the other, raising Money by Troops of Horse, which has been try'd in *England,* to the Destruction of the Contrivers; *and what has been,* he says, *will always be again.*

From this he proceeds to an insolent saucy Banter[47] on his Majesty's Person, *whose Vertue,* he says, *we ought not to hazard by leading it into Temptation:*[48] *Our Heroes,* he says, *are of a coarse Allay,* and he has observed most Men to do all the Mischief they can, and therefore he is for dealing with them as with Children and Mad Men, that is, take away all Weapons from them, by which they may do either themselves or others any Mischief: *as the Sheep who addrest to* Apollo, *that for the future the Wolves might have no Teeth.*[49]

His placing this in the Plural, the Courtiers, is too thin a Screen to blind any Man's Eyes; but 'tis as plain as if it had been said in so many Words, that all this is meant directly of the King; for who is it we have been speaking of? *'tis the King, who is not to be trusted with an Army, or*

44. An ancient tax levied in time of war on the ports and maritime towns, cities, and counties of England to provide ships for the king's service. It was revived by Charles I (with an extended application to inland counties), but was finally abolished by statute in 1640 (*OED,* s.v. "ship-money"). Cf. the Grand Remonstrance (Appendix B, below, p. 599); Neville, *Plato Redivivus,* pp. 125–26; May, *History,* lib. 1, pp. 16 and 84; and Ludlow, *Memoirs,* 1:6.

45. See above, p. 32, n. 77.

46. In the form of minted money (*OED,* s.v. "specie," 3b).

47. See above, p. 73, n. 5.

48. See above, p. 32, n. 79.

49. See above, p. 33, n. 80.

with the Arms of the Kingdom; 'tis the King who must be the Tyrant, and must raise Money, and shut up the Exchequer, and the like; and he speaks here of nothing but what the King only can be supposed to do.

In Confutation of his 18th Page, I could very plainly demonstrate, that even a Slavery under a Protestant Army would differ very much from a Slavery under a Popish and French Army. *England* has felt the First, [12] and seen others feel the last: there is a Difference in Slavery, *Algiers* is better than *Sally;*[50] and there are Degrees of Misery; and this is not putting an Epethite upon Tyranny, ask the Protestants of *Languedoc* if the *French Dragoons* were not worse than the *Spanish Inquisition.*[51] But this is Foreign to the Point, it does not appear to any considerate Person, that

50. Salé is a coastal city in northwest Morocco. In the seventeenth century it became an independent republic and was the home port of a fleet of pirates, the so-called Sallee Rovers. The treatment received by their prisoners was reputed to be exceptionally harsh: see, e.g., Anonymous, *A Description of the Nature of Slavery Among the Moors and the Cruel Sufferings of those that fall into it* (1721). Robinson Crusoe is briefly the slave of a Sallee Rover (Defoe, *Robinson Crusoe*, pp. 18–23); so too is the old woman in Voltaire's *Candide* (chap. 11). Other writers at this time drew a distinction between the kinds and degrees of harshness of slavery that might be encountered in the various regions of North Africa, and underlined the comparative humanity of Algierian slavery:

> It must be observ'd, there is a vast Difference between those who are *Slaves* at *Macqueness*, and those who are carry'd into *Slavery* at *Tunis, Tripoli, Algiers*, or other Parts of the *Turkish* Dominions. For the former are *Slaves* only to a *great Prince*, who forces them to constant and intolerable Services, with the poor Allowance only of Bread and Water; and if they work themselves to Death he is not in the least concern'd: But the latter are usually expos'd, like Beasts, to Sale in the Market-place, and are purchas'd by private Persons, who are generally call'd their *Patteroons*. Now 'tis the Interest of these to preserve the Lives of their *Slaves*, and many of these *Barbarians* (I am sorry and asham'd to relate it) are more kind and merciful to them, than many, in other Countries, who call themselves *Christians*, are to their *Apprentices* and *Servants*. (Thomas Pocock, *The Relief of Captives* [1720], pp. 22–23)

51. An allusion to Louis XIV's policy of "dragonnades," begun in 1681, which involved quartering ill-disciplined dragoons in Protestant households to intimidate them into converting to Roman Catholicism. Although the Spanish Inquisition has become a byword for religious oppression, in fact it did not greatly affect Protestants.

here is any of these Slaveries in view, and therefore, I thank God, we are not put to the Choice.

I shall leave him now, and discourse a little in Particular of the thing it self, and what other Pretensions he makes will meet their Answer in the process of the Story as they come in my way.

As I said at the Beginning, *what's all this to us?* We who are *English Men* have the least Reason of any People in the World, to complain of any of our Laws, or of any Publick Affairs, because nothing is or can be done, but I, and every *individual Free holder* in *England*, do it our selves, we consent to it, and tacitly do it by our *Representatives* in the Parliament; and since then our Liberties, aye and our Lives are committed to them, who are you, Sir? that you shou'd run before you are sent, and dictate to the *Collective Body of the Nation*, what they ought or ought not to do? if *the House of Commons* think fit to continue 50000 Men, there is no doubt but they will find ways so to keep them at their dispose, that even that Army shall be the Preserver of our Liberties, not the Destroyer of them, and to them let us leave it.

But 'tis the King is the Bugbear,[52] *a Royal Army shall destroy us, but a Parliament Army shall protect us.* Page II. *Commonwealths,* he says, *may have Armies, but Kings may not.* Now if putting Arms into the Hands of Servants is so fatal, why it's as dangerous to make a general Muster of the Militia, as 'twas to the *French*[53] in [13] the *West-Indies,* to give their Arms to their Servants, a standing Militia regulated and disciplin'd, such as the *Vaudois* or *Miquelets,*[54] why that's *a Standing Army, and shall be as insolent as they, if you give them an Opportunity, and a Standing Army,* as they may be regulated, *shall be as safe and as far from Tyrannizing as they.*

And with this Gentleman's leave, I believe I could form a Proposal how an Army of 20000 Men might be kept in *England,* which should be so far from being destructive of, that, they should on all Occasions be the Preservers and Protectors of the Peoples Liberties, in case of a *Court Invasion,* for that is the Out-cry; I confess, I do rather beg the Question

52. See above, p. 36, n. 88.
53. See above, p. 22, n. 52.
54. See above, p. 38, nn. 94 and 95.

here, than produce my Schemes of that Nature, because I do not think it becomes me to dictate to my Superiors, who without Question, know better what to do in that great Concern of the Government, than I could direct.

The Question here may be more properly, What sort of an Army we talk of? If 'twere an Army Independant of the People, to be paid by the King, and so entirely at his absolute dispose. If 'twere to be an Army of 50000 Men, why then something may be said; but our Gentleman has not talk'd of above 20000, and I presume he speaks of that without any Authority too, and at the same time talks of the Valour and Performances of the Militia, and wou'd have Sixty thousand of them settled and regulated. This Argument of the Militia is strangely turn'd about by him; sometimes they are such Hero's that they are able to defend us, and why should they not, and the like, *page* 20, 21. and sometimes so weak that 20000 Men *will ruine us all;* nay, any thing of an Army. If they are strong enough to defend us from all the World, a small number of standing Troops cannot hurt us; if they are not, then we must [14] have an Army, or be exposed to every Invader.

I wonder therefore this Gentleman does not descend to show us a time when the Militia of any Country did any Service *singly*, without the help of the Regulated Troops; I can give him a great many Instances when they did not. The best time that ever the Militia of *England* can boast of doing any Service, was in our Civil War; and yet I can name a Gentleman, who is now alive, who was an Officer of Horse in the Parliament Army, he was posted by the General at *a Defile*,[55] to dispute the Passage of some of the King's Horse, who advanc'd from *Warrington Bridge* in *Cheshire,* finding himself prest, he sent away to the General for some Foot to support him: He sent him a Company of Foot of the Militia, and a Detachment of Dragoons; the Foot were plac'd behind the Hedges to line the Pass where they might have fir'd almost under Covert, as behind a Breast-work;[56] but as soon as ever the King's Horse appear'd, without

55. A narrow passage which requires troops to march in single file.

56. A fieldwork, usually improvised, a few feet in height intended to serve as a defense against an enemy (*OED*, s.v. "breastwork").

firing one shot, they run all away.[57] These were Regulated Militia. But our Author gives us three Instances of Countries, whose Militia defend them; and three more of the bravery of a Country Militia, which Instances I must a little examine.

Poland, Switzerland, and the *Grisons*[58] are an Instance of Nations who defend themselves against powerful Neighbours without a standing Army. As to *Poland*, I have *shown already* at what a rate they have defended themselves. The *Swiss* and *Grisons* subsist between formidable Enemies, just as the Duke of *Savoy*[59] defends himself between the *French* and the *Spaniards*, or as *Hamburgh* between the *Danes* and the Dukes of *Zel*,[60] or as *Geneva* between the *French* and the *Savoyard*; not but that either side is able to devour them, but because when ever one side Attaques them, the others defend them; for 'tis [15] neither sides Interest to see the others have them.

But now we come to the Militia, the *London* Apprentices in the late War, and the *Vaudois* and *Miquelets*[61] in this. As to the *London* Auxiliaries, which they call Apprentices, they behav'd themselves very well, but it was in Conjunction with the Regulated Troops, when I must also say, the King's Army at that time were but raw, and not much better than themselves.

The *Vaudois* are *Les Enfans perdus*,[62] a People grown desperate by all the Extremities which make Cowards fight; a small handful of Ruin'd Men, exasperated by the Murder of their Families, and loss of their Estates, and are to be lookt upon as Men metamorphised into Dragons and Furies; and yet even the *Vaudois* have never fought but on Parties, Skirmishes, Surprizes, Beating up Quarters, and the like, back'd with

57. Defoe later reshaped and reimagined this episode in his *Memoirs of a Cavalier* (Defoe, *Cavalier*, pp. 152–53; cf. Ludlow, *Memoirs*, 1:44–45, 47, 49–50).

58. See above, p. 24, n. 55.

59. In the seventeenth century the dukes of Savoy ruled over what is now a region of southeast France and northwest Italy, and preserved their independence by means of skill in both warfare and diplomacy.

60. One of the hereditary titles of the House of Hanover, which in the person of George I would succeed to the English throne in 1714.

61. See above, p. 38, nn. 94 and 95.

62. Literally, "lost children"; thus, a forlorn hope.

Retreats into inaccessible Rocks, and skulking behind the Cliffs, from whence, like Lightning, they break out on the Enemy, and are gone before they could well find where they were.

The *Miquelets* in *Catalonia* are another Instance, and these are but People, who by the Advantages of the Mountains, lye in wait to intercept Convoys, and surprize Parties, and have done the *French* exceeding Dammage, on account of the Distance of the *French* Armies in that Country from their Magazines;[63] for 'tis necessary to state Matters very exactly, to debate with so cunning a Disputant. But for the Service of either the *Vaudois* or *Miquelets* in the open Field, it has not been extraordinary. As to the Militia in *Ireland*, all their Fame is owing to the despicable wretched Conduct of the *Irish;* for what Army but that of a Rabble of *Irish*, could *Iniskilling*[64] and *London-Derry*[65] have stood out against, at the rate they did. So that these Wonders of the Militia are all Phantosms, [16] and not applicable to the present Case at all.

I shall a little urge here by way of Reply, That there seems to be a Necessity upon the People of *England* at this time, to stand in a Posture of Defence more than usually; if I cannot prove this, then I say nothing.

---

63. I.e., military stores.

64. See above, p. 38, n. 96. Burnet praised the resolve of the inhabitants of Enniskillen: "The Inhabitants entred into Resolutions of suffering any thing, rather than fall into the hands of the *Irish*: A considerable Force was sent against them: but thro' their courage, and the cowardice of the *Irish*, they held out" (Burnet, *History*, 2:19). Boyer also praised their prowess:

> On the 24th of *April* a Detachment of the Garrison of *Inniskillin*, headed by Lieutenant Collonel *Lloyd*, made an Excursion into the Enemies Country, took and demolish'd the Castle at *Anghor*, and return'd home with a considerable Booty. Several other Skirmishes and Rencounters pass'd between the two Parties, wherein the *Inniskilliners* signaliz'd their Valour, and always came off with Advantage; but none of those Actions was so remarkable as that which happen'd, as it were by a particular Appointment of Providence, on the same Day *London-Derry* was reliev'd, wherein 2000 *Inniskilliners* fought and routed 6000 *Irish*, at a place call'd *Newton Butler*, and took their Commander *Mackarty*, with the loss only of 20 Men kill'd, and 50 wounded. (Boyer, *William III*, 2:69–70; cf. Jones, *History of Europe*, p. 370)

65. See below, p. 319, n. 165.

First, This Necessity arises from the Posture of our Neighbours: *In former times*, says our Authour, *there was no difference between the Citizen, the Souldier, and the Husband-man*;[66] but 'tis otherwise now, *Sir*, War is become a Science, and Arms an Employment, and all our Neighbours keep standing Forces, Troops of *Veteran* Experienced Soldiers; and we must be strangely expos'd if we do not.

In former times the way of Fighting was Common to all, and if Men ran from the Field to the Camp, so did their Neighbours, and 'twas as good for one as another. But how did the *Romans* preserve their *Frontiers*, and plant their Colonies? That was not done by Citizens of *Rome*, but by Legionary Troops;[67] and shall we Disarm, while our Neighbours keep standing Armies of Disciplin'd Souldiers on foot? Who shall secure us against a sudden Rupture? Whoever will give himself the trouble to look into the Treaties of *Westphalia* and *Nimeguen*,[68] and to Examine the Conduct of the *French* King, they will find, He did not then account Leagues such Sacred things as to bind him against a visible Advantage; and why should *we lead him into Temptation?*[69] Let any one but reflect on the several Treaties between him and the Duke of *Lorrain*,[70] the Duke of

66. A man who tills or cultivates the soil; a farmer (*OED*, s.v. "husband-man," 1a).

67. Possibly a historical error on Defoe's part. During the expansion of the Roman Republic (509–27 B.C.) her conquests were indeed made by legionary troops, but these were technically a militia, not a permanent professional army. When Rome became an empire her forces had become a professional standing army. See the introduction, above, pp. xlii–xlviii.

68. The Peace of Westphalia was signed in two parts, on 30 January (Spain and the Low Countries) and 24 October (the German states, France, and Sweden) 1648; it concluded the Eighty Years' War between Spain and the Low Countries, and the German phase of the Thirty Years' War. By this treaty France gained Alsace, and was confirmed in its possession of Metz, Toul, and Verdun, thus establishing a firm frontier west of the Rhine. The Treaties of Nijmegen (1678–79) ended the Dutch War, in which France had opposed Spain and the Dutch Republic. Once again, French territory was considerably increased by the provisions of these treaties. See Jones, *History of Europe*, pp. 1–27.

69. Cf. above, p. 32, n. 79. Primarily a clear reference to the language of the Lord's Prayer (Matthew 6:13; Luke 11:4) but also, in the context of this pamphlet, a glance at the technical theological sense of "scandalous"; cf. above, p. 77, n. 12.

70. Charles III (or IV) (1604–75), Duke of Lorraine; resolute adversary of France on its northern borders. In 1641 Charles had signed the Treaty of

Savoy,[71] and the *Spaniards*; after which ensued, the Prize of all *Lorrain*, the taking of all *Savoy*, and the taking of the City and Country of *Luxemburgh*; let them look on his surpri[17]sing the Principality of *Orange,*[72] directly contrary to the Peace of *Nimeguen*, and the like, and is this a Neighbour to live by Naked and without an Army? Who shall be Guarantee that the *French* shall not insult us, if he finds us utterly Disarmed.

To answer this Necessity says this wise Gentleman, *We will have an Equivalent; why, we will not have a Land Army, but we will have a Sea Army,* that is, *a good Fleet.* A fine Tale truly, and is not this some of Mr. *Johnson's* false Heraldry,[73] as well as 'tother? Is it not all one to be Slaves to an Army of Musqueteers, as a Rabble of Tarrs.[74] Our very Scituation, which the Author is in his Altitudes about, and blesses his *God Neptune for* at such a rate; that very Scituation exposes us to more Tyranny *from a Navy, than from an Army:* Nay I would undertake, if I were Admiral of a good Fleet, to Tyrannize more over this Nation, than I should if I were General of

---

Saint-Germain with France, which stipulated that his duchies would be forfeited by any future aggression against France. He eventually sold his estates to Louis XIV in 1662, but continued to wage war against France.

71. Vittorio Amedeo Sebastiano (1666–1732), Duke of Savoy; initially a client of Louis XIV, he subsequently broke away from French tutelage, joining the Grand Alliance in 1690. Possessed of a faint claim to the Spanish throne on the death of Carlos II (it depended on the nonpayment of the dowry of his great-grandmother the Infanta Catherine Michelle of Spain), he expected French support in his claim for the Duchy of Milan in lieu, but after the Treaty of Vigevano (1696) Louis XIV withdrew his support.

72. Lorraine had been sold to Louis XIV in 1662, although the heirs of Charles III had the sale annulled by the Treaty of Nomény (1663); it was handed back under the terms of the Treaty of Ryswick (1697) (Burnet, *History*, 2:202). France did not in fact annex Savoy until 1792, under the first French Republic, although during the War of the League of Augsburg (1688–97) France had made deep inroads into Savoyard territory, and the marquis de St. Ruth (see below, p. 96, n. 78) occupied most of the Duchy of Savoy (which, however, comprised only the northwest portion of the Principality of Savoy). Louis XIV had made incursions into Luxembourg from 1679, and in 1684 had completed his conquest by capturing Luxembourg city (Jones, *History of Europe*, p. 180). However, under the terms of the Treaty of Ryswick (1697), Luxembourg had been restored to Spain. In 1660 Louis XIV had captured Orange and destroyed its fortifications. It was finally ceded to France by the Treaty of Utrecht (1713).

73. See above, p. 33, n. 81.

74. I.e., sailors.

40000 Men. I remember 'twas a great cry among the *Jacobite Party*, about four Year ago; what a vast Charge are we at about a War for the Confederates, *Damn the Confederates*,[75] let us keep a good Fleet, and we are able to defend our selves against all the World; let who will go down, and who will go up, no Body will dare to meddle with us: But God be thanked, the King knew better than these, what was the true Interest of *England*; a War in *Flanders* is a War in *England*, let who will be the Invaders; for a good Barrier between a Kingdom and a powerful Enemy, is a thing of such Consequence, that the *Dutch* always thought it well worth the Charges of a War to assist the *Spaniard*; for thereby they kept the War from their own Borders and so do we.

In defending this silly Equivalent of a Fleet, he has the Vanity to say, *If our Fleet be well mann'd, 'tis a ri[18]diculous thing to think of any Princes Invading us*; and yet we found it otherwise. This very War we found King *James* invaded *Ireland*, and the *French* sent him an Aid of 8000 Men,[76] who stood their Ground so well at the Battle of the *Boyn*,[77] that if King *James* had done his part as well, it might have been a dearer Victory than it was; after this he fetch'd those 8000 off again; and after that sent Monsieur St. *Ruth*;[78] and after that a Relief to *Limerick*, tho' it came too late; and all this notwithstanding we had the greatest Fleet at Sea, that ever *England* had before that time, since it was a Nation.

Thus Experience Baffles this foolish Equivalent, for Armies are not Transported with so much Difficulty; and the Six hundred Sail the P. of

---

75. I.e., England's allies in the League of Augsburg.

76. Burnet numbers the French troops sent to Ireland to assist James II in 1689 at 5,000 and estimates James's total forces at 30,000 foot and 8,000 horse (Burnet, *History*, 2:17, 18). Boyer reports that James embarked for Ireland from Brest with no more than "1500 Men, commanded by experienc'd *French*, *Scotch* and *Irish* Officers" (Boyer, *William III*, 2:57).

77. See above, p. 38, n. 96.

78. Charles Chalmont (ca. 1650–91), marquis de St. Ruth; French general sent by Louis XIV to command in Ireland. The previous year St. Ruth had been vigorous in his oppression of the Protestants of Savoy, as Burnet remarks: "St. *Ruth*, one of the violentest of all the Persecutors of the Protestants in *France*, was sent over with two hundred Officers to command the *Irish* army" (Burnet, *History*, 2:78). St. Ruth died at the Battle of Aughrim (12 June, 1691), where he was hit by a cannonball.

Orange brought with him, had not been absolutely necessary for 14000 Men; but there were vast Stores, Artillery, Arms, and heavy Baggage with them,[79] which are not always necessary; for we know Monsieur *Pointy* carried 4500 Men with him, on his Expedition to *Cartagena* in but 16 Ships;[80] and the 8000 Men before-mentioned, sent to *Ireland*, were carried in not above 35 or 38 Sail.

Another wretched Equivalent, which this Author would have us trust to, is the *Militia*; and these he magnifies, as sufficient to defend us against all the Enemies in the World; and yet at the same time so Debases them, as to make them nothing in Comparison of a small Army: Nay, he owns, that *notwithstanding these we are undone, and our Liberties destroyed, if the King be trusted but with a few Guards.* This is such a piece of Logick as no Man can understand.

If a Militia be regulated and *Disciplin'd*, I say they may enslave us as well as an Army; and if not, they cannot be able to defend us; if they are unable to Defend us, they are insignificant; and if able, dangerous; [19] *But*, says the Author, *there is no danger from the Militia, for they are our selves, and their Officers are Country Gentlemen of Estates:* And is not our Army full of *English* Gentlemen, of Estates and Fortunes; and have we not found them as inflexible to the Charms of Tyranny, when closetted in the late Reign;[81] and as true to the Protestant Interest and Liberties of *England*, as any Country Gentlemen, or Freeholders, or Citizens in *England*. Did

---

79. See above, p. 34, n. 82.

80. Jean Bernard Louis Desjean (1645–1707), baron de Pointis; naval officer. In 1697 the Spanish port of Cartagena on the coast of Colombia had been attacked and looted by Pointis and his associate, Jean Baptiste Ducasse (Jones, *Theatre of Wars*, p. 98). In January 1690 Pointis had been sent to Ireland by Louis XIV to assess the chances of a Jacobite victory, and had reported back positively, saying that the Irish were disorganized but enthusiastic (Miller, *James II*, pp. 220–21).

81. A term coined to describe James II's browbeating of his political opponents. Burnet explains the word's origins: "All those, who had either spoken or voted for the Test [i.e., the Test Act: see below, p. 558, n. 38], were soon after this disgraced, and turned out of their places, tho' many of these had served the King hitherto with great obsequiousness and much zeal. He called for many of them, and spoke to them very earnestly upon that subject in his closet: Upon which the term of closeting was much tossed about" (Burnet, *History*, 1:667). Cf. Miller, *James II*, pp. 163–64, and Jones, *Secret History*, pp. "45–48" (sigs. Cccccc7^r–Cccccc8^v).

they not lay down their Commissions, did they not venture to disobey his illegal Commands? when the Cowardly Citizens address'd him with their nauseous Flattering, fulsome Harrangues; thank'd him for their Bondage, and gave up their Charters and Priviledges,[82] even before he ask'd for them; *These are the Persons that must guard our Liberties*; and they would be finely Guarded, *God help us.* I remember a Speech which I have to show in *Manuscript* of Sir *Walter Rawleigh*,[83] on the Subject of the *Spanish* Invasion, which comes directly to this Case. The Author of this Pamphlet, to instance in the prodigious Navy that is necessary to bring over a small Army, tells us, the *Spanish Armado* Embark'd but 18000 Men, but he forgot that they were to take the Prince of *Parma* on Board from *Flanders* with 28000 old Low Country Soldiers more, with which Army, as Sir *Walter Rawleigh* observ'd to that Gentleman, it was no improbable thing to think of Conquering this Kingdom; and Queen *Elizabeth* was so sensible of it, that she often told Sir *Walter*, that if they had not been beaten at Sea, they had been all undone, for her Armies were all Tumultuary Troops,[84] Militia, and the like.[85]

To proceed, I'll grant all the Improbabilities which he suggests of the *French King's* reviving a War, which has been so fatal to him: And as to King *James* Coming, [20] truly I'll allow the Militia are fittest at all times to deal with him; but to use his own Method of *Supposing the worst*, I'll *suppose* the *French King* waving the Ceremony of a *League*, and

82. In November 1687 James II had set up a commission to regulate corporations. Over the ensuing months the commissioners carried out a number of purges of boroughs represented in Parliament. Some corporations were regulated several times. In many cases Anglicans were replaced by Catholics and dissenters. The commissions of the peace in the counties were similarly weeded (*ODNB*). Defoe here echoes the language of William's *Declaration* of 1688, in which one of James's misdemeanors is to have "invaded the Priviledges, and seised on the Charters of most of those Towns that have a right to be represented by their Burgesses in Parliament: and have procured surrenders to be made of them, by which the Magistrates in them have delivered up all their Rights, and Priviledges, to be disposed of" (see Appendix C, below, p. 615).

83. Sir Walter Raleigh (or Ralegh) (1554?–1618), explorer, soldier, courtier, and poet; a favorite of Elizabeth I and captain of the Queen's Guard.

84. Gathered hastily and promiscuously, without order or system; irregular, undisciplined (*OED*, s.v. "tumultuary," 1).

85. Untraced.

a *Declaration of War*, when he has recovered Breath a little, shou'd as much on a sudden as can be, break with us single, and pour in an Army of 50000 Men upon us; I'll suppose our Fleet may be by accident so lockt in, as King *James's* was,[86] *for what has been may be*, and they take that Opportunity, and get on Shore, and to oppose their Army, truly we raise the Militia, a Fine Shew they wou'd make, but what wou'd they do against 60 Batalians of *French* and *Swiss* Infantry? wou'd this Gentleman *venture to be hang'd if they run all away and did not fire a Gun at them?* I am sure I wou'd not.

But on the other Hand, if the Militia are a sufficient Guard against a *Foreign Power*, so they are against a *Home Power*, especially since this *Home Power* may be kept down to a due Ballance, so as may but suffice to keep us from being insulted by a *Foreign Enemy;* for Instance, suppose the King were to entertain in constant Pay, 20000 Men, including his Guards and Garrisons, the Militia of *England* Regulated and Disciplin'd, join'd to these, might do somewhat, but by themselves nothing. I can give him innumerable Instances of the Services of the Militia, but I never heard or read of any real Bravery from them, but when join'd with Regular Troops.

To Instance once for all, 'tis notorious that when the Prince of *Conde* attackt the Citizens of *Paris* at *Charenton*, that Populous City being all in an Uproar, sent a Detachment of 20000 Men to dislodge the Prince, who with 1500 Horse and Dragoons, drove them all away, and they never lookt behind them, till they got within the City Wall.[87]

[21] Another Necessity for keeping up a certain Number of Troops, is the vast Expence and Difficulty of making a New-rais'd Army fit for Service; I am bold to say, as the Nature of Fighting is now chang'd, and the Art of War improv'd, were the King now to raise a New Army, and to be Commanded by New Officers, Gentlemen who had seen no Service,

86. See above, p. 34, n. 84.

87. Louis II de Bourbon (1621–86), prince de Condé, duc d'Enghien, known as "le Grand Condé"; prince of the blood, leader of the last of the aristocratic uprisings known as the Fronde (1648–53); an extremely accomplished general. During the first Fronde Condé conducted the siege of Paris on behalf of the government (January–March 1649). Charenton is a suburb on the southeastern edge of Paris, approximately four miles from the city center. In the seventeenth century it was the headquarters of the Huguenot churches.

it should cost him Three Years Time, and 30000 Mens Lives to bring them into a Capacity to face an Enemy. *Fighting is not like what it has been*; I find our Author is but a *Book Soldier*, for he says, *Men may learn to be Engineers out of a Book*; but I never heard that a *Book Gunner* could *Bombard a Town*; the Philosophy of it may be Demonstrated in Scales and *Diagrams*, but 'tis the Practice that produces the Experiments;[88] 'tis not handling a Musket, and knowing the Words of Command, will raise a Man's Spirit, and teach him to Storm a Counterscarp;[89] Men must make the Terrors of the War familiar to them by Custom, before they can be brought to those Degrees of Gallantry. Not that there is an intrinsick Value in a *Red Coat*;[90] and yet the Argument is not at all enforced by the Foul Language he gives the Souldiers, while they are fighting in *Flanders*, and laying down their Lives in the Face of the Enemy to purchase our Liberty; 'tis hard and unkind to be treated by a rascally Pamphleteer with the scandalous Term of *Ragamuffins*, and *Henroost Robbers*. I am no Soldier, nor never was,[91] but I am sensible we enjoy the present Liberty, the King his Crown, and the Nation their Peace, bought with the Price of the Blood of these *Ragamuffins*, as he calls them, and I am for being civil to them at least.

I might descend a little to examine what a strange Country *England* would be, when quite dismantled of all her Heroes (as he calls them); truly were I but a [22] Pirate with a Thousand Men, I wou'd engage to keep the Coast in a Constant Alarm. We must never pretend to bear any Reputation in the World: No Nation would value our Friendship, or fear to affront us. Not our Trade Abroad would be secure, nor our Trade at Home. *Our Peace*, which we see now establish'd on a good Foundation, what has procur'd it? a War, and the Valour of our Arms, speaking of

---

88. I.e., experience.

89. In a fortification, the outer wall or slope of the ditch, which supports the covered way; sometimes extended to include the covered way and glacis (*OED*, s.v. "counterscarp").

90. Since the early seventeenth century the uniform of some English forces had included a red coat.

91. Except at the defeat of the Duke of Monmouth's forces at Sedgemoor in 1685 (Novak, *Defoe*, pp. 82–86; Richetti, *Defoe*, p. 10; Backscheider, *Defoe*, pp. 35–40).

Second Causes.[92] And what will preserve it? truly nothing but the Reputation of the same Force; and if that be sunk, how long will it continue? Take away the Cause, and our Peace, which is the Effect, will certainly follow.

Let me now a little examine the History of Nations who have run the same risque this Gentleman would have us do, and not to go back to remote Stories of the *Carthaginians*,[93] who the *Romans* could never vanquish till they got them to dismiss their *Auxiliary Troops*, the Citizens of *Constantinople*, who always deny'd their Emperor the Assistance of an Army, were presently ruin'd by the *Turks*.[94] We will come nearer home: The Emperor *Ferdinand* II. over-run the whole Protestant Part of *Germany*, and was at the point of Dissolving the very Constitution of their Government, and all for want of their having a *Competent Force* on foot to defend themselves; and if they had not been deliver'd by the Great *Gustavus Adolphus, God Almighty must have wrought a Miracle to have sav'd them.*[95] Next look into *Poland*, which our Author reckons to be one of the *Free Countries who defend themselves without a standing Army.* First he must understand, for I perceive he knows little of the Matter, that *Poland*

92. I.e., the primary cause is the divine favor enjoyed by the English and the rest of the Grand Alliance as a consequence of fighting against Catholic France in a just and religious war.

93. Defoe refers to *A Notable and Memorable Story of the Cruel War between the Carthaginians and their own Mercenaries* (1647), a pamphlet purporting to be an extract from Raleigh's *History of the World*, in which ancient history was adapted to the circumstances of the English Civil War, and which had contributed to some of the attitudes which informed the standing army controversy of the late 1690s.

94. Mahomet II conquered Constantinople in 1453, finally entering the city on 29 May. The emperors of Constantinople during the decay of the eastern empire after the tenth century tended to rely on foreign mercenaries from northern Europe. The military spirit of the Greeks had become enfeebled by refinement and religion; the canons of St. Basil stipulated that soldiers should be separated for a period of three years from the community of the faithful (Gibbon, *Decline and Fall*, 3:409).

95. Ferdinand II (1578–1637), Holy Roman Emperor from 1619, archduke of Austria, king of Bohemia (1617–19; 1620–27), king of Hungary (1618–25); leader of the Roman Catholic Counter Reformation and champion of absolutism in the Thirty Years' War (1618–48), the main developments of which Defoe summarizes here. In 1720 Defoe would return to the Thirty Years' War and use it as the setting for part 1 of his *Memoirs of a Cavalier*.

has not defended it self; or if it has, it has been at a very sorry rate, God knows, much such a one as we should do without an Army, or at much such a rate as we did of old, when the *Picts* and *Scots* were our Hostile Neigh[23]bours. Pray let us see how *Poland*, which enjoys its freedom without a standing Army, has defended it self: First, It has been ravag'd on the side of *Lithuania* by the Effeminate *Muscovites*, and tho' the *Poles* always beat them in the Field, yet they had devoured their Country first before the *Polanders* Militia could get together. On the other hand, the *Tartars*, in several volant[96] Excursions, have over-run all *Upper Poland*, *Ukrania* and *Volhinia*, even to the Gates of *Crakow;* and in about Fifty years 'tis allow'd they have carried away a Million of this *wretchedly free People* into Slavery, so that all *Asia* was full of *Polish* Slaves.

On the East side *Carolus Gustavus*, King of *Sweden*, over-run the whole Kingdom, took *Warsaw, Crackow*, and beat King *Casimir* out of the Country into *Silesia*, and all in one Campaign, and only indeed for want of a *Force ready* to meet him upon the Frontiers; for as soon as *Casimir* had time to recover himself, and Collect an Army, he lookt him in the Face, and with an Invincible Resolution fought him wherever he met him: But the ruin of the Country was irreparable in an Age.[97]

96. I.e., flying, rapid (*OED*, s.v. "volant," 1b).

97. Defoe is here summarizing the major events of Polish history in the mid-seventeenth century. In 1648 Bohdan Khmelnytsky had become leader of the Zaporozhian Cossacks (Defoe's "Tartars"). He defeated Polish troops in a series of engagements and became master of the Ukraine. In 1654 Khmelnytsky reached an agreement with Tsar Alexis, and Muscovite troops invaded Lithuania, occupying its capital, Wilno, in 1655. Charles X of Sweden, anxious to counterpoise growing Muscovite power in the Baltic, invaded Poland, which capitulated to him in July 1655, and King John II Casimir Vasa was exiled to Silesia. Gradually, however, the Swedes were driven out of Poland, and the Treaty of Oliwa (1660) restored the territorial status quo ante the Swedish invasion. Poland was a byword for constitutional confusion in England at this time:

> Poland is both governed and possessed by some very great persons or potentates, called palatines, and under them by a very numerous gentry. For the king is not only elective, but so limited, that he has little or no power but to command their armies in time of war; which makes them often choose foreigners of great fame for military exploits: and as for the commonalty or countrymen, they are absolutely slaves, or villains. This government is extremely confused; by reason of the numerousness of the gentry: who do not

To come nearer home, and nearer to the Matter in hand, our Neighbours the *Dutch,* in the Minority of the present King, and under the manage of *Barnavelt*'s Principles reviv'd in the Persons of the *De Witts,* to preserve their Liberties, as they pretended they would suppress the Power of the House of *Orange,* and Disband their old Army which had establish't their Freedom by the Terror of their Arms; and to secure themselves, they came to a regulated Militia, the very thing this Gentleman talks of: Nay, this Militia had the Face of an Army, and were entertain'd in Pay; but the Commissions were given to the Sons of the principal Burghers, and the Towns had Governors from among themselves. [24] This is just what our Gentleman wou'd have; and what came of this? These brave Troops were plac'd in Garrisons in the Frontier Towns: And in the Year 1672, the *French* King, this *very individual French King now regnant,* during the continuance of the *Sacred Peace of Westphalia,*[98] enters the Country at the Head of *two dreadful Armies,* and these Soldiers, that were the Bulwark of the Peoples Liberties, surrendred the most impregnable Towns, garrison'd some with 2000, some 3000 Men, nay some with 6000, without striking a stroke, nay faster than the *French* cou'd well take Possession of them; so that in about Forty days he had taken 42 strong Towns, which would cost him Seven years to take now, tho' no Army were in the Field to disturb him; and then the People saw their Error, and gave themselves the Satisfaction of Tearing to Pieces the Authors of that pernicious Advice.[99]

---

always meet by way of representation as in other kingdoms; but sometimes, for the choice of their king and upon other great occasions, collectively in the field. (Neville, *Plato Redivivus,* p. 144)

A few years later, in *The Dyet of Poland* (1705), Defoe would return to seventeenth-century Polish history, and exploit it and the characters prominent within it as sources of innuendo with which to satirize English politics of the period 1688–1705.

98. See above, p. 94, n. 68.

99. An abbreviated (and, as one would expect from Defoe, a pungently Orangist) account of Dutch history in the mid-seventeenth century. Johan van Oldenbarnevelt (1547–1619), lawyer and statesman, was one of the founders of an independent Netherlands. He mobilized resistance to Spain, and in 1596 devised the anti-Spanish Triple Alliance with France and England. Johan de Witt (1625–72) was a statesman of a younger generation who pursued Oldenbarnevelt's policy of

And truly, I think these Instances are so lively, that I wonder our Author, who I perceive is not so ignorant, as not to know these things, shou'd not have provided some Answer to it, for he could not but expect it in any Reply to him.

These things may a little tell us what is the *Effects of a Nations being disarm'd* while their Neighbours are in Arms, and all this must be answer'd with *a Fleet;* and that may be answer'd with this, *We may be invaded not-withstanding a Fleet*, unless you can keep up such a Fleet as can Command the Seas in all parts at the same time, or can, as Queen *Elizabeth* did, forbid your Neighbours to build Ships. But the *French* King is none of those, and his Power at Sea is not to be slighted: Nor is it so small, but it may with *too much ease* protect an Invasion, *and it is not safe to put it to that hazard.*

Another Necessity of an Army seems to me to lye a[25]mong our selves: There are Accidents which require the help of an Army, tho' the King and People were all of a Mind, *and all of a side.* King *James* and his Parliament had a full understanding, and they were as Vigorous for him, as ever Parliament was for a King, and yet what had become of both if he had not had *Regular Troops* to have resisted the Duke of *Monmouth?*[100] If they had been to be raised *then*, he must have gone to *France* then, as he did now, or have stay'd at home and have far'd worse, for they wou'd hardly have us'd him so tenderly as the present King did to my knowledge.

I am loth to mention the *Jacobite Party* as an Argument worth while, to maintain any thing of force, but just enough to prevent *Assassinations and private Murthers on the King's Person;* for as they never dar'd *look him*

---

independence for the Netherlands. During the minority of William III de Witt was the leading figure in Dutch politics, restoring the finances of the United Provinces and consolidating its commercial dominance in the East Indies. However, when Louis XIV invaded the United Provinces in 1672 and made devastating inroads, there was popular clamor for William III (whom de Witt had carefully excluded from real political or military power) to be placed at the head of affairs. On 24 July 1672 de Witt's elder brother, Cornelis de Witt (1623–72), was arrested on a charge of conspiracy against William, and tortured. When his brother visited Cornelis in the Gevangenpoort at The Hague, an Orangist lynch mob burst in and tore both brothers to pieces. See Coke, *Detection*, pp. 484–87; Jones, *Secret History*, pp. "56–60" (sigs. Dd4ᵛ–Dd6ᵛ); Sidney, *Discourses*, pp. 207–8; and Temple, *Memoirs*, pp. 20–22.

100. See above, p. 28, n. 68.

in the face when powerfully assisted by the *French;* so I dare say they will never have the Courage to disturb our Peace *with Sword in hand;* what they do, will be by Caballing[101] to foment Distrusts and Discontents to embroil, if possible, the King with his People, or by private villainous Assassinates[102] to destroy him, and by that means to involve the whole Nation in *Blood and Disorder.*

I allow the Speech of Queen *Elizabeth* to the Duke *D'Alancon* was very great and brave in her;[103] but pray had Queen *Elizabeth* no *standing Army?* On the contrary, she was never without them; she never had less in the *Low Countreys,* in aid of the *Dutch,* in *France* in aid of the King of *Navar,*[104] and in her Wars in *Ireland,* than 30000 Men; and all the difference was, that she kept them abroad, employ'd for the Assistance of her Neighbours, and had them absolutely at Command; and so sensible she was of the want of them on the approach of the *Spanish Armado,* that she never left her self so bare of them afterwards: and therefore to compare her Enemies and ours, and her Force with ours, without an Army, as he does [26] *p.* 19. is a *Deceptio visus*[105] upon our Understanding, and a presumption that no body has read any History but himself.

101. To conspire for some secret, private, and usually mischievous end (*OED,* s.v. "cabal"). In the recent English past the term "Cabal" (which had been coined earlier in the seventeenth century, and which derives from the term for the Jewish mystical tradition of interpretation of the Old Testament) had been applied to the five ministers of Charles II who had signed the Treaty of Alliance with France for war against Holland in 1672. These were Clifford, Arlington, Buckingham, Ashley Cooper, and Lauderdale, the initials of whose names coincidentally spelled "cabal." See Coke, *Detection,* p. 478, and Jones, *Secret History,* pp. "37–40" (sigs. Cc3^r–Cc4^v).

102. I.e., assassins (*OED,* s.v. "assassinate," 2a).

103. See p. 44, n. 109.

104. Henri de Navarre or de Bourbon (1553–1610); as Henri IV, king of France from 1589; leader of the Huguenots during the French Wars of Religion; recipient of aid from his coreligionist Elizabeth I of England until his conversion to Roman Catholicism in 1593.

105. A deceitful appearance or trick of legerdemain. The phrase occurs frequently in English writing of the earlier seventeenth century: e.g., "a gross *Delusion;* a kind of *deceptio visus,* a filling the Eye with phantastick *Aerial* Images, which have no *solid* Being" (Richard Allestree, *The Causes of the Decay of Christian Piety* [1667], p. 83). It is a phrase of which Defoe was at this time fond, since he had used it earlier in 1697 in his *An Essay Upon Projects,* when urging his reader to

Then we come to K. *Charles* the Second's time in *p. 26.* and *then*, he says, *we thought a much less Army than is now contended for a grievance.* To which I answer, *Quatenus*[106] *an Army*, they were not thought a Grievance, but attended with the Circumstances of Popish Confederacies and Leagues, and *a Popish Successor in view*,[107] and then *visibly managing them* they might be thought so; and yet the *Grand Jury*[108] presenting them, made them no more a Grievance than if they had presented the Parliament which granted an establisht number of Troops to King *Charles*.

Another bold Assertion he makes *p. 27. That a standing Army is the only way to bring in K.* James. This is a strange preposterous Supposition, and has no Argument brought to prove it, but the uncertain capricious Humour of the Souldiery, who in all Ages have produc'd violent Revolutions, may bring it to pass; that is in short, *the Thing is possible*, and that is all he can say; and 'tis every jot as possible, that K. *William* himself should change his Mind, *Abdicate the Throne*, and *Call in K. James again*, therefore *pray let us have no King at all*, for really when all is done *these Kings are strange things, and have occasion'd more violent Revolutions in the World than ever have been known in unarm'd Governments.* Besides, if we had no King, then a *standing Army* might be safe enough; for he tells you, *in Commonwealths they may be allow'd*, p. 11. *but in Monarchies they are the Devil and all:* Nay he gives two Instances when we had Armies turn'd out their Masters, *Oliver Cromwel* and *General Monk*,[109] and yet both these were in the time of *a Commonwealth*. Now I would know if ever an Army turn'd out their King; as for K. *James*, his instance is false, he really run away from his Army, his Army did not turn him out; 'tis true, part of it deserted: but I am bold to say, had K. *James*, with the Remainder, made [27] good his Retreat, *Souldier like*, either to *London*, or

---

distinguish between "Improvement of Manufactures or Lands, which tend to the immediate Benefit of the Publick, and Imploying of the Poor; and Projects fram'd by subtle Heads, with a sort of a *Deceptio Visus*, and *Legerdemain*, to bring People to run needless and unusual hazards" (p. 15).

106. As far as, or "to the extent that they were [an army]."

107. I.e., the future James II, then Duke of York, who had converted to Roman Catholicism by 1676.

108. See above, p. 45, n. 111.

109. See above, p. 48, nn. 118 and 119.

under the *Canon of Portsmouth,* or to both, which he might ha' done, for no Body pursued him, till the *French King* had reliev'd him, *it might have been a Civil War to this Hour.*

And thus I have followed him to his last Page, I think I have not omitted any of his material Arguments or Examples; whether he is answered or not, in point of Argument, I leave to the Reader: what I have discovered in his Sophistical straining of Arguments, and misapplying his Quotations to gild by his Wit the want of his Proof, is what I thought needful; his malicious Spirit every where discovers it self, and to me he seems to be a discontented unsatisfied sort of a Person,[110] that is for any thing but what shou'd be, and borrows the Pretence of Liberty, to vent his Malice at the Government: Nor is it a new Invention, when ever any Person had a mind to disturb the *Roman Government,* Liberty was always the Word, and so it is now.

Conclusion

I shall say no more as to Argument, but desire the Favour of a Word in General, as to the present Controversy.

To me it seems one of the most impudent Actions that ever was suffered in this Age, that a Private Person shou'd thus attack the King, after all that he has done for the Preservation of our Liberties and the Establishing our Peace, after all the Hazards of his Person and Family, and the Fatigues of a bloody War, to be represented at his Return, as a *Person now as much to be feared as King* James *was; to be trusted no more than a Mad Man,* and the like, before he so much as knows whether there shall ever be any Dispute about the Matter, or no.

Has the King demanded a Standing Army?[111] Has he propos'd it? Does he insist upon it? How if no such thought be in him? 'Tis a Sign what a Government we live under, and 'tis a Sign what Spirit governs some Men, who will abuse the most indulgent Goodness. It had been but time

110. See above, p. 78, n. 15.
111. Burnet is clear on this point: "At the opening the Session of Parliament [in 1697], the King told them, that in his opinion, a standing Land Force was necessary" (Burnet, *History,* 2:206; cf. Boyer, *William III,* 3:287).

to have wrote such an Invective upon the King and the Army, when we had found the Parliament of *England* strugling to disband them, and the King resolute to maintain them: But *This!* when the King and the House are all Union and Harmony![112] 'tis intollerable, and the King ought to have some Satisfaction made him, and I doubt not but he will.

I am not, nor, I think, I have no where shown as if I [28] were for the Government by an Army; but I cannot but suppose, with Submission to the House of Commons, that they will find it necessary to keep us in a Posture of Defence sufficient to maintain that Peace which has cost so much Blood and Treasure to procure, and I leave the Method to them, and so I think this Author ought to have done. I do not question but in that great Assembly all things will be done for the Maintenance of our Liberty with a due respect to the Honour and Safety of his Majesty, that is possible: They have shown themselves the most steady and Zealous for his Interest and the Publick, of any Body that ever filled that House; and I could never see, and yet I have not been a slight observer of Affairs neither. I say, I could never see the least symptom of an Inclination in the King's Actions, to dislike or contradict what they offered: has he not left them to be the entire judges of their own Grievances, and freely left them to be as entire judges of the Remedies? Has he ever skreened a Malefactor from their Justice, or a Favourite from their Displeasure? Has he ever infring'd their Priviledges? and as to who shall come after, we have his Royal Declaration at his coming to these Kingdoms; *That his Design was to establish our Liberties on such Foundations, as that it might not be in the power of any Prince for the future to invade them,* and he has never yet attempted to break it;[113] And how is this to be done? not at the direction of a Pamphlet, but by the King, Lords and Commons, who have not taken a false Step yet in the Matter; To them let it be left, and if they agree, be it *with an Army,* or *without an Army;* be it *by a Militia regulated,* or *by an Army regulated,* what is that to him?

112. For Boyer's contrasting analysis of the deep divisions in this Parliament, see below, p. 326, n. 185.

113. A précis of part of William's addition to his *Declaration* (cf. Boyer, *William III,* 1:225–26; see Appendix C, below, p. 622).

I have indeed heard much of *a Militia regulated into an Army*, and truly I doubt not, but *an Army might be regulated into a Militia*, with Safety and Honour to the King, and the Peoples Liberties. But as I have said, *I leave that to the Government to determine*, and conclude with only this Observation; If ever the Gentleman who is the Author of this Pamphlet be trac'd, I verily believe he will appear to be one, who thinking he has deserv'd more Respect from the Government than he has found, has taken this Way to let them know, they ought to have us'd him better or us'd him worse.

FINIS.

Walter Moyle

The Second Part of an Argument

1697

1. "His neighbor Ucalegon is ablaze" (Virgil, *Aeneid*, II.311–12). The quotation comes from Aeneas's description of the sack of Troy.

THE
SECOND PART
OF AN
ARGUMENT,
Shewing, that a

Standing Army

Is inconsistent with
A Free Government, and absolutely
destructive to the Constitution of
the English Monarchy.

With Remarks on the late published LIST of
King *JAMES*'s Irish Forces in France.

Proximus ardet Ucalegon.[1]
Virgil. Aen. l. 2.

London, Printed in the Year, *1697*.

The Preface

The following Considerations were written, and designed to be published soon after the Argument *against a* Standing Army *appeared. But a Report being given out, That the Advocates for a* Standing Army *would do Wonders on that Subject, 'twas thought convenient to expect Their Atchievements, that if their Success should prove in any measure answerable to their Confidence, the Publick might have been no farther importuned about the Matter. I think I may justly say, This Mountain, after all its Pangs and Convulsions, has brought forth nothing but a ridiculous Mouse.[2] And therefore I shall submit to the Judgment of all impartial Englishmen, what is here said in confirmation of the* Argument: *Which I hope will be of the greater weight, because taken from our own History.*

2. An allusion to Horace's famous image of the bathos: "Parturient montes, nascetur ridiculus mus" (*De Arte Poetica*, l. 139).

An Argument, &c.

PART II

We have much talk of a Standing Army which is to be in time of Peace, but no body can tell us what they are to do: We know their usual Commission is to kill and slay; But where is the Enemy? Men talk of this with as much certainty, as if they were already established. Which is yet the more surprizing, if we reflect on one of the Articles of Charge against the late King *James*.[3] It is plain therefore that all this is Practice, and that these bold Forestallers of Parliaments would fain Enact that without Doors,[4] which from the Foundation of this Kingdom was never attempted within.

These Gentlemen are also pleased to affirm it necessary to have a vast Body of Forces continued on foot: Whereas the first Project we find for a Standing Army, in the Year 1629, requires only three thousand Foot in constant Pay, to bridle the Impertinence of Parliaments; to overaw the Parliament and Nation; to make Edicts to be [6] Laws; to force upon the People vast numbers of Excises; and in short, to overturn the whole Frame of this noble English Government. Whoever has a mind to peruse

---

3. Presumably the allegation that he maintained a standing army. The preamble to the Bill of Rights (1689) lists among James's transgressions that he was guilty of "raising and keeping a standing army within this kingdom in time of peace without consent of Parliament, and quartering soldiers contrary to law" (see Appendix D, below, p. 628).

4. I.e., outside Parliament; cf. above, p. 65 and n. 23.

that dangerous Scheme in *Rushworth's Appendix*, pag. 12. and what he says of it in his History, will see enough.[5]

I marvel whose Advocates these Men are in this Matter: For I am satisfied none of those brave Englishmen, who have fought honourably abroad, ever meant, when the Service was over, to be a Charge, Burden and Terror at home to their own Country; nor to disfranchise us of two of our Native Liberties, Freedom from Martial Law, and Billeting of Souldiers; and thereby directly to take away from themselves, as well as from their Fellow-subjects, one half of the Benefit of the *Petition of Right*,[6]

---

5. Moyle refers to a policy document presented in Star Chamber in 1629 which aimed to strengthen the internal police of the kingdom and also to raise taxes. It had been reprinted in the appendix to Rushworth, *Historical Collections*, pp. 12–17. The proposal had two goals: "to secure your State, and to bridle the impertinency of Parliaments: the other, to increase your Majesties Revenue, much more then it is." The former was to be achieved by the erection of "a Fortress in every chief Town," for which it was calculated that a total force for the kingdom of "three thousand men will be sufficient" (Rushworth, *Collections*, pp. 12–13). The proposal recalls the marks of a tyrant as explained in early modern resistance theory: "A tyrant places foreigners in garrisons, and constructs fortresses against the citizens. He disarms the people, and expels it from fortifications. He surrounds himself with barbarous and servile guards, and with public funds hires spies and informers against his subjects, like scouts against an enemy" (*Vindiciae*, p. 145).

6. The Petition of Right was passed on 7 June 1628, and restricts non-Parliamentary taxation, forced billeting of soldiers, imprisonment without cause, and the use of martial law. It concludes as follows:

> That no man hereafter be compelled to make or yield any gift, loan, benevolence, tax, or such like charge, without common consent by act of parliament; and that none be called to make answer, or take such oath, or to give attendance, or be confined, or otherwise molested or disquieted concerning the same or for refusal thereof; and that no freeman, in any such manner as is before mentioned, be imprisoned or detained; and that your Majesty would be pleased to remove the said soldiers and mariners, and that your people may not be so burdened in time to come; and that the aforesaid commissions, for proceeding by martial law, may be revoked and annulled; and that hereafter no commissions of like nature may issue forth to any person or persons whatsoever to be executed as aforesaid, lest by color of them any of your Majesty's subjects be destroyed or put to death contrary to the laws and franchise of the land.

For the full text, see Appendix A, below, pp. 577–80.

and in consequence the other half too, The Freedom of their Persons and Estates.

I shall therefore consider of a Standing Army, without minding who is for it, or who is against it in this Age, and only shew what are like to be the Consequences of it in future Reigns. And I have reason to do thus, because if the Parliament give the best King a Standing Army, the worst King shall hereafter claim and have it.

We have many Instances where Parliaments in a kind Fit, by one sudden Grant, have entailed a World of lasting Misery upon the Nation. I will mention but one; The Kingdom was newly delivered from a bitter Tyrant, I mean King *John*, and had likewise got rid of their perfidious Deliverer the Dauphin of *France;*[7] who [7] after the English had accepted him for their King, had secretly vowed their Extirpation, which the* *Viscount of Melun*,[8] a Frenchman, being at the point of Death, disclosed; they were moreover blessed with a young Prince,[9] of whom they conceived mighty Hopes, in the Hands of a very wise and honest Council. This was Life from the Dead, and a true Revolution. In the Transport of all

---

* *Daniel*, pag. 148.

7. John (1167–1216), king of England. In 1215 Prince Louis, the French dauphin, was offered the English throne by a group of rebellious barons, and sent an advance guard of French troops to London in December of that year. John died the following year while trying to suppress rebellions on several fronts.

8. The chronicles record that a French nobleman, the viscount Melun, disclosed at the point of death that Louis intended to massacre the English rebels who had invited him to invade. Shakespeare dramatized this episode in *King John*, V.iv.10–20. Moyle's footnote refers to the following passage in Daniel:

> The popular bruit generally divulged concerning the confession of the Viscont *Melun* a Frenchman, who, lying at the point of death, toucht with compunction, is said to reueale the intention, & vow of *Louys* (which was vtterly to extinguish the English nation, whom he held vile, & neuer to be trusted, hauing forsaken their own Soueraign Lord) wrought a great auersion in the hearts of the English, which whither it were indeed vttered, or giuen out of purpose, it was so to be expected, according to the precedents of all inbrought farreiners vpon the deuisions of a distracted people. (Samuel Daniel, *The Collection of the Historie of England* [1618], p. 125)

9. I.e., Henry III (1207–72).

this Happiness, about the *7th* Year of this new King *Henr.* 3. the Parliament granted him the Wardship of their Heirs. *Knighton*, pag. 2430, records it thus; *Magnates Angliae concesserunt Regi Henrico Wardas Haeredum & terrarum suarum, quod fuit initium multorum malorum in Anglia.*[10] He says this Grant was the beginning of many Mischiefs in *England*. In the Year 1222 these Mischiefs had their Rise and Beginning; but where they ended, no old Chronicle could ever tell: For after this intolerable Bondage had continued above four hundred Years, the Nation at last ransomed themselves in our time by giving the Excise.[11] It is a grief to all after Ages to find a Parliament so miserably overseen, for they both mistook their Man; and the hopeful Prince proved as bad, as if the very Soul of his Father *John* had passed into him, which is the common Character given him by all the Antient Historians:[12] And then they utterly mistook the Nature of the Grant, and did not foresee what a Misery

10. "The English nobles granted to King Henry wardship of their heirs and estates, which was the source of many evils in England." Henry Knighton (d. ca. 1396), chronicler and Augustinian canon. The quotation comes from Sir Roger Twysden's compilation of early chronicle histories of England, *Historiae Anglicanae Scriptores X* (1652), p. 2430. The Court of Wards had become extremely unpopular during the reign of James I, acquiring the stigma of being an instrument of oppressive rule. In 1610 James had offered to abolish it in return for a revenue from Parliament of £200,000 per annum (see Ludlow, *Memoirs*, 1:5, and Sidney, *Discourses*, pp. 64–65). The Court had ceased to function when the Long Parliament had abolished feudal tenures in February 1646. It was formally abolished by the Tenures Abolition Act of 1660. For commentary, see H. E. Bell, *An Introduction to the History and Records of the Court of Wards & Liveries* (Cambridge: Cambridge University Press, 1953).

11. A duty charged on home goods, levied either in the course of their manufacture or at point of sale (*OED*, s.v. "excise," 2). An excise was first adopted in England on 22 July 1643. It long provoked resentment, as Johnson's pungent definition shows: "*Excise*, a hateful tax levied upon commodities, and adjudged not by the common judges of property, but wretches hired by those to whom excise is paid."

12. Moyle blackens Henry's character. Sir Robert Cotton had described him as "a Child . . . mild and gracious, but easie of nature, whose Innocency and natural goodness led him safe along the various dangers of his Fathers Reign" ("A Short View of the Long Reign of King Henry III," in *An Answer to Such Motives* [1675], p. 104). It is a view endorsed by modern historians, who see Henry as "a *vir simplex*, an uncomplicated, almost naïve man, pious, and a lover of peace" (*ODNB*).

and Vassalage[13] it might prove to their Posterity. I appeal to all [8] the Antient Nobility and Gentry, who know any thing of the Affairs of their own Families, whether it was so or not: And yet these were honest and brave Men, who would rather have died than have been the Authors of so much Mischief: but they were led by false Appearances, that by having the King Guardian of their Children, they could not be wronged; they would have the best Education at Court, stand fair for future Preferment, and that a happier Provision for their Posterity could not be made: Neither could it, for the very Learning which this instructive Passage has given to their late Posterity, countervails all the Mischiefs that are past.

But the Advocates for a Standing Army tell us, That tho the Wards by being annexed to the Crown, and so becoming a Prerogative, could not be parted with, which was the cause of the long continuance of that Mischief, after it was known and felt to be so; yet all this is cured by making the Act Temporary, and setling a Standing Army only during his Majesty's Reign, or for Years, or they know not how. I find they have a great mind to their Cucumber,[14] for they are content to have it dressed and pickled any way.

I answer, That succeeding Princes, if they find an Army, will keep it, and will not trouble themselves whether the Law be Temporary or Perpetual. A plain Instance we have of this in the Customs: For tho Tunnage and Poundage,[15] and the other Impositions, are a Subsidy and free Gift, and the King's Answer to the Bill thanks the [9] Subjects for their Good-wills. And tho Parliaments have always used such Cautions and

13. Subjection or servitude (*OED*, s.v. "vassalage," 3a).

14. The meaning of this curious saying is clear enough (i.e., to be determined on a course of action, no matter what the cost), but I have been unable to find any other instances of its use.

15. "Tonnage" is a tax or duty formerly levied upon wine imported in tuns or casks, at the rate of so much for every tun (*OED*, s.v. "tonnage," 1). "Poundage" is a duty or tax of so much per pound sterling on merchandise, and in particular a subsidy, usually of twelve pence in the pound, formerly granted by Parliament to the Crown, on all imports and exports except bullion and commodities paying tonnage (*OED*, s.v. "Poundage," 1a).

Limitations in those Grants, as might prevent any Claim, and heretofore limited them to a short time, as for a Year or two; and if they were continued longer, they have directed a certain space of Cessation, or Intermission, that so the Right of the Subject might be the more evident; at other times they have been granted upon occasion of War for a certain number of Years, with Proviso, that if the War were ended in the mean time, then the Grant should cease; and of course they have been sequestred into the hands of some Subjects for the guarding of the Seas.

Notwithstanding all this, tho the Parliament so carefully guarded their Grants, yet King *Charles* the First took this Subsidy without any Grant at all, for sixteen Years together; tho several Parliaments in the mean time forbad the payment of it, and voted all those to be publick Enemies that did not refuse it.[16] The like did his Son the late King *James* till his Parliament gave it him: and in his first Speech to them he demanded it as his own, by the name of *my Revenue*.[17] And why then shall

---

16. Tonnage and poundage was technically a free gift to the monarch from the Commons, rather than a tax to which the Crown was entitled, as Selden had explained in the House on 16 June 1628 (Rushworth, *Collections*, p. 640). Charles had collected tonnage and poundage from the beginning of his reign, but had done so without the authority of a parliamentary grant. In 1628 the Commons sent Charles a "Remonstrance" in which their view of the constitutional position was made clear:

> Although Your Royal Predecessors the Kings of this Realm have often had such Subsidies, and Impositions Granted unto them, upon divers occasions, especially for the guarding of the Seas, and safeguard of Merchants; Yet the Subjects have been ever careful to use such Cautions, and Limitations in those Grants, as might prevent any claim to be made, that such Subsidies do proceed from duty, and not from the free gift of the Subject; And that they have heretofore used to limit a time in such Grants, and for the most part but short, as for a year or two, and if it were continued longer, they have sometimes directed a certain space of Cessation, or intermission, that so the right of the subject might be more evident. (Rushworth, *Collections*, p. 641)

On 22 June 1641 Charles gave his assent to a bill to abolish tonnage and poundage.

17. Following the death of his brother Charles II on 6 February 1685, James II addressed Parliament on 22 May. After promising to "Defend and Support" the Church of England "as it is now by Law Established," he went on to ask them to apply their minds to "the Settling of My Revenue, and Continuing it during my

not another Prince come and say the same, Give me my Army, if he ever have a Parliament to ask? To limit a Prince with Laws where there is an Army, is to bind *Sampson* with his Locks on.[18]

Having made appear that an Army now will be an Army always, I come in the next place to show what the Consequences of it will be, both [10] by the Experience of former Ages, and by the Nature of the Thing.

In all Ages and parts of the World, a Standing Army has been the never-failing Instrument of enslaving a Nation; which *Richard* the Second,[19] (*Walsing.* pag. 354.) compassing to do here in *England*, accordingly used the Means. For the Safety of his Person, he assembled together (*multos Malefactores*) a great number of profligate Persons out of the County of *Chester*, who should keep watch and ward continually about him in their turns. This Life-guard of his consisted of four thousand Archers; who committed such Outrages amongst the People, overawed the Parliament, and aided him in his Tyrannical Proceedings in such a manner, as could

---

Life, as it was in the Time of the King My Brother," and he concluded his address, having referred to Argyle's rebellion in Scotland, by reminding them to "give Me My Revenue" (*His Majesties Most Gracious Speech to both Houses of Parliament* [1685], pp. 4, 5, 7).

> Three days after Charles died, James announced his intention to summon a Parliament. He also announced that he would continue to collect the revenues voted to Charles for life and that he had no doubt that Parliament would vote the same to him. Some thought this very irregular. It was normal for a new king to collect the customs before his first Parliament met, but Charles II had been the first king to be granted the excise, so there were no precedents for its collection at a new king's accession. For this reason, a new contract for the collection of the excise had been sealed the day before Charles died and the judges ruled (by a majority of eight to four) that the contract was valid. On 16th February [1685] James issued a proclamation publicizing this ruling and, despite a few grumbles, found little difficulty in collecting Charles's revenues. (Miller, *James II*, p. 135)

18. I.e., with his strength undiminished, and therefore to no purpose. Milton's *Samson Agonistes* had been first published in 1671.

19. Cf. Twysden, *Scriptores*, p. 2748.

not be believed, if it were not witnessed by a whole Parliament, and his own Confession,* *Artic.* the *5th.*

* Item, Tempore quo idem Rex in Parliamento suo fecit adjudicari Ducem Gloucestriae, & Comites Arundell & Warwick ut liberius possit exercere Crudelitatem in eosdem, & voluntatem suam injuriosam in aliis adimplere, sibi attraxit multitudinem magnam Malefactorum de Comitatu Cestriae, quorum quidam cum transeuntes per Regnum, tam infra Regis hospitium quam extra, Ligeos Regni crudeliter occiderunt, & quosdam verberaverunt, vulneraverunt, & depraedarunt bona populi, & pro suis victualibus solvere recusarunt, & Uxores & alias mulieres rapuerunt, & violaverant, & licet super eorum hujusmodi excessibus graves querimoniae deferebantur ad audientiam dicti Domini Regis, Idem tamen Rex super his justitiam, seu remedium facere non curavit, sed favebat iisdem gentibus in maleficiis eorum; Confidens in iis & eorum praesidio, contra quoscunq; alios Regni, propter quod fideles regni sui magnam commotionis & indignationis materiam habuerunt. *Decem. Scrip. Col.* 2748.[20]

20. The quotation comes from the bill of complaint drawn up as part of the deposition of Richard II by Henry Bolingbroke in 1399. Moyle has carelessly transcribed the passage from Sir Roger Twysden's *Historiae Anglicanae Scriptores X* (1652) so as to obscure the sense. In Twysden it reads:

> *Item,* Tempore quo idem Rex in Parliamento suo fecit adjudicari Ducem *Gloucestriae,* & Comites *Arundell,* & *Warwick,* ut liberius possit exercere crudelitatem in eosdem, & voluntatem suam injuriosam in aliis adimplere, sibi attraxit multitudinem magnam malefactorum de Comitatu *Cestriae,* quorum quidam cum Rege transeuntes per regnum, tam infra [intra?] hospitium Regis, quam extra ligeos regni crudeliter occiderunt, & quosdam verberaverunt, vulneraverunt, & depraedarunt bona populi & pro suis victualibus solvere recusarunt, & uxores & alias mulieres rapuerunt, & violaverunt, & licet super eorum hujusmodi excessibus graves querimoniae deferebantur ad audientiam dicti Domini Regis, idem tamen Rex super hiis justitiam, seu remedium facere non curavit, sed favebat iisdem gentibus in maleficiis eorundem, confidens in eis, & eorum praesidio contra quoscunq; alios regni sui, propter quod fideles regni sui magnam commotionis & indignationis materiam habuerunt. (Twysden, *Scriptores*, col. 2748)

It translates as:

> At which time the king caused the Duke of Gloucester and the Earls of Arundel and Warwick to be impeached in Parliament so that he might the more freely persecute them. And to gratify his malicious intentions toward others, he gathered around him a great multitude of criminals from the county of Chester, some of whom, as they traveled through the kingdom in the company of the king, cruelly slew freemen of the kingdom whether or not they were the king's guests. Some they scourged and wounded. They plundered the people's possessions, and they refused to pay for their food. They raped and outraged men's wives and other women, and even though

[11] In short, tho many of those *Cheshire*-men plundered and lived upon Free-quarter;[21] beat, wounded, killed and ravished where-ever they came: Yet because they enabled him to execute all his cruel and arbitrary Designs in Parliament, he countenanced them in all their Crimes, as confiding in them, and trusting in their defence of him against all the Realm beside: For which cause all the Lieges of his Realm had great matter of Commotion and Indignation.

This Parliament was in the 21*st* of his Reign,[22] and in it the Frame of this English Government was quite destroyed. I need not shew in what Particulars, for that is done already by *Bacon*,[23] and many other Lawyers. But in short, the King was made absolute, and the whole Power of Parliament, which might remedy things afterwards, was given up: For it was

---

serious complaints about these and similar excesses were brought to the attention of their sovereign lord, he however was unconcerned either to bring them to justice, or to make amends. Rather, he smiled upon them in their wrongdoing, reposing confidence in them and seeing them as his defense against all his other subjects; on account of which his loyal subjects had great reason to feel indignation and disquiet.

21. The right of troops to be billeted in free quarters; the necessity for troops of having to find free quarters; the obligation or imposition of having to provide free board and lodging for troops (*OED*, s.v. "free-quarter"). It came to be resented as in effect a non-Parliamentary tax on the property of the subject: see Henry Care, *English Liberties* (1680), p. 145.

22. I.e., 1397.

Parliament opened at Westminster on 17 September 1397. The monk of Evesham describes how the building was surrounded by 200 of the king's Cheshire archers, and both he and Adam Usk convey the sense of terror they were evidently intended to induce. The chancellor, Edmund Stafford, set the tone for the parliament by preaching a sermon in which he declared that the power of the king lay singly and wholly with the king, and that those who usurped or plotted against it were worthy of the penalties of the law. (*ODNB*)

23. Nathaniel Bacon (1593–1660), politician and author; prominent in the opposition to Charles I; refused to pay the forced loan in 1628; active in the Parliamentarian cause during the Civil Wars. Bacon's *An Historicall Discourse of the Uniformity of the Government of England* (1647) was a justification of the proceedings of the Long Parliament against Charles I which developed and deployed the idea of an "ancient constitution" to devastating effect. Bacon's analysis of the reign of Richard II occurs in the first chapter of his *The Continuation of an Historicall Discourse of the Government of England* (1651).

made Treason for any Man to endeavour to repeal any of the Arbitrary Constitutions that were then made.

I am even ashamed, when I observe former Princes so zealous for oppressing and wronging a Nation, and so bent upon it, to reflect how cold and remiss many Subjects have been in all times, and how unconcerned to preserve their indispensible Rights, which are the very Being both of themselves and their Posterity: To see King *John* ready to pawn his Soul, and offer *Miramolim* the Emperor of *Morocco* to turn Turk, and to make his Kingdom tributary to him only, to get his Assistance to enslave this Nation, and Subjects to take no care of their English Liberties;[24] [12] which certainly are proved to be worth keeping by the eagerness of bad Princes to take them away.

But to return to our *Cheshire*-men, and to the Parliament which they had in charge, *Sagittariis inumerabilibus vallato*,[25] walled about with an infinite number of Archers, as it is described *Artic.* 4. The Parliament was hereby so overawed, that in what they did they were *Magis timore Regis ducti quam mentium ratione*,[26] led more by fear of the King than their Consciences; their Souls were not their own. And besides the Standing Awe and Terror which this Guard was to both Houses during their Session, there happened a Passage at last which put them all into a very great Fright: It is thus set down by *Stow*,[27] p. 316. "And then licence being had

24. A rumor about John reported in the early chronicles of his reign, but now dismissed by historians as a monkish calumny (*ODNB*). Moyle may have read it in Daniel's *Collection* (from which he has already quoted: see above p. 119, n. 8):

> And to shew the desperate malice of this king (who, rather then not to haue an absolute domination ouer his people, to doe what he listed, would be any thing himselfe vnder any other that would but support him in his violences) there is recorded an Ambassage (the most base & impious that euer yet was sent by any free and Christian Prince) vnto *Miramumalim* the *Moore* . . . wherein he offred to render vnto him his kingdom, and to hold the same by tribute from him, as his Souraigne Lord: To forgoe the Christian faith (which he held vayne) and receiue that of *Mahomet*. (Daniel, *Collection*, p. 119)

25. I.e., "besieged by countless archers."
26. "Guided more by their fear of the king than by the reason of their minds."
27. Also it was enacted, that criminall causes from thenceforth should be determined in euery Parliament, and then licence being had to depart, a

to depart, a great stir was made, as is used; Whereupon the King's Archers, in number 4000, compassed the Parliament-House (thinking there had been in the House some Broil by fighting) with their Bows bent, their Arrows notched, and drawing ready to shoot, to the terror of all that were there; but the King herewith coming, pacified them."

These Men did the King such acceptable Service, that he could do no less than make some return to his Implements,[28] which he did in honouring *Cheshire* for their sakes. In this Session of Parliament he made it a Principality, *Cap.* 9. and himself Prince of *Chester:* And so as *Bacon* says,[29] *Counties go up, and Kingdoms go down:* This had never risen again but by a happy Revo[13]lution, which followed in less than two Years. So much for the *Cheshire*-men.

But what signify the Proceedings of this villanous[30] Crew to an Army, who are all of them Men of Honour, and perhaps in Parliament-time shall be ordered a hundred miles off? these cannot wall in, surround, begirt and beset a Parliament, nor consequently hinder it from being a Free Parliament. That I deny, for I hope such an Army may differ in Judgment, and can petition a Parliament at that distance; and we very well know that their Desires are always Commands. The Parliament in 41, long before there was any breach with the King, were in a fair way to have been petitioned out of doors[31] by an Army 150 miles off, tho there was the Clog[32] of a Scotch Army at the heels of them, who upon the least Motion would certainly have followed. And if *Denzill Holles* had not locked the Doors, and communicated the Matter to the House, who immediately fell upon

---

great sturre was made as is vsed, wherevpon the Kings Archers, in number four thousand, compassed the Parliament house, thinking there had bin in the house some broyle or fighting, with their bowes bent, their arrowes set in them, and drawing, readie to shoote, to the terrour of all that were there, but the King heerewith comming, pacified them. (John Stow, *Chronicles* [1580], p. 521)

28. As applied to persons, a tool or implement (*OED*, s.v. "implement," 2b).

29. "*Cheshire* for this service is made a Principality; & thus goes *Counties* up, and *Kingdoms* down" (Nathaniel Bacon, *The Continuation of an Historicall Discourse of the Government of England* [1651], p. 11).

30. Here meaning both morally repugnant and servile.

31. See p. 117, n. 4.

32. Hindrance (*OED*, s.v. "clog," 3).

the Officers that were Members, Colonel *Ashburnham*, *Willmot*, *Pollard*, &c. and quashed the Design, it had brought the whole Nation into great Confusion.[33] The Petition of an Army is like that of the Cornish-men in *Henry* the Seventh's Time; it is always a strong Petition.[34]

33. Denzil Holles (1598–1680), first Baron Holles; Parliamentarian and politician. The other named members were all conspirators in the Army plots of 1641, which were intended to bend Parliament to the will of the king: William Ashburnham (1604/5–1679), army officer and politician; Henry Wilmot (1613–58), first Earl of Rochester, Royalist army officer; Sir Hugh Pollard (1603–66), Royalist army officer and courtier. See Conrad Russell, "The First Army Plot of 1641," *Transactions of the Royal Historical Society* 38 (1988): 85–106.

34. An allusion to some of the language alleged to have been used by Cornish rebels in 1496:

> For no sooner beganne the *Subsidie* to bee leuied in *Corne-wall*, but the People there began to grudge and murmure. The *Cornish* being a Race of Men, stout of stomacke, mighty of Bodie and Limme, and that liued hardly in a barren Countrey, and many of them could (for a neede) liue vnder ground, that were *Tinners;* they muttered extreamely, that it was a thing not to be suffered, that for a little stirre of the *Scots,* soone blowne ouer, they should be thus grinded to Powder with *Payments:* And said, it was for them to pay, that had too much, and liued idly. But they would eate the bread they got with the sweat of their browes, and no man should take it from them. And as in the *Tides* of *People* once vp, there want not commonly stirring *Windes* to make them more rough: So this *People* did light vpon two *Ring-leaders,* or Captaines of the *Rout.* The one was one MICHAEL IOSEPH, a *Black-smith* or *Farrier* of *Bodmin;* a notable talking Fellow, and no lesse desirous to bee talked of. The other was THOMAS FLAMMOCKE, a *Lawyer;* who by telling his neighbours commonly vpon any occasion, that the *Law* was on their side, had gotten great sway amongst them. This Man talked learnedly, and as if he could tell how to make a *Rebellion,* and neuer breake the *Peace.* Hee told the *People,* that *Subsidies* were not to be granted nor leuied in this case; that is, for *Warres* of *Scotland* (for that the *Law* had prouided another course, by seruice of *Escuage,* for those Iourneyes) much lesse when all was quiet, and Warre was made but a *Pretence* to poll and pill the *People:* And therefore that it was good, they should not stand now like Sheepe before the Shearers, but put on Harnesse, and take Weapons in their hands: Yet to doe no creature hurt; but goe and deliuer the King a *Strong Petition,* for the laying downe of those grieuous *Payments,* and for the punishment of those that had giuen him that Counsell; to make others beware how they did the like in time to come: And said, for his part hee did not see how they could doe the duetie of true *English-men,* and good *Liege-men,* except they did deliuer the King from such wicked Ones that would destroy both Him and the Countrey. (Francis Bacon, *The Historie of the Reigne of King Henry the Seuenth* [1629], pp. 163–64)

Nay, an Army could not go out in this humble way to over-rule a Parliament. If they are in being, they influence; and in *Cesar's* easy way they conquer, by looking on.[35] The very Reputation of a Force to back them, will make all Court-Proposals speak big, tho never so contrary to [14] the Interest of the Nation. For there is no debating nor disputing against Legions. It will tempt them to do many things they durst not otherwise think of: What is much out of our reach, rarely is the Object of our Thoughts; but the Facility of Execution is generally the first Motives to an Attempt. Now it is abundantly the Interest of Court-Flatterers to live under a corrupt Reign. Then Bribes and Confiscations fill their Coffers. No Man's Wife or Daughter is free from their Lust, or Estate from their Avarice. They extort Presents from the Nobility, Goods from the Tradesmen, and Labour from the Poor. In short, all is their own. And 'tis to be feared, these Gentlemen (unless they have more Vertue than usually falls to their share) will put Princes upon such Counsels as promote their own Advantage. They will tell them how mean it is to be awed by a few Country Gentlemen, when all the Kings in *Europe* besides are got out of Pupilage, as *Lewis* XI called it.[36] They will fill their heads with a

35. An allusion to the famous laconic brag of Julius Caesar after his rapid victory over Pharnaces II of Pontus in 47 B.C., "Veni, vidi, vici"; "I came, I saw, I conquered." The phrase had recently been revived and Christianized in a European context when after his victory in the Battle of Vienna (11 and 12 September 1683) King Jan III of Poland is reported to have said, "Venimus, vidimus, Deus vicit."

36. Louis XI (1423–83), king of France.

> The Warre which they undertook against him, they entituled, *the Warre of the Weale publick*, because the occasion of their taking Armes was for the liberty of the Countrey and the People, both whom the *King* had beyond measure oppressed. True it is, they had also their particular purposes, but this was the main, and failing in the expected event of it, all that they did was to confirme the bondage of the Realm by their owne overthrow. These *Princes* once disbanded, and severally broken, none durst ever afterwards enter into the action: for which reason King *Lewis* used to say that he had brought the *Kings* of *France Hors Pupillage* out of their Wardship: a speech of more Brag than Truth. (Peter Heylyn, *France Painted to the Life* [1656], pp. 259–60)

Louis XI was a villain in the eyes of commonwealth Whigs, as the monarch who had forged, and demonstrated the use of, many of the most effective instruments

thousand trifling Jealousies of Monsters, Commonwealths, and such like Bug-bears:[37] and it hath been difficult even for the wisest Princes to free themselves from this sort of Cattle.[38] *False Prophets shall arise that shall deceive even the Elect.*[39] Nothing but the Fear of Punishment, and the being made a Sacrifice to the Peoples just Revenge, can make such Men honest: But if they have an Army to protect them, all these Considerations are laid aside, and all Arguments are answered in a word, *The King has an Army. The King has an Army*, stops all Mouths, [15] and cuts off all Reply. It is as if it should be said, Set your hearts at rest, for the King has all Power in his hands, and you have none: He has all your Estates, Lives and Liberties, under his Girdle: Slaves, and talk! The King has an Army, is a confuting Answer to every thing but a better Army, which Thanks

---

of absolutism: "The mischievous sagacity of . . . Lewis the 11th, which is now called king-craft, was wholly exerted in the subversion of the laws of France" (Sidney, *Discourses*, p. 575).

37. See above, p. 36, n. 88.

38. By extension from the literal sense of property, particularly in the sense of property as livestock, here referring metaphorically to personal slaves (*OED*, s.v. "cattle," 4e, 7b). The claim that monarchs do not preside over their subjects "by some excellence of nature, as men do with sheep or cattle" occurs in early modern resistance theory (e.g., *Vindiciae*, p. 68; see also pp. 75, 110). The term had more recently been powerfully deployed by John Locke, who in his *Two Treatises* had berated Filmer for speaking of men "as if God had no care of any part of them, but only of their Monarchs, and that the rest of the People, the Societies of Men, were made as so many Herds of Cattle, only for the Service, Use, and Pleasure of their Princes" (Locke, *Treatises*, p. 256, § 156; cf. also above, p. 33, n. 80). In 1698 Edmund Ludlow would define the point of dispute between Charles I and the Parliament as "*Whether the King should govern as a God by his Will, and the Nation be governed by Force like Beasts: or whether the People should be governed by Laws made by themselves, and live under a Government derived from their own Consent*" (Ludlow, *Memoirs*, 1:267; cf. Sidney, *Discourses*, p. 133). For a later instance of the trope, see Gibbon, *Decline and Fall*, 1:187. The point of political theory at stake is whether or not a kingdom (and all that it contains) is the private property of the king. Bartolus of Sassoferrato had maintained that there were some kingdoms "which can be conveyed like our other goods and rights" ("On the Government of a City"). But the strengthening tradition thereafter was that a monarch's rights over his kingdom were different in kind from the rights a person enjoyed over their private property.

39. Matthew 24:11, 24; Mark 13:22.

be to God and his present Majesty we have found. But as we are not to live upon Miracles, so we are not to tempt Dangers.[40]

I have stayed the longer upon this Point, in shewing how inconsistent an Army is with the Freedom of Parliament, because they being the Keepers of our English Liberties, can ill perform that Office, when they have parted with their Power into other hands. They are the last Resort of the Subject for the Redress of their Grievances. But how shall they relieve the poor *Royston*-men;[41] for instance, from the Oppression and Insolences of the Souldiery, when perhaps they shall be subject to the like themselves? The Projectors are aware of this terrible Inconvenience, and therefore they propose an Expedient, That it shall be the King's Army, but the Parliament shall have the paying of them; whereby they shall be as much the Parliament's humble Servants, as the Parliament their proper Masters.

Much at one I believe.[42] For the Long Parliament had not such a King and Parliament Army as this, but an Army that was all their own, their Creatures, as the Court-word is; raised, listed, commissioned, and paid wholly by them[16]selves, and not in Partnership; and that had manfully fought all their Battels: And yet upon the first Distaste[43] they were pleased

40. Cf. above, p. 32, n. 79, and p. 94, n. 69.

41. In June 1647 the Parliamentarian General Fairfax was presented with a petition signed by over a thousand inhabitants of Royston. Fearing that "after we have, by the blessing of the Almighty upon this Army, been rescued from many oppressions which lay heavie upon us, we are now like to be vassalaged and enslaved in the Norman Laws, and Prerogative clutches of an ambitious party in the Nation," the men of Royston asked Fairfax not to disband the army until "such time as you see these and the Kingdoms just and legal Requests imbraced" (*Four Petitions to his Excellency Sir Thomas Fairfax* [1647], pp. 4, 5). Their concern was over the imposition of martial law: cf. William Thompson, *Englands Freedome, Souldiers Rights* (1647), p. 8n; John Lilburne, *The peoples Prerogative and Priviledges, asserted and vindicated, (against all Tyranny whatsoever)* (1648), pp. 42, 50; and Anonymous, *A Plea for the late Agents of the Army, against the proceedings of the Gen. Officers to punish them by Martiall Law* (1647).

42. I.e., there is no difference between this case and the alternative whereby Parliament are not the paymasters of the army (*OED*, s.v. "at one," 4).

43. A reference to the suspicions of the Long Parliament entertained by the army in the spring and summer of 1647: "the army had no dread of the authority and power of the Parliament, which they knew had been so far prostituted that it had lost most of its reverence with the people; but it had great apprehension that

to take, they distressed their own Masters, and with a high hand forced them to banish eleven of their principal Members, *Denzil Holles*, Sir *Philip Stapylton*,[44] *Glyn*,[45] and such other great Men. Sir *Philip Stapylton* died in his Banishment.[46] At another time they would not suffer near a

---

by its conjunction with the city it might indeed recover credit with the kingdom, and withhold the pay of the army, and thereby make some division amongst them" (Clarendon, *History*, 4:235).

44. Sir Philip Stapleton (1603–47), politician and army officer. Stapleton was elected MP for Hedon in the Short Parliament and in June 1640 signed the petition of the Yorkshire gentry against the forced billeting of royal soldiers in the county. His involvement in antiarmy propaganda and his activism in advocating the army's disbandment ahead of satisfactory arrangements for settling its pay arrears or dealing with other grievances aroused hostility from Fairfax and Cromwell. He attracted further animosity from the army by assaulting Major Tulidah, who presented an army petition which Parliament desired to suppress. Stapleton was among the eleven MPs impeached by Sir Thomas Fairfax in the name of the army on 16 June 1647. They were accused of incensing Parliament against the army, endeavoring to provoke another civil war, and obstructing the relief of Ireland. The eleven members withdrew from the House rather than face impeachment. On 20 July passes were issued permitting their departure overseas but, heartened by the antiarmy riots in London on 26 July, Stapleton returned to Parliament. On 3 August Fairfax declared that he wanted Stapleton handed over to him to stand trial. On 6 August the resistance of the city collapsed, and Stapleton fled with five of the other impeached members. On 14 August they boarded a ship on the Essex coast bound for Calais, but they were overtaken and captured by a Captain Lamming. Vice-Admiral Batten subsequently allowed their release, and they landed at Calais on 17 August. Feverish and suffering from flux, Stapleton died at Calais in an inn called the Three Silver Lions on 18 August. As his illness was suspected to be plague, he was buried immediately in the Protestant burial ground (*ODNB*).

45. Sir John Glynne (1603–66), judge and politician; consummate political survivor. In the summer of 1647 Glynne had become involved with Sir Philip Stapleton, Denzil Holles, and other leading political Presbyterians at Westminster in the counterrevolutionary attempt to disband the army. As a result, he was one of the eleven members impeached by the army in June 1647; the following September he was unseated from the Commons and committed to the Tower. The charges laid against him focused in particular on his role in London's helping to foment a new war, encouraging the riotous invasion of the Houses on 26 July, and scheming with the committee of safety and the new Presbyterian-dominated city militia committee. He was released from custody by the Commons on 23 May 1648 (*ODNB*).

46. Moyle refers to the events of mid-June 1647. After Denzil Holles (see above, p. 128, n. 33) had affronted Ireton and challenged him to a duel, the army were so incensed "that they were resolved one way or other to be rid of him [i.e. Holles], who had that power in the House, and that reputation abroad, that when he could

hundred Members to enter into the House, whom they thought not well affected to the Business then in hand, and at the same time evil intreated and imprisoned about forty Members.[47] This they called purging the House. After they had thus handled them at several times, in conclusion, the Officers came and reprimanded the House, bid take away that Fool's Bawble the Mace, violently pulled the Speaker out of the Chair, drove out the Members, and locked up the Doors, and so good night to the Parliament.[48] The Wisdom of that Parliament may have been very great,

---

not absolutely control their designs, he did so obstruct them that they could not advance to any conclusion" (Clarendon, *History*, 4:238). Accordingly Sir Thomas Fairfax prepared "an impeachment of high treason in general terms against Mr. Hollis and the persons mentioned before [Stapleton, Lewes, Glynne, Waller, Massy, and Browne], and others, to the number of eleven members of the House of Commons." The House of Commons

> answered positively that they neither would nor could sequester those members from the House, who had never said or done any thing in the House worthy of censure, till proof were made of such particulars as might render them guilty. . . . However the Parliament seemed resolute, the accused persons themselves, who best knew their temper, thought it safer for them to retire, and by forbearing to be present in the House, to allay the heat of the present contest. (Clarendon, *History*, 4:239)

47. A reference to the events of 6 December 1648 and their aftermath: "The next morning there was a guard of musketeers placed at the entry into and door of the House; and the officers thereof having a list in their hands of the names of those who should be restrained from going into the House, all those were stopped, one by one, as they came, and sent into the court of wards, where they were kept together for many hours, under a guard, to the number of near one hundred" (Clarendon, *History*, 4: 465–66). In fact, 143 members were detained, of whom 47 were subsequently imprisoned.

48. A reference to Cromwell's dissolution of the Rump Parliament on 20 April 1653:

> Having adjusted all things with his chief officers of the army, who were at his devotion, in the month of April that was in the year 1653, he [Cromwell] came into the House of Parliament, in a morning when it was sitting, attended with the officers who were likewise members of the House, and told them that he came thither to put an end to their power and authority, which they had managed so ill that the nation could be no otherwise preserved than by their dissolution, which he advised them, without farther debate, quietly to submit unto. And thereupon another officer, with some files of musketeers, entered into the House, and stayed there till all members walked out; Cromwell reproaching many of the members by name, as they went out of

but it was Nonsense for them to think, that an Army does not know its own Strength. For without dear-bought Experience any body may know beforehand what will be the natural Consequences of a Standing Army. From the day you set them up, you set up your Masters; you put your selves wholly into their hands, and are at their discretion. It is the Conquest of the Nation in the silentest, shortest, and surest way. They are able to dispose of your Lives and Estates at Will and Pleasure: And what can a foreign Conqueror do more? If after this we live and possess any thing, [17] 'tis because they let us: and how long that shall be, neither we, no nor they themselves, know.

Nay, in many respects an authorized Standing Army is far worse than a foreign Invasion, and a Conquest from abroad. For there we have a chance for it: but this is a Conquest in cold Blood, which may not be resisted. And we lose the inseparable Rights of the Conquered, which is to rescue and deliver themselves, and to throw off the Yoke[49] as soon as they can. It is likewise a great Aggravation of our Misery, to be enslaved at our own Cost and Charges: Besides the bitter Resentments of Unkindness and Breach of Trust, if it be done by those who ought to protect us, and provide better for us; at least should not leave us in a worse Condition than they found us. But above all, if we contribute to our own Thraldom by our Folly, Flattery and little self-seeking; if the Destruction of us and our Posterity be of our selves, that Reflection hereafter will have a Sting in it; and it will not be enough to say, Who would have thought it?

Now in being over-powered and conquered by a Foreign Enemy, we contract none of this Guilt, and suffer it as a bare Calamity. But there is no great fear of that, for the Duke *de Rohan* is our Guarantee that we

the House, with their vices and corruptions, and amongst the rest, sir Harry Vane with his breach of faith and corruption; and having given the mace to an officer to be safely kept, he caused the doors to be locked up; and so dissolved that assembly which had sat almost thirteen years, and under whose name he had wrought so much mischieve, and reduced three kingdoms to his own entire obedience and subjection. . . . (Clarendon, *History*, 5:277–78)

Cromwell is supposed to have referred to the mace (the symbol of Parliament's authority) as "that bauble."

49. The symbol of servitude; see above, p. 75, n. 10.

cannot be conquered from abroad; who in a spiteful Description of *England* says, it is a great Animal that can be destroyed by nothing but it self.[50] Every body must die when their time is come: and Empires as well as private Men must submit to Time and Fate; Governments have their Infancy, their Meridian [18] and their Decay; and the Preludes to their Destruction are generally Luxury, Pride, Sloth, Prodigality, Cowardice, Irreligion, Self-interest, and an universal Neglect of the Publick. God grant this be not the Condition of a Nation I know.

Well, 'tis all one; for let a Standing Army be what it will, still we must have it for this unanswerable Reason, *viz. The Defence of the Nation from a sudden Invasion: for unless*, say they, *you have an Army to lie leiger,*[51] *you are liable to be overrun by a foreign Enemy e're you are aware; and you will shew less Wit than* Aesop's *Rhinoceros;*[52] *you will have your Men to raise, and your Teeth to whet, when you should use them.* This Thought I confess is very natural and obvious, and therefore could not possibly escape our wise Forefathers; yet we cannot learn that ever they put it in practice, which is a great sign they did not like it. No, we are well assured that they would not have suffered a Mercenary Army to defend the Nation if they

50. Henri, duc de Rohan (1579–1638); soldier, writer, and a leader of the Huguenots during the French Wars of Religion. In his *A treatise of the interest of the princes and states of Christendome* (1640), Rohan cited a maxim he attributed to Elizabeth I: "Queene ELIZABETH (who by her prudent gouernment has equall'd the greatest *Kings* of *Christendome*) shee knowing well the disposition of her *State*, beleeued that the true interest thereof consisted, *First* in holding a firme vnion in it selfe, atcheiuing to smother the reliques of precedent factions, deeming (as it is most true) that *England is a mightie Animal, which can neuer dye except it kill it selfe*" (pp. 34–35).

51. I.e., to remain encamped in arms (*OED*, s.v. "leaguer," 3).

52. See Fable 197 in *Aesop's Fables, with their Morals* (1706): "*Rhinoceros* his dulled Teeth did whet / Upon the hard'ned Tree, thereon to set / A keener edge, But *Reynard* passing by, / Asks the *Rhinoceros* the reason why / He whet his Teeth, confronted by no Foe, / Nor any danger; Why then did he so? / The Brute replies, Good reason why, for when / Dangers assault me, sure I ought not then / Be to set edge upon my Teeth employ'd, / But use their sharpness, lest I be annoy'd"; to which the moral is, "*Men must be arm'd 'gainst Ills that may ensue, / And future Dangers, else they soon may rue*" (p. 272). It is a fable much in the spirit of Machiavelli's remarks in chapt. 3 of *The Prince*, to the effect that dangers must be anticipated: "Once evils are recognised ahead of time, they may be easily cured; but if you wait for them to come upon you, the medicine will be too late, because the disease will have become incurable" (Machiavelli, *The Prince*, p. 12).

would have done it *gratis*.[53] They would rather have mistrusted it would double the Invasion, and make it as big again as it was. I do not speak this by guess, but have it from the wise Sir *Robert Cotton*, who being consulted, *3 Caroli*, in a difficult State of Affairs, amongst other things gave this Advice at the Council-Table: *Rushworth*, pag. 469. *There must be, to withstand a Foreign Invasion, a proportion of Sea and Land Forces. And it is to be considered, that no March by Land can be of that speed to make head against the landing of an Enemy: Then that follows, That there is no such Prevention as to be Master of the Sea.*

[19] *For the Land Forces, if it were for an offensive War, the Men of less Livelihood were best spared; and we used formerly to make such Wars* Purgamenta Reipublicae,[54] *if we made no farther Purchase by it. But for the Safety of the Commonwealth, the Wisdom of all times did never intrust the Publick Cause to any other than to such as had a Portion in the Publick Adventure. And that we saw in eighty eight, when the Care of the Queen and of the Council did make the Body of that large Army no other than of the Trained Bands.*[55]

In the same Advice to the King he lets him know how the People resented his keeping up an Army in the Winter, tho we were then in War both with *France* and *Spain*. The words are these:

And the dangerous Distastes to the People are not a little improved by the unexampled Course, as they conceive, of retaining an Inland Army in Winter Season, when former Times of general Fear, as in eighty eight, produced none such; and makes them in their distracted Fears conjecture idly, it was raised wholly to subject their Fortunes to the Will of Power rather than of Law, and to make good some farther Breach upon their Liberties and Freedoms at home, rather than defend us from any Force abroad. And tells the King the Consequences of these Jealousies is worthy a prudent and preventing Care.[56]

But *what signify the Proceedings of former Ages to us?* say the Projectors,[57] *the World is strangely altered, and the Power of* France *is become so formidable,*

---

53. I.e., free of charge.
54. "For the cleansing of the commonwealth."
55. For the whole text of Cotton's advice to the king, see Rushworth, *Collections*, pp. 471–76; quotation on p. 473.
56. Rushworth, *Collections*, pp. 475–76.
57. A jab at Defoe, whose *An Essay Upon Projects* had been published earlier in 1697.

that it can never be opposed in the Elizabeth *way.* They still keep up an Army of three or four hundred thousand Men, and how shall us [20] defend our selves against all those, without ten or fifteen thousand disciplined Troops?

I think the Author of the *Argument*, page 18 and 19, hath sufficiently shewed the Difficulty, if not Impossibility, of a Foreign Invasion, whilst we are superior at Sea; the great improbability the French King should engage in such a Design, and much greater he should succeed in it. But that we may for ever lay this Goblin,[58] we will admit our Fleets to be kidnapp'd by an unlucky Wind, whilst the French land twenty thousand Men in our Country. Tho in gratitude for this Concession, I hope my Adversaries will grant that their Fleet cannot get back again without our meeting with them, (since the same Wind that carries them home, will carry us out); or if they will not be so good-natur'd as to allow this, I will undertake for them (for we live in an undertaking Age) that they will agree we shall intercept their Supplies. Then the Case is thus, That twenty thousand Men, of which few can be Horse, are landed in *England*, without any humane probability of being supplied from abroad.

I say, this Army shall never march twenty miles into the Country; for they cannot put themselves in a marching posture in less than a fortnight or three weeks; and by that time we may have 100000 Militia drawn down upon them, whereof ten thousand shall be Horse, and as many Dragoons as we please: And if this Militia does nothing else but drive the Country, cut off their Foragers and Straglers, possess themselves of the Defilees,[59] and intercept Provisions, their Ar[21]my must be destroyed in a small time.

Of this kind I could give many Instances out of History: but because Antient ones, they say, will not fit our purpose, I will give you a late one out of *Ireland*.

58. Metaphorically, an unfounded belief (*OED*, s.v. "goblin"); cf. Samuel Parker (trans.), *Eusebius Pamphilus His Ten Books of Ecclesiastical History* (1703), p. 111, referring to the heresy of the Helcesaites, who eliminated doctrine from faith and reduced it to a mere matter of sincere belief: "But this Goblin disappear'd in an instant."

59. A narrow way or passage along which troops can march only by files or with a narrow front; a narrow pass or gorge between mountains (*OED*, s.v. "defile," 1).

1st, I think it will be readily agreed, there are ten Men in *England* for one in *Ireland*.

2dly, That King *William* had more English and Scotch to join with him in *Ireland*, than the F. K.[60] hath Malecontents in *England*.

3dly, That even our Militia have more Courage than Irishmen. And yet tho we had eight thousand Horse, and above thirty thousand Foot in *Ireland*, and a great part of the Country in our possession, yet we were more than four Years in conquering the rest, and almost a Miracle we did it then. And I believe no Man will deny, if we could not have supplied our Army from *England*, but they had all there perished; such is the Advantage of fighting upon one's own Dunghil.

And to shew what Treatment the French are like to meet with in *England*, I will put you in mind of the *Purbeck* Invasion,[61] which was so

60. I.e., French king.

61. On 15 December 1678 (O.S.) there was a false alarm of a French landing on the Isle of Purbeck on the south coast of England: "'Tis true, we have some Grounds to be Jealous, least a *French Armade* may too soon come over, and attaque us; but, admit the worst, that it should dare to invade us, they cannot any where Land so considerable a number both of Horse and men, as there ought to be for such a design, in so short a time as that the Country would not be Allarm'd at it, and be presently up to quell so adventurous a Motion; as we may be sure of, by what happened about a year since in the Isle of *Purbeck* in *Dorsetshire*" (Anonymous, *A Letter to a Friend* [1679], p. 7). Cf. Isaac Sharpe, *Animadversions* (1704), p. 2; Thomas Baker, *The Head of the Nile* (1681), p. 4; Samuel Clarke, *The Historian's Guide* (1690), p. 102; Nathaniel Johnston, *The Excellency of Monarchical Government* (1686), p. 413; Richard Kingston, *Vivat Rex* (1683), p. 38; Sir Roger L'Estrange, *The Answer to the Appeal Expounded* (1680), p. 10; Sir Roger L'Estrange, *A Brief History of the Times* (1687), p. 136; Sir Roger L'Estrange, *The Case Put* (1679), p. 35; Sir Roger L'Estrange, *Lestrange's Narrative of the Plot* (1680), p. 15; John Northleigh, *The Parallel* (1682), p. 16; Titus Oates, *Dr. Oates's Answer* (1683), p. 2; Sir William Petty, *The Politician Discovered* (1681), p. 9; John Rainstorp, *Loyalty Recommended* (1684), p. 19; Elkanah Settle, *The Present State of England* (1684), p. 4. The militia arrangements for the Isle of Purbeck were anomalous, as the 1662 Militia Act had recognized:

> That the Militia of the Island of Purbeck shall remaine separate from the County of Dorsett as heretofore hath beene used And that His Majesties Leiutenant of the said Island and his Deputies or any three or more of them for the time being shall have power for the levying arraying mustering and conducting of such number of Foot for the defence of the said Island in such manner and by such wayes and meanes as heretofore hath beene used And

private, that it was seen only by an old Man and a Boy: And yet tho the Country thought the Government against them, we had above forty thousand Voluntiers in Arms[62] in two or three days time, who came thither on their own accord to give them the meeting; and if they had been there, I doubt not would have given a good account of them. Our Court when it was over, shewed their dislike of it, and questioned the [22] Sheriff of *Dorsetshire* about it. And tho we have forgot it, yet I believe the French will remember *Purbeck;* for it shewed the true Spirit and Genius of the English Nation.

To conclude, The whole management of this Project is ridiculous; but the fatal Consequences of it require deeper thought: For when we have fool'd our selves into the Bondage of a Standing Army, how shall we ever get out of it again? Not as the Nation freed themselves from the Court of

---

alsoe to use and execute within the said Island all and every the Powers which by the true Intent of this Act any of His Majesties Leiutenants or his or theire Deputies or any of them might in any respective County use or execute. (§ XXI)

Toland notes this anomaly (below, p. 222) and says that as a result of these special measures the militias of the Isle of Purbeck, the Isle of Wight, and Guernsey and Jersey were acknowledged to be the equal of regular troops.

62. The prompt response to the rumor of a French landing was captured, and perhaps exaggerated, in a later contribution to the standing army controversy:

I remember I was at an Anchor in *Studland Bay,* when there was just such another Invasion in the Isle of *Purbeck,* as you Folk expect. If there was then any Standing Army, they were guarding the Royal Ducks in St. *James* Park, or otherwise employ'd; but I am sure they were not there. Now without any Royal Mandate, Commission, or any Order from above, the bold *Brittons* assembled in a hostile maner with all the Weapons of Defence the Country could afford and without any Ceremony march'd to the Place of landing. The Rumour of the French Numbers was Ten thousand, and in 48 hours there were a Hundred thousand in Arms in *Dorsetshire,* and the adjoining Counties, who came down time enough to the Sea side to engage the Invaders. I believe [if] these Hodmandods, Raw-heads and Bloody-bones, with which the Children of *England* are now scar'd, should appear, we shall be in a good posture of defence, without Twenty thousand Red Coats, which are morr terrifying thun an Idvasion. (Anonymous, *The Seaman's Opinion of a Standing Army in England* [1699], p. 5; the unusual orthography is presumably intended to mimic the accent of a seafarer)

Wards. We cannot buy it off for two very good Reasons: No Money will be taken for it; and we shall have nothing to give which is not theirs already: Our Estates, Lives and Liberties will be all at their Command. They will have the Keys of our Money, and the Titles to our Lands in their Power.

This last and irreparable Mischief and Misery the Projectors[63] had prepared for us. But under a Gracious King and a Wise Parliament, I hope we shall never see it. His Majesty's Declaration is directly against a Standing Army, *as a means to assist all Arbitrary Designs, and thereby enslave the Nation;* directly against all wicked Attempts of Conquest, and all Despotick Government; 'tis full of Liberty and Property in every part: So that we are sure to be safe on that side. And this Declaration was so highly valued, and so wholly relied upon by the Parliament, that it is incorporated into our Laws as the only redress of our past Grievances and Oppressions, and the best Foundation of our future Happiness: And with entire [23] confidence that his Majesty would continue to act in pursuance of that Declaration, the Parliament resolved that he should be, and be declared King. So that it is to be accounted the *Pacta Conventa*[64] of this Government.

Here I know the Projectors[65] will say, That the Army condemned by the Declaration, was the late K. *James*'s Army, kept up in time of Peace without Consent of Parliament: whereas this Standing Army is to be kept up with their Consent.[66]

True it was so, and therefore it was a Riot and unlawful Assembly every hour it stood; and having no Law for it, it might have been presented or indicted; to no purpose indeed: But as an Invasion upon the Subject it might be resisted and pulled down as a Nuisance, when-ever the Nation found themselves able. But suppose this Army had been made part of the Constitution, and had obtained an Act of Parliament for it, which is as much as we can have for a King or a Queen; what then had become of us? They were Aids and Instruments of Arbitrary Government

63. See above, p. 136, n. 57.
64. I.e., the agreed covenant.
65. See above, p. 136, n. 57.
66. See above, p. 50, n. 123.

before, but then they had been legal Instruments, and had enslaved us by Authority. In short, we could not have relieved our selves from them, nor any one else in our behalf, because our own Act and Deed would have always been good against us. The delightful Notion we know his Majesty by, is that of our Deliverer which he was upon this occasion. But these mischievous Projectors[67] would turn it into such a Deliverance, as if we [24] had been helpt over a Ford, to be afterwards lost in the Sea. And as to the Parliament, we are safe on that side, for a Reason amongst others which is in the *Declaration* in these words; *And it cannot be imagined that those who have invited us, or those that have already come to assist us, will join in a wicked Design of Conquest, to make void their own Titles to their Honours, Estates and Interests.*[68]

67. See above, p. 136, n. 57.
68. From the "Additionall Declaration" appended to the main text (William, *Declaration*, p. 8; see Appendix C, below, p. 625).

*A Postscript, with Remarks on a late
published List of Irish Papists now in the
French King's Service*

The Advocates for a Standing Army having lately published a List[69] of an Army of Irish and other Papists now in the French King's Service, which they say are ready when called for, I could not let that Paper go without some Remarks; because it informs us of some things, that, if I mistake not, deserve the Consideration of all true English Men, and are as followeth.

1. That there is in *France* an Army of eighteen thousand Irish and other Papists, with K. *James* at the Head of them.

2. That they are ready to be transported hither when called for.

3. They give broad Hints that there is a sort of Men amongst us, who will call for them.

4. That these Irish and their Correspondents will answer whatever has been or shall be written against a standing Army.

To the first I answer, that tho the Irish are the best Troops in the World to plunder, murder, and massacre the innocent and defenceless People, [26] yet they are the worst of all Souldiers when they meet with Resistance. The late War in *Ireland*, particularly the Siege of *London-derry*, and the routing of *Justin Maccarty*, one of their best Officers, who was at the Head of a considerable Army, by a small Number of the despised Militia, has abundantly demonstrated this Truth.[70] And it deserves

69. Anonymous, *A List of King James's Irish and Popish Forces in France* (1697).
70. See above, p. 38, n. 96, and below, p. 323, nn. 177 and 178.

the Resentment of the English Nation, to find the Enemies of their Country endeavouring at last to fright them with that despicable Crew, when the Terror they would have given us of the French Armies has proved ineffectual. Besides, the French King is in possession of these Irish Troops; they serve him, and are paid by him: and no Man but a Publick *Boutefeu*[71] would have the Confidence to say, He will lend them to King *James* to invade us: For what will that be less than declaring a new War? And they who think it in the Power of the French King to assist King *James* against us, without any Breach of the late Treaty, do in effect say, That due Care has not been taken of the Nation, than which there cannot be a more scandalous Reflection on his Majesty.

To the second and third of their Menaces I shall only say, That 'tis somewhat extraordinary, that Men should dare publickly to avow their Correspondence with our Enemies, to own themselves acquainted with their Designs against us, to threaten the People with an Army of Irish *Banditi*, and to let us know that there are some amongst us ready to join them. But the Great Council of the Nation being now assembled, will [27] undoubtedly make such Provision for our Safety, that neither they nor their Correspondents shall be able to hurt us.

In the last place they tell us, that this is an Answer to *the Argument against a Standing Army*, and to all that has been or shall be written on that Subject. Here's thorow Work indeed: and 'tis pity it should want a Place in the next Edition of the *Irish Wisdom*.[72] Mr. *Bayes*'s fighting singly against whole Armies is nothing to it:[73] For he like a modest Man, was only for routing such as should be raised, and never once dreamt of destroying them before they had a Being.

71. An incendiary, a firebrand; one who kindles discontent and strife (*OED*, s.v. "boutefeu").

72. I.e., folly.

73. An allusion to Buckingham's burlesque of heroic drama, *The Rehearsal* (1672). In act 4, scene 1 the playwright, "Mr. Bayes" (a satire on Dryden) creates a hero, "Drawcansir," who "frights his Mistriss, snubs up Kings, baffles Armies, and does what he will, without regard to good manners, justice or numbers." When the humanity, justice, and plausibility of this character are queried, Bayes explains that "I prefer that one quality of singly beating of whole Armies, above all your moral vertues put together, I gad" (Buckingham, *Plays*, 1:433). Cf. above, p. 47 and n. 116.

'Tis hoped therefore that this last Goblin[74] will do us no more hurt than all the rest that have been industriously raised to terrify the People, and to disturb the Publick Peace.

THE END.

Andrew Fletcher

*A Discourse Concerning Militia's
and Standing Armies*

1697

1. "It is a perilous thing to entrust the supreme power of the state to mercenaries—men who lack both property and hope, and who would attempt anything for money; men whose deep greed catches fire at the chance of a revolution, and whose fidelity fluctuates with fortune" (Jacques-Auguste de Thou, *Historiarum sui temporis tomus primus* [London, 1733], lib. 17, § 2, p. 576). Jacques-Auguste de Thou (1553–1617), French statesman, historian, and bibliophile; author of *Historia sui temporis* (A history of his own time), published in five parts between 1604 and 1620. In bk. 1 of *The Art of War* Machiavelli had written in similar terms about the tendency of professional soldiers to create disorder in a state (Machiavelli, *Chief Works*, 2:579).

A

DISCOURSE

Concerning

MILITIA'S

AND

Standing Armies.

With relation to the Past and Present
Governments of *EUROPE*,

AND OF

ENGLAND in particular.

---

*Res est periculi plena, summam Rei Publicae hominibus
Mercenariis, sine re, sine spe, quidvis ob pecuniam
ausuris, committere; quorum profundam avaritiam
incendat ad nova molienda occasio, & fortuna secum
fidem circumagat.* Thuan. Hist.[1]

London, Printed in the Year 1697.

A Discourse Concerning
Militia's and *Standing Armies*

There is not perhaps in humane Affairs any thing so unaccountable as the Indignity and Cruelty with which the far greater part of Mankind suffer themselves to be used under pretence of Government. For some Men falsly perswading themselves that bad Governments are advantageous to them, as most conducing to gratify their Ambition, Avarice and Luxury, set themselves with the utmost Art and Violence to procure their Establishment: and almost the whole World has been trampled under foot, and subjected to Tyranny, for want of understanding by what Methods they were brought into it. For tho Mankind take great Care and Pains to instruct themselves in other Arts and Sciences, yet very few apply themselves to consider the Nature of Government, an Enquiry so useful and necessary both [4] to Magistrate and People. Nay, in most Countries the Arts of State being altogether directed either to enslave the People, or to keep them under Slavery, it is become almost every where a Crime to reason about Matters of Government. But if Men would bestow a small part of the Time and Application which they throw away upon curious but useless Studies, or endless Gaming, in perusing those excellent Rules of Government which the Antients have left us, they would be enabled to discover all such Abuses and Corruptions as tend to the Ruine of Publick Societies. 'Tis therefore very strange that they should think Study and Knowledg necessary in every thing they go about, except in the noblest and most useful of all Applications, The Art of Government.

Now if any Man in compassion to the Miseries of a People should endeavour to disabuse them in any thing relating to Government, he will certainly incur the Displeasure, and perhaps be pursued by the Rage of those, who think they find their Account in the Oppression of the World; but will hardly succeed in his Endeavours to undeceive the Multitude. For the Generality of all Ranks of Men are cheated by Words and Names; and provided the antient Terms and outward Forms of any Government be retained, let the Nature of it be never so much altered, they continue to dream that they shall still enjoy their former Liberty, and are not to be awakned till it prove too late. Of this there are many remarkable Examples in History; but that parti[5]cular Instance which I have chosen to insist on, as most sutable to my purpose, is, the Alteration of Government which happened in most Countries of *Europe* about the Year 1500.[2] And 'tis worth Observation, that tho this Change was fatal to their Liberty, yet it was not introduced by the Contrivance of ill-designing Men; nor were the mischievous Consequences perceived, unless by a few wise Men, who, if they saw it, wanted Power to prevent it.

Two hundred Years being already passed since this Alteration began, *Europe* has felt the Effects of it by sad Experience; and the true Causes of the Change are now become more visible.

To lay open this Matter in its full Extent, it will be necessary to look farther back, and examin the Original and Constitution of those Governments that were established in *Europe* about the Year 400, and continued till this Alteration.[3]

When the Goths, Vandals, and other warlike Nations, had at different Times, and under different Leaders, over-run the Western Parts of the Roman Empire, they introduced the following Form of Government into all the Nations they subdued. The General of the Army became King of the Conquered Country; and the Conquest being absolute, he

---

2. Fletcher refers to the rise of monarchical absolutism.

3. I.e., the feudal governments established by the northern barbarians in the former provinces of the Roman Empire in the west. Harrington had identified the "inundations of Goths, Vandals, Huns and Lombards that overwhelmed the Roman Empire" as marking the point of origin of "modern prudence" (Harrington, *Oceana*, p. 43).

divided the Lands amongst the Great Officers of his Army, afterwards called *Barons*; who again parcelled out their several Territories in smaller Portions to the inferiour Souldiers that had followed them in the Wars, and who then became their Vassals, [6] enjoying those Lands for Military Service. The King reserved to himself some Demeasnes[4] for the Maintenance of his Court and Attendance. When this was done, there was no longer any standing Army kept on foot, but every Man went to live upon his own Lands, and when the Defence of the Country required an Army, the King summoned the Barons to his Standard, who came attended with their Vassals. Thus were the Armies of *Europe* composed for about eleven hundred Years, and this Constitution of Government put the Sword into the hands of the Subject, because the Vassals depended more immediately on the Barons, than on the King; which effectually secured the Freedom of those Governments. For the Barons could not make use of their Power to destroy those limited Monarchies, without destroying their own Grandeur; nor could the King invade their Privileges, having no other Forces than the Vassals of his own Demeasnes to rely upon for his Support in such an Attempt.

I lay no great stress on any other Limitations of those Monarchies; nor do I think any so essential to the Liberties of the People, as that which placed the Sword in the hands of the Subject. But since in our time most Princes of *Europe* are in possession of the Sword, by standing Mercenary Forces kept up in time of Peace,[5] and absolutely depending upon them, I say that all such Governments are changed from Monarchies to Tyrannies. Nor can the Power of granting or refusing Money, tho vested in the Subject, be a sufficient Security for Liberty, where a standing Mer[7]cenary Army is kept up in time of Peace: For he that is arm'd, is always Master of the Purse of him that is unarm'd. And not only that Government is Tyrannical, which is tyrannically exercised; but all Governments are

---

4. Property attached to the Crown (*OED*, s.v. "demesne," 5a).

5. Note that here Fletcher confounds two things which may exist separately, namely a standing army and a mercenary army. Standing armies, although professional in the sense of being paid, need not consist of mercenaries (that is to say, soldiers who will hire themselves out to any master).

Tyrannical, which have not in their Constitution a sufficient Security against the Arbitrary Power of the Prince.

I do not deny that these limited Monarchies during the greatness of the Barons, had some Defects: I know few Governments free from them. But after all, there was a Balance that kept those Governments steady, and an effectual Provision against the Encroachments of the Crown. I do less pretend that the present Governments can be restored to the Constitution before mentioned. The following Discourse will show the impossibility of it. My Design is, first of all to explain the Nature of the past and present Governments of *Europe*, and to disabuse those who think them the same, because they are called by the same Names; and who ignorantly clamour against such as would preserve that Liberty which is yet left.

In order to this, and for a further and clearer Illustration of the Matter, I shall deduce from their Original the Causes, Occasions, and the Complication of those many unforeseen Accidents, which falling out much about the same time, produced so great a Change. And it will at first sight seem very strange, when I shall name the Restoration of Learning, the Invention of Printing, of the Needle and of Gunpowder, as the chief of [8] them; things in themselves so excellent, and which, the last only excepted, might have proved of infinite Advantage to the World, if their remote Influence upon Government had been obviated by sutable Remedies. Such odd Consequences, and of such a different Nature, accompany extraordinary Inventions of any kind.

Constantinople being taken by *Mahomet* the Second, in the Year 1453,[6] many Learned Greeks fled over into *Italy;* where the favourable reception they found from the Popes, Princes, and Republicks of that Country, soon introduced amongst the better sort of Men, the study of the Greek Tongue, and the Antient Authors in that Language. About the same time likewise some Learned Men began to restore the Purity of the Latin Tongue. But that which most contributed to the Advancement of all kind of Learning, and especially the study of the Antients, was the Art of Printing; which was brought to a great degree of Perfection a few Years after. By this means their Books became common, and their Arts generally

6. See above, p. 101, n. 94.

understood and admired. But as Mankind from a natural propension to Pleasure, is always ready to chuse out of every thing what may most gratify their vicious Appetites; so the Arts which the Italians first applied themselves to improve, were principally those that had been subservient to the Luxury of the Antients in the most corrupt Ages, of which they had many Monuments still remaining. *Italy* was presently filled with Architects, Painters and Sculptors; and a prodigious Expence was made in Buildings, [9] Pictures and Statues. Thus the Italians began to come off from their frugal and military way of living, and addicted themselves to the pursuit of refined and expensive Pleasures, as much as the Wars of those times would permit. This Infection spread it self by degrees into the Neighbouring Nations. But these things alone had not been sufficient to work so great a Change in Government, if a preceding Invention, brought into common use about that time, had not produced more new and extraordinary Effects than any had ever done before; which probably may have many Consequences yet unforeseen, and a farther Influence upon the Manners of Men, as long as the World lasts: I mean, the Invention of the Needle, by the help of which Navigation was greatly improved; a Passage opened by Sea to the *East-Indies*, and a new World discovered. By this means the Luxury of *Asia* and *America* was added to that of the Antients; and all Ages, and all Countries concurred to sink *Europe* into an Abyss of Pleasures; which were rendred the more expensive by a perpetual Change of the Fashions in Clothes, Equipage and Furniture of Houses.

These things brought a total Alteration in the way of living, upon which all Government depends. 'Tis true, Knowledg being mightily increased, and a great Curiosity and Nicety in every thing introduced, Men imagined themselves to be gainers in all Points, by changing from their frugal and military way of living, which I must confess had some mixture of Rudeness and Ignorance in it, tho not inseparable from it. But at [10] the same time they did not consider the unspeakable Evils that are altogether inseparable from an expensive way of living.

To touch upon all these, tho slightly, would carry me too far from my Subject; I shall therefore content my self to apply what has been said, to the immediate Design of this Discourse.

The far greater share of all those Expences fell upon the Barons; for they were the Persons most able to make them, and their Dignity seemed to challenge whatever might distinguish them from other Men. This plunged them on a sudden into so great Debts, that if they did not sell, or otherwise alienate their Lands, they found themselves at least obliged to turn the military Service their Vassals owed them, into Money; partly by way of Rent, and partly by way of Lease, or Fine for paiment of their Creditors. And by this means the Vassal having his Lands no longer at so easy a Rate as before, could no more be obliged to military Service, and so became a Tenant. Thus the Armies, which in preceding times had been always composed of such Men as these, ceased of course, and the Sword fell out of the hands of the Barons. But there being always a necessity to provide for the Defence of every Country, Princes were afterwards allowed to raise Armies of Volunteers and Mercenaries. And great Sums were given by Diets[7] and Parliaments for their Maintenance, to be levied upon the People grown rich by Trade, and dispirited for want of Military Exercise. [11] Such Forces were at first only raised for present Exigencies, and continued no longer on foot than the Occasions lasted. But Princes soon found Pretences to make them perpetual, the chief of which was the garisoning Frontier Towns and Fortresses, the Methods of War being altered to the tedious and chargeable way of Sieges, principally by the Invention of Gunpowder. The Officers and Souldiers of these Mercenary Armies depending for their Subsistence and Preferment, as immediately upon the Prince, as the former Militia's did upon the Barons, the Power of the Sword was transferred from the Subject to the King, and War grew a constant Trade to live by. Nay, many of the Barons themselves being reduced to Poverty by their expensive way of living, took Commands in those Mercenary Troops; and being still continued Hereditary Members of Diets, and other Assemblies of State, after the loss of their Vassals, whom they formerly represented, they were now the readiest of all others to load the People with heavy Taxes, which were employed to increase the Prince's Military Power, by Guards, Armies, and Citadels, beyond Bounds or Remedy.

7. The regular meetings of the estates of a realm or confederation; hence also collectively the estates or representatives so meeting (*OED*, s.v. "diet," n. 2, 5b).

I am not ignorant that before this Change, Subsidies were often given by Diets, States and Parliaments for maintaining Wars; but these were small, and no way sufficient to subsist such numerous Armies as those of the Barons Militia.

[12] What I have said hitherto has been always with regard to one or other, and often to most Countries in *Europe*. What follows will have a more particular regard to *England*; where, tho the Power of the Barons be ceased, yet no mercenary Troops are yet established. The Reason of which is, that *England* had before this great Alteration lost all her Conquests in *France*,[8] the Town of *Calais* only excepted;[9] and that also was taken by the French, before the Change was thorowly introduced. So that the Kings of *England* had no Pretence to keep up Standing Forces, either to defend Conquests abroad, or to garrison a Frontier towards *France*, which was their formidable Enemy, since the Sea was now become the only Frontier between those two Countries.

Henry the Seventh seems to have perceived the Alteration before-mentioned more than any Prince of his time, and obtained several Laws to favour and facilitate it. But the succeeding Princes were altogether improper to second him: For *Henry* the Eighth was an unthinking Prince. The Reigns of *Edward* the Sixth, and Queen *Mary*, were short, and Queen *Elizabeth* loved her People too well to attempt it. King *James* the First was a Stranger, and of no Interest abroad. King *Charles* the First did indeed endeavour to make himself Absolute, tho somewhat preposterously; for he attempted to seize the Purse, before he was Master of the Sword. But very wise Men have been of Opinion, that if he had been possessed of as numerous Troops as those which were [13] afterwards raised, and constantly kept up by King *Charles* the Second, he might easily have succeeded in his Enterprize.[10] For we see that in those Struggles which the Country Party had with King *Charles* the Second, and in those Endeavours they used to bring about that Revolution which was afterwards compassed by a Foreign Power,[11] the chief and insuperable

8. English power in France was destroyed at the end of the Hundred Years' War in 1453, when Charles VII completed the French conquest of Aquitaine.

9. Calais remained in English hands until 1558.

10. This is Trenchard's opinion; see above, p. 27.

11. I.e., 1688.

Difficulty they met with, was from those Forces. And tho King *James* the Second had provoked the Nation to the last degree, and made his own Game as hard as possible, not only by invading our Civil Liberties, but likewise by endeavouring to change the Established Religion for another which the People abhorred, whereby he lost their Affections, and even those of a great part of his Army; yet notwithstanding all this Misman-agement, *England* stood in need of a foreign Force to save it; and how dangerous a Remedy that is, the Histories of all Ages can witness. 'Tis true, this Circumstance was favourable to the Nation, that a Prince who had married the next Heir to the Crown,[12] was at the Head of our Deliv-erance; yet did it engage us in a long and expensive War.[13] And now that we are much impoverished, and by means of our former Riches and pre-sent Poverty, fallen into all the Corruptions which those great Enemies of Vertue want, and Excess of Riches can produce; that there are such Numbers of Mercenary Forces on foot at home and abroad; that the great-est part of the Officers have no other way to subsist; that they are com-manded by a wise [14] and active King, who has at his Disposal the formidable Land and Sea Forces of a Neighbouring Nation, the great Rival of our Trade:[14] A King, who by Blood, Relation, other particular Ties, and common Interest, has the House of *Austria*, most of the Princes of *Germany*, and Potentates of the North, for his Friends and Allies; who can, whatever Interest he join with, do what he thinks fit in *Europe:* I say, if a Mercenary Standing Army be kept up, (the first of that kind, except those of the Usurper *Cromwel*[15] and the late King *James*, that *England* has seen for thirteen hundred Years) I desire to know, where the Security of the Liberties of *England* lies, unless in the good Will and Pleasure of the King: I desire to know, what real Security can be had against a Standing Army of Mercenaries, backed by the Corruption of a Nation, the Ten-dency of the way of Living, the Genius of the Age, and the Example of the World.

12. In 1677 William of Orange had married Mary, the daughter of James II (then Duke of York).

13. See above, p. 9, n. 13 and p. 26, n. 64.

14. I.e., the Low Countries.

15. See above, p. 22, n. 51, and p. 48, n. 118.

Having shown the Difference between the past and present Government of *England*, how precarious our Liberties are, and how from having the best Security for them we are in hazard of having none at all; 'tis to be hoped that those who are for a Standing Army, and losing no occasion of advancing and extending the Prerogative, from a mistaken Opinion that they establish the antient Government of *England*, will see what sort of Patriots they are.

[15] But we are told, that only Standing Mercenary Forces can defend *England* from the perpetual Standing Armies of *France*. However frivolous this Assertion be, as indeed no good Argument can be brought to support it, either from Reason or Experience; yet allowing it to be good, what Security can the Nation have, that these Standing Forces shall not at some time or other be made use of to suppress the Liberties of the People, tho not in this King's time, to whom we owe their Preservation? For I hope there is no Man so weak to think, that keeping up the Army for a Year, or for any longer time than the Parliament shall have engaged the Publick Faith to make good all Deficiencies of Funds granted for their Maintenance, is not the keeping them up for ever. 'Tis a pitiful shift in the Undertakers for a Standing Army, to say, We are not for a Standing Army; We are only for an Army from Year to Year, or till the Militia be made useful. For *England* cannot be in any hazard from *France;* at least, till that Kingdom, so much exhausted by War and Persecution, shall have a breathing space to recover. Before that time our Militia will be in order; and in the mean time our Fleets. Besides, no Prince ever surrendred so great Countries, and so many strong Places, I shall not say, in order to make a new War; but, as these Men will have it, to continue the same. The French King is old and diseased,[16] and was never willing to hazard much by any [16] bold Attempt. If he, or the Dauphin;[17] upon his Decease, may be suspected of any farther Design, it must be upon the

---

16. In fact, Louis XIV did not die until 1 September 1715.

17. The customary title of the heir apparent to the French throne. In this instance, Louis de France, or le Grand Dauphin, or more simply Monseigneur (1661–1711), the son of Louis XIV and Marie-Thérèse of Austria. He predeceased his father, and so never became king of France.

Spanish Monarchy,[18] in case of the Death of that King. And if it be objected, that we shall stand in need of an Army, in such a Conjuncture; I answer, that our Part in that, or in any other foreign War, will be best managed by Sea, as shall be shown hereafter.

Let us then see if Mercenary Armies be not exactly calculated to enslave a Nation. Which I think may be easily proved, if we consider that such Troops are generally composed of Men who make a Trade of War, and having little or no Patrimony, or spent what they once had, enter into that Employment in hopes of its Continuance during Life, not at all thinking how to make themselves capable of any other. By which means heavy and perpetual Taxes must be entail'd for ever upon the People for their Subsistence; and since all their Relations stand engaged to support their Interest, let all Men judg, if this will not prove a very united and formidable Party in a Nation. But the Undertakers for a Standing Army will say; Will you turn so many Gentlemen out to starve, who have faithfully served the Government? This Question I allow to be founded upon some Reason. For it ought to be acknowledged in Justice to our Army, that on all Occasions, and in all Actions, both Officers and Souldiers have done their part. And therefore I think it may be rea[17]sonable, that all Officers and Souldiers of above forty Years, in consideration of their Unfitness to apply themselves at that Age to any other Employment, should be recommended to the Bounty of the Parliament.

But the Undertakers must pardon me if I tell them, That no well-constituted Government ever suffered any such Men in it, whose Interest leads them to imbroil the State in War, and are an useless and insupportable Burden in time of Peace. *Carthage*, after the first Roman War, found

18. As indeed happened on the death of Carlos II of Spain on 1 November 1700. Carlos left a will bequeathing his territories to Philip of Anjou, the grandson of Louis XIV. In defiance both of the Partition Treaties of 1698 and of the solemn vow of renunciation he had made on his marriage to the Infanta Maria Theresa, Louis accepted the will and thus created the alarming possibility of the union of the French and Spanish crowns. Preventing the realization of this prospect was the casus belli of the War of the Spanish Succession (1702–13), in which an alliance of Britain, the Low Countries, and the emperor Leopold I resisted French ambition. See Macaulay, *History*, 6:2809–34.

how dangerous they were:[19] And *Holland*, in the Year 1672, how useless to defend them.[20] If ever any Government stood in need of such a sort of Men, 'twas that of antient *Rome*, because they were engaged in perpetual War. The Argument can never be so strong in any other Case. But the Romans well knowing such Men and Liberty to be incompatible, and yet, being under a necessity of having Armies constantly on foot, made frequent Changes of the Men that served in them; who, when they had been some time in the Army, were permitted to return to their Possessions, Trades, or other Employments. [21] And to show how true a Judgment

19. On the conclusion of the First Punic War in 241 B.C. the Carthaginian mercenaries, exasperated by being denied their pay, rebelled against their masters, and in 237 B.C. were eventually defeated by Hamilcar Barca after four years of atrocious fighting. The events of the so-called Mercenaries War would provide the lurid backdrop to Flaubert's *Salammbô* (1862). Fletcher is here almost translating Machiavelli, who in chap. 12 of *The Prince* wrote: "Delle armi mercenarie antiche in exemplis sono e Cartaginesi, li quali furono per essere oppressi da' loro soldati mercenarii finita la prima guerra con li Romani, ancora che e Cartaginesi avessino per capi loro proprii cittadini"; "An example from antiquity of the use of mercenary troops is the Carthaginians. They were almost overcome by their own mercenary soldiers after the first war with the Romans, even though the Carthaginians had their own citizens as officers" (Machiavelli, *Opere*, p. 40; Machiavelli, *The Prince*, p. 44). See also *L'arte della guerra* (Machiavelli, *Opere*, p. 504; Machiavelli, *Chief Works*, 2:574) and Harrington, *Oceana*, p. 76.

20. In 1672 French forces had invaded the United Provinces and had made rapid advances: "I need not recite . . . the Success he [Louis XIV] met with in his Enterprize, and how like a Torrent he carried all before him; how *Rhinburg, Dossery, Deudekom, Rees, Wesel, Emerick, Doesburg, Turesume, Nimeguen, Swoll, Daventer, Grave, Arnheim, Skinenschon, Creveceer,* fell quickly into his hands" (Jones, *Secret History*, p. "51" [sig. Dd2ʳ]; cf. Temple, *Memoirs*, pp. 19–20). Note that Defoe has also cited the devastating success of French arms in 1672 as support for his opposing arguments (above, p. 103 and n. 99).

21. Initially under the Republic, the Roman army was a militia, and would be disbanded on the cessation of hostilities. Over time a professional military establishment arose, which was formalized under Gaius Marius (157–86 B.C.). The normal period of enlistment was twenty years, and the annual pay was 120 denarii, from which was deducted the cost of rations. Fletcher is repeating a principle stated by Machiavelli in *L'arte della guerra*: "Tal che, se uno re non si ordina in modo che i suoi fanti a tempo di pace stieno contenti tornarsi a casa e vivere delle loro arti, conviene di necessità che rovini. . . ."; "So that, if a king does not so arrange things that his infantry are content to return home and live off their trades during times of peace, he will necessarily come to ruin. . . ." (Machiavelli, *Opere*,

that wise State made of this Matter, it is sufficient to observe, that those who subverted that Government,[22] the greatest that ever was amongst Men, found themselves obliged to continue the same Souldiers always in constant Pay and Service.

[18] There is another thing which I would not mention if it were not absolutely necessary to my present purpose; and that is, the usual Manners of those who are engaged in Mercenary Armies. I speak now of Officers in other Parts of *Europe*, and not of those in our Army, allowing them to be the best; and if they will have it so, quite different from all others. I will not apply to them any part of what I shall say concerning the rest. They themselves best know how far any thing of that Nature may be applicable to them. I say then, most Princes of *Europe* having put themselves upon the foot of keeping up Forces, rather numerous, than well entertain'd, can give but small Allowance to Officers, whom, notwithstanding, they permit to live in all that Extravagancy which mutual Example and Emulation prompts them to. By which means the Officers become insensibly engaged in numberless Oppressions and Cruelties, the Colonels against the Captains, and the Captains against the inferior Souldiers. So that there is hardly any sort of Men who are less Men of Honour than the Officers of Mercenary Forces: and indeed Honour has now no other Signification amongst them than Courage. Besides, most Men that enter into those Armies, whether Officers or Souldiers, as if they were obliged to show themselves new Creatures, and perfectly regenerate, if before they were modest or sober, immediately turn themselves to all manner of Debauchery and Wickedness, [19] committing all kind of Injustice and Barbarity against poor and defenceless People. Now tho the natural Temper of our Men be more just and honest than that of the French, or of any other People, yet may it not be feared, that such bad Manners may prove contagious? And if such Manners do not fit Men to

---

p. 507). Machiavelli had identified Marius as the instigator of Roman corruption (*Discourses*, bk. 1, chap. 17).

22. A reference in the first instance to Julius Caesar (102–44 B.C.), who waged war on the Republic and who increased the annual pay of the soldiery from 120 to 225 denarii. Augustus (63 B.C.–A.D. 14), the first *princeps* of Rome, created a standing army of twenty-five legions with fixed stations and names.

enslave a Nation, Devils only must do it. On the other hand, if it should happen that the Officers of a Standing Army in *England* should live with greater Regularity and Modesty than was ever yet seen in that sort of Men, it might very probably fall out, that being quarter'd in all Parts of the Country, they might be returned Members of Parliament for most of the Electing Boroughs; and of what Consequence that would be, I leave all Men to judg.[23] So that whatever be the Conduct of a Mercenary Army, we can never be secure as long as any such Force is kept up in *England;* and I confess I do not see by what Rules of good Policy any Mercenary Forces have been connived at either in *England* or elsewhere. Sure, 'tis allowing the Dispensing Power[24] in the most essential Point of the Constitution.

23. Fletcher alludes to the corruption of the independence of the House of Commons which would arise were a substantial number of its members also to be in the pay of the Crown. Cf. above, p. 40, n. 99.

24. The Crown's power of dispensing with or suspending the laws of church or state in special cases (*OED*, s.v. "dispensing"). It had been declared contrary to law by the English and the Scottish Parliaments in 1689 following its notorious use by James II. Sir Edward Hales was a Catholic who held a commission in the army in defiance of the Test Act, claiming that he held letters under the great seal dispensing with the statute's obligation to take communion in the Church of England. Instigated by the Crown, Hales's coachman, Godden, brought a collusive action against him to test the validity of this dispensation. In 1686 it was heard on appeal by the twelve judges of the common-law courts, all but one of whom found in favor of the king's dispensing power. On the authority of this decision James issued dispensations appointing more and more Catholics to places under the crown (*ODNB*). William of Orange had placed James's use of the dispensing power prominently in the list of grievances which prompted the invasion of 1688:

> Evill Councellours ... did Invent and set on foot, the Kings *Dispencing power,* by vertue of which, they pretend that according to *Law,* he can *Suspend* and *Dispence* with the Execution of the *Lawes,* that have been enacted by the Authority, of the King and Parliament, for the security and happines of the Subject and so have rendered those Lawes of no effect: Tho there is nothing more certain, then that as no Lawes can be made, but by the joint concurrence of King and Parliament, so likewise lawes so enacted, which secure the Publike peace, and safety of the Nation, and the lives and liberties of every subject in it, can not be repealed or suspended, but by the same authority. (See Appendix C, below, p. 610.)

For contemporary commentary, see Jones, *Secret History*, pp. "35–37" (sigs. Ccccc2ʳ–Ccccc3ʳ).

The Subjects formerly had a real Security for their Liberty, by having the Sword in their own hands. That Security, which is the greatest of all others, is lost; and not only so, but the Sword is put into the Hand of the King by his Power over the Militia.[25] All this is not enough; but we must have a Standing Army of Mercenaries, who for the most part have no [20] other way to subsist, and consequently are capable to execute any Commands. And yet every Man must think his Liberties as safe as ever, under pain of being thought disaffected to the Monarchy. But sure it must not be the antient Limited and Legal Monarchy of *England*, that these Gentlemen mean. It must be a French Fashion of Monarchy, where the King has Power to do what he pleases, and the People no Security for any thing they possess. We have quitted our antient Security, and put the Militia into the Power of the King. The only remaining Security we have is, That no Standing Army was ever yet allowed in time of Peace, the Parliament having so often and so expresly declared it to be contrary to Law.[26] If a Standing Army be allow'd, what Difference will there be between the Government we shall then live under, and any kind of Government under a good Prince? Of which there have been some in the most despotick Tyrannies. If this be a Limited and not an Absolute Monarchy, then, as there are Conditions, so there ought to be Securities

25. The preamble to the Militia Act of 1661 (13 Car. II, c. 6) begins:

Forasmuch as within all his Majesty's realms and dominions the sole supreme government, command and disposition of the militia and of all forces by sea and land and of all forts and places of strength is and by the laws of England ever was the undoubted right of his Majesty and his royal predecessors, Kings and Queens of England, and that both or either of the Houses of Parliament cannot nor ought to pretend to the same, nor can nor lawfully may raise or levy any war, offensive or defensive, against his Majesty, his heirs or lawful successors, and yet the contrary thereof hath of late years been practised, almost to the ruin and destruction of this kingdom, and during the late usurped governments many evil and rebellious principles have been distilled into the minds of the people of this kingdom, which unless prevented may break forth, to the disturbance of the peace and quiet thereof. . . . (*Stuart Constitution*, p. 374)

26. The maintenance of a standing army had been declared contrary to law in the Bill of Rights of 1689; see above, p. 50, n. 123, and Appendix D (below, p. 629).

on both sides. The Barons never pretended that their Militia's should be constantly on foot, and together in Bodies, in times of Peace. 'Tis evident that would have subverted the Constitution, and made every one of them a Petty Tyrant. And 'tis as evident, that Standing Forces are the fittest Instruments to make a Tyrant, tho not of so gracious a Prince as we now live under, yet, to be [21] sure, of some of his Successors. Whoever is for making the King's Power too great or too little, is an Enemy to the Monarchy. But to give him a Standing Army, puts his Power beyond Controul, and consequently makes him Absolute. If the People had any other real Security for their Liberty than that there be no Standing Army in time of Peace, there might be some colour to demand it. But if that only remaining Security be taken away from the People, we have destroyed the Monarchy.

'Tis pretended, we are in hazard of being invaded by a powerful Enemy; Shall we therefore destroy our Constitution? What is it then that we would defend? Is it our Persons, by the Ruine of our Constitution? In what then shall we be Gainers? In saving our Lives by the Loss of our Liberties? If our Pleasures and Luxury make us live like Brutes, it seems we must not pretend to reason any better than they. I would fain know, if there be any other way of making a Prince Absolute, than by allowing him a Standing Army: If by it all Princes have not been made Absolute; If without it, any. Whether our Enemies shall conquer us is uncertain. But whether a Standing Army will enslave us, neither Reason nor Experience will suffer us to doubt. 'Tis therefore evident, that no Pretence of Danger from abroad, can be an Argument to keep up a Standing Army, or any Mercenary Forces.

[22] Let us now consider whether we may not be able to defend our selves by a well-regulated Militia against any Foreign Force, tho never so formidably; that the Nation may be free from the Fears of Invasion from abroad, as well as from the Danger of Slavery at home.

'Tis well known, that after the Barons had lost the Military Service of their Vassals, Militia's of some kind or other were established in most parts of *Europe*. But the Prince having the Power of naming and preferring the Officers of these Militia's, they could be no Balance in Government as the former were. And he that will consider what has been said in this Discourse, will easily perceive that the essential Quality requisite to such a Militia, as might fully answer the Ends of the former, must be that the Officers should be named and preferr'd, as well as they and the Souldiers paid, by the People that set them out. So that if Princes look upon the present Militia's as not capable of defending a Nation against Foreign Armies; the People have little reason to entrust them with the Defence of their Liberties.

'Tis as well known that after the dissolution of that Antient Militia under the Barons, which made this Nation so Great and Glorious, tho, by setting up Militia's generally through *Europe*, the Sword came not into the Hands of the Commons; which was the only thing could have con[23] tinued the former Balance of Government, but was every where put into the Hands of the King: nevertheless ambitious Princes, who aimed at absolute Power, thinking they could never use it effectually to that end, unless it were wielded by Mercenaries, and Men that had no other Interest in the Common-wealth than their Pay, have still endeavoured by all means to discredit Militia's, and render them burdensome to the People, by never suffering them to be upon any Right, or so much as tolerable Foot, and all to perswade the Necessity of standing Forces.[27] And indeed they have succeeded too well in this Design: For the greatest part of the World has been fool'd into an opinion, That a Militia cannot be made serviceable. I shall not say 'twas only Militia's could conquer the World; and that Princes to have succeeded fully in the Design before-mentioned, must have destroyed all the History and Memory of Antient Governments, where the Accounts of so many excellent Models of Militia are yet extant. I know the Prejudice and Ignorance of the World concerning the Art of War, as it was practised by the Antients; tho what remains of that Knowledg in their Writings be sufficient to give a mean Opinion of the Modern Discipline. For this Reason I shall examine, by what has passed of late Years in this Nation, whether Experience have convinced us, that Officers bred in Foreign Wars, be so far preferable to others who have been under no other Discipline than that of an [24] ordinary and ill-regulated Militia; and if the Commonalty of *England* at their first

27. For examples of disparagement of the militia, see above, p. 36, n. 89.

entrance upon Service, be not as capable of a resolute Military Action, as any standing Forces. The Battel of *Naseby*[28] will fully resolve this Doubt, which is generally thought to have been the deciding Action of the late Civil War. The Number of Forces was equal on both sides;[29] nor was there any Advantage in the Ground, or extraordinary Accident that happened during the Fight, which could be of considerable importance to either side. In the Army of the Parliament, nine only of the Officers had served abroad, and most of the Souldiers were Prentices drawn out of *London* but two months before. In the King's Army there was above a thousand Officers that had served in foreign Parts: Yet were they routed and broken by those new-raised Prentices; who were observed to be obedient to Command, and brave in Fight; not only in that Action, but on all Occasions during that active Campagn. The People of this Nation are not a dastardly Crew, like those born in Misery under Oppression and Slavery, who must have time to rub off that Fear, Cowardice and Stupidity which they bring from home. And tho Officers seem to stand in more need of Experience than private Souldiers, yet in that Battel it was seen, that the Sobriety, and Principle of the Officers on the one side, prevailed over the Experience of those on the other.

[25] 'Tis well known that divers Regiments of our Army lately in *Flanders*[30] have never been once in Action, and not one half of them above thrice, nor any of them five times during the whole War. O, but they have been under Discipline, and accustomed to obey! And so may Men in Militia's. We have had to do with an Enemy, who, tho abounding in Numbers of excellent Officers, yet durst never fight us without a visible Advantage. Is that Enemy like to invade us, when he must be unavoidably

28. A momentous encounter between Royalist and Parliamentary forces twenty miles south of Leicester on 14 June 1645. Despite the initial success of the Royalist cavalry under Prince Rupert, the Parliamentary forces showed superior discipline and were able to rout the Royalist infantry and capture the Royalist artillery— losses which destroyed Charles I's ability subsequently to wage war. See Ludlow, *Memoirs*, 1:153.

29. In fact the Royalist forces were outnumbered 10,000 to 14,000.

30. During the War of the League of Augsburg, also called the War of the Grand Alliance (1689–97), the main theater of war was in the Low Countries, with less important activity also in Spain and Italy.

necessitated to put all to hazard in ten days, or starve, unless we will suppose we are to have no Fleet at all?

But to come to some of the Capital Errors committed by those that established the Modern Militia's, besides what has been already mentioned; One of the chief was, the discontinuing to exercise the whole People, for which there were many excellent and wholsome Laws in this Nation, and almost every where else. Another Error was, the taking Men without distinction, and, for the most part, the Scum of the People into that small number which they listed and exercised. Whereas if a small number only was to be exercised, no Man of Quality or Riches ought to be excused from that Duty.[31] Thus it was, that these Militia's fell into contempt; and Men of Quality and Estates having Power to send any wretched Servant in their place, became themselves abject and ti[26]morous, by being disused to handle Arms, 'Tis well observed by a Judicious Author,[32] that 'tis easier to exercise a greater Number than a less; and

31. The Militia Act of 1662 (more correctly, An Act for ordering the Forces in the several Counties of this Kingdom) established high property qualifications for the militia:

> No person shall be charged with finding a Horse Horseman and Armes unless such person or persons have a Revenue of Five hundred pounds by the yeare in possession or have an Estate of Six thousand pounds in goods or money besides the furniture of his or theire houses and so proportionably for a greater Estate in lands in possession or goods as the respective Lieutenants and theire Deputies as aforesaid in theire discretions shall see cause and thinke reasonable And they are not to charge any person with finding a Foot Souldier and Armes that hath not a yearely Revenue of Fifty pounds in possession or a personal Estate of Six hundred pounds in goods or moneys (other then the stocke upon the ground) and after the aforesaid rate proportionably for a greater or lesser Revenue or Estate Nor shall they charge any person with the finding both of Horse and Foot in the same County. (14 Car. II, c.3)

However, as Toland was to point out (below, p. 189), these people did not have to serve in person, but could send a substitute in their stead.

32. In bk. 1 of *The Art of War*, Machiavelli extolls the superiority of large militias over small: "Senza dubbio egli è migliore e piu necessario il numero grosso che il piccolo: anzi a' dire meglio, dove non se ne può ordinare gran quantità, non si può ordinare una ordinanza perfetta. . . ."; "Seeing it is your desire to be satisfied, which is best, a great number or a small; without doubt a great number is best, and not only more necessary, but (to speak frankly) a compleat and perfect Militia is

consequently all that are able to bear Arms in a Nation, than a small Number pickt out of a wide Country; who must march far, and be from home several days at each Exercise. And perhaps it might be found an unnecessary trouble and burden, to have certain numbers of Men listed and formed into Bodies in time of Peace, if the whole People were exercised, and an easy Method laid down, by which such numbers of Men as shall be thought convenient, may always be drawn out, even upon the most sudden Occasion. For by this means the Choice will be greater, as it ought to be, that so Trade, Manufactures and Husbandry may be as little disturbed as possible, since the Impediments of the several Conditions of Men are so many and so various.

'Twill be said, That I insist much upon the Errors of the present Militia, and do not propose a new Model[33] by which they may be amended. I answer, A Parliament only can do that. The People are to tell wherein they are agrieved, and what is amiss: It belongs only to that Wise Council to apply sutable Remedies: Which cannot be difficult when the Causes of the Disease are discovered. And there are many Models of Militia, both Antient and Modern, from which divers useful things may be taken.

[27] Of the Fleet I shall say little, having chiefly undertaken to speak of Militia's and standing Forces. But surely *England* cannot justly apprehend an Invasion, if the Fleet alone were in such order as it ought to be. And it can never be the Interest of this Nation to take any other share in preserving the Balance of *Europe*, than what may be performed by our Fleets. By which means our Money will be spent amongst our selves, our Trade preserved to support the Charge of our Navy; our Enemies totally driven out of the Sea, and great numbers of their Forces diverted from opposing the Armies of our Allies abroad, to the defence of their own Coasts.

If this Method had been taken in the late War, I presume it would have proved, not only more advantagious to us, but also more serviceable

---

not to be had in any place where there is not great plenty of men. . . ." (Machiavelli, *Tutte l'opere*, 2:332; Machiavelli, *Works*, p. 447).

33. In the second edition of this text, published in 1698 as *A Discourse of Government with Relation to Militia's*, Fletcher did offer a blueprint for a militia; see Fletcher, *Political Works*, pp. 24–29.

to our Allies than that which was followed. And 'tis in vain to say, that at this rate we shall have no Allies at all: For the weaker Party on the Continent must be contented to accept our Assistance in the manner we think fit to give it, or inevitably perish. But if we send Mercenary Forces beyond the Seas to join those of our Allies, then, at the end of every War, the present struggle will recur, and at one time or other the Nation will be betrayed, and a Standing [28] Army established: So that nothing can save us from following the Fate of all the other Kingdoms in *Europe*, but putting our Trust altogether in our Fleets and Militia's, and having no other Forces than these. The Sea is the only Empire which can naturally belong to us. Conquest is not our Interest, much less to consume our People and Treasure in conquering for others.[34]

To conclude;

If we seriously consider the happy Condition of this Nation, who have lived for many Ages under the Blessings of Liberty, we cannot but be affected with the most tender Compassion to think that a Country, whose Fields are every where well cultivated and improved by the Industry of rich Husbandmen; Her Rivers and Harbours filled with Ships; Her Cities, Towns, and Villages, enrich'd with Manufactures; where Men possessing vast Estates, are not hated and abhorred as in other Countries, but deservedly blessed, by the poorer sort of People; whose Merchants live in as great Splendor as the Nobility of other Nations, and whose Commonalty not only surpasses all those of that degree which the World can now boast of, but also those of all former Ages, in Courage, Honesty, good Sense, Industry, and Generosity of Temper; in whose very Looks there are such visible [29] Marks of a free and liberal Education, which Advantages cannot be imputed to the Climate, or to any other Cause, but the Freedom of the Government under which they live: I say, it cannot but make the Hearts of all honest Men bleed to think, that in their days the Felicity of such a Country must come to a Period, if the Parliament do not prevent it, and his Majesty be not prevailed upon to lay aside the Thoughts of a Mercenary Army, which tho it may seem a Security in his

34. A jab at William III's policy of committing English forces in Continental wars.

time, yet by being continued, as will inevitably come to pass, must pro-duce, under his Successors, those fatal Consequences that have always attended such Forces in the other Kingdoms of *Europe;* Violation of Property, Decay of Trade, Oppression of the Country by heavy Taxes and Quarters, the utmost Misery and Slavery of the poorer sort, the Ruine of the Nobility and Gentry by their Expences in Court and Army, Deceit and Treachery in all Ranks of Men, occasioned by Want and Necessity. Then shall we see our once happy Commonalty become base and abject, by being continually exposed to the brutal Insolence of the Souldiers, our Women debauch'd by their Lust, ugly and nasty through Poverty, and the want of things necessary to preserve their natural Beauty. Then shall we see that great City, the Pride and Glory not only of our Island, but of the World, subjected to the excessive Impositions [30] *Paris* now lies under, and reduced to a Pedling Trade, serving only to foment the Luxury of a Court. Then will *England* know what Obligations she has to those who are for Mercenary Armies.

FINIS.

John Toland

The Militia Reform'd

1698

1. Literally, "as apt for Mars as for Mercury" (in Roman mythology, the gods of war and eloquence respectively); hence, "as apt for warfare as for learning." Cf. below, p. 215, n. 60. The phrase had a proverbial force in early modern English literature and was (for instance) the motto of the poet George Gascoigne. In *Oceana*, Hermes de Caduceo praises the marriage of "arms and councils, in the mutual embraces whereof consisteth your whole commonwealth" (Harrington, *Oceana*, p. 97).

The Militia Reform'd;

OR AN

EASY SCHEME

OF

Furnishing *ENGLAND* with a Constant
LAND-FORCE, capable to *prevent* or to
subdue any Forein Power; and to maintain
perpetual QUIET at Home, without endangering
the PUBLICK LIBERTY.

Tam Marte quam Mercurio.[1]

LONDON;
Printed by John Darby in Bartholomew Close:
and sold by Andrew Bell at the Cross-Keys and Bible
in Cornhil, MDCXCVIII.

The Militia Reform'd, &c.

The following Discourse (most Noble LORD[2]) begun at your Request, and finish'd within the short time You prescrib'd, is now made a Present to the World; which, if the Favour deserves any Return, is oblig'd to your Lordship for the Publication. You have long since justly acquir'd the Esteem of all good Men; and the known measure of their Prayers, when they wish their Relations happy, is that they may equal your Lordship's Probity and Understanding. But tho you neither want, nor desire the regards of any besides the *Vertuous*;[3] yet no News can be more pleasing, than to hear of a constant [4] Addition to your Friends, this being an infallible Sign, that the Number of Publick-spirited Men increases: For he must needs be your sworn Enemy, who is not a hearty lover of his Country. I purposely forbear to express your Name, or to enlarge an Encomium, which, I know, will not be grateful, tho unsuspected of Flattery; and therefore I leave your Lordship to be entertain'd by mine, or your own more solid Observations.

1. To employ one's Thoughts on what he pleases, and to speak as freely as he thinks, is the greatest Advantage of living in a free Government; the next to this is being Master of what you possess from the Favour of others, or by your own Industry; and then, that Merit is indifferently rewarded in Persons of all Conditions and Degrees. Their due Value is ordinarily set upon [5] the two last by most Men, and Life it self should be

2. Unidentified; possibly an enabling fiction.
3. Here meaning not only morally righteous (*OED*, s.v. "virtuous," 2a) but also learned (*OED*, s.v. "virtuous," 6).

readily expos'd to maintain or acquire the first; for, without it to live, is, in my Opinion, worse than any Death. Under Despotick Princes none dares mutter at his own, or the Sufferings of his Fellows; much less put so much Confidence in his dearest Friend, as to condole their common Slavery, where the Informer is tempted with immense Rewards, and certain Death or Disgrace attend the Accus'd. This is the bless'd Unity of that Constitution which some admire so much, because no Complaints are heard in it; whence they would persuade us, that it is also free from all Grievances. But where Laws secure the Rights of the SUBJECT, with the same Care as the Privileges of the MAGISTRATE, no sooner is any pinch'd but he cries out; and the Authors of the Peoples Oppression are oblig'd to change their Conduct, or to rectify their Mistakes. Either the PRINCE is disabus'd, when his MINISTERS have seduc'd him by false Representations; or sometimes the MINISTERS refuse to act, if the PRINCE be resolv'd upon Arbitrary Courses. Now, 'tis our peculiar Hap[6]piness in *England,* that no other Government in *Europe* is equal to us, whether the DIGNITY of the Magistracy, or the LIBERTY of the People be consider'd. But particularly in all dubious Affairs of Publick Concern, 'tis every Man's Duty to assist his Country by his Advice, as well as with his Hand in time of Danger: And Matters are as freely debated among us abroad, as within their own Walls by our Senators, who likewise in their printed Votes inform us of all their Resolutions and Proceedings. These Considerations, join'd with the Request of a Person I honour,[4] have prevail'd with me to deliver my Opinion at this time concerning the modelling and disciplining of our MILITIA; and I question not but it will by our Wise and August *Parliament* be establish'd on such a foot as shall effectually defend us hereafter against all Foreign Force, and constantly preserve our Freedom and Peace at home.

2. But before I descend to any Particulars, I must premise something concerning the present Factions that unfortunately divide us, and which discover their fatal Effects too much upon the present Occasion. One says, the TORIES [7] will never heartily consent to any Model that makes the MILITIA useful: Another replies, that this is only an ill-natur'd

---

4. Presumably the unidentified "Noble LORD" of n. 2 above.

Insinuation, while some of the WHIGS oppose the thing openly, and are glad of any Pretence to conceal their true Reasons. But these Names are now of a very doubtful signification.[5] We hear of Court and Country, of Apostate and Adhering WHIGS; nor are the TORIES more united among themselves. 'Tis observable that no Man, however otherwise negligent of his Conduct, is willing to own that without any reason at all he differs from others in Word or Action: but whether he dissembles, or ingenuously tells the Cause of his Dissent, yet *Interest* or *Conscience* (real or mistaken) are the two principal Springs of all Divisions. Indeed we find by frequent Experience, that where *Interest* secretly governs, *Conscience* is openly pretended; but in this case no body's bare Profession is to be regarded, his Actions being the most certain Interpreter of his Thoughts. If one therefore, who would pass for a *Patriot*, has any Interest separate from that of the Publick, he's no longer entitl'd to this Denomination; [8] but is a real Hypocrite that's ready to sacrifice the Common Good to his Private Gain, than which no worse can be said of any particular Faction. Now such Distinctions as these of WHIG and TORY, cannot miss of being often made with a great deal of Partiality and Injustice; for, according to your predominant Passion, he's a WHIG whom you love, and he that you hate's a TORY; and so on the contrary, as you happen to be engag'd in either Party. Notwithstanding, 'tis sometimes a mighty easy

---

5. In his *A Dissertation Upon Parties* (1735) Bolingbroke would comment on the instability of party identities: "These associations are broken; these distinct sets of ideas are shuffled out of their order; new combinations force themselves upon us; and it would actually be as absurd to impute to the Tories the principles, which were laid to their charge formerly, as it would be to ascribe to the projector and his faction the name of Whigs, whilst they daily forfeit that character by their actions" (Bolingbroke, p. 5). Under Hanoverian Whig administrations, the language of a Tory opposition could sound very similar to that of the Old Whigs during the reign of James II. As John Pocock observes, "Tory language, which ought to have been and often was High Church and Jacobite, ought not to have been but often was radical and republican, Commonwealth as well as country. There are Jacobite manifestos of 1745 that sound not unlike Monmouth's manifestos of 1685" (J. G. A. Pocock, "Varieties of Whiggism," in *Virtue, Commerce, and History* [Cambridge: Cambridge University Press, 1985], p. 245). As Swift himself wrote in *The Examiner*, 33 (22 March 1710), "I am not sensible of any material Difference there is between those who call themselves the *Old Whigs*, and a great Majority of the present *Tories*."

thing to see through all these feign'd Pretences. Should one, for Example, who was formerly taken for a Friend to LIBERTY, now that he has got or expects Preferment, neglect or oppose any Publick Good, in promoting which he might be disappointed or depriv'd of his Post; this Man must not think to live always upon the Credit of the old Stock, when it appears that either he has entirely chang'd his Sentiments, or was never sincere; and that he resisted the former Powers, because they were not kind enough to him, but not out of any fix'd Enmity to SLAVERY. Some Folks there be who seem'd at the beginning to favour [9] the REVOLUTION, yet ever since oppos'd the Government, because they think their real or fanci'd Merit not sufficiently rewarded[6] by the King, to whom it is impossible to heap Preferments upon every Body tho never so deserving, unless they would be all Commanders without any to obey them. But we likewise know others who from Enemies to King *WILLIAM*, are become his Friends; and this of all Changes is the most natural and commendable, that one who by Education, Example, or otherwise, was once engag'd against the Interest of his Country, should upon better consideration desert a Party to join with the Publick. Several of these, it may be, never thought during one hour of the Original or End of Societies, till the late Differences gave 'em an opportunity and incouragement to do it: And if the Discovery of Truth proves to be the Result of their Study, we ought not to reject their Reasons now, because we justly disallow'd their Errors before. Certainly a true PATRIOT can be of no Faction, nor consequently for excluding any from sharing the Blessings of that LIBERTY they are willing to support. [10] If the *Romans* admitted their vanquish'd Enemies to an equal participation of their Laws and Privileges, how much more readily should we embrace our own Country-men with both Arms, and welcome the return of our prodigal Brethren to their Duty towards our common Mother? But granting that in this Business of the MILITIA, some of those who promote it are not sincere, tho Charity commands us to hope the best, we need not be sollicitous whether they are or not, so long as the thing is good in it self, and they concur with us in establishing a Constitution they cannot afterwards resist if they would,

---

6. E.g., Robert Ferguson (above, p. 75, n. 7, and p. 78, n. 16).

nor, I hope, be willing, if they could. This is the highest Mark of Sincerity; and, for my part, I shall never think him a Fo to *England* that has a hand in it. But if any continue still scrupulous, let him not be asham'd to imitate the Prudence of the great *Apostle*,[7] who said, *Some preach* Christ *even out of Envy and Strife, and some also out of good Will; The one preach* Christ *out of Contention, not sincerely;—but the other out of love.—What then? Notwithstanding, everyway, whether in Pretence, or in Truth,* Christ *is preach'd;* [11] *and I therein do rejoice, yea and will rejoice.* Now what's judg'd lawful in *Religion*, and by an Apostle too, may, I think, with a very good Grace be admitted in *Politicks*. After all, I am the farthest imaginable from being an Advocate for any disaffected Persons. The Government is under no Obligation to indulge Men continuing in opposition to it; nor should those, who are resolv'd upon adhering to the late King, think upon abusing the Lenity of the present, if the Immortal BRUTUS[8] spar'd not his own Sons, when they were found plotting the Restoration of the *Abdicated* Tyrant.

3. Another thing I am sorry to hear out of a great many peoples Mouths, is, that we have not Vertue enough to agree upon any tolerable Model of training our MILITIA, and that it's almost impossible we should ever recover our former Reputation of Valour. But this Argument is nothing the less weak for being so common; and the true Intent of such as always cry none but good Men can make good Laws, is (besides affronting others) to place all Power in the hands of their own Party, who with them are the only good Men. [12] 'Tis Government or Education makes all the Difference among Nations as to Military and Civil Discipline, foreign Commerce, domestick Oeconomy, or the like. Upon the first Discovery of this Island by the *Romans*, its Inhabitants were found as savage as we know the *Americans* to be now. The Climate of *Rome* is still the same, the Bodies

7. I.e., St. Paul. Toland quotes from Philippians 1:15–18.

8. I.e., Lucius Junius Brutus, the founder of the Roman Republic, who condemned his sons to death when it was discovered that they were plotting to reintroduce the royal family of the Tarquins to Rome. The innuendo of *"Abdicated"* applies this episode of Roman history to modern-day Jacobites hoping to restore the Stuarts. For a discussion of the importance of theories of abdication in the Glorious Revolution, see J. P. Kenyon, *Revolution Principles: The Politics of Party 1689–1720* (Cambridge: Cambridge University Press, 1977).

of its Citizens, and the Distances of other Places remain the same; yet they have wholly lost the Secret of conquering the World, and are become as poor and mean spirited as their Ancestors were gallant and brave: for the latter were free, and the former are ignorant Slaves.[9] To come nearer home, all the Pains imaginable have been taken for a considerable space to render our selves luxurious and illiterate, the better to dispose us to favour the tyrannical Designs of our late Kings; but have we not so retriev'd our Credit in *Europe* under the Administration of his present Majesty, as if we had voluntarily suffer'd it to be eclips'd a while, that it might shine the brighter ever after? And to apply this more particularly still, I readily own that the MILITIA, as now regulated, is burdensom and useless; but it follows [13] not that all are necessarily so, the contrary being plain from the Histories of every Age as well as from present Experience. And before I have done I shall give a Demonstration that the Frame of our Militia could not be more successfully contriv'd to render it the Object of the Peoples Contempt and Aversion, with a Design to create in them a good Opinion of Mercenaries, and to make 'em believe a necessity of always keeping up a Standing Force of such. In a word, when our Men are better train'd, they will not make such a ridiculous Figure under their Arms; and when the Charge is less felt or laid out to better purpose, it will be more cheerfully paid.

4. But we are still encompass'd with many Dangers. It's said that those Souldiers who have so bravely fought for ours and the Liberties of *Europe*, declare it is not from any private Interest of their own, but out of regard to our future Safety, they desir'd to be kept on foot; and that in Honour we ought not to discharge Men who suffer'd so much for our sakes. We are to blame indeed if we don't sufficiently provide for our own Security; but as to the [14] Souldier's Merits, I answer first, that their

9. Early modern and eighteenth-century travelers frequently commented on the contrast between the heroic ancient Romans and their base modern descendants. Montesquieu's comments are representative: "La majesté du peuple romain, dont parle tant Tite-Live, est fort avilie. . . . A présent le peuple romain *est gens aeterna, in qua nemo nascitur* [an eternal people where there are no births], à quelques bâtards près. On a interpreté le S.P.Q.R.: *Sanno puttare queste Romane* [these Romans know how to prostitute themselves]" (*Voyage de Gratz à la Haye*, in *Oeuvres complètes*, p. 260).

past Service is duly acknowledg'd, and order'd to be rewarded. Secondly, That such as never saw our Enemies, are more clamorous than those who beat them. And, Thirdly, That this unreasonable Demand was not made by the Body of the common Souldiers, who are generally desirous of returning home to their Wives, or their Relations, or their Callings; and more particularly at this time, because that hitherto they have known nothing but the Danger, Want, or Fatigue of the War; whereas, once tasting the Pleasures of Idleness and Ease, they will every day become less willing to disband. And now the Question all this while ought not to have been, whether these Gentlemen mean what they say, or only pretend it; but what's most for the Advantage of the Nation. This was the Motive of raising them, and should be that of establishing or laying them aside. War being their Trade, 'tis no wonder if they be always for continuing it; nor can it ever happen to be otherwise, should they be wholly left to themselves, no more than any other Persons, without the Intervention of the Civil Au[15]thority, would reform the Abuses of their own Professions. But the *Parliament* has now put an end to this Dispute; and, to the great Satisfaction of all good Men, granted to his Majesty a sufficient *Guard* both for the Honour and Safety of his Person, with a competent Number besides to secure some important Places till the New MILITIA is regulated, which, I hope, in a little time may be happily effected.[10] In the following Model Provision is made for several hundreds of the disbanded Army, and I daresay the Change propos'd in their Condition will give most of 'em Satisfaction; tho, by the way, they ought to be content, should the *Parliament* proceed no further to gratify them than they have already resolv'd. The most stupid Souldier knows very well an Army has nothing in it so charming that could induce the Nation to raise one, but upon some pressing Necessity, and not to keep it up perpetually; nor can the Service perform'd be ever so great, as not to be requited under such a Return. I cannot determin whether it would occasion more Indignation or Mirth to hear a Man contending, that because the Souldiers defend[16]ed our Liberty at the publick Charge for nine Years against the

10. Toland refers to the decision of Parliament on 11 December 1697 to disband all the forces raised since 1680, which effectively reduced the land force to 8,000 (Burnet, *History*, 2:207; Boyer, *William III*, 3:302).

French,[11] we can do no less than become their Slaves for ever. This Paradox is too gross for any to maintain, or perhaps to intend; yet every considering and indifferent Person must perceive the Consequence to be true. I shall therefore, to avoid the Labour of proving what is self-evident, put you only in mind of the Gentleman, who, having engag'd the Maid to speak a good Word for him to her Mistriss, would needs when the Lady consented quit her, and marry the Maid, out of pure Gratitude for the pains she had taken on his behalf.

5. But the Honour and Safety of the Nation is the commendable Design of all sides; wherein they are certainly in the right, since all Countries must have some Force to defend them against foreign Invasions and domestick Tumults: for as it was their own Good and Security which occasion'd Men first to quit the State of Nature, and to associate themselves into Governments;[12] so the Raising and Regulation of their Forces must be directed and accommodated to the same ends. An Island is best situated for Preservation, as having need [17] of little other Force, either to infest foreign Coasts, or to protect its own, besides a numerous Fleet which it can never want. But if it be likewise a Government for Encrease,[13]

---

11. I.e., in the War of the League of Augsburg, also called the War of the Grand Alliance (1689–97).

12. Cf. Hobbes, *Leviathan:* "The finall Cause, End, or Designe of men, (who naturally love Liberty, and Dominion over others,) in the introduction of that restraint upon themselves, (in which wee see them live in Commonwealths,) is the foresight of their own preservation, and of a more contented life thereby; that is to say, of getting themselves out from that miserable condition of Warre. . . ." (pt. 2, chap. 17; Hobbes, *Leviathan*, p. 117); and Locke, *Two Treatises:* "I easily grant, that Civil Government is the proper Remedy for the Inconveniences of the State of Nature" (bk. 2, chap. 2, § 13; Locke, *Treatises*, p. 276).

13. The distinction between governments of increase and governments of preservation goes back to Machiavelli (*Discourses*, bk. 1, chap. 6, and bk. 2, chap. 19) and (in an English context) more proximately to Machiavelli's English disciple, James Harrington (Harrington, *Oceana*, pp. 7, 32–33, 155–57, 217–19). The distinction had been revived and explored in the 1690s in the political economy of Charles Davenant. For context and commentary, see John Robertson, "Universal Monarchy and the Liberties of Europe: David Hume's Critique of an English Whig Doctrine," in *Political Discourse in Early Modern Britain*, ed. N. Phillipson and Q. Skinner (Cambridge: Cambridge University Press, 1993), pp. 349–73.

such as ours, its Situation naturally leading it to Trade and planting of Colonies; and if it has the noble Ambition of holding the Balance steddy between other Governments, of succouring the Distress'd, and grudging Liberty to none, then it must be always provided with a considerable *Land-Force*. Of this there's no Dispute. Then the only Question is, Whether it be safest to trust Arms continually in the hands of ignorant, idle, and needy Persons; or, only when there's occasion for it, in the hands of sober, industrious, and understanding Freemen. That the latter can never be dangerous to our Liberty and Property at home, and will be infinitely more effectual against an Enemy attacking, or invaded by us, I am now going to prove; and at the same time to deliver an intelligible and practicable MODEL of disciplining and maintaining such a Force with very little Charge, and no Trouble at all. My Method shall be to lay down a few *Propositions*, and those [18] very short, to each of which I subjoin a *Discourse* confirming or explaining it, and containing what other Remarks might be naturally made in that Place. But I am so far from writing all I have read or observ'd upon this Subject, that I shall omit several useful things wherein the World seems to be already well satisfy'd, or that are not absolutely essential to my purpose. As I expect the common Fate of all Writers, that some probably out of Ignorance or Malice, and others, perhaps, from substantial Reasons may except against my Performance; so I desire (as in Justice I am bound) that all real Imperfections, or whatever the Injudicious and Envious may mistake for such, be wholly laid at my own door, and not charg'd upon the Subject, which ought not to suffer under the Disadvantage of unskilful Management.

6. Now my First Proposition shall be, THAT *ENGLAND* CONSISTING OF FREEMEN AND SERVANTS, NONE BE CAPABLE OF SERVING IN THE MILITIA BUT THE FORMER. By FREEMEN I understand Men of Property, or Persons that are able to live of themselves; and those who cannot subsist in this Inde[19]pendence I call SERVANTS. The bare Explication of the Terms should, one would think, be sufficient to perswade any Man of Sense that the former should not only be sooner trusted with Arms than the latter; but that they must needs use 'em likewise to better purpose. For besides that all the Endowments which Nature has made

common to both are improv'd in FREEMEN, the very Temper of their Bodies being much stronger and livelier by better feeding, which is no little Ingredient to Courage, they fight also for their Liberty and Property; whereas the other have nothing to lose but their Lives, which are likewise infinitely dearer to those whose Circumstances render 'em more agreeable and easy. The *Romans*, who understood the Art of War beyond all the World, did not make SOLDIERY a Refuge to Poverty and Idleness; for none but Men of Fortune and Property, whose private Interest firmly engag'd them to the Publick Good, had the Honour of serving in their Armies. Nay, so far were they from employing the poor and servile sort, that unless a Man was worth a certain Sum appointed by Law, he was [20] excluded from military Duties, which in that Government was thought no reputable Privilege. All that enjoy'd not the Property assign'd they partly call'd *POLMEN, as being return'd for nothing but their Heads in the publick Taxation; and partly †BREEDERS, as being no other way useful to *Rome*, but by encreasing the Number of its Citizens. ‡*Seeing a Man's real or personal Estate, says AULUS GELLIUS, are a sure Pledg and Hostage for his Fidelity to the Government, and that these Enjoyments seem to be the ground of one's Love to his Country, therefore neither the* BREEDERS *nor the* POLMEN *were listed as Souldiers, but in case of extraordinary Tumults*

---

* Capitecensi (à Capitis censione) vocabantur qui nullo aut perquam parvo aere censebantur. *A. Gellius, l. 16. c. 10.*[14]

† Proletarii, à munere officioque prolis edendae appellati sunt. *Id. ibid.*[15]

‡ Quoniam res pecuniaque familiaris obsidis vicem pignorisque esse apud Rempublicam videbantur; amorisque in patriam sides quaedam in ea firmamentumque erat; neque Proletarii neque Capitecensi, Milites, nisi in tumultu maximo, scribebantur. *Id. ibid.*[16]

14. "Qui vero nullo aut perquam parvo aere censebantur, 'capite censi' vocabuntur"; "Those who were estimated to have no property at all, or next to none, were called 'capite censi' (that is to say, 'counted by head')" (Aulus Gellius, XVI.x.10).

15. "[Proletarii] a munere officioque prolis edendae appellati sunt"; "[The proletarii] were named after their duty and function of producing offspring" (Aulus Gellius, XVI.x.13).

16. "But since property and money were regarded as a hostage and pledge of loyalty to the State, and since there was in them a kind of guarantee and assurance of patriotism, neither the proletarii nor the capite censi were enrolled as soldiers except in some extraordinary crisis" (Aulus Gellius, XVI.x.11). Cf. Giovanni Botero, *Della ragion di stato* (1589), IV.7.

or Insurrections. But they were arm'd upon those Occasions by [21] the *Publick, and rather employ'd in keeping watch and ward at home, than led into the Field against the Enemy. We find that all those who aspir'd at Tyranny or any unlimited Power above the Laws, as †*MARIUS*[17] for example, did constantly make Levies of the poorer sort, putting Arms into the hands of those that had no stake to lose, and who for that Reason would be sure not to design the Good of the Commonwealth, but only his Profit that employ'd them: nor will they be more faithful to the latter than to the Government when any other makes them a more advantageous Offer. Now, all this is natural enough, and should not surprize anybody: for the same Reason that prevails with the *Rich* to fight for that Government, whose excellent Constitution secures his Property to him, moves the *Indigent* to serve against it; and that is [22] to make both their Lives more easy; whence it may be concluded that Citizens will always appear for Liberty, and Servants fight for Bread. 'Tis well known, that all the World over, where-ever the Sword is in the hands of the *People*, it is a free Government be it of one or of many; and on the

---

* Armaque iis sumptu publico praebebantur. *Id. ibid.*

    Proletarius publicitus scutisque feroque
    Ornatur ferro, Muros, Urbemque, Forumque,
    Excubiis curat. *Ennius.*[18]

† Ipse (Marius) milites scribere non more majorum neque ex classibus, sed uti libido cujusque erat, Capitecensos plerosque;—Quod ab eo genere celebratus auctusque erat: & homini potentiam quarenti egentissimus quisque opportunissimus. *Salust. in Bello Jugurt.*[19]

17. Cf. above, p. 19, n. 44, p. 86, n. 40, and p. 161, n. 21.

18. "Arms were provided for them at the public expense" (Aulus Gellius, XVI.x.13); "With shield and savage sword is Proletarius armed / At public cost; they guard our walls, our market, and our town" (Ennius, quoted in Aulus Gellius, XVI.x.1).

19. "He himself [Marius] in the meantime enrolled soldiers, not according to the classes in the manner of our forefathers, but allowing anyone to volunteer, for the most part the proletariat . . . because that class had given him honor and rank; and to one who aspires to power the poorest man is the most useful" (Sallust, *Bellum Jugurthinum*, LXXXVI). For Machiavelli's comments on the military utility of the ancient Roman division into classes, see *The Art of War*, bk. 1 (Machiavelli, *Chief Works*, 2:587).

contrary, all Tyrannies are supported by *Mercenaries:* nor is there any thing peculiar in our Soil, our Air, or in our Persons to hinder the same Circumstances from producing the like Effects. It is likewise to be consider'd, that all Wars carri'd on by FREEMEN are suddenly finish'd, because, not being instigated by Want or the desire of Rapine, they are ever longing to return home to reap the Pleasure of their own Possessions, together with the agreeable Society of their Families, Relations, and Friends. But all Wars manag'd by MERCENARIES prove extremely tedious and burdensom, for they never end till the Country that employs them be exhausted of all its Treasure, which is their sole Motive of making Peace. It ought to be also remark'd, that a MILITIA of *Freeholders* is not only harder to be conquer'd than that of *Servants* or *Mer*[23]*cenaries*, but must be even superior to an Army wholly compos'd of *Gentlemen* under an Arbitrary Monarch: for the latter, notwithstanding their Honors and Privileges, are not absolutely free, but retain'd on the behalf of Tyranny; whereas Men of Property being all disciplin'd (as we propose) and having Arms in their hands for the Defence of *Liberty*, upon which from their Infancy they are taught to value themselves, and to prefer it to all other Conditions (Life, Riches, and Honors without it being not only precarious, but of no other use except to prolong a miserable and infamous *Slavery;*) FREEMEN, I say, thus train'd, excel all others in Greatness of Soul and Courage: Nor are their haughty Spirits ever to be subdu'd, especially when they consider they are fighting for their own, and not otherwise employ'd for their Fellows than these are for them, their common Endeavours being to secure every Man's private Property. Such a Constitution, where all Persons are equally educated in Civil and Military Discipline, was never conquer'd by any Standing Armies, unless previously weaken'd by some intestine Divisions. [24] On the other hand, of two Free Governments 'tis possible indeed for the greatest to overcome the least; but then we find (to use the Words of a most observing Man)[20] that the Walls and Towers of such a Government become its Funeral Piles, and that it expires in its own Flames, leaving nothing to the

---

20. Cf. Machiavelli, *The Prince*, chap. 5.

Conqueror but its Ashes; witness *Saguntum*[21] when master'd by *Carthage*, and *Numantia*[22] by *Rome*. I need not longer insist upon this Matter, and therefore shall remark in the last place, that whenever any free Empire degenerated into Tyranny, as that of *Rome* is known to have done, then Men of Property were not enjoin'd or encourag'd to serve themselves, but either permitted to find others that would go out in their room, or to pay down so much ready Money; upon which occasion says one, speaking of the *Romans,* **They sent those to defend them in the Field, whom they would scorn to admit into their domestick Service.* Indeed some of the Emperors perceiv'd this Error, and endeavor'd to correct it, but in vain, since at the same [25] time they resolv'd to continue arbitrary. But however the following Order was publish'd by GRATIAN, VALENTINIAN, and THEO-DOSIUS: †*We decree,* say they, *that in our best Troops there be no Slave enroll'd, nor any Servants out of Houses of Entertainment, nor any from Places of infamous resort, nor out of Eating-houses, the Houses of Correction, or other such infamous Fellows.* Yet we are so far from observing this Rule of listing FREEMEN only, that in the ‡Act now in force for regulating our MILITIA,[23]

---

* Talesque sociantur armis, quales Domini habere fastidiunt. *Vegetius, l.* I. *c.* 7.

† Inter optimas lectissimorum militum turmas, neminem è numero servorum dandum esse decernimus, nevè ex Caupona ductum, vel ex famosarum ministris tabernarum, aut ex cocorum aut pistorum numero, vel etiam eo quem obsequii deformitas Militia secernit, nec tracta de Ergastulis nomina. *Cod. Theodos.* l. 7. tit. 13.

‡ 14 Car. 2. §. 25.

21. Modern day Sagunto, in eastern Spain. The Romans had agreed with the Carthaginians that Saguntum would remain independent. But in 219 B.C. the town was taken by Hannibal after prolonged resistance, and this was the immediate cause of the Second Punic War (218–201 B.C.). Saguntum was recaptured by Rome in 214 B.C.

22. An important town near modern Soria in Spain. Numantia was the center of Celtiberian resistance to Roman expansion, and successfully repulsed a series of Roman attacks before succumbing to Scipio Aemilianus in 133 B.C. after an eight-month siege.

23. The English Militia acts did not require service in person, but rather imposed a duty to supply and equip either a horse man or an infantry man depending on wealth:

no Man is oblig'd to serve in Person, but may send whom he pleases to appear for him, tho never so poor and weak, or ignorant of the use of Arms, and all other Arts.

7. Thus far have I discours'd of the Persons who are to constitute our MILITIA, and now I come to the Method of *training* them; after which I shall [26] orderly proceed to their Number, Charge, Age, and other necessary Considerations. My Second Proposition therefore is, THAT ONE AFTERNOON EVERY WEEK THERE BE A PAROCHIAL EXERCISE OF ALL MALES, AS WELL SERVANTS AS FREEMEN, FROM 16 TO 40 YEARS OF AGE. Whether this be done on Mondays, or Thursdays, or Saturdays, is indifferent; and I must not forget that the *Switzers* think no Day so proper for it as SUNDAY, from the following Reasons, *viz*. First, because no other Business is interrupted by the Exercise propos'd, all Labor being already prohibited on that Day; so that Servants and their Masters have equal Leisure, none are hinder'd from going to Fairs or Markets, nor any Meetings or Bargains interrupted. Secondly, There needs not a more frequent repetition of the Parochial Exercise, no Mercenary Souldiers in the World (whatever is boasted of their Discipline) being train'd near so many Days in the Year, tho no Duty be perform'd in foul Weather. And thirdly, because after the Publick Service of GOD is over, People are thus restrain'd from idle Santring[24] or immoral Courses, and em[27]ploy'd, as the *Switzers* think, in the next Work most becoming good Men, the publick service of their COUNTRY. But I prescribe no time, all that I aim at being to have as many Days in the Year appointed as will be sufficient, and also convenient. Every Saturday then, or Sunday in the Afternoon (for so I may suppose) all the Men of every Parish are to

---

No person charged with the finding of Horse or Foote or with contributing thereunto as aforesaid shall be compellable to serve in his or their proper person but may according to such proportion as they are or shall respectively be charged by this Act find one or more fitt or sufficient man or men qualified according to this Act to be approved by his or theire Captain respectively subject neverthelesse to be altered upon appeal to the Leiutenant or in his absence as aforesaid to his Deputy Leiutenants or any two of them as there shall be cause. (An Act for ordering the Forces in the several Counties of this Kingdom [1662], § XXIV; cf. 14 Car. II, c. 3, § XIX)

24. Dawdling, idling (*OED*, s.v. "saunter," 3).

assemble on some Green or Plain, it may be where the *Buts*[25] were of old, and instead of Tipling, Gaming, and other Diversions equally pernicious to their Minds and Bodies, they learn the use of Arms; wherein, as we see by Experience, they will be imitated by the very Children, who by that time their Age obliges them to appear in the same place, will be superior to their Fathers, and need so little Exhortation, that they cannot be prevented from acquiring this Art. To this publick Meeting will all the superannuated and experienc'd Men, all the marri'd and single Women resort, and create in those that are to exercise a noble Emulation of excelling one another in Agility or Skill, as every one is dispos'd to merit the Affection or Applause of the Spectators. This weekly Exer[28]cise will not only be to all People a grateful Pastime, and relaxation from their ordinary Labor or Busness, but also greatly influence their very Constitutions, by rendring them more robust, nimble, healthy, and accustom'd to all manner of Fatigue. When 'tis once settl'd, we can easily imagin how it may be perpetuated: But to effect the former, we have now a happy Occasion put into our hands of rewarding no small number of those Persons who have been imploy'd in our Service abroad these several Years past: For let all the *Serjeants* of the disbanded Army, and, if their Number be not sufficient, several of the *Corporals* or other expert Souldiers, be distributed one a piece over all the Parishes of *England*, and enjoy half Pay, or what the *Parliament* shall judg more convenient for one Year; during which time they shall be oblig'd to discipline the People on the Days and Place appointed. And for their further Encouragement, let it be provided also that they may have free Licence to follow what lawful Callings they please in that Country or Town during their Lives. Thus King CHARLES the First, when he was in the good Hu[29]mor of issuing out a Proclamation *to instruct and exercise the Train'd Bands, as well*

---

* Rushworth's *Collect. Vol.* I. *Pag.* 197.[26]

25. I.e., the targets in archery.

26. "Furthermore, for the instructing and exercising of the Trained Bands as well Officers as Soldiers, by Men experienced in Military Exercises, The King gave Commandment, that divers Low-Countrey Souldiers should be assigned to the several Counties, and that the Trained-Bands should be ready at the times appointed, for their Directions in their Postures and use of Arms" (Rushworth, *Collections*, p. "155," i.e., p. 197).

Officers as Soldiers, by Men experienc'd in Military Exercises, order'd *that divers Low-Country Soldiers should be assign'd to the Several Counties for this end.* But how this good Design was put in execution every one knows; nor are we more ignorant how the MILITIA was render'd useless under his Successor, when it was enacted that single Companies should be exercis'd but †four times a Year;[27] and this Exercise not to continue above two Days at a time, whereby they were likely to prove glorious Soldiers. Now, it is plain that all the People of *England* may be *parochially* exercis'd in the Use of Arms one Afternoon in every Week throughout the Year (unless prevented by bad Weather) without any Expence but the pay of one Man for the first Year only; and without any trouble at all, but on the contrary, to the great Satisfaction and Recreation of the People. Here it may be objected, that this second Proposition of Exercising all [30] without any distinction, seems to contradict the first, which ordains that only Men of Property be of the MILITIA. To this I answer, that there is a vast difference between training all to Arms, and having every body of the Army. I am still of the same Opinion, that none but FREEMEN be of the MILITIA; and yet I am for training the *Poor* and *Servants.* First, there's no trouble in doing it, they being to appear with their Landlords or Masters; and tho they belong not to the Number of the Companies, yet they may well be exercis'd in them. Neither is there any danger in it, seeing their Arms are only deliver'd to them on those publick Days by the *Overseers* in whose custody they are all the Week; for I suppose a little *Armory* in every Parish. Besides, the FREEMEN are always arm'd themselves, and ready to suppress the others upon the least appearance of

† 14 Car. 2. §. 21.

27. The time commitment required by the militia was not onerous:

The ordinary times for training exerciseing and mustering the Forces to be raised by vertue of this Act shall be these following (that is to say) the General Muster and Exercise of Regiments not above once a Yeare the training and exerciseing of single Companies not above foure times a Yeare unlesse speciall Directions be given by His Majestie or His Privy Council And that such single Companies and Troopes shall not att any one time be continued in Exercise above the space of two dayes And that att a Generall Muster and Exercise of Regiments no Officer or Souldier shall be constrained to stay for above foure dayes togeather from theire respective habitac[i]ons. (An Act for ordering the Forces in the several Counties of this Kingdom [1662], § XX)

Disorder. Thus every Person in the Kingdom becomes a Soldier; for tho a Servant changes his County, his Master, his Work, or Treatment, yet wherever he comes there he's train'd, and has no exemption from Exercise. The Design of this is three[31]fold; First, because when the POOR and SERVANTS become FREEMEN themselves (as, thanks to our *Liberty*, it happens every day) they may not be ignorant of Military Duties. Secondly, That if the Nation is not dispos'd to send part of their MILITIA upon any Foreign Expedition, their *Voluntiers* may not be raw undisciplin'd Fellows, but ready train'd to their hands; nor any thing wanting but to appoint 'em Officers, and to distribute 'em into Regiments. Thirdly, Upon any sudden Invasion from abroad, or in case of some Domestick Insurrection, they may be added as AUXILIARIES to the MILITIA (by which name I shall always design them hereafter) and be appointed either to serve in the Field, or to keep in Garisons, as shall be judg'd most expedient in such Circumstances. The *Romans* made use of 'em upon all these Occasions, and call'd 'em **Subitaneous Souldiers*, or a *Tumultuary Army*,[28] from the sudden and tumultuary manner or cause of raising them. The *Parochial Assemblies* to treat of Civil or Military Affairs, are answerable [32] to the COMITIA CURIATA [29] of Antient *Rome;* and, by the way, seeing some Parishes may be very thinly inhabited, let every such be join'd to the nearest, and both be reputed as one.

8. Having thus laid the Foundation of all *Discipline* in the Parishes, my Third Proposition is, THAT THE FORCES OF EVERY HUNDRED ASSEMBLE AT THE CAPITAL THEREOF FOUR TIMES A YEAR, BOTH FOR PUBLICK EXERCISE, AND TO DISPUTE GAMES AND PRIZES. These Meetings answer in some sort the COMITIA CENTURIATA [30] of the *Romans*, wherefore I shall make bold to call them *Centuriate Assemblies;* for our

* Subitarii Milites, exercitus tumultuarius.

28. See above, p. 98, n. 84.

29. The assembly of the "curiae," or wards, at Rome; the primitive assembly of the Roman people. Before the expulsion of the Tarquins the comitia elected the Roman kings, and is said to have voted on questions of war and peace. During the Republic it ratified the conferment of power on new magistrates. In the late Republican period its meetings were purely formal. Cf. Harrington, *Oceana*, pp. 73–75.

30. The assembly of the Roman people in "hundreds," the military divisions created by Servius Tullius. The organization of this assembly gave power to the wealthy. It elected the chief magistrates in the Republic, had the power of legislation, and heard appeals in capital cases. Cf. Harrington, *Oceana*, pp. 73–75.

Hundred, Cantred, or *Wapentake,* is term'd *Centuria* by the politest Historians that wrote of our Affairs in Latin. It is then easily understood,
that in those *Centuriate Assemblies* the People meet not to learn the bare
handling of their Weapons, that being already perform'd in the *Parochial
Exercises;* but to shew their Experience, and the Progress they have made
at home. Here also they are form'd into greater Bodies, and taught all
that is peculiar to such, or different from their Duty in single Com[33]
panies. As for the *Games* and *Prizes,* all wise Nations have instituted the
like, sometimes for promoting of Trade, or only for breeding good
Horses; but generally to educate their People in the love and practice of
Arms, or other Exercises tending to fit and dispose 'em to a Martial Genius, such as Racing, Fencing, Wrestling, throwing the Bar, or the like;
of which you may find various Examples in the Governments of Antient
Greece and *Italy.* Let the *Prizes* in themselves be never so inconsiderable,
yet once that Honor and Reputation are annex'd to them, Men will as
eagerly contend for 'em, as if they were the highest Lucre in the World. It
has been observ'd in all Ages, that nothing is so effectual to make one
undertake or quit any Enterprize, as the *Commendation* or *Disgrace* attending it; yet these have fail'd sometimes, but a prospect of *Gain* seldom
or never. Now our PRIZES are not without their Profit, as well as Use and
Delight; for, besides the real Value of what is got, the Winner likewise
stands fairest for Preferment, where Places are dispos'd according to
Merit. As for the [34] Charge of those GAMES it may be made very easy,
an Annual Revenue being establish'd for that purpose. 'Tis so much the
Interest of the *Hundreds* to concur in it, that rather than it should not
be done, the Capital Town, where the Meeting is to be, will gladly raise
the Sum in consideration of the brisk Trade it must occasion at those times:
But all such Expences ought to be collected from the Inhabitants according to their real or personal Estates. And they'l contribute to no Tax, tho
never so necessary, so willingly as to this; because in the first place it is
not bestow'd, as the best part of some other Revenues, on Men of no
Merit: Secondly, because it is not carri'd out of the Country: And thirdly,
because every Man has his lucky Hit for the PRIZE to fall to his own
share. Now, 'tis all one wherein the PRIZE consists, whether it be a Silver
Chain, a Medal, or any sort of Plate; for the Disputes in other Places
were not less eager to obtain Garlands of Oak or Laurel. But the most

proper, in my Opinion, are some good and beautiful *Arms;* for the Conqueror, and his Heir after him, [35] will be as loth to part with them in Fight, as proud of wearing them in time of Peace. And this is indisputably more natural, and will prove far more effectual than the Policy of JULIUS CESAR,[31] who us'd to adorn the Arms of his Men with Gold, Silver, and Gems, that they might the less tamely quit such precious things to the Enemy. There must be also a proportionable difference between the PRIZES, the same neither in Kind nor Value belonging to the Horse and Foot, or to him that hits the Mark in shooting, and to another that wins at some other Game; for I would have them of all useful sorts, and a Field-piece likewise in every *Hundred* to breed expert Gunners, with Magazines of Powder, Bullets, and all other requisite Ammunition in every *County.* Lastly, I would have it ordain'd that he who at these GAMES has got one PRIZE, should not be permitted to stand for any other at that time; and that the Names of all the Winners be carefully register'd, as well out of regard to the Reputation of particular Persons, as that the Publick may know where to find able Men in [36] time of need. What a Change this Institution will beget in all the Kingdom; what Trade it will occasion in the Country; and what Emulation between the Inhabitants of every *Hundred* (to speak nothing of the principal Design) can scarcely be imagin'd by such as have never experienc'd any thing like it; and yet there's nothing new or notional in all this, the same having been successfully practis'd either wholly or partly in many other Places of the World. I shall add no more of the *Hundreds,* but that every *City* being a County of it self, and other populous *Corporations,* may hold their *Centuriate Assemblies* within their own Precincts, and be not oblig'd to any Exercise abroad, except the *Annual Encampment,* whereof I am now going to treat.

9. Tho it be of the highest Importance to have all Persons in our Nation *parochially* exercis'd, and accustom'd in the Hundreds to muster

---

31. "Nec milites eos pro contione, sed blandiore nomine commilitones appellabat habebatque tam cultos, ut argento et auro politis armis ornaret, simul et ad speciem et quo tenaciores eorum in proelio essent metu damni"; "When assembled he [Caesar] addressed them not as 'soldiers' but with the milder term of 'comrades,' and he looked after them well, providing them with weapons inlaid with silver and gold, both for the show of the thing, and also so that they would hold on to them more tenaciously in battle, for fear of losing them" (Suetonius, "Divus Iulius," LXVII.2).

in larger Bodies; yet they may be still ignorant of the Discipline of a compleat *Army*, to which all they have hitherto done is only subservient, as we first learn the Names of the Letters, and then to join them into [37] Syllables, in order to read and understand a Book. My Fourth Proposition is therefore, THAT *ENGLAND* BE DIVIDED INTO THREE EQUAL DISTRICTS, CALL'D THE NORTHERN, MIDDLE, AND WESTERN CLASSES; AND THAT THE STANDING MILITIA OF THE WHOLE CONSISTING OF SIXTY THOUSAND MEN, TWENTY THOUSAND THEREOF DO ANNUALLY ENCAMP FOR THE SPACE OF THREE WEEKS IN SOME ONE OF THE CLASSES; AND SO TO SUCCEED BY TRIENNIAL ROTATION, WHICH RULE IS ALSO TO BE OBSERV'D IN THE COUNTIES PROPORTIONABLY. This military Division of the whole Kingdom may be as easily imagin'd or perform'd, as the Circuits appointed for distributing of Justice. Nor is there any Difficulty in apprehending the *Triennial Rotation;* Suppose, for example, that in the Month of *July*, 1698, the twenty thousand Men, which is the Portion of the Western *Class*, encamp somewhere in *Cornwal*, those of the middle *Class* in *July*, [38] 1699, at any Place in *Hartfordshire*, and those of the Northern *Class* in *July*, 1700, in some part of *Yorkshire:* Then you return again in *July*, 1701, to *Devonshire*, the Year after to *Surrey*, the sixth Year to *Cumberland*, and so perpetually round. The *Rotation* in the *Counties*, or changing the Place of Encampment, is grounded upon the clearest Equity; for if the CAMP proves a Trouble (as 'tis impossible it should) to the County where it is, then Justice requires that all should bear their share of it: And if on the contrary it be highly profitable by the vast Trade it must occasion in the Consumption of Provisions, or otherwise; and considering too that ready Money will be paid for every thing, then 'tis as reasonable that all should enjoy the Benefit in their turns. As for the Order to be observ'd, to take away all occasions of Dispute, there needs no more but to cast Lots at the beginning in every *Class*, to know what County shall be the first, second, third, and so on. But if an Objection should be rais'd by any against the Number of the *Classes*, from the Largeness of their Bounds, and consequently the great [39] Distance in many Parts from the Place of Encampment; I answer, that 'tis not the precise Number, but the Distribution for which I contend: for the Kingdom may as well be divided into six *Classes*, each containing 10000 of the MILITIA, and annual CAMPS in any two of 'em at a time. Thus still the

Triennial Rotation remains the same, and we have every Year 20000 Men (besides the *London-Militia*) encamp'd somewhere in the Kingdom, to the great Terror of all our Enemies, and to our own unspeakable Advantage and Reputation; we have an Army of sixty thousand FREEMEN to defend the whole Nation, and yet every part of it always provided with a sufficient Number, either absolutely to defend themselves, or to stop any Enemy till our whole Forces draw together. But then this wheeling Number of sixty Thousand is very inconsiderable, in comparison of many thousand FREEMEN more, that are always ready to relieve, to repair, to succeed, or to join them upon occasion; to speak nothing of those *exempted from Duty*, nor of the *poor* and *servile*; all which Orders of [40] Men are not only well disciplin'd, but oblig'd also to serve upon uncommon Emergencies. But to return to our CAMP, there our MILITIA learns the highest Perfection of Discipline, and is taught to make regular Sieges and Attacks in all Forms, to storm Castles, to fight Battles, to gain advantageous Posts, to make honorable Retreats, to intrench themselves, to forage, decamp,[32] and, in one word, to perform all the other Duties of an *Army*. Now, besides the Necessity and Usefulness of all these Exercises, they will be extraordinary entertaining too. The whole Country round will come to divert themselves in this Place, and pass that Season the most agreeably of all the Year. It would be a superfluous Labour to spend more Words in Commendation of this part of our MODEL; and so I come to make one Remark concerning the Expences, after taking notice that the yearly general Exercise, prescrib'd by the Act for regulating our MILITIA,[33] yet in force, is to continue but only the space of *four Days. [41] The *Assessments* laid by this same Act are so grievous as well as useless, that a long Experience, and the general Outcry against them, spare me the pains of shewing their Defects; nor will I for the same Reasons make any stop at the Abuse of calling People so often from their Business, for no other end but to fill the *Muster-master's*[34] Pockets; neither will I insist

---

* 14 Car. 2. cap. 3. §. 21.

32. To break up a camp (*OED*, s.v. "decamp"; first recorded usage, 1678).

33. See above, p. 192, n. 27.

34. The officer in charge of the muster roll of part of an army (*OED*, s.v. "muster-master").

upon the intolerable Grievance of *Trophy-money*;[35] all those things, as I said before, being so universally known, that every body can prescribe a proper Remedy. I propos'd three Weeks (and I still think it time enough) for the *Annual Encampment*, *viz.* a Fortnight for actual Service, and the other eight days, upon the supposition of three *Classes*, for coming and going; and fewer will do, if the *Classes* be six in Number. But suppose another Week be added, then 'tis plain that the Charge of a hundred and twenty thousand Men during one Month, is no more than the Pay of ten Thousand for a Year; whence every body may infer how much cheaper we may entertain twenty thousand FREEMEN for a Fortnight or three Weeks, than ten thou[42]sand MERCENARIES for a Twelvemonth, making all reasonable Allowance in the Difference of their Pay. The Expence in our MODEL then is both laid out to much better purpose, and made a great deal easier than any of this nature heretofore. Nay the very *Rotation* should recommend it self to all Mens Approbation, seeing it comes with respect to the *Charge* but every third Year to the turn of each *County*, and as to the *Duty* much seldomer to particular Persons; whereas the *Rotation* of the *Jews* was monthly, and took in the whole People in a Year: They had 24000 Men under Arms every Month, and I don't propose twenty thousand for one Month in twelve. But the *Jewish* MILITIA kept Guards and Garisons too; *Now the Children of Israel after their Names*, (says the Author of the first Book of their Chronicles) *the chief Fathers, and the Captains of Thousands and Hundreds, and their Officers that serv'd the King in any Matter of the Courses, which came in and went out Month by Month throughout all the Months of the Year, of every Course were twenty and four thousand.*[36] There needs [43] no more to be said on this Head, only that the Cities of *London* and *Westminster*, with their Suburbs and Liberties,[37] together with the Borough of *Southwark*, are not to be comprehended within any of the *Classes*, but to have their own CAMP annually in some convenient Place adjacent.

35. A tax formerly levied in each county for incidental expenses connected with the militia (*OED*, s.v. "trophy").

36. 1 Chronicles 27:1.

37. The districts outside a city over which its jurisdiction nevertheless extends (*OED*, s.v. "liberty," 6c[b]).

10. So far of the Persons qualified to serve in the MILITIA, and the several degrees of *training* them: Now we shall speak of their AGE; for although this Particular is generally neglected in *Mercenary* Armies, yet it has been ever carefully consider'd in all *free* Governments: because the Design of these being to render the People happy, they impartially assign Labor and Ease to those Periods of Life to which they are most sutable. Then my Fifth Proposition is, THAT EVERY FREEMAN, WHEN HIS TURN COMES, BE OBLIG'D TO PERSONAL SERVICE IN THE MILITIA FROM THE EIGHTEENTH TO THE FIFTIETH YEAR OF HIS AGE; AND THAT ALL ABOVE OR UNDER THESE YEARS BE EXEMPTED FROM THE SERVICE, THO NOT [44] FROM THE CHARGE. The *Romans* oblig'd their Citizens to Arms from the *seventeenth to the six and fortieth Year of their Age, in which time every Man was to go upon the Service of the Commonwealth, (in case of need) if he were of the Horse ten, or of the Foot †twenty times; and if he was hinder'd by Sickness or otherwise from compleating this Number, he might be compell'd to do it until he was fifty. But all under seventeen or above fifty were absolutely ‡excus'd, unless upon those extraordinary Occasions whereof we spoke before; and then the *Veterans* and *Emeriti* (for so they call'd the superannuated Soldiers) might not only be forc'd to take up Arms, but they ordinarily came in of themselves

* Servius (Rex Pop. Romani) ab anno septimo decimo, quod idoneos jam esse Reipublicae arbitraretur, Milites scripsisse dicitur à Tuberone Historico apud A. Gellium (l. 10. c. 28.) eosque ad annum quadragesimum sextum juniores, supraque eum annum seniores appellasse.[38]

† τοὺς μὲν ἱππεῖς δέκα, τοὺς δὲ πεζοὺς ἓξ καὶ δέκα δεῖ στρατείας τελεῖν κατ' ἀνάγκην ἐν τοῖς τετταράκοντα καὶ ἓξ ἔτεσιν ἀπὸ γενεᾶς. Polyb. de Militia Romana.[39]

‡ Lex à quinquagesimo anno Militem non cogit. *Seneca de Brevitate vitae, c. ult.*[40]

38. A précis of Aulus Gellius X.xxviii.1: "In Aulus Gellius (X.xxviii) it is reported by the historian Tubero that Servius the king of the Romans conscripted as soldiers those who were seventeen, because it was now thought that they were suited to public affairs, and to call them juniors until they were forty-six, and after that to call them seniors."

39. "A cavalryman must serve for ten years in all and an infantryman for sixteen years before reaching the age of forty-six" (Polybius, VI.xix.2). For Machiavelli's ideas about military age, see *The Art of War*, bk. 1 (Machiavelli, *Chief Works*, 2:583).

40. "The law does not require military service from those over fifty" (Seneca, *De Brevitate Vitae*, XX.iv).

[45] when their Country was in danger, and by their Valor and Experience did often save it from Destruction. In like manner, when any General of great Reputation was to go upon some glorious Expedition, several *Veterans us'd to offer him their Service voluntarily, which was very acceptable, being most useful both by their Example to the rest, and their own personal Exploits. But I expect to be told, that GENTLEMEN will never consent their Sons should be train'd like *Common Souldiers*. Now it may be easily perceiv'd, that this Contemt upon the most honorable Profession of *Arms* is purely accidental, and altogether occasion'd by the *Mercenary Soldiers* abroad, who, excepting some Officers and a few Voluntiers, being most of 'em the Scum of Mankind, consisting of ignorant, brutish, mean, beggerly, and idle Fellows, that live only upon a scanty Hire, which is [46] seldom punctually paid, they must necessarily have recourse to Stealing, Robbing, Plundring, Assassinating, and the like flagitious Practices; and what's still worse, the *Arbitrary Princes* who maintain them, must e'en let them live upon their shifts, by countenancing or conniving at these Disorders: for there's no Remedy unless they be duly paid, which is never done except in Free Governments, such as ours and *Holland*. But in a well-regulated MILITIA Gentlemen make their Discipline to be properly an Exercise or Diversion in time of Peace; and in War they fight not only to preserve their own Liberty and Fortunes, but also to become the best Men in their Country. Nor are they any thing influenc'd by that PAY which the Government justly allows them: for as they who sit quietly at home should bear their Charges who serve 'em abroad, and not let those be Losers in their private Affairs, whose Valour provides Security to theirs; so on the other hand, when it becomes their turn who are now employ'd to keep at home, they will as cheerfully

---

* Licinius quoque veteres scribebat Milites Centurionesque, & multi voluntate nomina dabant. *Livius, l.* 42. *c.* 32. Militares hominess & stipendia justa, & corpora aetate & assiduis laboribus confecta habere; nihil recusare tamen, quo minus operam Reipublicae dent. *Id. ibid. c.* 33.[41]

41. "Licinius was also enrolling the veteran soldiers and centurions; likewise many enlisted of their own free will" (Livy, XLII.xxxii.6); "These martial men had completed their military service and had also exhausted their physical vigor as a result of age and diligent labor; however, they did not object to contributing their labor to the state" (Livy, XLII.xxxiii.3).

contribute to maintain those who suc[47]ceed 'em abroad, as they receiv'd their PAY before. There is no Weight at all then in the Objection, especially since no time is lost to Young or Old: and that there is none is very evident, for no body will say that either Gentlemen or Artizans lose any time in the *Parochial Exercises*; all People allow more time upon their Pleasures every Year than is spent in the *Centuriate Assemblies;* and their turn in the CAMP returns so seldom as to admit of nothing to be said against it. After all, if *Gentlemen* will be at the pains of fighting for their own, (and who can doubt but they will?) 'tis surely worth their while to learn the Art of doing it; but of this by and by in a more proper Place.

    II. The AGE of the Persons constituting our MILITIA being thus determin'd, we proceed next to their COMMANDERS, who make the Subject of the Sixth Proposition, which is, THAT ALL THE COMMISSION'D OFFICERS OF THE MILITIA HAVE REAL OR PERSONAL ESTATES PROPORTIONABLE TO THEIR SEVERAL DEGREES; AND [48] THAT ALL PERSONS THUS RIGHTLY QUALIFI'D IN EVERY COUNTY SUCCEED ONE ANOTHER BY TRIENNIAL ROTATION, THE LORDS LIEUTENANTS ONLY EXCEPTED, WHO, BEING GENERAL OFFICERS, ARE NOT TO BE CHANG'D WHILE THE KING IS PLEAS'D TO CONTINUE 'EM IN THEIR POSTS. The Reasons for qualifying the OFFICERS by their *Property* are the same with those I have offer'd under the first Proposition for admitting FREEMEN only to serve in the MILITIA, which spares me the Labour of Repetition in this place. As for the *Rotation* of *Officers* propos'd, it is grounded upon uncontested Experience and Equity. All good Politicians have ever allow'd that to be the best and noblest Government where Men learn alternately to *command* and to *obey;* because at this rate they are not only fitted to serve their Country upon all occasions, but likewise made competent Judges of the Merit or Miscarriage of others. This was the known Practice of the *Romans*, whose *General Officers* were, in the ordinary Course of [49] their Government, annually elected, no body thinking it a Disgrace to serve under him this Year, whom he had commanded the last, nor to be afterwards an inferior Officer in that Army whose Exploits were the Effects of his Conduct before. And truly this sort of *Rotation* seems to me a Duty requir'd by the Light of Nature: for keeping an equal Balance between those of the same Qualifications contributes above all things to keep 'em in Peace and Friendship. If the *Offices* shall be thought honorable, pleasant, or profitable, no body envies another, because they are all to enjoy 'em in their turns: And if on the other hand they should be found a Charge or Trouble, then doubtless every one ought to bear his share of the Burden; nor is it at all material, whether they be elected by LOT, or successively appointed by the KING. The PEERS, who are commonly the Lords Lieutenants of Counties, are by this *Model* restor'd to all the Privileges that were truly good and excellent in their first Institution, the immediate Command of [50] all the FREEMEN in *England* under the KING being their proper Charge; and the eternal Fame which some of their Ancestors have worthily acquir'd, is wholly owing to the glorious Actions they perform'd in this Quality on the behalf of their Country; and not in the least to that immoderate Power they might then exercise over the PEOPLE, who, if they record any *Nobleman* upon this account, do it as an Example they execrate and abhor, and not out of Gratitude or Love, as in the former case. To the only Objection I apprehend against this Proposition, which is, that it seems to limit his *Majesty's* Authority, I answer, That no Man can trust him with a greater Power of doing Good (for he would neither accept nor use any other) than I am willing to do; seeing in the Opinion I entertain of his Justice, Valor, and Wisdom, I believe my self not inferior to any: which Declaration ought to be esteem'd the more sincere, inasmuch as I never had nor expect any particular Favor from him besides *Liberty* and *Safety*, [51] the common Blessings of his Government. He knows already that all the *Power* he has is bounded by Laws,[42] and we are convinc'd by Experience that he refuses no Limitation

42. A precipitating factor in the run-up to the Glorious Revolution had been James II's attempts to place the power of the Crown above the law. By means of the collusive action of *Godden v. Hales* (1686) (see above, p. 163, n. 24) and a hand-picked bench, James had established in the courts "that the government of *England* was entirely in the King: That the Crown was an Imperial Crown, the importance of which was, that it was absolute: All penal laws were powers lodged in the Crown to enable the King to force the execution of the law, but were not bars to limit or bind up the King's power: The King could pardon all offences against the law, and forgive the penalties: And why could he not as well dispense with them?" (Burnet, *History*, 1:669–70). It should not be forgotten that William III was himself a Stuart, and moreover a Stuart whose ideas of monarchical authority were hardly less high than those of his uncle. William had been raised in the autocratic

to it when he judges it to be for the Advantage of the Nation. Thus have the Act for *Triennial Parliaments*, and that of *regulating Trials in cases of High Treason* (to mention no more) past by his Authority; whereas no Prince that design'd to injure his Subjects, would ever give his Assent to either of them. A Person of his Sagacity and Prudence will not easily be deluded by the mean Obsequiousness of any MINISTERS, who make their Court with gratifying what they take to be their Master's *Inclinations;* and, without any regard to his or the Nation's real Interest, lay out all their Efforts to gain him some *invidious Point:* for it is a setl'd Maxim with most of this Race, That ALL KINGS WHATSOEVER WOULD BE ABSOLUTE; presuming on which pernicious Doctrine they bring a certain Ruin on the Affairs of *Princes*, if not happily prevented by [52] their own timely Fall, which commonly happens in *Free Governments*. But a good KING, instead of lessening his own Power by Concessions of this nature, gains more Security, Respect, and Glory, than could be obtain'd by the most numerous *Armies*. I cannot upon this occasion but relate the remarkable Story of THEOPOMPUS King of *Sparta, who,* as VALERIUS MAXIMUS *writes, when he first ordain'd that the* EPHORI, *or Overseers, should be created at* Lacedemon, *to be such a Restraint upon the Kings there, as the Tribunes were upon the Consuls at* Rome, *the Queen complain'd to him, that by this means he transmitted the Royal Authority greatly diminish'd to his*

---

traditions of the Brabant aristocracy, and he was vigilant to defend the absolute character of his own rule. However they were later redescribed, and whatever was claimed on his behalf in his various manifestoes, William's motives for involving himself in the affairs of England in 1688 had little to do with securing the liberties of Englishmen (in the early years of his reign he was very careful to keep the Whigs at a distance) and much more to do with securing his own dynastic interests and those of his wife. Toland here is perhaps employing the panegyrical trope of *laudando praecipere;* that is, praising someone for a virtue they ought to possess, but actually lack.

* Cum primus instituisset (Theopompus Spartanorum Rex) ut Ephori Lacedaemone crearentur, ita futuri Regiae potestati oppositi quemadmodum Romae Consulari Imperio Tribuni plebis sunt objecti; atque illi uxor dixisset, id egisse illum ut filiis minorem potestatem relinqueret; Relinquam, inquit, sed diuturniorm. Optimè quidem; ea enim demum tuta est potentia, quae viribus suis modum imponit. Theopompus igitur, legitimis regnum vinculis constringendo, quo longius à Licencia retraxit hoc propius ad benevolentiam Civium admovit, *L.* 4. *c.* 1. *de externis,* § 8.

Chil[53]*dren: I leave it indeed less,* answer'd he, *but more lasting. And this,* adds our Author, *was excellently said; for that Power only is safe, which is limited from doing Hurt.* THEOPOMPUS *therefore,* continues he, *by confining the Kingly Power within the Bounds of the Laws, did recommend it by so much to the People's Affection as he remov'd it from being Arbitrary.*[43] But, lest I might seem to digress, I demand, What Power is taken out of the KING's hand by our Proposition? For in the present *Militia* the Colonels, Majors, Captains, and other Officers are to be appointed by the *Lord Lieutenant;[44] and I would have 'em chosen by his *Majesty* himself,

---

* 14 Car. 2. cap. 3. §. 2.

43. [Theopompus] first instituted the creation of ephors in Lacedaemon, who would stand in opposition to the regal power as in Rome the Tribunes of the Plebs were set up to counter the authority of the consuls. When his wife told him that he had managed matters so as to leave less power to his sons, "Ay," he said, "but longer lasting." Very right he was, for power is safe only if it imposes limits on its own strength. Therefore by confining the royal prerogative in legitimate constraints Theopompus placed it nearer the good will of the citizens the further he drew it back from license. (Valerius Maximus, IV.i.ext. 8)

This example of wise moderation in a prince had recently been quoted approvingly by Henry Neville (Neville, *Plato Redivivus*, p. 178).

44. Bee it therefore declared and enacted . . . That the Kings most Excellent Majestie His Heires and Successors shall and may from time to time as occasion shall require issue forth severall Commissions of Lieutenancy to such persons as His Majesty His Heires and Successors shall thinke fit to be His Majesties Leiutenants . . . which Leiutenants shall have full power and authority to call togeather all such persons at such times and to arm and array them in such manner as is hereafter experessed and declared and to form them into Companies Troops and Regiments and in case of Insurrection Rebellion or Invasion them to lead conduct and imploy or cause to be conducted and imployed as well within the said severall Counties Cities and places for which they shall be commissionated respectively as alsoe into any other the Counties and places aforesaid for suppressing of all such Insurrections and Rebelions and repelling of Invasions as may happen to bee according as they shall from time to time receive directions from His Majesty His Heires and Successors and that the said respective Leiutenants shall have full power and authority from time to time to constitute appointe and give Commissions to such persons as they shall thinke fitt to be Colonels Majors Captaines and other Commission Officers of the said persons so to be armed arrayed

or whom he pleases to depute, but only *qualify'd* to serve their Prince and Country more effectually: Nor can the Nomination be any where more safely lodg'd than in the KING for his Life, provided the Act restrains it to Election under his *Successors*, who will enjoy all reasonable Power, since [54] they may appoint or continue the General Officers at their pleasure. And, besides the foregoing Considerations, nothing can render his present *Majesty* more easy than this part of the *Model*, seeing that by it he has an admirable Opportunity of gratifying all Sides, and disobliging none; for if he should put any TORIES in Commission, the WHIGS would presently cry, that he was committing himself solely into their Enemies Hands; and should the WHIGS be the only Persons intrusted, the TORIES would justly continue still disaffected: Whereas on the foot of the *Rotation* propos'd he may fairly employ those of both Parties duly qualify'd to serve their Country. And indeed I may venture to affirm, that this impartial Distribution of *Honor* and *Profit* is the only way possible to heal ours, or the Divisions of any other Government: for such as are not admitted to *Confidence* and *Preferment*, are most of 'em offended upon no other score; and they who are in possession of those *Advantages* will [55] be always for retaining and engrossing them, either by the Exclusion or absolute Ruin of their Adversaries. But as in *War* the KING has equally protected all his Subjects, so I hope in *Peace* he'll abolish their infamous *Distinctions*, and render *England* the Glory and Terror of the World.

12. The most excellent *Institution* imaginable cannot be of any considerable Duration, unless extraordinary Care be taken about the Education of YOUTH, which is shamefully neglected in this Age; for very few are at those Pains and Expence in forming the Manners of their own Children, as they freely bestow to breed up Setting-dogs and Race-horses, or on things altogether as frivolous and indifferent. The sad Effects of this Disorder are visible enough every where, and were ever carefully prevented in *wise Governments*. All *Legislators* had a particular regard[45] in their

---

and weaponed. (An Act for ordering the Forces in the several Counties of this Kingdom [1662], preamble)

45. For Lycurgus's ideas on Spartan education, and the importance he attached to it, see Plutarch, "Lycurgus," XIV–XIX. Toland himself wrote "A Letter

Laws to the breeding of the *Young*, well knowing that such as they were, such the *Government* would prove to be. [56] What's amiss in this respect among our selves is more easily discover'd, than reform'd. I shall therefore at this time content my self with offering a Remedy in what immediately concerns my Subject, and so the Seventh Proposition of this *Scheme* shall be, THAT ALL NOW UNDER THE AGE OF EIGHTEEN YEARS, OR THAT SHALL BE BORN HEREAFTER, BE INCAPABLE OF HOLDING ANY POST OF HONOR OR PROFIT UNDER THE GOVERNMENT (EXCEPTING IN THE PROFESSIONS OF DIVINITY, LAW, AND PHYSICK) UNLESS THEY FIRST QUALIFY THEMSELVES BY SERVING TWO CAMPAIGNS BY LAND OR SEA. By this Proposition none already arriv'd to the complete Age of *Manhood* are excluded from bearing Offices; and they who are now full *Eighteen*, are only kept back till they are Twenty, before which time they could scarcely expect Employment even as Matters now stand. I cannot therefore foresee that any [57] Opposition will be made to this part of the *Model*, seeing it neither affects them who are actually engag'd in Business, nor such as stand Candidates for Preferment: For the blame of being unqualifi'd, as propos'd, ought to be attributed to a Defect in our *Constitution*, and not to any want of *Merit* in particular Persons. The YOUTH themselves (if we can imagin 'em so basely dispos'd) are not in a Condition to obstruct it; and if it happens to pass, it becomes as familiar to those who shall be born hereafter as the other parts of our Government. There remain then no Adversaries in all probability, unless some People should envy the happy Effects of it to their *Country*, which we may better judg impossible than SOLON that no *Parricide* could be perpetrated in his Republick, which is the Reason that he ordain'd no Punishment for this horrid Crime.[46] The most unthinking among us

---

Concerning the Roman Education"; see *The Miscellaneous Works of Mr. John Toland*, 2 vols. (1747), 2:1–11.

46. Solon (ca. 640–ca. 558 B.C.), Athenian aristocrat, statesman, legislator, and poet; his laws were incorporated into the Twelve Tables of Roman law; cf. Neville, *Plato Redivivus*, p. 200. "He [Romulus] made many good and profitable Laws, most of which were unwritten. . . . He appointed no Punishment for real *Parricide*, but call'd all Murder by that Name; thinking the latter a detestable Crime, but the other impossible: And it was indeed a Crime never known in *Rome* for

must perceive that no other Method can be so effectual to render our *Country* famous, and our *Government* lasting. When the *Young Men* (of all [58] others the most ambitious of Glory and Honor) are once convinc'd that this is the only Road to Preferment, they will timely qualify themselves, and so all Posts will be suppli'd with Persons of known Experience. Whoever has read the preceding part of this Piece, cannot mistake my Sense about the *Land-Campaigns;* but as to the SEA, he that is two Summers aboard any Man of War in our ordinary Guards, or that goes twice in any Vessel into the *Baltick, Mediterranean,* or the *West-Indies,* and once to any part of the *East-Indies,* shall be deem'd rightly qualifi'd. It signifies nothing whether it be in War or Peace; for the principal Design is to acquaint 'em with the Nature of this Service so important to our Island, and to give 'em an opportunity of seeing Forein Countries in order to put a true Value upon their own. When one that has thus past a part of his time is afterwards a Member of the House of *Lords* or *Commons,* of the *Admiralty* or *Navy,* he must needs speak more pertinently, and be less [59] easily deceiv'd in the usual Disputes, whether any Miscarriage is occasion'd by Treachery or Accident; he can discern the Guilt or Merit of the Seamen; he can judg of Victualling, Manning, or otherwise fitting out our ships; and determin the proper Seasons for every Action far better than another that never was at Sea unless in a Ferry-boat to *Calais* or the *Bril.*[47] We know likewise by the great Care the KING has taken to supply his Ships with able Masters, and by what we may observe in the Accomplishments of several Persons who sail'd in them, that there is not a properer place of learning most part of the *Mathematicks,* there being no doubt to be made about the particular Art of *Navigation.* And to speak no more of the Marine (for to hint these things is enough) when *Gentlemen* are so long debar'd all their ordinary Land-Exercises, they have an excellent opportunity of studying *Geography* or *Astronomy,* and mastering the best part of Antient and Modern *History:* for they must

---

600 Years" (Laurence Echard, *The Roman History* [1696], p. 16). Cf. the Cornelian law *de parricidis.*

47. Modern-day Brielle in the Netherlands; the place from which William of Orange had set sail to invade England in 1688.

read [60] something in their own defence against *Idleness*, the most painful Condition in the World; and they may keep Books as conveniently in
their Cabins, as in their Studies at home. After a considerable number
are thus initiated at Sea, while others by Land make the ordinary Tour of
Holland, Germany, Italy, and *France;* and that several, perhaps, have
travell'd both by Land and Sea, no Government in the World can be so
well suppli'd with Learn'd, Polite, and able Men to fil all sorts of Stations.
The *Romans* did after this manner educate their Children from their very
Cradles in the Theory and Practice of those things wherein they were
afterwards to make a glorious Figure in the Service of their Country.
They, to whom the particular Inspection of the YOUTH was committed,
were not Persons retir'd, and strangers to Business; but Men of nice
Breeding, and that understood Mankind as well as the Liberal Arts and
Sciences. They inform'd their Pupils (to whom they were rather Com-
pani[61]ons than Masters) in the Duties of grown Age, before they arriv'd
to it; and, having no Interest to keep 'em more ignorant than themselves,
they did not waste their time by teaching 'em any barbarous Jargon, trifling Notions, or useless Speculations, which they must unlearn again if
they would be understood, or not be counted ridiculous when they come
abroad into the World. *The Young Men,* says *PLINY, were early accustom'd
to Arms in the Field, that they might learn by obeying to command, and to act
the part of a General while they follow'd one. Aspiring likewise to Civil Dignities, they stood by the Door of the Senate House, and were Spectators of the
Publick Assembly before they were Members of it.* The *Young Gentlemen* also
us'd to chuse to themselves *Patrons* of the most eminent Persons in the
City, whose great Actions they diligently observ'd, and [62] propos'd not
so much to imitate, as to exceed them. Every Morning they went to their

---

* Adolescentuli statim Castrensibus stipendiis imbuebantur, ut imperare
parendo, duces agere dum sequuntur, assuescerent: Inde Honores petituri assiste-
bant curiae foribus, & concilii publici spectatores, antequam consortes erant. *Epist.*
14. l. 8.[48]

48. "Hence young men began their early training with military service, so that
they might grow accustomed to command by obeying, and learn how to lead by
following others; hence as candidates for office they stood at the door of the Senate
house and watched the course of state councils before taking part in them" (Pliny,
Letters, VIII.xiv.5).

Levée, and thence accompani'd them to the FORUM and other publick Places, where they patiently bore Hunger, Thirst, and all manner of Fatigue, that they might attain to the highest pitch of *Eloquence*, and be throughly vers'd in *Civil Affairs*. When the Business of the Day was over, they dutifully waited home upon their Patrons, and these again on their part took abundance of care to improve the *Youth*. They were as cautious to give 'em any ill Examples in Words or Action, as to their own Children. They entertain'd them with the greatest familiarity, and the general Subject of their Discourse was about framing good Laws, and the several kinds of Government; in their own, they taught 'em wherein consisted the *Magistrates Power, and *the Liberty of the People;* they explain'd the Art of War, and read Divine Lec[63]tures concerning the Excellency of Vertue; never forgetting to inculcate upon every occasion the Love of their Country as the Foundation of all their future Actions at Home or Abroad: Nor did the Conversation want facetious and pleasant Intervals to make it easier to both sides. This was the true Source, not only of that unparallel'd Friendship, Valour, Prudence, Justice, Eloquence, and Generosity wherein that bravest People of the Universe excel'd; but even the preeminence of their *Historians* above all the Modern proceeds from hence: For the *Young Gentlemen* being so intimately acquainted with the Actions of their *Patrons*, and writing down their remarkable Sayings, or copying their most finish'd Compositions, they afterwards frequently mention'd or quoted them; so that all the best and vertuous Examples became commonly known. But of this Subject I shall speak more copiously in my BRUTUS,[50] or THE HISTORY OF LIBERTY AND TYRANNY which I am now digesting, with a Design, whenever [64] finish'd, to publish it in †*Latin* and *English*. In this Work I endeavor to copy the People whereof I treat, and will confirm my Subject with the most beautiful Passages of the Antients, as well as illustrate it by Modern Examples, both of the Dead and the Living. As to the latter I shall make little

---

* Quae Vis magistratibus, quae caeteris Libertas. *Id. ibid.*[49]

† *BRUTUS, sive Libertatis & Tyrannidis Historia.*

49. "What power belongs to magistrates, and what freedom to the rest" (Pliny, *Letters*, VIII.xiv.6).

50. Never in fact published.

mention of the worse sort, thinking to dishonor 'em more by silencing their Names, should my History last to Posterity, than by relating their infamous Actions; and if my Book miscarries, they are but in obscurity still. That the number of extraordinary Men is very small in our Age, we need not desire a clearer Demonstration than to find so few Histories tolerably pen'd; for 'tis want of Matter, and consequently of Encouragement, but not of Ability, which makes our Writers so much inferior to those of past times, when CICERO himself courts to be immortaliz'd by the [65] *Pen of LUCCEIUS. PLINY, who liv'd in the decay of the *Roman* Empire and Manners, tells us what Honors were formerly confer'd on those who wrote the Histories of Governments or Great Persons: †*But in our time,* says he, *this Custom, as several good and excellent things, is quite abolish'd; for since we left off to do commendable Actions, we think it impertinent to be commended.* This Digression (if any thing that makes for my purpose may be so cal'd) is intended to excite our *Youth* to pursue Fame by noble and useful Performances. TULLY, whole Elo[66]quence and Quality of a *Roman* Senator made him an Advocate for Kings, disdains not to acknowledg that he wrote the best part of his incomparable Works

---

* Ardeo cupiditate incredibili, neque, ut ego arbitror, reprehendenda, nomen ut nostrum scriptis illustretur, & celebretur tuis.—Neque enim me solum commemoratio posteritatis ad spem quandam Immortalitatis rapit: sed etiam illa cupiditas, ut vel auctoritate testimonii tui, vel indicio Benevolentiae, vel suavitate Ingenii, vivi perfruamur. *Epist. Famil. l. 5. Ep.* 12.[51]

† Fuit moris antiqui, eos qui vel singulorum Laudes vel urbium scripserant, aut Honoribus aut Pecunia ornare: nostris vero temporibus, ut alia speciosa & egregia, ita hoc in primis exolevit. Nam postquam desimus facere Laudanda, laudari quoque ineptum putamus. *L.* 3. *Ep.* 21.[52]

51. "I have a burning desire, of a strength you will hardly credit but ought not, I think, to censure, that my name should gain luster and celebrity through your works. . . . The thought that posterity will talk of me and the hope, one might say, of immortality hurries me on, but so too does the desire to enjoy in my lifetime the support of your weighty testimony, the evidence of your good will, and the charm of your literary talent" (Cicero, *Ad Familiares*, V.xii.1 [Letter 22]).

52. "It was the custom of antiquity to reward poets who had sung the praises of cities or individuals with gifts of office or money, but in our day this was one of the first things to fall out of fashion along with many other fine and honorable practices; for, now that we do nothing to merit a poet's tribute, it seems foolish to receive one" (Pliny, *Letters*, III.xxi.3).

to reform and *instruct the *Youth;* which in that declining State of the Commonwealth, was strangely corrupted. The two Years of Action which I add to their Sedentary Studies, will not, I hope, seem tedious, if in their reading they observe that the *Romans* were to serve ten times to become capable of certain Posts, seven times for others, and four e're they could fill any place almost in the Government.

13. Hitherto the whole Discourse related to our own DEFENCE against Invasions; but sometimes we are oblig'd to transport Armies beyond the Seas, either to ASSERT our own Rights against insolent and [67] treacherous Enemies, or else to ASSIST our Friends and Allies. That such Occasions may frequently happen, none will go about to deny; yet Multitudes (I'm afraid) will dislike the Methods I would have observ'd in the management of our *Forein Wars.* But my Assertions are not the less solid because some People are Cowards, and others now unaccustom'd to what their Ancestors successfully practis'd heretofore: Nor ought the rest of the *Scheme,* should any reject this part of it, be counted the more weak or inconsistent. So my Eighth Proposition is, THAT THE MAIN BODY OF OUR ARMIES ABROAD BE WHOLLY COMPOS'D OF THE FREE MILITIA, THE ONE HALF TO BE ANNUALLY RELIEV'D BY SUCCESSIVE LEVIES IN THE CLASSES; AND BE ALWAYS CORROBORATED WITH A SUFFICIENT NUMBER OF AUXILIARIES. We prov'd before under the First Proposition, that FREEMEN will fight better than [68] SERVANTS, that all Wars carri'd on by the former are quickly finish'd, that wherever the Sword is in their Hands that Government is free, and that they are consequently disus'd or discourag'd from bearing Arms by such as design to set up a Tyrannical Power. Now, all these Reasons should prevail with us to send our MILITIA of *Citizens* abroad instead of *Mercenaries.* The *Romans* in

---

* Quod enim munus Reipublicae afferre majus meliusne possumus, quam si docemus atque erudimus Juventutem? his praesertim moribus atque temporibus, quibus ita prolapsa est, ut omnium opibus refrenanda ac coercenda sit, &c. *De Divinatione l.* 2. *c.* 2.[53]

53. "For what greater or better service can I render to the commonwealth than to instruct and train its youth—especially in view of the fact that our young men have gone so far astray because of the present moral laxity that the utmost effort will be needed to hold them in check and direct them in the right way?" (Cicero, *De Divinatione,* II.ii.4).

point of War are the best Example, with respect to Success or Safety, that any Nation can imitate; and while they strictly adher'd to this Rule, they were both invincible themselves, and no People on Earth could resist the Force of their Arms. But when their Antient Orders were neglected or abolish'd, then they became an easy Prey to all that invaded them. Thus the *Eastern* Nations, tho infinitely superior in Numbers and Territories, yet by reason of their luxurious living, and that they plac'd their chief Strength in mighty Bodies of *Mercenaries*, they were quickly subdu'd by the MILITIA of *Italy*; nor would the Inhabitants [69] of that Country perform less at this present time, were they under the same Discipline. The *Gauls, Germans,* and *Brittons* were more valiant, it's true, than the *Asiatic* Nations, and better order'd (for they were a kind of MILITIA) but they were also finally subdu'd and broken by the *Roman* Legions. On the other hand, when the Sword was taken from the *Citizens* or *Freemen*, and put into the Hands of *Servants* by the Arbitrary Emperors who durst not trust Men of Property, the Oriental Countries not only shook off the *Roman* Empire; but likewise the *Lombards* and *Goths* invaded *Italy* it self; and tho not exceeding the old *Gauls* and *Germans* in Courage or Conduct, yet they absolutely conquer'd the Conquerors of the World. In short, the *Romans* lost their LIBERTY and PROPERTY, and with them all that ardent LOVE to their Country, which made them so freely bleed in its Defence before. And indeed no Man of sense ever meant any other thing by that Inclination for one's Coun[70]try, so much celebrated in the Works of Orators and Poets, but only the good Government of it. *Dimicare pro Aris & Focis*[54] was a synonymous Expression in the mouth of a *Roman,* for *pugnare pro Patria.*[55] Hence it is that BRUTUS reproaching CICERO for the servile Court he made to OCTAVIUS, speaks to him in these Terms; *Do you believe then,* says he, *that we receive Security when our

---

* Videmur ergo tibi Salutem accepturi, cum vitam acceperimus? Quam, si prius dimittimus Dignitatem & Libertatem, quî possumus accipere? An tu Romae habitare, id putas incolumem esse? Res non Locus oportet praestet istuc mihi? *Lib. ad Brut. Ep.* 16.[56]

54. To struggle for their altars and hearths (metonyms for religion and home).
55. To fight for their homeland.

Lives are spar'd? Or how can we accept of the latter, if first we must part with our Liberty and Dignity? Do you think that to be safe, it is enough to live at Rome? The Thing and not the Place can only put me in that condition. And afterwards he adds, †*Either I shall reduce those to their Duty who oppress their Country, or remove to a* [71] *great distance from you that are willing to be Slaves, and, wherever I may be free, there think my self in* Rome. We likewise are taught to love our Country above all others, valuing our selves every moment upon being ENGLISH MEN; and that most deservedly, for we cannot speak too magnificently of our Felicity. But we never mean our Soil or Climate, seeing these are much excel'd by several others in the World; therefore it must be our Government that makes the Scale heavier on our side. A partial Affection to the Land where we first drew our Breath, abstracted from other Considerations, is but a childish Prejudice, not less ridiculous than that of some elder Persons, who think it an extraordinary Blessing to be laid in the same Graves with their Relations. The *Romans* then were always possess'd with a hearty Kindness for their Country; and being earnestly desirous of returning to it in Peace, as well as certain of receiving the Rewards and Applause due to their Merit, they perform'd Wonders abroad. [72] The Reason why no other People did as much is, because the Government of no other Place was so well constituted.[58] Here was no difference between the *Citizen* and the

† —Aut longe à servientibus abero, mihique esse judicabo Romam, ubicunque liberum esse licebit. *Id. ibid.*[57]

56. "Do you think we are getting welfare if we are allowed to live? How can we have welfare if we let status and liberty go? Or do you think that merely to live in Rome is to be a citizen? It seems to me that to be a Roman is a matter of condition, not of place" (Cicero, *Letters to Brutus*, I.xvi.5–6 [Letter 25]).

57. "Or else I shall stay far away from the servile herd, and wherever I can live as a free man—there, for me, will be Rome" (Cicero, *Letters to Brutus*, I.xvi.8 [Letter 25]).

58. Toland echoes Machiavelli's admiration for the benign consequences of the Roman government at the opening of the first chapter of book 2 of the *Discourses*: "For if there is nowhere to be found a republic so successful as was Rome, this is because there is nowhere to be found a republic so constituted as to be able to make the conquests Rome made. For it was the virtue of her armies that caused Rome to acquire an empire, and it was her constitutional procedure and the peculiar customs which she owed to her first legislator that enabled her to maintain

Statesman, between the *Husbandman* and the *Soldier;* whence the Minds of the Inhabitants were enlarg'd to that degree, that they became capable of designing and effecting every thing. Their KNOWLEDG and POLITENESS made them sensible of the Excellency of their Constitution, which still encreas'd their Fondness of it, and render'd 'em so valiant to preserve it. Their City and Territory were divided into several TRIBES, not unlike our Counties, and their Assemblies call'd COMITIA TRIBUTA. Their People again were distributed into six *Classes,* besides the lesser Divisions of *Centuries,* and *Curiae* or *Parishes.* Now, their MILITIA going always abroad by *Rotation* out of the *Tribes* and *Colonies,* together not seldom with their *Allies,* whenever they were beaten (as in the dubious Events of War it must happen sometimes) they were im[73]mediately repair'd; and so one Army constantly sent after another, which could not fail where the People were all disciplin'd, till no Force whatsoever was able to stand before them. But when a *Mercenary* Army is once routed and dispers'd, then all is irrecoverably lost, because that either you cannot presently take the Field again, or you only oppose the Enemy with undisciplin'd Multitudes.[59] Now we may easily conceive why a MILITIA of *Freemen* are for venturing a Battle whenever they are favor'd with an Opportunity of doing it, whereas MERCENARIES are observ'd to decline fighting as much as they can; for, to speak nothing of what we said before concerning their different Dispositions, the first are sure of making good their Losses by a *Rotation* of their Fellows, and the latter wait for Advantages, because the Loss of one Battle is often enough to ruin them. From all that is premis'd, I think I may conclude, that to make successive Levies of our own FREE MILITIA out of the several Parts of [74] *England,* and corroborated with

---

what she had acquired, as will be explained at length in many of the discourses which follow"; "Perché se non si è trovata mai republica che abbi fatti i profitti che Roma, è nato che non si è trovato mai republica che sia stata ordinata a potere acquistare come Roma. Perché la virtù degli eserciti gli fecero acquistare lo imperio: e l'ordine del procedere ed il modo suo proprio e trovato dal suo primo latore delle leggi, gli fece mantenere lo acquistato, come di sotto largamente in più discorsi si narrerà" (Machiavelli, *Opere,* p. 221). A classical precedent for Machiavelli's praise of the Roman constitution is to be found in Polybius, VI.1.

59. For similar laments over the uselessness of mercenaries, of which Toland here seems to be offering a précis, see Machiavelli, *The Prince,* chap. 12.

some AUXILIARY REGIMENTS, is the best Method of waging the Wars abroad, whether we design to bring 'em to a speedy Period, or to spread wider the Terror of our Fame and Arms. The Names of all Persons capable of Military Duties in every County must be carefully registr'd to facilitate the *Rotation*, as was done in the *Roman* Tribes, where every Man was sworn (both in regard of the Charge and Service) to conceal neither the Name, Age, Condition, or Quality of any in his Family, that every one, who was able, might by his Purse or Person contribute to the Publick Good. The Regiments may likewise be denominated from the *Countries* or Places that send them, which will create an Emulation in the several Parts of the Kingdom to outdo each other's Actions. They will be as eager sometimes for regaining the Honor which one lost, as fearful to lose what the other won. Thus Men of ARTS and ARMS[60] will be the very same Species among us, whereas now they are extremely [75] different in most Parts of the World; for the former are generally *Cowards*, and the latter *barbarous* and *rude*. From all these Considerations, I cannot be perswaded that any Man of *Property* will refuse to go in his turn (which can seldom happen) on forein Service. If he hires a mean Person to supply his Place, this is raising a *Mercenary Army*, whereby he makes his *Man* become his *Master*. And how little soever FREEMEN think of the matter, while such Creatures are out of the Kingdom, yet they'l find 'em wonderful troublesom on their Return, should there be no other Difficulty but that single one of disbanding 'em. 'Tis strange what a Confusion very small Numbers of 'em produce in a Country, as has been abundantly demonstrated by the Ingenious Author[61] of the unanswerable *Argument against a Standing Army*. The few Soldiers that return'd in King *CHARLES* the First's time from an unsuccessful Voyage to *Cadiz*, were not presently disbanded as they ought to have been, but quarter'd up and down in [76] several Parts of the Kingdom: And a Great Person, who was an Eyewitness tells us, "That these *Soldiers broke out into great Disorders; they MASTER'D the People, disturb'd the Peace of Families, and the Civil Government of the Land; there were frequent

* Ruthworth's *Collect*. *Vol*. I. *p*. 420.
60. Cf. the epigraph (above, p. 174, n. 1).
61. I.e., John Trenchard and Walter Moyle.

Robberies, Burglaries, Rapes, Rapines, Murders, and barbarous Cruelties; unto some PLACES they were sent as a PUNISHMENT; and wherever they came, there was a general Outcry. The High-ways were dangerous, and the Markets unfrequented; they were a Terror to all, and undoing to many."[62] I said before, that every *Roman Freeman* was oblig'd to bear Arms (if need were) twenty times from the seventeenth to the six and fortieth Year of his Age; that they were excus'd from Duty after fifty; and that in case of extraordinary Necessity the old Soldiers might be compel'd if they did not give in their Names when desir'd, but that [77] they did for the most part voluntarily offer their Service to their Country. This whole matter, with several other admirable Effects of their Discipline, is represented to the life in the Speech of a Farmer to LICINIUS a *Roman* General. When the War was declar'd against PERSEUS King of *Macedonia*,[63] several Veterans were listed and came in freely; but some of

---

62. I.e., John Rushworth himself (Rushworth, *Collections*, p. 420). John Rushworth (ca. 1612–90), historian and politician. In the preface to his *Historical Collections* Rushworth drew attention to his direct experience of the events he described from 1630 onward: "I did personally attend and observe all Occurrences of moment during that Interval in the *Star-Chamber*, *Court of Honour*, and *Exchequer-Chamber*, when all the Judges of *England* met there upon extraordinary Cases; at the Council-Table, when great Causes were heard before the King and Council: And when matters were agitated at a greater distance; I was there also, and went on purpose out of a curiosity to see and observe" (Rushworth, *Collections*, sigs. b2ᵛ–b3ʳ).

63. Livy, XLII.xxxiv.

* Spurius Ligustinus tribus Crustuminae ex Sabinis sum oriundus, Quirites. Pater mihi jugerum agri reliquit, & parvum tugurium in quo natus educatusque sum; hodieque ibi habito. Quum primum in aetatem veni, pater mihi uxorem fratris sui filiam dedit: quae secum nihil attulit praeter libertatem pudicitiamque, & cum his foecunditatem, quanta vel in diti domo satis esset. Sex filii nobis, duae filiae sunt; utraeque jam nuptae. Filii quatuor togas virile habent, duo praetextati sunt. Miles sum factus, P. Sulpitio, C. Aurelio Consulibus. In eo exercitu qui in Macedoniam est transportatus, biennium miles gregarius fui adversus Philippum regem: tertio anno virtutis causa mihi T. Quintius Flaminius decumum ordinem hastatum assignavit. Devicto Philippo Macedonibusque, quum in Italiam portati ac dimissi essemus, continuo Miles voluntarius cum M. Portio Consule in Hispaniam sum profectus. Neminem omnium Imperatorum, qui vivant, acriorem virtutis spectatorem ac judicem fuisse sciunt, qui & illum & alios duces longa militia experti sunt. Hic me Imperator dignum judicavit cui primum hastatum

'em were displeas'd, that they should be plac'd in any lower Order than they had formerly possess'd. This occasioning a Difference between the *Consuls* and the *Tribunes* of the People, out steps the Countryman, and bespeaks the Assembly in the following manner: *"I am Spurius Ligustinus, O *ROMANS*, of the *Crustumin* Tribe, and originally a *Sabin*. My Father left me a little spot of Land, with a small House, in which I was born and bred, and I dwell there at this time. As [78] soon as I was of Age, he gave me in Marriage his own Brother's Daughter, who, excepting her Chastity, and that she was free-born, brought me no other Dowry; yet fruitful enough to supply a richer Family. We have six Sons and two Daughters, the latter both marri'd. Of our Sons four are grown Men, and the other two yet Striplings. I first bore Arms in the Consulship of Publius Sulpitius, and Caius Aurelius. I was two Years a private Soldier in that Army which was transported into *Macedonia* against King *PHILIP:* The third Year *FLAMINIUS*, in regard of my Merit assign'd me the tenth Division of the Spearmen. [79] Philip and the *Macedonians* being conquer'd, when we were brought back into *Italy* and

---

prioris centuriae assignaret. Tertio iterum voluntarius miles factus sum in eum exercitum, qui adversus Aetolos & Antiochum regem est missus. A Man. Acilio mihi primus princeps prioris centuriae est assignatus. Expulso rege Antiocho, subactis Aetolis, reportati sumus in Italiam: & deinceps bis, quae annua merebant legiones, stipendia feci. Bis deinde in Hispania militavi, semel Q. Fulvio Flacco, iterum Ti. Sempronio Graccho Praetore. A Flacco inter caeteros, quos virtutis causa secum ex provincia ad triumphum deducebat, deductus sum. A Ti. Graccho rogatus, in provinciam ij. Quater intra paucos annos primum pilum duxi: quater & tricies virtutis causa donatus ab Imperatoribus sum: sex civicas coronas accepi: viginti duo stipendia annua in exercitu emeriti habeo: & major annis sum quinquaginta. Quod si mihi nec stipendia omnia emeriti essent, nec dum aetas vacationem daret, tamen quum quatuor milites pro me uno vobis dare, P. Licini, possem, aequum erat me dimitti. Sed haec pro causa mea dicta accipiatis velim: ipse me, quoad quisquam qui exercitus scribit, idoneum militem judicabit, nunquam sum excusaturus. Ordinem quo me dignum judicent Tribuni militum, ipsorum est potestatis: ne quis me virtute in exercitu praestet, dabo operam; ut semper ita fecisse me, & Imperatores mei, & qui una stipendia fecerunt, testes sunt. Vos quoque aequum est, Commilitones, etsi appellationis vobis usurpatis jus, quum adolescentes nihil adversus Magistratum Senatusq; autoritatem usquam feceritis, nunc quoque in potestate Senatus ac Consulum esse, & omnia honesta loca ducere, quibus Rempublicam defensuri sitis. *Livius l*. 42. *c*. 34.

disbanded, I went immediately a Voluntier under MARCUS PORTIUS the Consul into *Spain*. That of all Generals living, he was the most nice Considerer and Judg of Merit, is known to every one who has been any considerable time in the Field under him or other Commanders: Now, he thought me worthy to preside over the first Order of the first Century of the Spearmen. I went the third time a Voluntier in that Army which was sent against the *Etolians* and King ANTIOCHUS, when MANLIUS ACILIUS created [80] me first Commander of the first Century. But ANTIOCHUS being expel'd, and the *Etolians* reduc'd, we return'd into *Italy*, and there I serv'd two of those Campagns to which the Legions are annually oblig'd. Afterwards I was twice a Soldier in *Spain;* once under the Pretor QUINTUS FULVIUS FLACCUS, and again under TIBERIUS SEMPRONIUS GRACCHUS. I was brought home by FLACCUS among the rest of those whom he had chosen for their Courage to grace his Triumph; and return'd back into that Province at the request of TIBERIUS GRACCHUS. I was Captain of the first Company of the Regiment four [81] times within the space of a few Years: I was by my Generals rewarded four and thirty times for my Valour: I receiv'd six Civic Crowns for saving the Lives of so many Citizens: I have taken Pay, in a word, two and twenty times in the Army, and am now above fifty Years old. But if I had not compleated the Number appointed by Law, nor were to be excus'd from Duty by reason of my Age; yet since in my own room I could give you, LICINIUS, four Soldiers, it were just I should be discharg'd. But I would have all this understood only of the goodness of my Cause, were I dispos'd to plead it; for as long as [82] any General judges me an able Soldier, I shall never excuse my self. What Post the Tribunes will assign me, lies in their own breasts. And, that none in the Army exceed me in Courage, shall be my endeavour: for, that it has been always so, my superior Officers, and such as serv'd along with me, are witnesses. Now altho, Fellow-Soldiers, you claim to your selves the right of Appeal; yet since during the whole course of your Youth you never did any thing against the Authority of the Senate or Magistrates, 'tis fit that you now also pay Obedience to the Senate and Consuls, esteeming all [83] those Posts to be honorable, wherein you have an opportunity of defending your Country." Having thus harangu'd, the *Consul*, after commending him with many words, led him out of the Assembly into the Senate, where he receiv'd the Thanks of the House; and he was by the Military Tribunes prefer'd according to his desert: whereupon the other Centurions quitted their Appeal, and readily compli'd with the pleasure of their Superiors.

14. All Men would live somewhere eternally if they could, and they affect to become Immortal even here on Earth. To have their Names perpetuated, was the true Spring of several great Mens Actions; and for that only end, have they patiently undergon all manner of Toil and Danger. But this Inclination never discovers it self so plainly, as in the care Men take of their Posterity. Some are content to live Beggers all their Days, that their Children after them may be rich: for they look upon these as their own Persons multipli'd by Propagation; whence such [84] as had none themselves, adopted the Children of others to bear their Names. The Legislator of the *Israelites*, as well as he of *Sparta*,[64] had a peculiar regard to this natural Desire, which in no Country must be neglected for Reasons upon which I need not insist at this time: Wherefore the Ninth Proposition is, THAT NO MAN BE OBLIG'D TO GO UPON ANY FOREIN EXPEDITION DURING ONE YEAR AFTER HIS MARRIAGE; NOR ALL THE SONS OF ANY MAN AT ONCE; NOR AN ONLY SON EVER, UNLESS HE'S WILLING HIMSELF. The Design of this Proposition is made so plain already, that, without more to do, I may pass to the Tenth and last of our Scheme, which is, THAT ALL LEVIES PERMITTED TO FOREIN STATES IN THIS KINGDOM, OR ANY FORCES LENT TO THEM, DO ENTIRELY CONSIST OF AUXILIARIES; AND THAT NO FREEMAN HAVE LEAVE TO SERVE ABROAD UNLESS AS A VOLUN[85]TIER TO QUALIFY HIMSELF FOR IMPLOIMENT AT HOME. The Reasonableness of this Proposition is likewise so evident from what went before, that it wants no larger Commentary. I could add here several other Particulars, but they'l come to be establish'd of course, if this SCHEME prevails wholly, or for the best part. I shall therefore write nothing now concerning the Methods of Listing

64. I.e., Moses. Lycurgus was the legendary legislator of Sparta.

or Disbanding, of Paying or Clothing, nor of Rewards or Punishments; tho with respect to the last, I cannot omit one pleasant Passage: for the *Romans* among divers kinds of Penalties, such as Fine or Imprisonment, us'd upon certain Occasions to *let a Soldier Blood, as if it had been Madness or Folly in him to commit such Faults, and that he wanted Physick more than Correction.

[86] 15. If this *Scheme of Reforming the* MILITIA be so intelligible and coherent, as I flatter my self it may, it would be a superfluous Labor, and no Complement upon the Reader's Sagacity, to remark distinctly all the good Effects and Consequences of it. Yet one I find convenient to mention, not that I think it less obvious than the rest, for it appears most evident at first sight; but because some Gentlemen are pleas'd to oppose it, and it is that I am for ARMING ALL THE PEOPLE. Now this is, in my Opinion, so useful and necessary, that, should we obtain nothing besides, it were well worth our while to procure an Act for this alone: For what can better demonstrate the Confidence his Majesty places in the unquestionable Affection of his Subjects, or more encrease and confirm the Veneration these have for him, than that he puts 'em in a Condition of defending themselves against all his and their Enemies, without needing or expecting the Assistance of others? But notwithstanding I took all pos[87]sible care to be duly inform'd, I could never hear any weighty Objection made to this Proposition, tho two are commonly offer'd, and the first of 'em is, that there will be no end of *Robberies*, and *House-breakings* in the Country, if the common People be once arm'd. I perceive these Gentlemen design to be *popular*, and the Vulgar are hugely oblig'd to 'em for their good Opinion. But supposing the worst, *Robberies* will be so far from being more frequent than at this time, that this is the only right Method of totally suppressing all such Disorders. It is an ordinary thing

---

* Fuit haec quoque antiquitus militaris animadversio, jubere ignominia causa militi venam solvi et sanguinem dimitti;—ut non tam poena quam medicina videretur. *A. Gellius, l.* 10. *c.* 8.[65]

65. "This also was a military punishment in old times, to disgrace a soldier by ordering a vein to be opened, and letting blood. . . . apparently not so much as a punishment as a medical treatment" (Aulus Gellius, X.viii).

for two or three Fellows to commit a *Robbery* in sight of twenty People, stronger and stouter than themselves, but that are either without Arms, or know not how to use 'em; whereas, upon the foot of our MODEL, when any House or Persons are known to be attack'd, they are not only provided for their own Defence, but the Neighbours are all ready to come in to their Assistance, both with Arms in their hands, and as able to handle [88] 'em as *House-breakers* can be suppos'd to do. But if the objecting Gentlemen have any meaning, it is that *Rogues* only should have Arms, and honest Men none to oppose them: For when any are dispos'd to violate the Laws, they always take care to arm themselves without any deference to Publick Authority; nor do we find that Thieves ever want Weapons, notwithstanding any Prohibitions to the contrary, which they no more regard than they do those which forbid 'em to steal. But good Men, on the contrary, will yield Obedience to the Laws; and so be expos'd, if thus left naked and unarm'd, to the Insults and Assaults of the most determin'd Villains. The next Objection is, That if the People be arm'd, there's an end of all the GAME in the Kingdom. Now supposing this were true, I think of the two we should sooner expose a few Birds to the People, than the People to the French or other Enemies. But indeed the GAME is in no danger. Deer, for example, [89] might be destroy'd with Bows and Arrows, no less than with Guns; yet in old times Englishmen were not disarm'd, but restrain'd from shooting Deer only by Laws, which may be accommodated to Guns as well as to Bows. Hare, Partridg and Pheasant are the principal GAME for Gentlemens diversion; and every one knows that these are more conveniently and frequently destroy'd by Nets, Hounds, Setting-dogs, and other Methods, than by shooting. Severe Penalties, which those concern'd will be sure to see inflicted, will prevent anything of this nature; and I hope we'l never see the Nation disarm'd a second time, under pretence of preserving the GAME. But, perhaps, it will be said, that although FREEMEN may be trusted with Arms, there will be danger from the *Poor* and *Servile*. This Objection was sufficiently answer'd in the Discourse subjoin'd to the Second Proposition; and besides I may add, if that will satisfy, that *Servants* are not arm'd according to this Scheme, but only disciplin'd against a time of [90] Necessity. I suppos'd before an *Armory* in every Parish, out of which on the days of Exercise only the *Poor* and *Servants* are furnish'd. And here I would not forget to hint that all such Arms provided at the Parochial Charge should be try'd and approv'd at the Tower of *London*, without any Liberty left to the Overseers to purchase others for this end, and that they be likewise all distinguish'd by the Parish Mark. I had several Opportunities in this Discourse to shew the Defects of the Act now in force for regulating the MILITIA, and my last Remark upon it shall be, that the *Isles of Wight* and *Purbeck* are left to *train their People as formerly.[66] The *Tower-Hamlets* likewise *having been always* (as 'tis said in the Act) *under the Command of his Majesty's Constable or Lieutenant of the Tower for the Service and Preservation of that Fort*, are permitted to be disciplin'd in such manner and form as heretofore. [91] The Reason of this Clause is very plain; for those two Islands lying so much expos'd to forein Invasions, it was fit they should be extraordinarily well provided for Defence. And so the *Tower-Hamlets*, because they were to keep Guard in the Tower, and might from thence distress the City, tho, lest they might not prove so unkind to their Neighbours, they were neglected as the rest, and exercis'd according to the Act: but the other Parts of the Kingdom being most likely to disrelish the Measures of the COURT, were industriously made uncapable of Resistance. And that this Suspicion may not seem ill grounded or malicious, I would fain know which was the best Model of training the MILITIA, the New or the Old? if the former, why should the Benefit of it be deny'd to those Places that stood most in need of it? and if the latter, why ought not the whole Nation to be as sufficiently train'd as one or two Islands? But all Persons own that *Guernsey* and *Jersey*, *Wight* and *Purbeck*, are equal [92] in their Discipline to any Standing Forces. But of this enough; nor can I allow my self to question but all Parties will now unanimously join to render the MILITIA useful for the King's and our common Preservation: for that a *Standing Army* or a *Militia* is of absolute Necessity, is agreed on every side; but the *Army* is order'd to be disbanded, and should those who were for continuing it

* 14 Car. 2. cap. 3. §. 22, 30, 31.
66. Cf. above, p. 138, n. 61.

now oppose the regulating of the *Militia*, they give us a Demonstration that either they never thought us in so great Danger as they pretended, or that they would have us entirely lost, because we refus'd to be sav'd after their Method, tho our own be more effectual and less expensive. I should now conclude, seeing no Objection remains against *arming the whole Free People of* England; but I must first take notice, that our Ancestors in *Germany* did in the time of the *Roman* Empire practise the very same thing, and that they always came arm'd to their Publick [93] Assemblies. **The Germans transact no publick or private Affairs*, says *TACITUS, but under their Arms; yet is it not usual for any to carry Arms till the Community first allows him to be capable. Then some principal Person in the Assembly, or the young Man's own Father, or one of his Relations, gives him a Shield and Spear. This is their Ceremony of declaring them to be of Age, and this is the first Honor confer'd on Youth. They were consider'd only as belonging to a private Family before, but as a part of the Publick ever after.* That this was our own Original Constitution in the *Saxon* time, none can be ignorant who is never so little vers'd in our antient Customs and Writings. But we read particularly in King *EDWARD*'s Laws, that upon a Day and Place [94] appointed, all that ow'd Suit and Service to any *Hundred* came to meet their new Governor, who stuck his Lance in the Earth, and then took Fealty of them, which they perform'd by touching the Governor's Lance with their own (as the *Germans* us'd to give their Assent by

---

* Nihil autem neque publicae neque privatae rei, nisi armati agunt. Sed Arma sumere non ante cuiquam moris, quam Civitas suffecturum probaverit, Tum in ipso concilio vel principum aliquis, vel pater, vel propinquus Scuto Frameaque juvenem ornant. Haec apud illos Toga, hic primus juventae honos: ante hoc domus pars videntur, mox Reipublicae. *De moribus German. cap.* 13.[67]

67. "They do no business, public or private, without arms in their hands; yet the custom is that no one takes arms until the state has endorsed his future competence: then in the assembly itself one of the chiefs or his father or his relatives equip the young man with shield and spear: this corresponds with them to the toga, and is youth's first public distinction: hitherto he seems a member of the household, next a member of the state" (Tacitus, *Germania*, XIII.1).

clattering their Arms) whence the whole Place or Meeting was then, as it is now in some of the Northern Parts of *England*, call'd a *Wapentake*, from the touching of their Weapons.[68]

FINIS.

68. Et quod Angli vocant Hundredum, supradicti comitatus vocant Wapentachium: Et non sine causa: Cum quis enim accipiebat prefecturam Wapentachii, die statuto in loco vbi consueuerant congregari, omnes maiores natu contra eum conueniebant, & descendente eo de equo suo omnes assurgebant ei. Ipse vero erecta lancea sua ab omnibus secundum morem foedus accipiebat. Omnes enim quotquot venissent cum lanceis suis ipsius hastam tangebant, & ita se confirmabant per contactum armorum, pace palam concessa. (William Lambarde, *Archaionomia* [1568], fol. 134[r–v]; see also Coke, *Writings*, 2:922–23)

For, as we read it in King *Edward*'s Laws, when any one came to take upon him the Government of a *Wapentake,* upon a day appointed all that owed suit and service to that Hundred, came to meet their new Governour at the usual place of their Rendezvouz. He upon his arrival, lighting off his Horse, set up his Lance an end (a Custom used also among the *Romans* by the *Praetor* at the meetings of the *Centumviri*) and according to custom took fealty of them. The Ceremony of which was, that all who were present, touch't the Governours Lance with their Lances, in token of a confirmation: whereupon that whole meeting was called a *Wapentake,* inasmuch as by the mutual touch of one anothers Arms, they had entred into a confederacy and agreement to stand by one another. This fashion, they say, the *Saxons* took up from the *Macedonians* their Progenitors. Others will have it from *tac* to take, and give this account of it, that the Lord of the Hundred at his first entrance upon the place was used to take the Tenants Arms, surrendred and delivered up to him by themselves, in token of subjection by way of Homage. (John Selden, *The Reverse or Back-Face of the English Janus* [1682], pp. 111–12)

See also Edward Leigh, *A Philologicall Commentary* (1658), p. 236.

Daniel Defoe

*An Argument Shewing that a Standing
Army with Consent of Parliament Is Not
Inconsistent with a Free Government*

1698

AN

ARGUMENT

Shewing, That a

Standing Army,

With Consent of

PARLIAMENT,

Is not Inconsistent with a

Free Government, &c.

---

2 Chron. 9. 25.
And King Solomon *had four thousand Stalls for Horses and Chariots, and twelve thousand Horsemen; whom he bestowed in the Chariot–Cities, and with the King at* Jerusalem.

LONDON:
Printed for E. Whitlock near Stationers. 1698.

The Preface

The Present Pen and Ink War rais'd against a Standing Army, has more ill Consequences in it, than are at first Sight to be Discern'd. The Pretence is specious,[1] and the cry of Liberty is very pleasing; but the Principle is Mortally Contagious and Destructive of the Essential Safety of the Kingdom; Liberty and Property,[2] are the Glorious Attributes of the English *Nation; and the dearer they are to us, the less Danger we are in of Loosing them; but I cou'd never yet see it prov'd, that the danger of loosing them by a small Army was such as we shou'd expose our selves to all the World for it. Some People talk so big of our own Strength, that they think* England *able to Defend it self against all the World. I presume such talk without Book; I think the prudentest Course is to prevent the Trial, and that is only to hold the Ballance of* Europe *as the King now does; and if there be a War to keep it abroad. How these Gentlemen*

1. I.e., attractive; here used without any overtly negative connotation of *"misleadingly* attractive."

2. "Liberty and Property" was the slogan of that broadly Whiggish political ideology which, although at times cogently and energetically challenged, nevertheless achieved hegemony in British political life between the Glorious Revolution of 1688 and the Great Reform Bill of 1832. As Gilbert Burnet put it, in his "An Exhortation to Peace and Union": "We are all then Brethren, as we are *Englishmen* and *Freemen*, born under a Government that gives us all possible Securities for both Liberty and Property, the two chief earthly Blessings of human Nature, whose Persons can neither be restrained, nor punished beyond the bounds of Law; who can be charged with no Taxes but by their own Consent; and who can be subject to no Laws but what were prayed by themselves" (Burnet, *Tracts*, p. 8). "Liberty and Property," then, denoted not so much two discrete values, as a certain peculiarly English stroke of political good fortune: namely, the possession of liberty construed as the provision of certain safeguards for the tenure of property.

will do that with a Militia, *I shou'd be glad to see Proposed;* 'tis not the King *of* England *alone, but the Sword of* England *in the Hand of the King, that gives Laws of Peace and War now to* Europe; *And those who would thus write the Sword out of his Hand in time of Peace, bid the fairest of any Men in the World to renew the War.*

The Arguments against an Army have been strongly urg'd; and the Authors with an unusual Assurance, Boast already of their Conquest, tho' their Armour is not yet put off. I think their Triumph goes before their Victory; *and if Books and Writing will not, God be thanked the Parliament will Confute them, by taking care to maintain such Forces, and no more, as they think needful for our safety abroad, without danger at home, and leaving it to time to make it appear, that such an Army, with Consent of Parliament, is not inconsistent with a Free Government,* &c.

An Argument, *shewing, that a Standing Army,*
with Consent of Parliament, is not Inconsistent
with a Free Government, &c.

In the Great Debates about a Standing Army; and in all the Arguments us'd on one side and 'tother, in the Case it seems to me, that both Parties are Guilty of running into the Extreams of the Controversie.

Some have taken up such terrible Notions of an Army, that take it how you will, call it what you will; be it Rais'd, Paid or Commanded by whom you will, and let the Circumstances be alter'd never so much, the Term is synonimous, an Army is an Army; and if they don't Enslave us, the Thanks is not to our good Conduct; for so many Soldiers, so many Masters: They may do it if they will; and if they do not do it now, they may do it in another Reign, when a King shall arise who knows not *Joseph*,[3] and therefore the Risque is not to be run by any means: From hence they draw the Consequence, *That a Standing Army is Inconsistent with a Free Government,* &c. which is the Title to the Argument.

This we find back'd by a Discourse of *Militia's*, and by a Second part of the Argument, *&c.* and all these Three, which seem to me to be wrote by the same [2] Hand, agree in this Point in General, That the War being at an end, *no Forces at all* are to be kept in Pay, *no Men* to be Maintained whose Profession is bearing Arms, whose Commission is to Kill and Slay, as he has it in *the Second Part*; but they must be Dismist, as Men for whom there is no more Occasion against an Enemy, and are dangerous to be kept up, least they find Occasion against our selves.

3. Exodus 1:8; cf. Acts 7:18.

The Advocates for the Necessity of a *Standing Army*, seem to make light of all these Fears and Jealousies; and Plead the Circumstances of the Kingdom, with Relation to our Leagues and Confederacys abroad, the Strength of our Neighbours, a Pretender to the Crown in Being,[4] the Uncertainties of Leagues, and the like, as Arguments to prove an Army necessary. I must own these are no Arguments any longer than those Circumstances continue, and therefore can amount to no more than to argue the necessity of an Army for a time, which time none of them has ventured to Assign, nor to say how, being once Establish'd, we shall be sure to be rid of them, in case a new King shou'd succeed before the time be expir'd, who may not value our Liberty[5] at the rate his present Majesty has done.

I desire calmly to consider both these Extreams, and if it be possible, to find out the safe *Medium* which may please us all.

If there be any Person who has an ill Design in pushing thus against the Soldiery, I am not to expect, that less than a Disbanding the whole Army will satisfie him; but such who have no other End than preserving our Liberties entire, *and leaving them so to Posterity*, will be satisfied with what they know is sufficient to that End; *for he who is not content with* [3] *what will fully answer the End he proposes, has some other End than that which he proposes.* I make no Reflections upon any Party, but I propose to direct this Discourse to the Honest well meaning English-Freeholder, who has a share in the *Terra firma*,[6] and therefore is concern'd to preserve Freedom to the inhabitant that loves his Liberty better than his Life, and won't sell it for Money; and this is the Man who has the most reason to fear a Standing Army, for he has something to loose; as he is most concern'd for the Safety of a Ship, who has a Cargo on her Botom.

This Man is the hardest to be made believe that he cannot be safe without an Army, because he finds he is not easie with one. To this Man all the sad Instances of the Slavery of Nations, by Standing Armies, stand as so many Buoys to warn him of the Rocks which other Free Nations have split upon; and therefore 'tis to this Man we are to speak.

4. I.e., the exiled James II.
5. See above, p. 202, n. 42.
6. I.e., the solid land.

And in order to state the Case right, we are to distinguish first between *England* formerly, and *England* now; between a Standing Army able to enslave the Nation, and a certain Body of Forces enough to make us safe.

England now is in sundry Circumstances, different from *England* formerly, with respect to the Manner of Fighting, the Circumstances of our Neighbours, and of our Selves; and there are some Reasons why a Militia are not, and perhaps I might make it out cannot be made fit for the Uses of the present Wars. In the Ancient Times of *England*'s Power, we were for many years the Invaders of our Neighbours, and quite out of fear of Invasions at home; but before we arriv'd to that Magnitude in the World, 'tis to be observed we [4] were hardly ever invaded, but we were conquer'd, *William* the Conqueror was the last; and if the Spaniard did not do the same, 'twas because God set the Elements in Battel array against them, and they were prevented bringing over the Prince of *Parma*'s Army; which if they had done, 'twould have gone very hard with us; but we owe it wholly to Providence.[7]

I believe it may be said, that from that Time to this Day, the Kingdom has never been without some Standing Troops of Souldiers entertain'd in pay, and always either kept at Home or employ'd Abroad; and yet no evil Consequence follow'd, nor do I meet with any Votes of the Parliament against them as Grievances, or Motions made to Disband them, till the Days of King *Charles* the First. Queen *Elizabeth*, tho' she had no *Guard du Corps*, yet she had her *Guards du Terres*. She had even to her last hour several Armies, *I may call them*, in Pay among Forreign States and Princes, which upon any visible Occasion were ready to be call'd Home. King *James* the First had the same in *Holland*, in the Service of *Gustavus Adolphus* King of *Sweden*, and in the Unfortunate Service of the King of *Bohemia;* and that Scotch Regiment,[8] known by the name of *Douglass*'s Regiment, have been, (*they say*) a Regiment Two hundred and fifty Years.

---

7. See above, p. 34, n. 83; and p. 64.

8. More commonly known as the Royal Scots; the senior infantry regiment of the British army, now digested into the Royal Regiment of Scotland. Defoe exaggerates the antiquity of the regiment. It began in the service of Gustavus Adolphus. In 1637 Lord James Douglas became colonel of the regiment, and it became known as the Régiment de Douglas.

King *Charles* the First had the same in the several Expeditions for the Relief of *Rochel*,[9] and that fatal Descent upon the Isle of *Rhe*,[10] and in his Expeditions into *Scotland*;[11] and they would do well to reconcile their Discourse to it self, who say in one place, *If King* Charles *had had Five thousand Men, the Nation had never struct one stroak for their Liberties;* and in another, *That the Parliament were like to have been petitioned out of doors by an Army a hundred and fifty Miles off, tho' there was a* [5] *Scotch Army at the Heels of them:*[12] for to me it appears that King *Charles* the First had an Army then, and would have kept it, but that he had not the Purse to pay them, of which more may be said hereafter.

But *England* now stands in another Posture, our Peace at Home seems secure, and I believe it is so; but to maintain our Peace abroad, 'tis necessary to enter into Leagues and Confederacies: Here is one Neighbour grown too great for all the rest;[13] *as they are single States or Kingdoms*, and therefore to mate[14] him, several must joyn for mutual Assistance, according to the Scotch Law of Duelling, *that if one can't beat you ten shall.*

---

9. An English military debacle of 1627. In an attempt to destabilize Richelieu, the chief minister of Louis XIII, Charles I's favorite, George Villiers, Duke of Buckingham, planned a combined forces operation to relieve the Huguenots besieged in La Rochelle. Arriving off the southeastern tip of the island of Ré on 12 July 1627, the English troops were successfully landed, and invested the citadel of St. Martin into which the French defenders had withdrawn. By the end of September the garrison was close to capitulation. However, Richelieu, who had taken personal charge of the French forces on the nearby mainland, dispatched a convoy of small ships that slipped through the English blockading fleet and brought supplies to the starving garrison. There was no prospect now of a swift victory, and Buckingham gave the order for withdrawal, in the course of which the English suffered heavy casualties: see May, *History*, lib. 1, p. 9. Late seventeenth-century Whig historians regarded this fiasco with fierce indignation as an illustration of the fecklessness of the Stuarts: see, e.g., Jones, *Theatre of Wars*, pp. 82–89, and Ludlow, *Memoirs*, 1:3–5.

10. See above, n. 9.

11. Following the unsuccessful attempt to impose a prayer book on the Church of Scotland in 1637, Charles I had faced a virtual rebellion from his Scottish subjects. He raised an army and marched it north, but he was unable to fight the quick campaign he wanted, and the expedition resulted in failure.

12. See above, pp. 27 and 127.

13. I.e., France under Louis XIV.

14. Overcome, defeat, or subdue (*OED*, s.v. "mate").

These Alliances are under certain Stipulations and Agreements, with what Strength and in what Places, to aid and assist one another; and to perform these Stipulations, something of Force must be at hand if occasion require. That these Confederacies are of absolute and indispensible necessity, to preserve the Peace of a weaker against a stronger Prince, past Experience has taught us too plainly to need an Argument.

There is another constant Maxim of the present State of the War; and that is, *carry the War into your Enemies Country, and always keep it out of your own.* This is an Article has been very much opposed 'tis true; and some, who knew no better, would talk much of the fruitless Expence of a War abroad; as if it was not worth while to defend your Confederates Country, to make it a Barrier to your own. This is too weak an Argument also to need any trouble about; but this again makes it absolutely necessary to have always some Troops ready to send to the assistance of those Confederates if they are invaded. Thus at the [6] Peace of *Nimeguen,*[15] six Regiments were left in *Holland,* to continue there in time of Peace, to be ready in case of a Rupture. To say, that instead of this we will raise them for their assistance when wanted, would be something, if this potent Neighbour, were not the *French* King, whose Velocity of Motion[16] the *Dutch* well remember in 1672. But then, *say they,* we may send our Militia. First, *The King can't command them to go;* and Secondly, if he could, *no body wou'd accept them;* and if they would go, and would be accepted of, *they would be good for nothing:* If we have no Forces to assist a Confederate, who will value our Friendship, or assist us if we wanted it? To say we are Self-dependent, and shall never need the Assistance of our Neighbour, is to say what we are not sure of, and this is certain it is as needful to maintain the Reputation of *England* in the Esteem of our Neighbours, as 'tis to defend our Coasts in case of an Invasion; for keep up the Reputation of our Power, and we shall never be Invaded.

15. Treaties of Nijmegen (1678–79) which ended the Dutch War (1672–78) between France and Spain and the Dutch Republic.

16. The early months of the Dutch War in 1672 saw French forces swiftly occupy three of the seven provinces of the Dutch Republic. These French successes prompted the Dutch to open the dikes around Amsterdam, flooding a large area and thus halting the French advance, albeit at ruinous expense.

If our Defence from Insurrections or Invasions, were the only necessary part of a future War, I shou'd be the readier to grant the Point, and to think our Militia might be made useful; but our business is *Principiis Obsta*,[17] to beat the Enemy before he comes to our own door. Our Business in case of a Rupture, is to aid our Confederate Princes, that they may be able to stand between us and Danger: Our Business is to preserve *Flanders*, to Garrison the Frontier Towns, and be in the Field in Conjunction with the Confederate Armies: This is the way to prevent Invasions, and Descents: And when they can tell us that our Militia is proper for this work, then we will say something to it.

[7] I'll suppose for once what I hope may never fall out, That a Rupture of this Peace shou'd happen, and the *French*, according to Custom, break suddenly into *Flanders*, and over-run it, and after that *Holland*, what Condition wou'd such a Neighbourhood of such a Prince, reduce us to? If it be answer'd again, Soldiers may be raised to assist them. I answer, as before, let those who say so, read the History of the *French* King's Irruption into *Holland* in the year 1672. where he conquer'd Sixty strong fortified Towns in six Weeks time: And tell me what it will be to the purpose to raise Men, to fight an Enemy after the Conquest is made?

'Twill not be amiss to observe here that the Reputation and Influence the *English* Nation has had abroad among the Princes of *Christendom*, has been always more or less according as the Power of the Prince, to aid and assist, or to injure and offend, was Esteem'd. Thus Queen *Elizabeth* carried her Reputation abroad by the Courage of her *English* Souldiers and Seamen; and on the contrary, what a ridiculous Figure did King *James*, with his *Beati Pacifici*,[18] make in all the Courts of *Christendom?* How did the Spaniard and the Emperor *banter* and *buffoon* him? How was his Ambassador asham'd to treat for him, while Count *Colocedo* told Count *Mansfield, That his New Master* (meaning King *James*) *knew neither*

17. To resist from the very outset.

18. "Blessed are the peacemakers" (Matthew 5:9). James I took this Biblical phrase for his motto: "He was both a wise and learned Prince of disposition merciful and gracious, a great seeker of peace, according to that Motto which he ever used, *Beati pacifici*" (Edward Leigh, *Choice Observations of all the Kings of England* [1661], p. 204; see also May, *History*, lib. 1, p. 5). Whig historians tended to comment contemptuously on this choice of motto: e.g., Jones, *Theatre of Wars*, p. 82.

how to make Peace or War?[19] King *Charles* the First far'd much in the same manner: And how was it altered in the Case of *Oliver?*

> *Tho' his Government did a Tyrant resemble,*
> *He made* England *Great, and her Enemies tremble.*
>
> Dialogue of the Horses.[20]

And what is it places the present King at the Helm of the [8] Confederacies? Why do they commit their Armies to his Charge, and appoint the Congress of their Plenipotentiaries at his Court? Why do Distressed Princes seek his Mediation, as the Dukes of *Holstien, Savoy,* and the like? Why did the Emperor and the King of *Spain* leave the whole Management of the Peace to him?[21] 'Tis all the Reputation of his Conduct and the *English* Valour under him; and 'tis absolutely necessary to support this Character which *England* now bears in the World, for the great Advantages which may and will be made from it; and this Character can never Live, nor these Allyances be supported with no Force at Hand to perform the Conditions.

These are some Reasons why a Force is necessary, but the Question is, What Force? For I Grant, it does not follow from hence, that a great

19. Count Don Carlos Coloma (1566–1637), soldier, diplomat, and translator of Tacitus into Spanish (1629); Spanish ambassador to England, 1622–24 and 1630–34. Maxim untraced, but cf. the similar remark of the Cardinal of Rouen to Machiavelli recounted in chap. 3 of *The Prince* (Machiavelli, *The Prince,* p. 15). Peter Ernst (1580–1626), Count von Mansfeld; Roman Catholic mercenary who fought on the Protestant side in the Thirty Years' War (1618–48). In 1624 Mansfeld had gone to England to raise an army for an anti-Hapsburg coalition and levied 12,000 foot and two troops of horse. En route to their rendezvous at Dover the troops "commited great Spoils and Rapines" and outraged the local population. The unpopularity of the adventure was cemented when two-thirds of the troops died of pestilence in transit, and "the Design came to nothing" (Rushworth, *Collections,* pp. 152–54).

20. Sometimes attributed to Andrew Marvell, "A Dialogue between the Two Horses," ll. 139–40 (slightly misquoted).

21. References to the prominent role England had played in the negotiations leading up to the Treaty of Ryswick (1697); see Jacques Bernard, *The Acts and Negotiations, together with the Particular Articles at Large of the General Peace, Concluded at Ryswick* (1698), pp. 3–5. Christian Albert (1641–95), Duke of Holstein. For the Duke of Savoy, see above, p. 95, n. 71.

Army must be kept on Foot in time of Peace, as the Author of the Second Part of the Argument says is pleaded for.[22]

Since then no Army, and a great Army, are Extreams equally dangerous, the one to our Liberty at Home, and the other to our Reputation Abroad, and the Safety of our Confederates; it remains to Inquire what *Medium* is to be found out; or in plain *English*, what Army may, with Safety to our Liberties, be Maintained in *England*, or what Means may be found out to make such an Army serviceable for the Defence of us and our Allies, and yet not dangerous to our Constitution.

That any Army at all can be Safe, *the Argument denies*, but that cannot be made out; a Thousand Men is an Army as much as 100000; as the *Spanish* Armado is call'd, *An Armado*, tho' they seldom sit out above Four Men of War; and on this Account I must crave [9] leave to say, I do Confute the Assertion in the Title of the Argument, that a Standing Army is Inconsistent with a Free Government, and I shall further do it by the Authority of Parliament.

In the Claim of Right, presented to the present King, and which he Swore to observe, as the *Pacta Conventa*[23] of the Kingdom, it is declar'd, *in hac verba, That the Raising or Keeping a Standing Army within the Kingdom in time of Peace, unless it be by Consent of Parliament, is against Law.*[24]

This plainly lays the whole stress of the thing, not against the thing it self, *A Standing Army*, nor against the Season, *in time of Peace*, but against the Circumstance, *Consent of Parliament;* and I think nothing is more Rational than to Conclude from thence, that a Standing Army in time of Peace, with Consent of Parliament, is not against Law, and I may go on, nor is not Inconsistent with a Free Government, nor Destructive of the *English* Monarchy.

There are Two Distinctions necessary therefore in the present Debate, to bring the Question to a narrow Compass.

22. Cf. above, p. 117.

23. See above, p. 140, n. 64.

24. Defoe refers to the Bill of Rights (1689); cf. above, p. 50, n. 123. See Appendix D, below, p. 629.

First, *I distinguish between a Great Army and a small Army. And*

Secondly, *I distinguish between an Army kept on Foot without Consent of Parliament, and an Army with Consent of Parliament.*

And whereas we are told, an Army of Soldiers is an Army of Masters, and the Consent of Parliament don't alter it, but they may turn them out of doors who Rais'd them, as they did the Long Parliament. The [10] First distinction answers that; for if a great Army may do it, a small Army can't; and then the Second Distinction regulates the First. For it cannot be supposed, but the Parliament when they give that Consent which can only make an Army Lawful, will not Consent to a larger Army then they can so Master, as that the Liberties or People of *England*, shall never be in danger from them.

No Man will say this cannot be, because the Number may be supposed as small as you please; but to avoid the Sophistry of an Argument, I'll suppose the very Troops which we see the Parliament have not Voted to be Disbanded; that is, those which were on Foot before the Year 1680.[25] No Man will deny them to be a Standing Army, and yet sure no Man will imagine any danger to our Liberties from them.

We are ask'd, if you establish an Army, and a Revenue to pay them, *How shall we be sure they will not continue themselves?* But will any Man ask that Question of such an Army as this? Can Six Thousand Men tell the Nation they won't Disband, but will continue themselves, and then Raise Money to do it? Can they Exact it by Military Execution? If they can, *our Militia must be very despicable.* The keeping such a Remnant of an Army does not hinder but the Militia may be made as useful as you please; and the more useful you make it, the less danger from this Army: And however it may have been the Business of our Kings to make the Militia as useless as they could, the present King never shew'd any Tokens of such a Design. Nor is it more than will be needful, for 6000 Men by themselves won't do, if the Invasion we speak of should ever be attempted. What has been said of the Appearance of the People on the

25. See below, p. 327, n. 190.

Purbeck fancied Invasion,[26] was very [11] true; but I must say, had it been a true One of Forty Thousand Regular Troops, all that Appearance cou'd have done nothing, but have drove the Country in order to starve them, and then have run away: I am apt enough to grant what has been said of the Impracticableness of any Invasion upon us, while we are Masters at Sea; but I am sure the Defence of *England*'s Peace, lies in making War in *Flanders.* Queen *Elizabeth* found it so, her way to beat the *Spaniards,* was by helping the *Dutch* to do it. And she as much Defended *England* in aiding Prince *Maurice,* to win the Great Battel of *Newport,* as she did in Defeating their *Invincible Armado.*[27] *Oliver Cromwel* took the same Course; for he no sooner declared War against *Spain,* but he Embark'd his Army for *Flanders:*[28] The late King *Charles* did the same against the *French,* when after the Peace of *Nimeguen,*[29] Six Regiments of *English* and *Scots* were always left in the Service of the *Dutch,* and the present War[30] is a further Testimony: For where has it been Fought; not in *England, God be thanked,* but in *Flanders?* And what are the Terms of the Peace, but more Frontier Towns in *Flanders?* And what is the Great Barrier of this Peace, but *Flanders;* the Consequence of this may be guess'd by the Answer King *William* gave when Prince of *Orange,* in the late Treaty of *Nimeguen;* when, to make the Terms the easier, 'twas offered, *That a Satisfaction shou'd be made to him by the* French, *for his Lands in* Luxemburgh;

26. Cf. above, p. 138, n. 61.

27. For the Armada, see above, p. 34, n. 83. Maurice (1567–1625), Prince of Orange; hereditary stadtholder of the United Provinces; an innovative and successful general who achieved a famous victory over the Spanish at Nieuwpoort on 2 July 1600. Praise of Elizabeth was a common trope in works critical of the Stuarts: see, e.g., May, *History,* lib. 1, pp. 1–4. For commentary, see Anne Barton, "Harking Back to Elizabeth: Jonson and Caroline Nostalgia," in her *Ben Jonson, Dramatist* (Cambridge: Cambridge University Press, 1984), pp. 300–320.

28. The conclusion of the First Anglo-Dutch War in April 1654 was followed, on 26 October 1655, by the publication of the Commonwealth's manifesto against the Spanish, which resulted in England's entering into a state of war with Spain in several theaters, including Flanders and the West Indies. An anti-Spanish treaty with France was concluded on 23 March 1657, and immediately English troops were sent to the Low Countries. On 3 July 1658 public thanksgiving was declared for the defeat of Spain.

29. Cf. above, p. 235, n. 15.

30. I.e., the War of the League of Augsburg (1689–97).

to which the Prince reply'd, *He would part with all his Lands in* Luxemburgh *to get the* Spaniards *one good Frontier Town in* Flanders.[31] The reason is plain; for every one of those Towns, tho' they were immediately the *Spaniards'*, were really Bulwarks to keep the *French* the further off from his own Country; and thus it is now: And [12] how our Militia can have any share in this part of the War, I cannot imagine. It seems strange to me to reconcile the Arguments made use of to magnifie the Serviceableness of the Militia, and the Arguments to enforce the Dread of a Standing Army; for they stand like two Batteries one against another, where the Shot from one dismounts the Cannon of the other: *If a small Army may enslave us, our Militia are good for nothing; if good for nothing, they cannot defend us,* and then an Army is necessary: *If they are good, and are able to defend us, then a small Army can never hurt us,* for what may defend us Abroad, may defend us at Home; and I wonder this is not consider'd. And what is plainer in the World than that the Parliament of *England* have all along agreed to this Point, That a Standing Army in time of Peace, *with Consent of Parliament*, is not against Law. The Establishment of the Forces in the time of K. *Charles* II, was not as I remember ever objected against in Parliament, at least we may say the Parliament permitted them if they did not establish them:[32] And the Present Parliament

---

31. A remark made in conversation with Charles II; for a slightly different version of it, see Boyer, *William III*, 1:99.

32. In fact the House of Commons did make attempts to disband armed forces during the reign of Charles II, for instance in 1678 after the signing of the Treaties of Nijmegen (30 Car. II, c. 1), of which the preamble begins:

> Wee Your Majestyes most loyall and obedient Subjects the Commons now in Parlyament assembled considering the great unnecessary Charge and Burthen and the many Inconveniencies to this Kingdome which Your Majestie sustaines by the Continuance of the Forces raised since the Nine and twentyeth of September One thousand six hundred seaventy and seaven and those brought since that time into this Kingdome from Forreigne Service from beyond the Seas and being desireous to enable Your Majestie to pay and disband the same Doe freely chearfully and unanimously present unto Your Majestie for the Ends and Purposes aforesaid the Summe of Two hundred and six thousand fower hundred sixty two pounds seaventeene shillings and three pence which wee beseech Your Majestie to accept of as a Testimony of our great Care for the Safety of Your Majestyes Person and the Peace and Prosperity of the Kingdome. . . .

seems enclin'd to continue the Army on the same foot, so far as may be suppos'd from their Vote to disband all the Forces raised since 1680.[33] To affirm then, *That a Standing Army*, (without any of the former Distinctions) *is Inconsistent*, &c. is to argue against the General Sense of the Nation, the Permission of the Parliament for 50 years past, and the Present apparent Resolutions of the best Composed House[34] that perhaps ever entred within those Walls.

To this House the whole Nation has left the Case, to act as they see cause; to them we have committed the Charge of our Liberties, nay the King himself has only told them His Opinion, with the Reasons for it, *without leading them at all;* and the Article of the *Claim of Right*,[35] is left in full force: For this Consent of Parli[13]ament is now left the whole and sole Judge, Whether *an Army* or *no Army*; and if it Votes an Army, 'tis left still the sole Judge of the Quantity, *how many*, or *how few*.

Here it remains to enquire the direct Meaning of those words, *Unless it be by Consent of Parliament*, and I humbly suppose they may, among other things, include these Particulars.

1. *That they be rais'd and continued not by a Tacit, but Explicite Consent of Parliament; or, to speak directly, by an Act of Parliament.*

2. *That they be continued no longer than such Explicite Consent shall limit and appoint.*

If these two Heads are granted in the word *Consent*, I am bold to affirm, Such an *Army is not Inconsistent with a Free Government*, &c.

I am as positively assur'd of the Safety of our Liberties under the Conduct of King and Parliament, while they concur, *as I am of the Salvation of Believers by the Passion of our Saviour;* and I hardly think 'tis fit for a private Man to impose his positive Rules on them for Method, any more than 'tis to limit the Holy Spirit, whose free Agency is beyond his Power:

33. See below, p. 327, n. 190.

34. For Boyer's analysis of the composition of this House of Commons, see below, p. 326, n. 185.

35. I.e., the Bill of Rights; see above, p. 238, n. 24, and Appendix D, below, pp. 627–34.

For the King, Lords and Commons, can never err while they agree; nor is an Army of 20 or 40000 Men *either* a Scarcrow enough to enslave us, while under that Union.

If this be allow'd, then the Question before us is, What may conduce to make the Harmony between the King, Lords and Commons eternal? And so the Debate about an Army ceases.

[14] But to leave that Question, since Frailty attends the best of Persons, and Kings have their *faux Pas*,[36] as well as other Men, we cannot expect the Harmony to be immortal; and therefore to provide for the worst, our Parliaments have made their own Consent the only Clause that can make an Army Legitimate: But to say that an Army directly as an Army, without these Distinctions, is destructive of the *English* Monarchy, and Inconsistent with a Free Government, *&c.* is to say then that the Parliament can destroy the *English* Monarchy, and can Establish that which is Inconsistent with a Free Government; which is ridiculous. But then we are told, that *the Power of the Sword was first placed in the Lords or Barons, and how they serv'd the King in his Wars with themselves and their Vassals, and that the King had no Power to Invade the Priviledges of the Barons, having no other Forces than the Vassals of his own Demeasnes to follow him:* And this Form is applauded as an extraordinary Constitution, *because there is no other Limitation of a Monarchy of any Signification than such as places the Sword in the hand of the Subject: And all such Governments where the Prince has the Power of the Sword, tho' the People have the Power of the Purse; are no more Monarchies but Tyrannies: For not only that Government is tyrannical which is tyrannically exercis'd, but all Governments are tyrannical which have not in their Constitution sufficient Security against the Arbitrary Power of their Prince;* that is, which have not the Power of the Sword to Imploy against him if need be.

Thus we come to the Argument: Which is not how many Troops may be allow'd, or how long; but in short, *No Mercenary-Troops at all can be maintain'd without Destroying our Constitution, and Metamorphizing our Government into a Tyranny.*

36. Errors or failings.

[15] I admire how the Maintainer of this Basis[37] came to omit giving us an Account of another Part of History very needful to examine, in handing down the True Notion of Government in this Nation, *viz.* of Parliaments. To supply which, and to make way for what follows, I must take leave to tell the Reader, that about the time, when this Service by Villenage and Vassalage[38] began to be resented by the People, and by Peace and Trade they grew rich, and the Power of the Barons being too great, frequent Commotions, Civil Wars, and Battels, were the Consequence, nay sometimes without concerning the King in the Quarrel: One Nobleman would Invade another, in which the weakest suffered most, *and the poor Man's Blood was the Price of all;* the People obtain'd Priviledges of their own, and oblig'd the King and the Barons to accept of an *Equilibrium;* this we call a Parliament: And from this the Due Ballance, we have so much heard of is deduced. I need not lead my Reader to the Times and Circumstances of this, but this Due Ballance is the Foundation on which we now stand, and which the Author of the Argument so highly applaudes as the best in the World; and I appeal to all Men to judge if this Balance be not a much nobler Constitution in all its Points, than the old *Gothick* Model of Government.[39]

In that the Tyranny of the Barons was intollerable, the Misery and Slavery of the Common People insupportable, their Blood and Labour was at the absolute Will of the Lord, *and often sacrifice to their private Quarrels:* They were as much at his beck as his Pack of Hounds were at the Sound of his Horne; whether [16] it was to march against a Forreign Enemy, or *against their own Natural Prince:* So that this was but exchanging one Tyrant for Three hundred, for so many the Barons of *England* were accounted at least. And this was the Effect of the Security vested in the People, against the Arbitrary Power of the King; which was to say

37. A set of principles laid down or agreed upon as the ground of negotiation, argument, or action (*OED*, s.v. "basis," 9c).

38. *Villenage:* the state or condition of a feudal villein; complete subjection to a feudal lord or superior; bondage, serfdom, servitude (*OED*, s.v. "villeinage," 2). *Vassalage:* the state or condition of a vassal; subordination, homage, or allegiance characteristic of, or resembling that of, a vassal (*OED*, s.v. "vassalage," 2a).

39. I.e., feudalism. See above, p. 152, n. 3.

the Barons took care to maintain their own Tyranny, and to prevent the Kings Tyrannizing over them.

But 'tis said, *the Barons growing poor by the Luxury of the Times, and the Common People growing rich, they exchang'd their Vassalage for Leases, Rents, Fines, and the like.* They did so, and thereby became entituled to the Service of themselves; and so overthrew the Settlement, and from hence came a *House of Commons:* And I hope *England* has reason to value the Alteration. Let them that think not reflect on the Freedoms the Commons enjoy in *Poland,*[40] where the *Gothick* Institution remains, and they will be satisfied.

In this Establishment of a Parliament, the Sword is indeed trusted in the Hands of the King, and *the Purse in the Hands of the People;* the People cannot make Peace or War without the King, nor the King cannot raise or maintain an Army without the People; and this is the True Ballance.

But we are told, *The Power of the Purse is not a sufficient Security without the Power of the Sword:* What! not against Ten thousand Men? To answer this, 'tis necessary to examine how far the Power of the Sword is in the Hands of the People already, and next whether the Matter of Fact be true.

[17] I say the Sword is in part in the Hands of the People already, by the Militia, who, as the Argument says *are the People themselves.* And how are they Ballanc'd? 'Tis true, they are Commissioned by the King, but they may refuse to meet twice, till the first Pay is reimburst to the Countrey: And where shall the King Raise it without a Parliament? that very Militia would prevent him. So that our Law therein Authorizing the Militia to refuse the Command of the King, tacitly puts the Sword into the Hands of the People.

I come now to Examine the Matter of Fact, *That the Purse is not an Equivalent to the Sword,* which I deny to be true; and here 'twill be necessary to Examine, How often our Kings of *England* have Raised Armies on their own Heads, but have been forced to Disband them for want of

40. In the seventeenth century the Polish constitution enshrined the principle of the "liberum veto," which meant that unanimity was necessary for any legislation. The liberum veto appeared to be a safeguard of the liberty of the ruled, but in practice it was just as likely to be wielded effectively by rulers. For the broader resonance of Poland in debates on English politics at this time, see above, p. 102, n. 97.

Moneys, nay, have been forced to call a Parliament to Raise Money to Disband them.

King *Charles* the First is an Instance of both these; for his First Army against the *Scots* he was forced to Dismiss for want of Pay; and then was forced to call a Parliament to Pay and Dismiss the *Scots;* and tho' he had an Army in the Field at the Pacification, and a Church Army too, yet he durst not attempt to Raise Money by them.[41]

I am therefore to affirm, *that the Power of the Purse is an Equivalent to the Power of the Sword;* and I believe I can make it appear, if I may be allowed to instance in those numerous Armies which *Gaspar Coligny,* Admiral of *France,* and *Henry* the Fourth King of *Navar,* and *William* the First P. of *Orange*[42] brought out [18] of *Germany* into *France,* and into the Low Countries, which all vanished, and could attempt nothing for want of a Purse to maintain them: But to come nearer, what made the Efforts of King *Charles* all Abortive, but *Want of the Purse?* Time was, he had the Sword in his Hand, when the Duke of *Buckingham* went on those Fruitless Voyages to *Rochell,*[43] and himself afterwards to *Scotland,*[44] he had Forces on Foot, a great many more than Five Thousand, which the Argument mentions, but he had not the Purse, at last he attempted to take it without a Parliament, *and that Ruin'd him.* King *Charles* the Second found the Power of the Purse, so much out-ballanced the Power of the Sword, that he sat still, and let the Parliament Disband his Army for him,[45] *almost whether he would or no.*

---

41. References to the events of the late 1630s, when Charles was forced to disband the defeated army he had sent against Scotland for want of money to pay them after the Short Parliament of April 1640 had refused to grant the large sum of twelve subsidies. The Scots then invaded England, defeated the English forces at Newburn on 28 August 1640, and took Newcastle (which they relinquished only a year later). Charles was forced to pay the Scots a subsidy of £25,000 per month (granted by the Long Parliament, which assembled on 3 November 1640).

42. Gaspard II de Coligny (1519–72), admiral of France and leader of the Huguenots during the early years of the French Wars of Religion (1562–98). Henri IV (1553–1610), king of France from 1589. William I (1533–84), Prince of Orange; first of the hereditary stadtholders (1572–84) of the United Provinces; leader of the revolt of the Netherlands against Spanish rule; byname "William the Silent."

43. See above, p. 234, n. 9.

44. See above, p. 234, n. 11.

45. In 1678, following the Treaties of Nijmegen (see above, p. 235, n. 15).

Besides the Power of the Purse in *England*, differs from what the same thing is in other Countries, because 'tis so Sacred a thing, that *no King ever touch'd at it but he found his Ruine in it*. Nay, 'tis so odious to the Nation, that whoever attempts it, must at the same time be able to make an Entire Conquest or nothing.

If then neither *the Consent of Parliament*, nor the *smalness of an Army proposed*, nor the Power of *the Sword in the Hands of the Militia*, which are the People themselves, nor *the Power of the Purse*, are not a sufficient Ballance against the Arbitrary Power of the King, what shall we say? Are Ten Thousand Men in Arms, without Money, without Parliament Authority, hem'd in with the whole Militia of *England*, and *Dam'd by the Laws?* Are they of such Force as to [19] break our Constitution? I cannot see any reason for such a Thought. The Parliament of *England* is a Body, of whom we may say, *That no Weapon Formed against them cou'd ever Prosper;* and they know their own Strength, and they know what Force is needful, and what hurtful, and they will certainly maintain the *First* and Disband the *Last*.

It may be said here, *'Tis not the fear of Ten Thousand Men, 'tis not the matter of an Army, but 'tis the* Thing *it self; grant a Revenue for Life, and the next King will call it,* My Revenue, *and so grant an Army for this King, and the next will say,* Give Me my Army.

To which I Answer, That these things have been no oftner ask'd in Parliament than deny'd; and we have so many Instances in our late Times of *the Power of the Purse,* that it seems strange to me, that it should not be allowed to be a sufficient Ballance.

King *Charles* the Second, as I hinted before, was very loath to part with his Army Rais'd in 1676. but he was forced to it[46] for want of Money to pay them; he durst not try whether when *Money had Raised an Army, an Army cou'd not Raise Money.* 'Tis true, his Revenues were large, but Frugality was not his Talent, and that ruin'd the Design. King *James* the Second was a good Husband,[47] and that very Husbandry had almost Ruin'd the Nation; for his Revenues being well managed, he maintain'd an Army out of it. For 'tis well known, the Parliament never gave him a Penny

---

46. Cf. above, p. 241, n. 32.
47. I.e., careful with money.

towards it; but he never attempted to make his Ar[20]my Raise any Money; if he had; 'tis probable his Work had been sooner done than it was.

But pray let us Examine abroad, if *the Purse has not Governed all the Wars of* Europe. The *Spaniards* were once the most powerful People in *Europe*; their Infantry were in the Days of the Prince of *Parma*,[48] the most Invincible Troops in the World. The *Dutch,* who were then his Subjects, and on whom he had Levied immense Sums of Money, had the 10th Penny demanded of them, and the Demand back'd by a great Army of these very *Spaniards,* which, among many other Reasons caused them to Revolt. The Duke *D'Alva*[49] afterwards attempted for his Master to raise this Tax by his Army, by which he lost the whole *Netherlands,* who are now the Richest People in the World; and the *Spaniard* is now become the meanest and most despicable People in *Europe,* and that only because they are the Poorest.

The present War[50] is another Instance, which having lasted Eight Years, is at last brought to this Conclusion. *That he who had the longest Sword has yielded to them who had the longest Purse.*

The late King *Charles* the First, is another most lively Instance of this Matter, to what lamentable Shifts did he drive himself? and how many despicable Steps did he take, rather than call a Parliament,[51] which he hated to think of. And yet, tho' he had an Army on Foot, he was forced to do it, *or starve all his Men;* had it been to be done, he wou'd have done it. 'Tis true, 'twas said the Earl of *Strafford* propos'd a Scheme, *to bring over an Army out* [21] *of* Ireland, *to force* England *to his Terms;* but the

48. Alessandro Farnese (1545–92), Duke of Parma and Piacenza; regent of the Netherlands, 1578–92.

49. Fernando Alvarez de Toledo y Pimentel (1507–82), third Duke of Alba (or Alva); governor-general of the Netherlands, 1567–73; notorious for his severities in that role, including the tax of the "tenth penny." Defoe is in error when he states that Alba followed the Duke of Parma as ruler of the Netherlands.

50. See above, p. 167, n. 30.

51. Charles I dissolved Parliament on 10 March 1629 and did not call another until April 1640; the intervening eleven years are referred to as the Personal Rule. Whig historians have tended to see these years as a provocative episode of incipient absolutism that stoked resentments ahead of the Civil War. For an exhaustive, subtle, and challenging counter-analysis, see Kevin Sharpe, *The Personal Rule of Charles I* (New Haven: Yale University Press, 1992).

Experiment was thought too desperate to be attempted, and the very Project Ruin'd the Projector;[52] such an ill Fate attends every Contrivance against the Parliament of *England*.

But I think I need go no further on that Head: The Power of Raising Money is wholly in the Parliament, as a Ballance to the Power of Raising Men, which is in the King; and all the Reply I can meet with is, *That this Ballance signifies nothing, for an Army can Raise Money, as well as Money Raise an Army; to which I Answer,* besides what has been said already; *I do not think it practicable in* England: The greatest Armies, in the Hands of the greatest Tyrants we ever had in *England*, never durst attempt it. We find several Kings in *England* have attempted to Raise Money without a Parliament, and have tryed all the means they could to bring it to pass; and they need not go back to *Richard* the Second, to *Edward* the Second,

---

52. Thomas Wentworth (1593–1641), lord lieutenant of Ireland and, eventually, Royalist ultra. See Thomas May's sketch of his character:

> He was a man of great parts, of a deepe reach, subtle wit, of spirit and industry, to carry on his businesse, and such a conscience as was fit for that worke he was designed to. He understood the right way, and the Liberty of his Country, as well as any man; for which in former Parliaments, he stood up stiffely, and seemed an excellent Patriot. For those abilities he was soone taken off by the King, and raised in honour, to be imployed in a contrary way, for inslaving of his Country, which his ambition easily drew him to undertake. (May, *History*, lib. 1, p. 20; see also lib. 1, pp. 53–54)

Following his appointment as chief councillor to Charles I in 1639, Strafford attempted to raise an army in Ireland to strengthen Charles's hand in his negotiations with his opponents in England, although in the first instance to fight the convenanters in Scotland. This new army was overwhelmingly Catholic, at least in the ranks, and this fact aggravated English fears about its possible deployment in England, as the Grand Remonstrance showed: "The Earl of Strafford passed into Ireland, caused the Parliament there to declare against the Scots, to give four subsidies towards that war, and to engage themselves, their lives and fortunes, for the prosecution of it, and gave directions for an army of eight thousand foot and one thousand horse to be levied there, which were for the most part Papists" (below, pp. 594–95). On 5 May 1640 Strafford is recorded to have told Charles in council that he had "an army in Ireland you may employ here to reduce this kingdom" (although it is not clear whether by "this kingdom" Strafford meant England or Scotland): see May, *History*, lib. 1, p. 93, and Ludlow, *Memoirs*, 1:9, 14. On 11 November 1640 Strafford was impeached for high treason, and after a dramatic state trial was executed on 12 May 1641.

to *Edward* the Fourth, to *Henry* the Eighth, or to *Charles* the First, to remind the Reader of what all Men who know any thing of History are acquainted with: But not a King ever yet attempted to Raise Money, by Military Execution, or Billetting Soldiers upon the Country. King *James* the Second had the greatest Army and the best, as to Discipline, that any King ever had; *and his desperate Attempts on our Liberties show'd his good Will,* yet he never came to that Point. I won't deny, but that our Kings have been willing to have Armies at Hand, to back them in their Arbitrary [22] Proceedings, and the Subjects may have been aw'd by them from a more early Resentment; but I must observe, that all the Invasion of our Rights, and all the Arbitrary Methods of our Governors, has been under pretences of Law. King *Charles* the First Levy'd Ship-Money[53] as his due, and the Proclamations for that purpose cite the pretended Law, that in Case of Danger from a Foreign Enemy, Ships shou'd be fitted out to Defend us, and all Men were bound to contribute to the Charge; *Coat* and *Conduct Money*[54] had the like Pretences; Charters were subverted by *Quo Warrantoes,*[55] and Proceedings at Law; Patriots were Murther'd[56] under Formal Prosecutions, and all was pretended to be done legally.

53. See above, p. 88, n. 44.

54. Respectively, money to provide a coat for each man furnished for military service and money to pay for the expense of conducting to the rendezvous at the coast each man furnished by a hundred to serve in the king's army. Charles I had attempted to levy both these taxes, and thereby provoked great resistance: see the Grand Remonstrance, Appendix B, below, p. 599; May, *History*, lib. 1, p. 16; and Ludlow, *Memoirs*, 1:6. For commentary, see Schwoerer, *Armies*, pp. 22–23.

55. Originally, a royal writ obliging a person to show by what warrant an office or franchise is held or claimed; later, and notoriously under James II, a legal information or action challenging an alleged right to hold an office or to exercise a power. James used *quo warrantoes* as a means of purging and intimidating corporations. See Boyer, *William III*, 2:87, 160.

56. Defoe presumably has in mind Algernon Sidney (1623–83) and Lord William Russell (1639–83), both of whom were executed after state trials for their part in the Rye House plot: see Jones, *History of Europe*, p. 147. He may, however, also be thinking of the Duke of Monmouth, for whom he had fought at Sedgemoor; although in Monmouth's case the act of attainder passed against him by Parliament on 16 June 1685 eliminated the need for a trial before he was executed after his capture.

I know but one Instance in all our *English* Story, where the Souldiery were employ'd as Souldiers, in open Defyance of Law, to destroy the Peoples Liberties by a Military Absolute Power, and that stands as an Everlasting Brand of Infamy upon our Militia; and is an Instance to prove, beyond the Power of a Reply, *That even our Militia, under a bad Government, let them be our selves, and the People, and all those fine things never so much* are under ill Officers and ill Management, *as dangerous as any Souldiery whatever,* will be as Insolent, and do the Drudgery of a Tyrant as effectually.

In the Year   when Mr. *Dubois* and Mr. *Papillon,* a Member of the Present Parliament, were chosen Sheriffs of *London,* and Sir *John Moor,* [23] under pretence of the Authority of the Chair, pretended to nominate one Sheriff himself, and leave the City to choose but one, and confirm the Choice of the Mayor, the Citizens struggled for their Right, and stood firm to their Choice, and several Adjournments were made to bring over the Majority of the Livery, but in vain: At length the Day came when the Sheriffs were to be sworn, and when the Livery-men assembled at *Guild-hall* to swear their Sheriffs, they found the Hall Garrison'd with a Company of Trained-Bands under Lieutenant Coll. *Quiney,* a Citizen himself, and most of the Soldiers, Citizens and Inhabitants; and by this Force the Ancient Livery-men were shut out, and several of them thrown down, and insolently used, and the Sheriffs thrust away from the Hustings, and who the Lord Mayor pleased was Sworn in an open Defiance of the Laws of the Kingdom, and Priviledges of the City.[57] *This was*

57. John Dubois (1622–84), local politician. Thomas Papillon (1623–1702), merchant and local politician. Sir John Moore (1620–1702), merchant and local politician; Lord Mayor of London. In 1681 Moore was next in seniority for the mayoralty, but, since he was regarded as friendly to the court, the Whigs attempted to prevent his election. The king and Sir Leoline Jenkins successfully intervened on his behalf by leaning on the tradesmen who catered to the court. The court now expected Moore to secure the election of a Tory sheriff in 1682. By ancient custom the lord mayor could nominate one of the sheriffs, but this right was contested and had been exercised irregularly and usually to raise revenue from fines. Moore drank to Dudley North at the bridgemasters' feast on 18 May 1682, and Ralph Box was put up as the second candidate. The Whigs, determined to retain jury selection in their hands, put up two of their own candidates, Thomas Papillon and John Dubois, for election by the whole livery. Although Moore declared North

done by the Militia to their Everlasting Glory, and I do not remember the like done by a Standing Army of Mercenaries, in this Age at least. Nor is a Military Tyranny practicable in *England,* if we consider the power the Laws have given to the Civil Magistrate, unless you at the same time imagine that Army large enough to subdue the whole *English* Nation at once, which if it can be effected by such an Army as the Parliament now seem enclined to permit, we are in a very mean Condition.

[24] I know it may be objected here, that the Forces which were on Foot before 1680. are not the Army in Debate, and that the Design of the Court was to have a much greater Force.

I do not know that, but this I know, that *those Forces were an Army,* and the Design of all these Opponents of an Army is in so many words, against *any Army at all,* small as well as great; a Tenet absolutely destructive of the present Interest of *England,* and of the Treaties and Alliances made by His Majesty with the Princes and States of *Europe,* who depend so much on his Aid in Guard of the present Peace.

The Power of making Peace or War is vested in the King: 'Tis part of his Prerogative, but 'tis implicitly in the People, because their Negative as to Payment, does really Influence all those Actions. Now If when the King makes War, the Subject shou'd refuse to assist him, the whole Nation would be ruin'd: Suppose in the Leagues and Confederacies His Present Majesty is engag'd in for the Maintenance of the present Peace, all the Confederates are bound in case of a Breach to assist one another

---

and Box duly elected at the common hall which he summoned on 19 June 1682, the Whig sheriffs then in office insisted on taking a poll. Moore responded by successive adjournments. When the Whig sheriffs declared Papillon and Dubois elected by a majority on 5 July, Moore conferred with the privy council. Secretary Jenkins instructed him to dissolve both common hall and the court of aldermen if necessary. Moore ordered another poll, and after more adjournments the court party eventually gained the day. North was declared sheriff on 14 July and Box on 15 July. Moore rejected petitions from the Whigs, and after Box was allowed to fine off on 5 September, Rich was declared sheriff in his place on 19 September. When Moore could not silence the clamor, he closed the Guildhall, and Rich and North were sworn in on 28 September. On 16 January 1683 common council passed a vote of thanks for Moore's handling of the crisis, but the struggle continued, and on 28 April 1683 Moore was arrested on the suit of Papillon and Dubois (*ODNB*). Cf. Burnet, *History,* 1:528–30, and Jones, *First Whigs,* pp. 202–6.

with so many Men, say Ten thousand for the *English* Quota, more or less, where shall they be found? *Must they stay till they are Rais'd?* To what purpose would it be then for any Confederate to depend upon *England* for Assistance?

[25] It may be said indeed, if you are so engag'd by Leagues or Treaties, you may hire Foreign Troops to assist till you can raise them. This Answer leads to several things which would take up too much room here.

Foreign Troops require Two things to procure them; Time to Negotiate for them, which may not be to be spar'd, for they may be almost as soon rais'd; Time for their March from *Germany*,[58] for there are none nearer to be hir'd, and Money to Hire them, which must be had by Parliament, or the King must have it ready: If by Parliament, that is a longer way still; if without, that opens a worse Gate to Slavery than t'other: For if a King have Money, he can raise Men or hire Men when he will; and you are in as much danger then, and more than you can be in now from a Standing Army: So that since giving Money is the same thing as giving Men, as it appear'd in the late K. *James*'s Reign, both must be prevented, or both may be allow'd.

But the Parliament we see needs no Instructions in this Matter, and therefore are providing to reduce the Forces to the same *Quota* they were in before 1680. by which means all the fear of Invading our Liberties will be at an end, the Army being so very small that 'tis impossible, and yet

---

58. Germany and the other states of Northern Europe were at this time reputed to be a source of mercenaries. Molesworth comments on this element in the economy of the northern European kingdoms in his *Account of Denmark*: "Souldiers are, through I know not what mistaken Policy, esteemed the Riches of the Northern Kings, and other German Princes . . . they are constrained to foment Quarrels between more potent Princes, that they may have the opportunity of selling to one or other those Forces which themselves cannot possibly maintain: so that at present Soldiers are grown to be as saleable Ware, as Sheep or Oxen, and are as little concern'd when they are sold" (Molesworth, *Denmark*, pp. 90–91). In pt. 4 of *Gulliver's Travels* (1726), Gulliver tells his Houyhnhnm master that there "is likewise a Kind of beggarly Princes in *Europe*, not able to make War by themselves, who hire out their Troops to richer Nations for so much a Day to each Man; of which they keep three Fourths to themselves, and it is the best Part of their Maintenance; such are those in many *Northern* Parts of *Europe*" (*Gulliver's Travels*, p. 365; manuscript evidence suggests that Swift may originally have written "Germany and other *Northern* Parts of *Europe*"). See also Defoe, *Cavalier*, p. 125.

the King will have always a Force at hand to assist his Neighbours, or defend himself till more can be Raised. The Forces before 1680. were an Army, [26] and if they were an Army by Consent of Parliament, they were a Legal Army; and if they were Legal, then they were not inconsistent *with a Free Government, &c.* for nothing can be Inconsistent with *a Free Government*, which is done according to the Laws of that Government: And if a *Standing Army* has been in *England* Legally, then I have proved, *That a Standing Army is not Inconsistent with a Free Government*, &c.

FINIS.

John Trenchard

A Short History of Standing Armies
in England

1698

1. "We were ensnared by guile and crocodile tears—we, whom neither the son of Tydeus nor Achilles of Larissa defeated, not ten years, not a thousand ships" (Virgil, *Aeneid*, II.196–98). These lines are taken from Aeneas's description of the sack of Troy (see above, p. 112, n. 1).

A Short
HISTORY
OF
Standing Armies
IN
ENGLAND

—Captiq; dolis, donisq; coacti,
Quos neq; Tydides, nec Larissaeus Achilles,
Non anni domuere decem, non mille Carinae.
Virg. Aen. ii.[1]

LONDON,
Printed in the Year MDCXCVIII.

The Preface

There is nothing in which the generality of Mankind are so much mistaken as when they talk of Government. The different Effects of it are obvious to every one, but few can trace its Causes. Most Men having indigested Ideas of the Nature of it, attribute all public Miscarriages to the corruption of Mankind. They think the whole Mass is infected, that it's impossible to make any Reformation, and so submit patiently to their Countries Calamities, or else share in the Spoil: whereas Complaints of this kind are as old as the World, and every Age has thought their own the worst. We have not only our own Experience, but the Example of all Times, to prove that Men in the same Circumstances will do the same things, call them by what names of distinction you please. A Government is a mere piece of Clockwork; and having such Springs and Wheels, must act after such a manner: and therfore the Art is to constitute it so that it must move to the public Advantage. It is certain that every Man will act for his own Interest; and all wise Governments are founded upon that Principle: So that this whole Mystery is only to make the Interest of the Governors and Governed the same. In an absolute Monarchy, where the whole Power is in one Man, his Interest will be only regarded: In an Aristocracy the Interest of a few; and in a free Government the Interest of every one. This would be the Case of England *if som Abuses that have lately crept into our Constitution were remov'd. The freedom of this Kingdom depends upon the Peoples chusing the House of Commons, who are a part of the Legislature, and have the sole power of giving Mony. Were this a true Representative, and free from external Force or privat* [iv] *Bribery, nothing could pass there but what they thought was for the public Advantage. For their own Interest is so interwoven with the Peoples, that if they act for themselves (which every one of them will do as near as he can) they must act for the common Interest of* England. *And if a few among them should find it their Interest to abuse their Power, it will be the Interest of all the rest to punish them for it: and then our Government would act mechanically, and a Rogue will as naturally be hang'd as a Clock strike twelve when the Hour is com. This is the Fountain-Head from whence the People expect all their Happiness, and the redress of their Grievances; and if we can preserve them free from Corruption, they will take care to keep every body else so. Our Constitution seems to have provided for it, by never suffering the King (till* Charles *the Second's Reign) to have a Mercenary Army to frighten them into a Compliance, nor Places or Revenues great enough to bribe them into it. The Places in the King's Gift were but few, and most of them Patent Places for Life, and the rest great Offices of State enjoy'd by single Persons, which seldom fell to the share of the Commons, such as the Lord Chancellor, Lord Treasurer, Privy-Seal, Lord High-Admiral,* &c. *and when these Offices were possess'd by the Lords, the Commons were severe Inquisitors into their Actions. Thus the Government of* England *continu'd from the time that the* Romans *quitted the Island, to the time of* Charles *the First, who was the first I have read of that made an Opposition to himself in the House of Commons the road to Prefer-ment; of which the Earl of* Strafford *and* Noy *were the most remarkable In-stances, who from great Patriots became the chief Assertors of Despotic Power.*[2] *But this serv'd only to exasperat the rest; for he had not Places enough for all that expected them, nor Mony enough to bribe them. 'Tis true, he rais'd great Sums of Mony upon the People; but it being without Authority of Parliament; and having no Army to back him, it met with such Difficulties* [v] *in the rais-ing, that it did him little good, and ended at last in his ruin, tho by the means of a long and miserable War,*[3] *which brought us from one Tyranny to another; for the Army had got all things into their Power, and govern'd the Nation by a Council of War, which made all Parties join in calling in* Charles *the Second: So that he came in with the general applause of the People, who in a kind fit*

---

2. For Strafford, see above, p. 249, n. 52. In the late 1620s Strafford had been an outspoken upholder of the liberties of the subject, and on 22 March 1628 had encouraged the House of Commons to "to vindicate 'our ancient, sober, vital lib-erties' in a speech that already contained much of the substance of the future peti-tion of right" (*ODNB*). For William Noy (or Noye), see below, p. 364, n. 3.

3. I.e., the English Civil War (1642–49).

gave him a vast Revenue for Life. By this he was enabled to raise an Army, and bribe the Parliament, which he did to the purpose: but being a luxurious Prince, he could not part with great Sums at once. He only fed them from hand to mouth: So that they found it as necessary to keep him in a constant Dependence upon them, as they had upon him. They knew he would give them ready Mony no longer than he had absolute necessity for them, and he had not Places enough in his disposal to secure a Majority in the House: for in those early days the art was not found out of splitting and multiplying Places; as instead of a Lord Tr——r to have Five Lords of the Tr——ry; instead of a Lord Ad——l to have Seven Lords of the Ad——ty; to have Seven Commissioners of the C——ms, Nine of the Ex——ze, Fourteen of the N——vy Office, Ten of the St——mp Office, Eight of the Pr——ze Office, Sixteen of the Commissioners of Tr——de, Two of the P——st⁴ Office, Four of the Transports, Four for Hackny Coaches, Four for Wine-Licenses, Four for the Victualling Office, and multitudes of other Offices which are endless to enumerat. I believe the Gentlemen who have the good Fortune to be in som of these Imployments, will think I complement them, if I should say they have not bin better executed since they were in so many hands, than when in fewer: and I must confess, I see no reason why they may not be made twice as many, and so ad infinitum, *unless the number be ascertain'd⁵ by Parliament: and what danger this may be to our Constitution, I think of with Horror. For if in Ages to com they should be all given to Parliament Men, what will be[vi]com of our so much boasted Liberty? what shall be don when the Criminal becoms the Judg, and the Malefactors are left to try themselves? We may be sure their common danger will unite them, and they will all stand by one another. I do not speak this by guess; for I have read of a Country where there was a constant Series of mismanagement for many Years together, and yet no body was punish'd: and even in our own Country I believe, som Men now alive can remember the time, when if the King had but twenty more Places in his disposal, or disposed of those he had to the best advantage, the Liberty of England had bin at an end. I would not be understood quite to exclude Parliament-men from having Places; for a Man may serve his Country in two Capacities: but I would not have it to be a*

4. Respectively Treasurer, Treasury, Admiral, Admiralty, Customs, Excise, Navy, Stamp, Prize, Trade, Post.

5. I.e., fixed.

Qualification for a Place; because a poor Borough thinks a Man fit to represent them, that therfore he must be a Statesman, a Lawyer, a Soldier, an Admiral, and what not? If this method should be taken in a future Reign, the People must not expect to see Men of Ability or Integrity in any Places, while they hold them by no other tenure than the disservice they do their Country in the House of Commons, and are sure to be turned out upon every prevalent Faction on the other side. They must then never expect to see the House of Commons act vigorously for the Interest either of King or People; but som will servilely comply with the Court to keep their Places, others will oppose it as unreasonably to get them: and those Gentlemen whose designs are for their Countries Interest, will grow weary of the best form of Government in the World, thinking by mistake the fault is in our Constitution. I have heard of a Country, where the Disputes about Offices to the value of thirty thousand Pounds per Annum, *have made six Millions ineffectual; what by som Mens prostitute compliance, and others openly clogging the Wheels, it has caus'd Want and Necessity in all kinds of Men, Bribery, Treachery, Profaneness, Atheism, Prodigality, Luxury, and* [vii] *all the Vices that attend a remiss and corrupt Administration, and a universal neglect of the Public. It is natural to run from one extreme to another; and this Policy will at last turn upon any Court that uses it: for if they should be resolv'd to give all Offices to Parliament-Men, the People will think themselves under a necessity to obtain a Law that they shall give none, which has bin more than once attemted in our own time. Indeed, tho there may be no great inconvenience in suffering a few Men that have Places to be in that House, such as com in naturally, without any indirect Means, yet it will be fatal to us to have many: for all wise Governments indeavor as much as possible to keep the Legislative and Executive Parts asunder, that they may be a check upon one another. Our Government trusts the King with no part of the Legislative but a Negative Voice, which is absolutely necessary to preserve the Executive. One part of the Duty of the House of Commons is to punish Offenders, and redress the Grievances occasion'd by the Executive part of the Government; and how can that be don if they should happen to be the same Persons, unless they would be public spirited enough to hang or drown themselves?*

But in my opinion, in another thing of no less importance, we deviated in Charles *the Second's time from our Constitution: for tho we were in a Capacity of punishing Offenders, yet we did not know legally who they were. The*

Law has bin always very tender of the Person of the King, and therfore has dispos'd the Executive part of the Government in such proper Channels, that whatsoever lesser Excesses are committed, they are not imputed to him, but his Ministers are accountable for them: his Great Seal is kept by his Chancellor, his Revenue by his Treasurer, his Laws are executed by his Judges, his Fleet is manag'd by his Lord High Admiral, who are all accountable for their Misbehavior. Formerly all matters of State and Discretion were debated and resolv'd in the Privy Council, where every [viii] *Man subscrib'd his Opinion, and was answerable for it. The late King* Charles *was the first who broke this most excellent part of our Constitution, by settling a Cabal or Cabinet Council,[6] where all matters of Consequence were debated and resolv'd, and then brought to the Privy Council to be confirmed. The first footsteps we have of this Council in any* European *Government were in* Charles *the Ninth's time of* France,[7] *when resolving to massacre the Protestants, he durst not trust his Council with it, but chose a few Men whom he call'd his Cabinet Council: and considering what a Genealogy it had, 'tis no wonder it has bin so fatal both to King and People. To the King: for whereas our Constitution has provided Ministers in the several parts of the Government to answer for Miscarriages, and to skreen him from the hatred of the People; this on the contrary protects the Ministers, and exposes the King to all the Complaints of his Subjects. And 'tis as dangerous to the People: for whatever Miscarriages there are, no Body can be punish'd for them; for they justify themselves by a Sign Manual,[8] or perhaps a privat Direction from the King: and then we have run it so far, that we can't follow it. The consequence of this must be continual Heartburnings between King and People; and no one can see the Event.[9]*

6. Generally speaking, any secret or extralegal council of the king, especially the foreign committee of the Privy Council. The term took on its present invidious meaning from a group of five ministers chosen in 1667 by King Charles II (Clifford, Arlington, Buckingham, Ashley Cooper, and Lauderdale), whose initial letters coincidentally spelled "cabal." However, it had fallen apart by 1672, and Ashley Cooper (later Earl of Shaftesbury) became one of Charles's most effective political opponents. See above, p. 105, n. 101.

7. Charles IX (1550–74), king of France; notorious for authorizing the massacre of Protestants at Paris on St. Bartholomew's Eve, 1572.

8. An autograph signature, especially that of the sovereign, serving to authenticate a document (*OED*, s.v. "sign-manual").

9. I.e., the outcome or conclusion.

A Short History of
Standing Armies in England

If any Man doubts whether a Standing Army is Slavery, Popery, Maho-metism, Paganism, Atheism, or any thing which they please, let him read,

First, The Story of *Matho* and *Spendius* at *Carthage*,[10] and the *Mamalukes* of *Egypt*.[11]

10. Commanders of the mercenary army which nearly defeated Carthage; see above, p. 161, n. 19.

11. Members of the regime established and maintained by emancipated white military slaves which ruled Egypt as a sultanate from 1250 until 1517, continuing as a ruling military caste of Egypt as a pashalik under Ottoman sovereignty until 1812, and of Syria from 1260 to 1516 (*OED*, s.v. "Mameluke"); "a light-horseman (in the Syrian and Arabian tongues) the Mamalukes were an order of valiant horse-men in the last Empire of Egypt" (Thomas Blount, *Glossographia* [1661], OED, s.v. "Mameluke"). The Mamalukes were renowned as an example of the conversion of military prowess into political ascendancy:

> It is woonderfull to tell vnto what a strength and glorie this order of the Mamalukes was in short time grown, by the care of the Aegyptian kings: By them they mannaged their greatest affaires, especially in time of wars; and by their valour, not onely defended their countrey, but gained many a faire victorie against their enemies, as they did now against the French. But as too much power in such mens hands, seldome or neuer wanteth danger, so fell it out now betwixt the late Sultan *Melech-sala*, and those masterfull Mamaluke slaues: who proud of their preferment, and forgetfull of their dutie, and seeing the greatest strength of the kingdome in their hands,

Secondly, The Historys of *Strada* and *Bentivolio,*[12] where he will find what work nine thousand *Spaniards* made in the 17 *Provinces,* tho the Country was full of fortified Towns, possessed by the Low Country Lords, and they had assistance from *Germany, England* and *France.*

Thirdly, The History of *Philip de Commines,* where he will find that *Lewis* the 11*th* inslaved the vast Country of *France* with 25000 [2] Men, and that the raising 500 Horse by *Philip* of *Burgundy* sirnamed the Good, was the ruin of those Provinces.[13]

---

traiterously slew *Melech-sala* their chiefe founder, setting vp in his place (as aforesaid) one *Turquiminus,* a base slaue, one of their owne order and seruile vocation, but indeed otherwise a man of a great spirit and valour. (Knolles, *Turkes,* p. 107; cf. Neville, *Plato Redivivus,* p. 181, and Sidney, *Discourses,* pp. 155, 197)

Like the Janissaries (see above, p. 28, n. 71), the Mamalukes were occasionally invoked pejoratively in the context of the English civil war:

The Eleven Impeached Members, before mentioned, who had superseded themselves, and were newly re-admitted, (the Army not being able to pro-duce their Charge, upon pretence of more weighty affairs) now altogether withdrew, and had Passes, (though some staid in *London*) some for beyond Sea, and other for their homes; in the way whither, one of them (Mr. *Nichols*) was seized on, and basely abused by *Cromwel:* another, Sir *Philip Stapleton,* one who had done them very good service, passed over to *Calice,* where fall-ing sick, as suspected, of the Plague, he was turned out of the Town, and perished in the way near to *Graveling*; whose end was inhumanely com-mented on by our *Mamaluke* like Saints, who inscribed it to the Divine Vengeance. (James Heath, *A Chronicle of the Late Intestine War* [1676], p. 142; see also Harrington, *Oceana,* pp. 17–18)

James Heath (1629?–64), son of the cutler to Charles I, was a historian of a pungently royalist character. This point of contact between his language of condemnation and that of a commonwealth Whig such as Trenchard reveals something of the volatility of political identities in the second half of the seventeenth century.

12. Famiano Strada (1572–1649), Italian historian; author of *De bello belgico* (1640), translated into English by Sir Robert Stapylton (1667), "that elegant Jesuit" (Thomas Browne, *Pseudodoxia Epidemica* [1646], p. 77). Guido Bentivoglio (1579–1644), Italian churchman, diplomat, and historian; author of *Relazioni in tempo delle sue nunziature* (1629) and *Della guerra di Fiandra* (1632–39).

13. Philippe de Commynes (ca. 1447–1511), French statesman and historian. Commynes was brought up in the Burgundian court, and was initially an adviser to Charles the Bold of Burgundy in his struggles with Louis XI of France. In 1472 Louis persuaded Commynes to desert Charles the Bold and to enter his service; see Bacon, *Essayes,* p. 83, "Of Frendship." Commynes's *Mémoires* were composed

Fourthly, Ludlow's Memoirs, where he will find that an Army raised to defend our Liberties, made footballs of that Parliament, at whose Actions all *Europe* stood amazed, and in a few Years set up ten several sorts of Government contrary to the Genius of the whole Nation, and the opinion of half their own Body: such is the influence of a General over an Army, that he can make them act like a piece of Mechanism, whatever their privat Opinions are.[14]

Lastly, Let him read the *Arguments against a Standing Army*, the *Discourse concerning Militias*, the *Militia Reform'd*, and the Answers to them:[15] but lest all this should not satisfy him, I will here give a short History of

---

1489–98 and were posthumously published in three parts from 1524 to 1528. During the seventeenth century in England Commynes's reputation as an astute commentator on politics was high: "Amongst modern Authours, *Philip de Commines* is famous; His *Memoires* are so exact, and withall so natural, that it appears, he was a great Agent in the affaires he treats of; Truth and Ingenuity are so much beholden to him, that he seems more tender to them, then to his own honour; for in discovering the policies then used, he makes himself a kind of Interloper, and leaves the Reader to judge, whether he served *Charls* or *Lewis* more faithfully" (Sir Thomas Culpeper, *Morall Discourses and Essayes* [1655], p. 49; cf. Edward Leigh, *Foelix Consortium* [1663], p. 167). Commynes's *Mémoires* were used by republican writers as an anatomy of tyranny written by an insider: see Sidney, *Discourses*, pp. 207, 247, 292, 488, 500. It is not surprising that Commynes is included in the emphatically Whiggish booklist included by Henry Neville in the second edition of his *Plato Redivivus* (1681).

14. Edmund Ludlow (1616/17–92), Parliamentarian army officer and regicide. After the Restoration, and in exile in Switzerland, Ludlow composed a huge autobiographical work, "A voyce from the watch tower." A surreptitiously rewritten and abbreviated version of "A voyce" appeared as the *Memoirs of Edmund Ludlow* in 1698–99 in three volumes, nominally published at Vevey but in reality printed by John Darby of Bartholomew Close, London. The editor was probably the deist and republican John Toland. The *Memoirs* belonged to a cluster of late seventeenth-century publications printed by Darby which included the *Discourses* of Algernon Sidney and the works of John Milton and James Harrington, and which took advantage of the standing army controversy that followed the Treaty of Ryswick in 1697 to promote the cause of the commonwealth and country Whigs. In Toland's version of the *Memoirs*, Ludlow's puritanism was eliminated, and his views overhauled so as to make him a republican of secular outlook and country party sympathies (*ODNB*). See Blair Worden's very detailed account of how this was done in the introduction to his edition of the surviving portion of the manuscript of Ludlow's memoir (Ludlow, *Voyce*, pp. 1–80).

15. All included in this volume; above, pp. 1–50, 111–45, 147–71, and 173–224.

Standing Armies in *England*, I will trace this mystery of Iniquity from the beginning, and show the several steps by which it has crept upon us.

The first footsteps I find of a Standing Army in *England* since the *Romans* left the Island, were in *Richard* the 2*d*'s time, who raised four thousand Archers in *Cheshire*, and suffered them to plunder, live upon free Quarter, beat, wound, ravish and kill wherever they went; and afterwards he called a Parliament, encompassed them with his Archers, forced them to give up the whole power of Parliaments, and make it Treason to endeavour to repeal any of the Arbitrary Constitutions that were then made: but being afterwards obliged to go to *Ireland* to suppress a Rebellion there, the People took advantage of it, and dethron'd him.[16]

The Nation had such a Specimen in this Reign of a Standing Army, that I don't find any King from him to *Charles* the 1*st*, that attemted keeping up any Forces in time of Peace, except the Yeomen of the Guard, who were constituted by *Henry* the 7*th:* and tho there were several Armies raised in that time for *French, Scotch, Irish*, other foren and domestic Wars; yet they were constantly disbanded as soon as the occasion was over. And in all the Wars of *York* and *Lancaster*, whatever party prevail'd, we don't find they ever attemted to keep up a Standing Army. Such was the virtue of those times, that they would rather run the hazard of forfeiting their Heads and Estates to the rage [3] of the opposit Party, than certainly inslave their Country, tho they themselves were to be the Tyrants.

Nor would they suffer our Kings to keep up an Army in *Ireland*, tho there were frequent Rebellions there, and by that means their Subjection very precarious; as well knowing they would be in *England* when called for. In the first three hundred Years that the *English* had possession of that Country, there were no Armies there but in times of War. The first Force that was establish'd was in the 14*th* of *Edward* the fourth, when 120 Archers on Horseback, 40 Horsemen, and 40 Pages were establish'd by Parliament there; which six Years after were reduc'd to 80 Archers, and 20 Spearmen on Horseback. Afterwards in *Henry* the Eighth's time, in the Year 1535, the Army in *Ireland* was 300; and in 1543, they were increased

16. See above, p. 125, n. 22.

to 380 Horse and 160 Foot, which was the Establishment then. I speak this of times of Peace: for when the *Irish* were in Rebellion, which was very frequent, the Armies were much more considerable. In Queen *Mary's* time the Standing Forces were about 1200. In most of Queen *Elizabeth's* Reign the *Irish* were in open Rebellion; but when they were all suppress'd, the Army establish'd was between 1500 and 2000: about which number they continued till the Army rais'd by *Strafford*[17] the *15th* of *Charles* the 1*st*.

In the Year 1602[18] dy'd Queen *Elizabeth*, and with her all the Virtue of the *Plantagenets*, and the *Tudors*. She made the *English* Glory sound thro the whole Earth: She first taught her Country the advantages of Trade; set bounds to the Ambition of *France* and *Spain;* assisted the *Dutch*, but would neither permit them or *France* to build any great Ships; kept the Keys of the Rivers *Maes* and *Scheld* in her own hands; and died with an uncontrol'd Dominion of the Seas, and Arbitress of Christendom. All this she did with a Revenue not exceeding 300000 pounds *per Annum;* and had but inconsiderable Taxes from her People.

No sooner was King *James* come to the Crown, but all the Reputation we had acquir'd in her glorious Reign was eclips'd, and we became the scorn of all Nations about us, contemned even by that State we had created,[19] who insulted us at Sea, seiz'd *Amboyna*, *Poleroon*, *Seran*, and other Places in the *East-Indies*,[20] by which they ingross'd that most

17. See above, p. 249, n. 52.

18. Elizabeth died on 24 March 1603. Under the Julian calendar, which was in use in England until 1752, the year began on 25 March, so by this reckoning Trenchard is correct to say that Elizabeth died in 1602, although since 1752 the year of her death has always been given as 1603.

19. I.e., the Low Countries, which Elizabeth had defended with armed force.

20. Ambon, an Indonesian island off the southwestern coast of Ceram (i.e., Seran); Polerone (or Pulorin or Pooleron) is another Indonesian island (see Lewes Roberts, *The Merchants Map of Commerce* [1700], p. 144). Attracted by Ambon's potential for the clove trade, the Portuguese had named and settled the island in 1521. The Dutch captured the Portuguese fort in 1605, took over the spice trade, and in 1623 destroyed an English settlement on the island. The Dutch local governor, Herman van Speult, believing that the English merchants, helped by Japanese mercenaries, planned to kill him and overwhelm the Dutch garrison as soon as an English ship arrived to support them, ordered the arrest of the alleged plotters. Under torture they admitted their guilt and were executed in February 1623. The so-called Amboyna Massacre (what Hobbes called "the old [but never to be

profitable Trade of Spices; fish'd up[4]on our Coasts without paying the customary Tribute, and at the same time prevail'd with the King to deliver up the Cautionary Towns of *Brill, Ramekins*, and *Flushing*,[21] for a very small Consideration, tho there were near six Millions Arrears. He squandred the public Treasure, discountenanc'd all the great Men who were rais'd in the glorious Reign of his Predecessor, cut off Sir *Walter*

---

forgotten] business of Amboyna": Hobbes, *Behemoth*, dialogue 4, p. 174) was even until the late seventeenth century a subject of enduring English resentment, which Dryden had exploited in his *Amboyna a Tragedy* (1673): see also Giovanni Battista Stoppa, *The Religion of the Dutch* (1680), pp. 50, 51, 52, 63; Elkanah Settle, *Insignia Bataviae* (1688), passim; John Hacket, *Scrinia Reserata* (1693), p. 53; Charles Leslie, *Delenda Carthago* (1695), p. 3; Lewes Roberts, *The Merchants Map of Commerce* (1700), p. 144. Amboyna, as a touchstone of anti-Dutch sentiment, was therefore very shrewdly referred to in the covertly Jacobite commentary on William of Orange's *Declaration* ("Gilbert Burnet," *The Prince of Orange his Declaration* [1688], p. 30). The conceding of Amboyna and Polerone to the Dutch by the treaty which ended the Third Anglo-Dutch War in 1674 was recalled, in the 1690s, as yet another instance of the weakness of Charles II (Coke, *Detection*, p. 497).

 21. In 1585 the Dutch had granted England the so-called cautionary towns as security for the large loan Elizabeth had made to the Dutch rebels in 1576:

> The rebellion was for many years chiefly maintain'd by forces from *England:* and the Queen making use to her advantage, of the evils as well of her confederates the *Dutch,* as of those of the *Spaniards* her enemies; she sent the Earl of *Lester* at that time into *Holland* with an entire Army, and demanded *Flushing,* and the *Ramakins* in *Holland,* and the *Brill* in *Zealand,* which are the chief Maretine keys of both those Provinces, to be assigned over to her as cautionary Towns, and to be garisoned by the *English.* (Bentivoglio, *Relations*, p. 41; cf. Edmund Bohun, *The Character of Queen Elizabeth* [1693], p. 157, and Coke, *Detection*, p. 482)

In 1616 the cautionary towns had been returned to the Dutch: "In the yeare 1616. the Hollanders upon a Composition made concerning the money lent by *Queene Elizabeth* upon the Cautionary townes, prevayled with King *Iames* to deliver up the Briel, Flushing and Rammekins after they had been 31. years in the possession of the English" ("E. W.," *Severall Remarkable Passages* [1673], pp. 3–4; cf. George Carew, *Fraud and Oppression Detected and Arraigned* [1676], p. 46; John Hall, *The Grounds & Reasons of Monarchy* [1650], pp. 120–21). There are references to the cautionary towns in Dryden's *Amboyna* (1673) (see above, n. 20), and memory of the cautionary towns was often deployed in anti-Dutch writings of the 1690s (e.g., Robert Ferguson, *A Brief Account of some of the late Incroachments and Depredations of the Dutch upon the English* [1695], p. 43).

Raleigh's Head,[22] advanc'd Favorites of his own, Men of no Merit, to the highest Preferment; and to maintain their Profuseness, he granted them Monopolies, infinit Projects, prostituted Honors for Mony, rais'd Benevolences and Loans without Authority of Parliament. And when these Grievances were complain'd of there, he committed many of the principal Members without Bail or Mainprise,[23] as he did afterwards for presuming to address him against the *Spanish* Match.[24] He pardon'd the Earl of *Somerset* and his Wife for Sir *Thomas Overbury's* Murder, after he had imprecated all the Curses of Heaven upon himself and his Posterity;[25]

22. Sir Walter Raleigh (1554?–1618), courtier, explorer, and author. Raleigh was suspected of treason by James I, and imprisoned in the Tower. On his release in 1616, he planned a voyage to Guiana, persuaded that he would find there immense amounts of gold. The voyage was a fiasco. On his return in the spring of 1618 Raleigh was again imprisoned, charged with treason, and executed on 29 October.

23. Procuring the release of a prisoner on someone's undertaking to stand surety for his or her appearance in court at a specified time (*OED*, s.v. "mainprize," 2a).

24. A reference to James I's project of marrying Charles, Prince of Wales, to the Infanta: "The grand business of State in the latter times of King *James*, was the Spanish Match, which had the King's heart in it, over-ruled all his Counsels, and had a mighty influence upon the universal state of *Christendom*" (Rushworth, *Collections*, p. 1). The proposed match was not popular with James's Protestant subjects. On 3 December 1621 Sir James Perrot (1571/72–1637) proposed that Parliament should petition the king to abandon the Spanish match. Perrot's views were widely shared in the Commons, which accordingly called upon the king to marry his son to a Protestant. James was so incensed at what he saw as an invasion of his prerogative that he reproached the House by letter (Rushworth, *Collections*, pp. 40–52, esp. pp. 43–44).

25. Sir Thomas Overbury (1581–1613), courtier and author. Overbury opposed the marriage between Robert Carr (subsequently Earl of Somerset) and Frances Howard (then Countess of Essex). James had Overbury imprisoned in the Tower, where he died on 15 September in circumstances that suggested poisoning at the hands of agents of Frances Howard.

Sir *Thomas* thus mew'd up, and excluded from the Sight of his nearest Relations and Servants, upon the *9th* of *May* was begun the Practice of poisoning Sir *Thomas,* in his Broth which *Weston* brought him; and this was continued with many Varieties of Poisoning, till the *14th* of *September,* when by a Glyster (for which the Administer had 20 *l.* Reward) he was dispatched: but the Malice against Sir *Thomas* did not end with his Death; for the Blanes and Blisters which the Poison had caused upon his Body, were interpreted to be the Effects of the *French-Pox,* and his Body was irreverently buried in a Pit digged in a very mean Place. (Coke, *Detection,* p. 69) and it was generally thought, because the Earl was Accessary to the poisoning Prince *Henry*.[26] He permitted his Son-in-law to be ejected out of his Principalities,[27] and the Protestant Interest to be run down in *Germany* and *France*, while he was bubled nine Years together with the hopes of the *Spanish* Match, and a great Fortune. Afterwards he made a dishonorable Treaty of Marriage with *France*, giving the Papists Liberty of Conscience:[28] and indeed, as he often declared, he was no otherwise an

26. Henry Frederick (1594–1612), Prince of Wales. Henry died on 6 November 1612 of what is now thought to have been typhoid, although poison was widely suspected at the time. "Never was any Prince's Death more universally and cordially lamented, and the more, by how much the Suddenness of his Death being known, before his Sickness was scarce heard of, was surprizing: As Mens Humours flowed they vented their Passions, some said, *A French Physician killed him*, others, *He was poisoned*; and it was observed, that poisoning was never more in fashion than at this time; others, *That he was bewitched*, &c." (Coke, *Detection*, p. 66).

27. In 1613 James's daughter, Elizabeth Stuart, had married Frederick V (1596–1632), elector Palatine of the Rhine and director of the Protestant Union. Following its adoption of Calvinism in the 1560s under Frederick III, the Palatinate had become the bulwark of the Protestant cause in Germany. Frederick V's acceptance of the crown of Bohemia in 1619 precipitated the Thirty Years' War, which was to prove disastrous to the Palatinate. Frederick was driven from Bohemia in 1620. In 1623 he was expelled from his German lands, deprived of his electoral dignity, and Catholic troops plundered the Palatinate. "Studious he [James] was of Peace somewhat overmuch for a King which many imputed to pusillanimity; and for certain, the thought of War was very terrible unto him; whereof there needs no further demonstration, than his management of the Cause of the *Palatinate:* For had he had the least scintillation of Animosity or Majestick Indignation, would he have so long endured his Son-in-law exterminated from his Patrimony. . . ." (Rushworth, *Collections*, p. 157; see also George Marcelline, *Vox Militis* [1625] and May, *History*, lib. 1, p. 6). The desertion of the cause of the Palatinate is mentioned in the Grand Remonstrance (Appendix B, below, p. 587).

28. On 1 May 1625 Charles I married by proxy Henrietta Maria (1609–69), the youngest daughter of Henri IV of France (Rushworth, *Collections*, pp. 169–70). The treaty had been signed in November 1624 before the sudden death of James I on 27 March 1625. It was unprecedented for a Catholic princess to be sent in marriage to a Protestant court, and this was reflected in the promises that Pope Urban VIII extracted from France in exchange for a papal dispensation. The marriage treaty therefore included commitments about the religious rights of the queen, her children, and her household; while in a separate secret document Charles promised to suspend operation of the penal laws against Catholics (Coke, *Detection*, p. 165).

In *France*, the Marriage-Treaty was not so fair, smooth, and plausible in the progress, as in the entrance. King *James* admiring the Alliance of mighty

Enemy to Popery, than for their deposing of Kings, and King-killing Doctrin.[29] In *Ireland* he gave them all the Incouragement he durst; which

Kings, though of a contrary Religion, as also fearing the disgrace of another breach, desired the Match unmeasurably; which the *French* well perceived, and abated of their forwardness, and enlarg'd their Demands in favour of Papists (as the *Spaniards* had done before them) and strained the King to the Concession of such Immunities, as he had promised to his Parliament he would never grant, upon the mediation of Forreign Princes. (Rushworth, *Collections*, p. 152; see also pp. 423–24)

29. Although the "monarchomachs" ("king-killers") tended to be Calvinists and revolutionaries, such as George Buchanan, there was also a strain of Roman Catholic political thought which deployed the concept of *imperium* to justify resistance by the subject against a tyrannical king, up to and including assassination. James would have encountered this strain of Catholic thought in the writings of Francisco Suárez (1548–1617), whose *Defence of the Catholic and Apostolic Faith* (1612) is in part an attack on James and his attempts to defend the English oath of allegiance against the criticisms made of it by Bellarmine and Clement VIII (Skinner, *Foundations*, 2:137–38, 177–78). But Catholic king-killing was not merely a point of political theory. The assassinations of Henri III on 1 August 1589 by Jacques Clément, a fanatical friar, and of Henri IV of France on 14 May 1610 by the Roman Catholic fanatic François Ravaillac had focused English attention on Roman Catholic willingness to sanction the assassination of monarchs:

What may I now say of theyr *Readinesse to Undertake* and *their Resolutenesse to Execute,* what act how dangerous and desperate soever, that may tend to the advauncement of theyr side or Order? I need not seeke farre back, nor farre off for examples. The late HENRY of Fraunce slaine by a Iacobine, and this man wounded by a Schollar of the Iesuites, the one for want of Zeale only in theyr violent courses; the other as misdoubted of sinceritie in his Conversion; may shew what measure theyr profest enemies were to attend, if they could obteine as open and ready accesse unto them. At this present this King hath gone in daunger of his life a long while from a Capuchine, having at the instigation as is sayd of certein Iesuites of Lorraine undertaken to dispatch him: whose Picture being brought hither by the MARQVIS DV PONT, caused search for him over all Paris, and at length hee is taken, and lastly also executed, together with an other Iacobine convicted of the same Crime. And what may it not be thought these men would do, being commanded by their Generalls whom they haue vowed to obey, and in the Popes necessary service, and with his expresse desire; who are caried with so desperate rage and furie, against whatsoever impediment theyr bare conceipts without warrant of higher Authoritie present unto them? (Sir Edwin Sandys, *Europae Speculum* [1629], p. 66)

It was an opinion powerfully echoed in 1677 by Andrew Marvell:

Nor is their [*sic*] any, whether Prince or Nation, that dissents from his Usurpations, but are marked out under the notion of *Hereticks* to ruine

Policy has bin follow'd by all his Successors since to this present Reign, and has serv'd 'em to two purposes: One is, by this they have had a pretence to keep up Standing Armies there to aw the Natives; and the other, that they might make use of the Natives against their English subjects. In this Reign that ridiculous Doctrin of Kings being *Jure Divino*[30] was coin'd, never before heard of even in the Eastern Tyrannies. The other parts of his Government had such a mixture of *Scharamuchi* and

---

and destruction whenever he [the Pope] shall give the signal. That word of *Heresy* misapplyed, hath served him for so many Ages to Justifie all the Executions, Assassinations, Wars, Massacres, and Devastations, whereby his Faith hath been propagated; of which our times also have not wanted Examples, and more is to be expected for the future. (Marvell, *Prose Works*, 2:231; see also pp. 233–34)

James's inclination toward Roman Catholicism, and its limitations, had already been noted by Rushworth, upon whom Trenchard is perhaps relying here: "This King affecting the name of a King of Peace, and Peace-maker, as his chief glory, had designed, what in him lay, the setling of a general Peace in Europe, and the reconciling of all Parties; and professed, that if the Papists would leave their *King-killing*, and some other grosser Errors, he was willing to meet them half-way" (Rushworth, *Collections*, p. 1; cf. the soothing letter from James to Pope Clement VIII which Rushworth reprints, pp. 162–64, and the parallel passage in Coke, *Detection*, p. 148. At this time it was treasonable for an Englishman to correspond with the Pope: Speck, *Revolutionaries*, p. 78). Thomas May offered a different explanation of James's willingness to seek an accommodation with Roman Catholicism: "It was feare for his own Person, that made him temporize with *Rome*, considering the boldnesse of Jesuiticall Assasines" (May, *History*, lib. 1, p. 5). The nightmare of Catholic-sponsored king-killing soaked deep into the English political imagination. The text of the oath of supremacy imposed in the eighteenth century required that "I do from my Heart Abhor, Detest, and Abjure, as Impious and Heretical, that damnable Doctrine and Position, *That Princes Excommunicated or Deprived by the Pope, or any Authority of the See of Rome, may be Deposed or Murthered by their Subjects, or any other whatsoever.*" During the hysteria over the Popish Plot in 1678 public awareness of the Catholic position on king-killing had supplied circumstantial corroboration to Oates's wild stories: "What the men of learning knew concerning their [the Jesuits'] principles, both of deposing of Kings, and of the lawfulness of murdering them when so deposed, made them easily conclude, that since they saw the Duke was so entirely theirs, and that the King was so little to be depended on, they might think the present conjuncture was not to be lost" (Burnet, *History*, 1:451). It was widely believed that Catholics condoned regicide if this would lead to reconversion (Speck, *Revolutionaries*, p. 168).

30. I.e., "divine right"; see above, p. 7, n. 10.

Harlequin,[31] that they ought not to be spoken of seriously, as Proclamations upon every Trifle, som against talking of News; Letters to the Parliament, telling them he was an old and wise King; that State Affairs were above their reach, and [5] therefore they must not meddle with them, and such like Trumpery. But our happiness was, that this Prince was a great Coward, and hated the sight of a Soldier; so that he could not do much against us by open force. At last he died (as many have believed) by Poison,[32] to make room for his Son *Charles* the First.

31. Stock characters in Italian commedia dell'arte, Scaramouch being a foolish, boastful coward who is beaten by Harlequin, the clever servant.

32. Although the rumor that James was poisoned is now discounted by historians, it was widely and luridly discussed at the time:

> The King being sicke of a tertian ague, and that in the spring which vvas of it selfe neuer found deadly, the Duke [of Buckingham] tooke his oportunitie when all the Kings Doctors of Physicke vvere at Dinner vpon the munday before the King dyed, without there knovvledge or consent, offered to the King a white povvder to take, the which the King longtime refused, but ouercome by his flattering importunitie at length tooke it, drunk it in wine, and immediatly became vvorse and vvorse, falling into many soundings and paynes, and violent fluxes of the belly so tormented, that his Maiestie cryed out aloud, o this white povvder! this white povvder! wold to God I had neuer taken it, it wil cost me my liffe. (George Eglisham, *The Forerunner of Reuenge* [1626], p. 21)

Roger Coke echoed and in some respects amplified this account while also making it more precisely circumstantial:

> Having had an Ague, the Duke of *Buckingham* did upon *Monday* the 21st before, when in the Judgment of the Physicians the Ague was in its Declination, apply Plaisters to the Wrists and Belly of the King, and also did deliver several quantities of Drink to the King, tho some of the King's Physicians did disallow thereof, and refused to meddle further with the King, until the said Plaisters were removed; and that the King found himself worse hereupon, and that Droughts, Raving, Fainting, and an intermitting Pulse, followed hereupon; and that the Drink was twice given by the Duke's own hands, and a third time refused: and the Physicians, to comfort him, telling him, that this second Impairment was from Cold taken, or some other Cause; *No, no*, said the King, *it is that which I had from* Buckingham. (Coke, *Detection*, p. 147; cf. Jones, *Tragical History*, pp. 319–24)

The thirteenth article of the House of Commons's impeachment of Buckingham on 8 May 1626 was the allegation that he had poisoned James I (Rushworth, *Collections*, pp. 350–53).

This King was a great Bigot, which made him the Darling of the Clergy; but having no great reach of his own, and being govern'd by the Priests (who have bin always unfortunat when they have meddled with Politics) with a true Ecclesiastic Fury he drove on to the destruction of all the Liberties of *England*. This King's whole Reign was one continued Act against the Laws. He dissolv'd his first Parliament[33] for presuming to inquire into his Father's Death, tho he lost a great Sum of Mony by it, which they had voted him: He entred at the same time into a War with *France* and *Spain*, upon the privat Piques of *Buckingham*,[34] who managed them to the eternal Dishonor and Reproach of the English Nation; witness the ridiculous Enterprizes upon *Cadiz* and the Isle of *Rhee*. He deliver'd *Pennington*'s Fleet into the *French* hands, betray'd the poor *Rochellers*, and suffered the Protestant Interest in *France* to be quite extirpated.[35] He

33. Charles opened his first Parliament on 18 June 1625 and dissolved it on 12 August, exasperated by what he took to be its reluctance to grant supply. By so doing, the two subsidies granted to Charles at the beginning of the session were forgone, and he was forced to raise money by other means: "The dissolution of Parliament preventing the Act of Subsidies, the King drew Supplies from the People, by borrowing of Persons able to lend, such competent sums of money, as might discharge the present occasions" (Rushworth, *Collections*, pp. 174, 192). The Grand Remonstrance construed the swift dissolution of this Parliament as a sign of undue Roman Catholic influence over the Crown (Appendix B, below, p. 586).

34. George Villiers (1592–1628), first Duke of Buckingham; royal favorite and courtier. The military expeditions of 1625 planned and recommended by him against Cadiz, led by Sir Edward Cecil, and for the relief of the Huguenots in La Rochelle, were embarrassing fiascos (see above, p. 234, n. 9). Both these military failures were mentioned in the Grand Remonstrance (Appendix B, below, p. 586). Rushworth records the impact these disasters had upon the morale of the nation: "And now when the unfortunate Action of *Rhee* was known and published throughout the Nation, the cry of the People was so great, and the Kings necessities so pressing, that it was in every mans mouth, a Parliament must needs be summoned" (Rushworth, *Collections*, p. 466; see also Neville, *Plato Redivivus*, p. 182).

35. Sir John Penington (1584?–1646), naval officer. Trenchard slightly misrepresents Penington's relationship with Buckingham. In the spring of 1625 Penington commanded a squadron promised as a loan to the French king, Louis XIII, to help quell the rebellion of the Count of Soubise. However, neither Charles I nor Buckingham actually wanted them to be employed to suppress French Protestantism. They hoped that by the time Penington's squadron reached France the Huguenots would have made peace with Louis, thereby allowing Penington's ships to be used in a combined Anglo-French military and naval operation against the Spanish satellite state of Genoa. Penington was accordingly given strict instructions to avoid involvement in France's civil wars. On his arrival at Dieppe in mid-June, however, he was

rais'd Loans, Excises, Coat and Conduct-mony,[36] Tunnage and Poundage,[37] Knighthood and Ship-mony,[38] without Authority of Parliament; impos'd new Oaths on the Subjects, to discover the value of their Estates;[39] imprisoned great numbers of the most considerable Gentry and Merchants for not paying his Arbitrary Taxes; som he sent beyond Sea, and the poorer sort he prest for Soldiers. He kept Soldiers upon free Quarter,[40] and

---

ordered by the admiral of France to transport 1,700 French troops to La Rochelle for service against the Huguenots. Penington was horrified and returned to England, an action approved of by his superiors. He was nevertheless ordered back to Dieppe in mid-July, whereupon he asked to be relieved of his command. Buckingham feigned anger at this request, which he refused, but was secretly delighted by his subordinate's reluctance to cooperate with the French, as there was as yet no confirmation of rumors that the Huguenots had agreed upon peace terms with Louis. Penington continued to give the duke secret cause for satisfaction, for at the end of July he connived at a mutiny by his crew which resulted in him returning to England for a second time. It was not until 5 August, when Buckingham and Charles were misled into thinking that Louis had made peace with the Huguenots, that Penington's ships (bar one) were transferred to French control (*ODNB*). See Rushworth, *Collections*, pp. 175–76, and May, *History*, lib. 1, pp. 8–9.

36. See above, p. 250, n. 54.

37. See above, p. 121, n. 15. These taxes were a point of friction between Charles I and his Parliaments; see above, p. 122, n. 16. See also Rushworth, *Collections*, pp. 645–48; May, *History*, lib. 1, p. 16; Coke, *Detection*, pp. 219–20; and the Grand Remonstrance (Appendix B; below, p. 589).

38. See above, p. 88, n. 44.

39. The commissioners charged with collecting the forced loan of 1626 were also empowered to question the recalcitrant on oath:

If any shall refuse to lend, and shall make delays, or excuses, and persist in their obstinacy, That they examine such persons upon Oath, whether they have been dealt withal to deny, or refuse to lend, or to make an excuse for not lending? Who hath dealt so with him, and what speeches or perswasions he or they have used to him, tending to that purpose? And that they shall also charge every such person in his Majesties name, upon his Allegiance, not to disclose to any other what his Answer was. (Rushworth, *Collections*, p. 423)

The imposition of these oaths is referred to in clause II of the Petition of Right (1628) (Appendix A; below, p. 578; Rushworth, *Collections*, p. 589). In the Grand Remonstrance it is complained that "New oaths have been forced upon the subject against law" (Appendix B; below, p. 591). For commentary see most recently Richard Cust, *The Forced Loan and English Politics: 1626–1628* (Oxford: Clarendon Press, 1987).

40. The right of troops to be billeted in free quarters; the obligation or imposition of having to provide free board and lodging for troops (*OED*, s.v. "free-quarter," p. 485, n. 21). "To the Imposition of Loan was added, the burthen of Billeting of Soldiers formerly returned from *Cadiz*, and the Moneys to discharge

executed Martial Law upon them. He granted Monopolies without number, and broke the bounds of the Forests.[41] He erected Arbitrary Courts, and inlarg'd others, as the High Commission-Court, the Star-Chamber, Court of Honor, Court of Requests, &c. and unspeakable Oppressions were committed in them, even to Men of the first Quality.[42] He commanded the Earl of *Bristol* and Bishop of *Lincoln* not to com to

---

their Quarters were for the present levied upon the Countrey, to be repaid out of Sums collected upon the general Loan" (Rushworth, *Collections*, p. 419; for Cadiz, see above, p. 276, n. 34). In 1628 a Petition Concerning the Billeting of Soulders was presented to the king, which complained that

> a new and almost unheard of way hath been invented and put in practice, to lay Souldiers upon them ["your Majesties Loyal Subjects"], scattered in companies here and there, even in the heart and bowels of this Kingdom; and to compel many of your Majesties Subjects to receive and lodge them in their own houses, and both themselves and others to contribute toward the maintenance of them, to the exceeding great disservice of your Majesty the general terror of all, and utter undoing of many your People (Rushworth, *Collections*, p. 542);

in consequence of which billeting was voted a grievance (Coke, *Detection*, pp. 207, 217). Billeting was recorded as a matter of resentment in the Grand Remonstrance (Appendix B, below, p. 587).

41. Enlarging the bounds of the forests, to bring more land within the scope of the forest laws, was one of the revenue-raising expedients of the Personal Rule.

> Once an area came under forest law, it was an offence to kill deer or keep dogs, keep guns, hunt foxes, to fence, destroy bushes, fell wood, pasture cattle, build or in any way encroach upon it. Officers of the forest could be fined in the Swanimote court for not fulfilling their duties or for appearing improperly dressed or equipped. Others who inhabited the forest, or exploited its timber for iron forging, could be offered the opportunity to pay to have their land disafforested, and so removed from forest jurisdiction, or could be fined for their encroachment. (Sharpe, *Personal Rule*, pp. 116–17; see also pp. 242–43; May, *History*, lib. 1, p. 16; Coke, *Detection*, pp. 124, 254, 266. See also the Grand Remonstrance [Appendix B, below, p. 589] and Blackstone, *Commentaries*, 4:429–31)

42. "It's scarce credible how the Business of this Court, the *Star-Chamber*, and Council-Table swelled, and what cruel and unheard of Censures were made, especially in the *Star-Chamber*, against all sorts of People, who did offend either against the King's Prerogative Royal, or the Arch-bishop's Injunctions" (Coke, *Detection*, p. 242). Cf. the Grand Remonstrance (Appendix B, below, pp. 590–92) and the complaint that "New judicatories [have been] erected without law." Cf. also Ludlow, *Memoirs*, 1:13, and Sidney, *Discourses*, p. 476.

Parliament;[43] committed and prosecuted a great many of the most eminent Members of the House of Commons for what they did there, som
for no cause at all, and would not let them have the benefit of *Habeas
Corpus;*[44] suspended and confin'd Arch-Bishop *Abbot*, because he would
not license a [6] Sermon that asserted Despotic Power, whatever other
cause was pretended.[45] He suspended the Bishop of *Glocester*, for refusing

43. John Digby (1580–1653), first Earl of Bristol; diplomat and politician. While
acting as English ambassador to the court of Madrid, Bristol had aroused the resentment of Charles and Buckingham. On the accession of Charles I in March 1625
Bristol was removed from the Privy Council, and in June Charles instructed him
not to attend Parliament. In January 1626 Bristol asked to attend Charles's coronation. The king retaliated by accusing Bristol of trying to make him convert to
Catholicism while in Madrid, and denied him a writ of summons to the Parliament that assembled in February 1626. On 22 March Bristol submitted a petition
to the House of Lords, requesting either to be summoned to Parliament or to be
placed on trial. The Lords' committee on privileges upheld his right to take his
seat, whereupon Charles reluctantly issued a writ of summons. John Williams
(1582–1650), archbishop of York, 1641; bishop of Lincoln, 1621; lord keeper, 1621.
Williams was commanded by Charles not to attend the Parliament of 1626, notwithstanding his entitlement as bishop of Lincoln to sit in the Lords. Williams
was the subject of a eulogistic memoir by his chaplain, John Hacket, *Scrinia Reserata* (1693). Both Digby and Williams were considered by Buckingham to be his
personal enemies (Coke, *Detection*, p. 174).

44. Literally, "you shall have the body"; technically, a writ issued by a court of
justice requiring the body of a person restrained of liberty to be brought before the
judge or into court, so that the lawfulness of the restraint may be investigated and
determined (*OED*, s.v. "habeas corpus"); more loosely, the principle which guaran-
tees to the subject the right of trial. In 1627 Parliament had debated the principle
of habeas corpus in relation to imprisonments arising from the forced loan (Rushworth, *Collections*, pp. 506–13; cf. Coke, *Detection*, p. 203). The Habeas Corpus Act
of 1679 (31 Car. II, c. 2) had confirmed and regularized the procedures relating to
this right. Cf. Neville, *Plato Redivivus*, pp. 188–89. For contemporary commentary,
see Henry Care, *English Liberties* (1680), pp. 129–31.

45. George Abbot (1562–1633), archbishop of Canterbury. Abbot was no favorite of Charles I, who preferred Laud (see below, p. 281, n. 48; and see May, *History*, lib. 1, p. 22). In the spring of 1627 the king had ordered Abbot to license a
sermon by Robert Sibthorpe in favor of the forced loan (see above, p. 277, n. 39).
Although Abbot had private reservations about the propriety of the loan, he pub-
licly supported its collection. However, Sibthorpe's arguments in favor of absolute
obedience Abbot would not endorse. In early July, Abbot was banished to his
manor of Ford in Kent. While at Ford Abbot preached regularly and wrote a narrative of the whole affair, placing the blame for his troubles on Buckingham. At
the opening of the Parliament of 1628 Abbot was warned by Charles to stay in

to swear never to consent to alter the Government of the Church;[46] supported all his Arbitrary Ministers against the Parliament, telling them he wondred at the foolish Impudence of any one to think he would part with the meanest of his Servants upon their account: and indeed in his Speeches, or rather Menaces, he treated them like his Footmen, calling them Undutiful, Seditious, and Vipers.[47] He brought unheard of Innovations into the Church; preferred Men of Arbitrary Principles, and

---

Kent, but he was recalled after petitioning from the Lords, and took his seat on 28 March. Abbot supported the Petition of Right and criticized the "new counsels" of 1626–28 that had precipitated the crisis between king and subject. In June he attacked "this miserable man" Roger Maynwaring (see below, p. 281, n. 48) who, like Sibthorpe, had preached "impious and false" doctrine in favor of the forced loan. The imposition of new taxes had been identified by Bartolus of Sassoferrato as one of the marks of a tyrant, although more recently Théodore Bèze in his *Du Droit des Magistrats sur Leurs Subiets* (1574) had questioned this:

> Suppose we are asked about a prince who oppresses his people with unjust taxes and subsidies. After remonstrations have been made, those having authority may and should restore order according to the laws of the realm, as we have indicated. But this also should be noted: a prince who exceeds his power in a matter like this should not be hastily judged a tyrant simply because he is extravagant, greedy, or given to some other vice. Tyranny implies confirmed wickedness involving general subversion of the political order and of the fundamental laws of a realm. (Franklin, *Constitutionalism*, pp. 131–32)

Cf. Sidney, *Discourses*, p. 11.

46. Godfrey Goodman (1583–1656), bishop of Gloucester. On 20 May 1640 Goodman refused to assent to the new ecclesiastical canons. When he did subscribe on 29 May, it was with some degree of reservation, for which he was suspended from his office and livings by a vote in both houses of convocation and imprisoned at the Gatehouse at Westminster. Goodman is a surprising (or unscrupulous) choice of victim for Trenchard to produce, since his reservations about the new canons were alleged to focus on those most hostile to a Roman Catholic understanding of the sacraments. Goodman had long been suspected of harboring sympathies toward Roman Catholicism.

47. A reference to Charles's short, bitter speech on the dissolution of Parliament on 10 March 1630. These terms of reproach had been wrung from the king by attacks on his religious policy:

> I thought it necessary to come here to day, and to declare to you and all the world, that it was meerly the undutiful and seditious carriage in the Lower House, that hath made the dissolution of this Parliament; . . . it being but some few Vipers among them that did cast this mist of undutifulness over most of their eyes: . . . To conclude, as those Vipers must look for their reward of punishment: so you, *My Lords*, must justly expect from me that

inclinable to Popery, especially those Firebrands, *Laud, Mountague,* and *Manwaring,*[48] one of whom had bin complain'd of in Parliament, another impeach'd for advancing Popery, and the third condemn'd in the House of Lords. He dispensed with the Laws against Papists,[49] and both encourag'd and prefer'd them. He called no Parliament[50] for twelve years

---

favour and protection, that a good King oweth to his loving and faithful Nobility. (Rushworth, *Collections,* p. 662; cf. Coke, *Detection,* p. 232)

48. William Laud (1573–1645), archbishop of Canterbury; chancellor of Oxford University. Charles I's favorite clergyman, and the architect of his Romanizing religious policy (see May, *History,* lib. 1, pp. 22–23). Impeached for high treason on 18 December 1640 by the Commons; executed 10 January 1645. Either Walter Montagu (1604/5–77), courtier and abbot of St Martin; apostate; condemned by the Commons to perpetual banishment on 31 August 1649; spiritual director to Henrietta Maria when in exile, and tutor to her son Henry, Duke of Gloucester; or (more probably) Richard Mountague (1575–1641), bishop of Norwich and religious controversialist; ally of archbishop Laud; impeached by the Commons for favoring Roman Catholicism. Roger Maynwaring (1589/90?–1653), bishop of St. David's; chaplain to Charles I; preacher of two inflammatory sermons in support of the forced loan (Rushworth, *Collections,* p. 423). Charles's indulgence toward these clergymen was a source of grievance:

> Bishop *Montague,* and Doctor *Manwaring,* procured a Royal Pardon of all Errors heretofore committed by them, either in speaking, writing, or printing, for which they might be hereafter questioned: And Doctor *Manwaring,* censured by the Lords in Parliament, and perpetually disabled from future Ecclesiastical Preferments in the Church of *England,* was immediately presented to the Rectory of *Stamford Rivers* in *Essex,* and had a Dispensation to hold it, together with the Rectory of St. *Giles's* in the Fields. (Rushworth, *Collections,* p. 635)

Algernon Sidney had included Laud and Maynwaring in his list of apologists for absolutism who were "the shame and misery of our age and country" (Sidney, *Discourses,* p. 11; see also May, *History,* lib. 1, p. 23).

49. "Then [1628] a Proclamation came forth, declaring the King's pleasure for proceedings with Popish Recusants, and directions to his Commissioners for making Compositions for two parts of three of their Estates, which, by Law, were due to his Majesty; nevertheless (for the most part) they got off upon easie terms, by reason of Compositions at undervalues, and by Letters of Grace and Protection, granted from time to time to most of the wealthiest of them" (Rushworth, *Collections,* p. 633).

50. The Personal Rule of Charles I ran from the dissolution of Parliament in 1630 until the summoning of the Short Parliament in the spring of 1640 (although it is normally calculated to have extended until the summoning of the Long Parliament early in 1641); see above, p. 248, n. 51.

together, and in that time govern'd as arbitrarily as the Grand Seignior.[51]

51. I.e., the Ottoman sultan; also known as the Great Turk or the Mogul (see below, p. 313, n. 141); for a roughly contemporary definition, see Henry Curzon, *The Universal Library*, 2 vols (1712), 1:194. Two recent works by Paul Rycaut, *The Present State of the Ottoman Empire*, 3rd ed. (1670) and *The History of the Turkish Empire* (1680), had supplied English readers with plentiful and often lurid information about the capricious, violent, and self-indulgent despotism practiced by the Ottoman sultans. Accordingly the Grand Seignior became a byword for despotic, autocratic rule, and had recently been specified as such by John Locke in his *Second Treatise*, § 91 (Locke, *Treatises*, p. 326; cf. Neville, *Plato Redivivus*, p. 123). It was with these connotations in mind that Charles II had assured the Earl of Essex in 1673 that "he did not wish to be like a Grand Signior, with some mutes about him, and bags of bow-strings to strangle men, as he had a mind to it" (Burnet, *History*, 1:345). See also "The Constitution of our English Government (the best in the World) is no Arbitrary *Tyranny*, like the Turkish Grand Seignior's, or the French King's, whose Wills (or rather *Lusts*) dispose of the Lives and Fortunes of their unhappy Subjects" (Henry Care, *English Liberties* [1680], p. 1; see also p. 149; see also Sidney, *Discourses*, p. 58; Anonymous, *The Picture of a High-Flyer* [1704], p. 2; Guy Miège, *Utrum Horum?* [1705], p. 15; Matthew Tindal, *Four Discourses* [1709], p. 12; George Hickes, *A Collection of Sermons* [1713], p. 14). In the West Country the suppression of Monmouth's rebellion by James II had been so severe that, according to Sir Robert Cotton speaking in the House of Commons on 14 May 1689, "those in the West did see such a shambles as made them think they had a Turk, rather than a Christian, to their King" (quoted in Speck, *Revolutionaries*, p. 55), and the language of Oriental despotism was applied by Whigs to the reigns of the later Stuart kings (e.g., Anonymous, *Secret History*, p. 38). Louis XIV was sometimes referred to as "the Grand Seignior of *Versailles*" (e.g., *A Collection of State Tracts*, 3 vols. [1705–7], 1:197), and in the 1730s this language could also be applied to Walpole and the Hanoverians, as shown by the title of the satirical pamphlet *A Specimen of Arbitrary Power; in a Speech made by the Grand Seignior to his Janizaries* (1731). The rule of the Grand Seignior was closely associated by English writers of this period with outrages and atrocities perpetrated by professional, standing troops:

> Tho' the Empire of the *Turks* be kept in one Family, yet it does not always descend to the first born or the next in blood, for the Reigning Emperour nominates and appoints one of his Sons, who is reckon'd fittest for Government, to be his Successor, passing by the rest of his Brethren. But he is not saluted Emperour, until that after his Father's death, he be confirmed by the Pretorian Bands commonly called Janizaries, and that they swear fealty to him; Then and not before he is Saluted their grand Seignior or Sultan. In this Interval these Janizaries commit horrid abuses, Spoil and pillage the Houses of all the Inhabitants at *Constantinople*, especially of the Christians there, Seize their effects; Murders, Adulteries, Rapes, and all Villainies Rage every where with impunity, and without check or controul. Nor wou'd

He abetted the *Irish* Massacre,[52] as appears by their producing a Commission under the Great Seal of *Scotland*,[53] by the Letter of *Charles* the 2*d*[54] in favor of the Marquess of *Antrim*, by his stopping the Succors that the Parliament sent to reduce *Ireland* six months under the Walls of *Chester*,[55] by his entring into a Treaty with the Rebels after he had ingaged his Faith to the Parliament to the contrary, and bringing over many thousands of them to fight against his People.[56] It is endless to

---

they pay Allegiance to their new Emperour till such time, as he swear to them Solemnly to indemnifie them for all past crimes. (Sir Thomas Craig, *Concerning the Right of Succession to the Kingdom of England* [1703], pp. 35–36)

52. On 22 October 1641 Sir Phelim O'Neill (ca. 1604–53), a member of the Irish Parliament, had seized Charlemont Castle in Ulster, claiming that his actions were authorized by Charles I. O'Neill's followers massacred hundreds of English colonists in Ulster. The General Declaration of the rebels claimed that they had taken up arms out of "*faithfull Duty and Loyalty to his incomparable Majesty*" (Sanderson, *History*, p. 443); see also May, *History*, lib. 2, pp. 34–37 and 121, where it is insinuated that Charles both connived at the massacre and then was deliberately slow and ineffective in suppressing the rebels.

53. The Irish produced what purported to be a commission from Charles to "use all politick Ways and Means possible to possess your selves (for our Use and Service) of all the Forts, Castles and Places of Strength and Defence . . . and also to arrest and seize the Goods, Estates and Person of all the English Protestants within the said Kingdom [of Ireland] to our use." This commission would be published in 1699 in the third volume of Ludlow's *Memoirs* (Ludlow, *Memoirs*, 3:335–36).

54. On 10 July 1663 Charles II wrote a letter in support of Randal MacDonnell (1609–83), Marquess of Antrim, exonerating him from any guilt arising from his actions in the Irish massacre on the grounds that "*what he did by way of Correspondence or Compliance with the Irish Rebels, was in order to the Service of our Royal Father and warranted by his Instructions, and the Trust reposed in him; and that the Benefit thereof accrued to the Service of the Crown*" (Ludlow, *Memoirs*, 3:357).

55. In September 1642 Robert Sidney, Earl of Leicester, complained to Algernon Percy, Earl of Northumberland, that Charles had commanded cavalry horses intended to suppress the rebels in Ireland to be handed over to the quarter-master general of the royalist army, Ralph Errington, who took them to Chester (Ludlow, *Memoirs*, 3:341–45; Sanderson, *History*, p. 561).

56. In 1645 Charles had empowered the Earl of Glamorgan

to treat and conclude with the confederate Roman *Catholicks in our Kingdom of* Ireland, *if upon necessitie any thing be condiscended unto, wherein our Lieutenant cannot so well be seen in, as not fit for us for the present publickly to own: therefore we charge you to proceed according to this our Warrant with all possible secrecie: and whatsoever you shall engage your self upon such valuable considerations as you in your*

enumerat all the Oppressions of his Reign; but having no Army to support him, his Tyranny was precarious, and at last his ruin. Tho he extorted great Sums from the People, yet it was with so much difficulty, that it did him little good. Besides, he spent so much in foolish Wars and Expeditions, that he was always behind-hand; yet he often attemted to raise an Army.

Upon pretence of the *Spanish* and *French* War he rais'd many thousand Men, who liv'd upon free Quarter, and rob'd and destroy'd wherever they came. But being unsuccessful in his Wars abroad, and prest by the Clamors of the People at home, he was forc'd to disband them. In 1627 he sent over 30000 *l.* to *Holland* to raise 3000 *German* Horse, to force his arbitrary Taxes; but this matter taking wind, and being examin'd by the Parliament, Orders were sent to countermand them.[57] In the 15*th* year [7] of his Reign he gave a Commission to *Strafford* to raise 8000 *Irish* to be brought into *England:* but before they could get hither, the *Scots* were in Arms for the like Oppressions, and marched into *Northumberland*, which forcing him to call a Parliament, prevented that design, and so that Army was disbanded.[58] Soon after he rais'd an Army in *England* to oppose the *Scots*, and tamper'd with them to march to *London*, and dissolve the Parliament: but this Army being composed for the most part of the Militia, and the matter being communicated to the House, who immediatly fell on the Officers that were Members, as *Ashburnham, Wilmot,*

---

judgment shall deem fit, We promise in the word of a King and Christian, to ratifie and perform the same of that which shall be granted by you, and under your Hand and Seal. The said confederate Catholicks having by their Supplies testified their zeal to our Service. (Sanderson, *History*, p. 855; cf. Coke, *Detection*, pp. 314–15)

In 1643 Irish forces had landed at Bristol to support the king (Sanderson, *History*, p. 650).

57. "The King, *January* the 30*th* [1627 O.S., i.e., 1628] granted a Privy-Seal to *Burlemach* [Philip Burlemac, a Dutch merchant operating in London], for 30000 *l.* to be returned to Sir *William Balfour*, and *John Dalbier*, for raising a thousand *German* Horse, with Arms both for Horse and Foot, to be sent into *England, February* the 28*th*, where was an Army already upon free Quarter, and after grants a Commission to 23 Lords and others to raise Money upon Impositions, or otherwise" (Coke, *Detection*, p. 200).

58. For Strafford, see above, p. 249, n. 52. Cf. Coke, *Detection*, p. 265.

Pollard,[59] &c. the design came to nothing. After this there was a Pacification between the King and the *Scots*; and in pursuance of it both Armies were disbanded. Then he went to *Scotland*, and indeavor'd to prevail with them to invade *England*; but that not doing, he sent a Message to the Parliament, desiring their concurrence in the raising 3000 *Irish* to be lent to the King of *Spain*; to which the Parliament refused to consent, believing he would make another use of them. When he came back to *London*, he pick'd out 3 or 400 dissolute Fellows out of Taverns, gaming and brothel-Houses, kept a Table for them; and with this goodly Guard all arm'd, he entred the House of Commons, sat down in the Speaker's Chair, demanding the delivery of 5 Members: But the Citizens coming down by Land and Water with Musquets upon their Shoulders to defend the Parliament, he attemted no further. This so inrag'd the House, that they chose a Guard to defend themselves against future Insults, and the King soon after left *London*.[60] Som time before this began the *Irish* Rebellion, where the *Irish* pretended the King's Authority, and shew'd the

59. John Ashburnham (1602/3–1671), courtier and politician; MP for Hastings; proceeded against by Parliament for contempt, 6 May 1642; discharged and disabled, 5 February 1644; estate sequestrated, 14 September 1644. Henry Wilmot (1613–58), first Earl of Rochester; Royalist army officer and courtier; MP for Tamworth; involved in the Army plots of 1641; committed to the Tower, 14 June 1641; expelled from the House, 9 December 1641. Sir Hugh Pollard (1603–66), royalist army officer and courtier; MP for Bere Alston; involved in the Army plots of 1641; proceeded against for misprision of treason, 9 December 1641; expelled from the House.

60. On 3 January 1642 Charles instructed the attorney-general, Sir Edward Herbert, to make a statement to the House of Commons accusing five members of the Commons and one member of the Lords of high treason. The following day he attempted to arrest the accused men as they sat in Parliament. But his intentions became apparent and the intended victims were forewarned. The MPs slipped away as the king, attended by about 100 troopers, entered the palace of Westminster. In the days that followed, Charles could not move out of the inner sanctums of Whitehall without hearing jeering, angry crowds, and he therefore withdrew: "The King now resident at *Hampton-Court*, seemed extremely distasted at the Citie, and pretended the reasons of his absence from Parliament to be fear for his Person, by reason of Tumults that might be raised: but true it is, after this time, he never could be brought neer the Citie or Parliament either in body or minde" (May, *History*, lib. 2, p. 41). Cf. Neville, *Plato Redivivus*, pp. 149–50; May, *History*, lib. 2, pp. 21–28; and Ludlow, *Memoirs*, 1:22–27.

Great Seal to justify themselves; which, whether true or false, raised such a jealousy in the People, that he was forced to consent to leave the management of that War to the Parliament: yet he afterwards sent a Message to them, telling them he would go to *Ireland* in Person; and acquainted them, that he had issued out Commissions for raising 2000 Foot and 200 Horse in *Cheshire* for his Guard, which they protested against, and prevented it. By this we may see what Force was thought sufficient in his Reign to inslave the Nation, and the frequent Attemts to get it.

Then the Civil Wars broke out between him and his People, in which many bloody Battels were fought; two of the most consi[8]derable were those of *Newbury* and *Naseby*,[61] both won by new Soldiers, the first by the *London* Militia, and the latter by an unexperienc'd Army, which the King used to call in derision the *New Nodel*.[62] And som years after, the Battel of *Worcester*[63] was in a great measure won by the Country Militia, for which *Cromwel* discharged them with anger and contemt, as knowing them Instruments unfit to promote his Tyrannical Designs. At last by the fate of the War the King became a Prisoner,[64] and the Parliament

61. There were two battles of Newbury in the Civil War. On 20 September 1643, 6,000 men fell in battle when the day was won by Parliamentary forces; on 27 October 1644, the Royalists overcame their Parliamentary opponents and went on to relieve Donnington Castle. Trenchard refers to the first of these battles. For the Battle of Naseby, see above, p. 167, n. 28.

62. A contemptuous play on the phrase "New Model": "The King's Party look'd upon the new Army and new Officers with such Contempt, that the *New Model* was by them in Scorn commonly call'd *The New Noddle*" (Laurence Echard, *The History of England*, 3 vols. [1718], 2:525). Charles's use of the phrase was notorious at the time. See also John Price, *Clerico-Classicum* (1649), pp. 54–55; Richard Hubberthorn, *The Common-Wealth's Remembrancer* (1659), pp. 15, 25; and Bulstrode Whitlocke, *Memorials of the English Affairs* (1682), p. 135. The memory of it endured among Whigs of a later generation; see John Oldmixon, *An Essay on Criticism* (1728), p. 46.

63. In 1651 Charles II, attempting to regain his throne, had assembled an army of Scots and had marched into England. By 22 August he had reached Worcester, where he was met by a numerically far superior Parliamentary army under the command of Cromwell, and was defeated on 4 September. Charles escaped from the battlefield and went into exile in France.

64. Trenchard has, slightly confusingly, now reverted to the events of the 1640s. Charles I was a prisoner from the spring of 1646 until his execution in 1649: first of the Scots at Newcastle (13 May 1646–3 February 1647); then of the English

treated with him while in that condition, and at the same time voted that som part of the Army should be disbanded, and others sent to *Ireland* to reduce that Kingdom; upon which the Army chose Agitators among themselves, who presented a Petition to both Houses,[65] that they would proceed to settle the Affairs of the Kingdom, and declare that no part of the Army should be disbanded till that was don. But finding their Petition resented, they sent and seiz'd the King's Person from the Parliaments Commissioners, drew up a Charge of High Treason against eleven Principal Members for indeavoring to disband the Army, entred into a privat Treaty with the King: but he not complying with their demands, they seized *London;* and notwithstanding the Parliament had voted the King's Concessions a ground for a future Settlement, they resolved to put him to Death, and in order therto purged the House, as they called it, that is, placed Guards upon them, and excluded all Members that were for agreeing with the King; and then they cut off his Head.

After this they let the Parliament govern for five years, who made their Name famous thro the whole Earth, conquered their Enemies in *England, Scotland* and *Ireland;* reduced the Kingdom of *Portugal* to their own Terms; recovered our Reputation at Sea; overcame the *Dutch* in several famous Battels; secured our Trade, and managed the public Expences with so much frugality, that no Estates were gained by privat Men upon the public Miseries; and at last were passing an Act for their own

---

Parliament at Holdenby House in Northamptonshire (7 February–4 June 1647); then of the New Model Army and its civilian allies at a series of great houses in East Anglia and Hertfordshire (4 June–24 August 1647); then at Hampton Court (24 August–11 November 1647); then on the Isle of Wight at Carisbrooke Castle and then Hurst Castle (16 November 1647–12 December 1648); and finally under strict guard in his palaces in and around London (15 December 1648–30 January 1649).

65. On 20 November 1648 six officers presented a remonstrance to the House of Commons. Inter alia it demanded that "an end might be put to this Parliament, and a new representative chosen of the people, for the governing and preserving the whole body of the nation; that no King might be hereafter admitted but upon election of the people, and as upon trust for the people, who should be likewise limited and restrained by the representative; with many other unpractical particulars, which troubled the Parliament the less for their incoherence, and impossibility to be reduced to practice" (Clarendon, *History*, 4:462–63).

Dissolution, and settling the Nation in a free and impartial Common-wealth; of which the Army being afraid, thought it necessary to dissolve them, and accordingly *Cromwel* next day[66] called two Files of Musque-teers into the House, and pulled the Speaker out of the Chair, behaving himself like a Madman, vilifying the Members, and calling one a Whoremaster, another a Drunkard, [9] bidding the Soldiers take away that fools bauble the Mace; and so good night to the Parliament.

When they had don this Act of violence, the Council of Officers set up a new form of Government,[67] and chose a certain number of Persons out of every County and City of *England, Scotland* and *Ireland:* and these they invested with the Supreme Power, but soon after expelled them, and then *Cromwel* set up himself,[68] and framed a new Instrument of

66. Trenchard describes the events of 19 April 1653, when Cromwell, exasper-ated by the Rump Parliament and aware of discontent among the army, cleared the chamber with the help of some forty musketeers and carried off the mace (the symbol of Parliament's authority) and all the papers on the table (i.e., under debate and consideration). Clarendon describes how Cromwell told Parliament "that he came thither to put an end to their power and authority" and that "thereupon an-other officer, with some files of musketeers, entered into the House, and stayed there till all members walked out; Cromwell reproaching many of the members by name, as they went out of the House, with their vices and corruptions . . . and having given the mace to an officer to be safely kept, he caused the doors to be locked up" (XIV.8–9; Clarendon, *History*, 5:277–78). Trenchard seems to be fol-lowing Roger Coke, who in his account of these events quoted Cromwell's notori-ous and contemptuous command to *"Take away that Fool's Bawble, the Mace"* (Coke, *Detection*, p. 362).

67. Following the expulsion of the Rump Parliament, the council of army offi-cers set up a council of state of seven senior officers (headed by Cromwell) and six civilians to run civil government and foreign policy on a day-to-day basis. At the same time, the council of officers themselves took responsibility for constitutional reform, eventually settling on a constituent assembly made up of a cross-section of men drawn from "the various forms of godliness in this nation." Gathered churches around the land spontaneously sent in lists of names, but the council of officers seems to have acted principally on its own knowledge in the final nomina-tion of 140 men to serve in the assembly. It was an assembly, not a parliament, and its task was to prepare the English people for self-government.

68. On 15 December 1653 Cromwell was sworn in as head of state. Trenchard exaggerates the authority bestowed on Cromwell by this new constitution, the Instrument of Government. In most matters of governance Cromwell was con-strained to act with and through the majority will of a council of state consisting of between thirteen and twenty-one members, over whose membership he had limited

Government by a Protector and a House of Commons, in pursuance of which he called a Parliament. But they not answering his Expectations, he excluded all that would not subscribe his Instrument; and those that remained, not proving for his purpose neither, he dissolved them with a great deal of opprobrious Language. He then divided *England* into several Districts or Divisions, and placed Major Generals or Intendents over them, who governed like so many Bashaws,[69] decimating[70] the Cavaliers, and raising Taxes at their pleasure.[71] Then forsooth he had a mind to

---

control. He and the council were given the authority to make law for the period before the next ensuing Parliament, after which he was required to make law in and through Parliament, with a limited power of veto over bills approved by them. The Instrument did, however, create a standing army: see the introduction, pp. xxi–xxii.

69. Turkish officers of high rank, such as military commanders or provincial governors (*OED*, s.v. "pasha").

70. A Roman military punishment, in which one in ten of a disgraced unit would be executed; here used more loosely to refer to severe and arbitrary punishment. Cf. Machiavelli, *The Art of War*, bk. 6 (Machiavelli, *Chief Works*, 2:690).

71. Trenchard's narrative has now advanced some eighteen months:

> The abject failure of the royalist risings in the spring of 1655 showed how acquiescent the English had become, but it also showed how little active support Cromwell could count upon among the county élites. If few rose in arms to challenge the regime, few rose in arms to support it. Everyone outside the army waited upon events. Cromwell was persuaded by Lambert to embark on a bold experiment. If people disliked the regime because there were too many soldiers and too much tax, then let both be halved and replaced by efficient, well-trained and equipped "select militias," made up mainly of demobilized veterans and paid for by a 10 per cent "decimation" tax on the income of all convicted royalists. And let the scheme be under the management of eleven senior officers (the major-generals) each responsible for a bloc of counties, and assisted by bodies of activist shire commissioners. (*ODNB*)

Cf. Clarendon:

> But that which troubled him [Cromwell] most was the distemper in his army, where he knew there were many troops more at the disposal of that party that would destroy him than at his own. . . . He resolved therefore upon an expedient which should provide for all inconveniences, as well amongst the people as in the army. He constituted out of the persons who he thought were most devoted to his person a body of major generals; that is, he assigned to such a single person so many counties, to be under his command as their major general: so that all England was put under the absolute power of twelve men, neither of them having any power in the jurisdiction of another, but every man in those counties which were committed to his

make himself King,[72] and called another Parliament to that purpose, after his usual manner secluding such Members as he did not like. To this Assembly he offered another Instrument of Government, which was by a Representative of the People, a 2*d* House composed of 70 Members in the nature of a House of Lords, and a single Person; and left a Blank for what name he should be called, which this worthy Assembly filled up with that of King, addressed to *Cromwel* that he would be pleased to accept it, and gave him power to nominat the Members of the Other House. This the great Officers of the Army resented, for it destroyed all their hopes of being Tyrants in their turn, and therefore addressed the Parliament against the Power and Government of a King, which made *Cromwel* decline that Title, and content himself with a greater Power[73] under the name of Protector. Afterwards he nam'd the *Other House*, as it

---

charge had all that authority which was before scattered among committee-men, justices of peace, and several other officers. (Clarendon, *History*, 6:16)

Cromwell defended the innovation, which entailed the raising of taxes without Parliamentary consent, in a speech of 17 September, 1656:

> I say there was a little thing invented, which was the erecting of your Major-Generals . . . we invented this, so justifiable to necessity, so honest in every respect. Truly, if ever I think anything were honest, this was, as anything that ever I knew; and I could as soon venture my life with it as anything I ever undertook. . . . And if there be any man that hath a face looking averse to this, I dare pronounce him to be a man against the interest of England. (Cromwell, *Speeches*, 4:269)

For further commentary, see Schwoerer, *Armies*, pp. 62–64.

72. Alderman Sir Christopher Packe proposed on 23 February 1657 that Cromwell be king under a contract that modified the terms of the Instrument, strengthening his personal authority as against that of the council but prescribing his power in relation to the ancient constitution and unshackled Parliaments. Cromwell was willing to accept everything except the title of king, which he regarded as "blasted" by God. In this Cromwell was perhaps both wily and pious, for the proposal that he should be made king, notwithstanding its apparent servility, was at bottom an attempt to specify and thus to ascertain the scope and jurisdiction of his office. The powers and duties of a king of England were well known; those of a Lord Protector remained to be defined.

73. As Lord Protector Cromwell enjoyed the power to nominate his successor, a power not possessed by any king of England either before or since. In other respects, however, the powers of the Lord Protector were modeled closely on those of the king.

was called, for the most part out of the Officers of the Army; but even this Parliament not pleasing him, he dissolved them in a fury, and govern'd the Nation without any Parliament at all till he died.

After his death the Army set up his Son *Richard*,[74] who called a new Parliament; but their procedings being not agreable to [10] the humor of the Soldiery, they forced the Protector to dissolve them: then they deposed him, and took the power into their own hands; but being unable to wield it, they restored the Commonwealth, and soon after expelled them again, because they would not settle the Military Sword Independent of the Civil: then they governed the Nation by a Council of War at *Wallingford*-House, and chose a Committee of Safety for the executive part of the Government; but that Whim lasted but a little time before they chose Conservators of Liberty; and that not doing neither, they agreed that every Regiment should choose two Representatives, and this worthy Council should settle the Nation; when they met, somtimes they were for calling a new Parliament, somtimes for restoring the old, which was at last don. By this means all things fell into Confusion,[75] which gave *Monk* an opportunity of marching into *England*, where he acted his part so dexterously, that he restor'd the King with part of that Army which had cut off his Father's Head.[76]

This is a true and lively Example of a Government with an Army; an Army that was raised in the cause, and for the sake of Liberty; composed for the most part of Men of Religion and Sobriety. If this Army could commit such violences upon a Parliament always successful, that had acquired so much Reputation both at home and abroad, at a time when the whole People were trained in Arms, and the Pulse of the Nation beat high for Liberty; what are we to expect if in a future Age an ambitious Prince should arise with a dissolute and debauched Army, a flattering

74. Richard Cromwell (1626–1712); Lord Protector of England, September 1658–May 1659. An object of Whiggish contempt: see Toland, *Restoring*, p. 16.

75. A compressed account of the chaotic short tenure of Richard Cromwell as Lord Protector, and the brief interim between his fall and the restoration of Charles II.

76. See above, p. 48, n. 119.

Clergy, a prostitute Ministry, a Bankrupt House of L——ds, a Pensioner House of C——ns,[77] and a slavish and corrupted Nation?

By this means came in *Charles* the Second, a luxurious effeminat Prince, a deep Dissembler, and if not a Papist himself, yet a great favorer of them: but the People had suffered so much from the Army, that he was received with the utmost Joy and Transport.[78] The Parliament in the Honymoon passed what Laws he pleased, gave a vast Revenue for life,[79] being three times as much as any of his Predecessors ever enjoyed, and several Millions besides to be spent in his Pleasures. This [11] made him conceive vaster hopes of Arbitrary Power than any that went before him; and in order to it he debauched and enervated the whole Kingdom: His Court was a scene of Adulteries, Drunkenness, and Irreligion, appearing more like Stews, or the Feasts of *Bacchus*,[80] than the Family of a Chief

77. See above, p. 40, n. 99.

78. See the entry in John Evelyn's diary for 29 May 1660:

This day came in his Majestie *Charles* the 2d to London after a sad, & long Exile, and Calamitous Suffering both of the King & Church: being 17 yeares: This was also his Birthday, and with a Triumph of above 20000 horse & foote, brandishing their swords and shouting with unexpressable joy: The wayes straw'd with flowers, the bells ringing, the streetes hung with Tapissry, fountaines running with wine: . . . I stood in the strand, & beheld it, & blessed God: And all this without one drop of bloud, & by that very army, which rebell'd against him: but it was the Lords doing, *et mirabile in oculis nostris*: for such a Restauration was never seene in the mention of any history, antient or modern, since the returne of the *Babylonian* Captivity, nor so joyfull a day, & so bright, ever seene in this nation: this happning when to expect or effect it, was past all humane policy. (Evelyn, *Diary*, 3:246; cf. Jones, *Tragical History*, pp. 373–74, and Ludlow, *Memoirs*, 3:1, 21)

79. In 1661 Parliament gave Charles II an income of (nominally) £1,200,000 per annum. However, the customs and excise duties on which the grant was based in fact yielded some £300,000 per annum less than this (Kenyon, *Stuart England*, p. 198). Ironically, given the tribulations of his father on that score, these grants included tonnage and poundage (see above, pp. 121–22, nn. 15 and 16).

80. Bacchus is one of the names of Dionysos, in Greek mythology the son of Zeus and Semele, and the god of wine. In ancient Greece the feasts of Bacchus (or bacchanalia) were orgiastic revels involving dancing, intoxication, violence, and sexual licence: see William Howell, *An Institution of General History* (1661), p. 679. They had spread to Italy by the second century B.C., and were suppressed by a decree of the Senate in 186 B.C. The sexual irregularity of Charles II's court was notorious, and the king himself reputed to be "almost Drowned in Voluptuousness

Magistrate: and in a little time the Contagion spread thro the whole Nation, that it was out of the fashion not to be leud, and scandalous not to be a public Enemy: which has bin the occasion of all the Miseries that have since happened, and I am afraid will not be extinguished but by our ruin. He was no sooner warm in his Seat,[81] but he rejected an advantageous Treaty of Commerce[82] which *Oliver* made with *France*, as don by a Usurper; suffer'd the *French* to lay Impositions upon all our Goods, which amounted to a Prohibition, insomuch that they got a Million a year from us in the overbalance of Trade. He sold that important Fortress of *Dunkirk*, let the *French* seize St. *Christophers* and other places in North *America*.[83]

---

and Sensual Delights" (Jones, *Secret History*, p. 52): cf. Pope, *Imitations of Horace*, Ep. II.i, ll. 139–54. Cf. also Machiavelli, *Discourses*, bk. 3, chap. 49.

81. I.e., comfortably settled into his position as king (*OED*, s.v. "warm," 7, and "seat," 8a).

82. Cromwell had sought and maintained an alliance with France as an element in his overall foreign policy of resisting Spain, and this alliance was renewed in the spring of 1658: "Tho *Cromwell* play'd the Fool in making War upon *Spain*, and Peace with *France*, yet he made a more advantageous Treaty of Commerce for the *English* to *France*, than before they had: I have not seen it, but had this from our *English* Merchants who traded to *France*" (Coke, *Detection*, p. 404; see also Toland, *Restoring*, p. 5, on the "preposterous Politicks" of Cromwell). Trenchard is here again relying on Roger Coke: "And the more to endear himself with his Brother of *France*, the King rejected the Advantageous Treaty of Commerce which *Oliver* made with *France*, as done by an Usurper" (Coke, *Detection*, p. 426).

83. In October 1662 the English government sold Dunkirk to the French for 5 million livres (according to some accounts, 2,500,000 livres [Jones, *Secret History*, p. 17]). It was a bitterly unpopular measure, which aroused dark suspicions concerning Charles's motives:

The Want of Money a little retarded the Marriage of the Princess with *Monsieur;* but this might be easily help'd, if the King would give up *Dunkirk* to the *French*, whereby he might pay 200000 *l*. for his Sister's Portion (which was more than his Father had with his Mother) and also receive 200000 *l*. more for himself. Nor was this all, he might save the Charges of maintaining a Garison there; yet the Parliament in the Hereditary Excise, allowed him 60000 *l*. *per Annum* for the Support of it. I do not find this mentioned in the Body of the Act, yet several Members assured me, it was so intended in the passing the Act. All this the King agreed to, and so *Dunkirk* and *Mardike* Fort were given up to the *French*, against all the Laws of *Humanity*, *Justice* and

He began a foolish and unjust War with the *Dutch;*[84] and tho the Parliament gave him vast Sums to maintain it, yet he spent so much upon his Vices,[85] that they got great advantages of us, and burnt our Fleet at *Chatham.*[86] At last he made as dishonorable a Peace with them, as he had

---

Prudence. (Coke, *Detection,* p. 429; see also Jones, *Secret History,* pp. 12–17; Jones, *Tragical History,* pp. 374, 376; and Ludlow, *Memoirs,* 3:118)

In the summer of 1666, the French had driven the English out of some of their territories in the West Indies: "The *English* and *Dutch* thus engaged at Wars at home, the *French* King, instead of sending his invisible Fleet into the Channel to assist the *Dutch,* sends a visible Fleet to the subduing the *English* in their Plantations in the *Leeward Islands,* and almost totally expell'd the *English* out of *St. Christophers,* and interrupted them in their Trade to their other Islands, and assumed a Soveraignty in those Seas" (Coke, *Detection,* p. 460).

84. The Second Anglo-Dutch War (1665–67). Cf. Sidney's bitterly sarcastic comments on the "justice of the war made against Holland in the year 1665" (Sidney, *Discourses,* p. 279).

85. The harmful impact of Charles's costly vices on the public finances was a topic in the satirical literature of the time. See, e.g., the opening of the parodic mock-speech to Parliament, sometimes attributed to Marvell, which had circulated in MS since 1675, and which would first be published in *Poems on Affairs of State,* vol. 3 (1704):

I can beare my owne straites with patience, but my Lord Treasurer doeth protest to mee, that ye Revenue, as it now standeth, will not serve him, & mee too; one of Us must pinch for it, if you do not helpe Us. I must speake freely to you, I am in incumbrances, for besides my Mistresses in present Service, my Reformado Mistresses lye hard upon mee. I have a pritty good Estate, I confesse; but God's-Fish I have a great charge upon itt. here is my Lord Treasurer can tell you, that all ye Money designed for ye next Summers Guard must of necessity be applyed to ye next yeares Cradles, & Swadling Clothes; what shall wee doe for Ships then? I onely hint it to you, for that is your businesse, & not mine: I know by experience, I can live without them. I lived ten yeares abroad without Ships, & had never better health in my life: but how you will doe without them I leave to your selves to judge, & therefore mention that onely by ye Bye, I do not insist upon itt. (Marvell, *Prose Works,* 1:461)

86. On 9 June 1667 the Dutch fleet entered the Thames and burned a number of ships of the Royal Navy:

The *Dutch* found an easy Passage, after they broke the Boom which lay cross the River; for no Fort was then finished at *Sheerness,* and that at *Upnor* ruin'd for want of Repair: however, the Duke [of Albemarle] put some Guns into it, which shooting high, little damaged the *Dutch* in the Passage:

don a War; a perpetual reproach to our Country, that our Reputation at Sea should be sunk to so low an eb as to be baffled by that Nation, who but a few years before had sent a blank Paper to the Parliament, to prescribe to them what Laws they pleased.[87] During this War the City of *London* was fired, not without violent suspicions that the Firebals were prepared at *Whitehall.*[88] Soon after this he entred into the Triple Alliance to oppose the growing greatness of *France,* and received a great Sum from the Parliament to maintain it, which he made use of to break the same League; sent Mr. *Coventry* to *Sweden* to dissolve it; and entred into a strict Alliance with *France,* which was sealed with his Sister's blood.[89] In

---

So the *Dutch* fired the *Royal James, London,* and *Royal Oak;* and the *Henry* being afloat, run so violently upon *Rochester-bridg,* the Tide forcing her, as endanger'd the breaking of it; and the *Royal Charles* was carried off by the *Dutch.* (Coke, *Detection,* p. 468; cf. Jones, *Secret History,* p. 65; Jones, *Tragical History,* p. 376; Sidney, *Discourses,* p. 209; and Ludlow, *Memoirs,* 3:200–202)

87. In 1654, at the conclusion of the First Anglo-Dutch War.
88. Trenchard refers to the Great Fire of London (2–5 September 1666).

The Firing of the City of *London* so soon succeeding the Division of the Fleet, caused a strange Consternation, not only in Mens Minds in *London,* but all the Nation over, That there were Designs to ruin the Nation on Shore as at Sea; whereupon infinite varieties of idle Tales and Stories were printed, as well as said; so as tho a general Fear of Plots against the Nation was evident, yet in this Confusion, the Cause from whence the City of *London* became fired was not only smothered, but the Means of searching into it prevented. (Coke, *Detection,* p. 461)

Trenchard's insinuation that Charles II was instrumental in causing the fire implicitly compares him with Nero, who had allegedly and infamously set fire to Rome in A.D. 64. David Jones attributed the fire to French influence operating through the Duke of York, who in 1666 was "brought quite over to the *French* Interest" (Jones, *Secret History,* pp. 25–26).

89. The Triple Alliance, an alliance between England, Holland, and Sweden, brokered by Arlington and Sir William Temple at The Hague in January 1668, and designed to check the expansionist policy of Louis XIV; see Marvell, *Prose Works,* 2:252, 336, 345, 359, and Toland, *Restoring,* p. 40. Henry Coventry (1617/18–1686), politician and diplomat.

The King who was so great in the Love of his Subjects and Parliament for the Triple League, and had received such vast Sums for it, now at the Instance of the *French* King sends Mr. *Henry Coventry* to the Court of *Sweden* to dissolve it, which he did so effectually, that that King not only stood

conjunction with them he made a new War upon *Holland*, to extirpat Liberty and the Protestant Religion; but knowing the Parliament were averse to the War, and would not support him in it, he attemted before any War declared to seize their *Smirna* Fleet,[90] shut up the Exchequer,[91]

Neuter at the beginning of the War with the *Dutch*, but in it joined with the *French* King against the Confederates; and this Success Mr. *Coventry* had, that for this Business which put all *Christendom* into a Flame, he was by the King made principal Secretary of State, and it may be presented with his fine Ranger's Place in *Enfield-Chase* too, and that perhaps with thrice more by the *French* King: Whereas Sir *William Temple*, who was the principal Instrument in the Peace at *Nimeguen*, lost 2200 *l.* by it, and his only Recompence was to be Secretary of State in Mr. *Coventry's* Place, if Sir *William* would give him 10000 *l.* for it. (Coke, *Detection*, pp. 477–78)

In March 1661, Charles's sister Henriette Anne (1644–70) had married the younger brother of Louis XIV, the duc d'Orléans (or "Monsieur," as he was known). The marriage was not a happy one, and on 29 June 1670 she suffered acute pain and claimed to have been poisoned by some iced chicory water. Almost certainly she died of peritonitis, but Trenchard alludes darkly to these rumors of poisoning. Once again, in this suspicion he follows Roger Coke (Coke, *Detection*, p. 474; see also Marvell, *Prose Works*, 2:243–44, and Jones, *Secret History*, pp. 67–79, esp. 78–79).

90. In the spring of 1672 the Dutch fleet from Smyrna, laden with a rich cargo, lay at anchor off the Isle of Wight. On 13 March Sir Robert Holmes (ca. 1622–92) attacked this fleet, and captured two vessels while also suffering severe losses. This action triggered the Third Anglo-Dutch War (1672–74), which was declared on 18 March. Coke saw this bungled operation, and the shutting up of the Exchequer, as the consequence of the policy of the Cabal (see above, p. 105, n. 101):

The first Result of this sacred Conclave, was the shutting up of the Exchequer, wherein the Bankers (who formerly had furnished the King with mighty Sums of Money at extorsive Interest) had lodged between 13 and 1400000 *l.* of the Subjects Money; this was in *January 167 1/2*. One would think these Monies added to the Aids granted in the last Session of Parliament, with those received from *France*, might have carried on the War against the *Dutch* on the King's Part; but to make sure, the Fleet for which the Parliament gave such vast Sums, to be equal with the *French* or *Dutch*, is set out under Sir *Robert Holmes* to surprize the *Dutch Smirna*-Fleet, which he vainly attempted the thirteenth and fourteenth of *March 1671/2*; and to sanctify so Heroick an Act; at this very time the Declaration of Indulgence was printed and published the fifteenth. (Coke, *Detection*, p. 478; see also Marvell, *Prose Works*, 2:255–56, and the mordant sarcasm of Sidney, *Discourses*, p. 279)

91. See above, p. 32, n. 77.

and became so mean as to be a Pensio[12]ner to *France*, [92] from whence his Predecessors with Swords in their hands had so often exacted Tribute. [93] He not only suffered, but assisted them to arrive at that pitch of Greatness, which all *Europe* since hath sufficiently felt and lamented. He sent over ten thousand Men to assist in subduing *Flanders* and *Germany*, by whose help they did several considerable Actions. [94] He sent them Timber, Seamen, Ship-Carpenters, and Models, contrary to the Policy of all Nations; which rais'd their Naval Force to a degree almost equal to our own: and for their exercise, he suffered them to take multitudes of *English* Ships by their Privateers, without so much as demanding satisfaction.

During this War he issued out a Declaration suspending the Penal Laws, which appears to be designed in favor of the Papists, by his directing a Bill afterwards to be stolen away out of the House of Lords, for indulging Protestant Dissenters, whom he persecuted violently most of

92. On 22 May 1670 Charles signed the secret Treaty of Dover with France, under the terms of which he received payments from Louis XIV in return for military help against the Dutch and a public declaration of his conversion to Roman Catholicism. See Jones, *Secret History*, p. 55.

93. A reference to English victories of the late middle ages, such as Crécy (1346), Poitiers (1356), and Agincourt (1415). Note Trenchard's careful choice of the word "Predecessors," rather than "forebears" or "ancestors"; the implicit denial of consanguinity makes the Stuarts exceptional among the otherwise heroic and martial English royal dynasties.

94. Charles had contributed soldiers to assist the French against the Dutch, and these troops had acquitted themselves well: "To these in the *French* Service does Sir *William* [Temple] and the *Germans* too ascribe the Glory of all the *French* Actions, who not only in *Turenne's* Life, but at his Death, saved the whole *French* Army" (Coke, *Detection*, p. 496). Marvell was indignant about the arrangement and detected a sinister covert purpose behind it:

> Therefore that such an absurdity as the ordering of Affairs abroad, according to the Interest of our Nation might be avoided, the English, Scotch and Irish Regiments, that were already in the French Service, were not only to be kept in their full Complement, but new numbers of Souldiers daily transported thither, making up in all, (as is related) at least a constant Body of *Ten thousand Men*, of his Majesties Subjects, and which oftentimes turned the Fortune of Battle on the French side by their Valour. . . . it was indeed a good way to train up an Army, under the French *Discipline* and *Principles*, who might be ready seasoned upon occasion in England, to be called back and execute the same Counsels. (Marvell, *Prose Works*, 2:278–79)

his Reign, while he both countenanced and preferred Papists, broke the Act of Settlement in *Ireland*, restored them to their Estates, issued forth a Proclamation giving the Papists liberty to inhabit in Corporations, and married the Duke of *York* not only to a Papist, but one in the *French* Interest, notwithstanding the repeated Addresses of the Parliament to the contrary.[95] It was in this Reign that that cursed and detestable Policy was much improved of bribing Parliaments,[96] by distributing all the great Imployments in *England* among them, and supplying the want of places with Grants of Lands and Mony. No Man could be preferred to any Imployment in Church or State, till he had declared himself an open Enemy to our Constitution, by asserting despotic Power under that nonsensical Phrase of *Passive Obedience*, which was more preach'd up than all the Laws of God and Man.[97] The Hellish Popish Plot was stifled, proved

95. Trenchard here attacks the religious policy of Charles II, which he depicts as favorable to Roman Catholicism. The future James II married Mary of Modena (1658–1718) on 30 September 1673. Modena was a client state of France. Coke saw this marriage as orchestrated by Louis XIV:

> But that the Catholick Design might take deeper Root and Continuance, the Duke of *York*'s Sons being dead, and the Princesses his Daughters being bred up in the Protestant Religion, Care must be taken to establish the Popish for the time to come; for which it was expedient the Duke should marry some Popish Princess, and to this end the Arch-Dutchess of *Inspruck* was propounded, and a Treaty entred into upon it. But tho the Princess's Religion pleased the *French* King, yet the Interest this Marriage would bring with it did not: So that tho the Treaty were far advanced, yet the *French* King (who ruled all the Roast) propounded the Princess of *Modena* (the Daughter of a little *Italian* Prince, and a Dependant of the *French* King's, yet had a great Interest in the Court of *Rome*) and this, against all Endeavours of the Parliament, and to the Dishonour of the Treaty with the Arch-Dutchess, prevailed, the *French* King having adopted her a Daughter of *France*, and given her a Portion. (Coke, *Detection*, pp. 476–77; see also pp. 499–500)

96. Charles's policy of procuring a compliant House of Commons by means of bribery was a frequent topic of Whig indignation: "For the Support of this holy Catholick Design, stood my Lord Treasurer *Clifford*, and a new Band of Parliament-Pensioners, never before heard of in *England*, at Board and Wages: but these being a kind of Land-Privateers, are to tax the Country to pay themselves, and to do whatsoever shall be commanded, or no Purchase no Pay" (Coke, *Detection*, p. 490; cf. Downie, *Harley*, p. 26). Cf. above, p. 40, n. 99.

97. For "passive obedience," see above, p. 6, n. 9.

since too true by fatal experience;[98] and in the room of it Protestant ones were forged, and Men trapan'd[99] into others, as the Meal-Tub, *Fitz Harris's*, the *Rye-House, Newmarket,* and *Black-Heath* Plots:[100] and by these Pretences, and the help of packt Judges and Juries, they butchered som of the best Men in *England*,[101] set immoderat Fines upon others, gave probable suspicion of cutting the Lord *Essex's* Throat:[102] and to finish our destruction, they took away the Char[13]ters, as fast as they were able, of

98. In 1678 Titus Oates (1649–1705), a renegade Anglican clergyman and inveterate impostor, alleged that Jesuits were planning the assassination of Charles II in order to bring his overtly Roman Catholic brother, the Duke of York (later James II), to the throne. The murder of the justice of the peace to whom Oates had made a sworn deposition of his evidence on 6 September 1678, Sir Edmund Berry Godfrey (1621–78), induced a moral panic that led to the execution of some 35 innocent people. For the suspicions surrounding the death of Charles II, see Jones, *Tragical History*, pp. 378–82.

99. Deceived, tricked, or otherwise misled (*OED*, s.v. "trepan"). On this "new coin'd word" see Sidney, *Discourses*, pp. 146, 195, 215.

100. The Meal-Tub plot (1680) and Fitz-Harris's plot (1681) were both attempts to implicate the dissenters in attempts to assassinate Charles II (see, respectively, Coke, *Detection*, pp. 546 and 562–64). The Rye House plot was an alleged Whig conspiracy in 1683 to assassinate Charles II on his way to Newmarket, when he would have to pass down a narrow lane by Rye House, in Hoddesdon, Hertfordshire. The leaders of the plot were the Duke of Monmouth (see above, p. 28, n. 68); Arthur Capel, Earl of Essex (see below, n. 102); Lord William Russell; Algernon Sidney (see above, p. 250, n. 56); Sir Thomas Armstrong (1633–84); Robert Ferguson (see above, p. 78, n. 16); and Lord William Howard (ca. 1630–94). The Newmarket plot was an earlier, abortive version of the Rye House plot (Anonymous, *A History of the New Plot* [1683]). The Black-Heath plot (1681) allegedly intended to raise a popular insurrection after a football match (Coke, *Detection*, p. 601; cf. Jones, *History of Europe*, p. 138).

101. Lord William Russell, Algernon Sidney, and Sir Thomas Armstrong were executed after the discovery of the Rye House plot.

102. Arthur Capel (1632–83), first Earl of Essex; politician and conspirator. Imprisoned in the Tower after the discovery of the Rye House plot, Capel was found with his throat cut on 13 July 1683. Although the coroner brought in a verdict of suicide, the fatal wound could not have been made with the small razor which was the only edged instrument Capel possessed (see Coke, *Detection*, p. 601). See also Robert Ferguson, *An Enquiry into, and Detection of the Barbarous Murther of the late Earl of Essex, or a Vindication of that Noble Person, from the Guilt and Infamy of having Destroyed Himself* (1689); Jones, *History of Europe*, pp. 138–39; and Jones, *Tragical History*, p. 378.

all the Corporations in *England*, that would not choose the Members prescribed them.[103]

103. Roger Coke explains the attempt made by the Court to remove the charter of the City of London:

> It was the latter End of *Michaelmas Term*, the great Inquest returned an *Ignoramus* upon the Bill of High Treason preferred against my Lord *Shafts-bury*, and in the Vacation all Wits were set on work how to take the Election of the Sheriffs of *London* out of the Power of the City, and no other Expedient could be found out but by taking away their Charter, which if it could be done, would not only entitle the Court to making of Sheriffs, but open a Gap to their making a House of Commons; for near 5/6 of the Commons are Burgesses and Barons of the Cinque Ports, who would not dare to contest their Charters, if the City of *London* could not hold theirs. So that in *Hilary Term* following, a *Quo Warranto* was brought against the City for two hainous Crimes, *viz.* That they had made an Address to the King for the Parliament to sit for Redress of Grievances, and to settle the Nation, (yet King *Charles* the First thought the Parliament's Vote of *non-Addresses* to him, was a Deposing of him) and that the City had raised Money towards repairing *Cheapside* Conduit, ruined by the Fire of *London*. (Coke, *Detection*, p. 600)

The policy was then quickly extended to other corporations:

> Though the City of *London*, and many other Cities in *England*, chose their Sheriffs; yet the Sheriffs of all the other Shires and Counties of *England* were named by the King: so that the King's next care was how to subvert the Constitution of *Parliament*, and like *Oliver Cromwel*, have a House of Commons of his own making: For the House of Commons is compounded of five hundred and thirteen Members, whereof but ninety two are Knights of Shires; so that near 5/6 are Burgesses, Citizens and Barons of the Cinque Ports: The Generality of the Corporations which send these Members are poor decayed places, and so not able as the City of *London* to contest their Charters, or if they could, they had little hope to keep them, now *London* could not hold theirs. Yet this would cost the Court a great deal of time to bring *Quo Warranto's* against above two hundred Corporations; and now all Hands are set at work to prevail upon these poor Inhabitants, and mighty Rewards are promised to those who should surrender them: but because Money was scarce, Bargains were made with Multitudes of them, to have Grants of Fairs for surrender of their Charters, and those which refused had *Quo Warranto's* brought against them. To humour the Court, and in perfect hope that in time the Mountains would bring forth, a Multitude of Corporations (or rather some loose vain Men, who assumed the Names of the Corporations) by heaps surrendred their Charters; and at excessive Rates (I cannot say renewed, but) took new ones, whereby the King reserved to himself the Power of disposing of all Places of Profit and Power, which at present was intrusted in their Hands who had betrayed their former Trust:

But he durst not have dreamt of all these Violations if he had not had an Army to justify them. He had thoughts at first of keeping up the Parliament-Army, which was several times in debate. But Chancellor *Hyde*[104] prevailed upon him by this Argument, that they were a body of Men that had cut off his Father's Head; that they had set up and pulled down ten several sorts of Government; and that it might be his own turn next. So that his fears prevailing over his ambition, he consented to disband them; but soon found how vain and abortive a thing Arbitrary Power would prove without an Army. He therefore try'd all ways to get one; and first he attemted it in *Scotland*, and by means of the Duke of *Lauderdale*,[105] got an Act passed there, wherby the Kingdom of *Scotland* was obliged to raise 20000 Foot and 2000 Horse at his Majesty's Call, to

---

nor did these Men care for the expence of purchasing their new Charter, tho it were to the starving the Poor of their Corporations, who should have been fed with the Monies expended in the Purchase. (Coke, *Detection*, p. 603; cf. Jones, *Tragical History*, p. 378, and Jones, *History of Europe*, pp. 154–55)

104. Edward Hyde (1609–74), first Earl of Clarendon; politician and historian; Lord Chancellor, 1658–67; thereafter disgraced, impeached, and exiled (Coke, *Detection*, p. 470). The accusation that he had recommended a standing army was prominent in the articles of impeachment (Schwoerer, *Armies*, pp. 72, 93).

105. John Maitland (1616–82), Duke of Lauderdale; politician and courtier; dominant figure in Scottish political life, 1667–79. In the mid-1660s Lauderdale had raised a Scottish army for Charles:

His *Highland Army*, which consisted of eight or nine thousand Men, not only lived upon Free Quarter, upon all sorts of the King's peaceable Subjects, but in most places levied great Sums of Money, under the Notion of Dry Quarters: they had only regard to the Duke's private Animosities; for the most part of the Places where they quartered and destroyed, had not been guilty of Field-Conventicles. The King's Subjects were denounced Rebels, and *Captions* issued out for seizing their Persons, for not entring into Bond, That neither they, nor any under them, shall go to Field-Conventicles; and the Nobility and Gentry were disarmed, who had ever been faithful to the King, and assisted in suppressing Field-Conventicles. Indictments were delivered in by the King's Advocate in the Evening, to be answered next Morning upon Oath, otherwise they were to be reputed guilty. These and many more of this kind, in the Matters relating to *Lauderdale*'s Administration of Affairs in *Scotland*, were represented to the King, and that by his Command; and are in *Lauderdale*'s and his Lady's Impeachment, which are all in Print. Notwithstanding all this, it was this *Lauderdale* who had procured an Act of Parliament [the Scottish Militia Act of 1669] to raise 20000

march into any part of his Dominions; and this Law is in being at this day. Much about the same time he rais'd Guards in *England*[106] (a thing unheard of before in our *English* Constitution) and by degrees increas'd them, till they became a formidable Army; for first they were but very few, but by adding insensibly more Men to a Troop or Company, and then more Troops or Companies to a Regiment, before the second *Dutch* War he had multiplied them to near 5000 Men.[107] He then began that War in conjunction with *France*, and the Parliament gave him two Millions and a half to maintain it, with part of which Mony he rais'd about 12000 Men, which were called the *Black-Heath Army* (appointing Marshal

---

Foot, and 2000 Horse, to march into *England* to serve the King upon all Occasions. (Coke, *Detection*, p. 491)

Cf. Schwoerer, *Armies*, p. 105.

106. Charles took a strong personal interest in the establishment of an effective permanent military force. A few thousand of the more reliable troops, plus the garrison of Dunkirk, had been retained as royal guards from the disbanded Commonwealth army. But a standing army aroused a powerful adverse reaction, and in late 1661 the government dropped an attempt to persuade Parliament to provide funding for a larger force. Nevertheless, a core permanent army had been created, whose existence and occasional enlargement to meet domestic or foreign crises or commitments was regarded with much apprehension in England (*ODNB*):

> *Henry* the Seventh was the first of our *English* Kings who used Guards, and he set up the Yeomen of the Guard, which was followed by all the Kings of *England* since: but tho the Convention had paid off and disbanded the *English* Armies, yet the King [Charles II] besides his Band of Pensioners, in imitation of the *French,* must have Guards of Horse and Foot, and the Parliament gave him Revenue enough to encrease these to what Number he pleased: But it had been better for him if he had imitated the *French* too, in preferring Men who were qualified, but few of these were to be found there: And tho he gave near double the Pay to these, yet was he much worse served than if Men of Merit had been there for half the Pay; for scarce one of the Officers but bought their Places; and this was so common, that the Prices were certain; so not he who deserved, but he which gave most was preferred; and when he was in, he owed the King no Service, having paid for what he had; and so his Business was how to improve his Bargain, not serve the King. And herein too the poor Cavaliers had the worst, they not having so much Money to buy as others had. (Coke, *Detection*, p. 427)

107. The Second Anglo-Dutch War began in 1665. The king possessed the power to increase the number of his guards at will (Coke, *Detection*, p. 535).

Shomberg to be their General, and *Fitz Gerald*[108] an *Irish* Papist their Lieutenant-General) and pretended he rais'd them to attack *Holland*; but instead of using them to that purpose, he kept them encamped upon *Black-Heath*, hovering over the City of *London*, which put both the Parliament and City in such confusion, that the King was forced at last to disband them. But there were several accidents contributed to it: First the ill success he had in the War with the *Dutch*, such Gallantries being not to be attemted but in the highest Raptures of Fortune: Next, the never to be forgotten Generosity of that great Man General *Shomberg*, whose mighty Genius scorn'd so [14] ignoble an Action as to put Chains upon a free People; and last of all, the Army themselves mutini'd for want of Pay: which added to the ill Humors that were then in the Nation, made the King willing to disband them. But at the same time, contrary to the Articles of Peace with the *Dutch*, he continu'd ten thousand Men in the *French* Service,[109] for the most part under Popish Officers, to be season'd there in slavish Principles, that they might be ready to execute any Commands when they were sent for over. The Parliament never met, but they address'd the King to recal these Forces out of *France*, and disband them;[110] and several times prepar'd Bills to that purpose, which

108. To compleat the miserable Condition of the *Dutch* Provinces, the King had raised an Army commanded by Marshal *Schomberg*, (who had done what he could for the *French* in *Portugal*, the Queen Regent of *Spain*, upon the *French* Irruption into the *Spanish Netherlands* in 1667, having made Peace with *Portugal)* and Col. *Fitz-Gerald*, an *Irish Papist*, Major-General: The Business of this Army was, as the Vogue went, That since the *French* King could not get that part of *Holland* which was drencht by Fresh Water, to souse it with Salt Water, by cutting down their Sea-Banks; but *Ponit Homo*. (Coke, *Detection*, p. 487)

For Schomberg, see below, p. 322, n. 174. Cf. Marvell, *Prose Works*, 2:270. The verse "History of Insipids" mocked "Our Blackheath host, without dispute / (Rais'd, put on board, why, no man knows) / Must Charles have render'd absolute / Over his subjects or his foes. . . .' (*POAS*, 1:248). In early modern resistance theory such behavior is said to be typical of a tyrant: "A tyrant . . . is always either preparing or threatening or pretending to be bent on war" (*Vindiciae*, p. 145). For commentary, see Schwoerer, *Armies*, pp. 101–3.

109. See above, p. 297, n. 94.

110. Parliament granted Charles money to pay off and disband his troops in, e.g., 1678.

the King always prevented by a Prorogation; but at last was prevail'd upon to issue forth a Proclamation to recal them, yet at the same time supply'd them with Recruits, incourag'd som to go voluntarily into that Service, and press'd, imprison'd, and carri'd over others by main Force: besides, he only disbanded the new rais'd Regiments, and not all them neither, for he kept up in *England* five thousand eight hundred and ninety privat Men, besides Officers, which was his Establishment in 1673.[111]

The King having two great designs to carry on together, *viz.* Popery and Arbitrary Power, thought this Force not enough to do his Business effectually; and therefore cast about how to get a new Army, and took the most plausible way, which was pretending to enter into a War with *France*; and to that purpose sent Mr. *Thyn* to *Holland*,[112] who made a strict League with the States: and immediately upon it the King call'd the Parliament,[113] who gave him 1200000 Pounds to enter into an actual War, with which Mony he rais'd an Army of between twenty and thirty thousand Men within less than forty Days, and sent part of them to *Flanders*. At the same time he continued his Forces in *France*, and took a Sum of Mony from that King to assist him in making a privat Peace with *Holland:* So that instead of a War with *France*, the Parliament had given a great Sum to raise an Army to enslave themselves. But it happen'd about this time that the Popish Plot[114] broke out, which put the Nation into such a Ferment, that there was no stemming the Tide; so that he was forc'd to call the Parliament, which met the 23*d* of *October* [15] 78, who immediatly fell upon the Popish Plot and the Land Army. Besides, there were discover'd 57 Commissions granted to Papists to raise Men,

---

111. See Coke, *Detection*, pp. 493–94.

112. Thomas Thynne (1640–1714), first Viscount Weymouth; politician and diplomat.

113. Parliament assembled on 28 January 1678. "The Houses thus met, the King acquainted them with the League he had made with *Holland,* and demanded Money of them to carry on the War against *France,* in case *France* did not comply with the League; whereupon the Parliament granted him a Tax by Poll, and otherways, which amounted to 1200000 *l.* not for Peace, but to enter into an actual War with *France:* But this Tax shall only beget another, to disband an Army raised upon that Pretence, tho no War was entred into against *France*" (Coke, *Detection*, p. 521).

114. See above, p. 299, n. 98.

countersigned *J. Will——son*; for which, and saying that the King might keep Guards if he could pay them, he was committed to the *Tower*.[115] This so inrag'd the Parliament, that they immediatly proceded to the disbanding of the Army, and pass'd an Act that all rais'd since the *29th* of *September* 77 should be disbanded,[116] and gave the King 693388 pounds to pay off their Arrears, which he made use of to keep them up, and dissolv'd the Parliament, but soon after called another, which pursu'd the same Counsels, and pass'd a second Act to disband the Army,[117] gave a new Sum for doing it, directed it to be paid into the Chamber of *London*, appointed Commissioners of their own, and pass'd a Vote,[118] *That the continuance of any Standing Forces in this Nation other than the Militia, was illegal, and a great Grievance and Vexation to the People*, so that Army was disbanded. Besides this, they complain'd of the Forces that were in *France*, and address'd the King again to recal them, which had som

115. And if the Parliament were thus amazed at their Sitting, it was no way lessened when as they found that in this very Month no less than 57 Commissions were discovered for raising Soldiers, granted to several Romish Recusants, with Warrants to muster without taking the *Oaths of Allegiance and Supremacy* and the *Test*, countersigned by Sir *J. W.* Secretary of State; whereupon, the Commons committed him to the *Tower*; yet the King next Day discharged him, with a Reprimand to the Commons: but upon the Commons Address to the King about it, the King, as before in his Declarations of Indulgence, promised to recal them. (Coke, *Detection*, p. 535)

For Sir Joseph Williamson, see above, p. 46, n. 113.

116. Trenchard refers to 29 Car. II, c. 1.

117. Trenchard refers to 30 Car. II, c. 1, An Act for granting a Supply to his Majesty (1678), the preamble to which reads:

We your Majesty's most loyal and obedient subjects the Commons now in Parliament assembled, perceiving that there is no further occasion for the Forces raised since 29 September last, and being sensible that the continuance of them must be a great burden and unnecessary charge to your Majesty, to the intent therefore that the said charge may not continue, and to enable your Majesty completely to pay and to disband all the said Forces as hereafter is mentioned and expressed, we . . . have given and granted . . . for the aims and purposes aforesaid . . . the sum of £206,462. 17s. 3d. (*Stuart Constitution*, p. 396)

118. The Commons passed this vote on 1 April 1679. They had passed an identically worded vote on 7 February 1674.

Effect; for he sent over no more Recruits, but suffer'd them to wear out by degrees. The Establishment upon the Dissolution of this Army, which was in the Year $16\frac{79}{80}$, were 5650 privat Soldiers, besides Officers. From this time he never agreed with his People, but dissolved three Parliaments[119] following for inquiring into the Popish Plot; and in the four last Years of his Reign call'd none at all. And to crown the Work, *Tangier* is demolish'd, and the Garison brought over, and plac'd in the most considerable Ports in *England*; which made the Establishment in $8\frac{3}{4}$ 8482 privat Men, besides Officers.[120] It's observable in this King's Reign, that there was not one Sessions but his Guards were attack'd, and never could get the least Countenance from Parliament; but to be even with them, the Court as much discountenanc'd the Militia,[121] and never would suffer it to be made useful. Thus we see the King husbanded a few

119. Charles dissolved Parliament on 25 January 1679 (this was the Long Parliament, which had sat since his Restoration in 1660); on 12 July 1679; and on 18 January 1681 (Coke, *Detection*, pp. 537–60). Coke asserts that the motive behind these dissolutions was "upon the Account of the Popish Lords and Popish Plot" (Coke, *Detection*, p. 537).

120. In 1662 Tangier had been transferred to the English Crown as part of the dowry of Catherine of Braganza (1638–1705), wife of Charles II. Although its fortifications were reinforced and improved, the cost of maintaining its defenses proved too great, and in 1684 it was abandoned. For contemporary comment, see Jones, *Secret History*, pp. 17–20. For the reputation and fate of its garrison, see below, p. 320, n. 168.

121. Stuart disparagement of the militia is given vivid expression in Dryden's "Cymon and Iphigenia" (1700): "The Country rings around with loud Alarms, / And raw in Fields the rude Militia swarms; / Mouths without Hands; maintain'd at vast Expence, / In Peace a Charge, in War a weak Defence: / Stout once a Month they march a blust'ring Band, / And ever, but in times of Need, at hand: / This was the Morn when issuing on the Guard, / Drawn up in Rank and File they stood prepar'd / Of seeming Arms to make a short essay, / Then hasten to be Drunk, the Business of the Day" (ll. 399–408). These memorable lines were also cited in the debates about a militia in the following century: see *Reflections on the Present State of Affairs* (1756), p. 10. Coke noted James's low opinion of the militia, following its poor performance against Monmouth in 1685: "He told them [Parliament], That the *Militia*, so much before depended on, was not sufficient for his Occasions, and that nothing could do but a good Force of well-disciplined Troops in constant Pay to defend us from such, as either at home or abroad are disposed to disturb us: That in Truth his Concern for the Peace and Quiet of his Subjects, as well as for the Safety of his Government, made him think it necessary to encrease the Number as he had done" (Coke, *Detection*, p. 625).

Guards so well, that in a small number of Years they grew to a formidable Army, notwithstanding all the endeavors of the Parliament to the contrary; so difficult it is to prevent the growing of an Evil, that dos not receive a check in the beginning.

[16] He increas'd the Establishment in *Ireland* to 7700 Men, Officers included; wheras they never exceded in any former Reign 2000, when there was more occasion for them: the *Irish* not long before having bin intirely reduced by *Cromwel*,[122] and could never have held up their Heads again without his Countenance. But the truth of it was, his Army was to support the *Irish*, and the fear of the *Irish* was to support his Army.

Towards the latter end of this King's Reign the Nation had so intirely lost all sense of Liberty, that they grew fond of their Chains; and if his Brother would have suffer'd him to have liv'd longer,[123] or had followed his Example, by this time we had bin as great Slaves as in *France*. But it was God's great Mercy to us that he was made in another Mould, Imperious, Obstinat, and a Bigot, push'd on by the Counsels of *France* and *Rome*, and the violence of his own Nature; so that he quickly run himself out of breath. As soon as he came to the Crown, he seiz'd the Customs and Excise[124] without Authority of

122. In May 1649 Cromwell had been appointed Lord Lieutenant of Ireland and general of the army there. Between 15 August 1649 and 26 May 1650 he cleared Munster of royalist garrisons in an energetic campaign marred by atrocities in Wexford and Drogheda.

123. I.e., the Duke of York, the future James II. Trenchard touches on the contemporary rumor that James had his brother poisoned in order to safeguard a Catholic succession. In fact, Charles appears to have died of the consequences of a major stroke.

124. Trenchard refers to James's having on his accession immediately claimed the revenues of the customs and excise (which were customarily granted to the Crown) without waiting for Parliament formally to grant them. Here once again Trenchard follows Roger Coke:

> The King's Father, *Charles* I, took the Customs before granted by Parliament; this King took both Customs and the Excise, granted only for the Life of his Brother, before they were given him by Parliament: How this corresponded with the King's Promise but the Week before, that he would never invade any Man's Property, I do not understand; for tho in every Government no Man has Property against the Supream Power, yet by the *English* Constitutions, the Supream Power of the Nation is in the Parliament, in Conjunction with the King: and the King's taking both the Customs and Temporary Excise for his Brother's Life, by his only Will and Pleasure, was

Parliament: He pick'd out the Scum and Scandals of the Law to make Judges upon the Bench;[125] and turn'd out all that would not sacrifice their Oaths to his Ambition, by which he discharg'd the Lords out of the *Tower*,[126] inflicted those barbarous Punishments on Dr. *Oates*, Mr. *Johnson*,[127] &c. butcher'd

---

as much a Violation upon the Property of the Subject, as if he had taken the rest of their Goods and Inheritances. (Coke, *Detection*, p. 610)

In continuing to claim these revenues, James was following the advice of George Jeffreys (see below, n. 125), and Parliament gave retrospective sanction to this action of the king's.

125. Principally the notorious George Jeffreys (1645–89). Jeffreys had in fact become chief justice of the King's Bench in 1683, but he was nevertheless a long-standing favorite of James II, who made him Lord Chancellor on 28 September 1685. Coke states the policy which guided James's scandalous promotions to the bench: "But this was but one Step towards this Holy Work; the King, to make a thorow Reformation, will make the Judges in *Westminster-Hall* to murder the Common Law, as well as the King and his Brother designed to murder the Parliament by it self; and to this end, the King, before he would make any Judges, would make a Bargain with them, that they should declare the King's Power of dispensing with the *Penal Laws* and *Tests* made against Recusants, out of Parliament" (Coke, *Detection*, p. 630).

126. On 25 October 1678, the House of Commons had impeached five Catholic peers for their alleged involvement in the Popish Plot: the Earl of Powis, Viscount Stafford, and Lords Arundel, Petre, and Belasyse. Stafford was executed on 29 December 1680; Petre died in prison on 5 January 1684; Arundel, Belasyse, and Powis were released on bail on 18 February 1684. Trenchard is therefore confused when he places their release in the reign of James II. The probable reason for the confusion is that Trenchard has been reading Coke's *Detection* hastily, for Coke does indeed discuss the release of the impeached lords at the beginning of his narrative of the reign of James II, but as part of a retrospective consideration of the events of the end of the reign of Charles II: "But the taking off the Heads of the *Whigs* was but half this Design; the impeached Lords in the *Tower* must be let loose, or the Game was but half play'd: This was so ticklish a Point, that neither *Pemberton* nor *Saunders* could be brought up to it; but *Saunders* dying, and *Pemberton* removed to the *Common Pleas*, Sir *Geo. Jeffries* was set up to do this Work, which he did to content, and so was initiated to do what other Journey-work the Court should order" (Coke, *Detection*, p. 611). In July 1686 James II admitted Arundel, Belasyse, and Powis to the Privy Council.

127. Titus Oates and Samuel Johnson were both subjected to vindictive prosecutions under James II. Oates had been arrested at the Amsterdam coffeehouse on 10 May 1684 on a charge of *scandalum magnatum* after a suit by the then Duke of York, whom Oates had called a traitor. Fined £100,000 after refusing to plead, Oates was placed in the Compter in default of payment and was later moved to the King's Bench prison. In October and December 1684 he was presented on charges of perjury. The trial was delayed by the death of Charles II on 6 February 1685 but finally took place on 8–9 May 1685. Oates was convicted on two counts: that he

many hundreds of Men in the *West*[128] after they had bin trapan'd into a Confession by promise of Pardon, murder'd *Cornish*,[129] got the Dispensing

---

had falsely sworn on 8–12 August 1678 to a "consult" of Jesuits at the White Horse tavern and that he had also falsely sworn to the presence of William Ireland in London on the same dates. A week later he was sentenced. He was to be imprisoned for life, divested of his canonical garb forever, and brought to Westminster Hall with a paper on his head with the inscription: "Titus Oates convicted upon full evidence of two horrid perjuries." He was also placed in the pillory in Palace Yard, Westminster, on 19 May and was pelted with eggs and other rubbish. This part of the sentence was to be repeated five times every year of his life in different parts of London. While a resident of King's Bench prison in 1684, Johnson had met Hugh Speke, a Whig agitator who was able to have Johnson's writings printed and distributed. In March 1686 Johnson and Speke decided to arouse the consciences of the Protestant soldiers serving in James II's army. Johnson's *A Humble and Hearty Address to All English Protestants in this Present Army* exhorted the soldiers to come to the defense of their religion rather than assist their Catholic officers in erecting a "popish-kingdom of darkness and desolation." The authorities were quick to suspect Johnson; he was convicted of high misdemeanor, sentenced to pay 500 marks, to stand in the pillory for three days, and to be flogged from Newgate to Tyburn. Johnson was also degraded from the priesthood. Roger Coke drew attention to the sufferings of both men (Coke, *Detection*, pp. 613, 638). For Oates and Johnson, see above, p. 299, n. 98, and p. 33, n. 81, respectively.

128. The defeat of Monmouth at Sedgemoor in 1685 was followed by savage reprisals orchestrated by George Jeffreys in his "Bloody Assizes." Roger Coke deplored the inhumanity of his proceedings:

> I will not dispute the Justice of these Executions; but I say, Justice ought to look forward, *viz.* to terrify others from committing like Crimes, never backward to take Pleasure in punishing; and a black Brand is set upon the Reigns of those Princes which shed much Blood: nor do we read in any Story, such a Sea of Blood flowed from Justice as did in less than eight Months after this King began his Reign: and that which rendred it more remarkable was the King's Profession to his Privy Council, and after to the Parliament, That he would imitate his good and gracious Brother, but above all, in his great Clemency and Tenderness to his People. (Coke, *Detection*, p. 621; cf. Jones, *History of Europe*, pp. 214–16)

See also above, p. 28, n. 68.

129. Henry Cornish (d. 1685), local Whig politician. Cornish had been implicated in some of the revelations about Whig plotting that were heard before the Privy Council during the summer of 1683. He was apprehended four times in the next two years, once on suspicion of distributing pamphlets that suggested the Earl of Essex had been murdered by the government (see above, p. 299, n. 102), and again during Monmouth's rebellion against James II. Arrested and found guilty in a hasty trial, he was executed on 23 October 1685 in front of his Cheapside house. Cornish's

Power [130] to be declar'd in *Westminster-Hall*, turn'd the Fellows of *Magdalen-College* out of their Freeholds to make way for a Seminary of Priests,[131] and hang'd Soldiers[132] for running away from their Colors. He erected the Ecclesiastical Commission, suspended the Bishop of *London*, because he would not inflict the same Punishment upon Dr. *Sharp* for preaching against Popery.[133]

---

persecution by James II was cited by Coke as one of his most outrageously tyrannical crimes (Coke, *Detection*, pp. 622–24; cf. Jones, *History of Europe*, p. 216).

130. See above, p. 163, n. 24.

131. On 4 September 1687 James summoned the fellows of Magdalen College to an audience at Christ Church, Oxford. In April he had instructed them to elect as their president a Roman Catholic, Anthony Farmer, but they had defied him by choosing John Hough instead. Hough's election had been declared void, and in July James had forbidden the fellows to make any new election. Farmer's candidacy for the presidency was dropped, and in his stead James ordered the fellows to elect Samuel Parker, bishop of Oxford. Once again they defied him. When they were again summoned to Christ Church, he demanded that they choose Parker. Yet again they refused. The ecclesiastical commission then visited Magdalen and stripped the fellows of their fellowships. Roger Coke gives extended consideration to James's attempt to intimidate the fellows of Magdalen, and concludes: "The Fellows thus expelled, the Statutes of the College are thrown out of Doors, to make room for a Seminary of Jesuits and Popish Priests, as much tending to the Subversion of the established Church of *England*, as the Statutes of the College" (Coke, *Detection*, p. 640). The key term Trenchard brandishes here is "Freeholds." At this time college fellowships were freehold property based on the college's endowment. Consequently James's ejection of the fellows of Magdalen was an invasion of property. As such it ran directly counter to the undertaking James had given on his accession that he would "never invade any man's property" (Miller, *James II*, p. 120). The ejection of the fellows of Magdalen demonstrated either that James had been insincere in making that promise or (more likely) that he had not fully understood what he was promising. Either way, the episode severely damaged James's credentials as king.

132. And though the King had no other Wars, but against the Laws and Constitutions of the Nation, yet he would have the Act of the *1, 2 Edw. 6. 2.* which makes it Felony, without Benefit of the Clergy, for any Souldier taking Pay in the King's Service, in his Wars beyond Sea, or upon Sea, or in *Scotland,* to desert from his Officer, to extend to this Army thus raised by the King: And because the Recorder of *London,* Sir *J. H.* would not expound this Law to the King's Design, he was put out of his Place, and so was Sir *Edward Herbert* from being Chief Justice of the *King's Bench,* to make room for Sir *Robert Wright,* to hang a poor Souldier upon this Statute; and afterward this Statute did the Work without any further dispute. (Coke, *Detection*, p. 643)

133. In 1686 James established an Ecclesiastical Commission with a very broad remit:

He closeted the Nobility and Gentry, turn'd all out of Imployment that would not promise to repeal the Test, put in Popish Privy-Counsellors, Judges, Deputy-Lieutenants, and Justices of Peace;[134] and to get all this confirm'd by the shew of Parliament, he prosecuted the Work his Brother had begun in taking away Charters,[135] and new model'd the Corporations by a sort of Vermin call'd Regulators.[136] He receiv'd a Nuntio from *Rome*, and sent an

to exercise, use, occupy, and execute under us all manner of Jurisdiction, Privileges and Preheminences in any wise touching, or concerning any Spiritual or Ecclesiastical Jurisdictions within this our Realm of *England*, and Dominion of *Wales;* and to visit, reform, redress, order, correct and amend all such Abuses, Offences, Contempts and Enormities whatsoever, which by the Spiritual or Ecclesiastical Laws of this Realm, can, or may be lawfully reformed, ordered, redressed, corrected, restrained or amended, to the Pleasure of Almighty God, and encrease of Vertue, and the Conservation of the Peace and Unity of this Realm. (Coke, *Detection*, pp. 632–33; cf. Jones, *History of Europe*, pp. 234–35)

John Sharp (1645?–1714), dean of Norwich and rector of St. Giles-in-the-Fields, London, had permitted himself some anti-Catholic remarks while preaching. James responded on 17 June 1686 by ordering the bishop of London, Henry Compton (1631/32–1713) to suspend him. Compton demurred on the grounds that Sharp could not be suspended without first being heard. As a result Compton was summoned before the recently created Ecclesiastical Commission on 9 August and was granted until 31 August to prepare his case. His counsel maintained that Compton had obeyed the king as far as he legally could. Nevertheless the verdict for his suspension was delivered on 6 September. The harsher sentence of deprivation was not imposed; this meant that Compton's episcopal revenues remained untouched, and therefore that the action taken against him could not be construed as aiming at his property. Coke expatiates on this episode (Coke, *Detection*, p. 639; see also Jones, *Secret History*, pp. "38–40" [sigs. Cccccc3^v–Cccccc4^v]).

134. See above, p. 97, n. 81.

135. See above, p. 98, n. 82, and p. 300, n. 103.

136. Regulators were members of a commission established in 1687 in order to influence the outcome of parliamentary elections by investigating and removing from borough corporations those members found to be disaffected to the king (*OED*, s.v. "regulator," 3). They were an object of resentment in the pamphlet literature of the time:

I must confess, there are some Dealings, that are enough to ferment even the Blood of a *Stoick:* to hear a Regulator Cant against Surrendring of Charters; to find a Man accused of holding Correspondence with Papists, by one that sat at Meat with the Pope's *Nuncio;* to see a late Addressor (who in spite of all Laws, would allow of the Dispensing Power) furious for some disputable Customs in particular Corporations; I say to see Men under these

Ambassador[137] [17] thither. He erected a Popish Seminary at the *Savoy*[138] to pervert Youth, suffer'd the Priests to go about in their Habits, made *Tyrconnel* Lord Lieutenant of *Ireland*, [139] turn'd all the Protestants out of the Army and most of the Civil Imployments there, and made *Fitton* (a Papist, and one

---

Circumstances prosecuting some few Miscarriages, which are so old, that nothing but Malice could remember; must tempt a Man to believe that either they have no sense of their own Faults, or else that they are afraid to be call'd to account, and so by putting others first, would willingly Postpone their Punishment. (John Lightfoot, *A Letter to a Member of Parliament* [1689], p. 1)

137. "My Lord *Castlemain* is sent Ambassador to the Pope, to render the King's Obedience to the *Holy* and *Apostolical See*, with great hopes of extirpating the Northern pestilent *Heresy*. In return whereof, the Pope sent his *Nuncio* to give the King his Holy *Benediction;* yet I do not find that he beforehand sent for Leave to enter the Kingdom, as was observed by Queen *Mary, Henry* VIII, and before" (Coke, *Detection*, p. 642; see also p. 647). A nuntio is a papal ambassador to a foreign court or government (*OED*, s.v. "nuncio," 1).

138. *Popish* Judges were made in *Westminster-Hall*, and *Popish* Justices of the Peace, and Deputy-Lieutenants all *England* over; the Privy Council was replenished with Popish Privy Counsellors; the *Savoy* was laid open to instruct Youth in the *Romish* Religion, and Popish Principles; and Schools for that purpose were encouraged in *London*, and all other Places in *England:* Four Foreign Popish Bishops, as *Vicars Apostolical*, were allowed in Ecclesiastical Jurisdiction all *England* and *Wales* over. (Coke, *Detection*, p. 642)

139. Richard Talbot (1630–91), first Earl of Tyrconnell and Jacobite Duke of Tyrconnell; army officer and politician. Talbot, a lucky survivor of the Drogheda massacre in 1649, served alongside the future James II when Duke of York in the later 1650s and remained close to him after the Restoration in 1660. With the accession of James II in 1685 Talbot began a meteoric rise that culminated in his appointment as Lord Deputy of Ireland on 8 January 1687. Before and during his tenure of office Talbot was an enthusiastic promoter of James's policy of promoting and rewarding Roman Catholics by giving them public offices and army commissions: "Tyrconnell's consistent objectives were to reverse the Act of Settlement so as to restore Catholics to their confiscated lands, to place the civil administration in Catholic hands, and to prevent any armed opposition to this by purging the army of protestants and by disarming the Protestant militia. The principal beneficiaries of these policies were to be the Old English, the Catholic gentry who had lost the most during the Cromwellian settlement" (*ODNB*). Following the landing of William of Orange in November 1688, Talbot organized Jacobite resistance to the new regime in Ireland and did his best to put heart into James II. He died of a stroke in August 1691 while organizing the defense of Limerick against Williamite forces under the command of Godard van Reede-Ginckel (1644–1703), first Earl of Athlone. Coke deplored the appointment and actions of Tyrconnell:

detected for Perjury) Chancellor of that Kingdom.[140] He issu'd out a Proclamation in *Scotland*, wherin he asserted his Absolute Power, which all his Subjects were to obey without reserve;[141] a Prerogative I think, never claim'd by the Great *Turk*, or the *Mogul*.[142] He issu'd out a Declaration for Liberty of Conscience,[143] order'd it to be read in all Churches, and imprison'd and try'd the seven Bishops[144] because they humbly offer'd their Reasons in a Petition

---

But the Toleration which the King allows his *Roman Catholick* Subjects in *Scotland*, he'll scarce permit to his Protestant Subjects in *Ireland;* for *Tyrconnel* (for so has *Talbot* merited for his Service in Reforming the Army) is not only made an Earl, but Lord Lieutenant of *Ireland*, in the room of my Lord *Clarendon*, and one *Fitton* (made Sir *Alexander*, an infamous Person, detected for Forgery, not only at *Westminster*, but at *Chester*, and fined in the House of Lords) was brought out of the *King's Bench* in *England*, to be Chancellor and Keeper of the King's Conscience in *Ireland*, in place of Sir *Charles Porter.* (Coke, *Detection*, p. 641)

140. Alexander Fitton (d. 1699), Jacobite Baron Fitton; politician and Jacobite sympathizer. Fitton's appointment as Lord Chancellor of Ireland was announced in January 1687. After 1688 Fitton eventually joined the exiled Jacobite court at St. Germain, where he would die in November 1699. Fitton had been "detected for perjury" in relation to a disputed property over which he had argued for his claim in a pamphlet titled *A True Narrative of the Proceedings in the Severall Suits in Law that Have Been Between the Rt. Hon. Charles Lord Gerard of Brandon and Alexander Fitton, Esq.* (1663). On 9 July 1663 the House of Lords had declared the *True Narrative* a scandalous libel, had fined Fitton £500, and had jailed him until he provided sureties.

141. "If the King were zealous in advancing his *Prerogative Royal* both in the Church and State of *England*, he will not be less in *Scotland;* whereupon the *12th* of *February 1686–87.* he issues out his Proclamation for *Toleration of Religion*, (which you may read in the *State Tracts*) wherein he asserts his Absolute Power, which he says, his Subjects ought to obey without reserve" (Coke, *Detection*, p. 641).

142. See above, p. 282, n. 51.

143. When the Judges had been above a Year propagating the King's Power in *Westminster-Hall*, and in their Circuits, of dispensing with the *Penal Laws* and *Tests* against Dissenters from the Church, upon the *25th* of *April 1687*, out comes the King's Declaration to all his Subjects for *Liberty of Conscience*, wherein the King declares, *That it had been a long time his constant Sense and Opinion, that* Conscience *ought not to be restrained, nor People forced in Matters of meer Religion; and that it was contrary to his Inclination, as he thought it to be the disinterest of the Government, by spoiling Trade, and depopulating Countries, &c.* (Coke, *Detection*, p. 641)

144. An order in council had been issued in May 1688 requiring the clergy to read the Declaration of Indulgence in their churches, and the bishops to distribute

against it: and to consummat all, that we might have no hopes of retrieving our Misfortunes, he impos'd a counterfeit Prince of *Wales*[145] upon the Nation.

Soon after he came to the Crown, the Duke of *Monmouth* landed,[146] and in a few weeks got together six or seven thousand Men: but they having neither Arms or Provisions, were easily defeated by not many more than 2000 of the King's Troops. Which leaves a sad prospect of the consequence of a Standing Army: for here was a Prince, the Darling of the common People, fighting against a bigotted Papist that was hated and abhor'd by them, and yet defeated by so small a number of Men, and many of them too his Friends; such is the force of Authority. King *James* took occasion from hence to increase his Army to between fifteen and sixteen thousand Men, and then unmask'd himself, call'd his Parliament, and in a haughty Speech told them, He had increas'd his Army, put in Officers not qualifi'd by the Test, and that he would not part with them.[147] He ask'd a Supply, and let them know he expected their

---

it throughout their dioceses. The archbishop of Canterbury and six bishops presented a petition to James on 18 May asking him not to insist on the distribution and reading of the proclamation. When the bishops published their petition, James prosecuted them for seditious libel. Because they refused to give recognizances to appear in court, he sent them to the Tower, where they spent a week before being bailed by twenty-one peers. At their trial the bishops denied the king's right to issue the Declaration of Indulgence. They were acquitted on 29 June: "Unless it were when *Monk* came into the City the *12th* of *February, 1659–60.* and Colonel *Cloberry* told the Citizens at *Guild-Hall* they should have a free Parliament, or when King *Charles* came into *London* the *29th* of *May* following, never were such loud Acclamations of Joy exprest, as upon the Acquittal of the Bishops" (Coke, *Detection*, p. 645).

145. An allusion to the events of the summer of 1688, when on 10 June James II's queen, Mary of Modena, had given birth to a son. Enemies of James II maintained that the pregnancy had been a sham and that the child presented as the heir to the throne had in fact been smuggled into the birthing chamber in a warming pan.

146. See above, p. 28, n. 68.

147. Justice, Judgment, and Righteousness support the Thrones of Princes, but these were Strangers to this King's ways, other Means must be found out to support and carry them through; a standing Army is judged the best Expedient: and as the King told the Parliament at their second Meeting, he had encreased his Army to double what it was before, so he made his Word good, that he would employ Men in it not qualified by the late *Tests;* and to this end, *Tyrconnel* having disbanded the *English* Army in *Ireland,*

compliance. This was very unexpected to those Loyal Gentlemen, who had given him such a vast Revenue for Life, who refus'd to take any Security but his Majesty's never-failing Word for the Protestant Religion, and indeed had don for him whatever he ask'd; which yet was not very extraordinary, since he had the choosing of most of them himself. But even this Parliament turn'd short upon an Army: which puts me in mind of a saying of *Macchiavel*,[148] viz. *That it is as* [18] *hard a matter for a Man to be perfectly bad as perfectly good*; tho if he had liv'd at this time, I believe he had chang'd his Opinion. The Court labor'd the matter very much; and to shew that good Wits jump,[149] they told us[150] that *France* was grown

---

qualified by the *Tests*, sends over an Army of *Irish* not qualified by the *Tests*, to encrease the Army in *England*. (Coke, *Detection*, p. 642)

See also below, p. 315, n. 150.

148. Cf. Machiavelli, *Discourses*, bk. 1, chap. 27, "Sanno rarissime volte gli uomini essere al tutto cattivi o al tutto buoni"; "Very rarely do men know how to be either wholly good or wholly bad."

149. Pass abruptly from one thing or state to another, with omission of intermediate stages (*OED*, s.v. "jump," 3a).

150. Trenchard refers to James's speech to Parliament on 9 November 1685, in which, following the suppression of Monmouth's rebellion, he stated that

the Militia, which hath hitherto been so much depended on, is not sufficient for such Occasions; and that there is nothing but a good Force of well disciplined Troops in constant Pay, that can defend us from such, as, either at Home or Abroad, are disposed to disturb us: And in truth, My Concern for the Peace and Quiet of My Subjects, as well as for the Safety of the Government, made Me think it necessary to increase the Number to the Proportion I have done: This I owed as well to the Honour as the Security of the Nation; whose Reputation was so infinitely exposed to all our Neighbours, by having so evidently lain open to this late wretched Attempt, that it is not to be repaired without keeping such a Body of Men on foot, that none may ever have the Thought again of finding us so miserably unprovided. It is for the Support of this great Charge, which is now more than double to what it was, that I ask your Assistance in giving Me a Supply answerable to the Expence it brings along with it: And I cannot doubt, but what I have begun so much for the Honour and Defence of the Government, will be continued by you with all the Cheerfulness that is requisite for a Work of so great Importance. Let no Man take Exception, that there are some Officers in the Army, not qualified, according to the late Tests, for their Employments: The Gentlemen, I must tell you, are most of them well known to Me: And, having formerly served with Me in several Occasions, and always approved the

formidable, that the *Dutch* Forces were much increas'd, that we must be strong in proportion for the preservation of our selves and *Flanders,* and that there was no dependence upon the Militia.[151] But this shallow Rhetoric would not pass upon them. They answer'd, that we had defended our selves for above a thousand Years without an Army; that a King's truest Strength is the Love of his People; that they would make the Militia useful, and order'd a Bill to be brought in to that purpose. But all this serv'd only to fulfill their Iniquity;[152] for they had don their own Business[153] before, and now he would keep an Army up in spite of them: so he prorogu'd[154] them, and call'd no other Parliament during his Reign; but to frighten the City of *London,* kept his Army encamp'd at *Hounslow-Heath* when the Season would permit, which put not only them but the whole Nation into the utmost Terror and Confusion. Towards the latter end of his Reign he had increas'd his Army in *England* to above twenty thousand Men, and in *Ireland* to eight thousand seven hundred and odd.

Loyalty of their Principles by their Practice, I think fit now to be employed under Me: And I will deal plainly with you, that, after having had the Benefit of their Service in such Time of Need and Danger, I will neither expose them to Disgrace, nor Myself to Want of them, if there should be another Rebellion to make them necessary for Me. (Grey, *Debates,* 8: pp. 353–54)

151. See above, p. 306, n. 121.

152. An allusion to the language of Christ's bitter denunciation of the Pharisees (Matthew 23:1–39, esp. 23:32: "Fill ye up then the measure of your fathers [iniquity]"). By means of that allusion Trenchard applies Christ's distinction between inward and outward religion and his attack on the spiritual hollowness of the Pharisees to the political hypocrisy and unwisdom of members of Parliament in the reign of James II. Trenchard also associates his pamphlet with a powerful tradition of righteous vehemence, e.g.:

Woe unto you, scribes and Pharisees, hypocrites! for ye pay tithe of mint and anise and cummin, and have omitted the weightier matters of the law, judgment, mercy, and faith: these ought ye to have done, and not to leave the other undone. Ye blind guides, which strain at a gnat, and swallow a camel. Woe unto you, scribes and Pharisees, hypocrites! for ye make clean the outside of the cup and of the platter, but within they are full of extortion and excess. (Matthew 23:23–25)

153. Ruined themselves (*OED,* s.v. "business," P10).

154. The technical term for the adjournment of a Parliament (*OED,* s.v. "prorogue," 3a, 3b).

This King committed two fatal Errors in his Politics. The first was his falling out with his old Chronies[155] the Priests, who brought him to the Crown in spite of his Religion, and would have supported him in Arbitrary Government to the utmost; nay, Popery (especially the worst part of it, *viz.* the Domination of the Church) was not so formidable a thing to them, but with a little Cookery[156] it might have bin rendred palatable. But he had Priests of another sort that were to rise upon their Ruins; and he thought to play an easier Game by caressing the Dissenters,[157] imploying them, and giving them Liberty of Conscience: which kindness lookt so preposterous, that the wise and sober Men among them could never heartily believe it, and when the Prince of *Orange* landed, turn'd against him.

His second Error was the disobliging his own Army, by bringing over Regiments from *Ireland*, and ordering every Com[19]pany to take in so many *Irish* Papists; by which they plainly saw he was reforming his Army, and would cashire them all as fast as he could get Papists to supply their room.[158] So that he violated the Rights of the People, fell out with the Church of *England*, made uncertain Friends of the Dissenters, and disoblig'd his own Army; by which means they all united against him,

155. Intimate friends or associates. In 1698 this was a recently coined word (*OED*, s.v. "crony"; earliest occurrence 1665, Samuel Pepys).

156. Falsification or concealment (*OED*, s.v. "cookery," 5; earliest occurrence 1709, Richard Steele). So this is another example of Trenchard's adoption of— even, perhaps, his coinage of—a newfangled vocabulary to balance the overwhelming appeal to history and tradition in the substance of his argument against standing armies, and to counteract (at least at the level of diction) the challenge of modernists such as Defoe that the anti–standing army position was estranged from current realities.

157. James pursued a policy of apparently even-handed religious toleration toward both Roman Catholics and Dissenters, although members of the Church of England suspected that the toleration of the latter was merely a feint to make the toleration of James's coreligionists seem less objectionable: cf. above, p. 312, n. 139. As Halifax observed, the Dissenters were being hugged now the better to be squeezed hereafter.

158. See above, p. 314, n. 147. "At this time there was not only a high Ferment in all the Nation against the King's Proceedings, but in the Army against its mixture with *Irish* Officers and Soldiers; which put the King into a great Agony, which was increased by the *Dutch* Preparation" (Coke, *Detection*, p. 649).

and invited the Prince of *Orange* to assist them: which Invitation he accepted, and landed at *Torbay* the 5*th* of *November* 1688. publishing a Declaration,[159] which set forth all the Oppressions of the last Reign [but the keeping up a Standing Army] declared for a free Parliament, in which things were to be so settled that there should be no danger of falling again into Slavery, and promis'd to send back all his foren Forces[160] as soon as this was don.

When the News of his Landing was spread thro *England,* he was welcom'd by the universal Acclamations of the People. He had the Hands, the Hearts, and the Prayers of all honest Men in the Nation: Every one thought the long wish'd for time of their Deliverance was com. King *James* was deserted by his own Family, his Court, and his Army. The Ground he stood upon mouldred under him; so that he sent his Queen and Foundling to *France*[161] before him, and himself followed soon after. When the Prince came to *London,* he disbanded most of those Regiments that were rais'd from the time he landed; and King *James*'s Army that were disbanded by *Feversham,*[162] were order'd to repair all again to their Colors: which was thought by som a false step, believing it would have bin more our Interest to have kept those Regiments which came in upon the Principle on which this Revolution is founded, than Forces that were rais'd in violation of the Laws, and to support a Tyrannical Government: besides, the

159. See Appendix C, below, pp. 611–25.

160. I.e., his native Dutch troops.

161. Disguised as a laundry woman, Mary of Modena, accompanied by the infant Prince James, had left London on 10 December 1688. They arrived in Calais on 11 December and reached Chatou for an audience with Louis XIV on 27 December.

162. Louis Duras (1641–1709), second Earl of Feversham; soldier and diplomat. Born in France, Duras came to England in the early 1660s and had entered the service of the Duke of York, later James II. On James's accession Feversham had been appointed to the Privy Council. He had commanded the royal forces which defeated Monmouth at Sedgemoor in 1685 and also the royal forces which advanced to meet William of Orange at Salisbury in November 1688. Under orders from James not to resist "a foreign army and a poisoned nation," Feversham disbanded the army on 10 December. After the establishment of the new regime Feversham did not go into exile, but remained in England and continued to attend the Lords. See Schwoerer, *Armies,* p. 146.

miserable Condition of *Ireland*[163] requir'd our speedy Assistance, and these Men might have bin trusted to do that work.

Within a few days after he came to Town, he summon'd the Lords, and not long after the Members of the three last Parliaments of King *Charles* the 2*d*, and was address'd to by both Houses to take upon him the Administration of the Government, to take into his particular care the then present [20] Condition of *Ireland*, and to issue forth Circulatory Letters for the choosing a Convention of Estates.[164] All this time *Ireland* lay bleeding, and *Tyrconnel* was raising an Army, disarming the Protestants, and dispossessing them of all the Places they held in *Leinster*, *Munster*, and *Connaught*:[165] which occasion'd frequent Applications here for Relief, tho it was to send them but one or two Regiments; and if that could not be don, to send them Arms and Commissions, which in all probability would have made the Reduction of that Kingdom very easy: yet tho the Prince's and King *James* his Army were both in *England*, no relief was sent, by which means the *Irish* got possession of the whole Kingdom but *Londonderry* and *Inniskilling*, the former of which Towns shut up its Gates the ninth of *December*, declaring for the Prince of Orange, and address'd for immediat Relief, yet could neither get Arms or Ammunition till the 20*th* of *March*; and the Forces that were sent with *Cunningham* and *Richards*[166] arrived not there till the 15*th* of *April*, and immediatly after deserted the Service, and came back again, bringing

---

163. Where Jacobite resistance would still continue for a number of years; see above, p. 312, n. 139.

164. The throne being vacant on the flight of James II to France, it was not possible to call a Parliament (of which an essential component is the monarch); hence this unusual terminology.

165. See above, p. 312, n. 139. Tyrconnell had resolved to fight as early as January 1689 and had induced James II to sail to Ireland to lead the resistance. Initially the war had gone well for James and Tyrconnell, who had succeeded in confining the Protestant rebels to Londonderry and Enniskillen. But by August 1689 the tide had begun to turn against the Jacobites, following the arrival in Ireland of an English army commanded by the Duke of Schomberg.

166. John Cunningham and Solomon Richards, both colonels commanding regiments in the English army, and both cashiered for their misconduct at the siege of Londonderry (Boyer, *William III*, 2:58–60; cf. Jones, *History of Europe*, p. 370).

Lundy the Governor[167] before appointed by his Majesty with them, and alledg'd for their Excuse, that it was impossible to defend the Town. But notwithstanding this Treachery, such was the resolution of the Besieged, that they continu'd to defend themselves with the utmost bravery, and sent again for Relief, which under *Kirk*[168] came not to them till the *7th* of *June*; nor were these poor Creatures actually reliev'd till the 30*th* of *July*, tho there appears no reason why he might not have don it when he first came into the Harbor, which was more than seven Weeks before.[169] Thus

167. Robert Lundy (d. before 1717), army officer. Lundy had served with gallantry in Tangier. His regiment was the garrison of Londonderry until November 1688 when it was recalled to make way for a Catholic regiment which, however, was refused entry by the populace. On 21 March 1689 Lundy privately swore an oath of allegiance to William and Mary and was appointed governor of Londonderry, but (says Boyer) "it soon appear'd how much His Majesty was mistaken in his Choice" (Boyer, *William III*, 2:58). On 20 April 1689, during the siege of the city by Jacobite forces, Lundy deserted his post and fled to Islay, where he was arrested and sent to London (Boyer, *William III*, 2:59–60). He was detained in the Tower until February 1690, when he was released on bail of £12,000. From 1704 until his death he served as adjutant-general to the king of Portugal. He is to this day commemorated in Londonderry by the annual burning of an effigy bearing the words "Lundy the Traitor."

168. Percy Kirke (d. 1691), army officer. In 1680 Kirke was given the command of Lord Plymouth's regiment of foot and posted to Tangier. In 1681 he was made governor of Tangier. His administration was notorious for brutality and corruption. After the evacuation of Tangier he returned to England, where his regiment was renamed the Queen's Regiment of Foot. Kirke commanded this regiment at Sedgemoor, and he was infamous in the aftermath of the battle for his inhumane treatment of captured rebels (for a lurid description, see Coke, *Detection*, p. 622). After the events of November 1688, Kirke promptly defected to William of Orange, who promoted him to major-general and gave him charge of the Londonderry relief force. He arrived in Lough Foyle on 11 June 1689. Although Kirke was initially tempted to wait matters out, on being commanded by Schomberg (see below, p. 322, n. 174) to attempt the relief, he attacked and prevailed on 31 July. However, Kirke's demeanor in the liberated city left much to be desired. Provoked by Kirke's disgraceful behavior, Sir James Caldwell asked "whether profest atheism and debauchery are fit weapons to beat down popery?" Nevertheless, after the relief of Londonderry Kirke continued to enjoy the favor of William III, for whom military effectiveness counted for more than suavity of manners.

169. James II laid siege to Londonderry on 20 April 1689. By early June the garrison and townspeople were reduced "to the last Extremity" (Boyer, *William III*, 2:63). It was not until 30 July that Kirke (see above, n. 168) was able to break the boom blockading the town's port, and on the following day lift the siege (Boyer,

we see the Resolution of these poor Men weari'd out all their Disappointments.

When the Convention met, they resolv'd upon twenty eight Articles, as the Preliminaries upon which they would dispose the Crown; but this design dwindled into a Declaration of our Rights,[170] which was in thirteen Articles, and the most considerable, *viz. That the raising and keeping up a Standing Army in times of Peace is contrary to Law,* had tag'd to it these words, *without Authority of Parliament;* as if the consent of the Parliament would not have made it Legal without those words, or that their Consent would make it less dangerous. This made [21] the *Jacobites* say in those early days, that som evil Counsellors design'd to play the same game again of a *Standing Army,* and attributed unjustly the neglect of *Ireland* to the same Cause, because by that omission it was made necessary to raise a greater Army to reduce it, with which the King acquainted the Parliament[171] the 8*th* of *March,* when speaking of the deplorable Condition of *Ireland,* he declar'd he thought it not advisable to attemt the reducing it with less than 20000 Horse and Foot. This was a bitter Pill to the Parliament, who thought they might have manag'd their share of the War with *France* at Sea; but there was no remedy, a greater Army must be rais'd,

---

William III, 2:67–68). For a contemporary eyewitness account, see George Walker, *A True Account of the Siege of London-Derry* (1689), which went through four reprintings in its year of publication. Walker had served as governor of the town jointly with Major Baker after the desertion of Lundy (see above, n. 167).

170. The Bill of Rights (1689) begins by listing the various ways in which James II had endeavored "to subvert and extirpate the Protestant Religion and the Lawes and Liberties of this Kingdome," then goes on to assert thirteen fundamental rights (see Appendix D, below, pp. 627–34).

171. On 8 March 1689 William's "Answer to the Address of both Houses" was read out in the House of Lords. In it William reminded Parliament of the situation of Ireland, and of the remedies it would probably require:

> I need not take Pains to tell you the deplorable Condition of *Ireland,* which, by the Zeal and Violence of the Popish Party there, and by the Assistance and Encouragements they have from *France,* 'tis brought to that Pass, that it is not advisable to attempt the reducing it, otherwise than by a very considerable Force, which I think ought not to be less than Twenty Thousand Horse and Foot; which, by the Blessing of God, will make the Work shorter, and in Consequence the Charge easier, though the First Expence must of Necessity be very great. (Boyer, *William III*, 2:16–17)

or *Ireland* lost; and to gild it, all the Courtiers usher'd in their Speeches with this Declaration, That they would be the first for disbanding them when the War was over; and this Declaration has bin made as often as an Army has bin debated since during the War, and I suppose punctually observ'd last Sessions. At last the thing was consented to,[172] and the King issu'd forth Commissions for the raising of Horse, Foot, and Dragoons. In this Army very few Gentlemen of Estates in *Ireland* could get Imployments, tho they were in a miserable Condition here, and made their utmost Application for them; it being a common objection by som Colonels, that a Man had an Estate there, which in all likelihood would have made him more vigorous in reducing the Kingdom. It was long after this Army was rais'd, before they could be ready to be transported;[173] and even then it was commonly said that *Shomberg*[174] found many things out of order; and

172. By An Act for raising Money by a Poll and otherwise towards the Reduceing of Ireland (1688), the preamble of which states:

> Wee Your Majestyes most Obedient and Loyall Subjects the Commons now in Parlyament Assembled being highly sensible of the deplorable Condition of Your Majestyes Protestant Subjects within Your Kingdome of Ireland occasioned by the Rebellion of the Earle of Tyrconnell and his Adherents with an humble and thankfull Acknowledgement of Your Majestyes favourable and tender Regard of Us Your Commons doe most humbly present unto Your Majesties a Free Gift of the severall Summes of Money hereafter specifyed towards the Reduceing Ireland to its due Obedience to be Levyed in such manner as hereafter is expressed and doe beseech Your Majestyes to accept thereof and that it may be Enacted. (William and Mary, 1688: An Act for raising Money by a Poll and otherwise towards the Reduceing of Ireland. [Chapter XIII. Rot. Parl. pt. 5. nu. 10.], *Statutes of the Realm: Volume 6: 1685–94* (1819), pp. 63–71)

173. On 3 August the House of Commons had presented an address to William stating: "1. That there had been Delays in the Succour of *Ireland*. 2. That there were not sufficient Preparations to transport the Forces to *Ireland*. And, 3. That several Ships had been taken for want of Guards, and Convoys to preserve them" (Boyer, *William III*, 2:126–27). Boyer also reports that the "Eighteen Regiments of Foot and Five of Horse design'd for the Reduction of *Ireland*, were rais'd in *England* with pretty good Success; but the Providing Ships to transport them, a Train of Artillery to attend them, and Provisions to maintain them, was manag'd with great Slowness and Supinity" (Boyer, *William III*, 2:132).

174. Frederick Herman de Schomberg, first Duke of Schomberg (1615–90); a professional soldier of mixed German and English descent who at different times served with great distinction in the armies of Saxe-Weimar, Brandenburg, France, England, and finally Holland. Schomberg had accompanied William III in his

when they were at last transported, which was about the middle of *August*,[175] they were not in a Condition to fight the Enemy, tho lately baffled before *Londonderry*, especially their Carriages coming not to them till the 24*th* of *September*, when it was high time to go into Winter-Quarters. By this means the *Irish* got Strength and Courage, and three fourths of our Army perish'd at the Camp at *Dundalk*.

But tho our Army could do nothing, yet the Militia of the Country, almost without Arms or Clothes, performed Miracles, witness that memorable Siege of *Londonderry*,[176] the defeat of General *Mackarty*,[177] who was intrench'd in a Bog with ten [22] thousand regular Troops, and attack'd by fifteen hundred *Inniskilling* men,[178] defeated, himself made a Prisoner, and three thousand of his Men kill'd; and a great many other gallant Actions they perform'd, for which they were dismiss'd by *Kirk* with Scorn and Ignominy, and most of their Officers left to starve. Thus the War in *Ireland* was nurs'd up either thro Chance, Inadvertency, or the necessity of our Affairs (for I am unwilling to think it was Design) till at last it was grown so big, that nothing less than his Majesty's great Genius, and the usual Success that has always attended his Conduct, could have overcom it.

---

invasion of England in 1688 and died in combat at the hands of Irish Jacobite cavalry during the Battle of the Boyne (1690).

175. On 12 August, according to Abel Boyer (Boyer, *William III*, 2:133).

176. See above, p. 320, n. 169.

177. Donough Maccarthy (1668–1734), fourth Earl of Clancarty; Jacobite army officer. Maccarthy played a leading part in the disastrous Irish campaign, eventually surrendering to Marlborough at the siege of Cork in October 1690. On Clancarty and the high drama surrounding him in 1698, see Macaulay, *History*, 6:2750–54.

178. The prowess of the Enniskillen militia during this war was celebrated:

The Duke of *Schomberg* . . . did . . . not restrain the *Inniskilliners* from making Excursions: Nor had he Reason to repent this Liberty he allow'd them, for on the 27th of *Septemb.* he receiv'd an Account that about a Thousand of them, headed by Collonel *Lloyd*, routed a Body of the *Irish* that were marching towards *Sligo*, consisting of about 5000 Men, of whom they kill'd 700, took *O Kelly* their Commander, and 40 other Officers Prisoners, besides a great Booty of Cattle, with the loss of very few of their Men. (Boyer, *William III*, 2:137)

When the Parliament met that Winter,[179] they fell upon the examination of the *Irish* Affairs; and finding Commissary *Shales*[180] was the cause of a great part of the Miscarriages, they address'd his Majesty that he would be pleas'd to acquaint the House who it was that advis'd the imploying him, which his Majesty did not remember. They then address'd, that he would be pleas'd to order him to be taken into Custody, and it was don accordingly; upon which *Shales* sent a Letter to the Speaker, desiring he might be brought over to *England*, where he would vindicat himself, and justify what he had don. Then the House address'd his Majesty again, that he might be brought over with all convenient speed; and the King was pleas'd to answer, that he had given such Orders already. Then the House refer'd the matter to a privat Committee; but before any Report made, or *Shales* could be brought to *England*, the Parliament was prorogu'd, and after dissolv'd; and soon after he fell sick and died.

The neglect of *Ireland* this Year made it necessary to raise more Forces, and increase our Establishment, which afterwards upon pretence of

179. Parliament debated the state of the nation, paying particular attention to Ireland, on 26–29 November 1689.

180. John Shales had been purveyor to James II's army, and in particular to the notorious standing army encamped on Hounslow Heath to intimidate London. After 1688 he had been retained in the royal service and was held to be responsible for the undersupply of Schomberg's Irish campaign (Claydon, *William III*, pp. 193, 200). On 26 November 1689 Sir Robert Howard said in the House of Commons:

> I never heard a Man speak well of *Shales*, nor do I believe I ever shall. He was very gracious with King *James*, and I am sorry he is employed by King *William*. You may kill two Birds with one Stone; and, to do something very plain, I would have an Address to the King to have Persons sent into *Ireland* to take Account of the Numbers of the Army, and the Provisions. I am plainly for Members of this House to go, who know their Duty to the Nation; that *Shales* may be secured there; and the Duke of *Schomberg* will inform them of all things, and *Shales*'s Books may be examined, that you may know the Number of the Army: You will then have a just Account of it, and I move for an Address of this Nature. (Grey, *Debates*, 9:451–52)

On 30 November William (who had refused to name the person who recommended Shales to him) bowed to the inevitable and asked Parliament to "recommend a number of Persons, not exceeding seven, to be commissioned by his Majesty to take care of the Provisions, and such other Preparations as shall be necessary for that service [the conquest of Ireland]." See Boyer, *William III*, 2:159–60.

invading *France* was advanc'd to eighty seven thousand six hundred ninety eight Men. At last by our great Armies and Fleets, and the constant expence of maintaining them, we were too hard for the Oeconomy, Skill, and Policy of *France;* and notwithstanding all our Difficulties, brought them to Terms both Safe and Honorable.[181]

It not being to the purpose of this Discourse, I shall omit giving any account of the Conduct of our Fleet during this [23] War, how few Advantages we reap'd by it, and how many Opportunities we lost of destroying the *French.* Only thus much I will observe, that tho a great part of it may be attributed to the Negligence, Ignorance, or Treachery of inferior Officers, yet it could not so universally happen thro the whole course of the War, and unpunish'd too, notwithstanding the clamors of the Merchants, and repeated complaints in Parliament, unless the cause had laid deeper: What that is, I shall not presume to enquire; but I am sure there has bin a very ill Argument drawn from it, viz. *That a Fleet is no security to us.*

As soon as the Peace was made, his Majesty discharg'd a great part of the foren Forces; and an Advertisement was publish'd in the Gazet, that ten Regiments should be forthwith disbanded; and we were told, as soon as it was don, that more should follow their example. But these Resolutions, it seems, were alter'd, and the modish Language was, that we must keep up a Standing Army.[182] Their Arguments were turn'd topsy turvy: for as during the War the People were prevail'd upon to keep up the Army in hopes of a Peace; so now we must keep them up for fear of a War. The Condition of *France*, which they had bin decrying for many Years, was now magnifi'd: we were told, that it was doubtful whether the *French* King would deliver up any of his Towns; that he was preparing a vast Fleet upon the Lord knows what Design; that it was impossible to make a Militia

---

181. By the Treaty of Ryswick (see above, p. 9, n. 13).

182. Parliament met on 3 December 1697 (Boyer, *William III*, 3:286). In his speech on that day William told Parliament that the "Circumstances of Affairs abroad are such, that I think my self obliged to tell you my Opinion, that for the present, *England cannot be safe without a Land-Force;* and I hope we shall not give those that mean Us ill, the opportunity of effecting that under the Notion of Peace, which they could not bring to pass by a War" (Boyer, *William III*, 3:287). See also Burnet, *History*, 2:206.

useful; that the warlike King *Jemmy*[183] had an Army of eighteen thousand *Irish* Hero's in *France*, who would be ready when call'd for; and that the King of *Spain* was dying.[184] The Members of Parliament were discours'd with as they came to Town;[185] 'twas whisper'd about, that the Whigs would be all turn'd out of Imployments: a new Plot was said to be discover'd for murdering the King, and searches were made at Midnight thro the whole City to the discovery of plenty of Fornication, but no Traiters. The Placemongers[186] consulted among themselves, and found by a wonderful Sympathy they were all of one Opinion; and if by any means they could get a few more to be of the same, the day was their own: so they were positive of suc[24]cess, and very sure they should carry it by above a hundred Voices.

183. I.e., James II. Trenchard's sarcasm is obvious.

184. Carlos II (1661–1700), king of Spain; known as "Charles the Mad" ("Carlos el Hechizado"): for a vivid portrait, see Macaulay, *History*, 6:2816–20. Carlos had no heir, and on his death he bequeathed his entire dominions to Philip of Anjou, the grandson of Louis XIV, thus precipitating the War of the Spanish Succession (1702–13). It had been realized for many years that the death of Carlos had the potential to detonate a continental crisis. See above, p. 160, n. 18.

185. Boyer's analysis of the various factions in the House of Commons is helpful to bear in mind when reading Trenchard's account of their proceedings:

> This House of Commons was compos'd of three sorts of Persons: The first were altogether in the Court Interest; not only because some of them had profitable Places in the Government, but also because they were all entirely satisfied, that King *William* had nothing but the Good of the Nation in Prospect; and that he would never encroach on their Liberties. The Second, Who stiled themselves the Country-Party, and most of whom the Court look'd upon as Disaffected, were such as never approved the Methods by which the Revolution was accomplish'd; who always entertain'd a Jealousie of King *William*, and therefore, upon several Occasions, endeavour'd to cross his Designs. The Third, and most dangerous, tho' fewest in Number, were those who hitherto had warmly stickled for the present Government; but who, at the same time, were secretly laying the Foundation of a Common-Wealth. 'Twas through the Encouragement of the latter, and the indefatigable Industry of some Men of desperate Fortunes and Principles, that the Nation was now over run with the Works of the boldest and most learned Advocates for a Republick. (Boyer, *William III*, 3:289–90)

Trenchard belonged to the third of these groups.

186. Those who trade in government places. *OED*'s earliest recorded occurrence is 1785 (s.v. "place"), so once again we can see Trenchard using a conspicuously modern vocabulary, or indeed perhaps even coining a word (cf. nn. 155, 156).

The House had not sat a week,[187] but this matter came to be debated; and the question in the Committee was, *Whether all Forces rais'd since the year 80 should be disbanded?* which was carried in the Affirmative, the Court being not able to bring it to a division; and the next day when it was reported, they did not attemt to set aside the Vote, but to recommit it, upon pretence it tied the King to the old Tory Regiments, (tho by the way, none of those Regiments have bin since disbanded) and som said they thought the Forces in 80 too many. I can safely say, tho I had frequent discourse with many of them, yet I never heard any one of them at that time pretend to be for a greater force than this Vote left the King: but let what will be their reasons, it was carried against them[188] by a majority of 37, the Affirmatives being 185, and the Negatives 148. I will not here take notice of what som People have said, *viz. That of the 148 who were for recommitting the Vote,* 116 *had Places,* because I doubt the fact, nor do I believe their Places would biass them.[189]

This was a thorow Victory, and required great skill and address to retrieve.[190] The fears of *France* were again multiplied; 'twas said there was a privat Article that King *James* was to leave *France,* which the *French* refused to perform; that *Boufflers* and the Earl of *Portland* had given one another the Lie;[191] that som of the latter's Retinue had bin kill'd; that the

---

187. For an account of the debates on a standing army beginning 10 December 1697, including a very long speech against standing armies rehearsing many of the topics cited by Trenchard, see Boyer, *William III*, 3:290–302 (Appendix E, below, pp. 635–50).

188. On 11 December 1697 (Boyer, *William III*, 3:302).

189. Mordant sarcasm.

190. Boyer explains William's affront at this vote: "The King was very much dissatisfied with these Resolutions; not but that his Majesty was willing to ease his *English* Subjects of the Charge, and free them from the Apprehensions of a Standing Army; . . . But his Majesty did not think it proper absolutely to comply with the Commons, as to the Licentiating [i.e., disbanding] all the Troops that had been raised since the Year 1680. whereby he must leave himself and his Kingdoms too much expos'd" (Boyer, *William III*, 3:302–3).

191. Louis-François (1644–1711), duc de Boufflers; French soldier and diplomat. Hans Willem Bentinck (1649–1709), first Earl of Portland; soldier and diplomat. Bentinck and Boufflers had befriended one another at the siege of Namur in 1695, although they were on opposing sides, and it had been Bentinck who had taken charge of Boufflers when he surrendered on 1 September (Jones, *History of Europe,*

pp. 596–97). That William and Louis XIV had appointed these two men as their representatives when the peace talks at Ryswick had become deadlocked in 1697 shows that both kings were negotiating in earnest. Bentinck and Boufflers met on 8 July 1697, and their discussions lasted three weeks, making such progress that the formal treaties could be signed in September. Boyer's comments on the meetings between the two men, and the speculations to which they gave rise, are worth quoting at length:

> His Majesty, wisely considering that the usual Forms, and incident *Chicaneries* of a solemn Negotiation, were no small hinderance to the Progress of the Treaty, thought fit to commit his Personal Interests, and those of his Dominions, to the Arbitration of Two Men of the Sword, to wit, the Earl of *Portland*, on his *Britannick*, and the Mareschal de *Bouflers*, on his most Christian Majesty's Part. . . . the Earl of *Portland*, as from himself, demanded a private Interview with Monsieur *de Boufflers*, which being readily granted, the two Generals met at an equal distance from their respective Camps, attended by the same number of Guards, and accompanied by several Officers of Note. This Preliminary Conference was soon follow'd by three others; at the last of which, the two Negotiators, after they had been some Time in the open Field, retir'd into a House in the Suburb of *Hall*, where they had Pen, Ink and Paper, and in an Hour, adjusted several Points, that the Plenipotentiaries at *Ryswick* would not have agreed upon in a Year. . . . The frequent Interviews between King *William*'s Favourite, and Mareschal *de Boufflers* occasion'd divers Speculations. On the one hand the *Jacobites*, who against all Reason flatter'd themselves, that tho' a Treaty of Peace was carried on at his Majesty's own Palace, yet he should be left out of it, saw by these Conferences their hopes entirely baffled; And on the other hand, a great many People, and even some of his Majesty's best Friends began to suspect that his Majesty had entred into a private Agreement with the King of *France*, in favour either of King *James*, or his Issue, upon Account of his *Britannick* Majesty's having the Peaceful enjoyment of his Dominions during Life; and being acknowledg'd as King of *Great Britain* by his most Christian Majesty: Which ill-grounded suspicion was three years after fully remov'd by King *William*'s effectual promoting the Settlement in the Protestant Line. Others gave out that my Lord *Portland*, and Monsieur *Boufflers*, had only agreed that King *James*'s Queen should have her Dowry paid her by *England*, in such a manner, as if her Husband was really Dead; but that afterwards she refus'd to accept it: And others again, have since imagin'd, not without some Probability, that in these Interviews was laid the first Foundation of the famous *Treaty of Partition*, which was afterwards concluded between King *William* and the King of France: But these are meer Conjectures; and will remain such, till the Earl of *Portland*, or the Mareschal *de Boufflers* are pleas'd to reveal what past betwixt them; which has been hitherto kept secret. (Boyer, *William III*, 3:265–66 [misnumbered 269]; cf. Jones, *History of Europe*, p. 655)

French Ambassador was stop'd, the King of *Spain* dead, and abundance more to this purpose. The Club was set up at the R——,[192] great Applications made, the Commission of the Excise was declared to be broke (by which nine Commissioners Places were to be disposed of, and above 40 Persons named for them) and many of the Country Gentlemen were gon home. Thus recruited, they were ready for a new Encounter: and since by the Rules of the House they could not set aside the former Vote directly, they would try to do it by a side wind;[193] which was by moving, that

---

Burnet is more forthcoming about the subject of those private conversations:

> The Marshal *Bouflers* desired a Conference with the Earl of *Portland*, and by the order of their Masters, they met four times, and were long alone: That Lord told me himself, that the subject of those Conferences, was concerning King *James:* The King desired to know, how the King of *France* intended to dispose of him, and how he could own him, and yet support the other: The King of *France* would not renounce the protecting him, by any Article of the Treaty: But it was agreed between them, that the King of *France* should give him no assistance, nor give the King any disturbance on his account: And that he should retire from the Court of *France*, either to *Avignon* or to *Italy:* On the other hand, his Queen should have Fifty thousand pounds a Year, which was her Jointure, settled after his Death, and that it should now be paid her, he being reckoned as dead to the Nation; and in this, the King very readily acquiesced: These Meetings made the Treaty go on with more dispatch, this tender point being once settled. (Burnet, *History*, 2:200–201)

Portland went as William's ambassador to France in January 1698 (Boyer, *William III*, 3:335–36). Cf. Macaulay, *History*, 6:2805–6, and Miller, *James II*, p. 239.

192. The Rota. Originally a club established in 1659 by James Harrington for the discussion of republican principles (to one of which—the rotation of offices—its title refers), and which met at the Sign of the Turk's Head in Palace Yard, Westminster, the Rota was revived later in the century. See the account in Aubrey's "Brief Life" of Harrington; William Baron, *Regicides, No Saints nor Martyrs* (1700), p. 15; *The Oceana of James Harrington*, ed. John Toland (1700), pp. xxviii–xxix; Anthony à Wood, *Athenae Oxonienses*, vol. 2 (1692), pp. 441, 591. For commentary, see Fink, *Classical Republicans*, pp. 87–89, and Ellis, *Coffee-House*, pp. 42–55. Although the name of the club refers primarily to the republican principle of rotation of offices (see, e.g., Harrington, *Oceana*, p. 123), it was perhaps also chosen not without a mischievous anticlerical glance at the papal court known as the Rota.

193. Indirectly or obliquely; with a connotation of underhandedness (*OED*, s.v. "side-wind," 2, 3).

directions might be given to the Committee of Ways and Means to consider of a supply for Guards and Garisons:[194] but the other side, to obviat this, offered these words as an Amend[25]ment, *viz. According to the Vote of the* 11th *of December.* This matter was much labored, and the Gentlemen that were against the Army explain'd themselves, and declar'd they were not for obliging the King to the Regiments in 80, but that they insisted only on the number, and he might choose what Regiments he pleased. By this means they carried it, but not without great opposition (tho I presume from none of those Gentlemen who declared in all Places they were for recommitting the former Vote only for the reasons before given) besides, they were forced to explain themselves out of a considerable part of it, for they allowed the King the *Dutch* Regiments, and the *Tangeriners;*[195] which in my opinion could not be well understood by the former Vote, the meaning of which seems to be, that the King should have all the Forces that *Charles* the 2*d* had in 80 in *England,* and these were not then here; the *Holland* Regiments being paid by the States, and their Soldiers; and the others 500 Leagues off at *Tangier.* But all this advantage would not satisfy the Army-Gentlemen: for in the Committee they indeavored again to set aside the Vote, by moving for a sum of 500000 pounds *per annum* for Guards and Garisons without naming any certain number (which would have maintain'd above 20000) but this could not be carried; therfore they came to a sort of Composition, to have but 10000, wherof a great number were to be Horse and Dragoons; and the Sum given to maintain them was 350000 pounds: but notwithstanding this they moved afterwards for 3000 Marines (alledging that these were not a Land-Force, but a Water-Force) which was carried.[196]

194. On 14 January 1698.

195. I.e., the troops that had formerly garrisoned Tangier before its abandonment in December 1684; see above, p. 320, n. 168.

196. On 14 January 1698. Boyer reports William's evasion and procrastination when faced with the demands of the House of Commons:

> They [the House of Commons] order'd, at the same time that a List be laid before them of such Commission-Officers as were to enjoy the Benefit of the preceding Resolution, but the Court, who was unwilling to let the Commons know how few of the Regiments were actually disbanded, took Care that this List was not presented to them; and when the Commons prest the King to it,

Here I will beg leave to observe one thing, that nothing would satisfy the Courtiers[197] at the beginning of the Winter but to have the Forces establish'd by the Parliament, and upon other Terms they would not accept them; and in all Companys said, that any Minister that advis'd the King to keep them up otherwise, or any Officer that continued his Commission ought to be attainted of High Treason: about which I shall not differ with these Gentlemen, nor do I arraign them for altering their opinion; for perhaps they may conceive that a Vote to give 350000 pounds for Guards and Garisons, is a sufficient [26] Authority against Law to

---

by an Address, his Majesty put them off by telling them, *He would comply with their Desire, as soon as conveniently he could*—(Boyer, *William III*, 3:304)

Burnet's summary of the dispute and William's response to it is also germane:

At the opening the Session of Parliament, the King told them, that in his opinion, a standing Land Force was necessary; The House of Commons carried the jealousy of a standing Army so high, that they would not bear the Motion, nor did they like the way the King took of offering them his opinion in the point: This seemed a prescription to them, and might biass some, in the Counsels they were to offer the King, and be a bar to the freedom of Debate; The Managers for the Court had no Orders to name any number; So the House came to a Resolution of paying off and disbanding all the Forces, that had been raised since the year 1680; This Vote brought the Army to be less than 8000: The Court was struck with this; and then they tried, by an after-game, to raise the number to 15000 Horse and Foot. If this had been proposed in time, it would probably have been carried without any difficulty; but the King was so long upon the reserve, that now, when he thought fit to speak out his mind, he found it was too late: So a Force not exceeding 10000 Horse and Foot was all that the House could be brought to. This gave the King the greatest distaste of any thing, that had befallen him in his whole Reign; He thought it would derogate much from him, and render his Alliance so inconsiderable, that he doubted whether he could carry on the Government, after it should be reduced to so weak and contemptible a state. He said, that if he could have imagined, that after all the service he should have done the Nation, he should have met with such returns, he would never have meddled in our Affairs; and that he was weary of governing a Nation, that was so jealous, as to lay itself open to an Enemy, rather than trust him, who had acted so faithfully during his whole Life, that he had never once deceived those who trusted him. He said this, with a great deal more to the same purpose, to my self; But he saw the necessity of submitting to that, which could not be helped. (Burnet, *History*, 2:206–7)

197. I.e., the first of the three groups into which Boyer divided the members of the House of Commons in this Parliament (above, p. 326, n. 185).

quarter Soldiers in all parts of *England*, as well out of Garisons, as in 'em, and as well at a distance from the King's Person, as about it.

Thus what our Courts for above a thousand years together had never Effrontery enough to ask; what the Pensioner Parliament[198] could not think of without astonishment; what King *James*'s Parliament (that was almost chosen by himself) could not hear debated with patience, we are likely to have the honor of establishing in our own age, even under a Deliverance.[199]

Now we will examin how far they have complied with the Resolutions of the House of Commons. Having so far gained upon the first Vote by the means before related, 'twas not easy to be imagined but they would nicely perform the rest, without any art or evasion: but instead of this, they reform'd a certain number of Men out of every Troop and Company, and kept up all the Officers, who are the most essential and chargeable part of an Army, the privat Soldiers being to be rais'd again in a few days whenever they please. This is such a disbanding as every Officer would have made in his Company for his privat advantage, and always did in *Charles* the 2*d*'s time, and even in this Reign when they were not in action: so that all the effect of such a Reform is to hinder the Officers from false Musters, and save the pay of a few common Soldiers.

But this would not satisfy the People, and therfore they disbanded som Regiments of Horse, Foot and Dragoons, and thought of that profound Expedient of sending a great many more to *Ireland*;[200] as if our grievance was not the fear of being enslav'd by them, but lest they should spend their Mony among us. I am sorry the Nation is grown so contemptible in these Gentlemens opinions, as to think that they can remove our fears of a Standing Army by sending them threescore miles off, from

198. See above, p. 40, n. 99.

199. I.e., by a formal act of Parliament (*OED*, s.v. "deliverance," 8a), though not without undertones of liberation, release, and rescue (*OED*, s.v. "deliverance," 1a) which reflect bitingly on William's reputation as the savior of the nation.

200. "[King William] had caus'd several Regiments of Horse, Dragoons and Foot to be disbanded; others to be reduced, and sent most of the latter either to *Scotland* or *Ireland*" (Boyer, *William III*, 3:302). As a separate kingdom, Ireland did not fall within the scope of the Bill of Rights and its prohibition of a standing army "in this kingdom" (i.e., England).

whence they may recal them upon a few days notice. Nay an Army kept in *Ireland*, is more dangerous to us than at home: for here by perpetual converse with their Relations and Acquaintance, som few of them perhaps may warp towards their Country; wheras in *Ireland* they are kept as it were in a Garison, where they are shut up from the communication of their Countrymen, and may be nurs'd up in another Interest. This is so [27] true, that 'tis a common Policy among Arbitrary Princes often to shift their Soldiers Quarters, lest they should contract friendship among the Natives, and by degrees fall into their Interest.

It may be said perhaps, That the People of *Ireland* will pay them; which makes the matter so much the worse, for they are less likely to have any regard to their Country. Besides, if we consider the Lords Justices Speech to that Parliament,[201] wherin they are let know that his Majesty *EXPECTS* that they will continue the Subsistence to the disbanded Officers, and support the present Establishment (which by the way is near three times as great as *Charles* the 2*d*'s) and this without any other ceremony or qualification of Time (with which his Majesty was pleas'd to express himself to his *English* and *Scotch* Parliaments) we may be convinc'd that they are not in a condition to dispute this matter; especially at a time when they apprehend Hardships will be put upon them in relation to their Trade:[202] and therefore we may be sure they will gratify the Court to the utmost of their Power, in hopes, if they can't prevent the passing a Law against them, to obtain a connivance in the execution. We may add; by this means they will keep their Mony in their own Country, a great part wherof came formerly to *England*, and have an opportunity of returning the

---

201. I.e., the Parliament of Ireland.

202. Although Ireland was at this time a separate kingdom from England, it did not enjoy self-government. Since 1495 Poyning's Law had stipulated that the Irish Parliament could not meet without royal license and had provided that all business of the Irish parliament required prior approval from the king and his council in England. In the mid-seventeenth century English control over Irish affairs had extended from politics to economics. The Navigation Acts controlled Irish trade and exports, while the Cattle Acts restricted the export of live cattle to England. In 1699 Charles Davenant would defend the necessity and justice of England's subjugation of Ireland by means of laws of trade: "But this holds more strongly, where the Seat of Dominion is in a great Emporium, for such a City will not only be the Head of Power but of Trade, governing all its Branches, and giving

Complement we design'd them last Year, if we don't prevent it by disbanding the Army there, as *Strafford*'s Army[203] in *Ireland* was formerly in the 15*th* of *Charles* the first, and lately another in 78[204] by our *English* Parliaments.

I can't avoid taking notice here, how different the modish Sentiments are in *Ireland* and *England*: for there the Language is, We must comply with the Court in keeping up the Army, or otherwise the Woollen Manufacture[205] is gon; and here the Men in fashion tell us, that an Army must be kept in *Ireland* to destroy the Woollen Manufacture, and execute the Laws we make against them; and in order to it the People of *Ireland* are to pay them.

This project of sending Men to *Ireland* was so transparent, that they durst not rely upon it; and therefore they told us, that as fast as Mony could be got, they would disband more [28] Regiments. The People were in great expectation when it would be don, and several times it was taken notice of in Parliament; and the Courtiers always assur'd them that nothing hindred it but the want of Mony to pay them off. 'Twas confidently said in all public places, that eighteen Regiments more would be disbanded, and the Regiments were nam'd; and I have heard it with great Assurance affirm'd by the Agents and Officers themselves, that the King had sign'd it in Council. Thus the Session was worn out, till the House of Commons tir'd with Expectation, address'd his Majesty, *That he would be pleas'd to give order that a List be laid before the House of the Army*

---

the Rules and Price; so that all Parts thereon depending, can deal but subordinately to it, till at last 'tis found that Provinces work but to enrich the Superior Kingdom" (Charles Davenant, *An Essay Upon the Probable Methods of Making a People Gainers in the Ballance of Trade,* 1699, p. 102). Davenant was replying to William Molyneux, who in his *The Case of Ireland's Being Bound by Acts of Parliament in England, Stated* (Dublin, 1698) had argued for a more lenient economic management of Ireland. However, the Declaratory Act of 1720 would cement Ireland's condition as a dependent kingdom, since it provided that Westminster could legislate for Ireland, and required that all bills passed by the Irish parliament be approved by Westminster.

203. See above, p. 249, n. 52.

204. See above, p. 305, n. 117.

205. Another very topical subject in 1698: "This Session likewise, upon Complaints made, that the Woollen Manufacture was carried on in *Ireland,* to the great Prejudice of that Staple Trade in *England,* the Commons took Care to stop the Progress of that growing Evil" (Boyer, *William III,* 3:330; see also p. 331). The address of the Commons to the King on this subject was made on 1 July 1698.

disbanded, and intended to be disbanded, and of the Officers Names who are to have half pay; and his Majesty was pleas'd to answer, *That he would comply with the desires of the House as soon as conveniently he could:* but the Parliament sitting not above a Month afterwards, his Majesty sent them no farther answer.[206]

At last the Parliament rose, and instead of disbanding they[207] brought over a great many foreign Regiments, and sent them to *Ireland*, as well as three more *English* ones. But even all this would not bring their Army in *England* down to ten thousand Men; so that they made another Reform, and since have incorporated the Officers of the disbanded Regiments in *Ireland* into the Standing Troops, by which means they have got an Army of Officers: wheras if these Gentlemen design their Army to defend us against a sudden Invasion, or to be in readiness against the King of *Spain's* Death, in my poor opinion they should have kept up the privat Soldiers, and disbanded all the Officers but such as are just necessary to exercise them; for Officers will be always ready to accept good Imployments, whereas the privat Soldiers will be very difficultly listed again in a new War, tho we all know they are easily to be got together when they are only to insult their Countrymen.

One good effect of this Army has already appear'd; for I presume every body has heard how prevailing an Argument it was in the late Elections, *That if we choose such a Man, we shall be free from Quarters:* and I wish this Argument dos not every day grow stronger. Nay, who knows but in another [29] Reign the Corporations may be told that his Majesty *expects* they will choose the Officers of the Army, and the Parliament be told that he *expects* they will maintain them?

But to set this matter in a full view, I will here put down the Establishment of King *Charles* the *Second* in 88, which was the foundation of the Vote of the 11*th* of *December*, as also his present Majesty's: and in this, as well as my other Computations, I do not pretend but I may be mistaken in many Particulars, tho I have taken what care I could not to be so; nor is it material to my purpose, so the variation from Truth is not considerable.

206. See above, p. 330, n. 196.
207. I.e., the Court.

I shall also set down King *William*'s Establishment as the Regiments were before the Reform,[208] because all the Officers still remain, and a great part of the privat Soldiers, which I take to be in effect full Regiments; the rest being to be rais'd again in a few days, if they are design'd for home Service, but, as I said before, the hardest to be got if they are designed for *Spain* or *Flanders*. But herein if any Man differs from me, he may make his own deductions.

The Establishment of Charles the 2d in England in the Year Eighty.

HORSE AND DRAGOONS IN ENGLAND.

	Troops and Companies.	Commis. Officers.	Non-Commis. Officers.	Private Men.	Total Number.
Troops of Guards	3	48	15	600	663
The Royal Regiment of Horse	8	34	40	400	474
A Troop of Dragoons raised in *July*, 1680.	1	4	8	40	52
Total Horse and Dragoons	12	86	63	1040	1189

FOOT IN ENGLAND.

	Troops and Companies.	Commis. Officers.	Non-Commis. Officers.	Private Men.	Total Number.
Gentlemen Pensioners	1	6	0	40	46
Yeomen of the Guard	1	7	0	100	107
The first Regiment of Foot-Guards	24	75	192	1440	1707
The *Coldstream* Regiment	12	39	96	720	855
The Duke of *York*'s Regiment	12	39	96	630	765
The *Holland* Regiment	12	39	96	600	735
Independent Companies	26	78	208	1260	1546
Total Foot in *England*	88	283	688	4790	5761

208. I.e., before the vote of 11 December 1697.

King Charles *the Second's Establishment in* Ireland *in the Year Eighty.*

	Troops and Companies.	Commis. Officers.	Non-Commis. Officers.	Private Men.	Total Number.
Troops of Horse	24	96	196	1080	1372

HIS FOOT IN IRELAND.

Yeomen of the Guard	1	3	0	60	63
A Regiment of Guards	12	40	99	1120	1259
Single Companies	74	222	444	4440	5166
Total Foot in *Ireland*	87	265	543	5620	6428

I have not here put down the Garison of *Tangier*, which was about three thousand Men, because that place is now lost, and consequently wants no Garison.

I will now set down his present Majesty's Establishment, and then compare them both together.

HORSE AND DRAGOONS UPON THE ENGLISH ESTABLISHMENT.

Three Troops of Horse Guards	3	48	15	600	663
One Troop of Dutch Guards	1	15	5	200	220
One Troop of Horse Granadiers	1	11	20	180	211
Lord *Oxford*'s Regiment	9	40	45	531	616
Lord *Portland*'s Horse Dutch Regiment	9	42	54	603	699
Lumley's Regiment	9	40	45	531	616

(Continued)

HORSE AND DRAGOONS UPON THE ENGLISH ESTABLISHMENT (cont.).

	Troops and Companies.	Commis. Officers.	Non-Commis. Officers.	Private Men.	Total Number.
Wood's	6	28	36	354	412
Arran's	6	28	36	354	412
Windham's	6	28	36	354	412
Schomberg's	6	28	36	354	412
Macclesfield's	6	28	36	354	412
Raby's Dragoons	8	37	72	480	589
Flood's Dragoons	8	37	72	480	589
Lord Essex's Dragoons	8	37	72	480	589
Total Horse and Dragoons in England	86	447	580	5855	6876

FOOT ON THE ENGLISH ESTABLISHMENT.

	Troops and Companies.	Commis. Officers.	Non-Commis. Officers.	Private Men.	Total Number.
Gentlemen Pensioners	1	6	0	40	46
Yeomen of the Guard	1	7	0	100	107
Lord Rumney's four Battalions	28	99	222	2240	2563
Lord Cutt's two Battalions	14	51	112	1120	1283
The blew Guards a Dutch Regiment, four Battalions	26	96	208	2366	2670
Earl of Orkney's a Scotch Regiment	26	88	208	1560	1656
Selwin's	13	44	104	780	928
Churchil's	13	44	104	780	928
Trelawny's	13	44	104	780	928
Earle's	13	44	104	780	928
Seymour's	13	44	104	780	928
Colt's	13	44	104	780	928
Mordant's	13	44	104	780	928

(Continued)

FOOT ON THE ENGLISH ESTABLISHMENT (cont.).

	Troops and Companies.	Commis. Officers.	Non-Commis. Officers.	Private Men.	Total Number.
Sir *David Collier*'s	13	44	104	780	928
Sir *Charles Hero*'s Fusileers in *Jersey*	13	46	104	780	930
Collingwood's	13	46	104	780	928
A Company at *Upnor* Castle	1	2	6	50	58
Total Foot in *England*	227	793	1796	15276	17865

HORSE AND DRAGOONS UPON THE *IRISH* ESTABLISHMENT.

Luson's	6	42	30	354	412
Langston's	6	42	30	354	412
Lord *Gallaway*'s a *French* Regiment	9	113	45	531	689
Ross's Dragoons	8	37	72	480	589
Ecklins's	8	37	72	480	589
Cunningham's	8	37	72	480	589
Mermon's a *French* Regiment	8	74	144	480	698
Total Horse and Dragoons in *Ireland*	53	338	465	3159	3962

FOOT UPON THE *IRISH* ESTABLISHMENT, WITH THE DISBANDED OFFICERS INCORPORATED.

Fairfax's	13	66	104	780	950
Collumbine's	13	66	104	780	950
Webb's	13	66	104	780	950
Granvill's	13	66	104	780	950
Brewer's	13	66	104	780	950
Jacob's	13	66	104	780	950
How's	13	66	104	780	950
Steward's	13	66	104	780	950
Hanmore's	13	66	104	780	950

(*Continued*)

FOOT UPON THE *IRISH* ESTABLISHMENT, WITH THE DISBANDED OFFICERS INCORPORATED *(cont.)*.

	Troops and Companies.	Commis. Officers.	Non-Commis. Officers.	Private Men.	Total Number.
Titcomb's	13	66	104	780	950
Stanley's	13	66	104	780	950
Bridges's	13	66	104	780	950
Fr. Hamilton's	13	66	104	780	950
Ingoldsby's	13	66	104	780	950
Pisar's	13	66	104	780	950
Bellasis's	13	66	104	780	950
Gustavus Hamilton's	13	66	104	780	950
Tiffany's	13	66	104	780	950
Martoon's a *French* Regiment	13	83	104	780	967
Lamellioneer's a *French* Regiment	13	83	104	780	967
Belcastle's a *French* Regiment	13	83	104	780	967
Holt's Regiment in the *West-Indies* which is not upon the *Irish* Establishment	13	44	104	780	928
Total Foot in *Ireland*	286	1481	2288	17160	20929

I will now compare both Establishments together.

Charles the 2*d's* Horse in Eighty in *England*	12	86	63	1040	1189
His Foot in *England*	88	283	688	4790	5761
His Horse and Foot in *England*	100	369	751	5830	6950

HIS ESTABLISHMENT IN IRELAND.

	Troops and Companies.	Commis. Officers.	Non-Commis. Officers.	Private Men.	Total Number.
His Horse in *Ireland*	24	96	196	1080	1372
His Foot in *Ireland*	87	265	543	5620	6428
His Horse and Foot in *Ireland*	111	361	739	6700	7800

ALL HIS ARMY IN ENGLAND AND IRELAND.

	Troops and Companies.	Commis. Officers.	Non-Commis. Officers.	Private Men.	Total Number.
His Horse in *England* and *Ireland*	36	182	259	2120	2561
His Foot in *England* and *Ireland*	175	548	1231	10410	12189
All his Army in *England* and *Ireland*	211	730	1490	12530	14750

King William's Establishment.

	Troops and Companies.	Commis. Officers.	Non-Commis. Officers.	Private Men.	Total Number.
His Horse in *England*	86	441	580	5855	6876
His Foot in *England*	227	793	1796	15276	17865
All his Forces in *England*	313	1234	2376	21131	24741

HIS ESTABLISHMENT IN IRELAND.

	Troops and Companies.	Commis. Officers.	Non-Commis. Officers.	Private Men.	Total Number.
His Horse in *Ireland*	53	338	465	3159	3962
His Foot in *Ireland*	286	1481	2288	17160	20929
All his Forces in *Ireland*	339	1819	2753	20319	24891

ALL HIS ARMY IN ENGLAND AND IRELAND.

	Troops and Companies	Commis. Officers.	Non-Commis. Officers.	Private Men.	Total Number.
His Horse and Dragoons in *England* and *Ireland*	139	779	1045	9014	10838
His Foot in *England* and *Ireland*	513	2274	4084	32436	38794
All his Army in *England* and *Ireland*	652	3053	5129	41450	49632

So that his present Majesty in *England* and *Ireland* alone has above three times as many Troops and Companies as *Charles* the Second had in the Year eighty, almost five times as many Commission Officers, near four times as many Non-Commission Officers; and when the Commanders shall have Orders to recruit their Companies, will have more than three times the number of common Soldiers, besides the disbanded Officers which are not [36] incorporated into other Regiments; and upon the Establishment they now stand, are as much Creatures to the Court, as if their Regiments were in being.

His Majesty's Forces in Scotland, *which in the Year Eighty consisted of 2806 Men.*

	Troops and Companies.	Commission Officers	Non-Commis. Officers.	Private Men.	Total Number.
The Troop of Guards	1	15	5	120	140
The Royal Regiment of Dragoons	8	37	72	320	429
Jedborough's Dragoons	6	27	54	240	321
The Royal Regiment of Foot Guards	16	51	128	912	1091
Rew's Fusileers	16	51	128	640	819
Collier or *Hamilton's*	16	51	128	640	819
Maitland's	16	51	128	640	819
In Garisons	4	12	24	295	331
All his Forces in *Scotland*	83	295	667	3807	4769

These Forces are as they are now reduc'd and allow'd by the Parliament of *Scotland*, for Reasons best known to themselves; which without doubt must be very good ones, since 'tis commonly said, that ten Privy Counsellors of that Kingdom, who appear'd against the Army, are turn'd out of the Council; which, if true, I presume will be a sufficient warning to our Gentlemen at home.

However, there is this use in the *Scotch* Army, that if the Parliament of *England* shall be prevail'd on to think any Forces necessary, a lesser Number will be sufficient.

His Majesty's Forces in Holland.

	Troops and Companies.	Commission Officers	Non-Commis. Officers.	Private Men.	Total Number.
Lawder's	13	44	104	780	928
William Collins	13	44	104	780	928
Murray's	13	44	104	780	928
Ferguson's	13	44	104	780	928
Stranaver's	13	44	104	780	928
	13	44	104	780	928
All the Forces in *Holland*	78	264	624	4680	5568
So that his Majesty's whole Army consists of	813	3612	6420	49937	59969

Of these seven thousand, eight hundred, and seventy seven, are Foreigners, which is the first foreign Army that ever set foot in *England* but as Enemies.

Since the writing of this I am informed, that *Brudenall's* Regiment is in being, and that *Eppinger's* Dragoons are in *English* Pay, which if true, will make the whole Army sixty odd thousand Men: but in this as well as many other Parts of the List I may be mistaken, for which I hope I shall be excused, when I acquaint the Reader that I was forced to pick it out from accidental Discourses with Officers, having apply'd to my Lord R——'s Office[209] without Success, tho I made such Interest for it as upon another occasion would not have bin refused.

209. Rochester. Laurence Hyde (1642–1711), first Earl of Rochester; courtier and politician. Although Hyde had, after 1688, initially been regarded by William

If the Prince of *Orange* in his Declaration, instead of telling us that we should be settled upon such a foundation that there should be no danger of our falling again into Slavery, and that he would send back all his Forces as soon as that was done, had promis'd us that after an eight Years War (which should leave us in Debt near twenty Millions) we should have a Standing Army establish'd, a great many of which should be Foreigners, I believe few Men would have thought such a Revolution worth the hazard of their Lives and Estates: but his mighty Soul was above such abject thoughts as these; his Declaration was his [38] own, these paltry Designs are our Undertakers, who would shelter their own Oppressions under his Sacred Name.

I would willingly know whether the late King *James* could have inslaved us but by an Army, and whether there is any way of securing us from falling again into Slavery but by disbanding them. It was in that sense I understood his Majesty's Declaration, and therefore did early take up Arms for him,[210] as I shall be always ready to do. It was this alone which made his assistance necessary to us, otherwise we had wanted none but the Hangman's.

I will venture to say, that if this Army dos not make us Slaves, we are the only People upon Earth in such Circumstances that ever escap'd it with the 4*th* part of their number. It is a greater force than *Alexander* conquer'd the East with,[211] than *Caesar* had in his Conquest of *Gaul*,[212] or indeed the whole *Roman* Empire;[213] double the number that any of our Ancestors

---

III with suspicion on account of his previous Stuart loyalism and his personal attachment to James II, by the end of William's reign rapprochement had taken place, and Hyde was given responsibility for the direction of Scottish affairs.

210. This seems to imply that Trenchard had joined William of Orange after he had landed in 1688, but this is not confirmed by any of his recent biographers.

211. Alexander the Great crossed the Dardanelles and invaded Asia in 334 B.C. with 30,000 infantry and 5,000 cavalry.

212. When Caesar took command of the province of Gaul in 58 B.C. he initially had four legions under his command, and in the course of his proconsulship he raised a further two legions. In the late republic the nominal strength of a legion was 6,000 men, although it often fell short of that number. So the maximum manpower available to Caesar during his conquest of Gaul, excluding native auxiliaries, was in the region of 36,000 men.

213. An error. The peacetime establishment of the Roman empire in the time of Hadrian would be calculated by Gibbon at thirty legions, totaling at that time

ever invaded *France* with,[214] *Agesilaus* the *Persians*,[215] or *Huniades*[216] and *Scanderbeg*[217] the *Turkish* Empire; as many again as was in any Battel

---

some 375,000 men (Gibbon, *Decline and Fall*, 1:46). Sidney had recently arrived at the same figure (Sidney, *Discourses*, p. 455).

214. Although reliable statistics are elusive, Edward III is said to have had an army of 32,000 at the siege of Calais (1346–47). Henry V invaded France in 1414 with an army of some 10,500 men and fought the Battle of Agincourt (1415) with approximately 6,000 men.

215. Agesilaus II (ca. 444–360 B.C.), king of Sparta; commander of the Spartan army through the period of its supremacy (404–371 B.C.); he invaded Phrygia in 396 and 394, and Lydia in 395. Reliable statistics for his forces are not available.

216. János Hunyadi (1407?–1456), Hungarian general; governor of the kingdom of Hungary, 1446–52; famous for his campaigns against the Turks, especially the so-called Long Campaign of 1443–44, in which his forces amounted to 30,000 men: "He was the first Christian captaine that shewed the Turkes were to be ouercome; and obtained more great victories against them than any one of the Christian princes before him. He was vnto that barbarous people a great terror, and with the spoile of them beautified his countrey" (Knolles, *Turkes*, pp. 266–358; quotation on p. 358). Hunyadi is a surprising name for Trenchard to mention, since he was one of the first European commanders to understand the inadequacy of feudal levies for modern warfare and in consequence built up a large regular army.

217. Or Skanderbeg; byname of Gjergj Kastrioti (1405–68), Albanian commander, who in the period 1444–66 repulsed thirteen Turkish invasions:

At this time amongst the distressed princes of MACEDONIA, and GRAECIA, one *Iohn Castrio* raigned in EPIRUS: who seeing how mightily the Turke preuailed against the princes his neighbours, and considering that hee was not able by any meanes to withstand so puissant an enemie; to obtaine peace, he was glad to deliuer into *Amurath* his possession, his foure sonnes, *Stanisius, Reposius, Constantine,* and *George,* for hostages: whom *Amurath* faithfully promised, well and honourably to intreat. But as soone as he had got them within his reach, he falsified his faith, and caused them to be circumcised after the Turkish manner, and to bee instructed in the Turkish superstition, to the great griefe of their Christian parents: . . . But *George* the youngest, whom the Turks named *Scander-beg* or lord *Alexander,* for his excellent feature, and pregnant wit, he alwaies entirely loued, and as some thought, more passionatly than he should haue loued a boy. Him he caused to be diligently instructed in all kind of actiuitie, and feats of warre, wherin he excelled al other his equals in *Amurath* his court; and rising by many degrees of honor, came at last (being yet but verie yong) to be a great Sanzack or gouernor of a prouince, and was many times appointed by *Amurath* to be generall of his armies; in which seruice hee so behaued himselfe, that he got the loue of all that knew him, and increased his credit with *Amurath:* vntill at last he found oportunitie by great policie and courage, to deliuer both himselfe and his

between the *Dutch* and *Spaniards* in forty Years War,[218] or betwixt the King and Parliament in *England;* four times as many as the Prince of *Orange* landed with in *England;*[219] and in short, as many as have bin on both sides in nine Battels of ten that were ever fought in the World. If this Army dos not inslave us, it is barely because we have a virtuous Prince that will not attemt it; and 'tis a most miserable thing to have no other Security for our Liberty, than the Will of a Man, tho the most just Man living: for that is not a free Government where there is a good Prince (for even the most arbitrary Governments have had sometimes a Relaxation of their Miseries) but where it is so constituted, that no one can be a Tyrant if he would.[220] *Cicero* says, tho a Master dos not tyrannize, yet 'tis a lamentable consideration that it is in his power to do so; and therfore such a Power is to be trusted to none, which if it dos not find a Tyrant, commonly makes one; and if not him, to be sure a Successor.[221]

---

natiue countrie, from the horrible slauerie of the Turkish tyrannie, as shall be afterwards declared. (Knolles, *Turkes*, pp. 260–404; quotation on pp. 260–61)

The references to Huniades and Scanderbeg were topical in 1698. At the end of the previous year in the Battle of Zenta, at the River Theisse in Hungary, Prince Eugene had defeated a Turkish army commanded by the Grand Seignior, thereby echoing their exploits (Burnet, *History*, 2:203–4; Jones, *History of Europe*, pp. 666–70). Narratives of confessional conflicts in eastern Europe at this time were commonly interleaved with accounts of Stuart misgovernment: e.g., Jones, *History of Europe*, pp. 156–79.

218. More commonly referred to as the Eighty Years' War (1568–1648), i.e., the Dutch struggle for independence from Spanish rule.

219. Boyer gives the strength of William's forces for the invasion of England as 3,660 cavalry and 10,692 infantry (Boyer, *William III*, 1:227). Burnet does not specify the size of William's army.

220. Trenchard here deploys a Roman concept of liberty, in which the criterion of whether or not a man is free is whether or not he is in the power, even potentially, of another (for which the technical Latin term was *obnoxius*, or "liable to punishment", i.e., the condition of a slave); see Quentin Skinner, *Liberty Before Liberalism* (Cambridge: Cambridge University Press, 1998), especially pp. 38–46. Cf. Algernon Sidney's similar understanding of liberty as "exemption from the dominion of another": "Liberty consists solely in an independency upon the will of another, and by the name of slave we understand a man, who can neither dispose of his person nor goods, but enjoys all at the will of his master" (Sidney, *Discourses*, pp. 57, 17).

221. Untraced.

If any one during the Reign of *Charles* the Second, when those that were call'd *Whigs*,[222] with a noble Spirit of Liberty, both in the Parliament House and in private Companies, oppos'd a few Guards as Badges of Tyranny, a Destruction to our Constitu[39]tion, and the Foundations of a Standing Army: I say, if any should have told them that a Deliverer should com and rescue them from the Oppressions under which they then labor'd; that *France* by a tedious and consumtive War should be reduc'd to half the Power it then had; and even at that time they should not only be passive, but use their utmost Interest, and distort their Reason to find out Arguments for keeping up so vast an Army, and make the Abuses of which they had bin all their lives complaining, Precedents to justify those Procedings; whoever would have told them this, must have bin very regardless of his Reputation, and bin thought to have had a great deal of ill nature. But the truth is, we have lived in an Age of Miracles, and there is nothing so extravagant that we may not expect to see, when surly Patriots grow servil Flatterers, old Commonwealthsmen declare for the Prerogative,[223] and Admirals against the Fleet.

But I wonder what Arguments in nature our Hirelings will think of for keeping up an Army this year. Good Reasons lie within a narrow Compass, and might be guessed at; but nonsense is infinit. The Arguments they chiefly insisted upon last year were, That it was uncertain

222. "Whig" is a contraction of "whiggamore," a term of abuse for Scottish Puritan rebels coined during the Civil War. However, it was not the armed conflicts of the 1640s but rather the Exclusion Crisis of 1679–81 that brought the words "Whig" and "Tory" into common use, where they referred to the two opposed camps in that crisis of state.

223. Trenchard alludes to the conversion of the Whigs from a party of revolution to a party of monarchical administration. Burnet notes that 1698 marked the turning point in their reputation with the nation: "It is certain, that this Act [the creation of the new East-India Company], together with the Inclinations which those of the Whigs, who were in good Posts, had expressed for keeping up a greater Land Force, did contribute to the blasting the reputation, they had hitherto maintained, of being good Patriots, and was made use of over *England* by the Tories, to disgrace both the King and them" (Burnet, *History*, 2:209). For a lively yet scholarly account of this evolution in the character of Whiggism, see J. P. Kenyon, *Revolution Principles: The Politics of Party*, 1689–1720 (Cambridge: Cambridge University Press, 1977).

whether the *French* King would deliver up any of his Towns if we disbanded our Army; that King *James* had 18000 Men at his devotion kept by the King of *France;* that a great Fleet was preparing there upon som unknown Design; that the King of *Spain* was dying;[224] that there was no Militia settled; and that they would keep them up only for a year to see how the world went. This with a few Lies about my Lord *Portland*'s and *Bouffler*'s quarrelling,[225] and som Prophecies of our being invaded in six months, was the substance of what was said or printed.

Now in fact the *French* King has deliver'd up *Giron, Roses, Belver, Barcelona,* and a great part of the Province of *Catalonia.* The Town and Province of *Luxemburg,* and the County of *Chiny,* the Towns of *Mons, Charleroy, Courtray,* and *Aeth* in the *Spanish* Provinces, to the King of *Spain.*

The Town of *Dinant* to the Bishop of *Leige.*

The Towns of *Pignerol, Cazal, Susa, Montmelian, Nice, Villa Franca,* all *Savoy,* and part of *Piemont* to the Duke of *Savoy.*

[40] The Cities of *Treves, Germensheim,* and the Palatinat; the County of *Spanheim, Veldentz,* and Dutchy of *Deuxponts,* the County of *Mombelliand,* and som possessions of *Burgundy;* the Forts of *Kiel, Friburg, St. Peterfort, Destoile;* the Town of *Philipsburg,* and most of *Alsace, Eberenburg,* and the Dutchy of *Lorrain* to the Empire: has demolished *Hunningen, Montroyal* and *Kernburg.*

He has delivered up the Principality of *Orange* to the King of *England.*

These are vast Countries, and contain in bigness as much ground as the Kingdom of *England,* and maintained the King of *France* above 100000 Men; besides, he had laid out vast Sums in the Fortifications he delivered up and demolished. Add to this, his Kingdom is miserably impoverished and depopulated by this War; his Manufactures much impaired; great numbers of Offices have bin erected, which like Leeches draw away the Peoples blood; prodigious Debts contracted, and a most beneficial Trade with *England* lost. These things being considered, there can be little danger of their shewing over much wantonness, especially for som years: and yet still we must be bullied by the name of *France,* and

224. See above, p. 326, n. 184.
225. See above, p. 327, n. 191.

the Fear of it must do what their Power could never yet effect: which is a little too gross, considering they were inslaved by the same means. For in *Lewis* the 11*th*'s time,[226] the *French* gave up their Liberties for fear of *England,* and now we must give up ours for fear of *France.*

Secondly, Most of King *James*'s *English* and *Irish* Forces which we have bin so often threatened with, are disbanded; and he is said to subsist upon his Majesty's Charity,[227] which will be a sufficient Caution for his good behaviour.

Thirdly, The *French* Fleet, which was another Bugbear, exceeded not this year 20 Sail, nor attemted any thing, tho we had no Fleet out to oppose them.

Fourthly, The King of *Spain* is not dead, nor in a more dangerous Condition than he has bin for som years; and we are not without hopes that his Majesty by his extraordinary Prudence[228] has taken such care as to prevent a new War in case he should die.

Fifthly, As to the Militia, I suppose every Man is now satis[41]fied that we must never expect to see it made useful till we have disbanded the Army. I would not be here understood to throw the whole odium of that matter upon the Court; for there are several other Parties in *England,* that are not over-zealous for a Militia. First, those who are for restoring K. *James*'s Trumpery,[229] and would have the Army disbanded, and no Force settled in the room of it. Next, there are a mungrel sort of Men

226. Louis XI (born 1423; king of France, 1461–83) exploited the threat posed by England to France during the Hundred Years' War to strengthen the power and authority of the French Crown. Louis XI was discussed in English political writing of the later seventeenth century as an example of one possible remedy for the perceived defects of the English constitution: namely, an enlargement of the powers of the Crown: see, e.g., Neville, *Plato Redivivus,* p. 174, and above, p. 129, n. 36.

227. I.e., the charity of William III; a reference to the payment of Mary of Modena's jointure of £50,000 per annum, which was agreed as part of the Treaty of Ryswick (see above, p. 327, n. 191).

228. In fact, Carlos II would die in 1700. Trenchard refers to the Partition Treaties, which were designed by William III to prevent a European war on the death of Carlos II, but which failed of their purpose when Louis XIV accepted the terms of Carlos's will; see above, p. 326, n. 184. For the Partition Treaties, see above, p. 160, n. 18.

229. I.e., the Jacobites.

who are not direct Enemies to the King, yet because their fancied merit is not rewarded at their own price,[230] they are so shagreen[231] that they will not let him have the Reputation of so noble an Establishment. Besides these, there are others that having no notion of any Militia but our own, and being utterly unacquainted with antient and modern History, think it impracticable:[232] and som wretched things are against it because of the Charge; whereas if their Mothers had taught them to cast account,[233] they would have found out that 52000 Men for a month will be but the same charge to the Subject as four thousand for a year, supposing the pay to be the same; and reckoning it to be a third part greater, it will be equivalent to the charge of 6000: and if we should allow them to be out a fortnight longer than was designed by the last Bill for exercising in lesser Bodies, then the utmost Charge of such a Militia will be no more than to keep up 9000 Men the year round. None of the Parties I mention'd will openly oppose a Militia, tho they would be all glad to drop it: and I believe no body will be so hardy as to deny, but if the Court would shew as much vigor in prosecuting it, as they did last year to keep up a Standing Army, that a Bill would pass; which they will certainly do if we disband the Army, and they think it necessary; and if they do not, we have no reason to think an Army so.[234] When they tell us we may be invaded in the mean time, they are not in earnest; for we all know if the King of *France* has any designs, they look another way: besides, he has provided no Transports,[235] nor is in any readiness to make an Invasion; and if he was, we have a Fleet to hinder him; nay, even the Militia we have in *London* and

230. E.g., Robert Ferguson and John Manley (see above, p. 78, nn. 16 and 17).

231. Grieved, vexed, or mortified (*OED*, s.v. "chagrin," 1, 2). It is perhaps interesting that this was precisely the word William III himself employed when on 16 December 1698 the House of Commons voted to reduce the army to 7,000 natural born Englishmen: "I am so chagrined . . . at what passes in the Lower House with regard to the troops, that I can scarce turn my thoughts to any other matter" (Schwoerer, *Armies*, p. 169).

232. See above, p. 306, n. 121.

233. To reckon or sum up; to perform the ordinary operations of arithmetic (*OED*, s.v. "cast," 37c).

234. I.e., think an army necessary.

235. Vessels for the conveyance of stores and troops (*OED*, s.v. "transport," 4).

som other Counties, are moderatly exercis'd:[236] and I believe those who speak most contemtibly of them will allow 'em to have natural Courage, and as good Limbs as other People; and [42] if they will allow nothing else, then here is an Army of a hundred or sixscore thousand Men, ready listed, regimented, horsed and armed: and if there should be any occasion, his Majesty can put what Officers he pleases of the old Army over them, and the Parliament will be sitting to give him what Powers shall be necessary. We may add to this, that the disbanded Soldiers in all probability will be part of this body; and then what fear can there be of a scambling[237] Invasion of a few Men?

I have avoided in this place discoursing of the nature of Militia's, that Subject having been so fully handled already; only thus much I will observe, that a Standing Army in Peace will grow more effeminat by living dissolutely in Quarters, than a Militia that for the most part will be exercised with hard labor. So that upon the whole matter, a Standing Army in Peace will be worse than a Militia; and in War a Militia will soon becom a disciplin'd Army.[238]

Sixthly, The Army has bin kept up for a Year, which is all was pretended to; and notwithstanding their Prophecies, we have had no Invasion, nor danger of one.

Lastly, The Earl of *Portland* and Marshal *Boufflers* were so far from quarrelling, that perhaps no *English* Ambassador was ever received in *France* with more Honor.[239]

But further, there is a Crisis in all Affairs, which when once lost, is never to be retrieved. Several Accidents concur to make the disbanding the Army practicable now, which may not happen again. We have a new

236. I.e., trained.

237. Slovenly or careless; ramshackle (*OED*, s.v. "scambling," 2).

238. A similar insight concerning the convertibility of a militia into a professional army, and vice versa, would later be amplified and deepened by Adam Smith in his discussion of national defense (Smith, *Wealth of Nations*, p. 703: V.i.a.33, 34).

239. For the elaborate ceremony of Portland's reception at Versailles, when he had made his public entry "with such extraordinary Splendor, as had never been seen at the Court of *France*," see Boyer, *William III*, 3:335–36. For a general account of Portland's embassy and of the strained relations with William III which preceded it, see Macaulay, *History*, 6:2794–2809.

Parliament, uncorrupted by the Intrigues of the Courtiers: besides, the Soldiers themselves hitherto have known little but the Fatigues of a War, and have bin so paid since, that the privat Men would be glad to be disbanded; and the Officers would not be very uneasy at it, considering they are to have half Pay, which we must not expect them hereafter when they have lived in Riot and Luxury. Add to this, we have a good Prince, whose Inclinations as well as Circumstances will oblige him to comply with the reasonable Desires of his People. But let us not flatter our selves, this will not be always so. If the Army should be continued a few years, they will be accounted part of the Prerogative,[240] and 'twill be thought as great a violation to attemt the disbanding them, as [43] the Guards in *Charles* the Second's time; it shall be interpreted a design to dethrone the King, and be made an Argument for the keeping them up.

But there are other Reasons yet: The public Necessities call upon us to contract our charge, that we may be the sooner out of debt,[241] and in a condition to make a new War; and 'tis not the keeping great Armies on foot that will inable us to do so, but putting our selves in a capacity to pay them. We have had the experience of this in eight years War; for we have not bin successful against *France* in one Battel, and yet we have weighed

240. See above, p. 13, n. 24.
241. A reference to the new principles of deficit financing employed by William III:

> Influenced by the economic thinking of Charles Montague, the government had made no serious effort, apart from the land tax, to meet the cost of the war . . . from direct taxation. Instead, it had used the income from indirect taxation to meet the interest payments on massive loans, and Montague's Act of 1693, enabling the public to buy annuities on a million-pound loan to be serviced by new excise duties imposed for ninety-nine years, betrayed the fact that the government envisaged not repaying the capital at all. . . . By the end of the war [1697] a National Debt had been created, standing at over thirteen and a half million pounds. . . . To the less sophisticated landowning gentry in Parliament it seemed immoral not to liquidate the National Debt, and they resented the fact that perpetual interest payments extended the financial burden of the war into peacetime. They may also have understood, however dimly, that this new system of deficit finance seriously undermined their capacity to control government by the imposition of fiscal pressure; to refuse taxation to service the debt would drive the country to bankruptcy and wreck the economy of the whole country. (Kenyon, *Stuart England*, pp. 284–85)

it down by mere natural Strength, as I have seen a heavy Country Booby somtimes do a nimble Wrestler: and by the same Method (not our Policy, Oeconomy, or Conduct) we must encounter them hereafter, and in order to it should put our selves in such Circumstances, that our Enemies may dread a new Quarrel, which can be no otherwise don, but by lessening our Expences, and paying off the public Ingagements as fast as we are able. 'Tis a miserable thing to consider that we pay near 4000000 *l.* a year upon the account of Funds, no part wherof can be apply'd to the public Service, unless they design to shut up the *Exchequer;*[242] which would not be very prudent to own. I would therfore ask som of our Men of Management; Suppose there should be a new War, how they propose to maintain it? For we all now know the end of our Line, we have nothing left but a Land-Tax, a Poll, and som few Excises, if the Parliament can be prevailed upon to consent to them. And for once I will suppose, that all together, with what will fall in a Twelvemonth, will amount to 3000000 *l.* and a half, which is not probable; and we will complement them, by supposing they shall not in case of a new War give above fourteen or fifteen *per cent.* for Premiums and Interest, then the Remainder will be 3000000 *l.* I believe I may venture to say, they will not be very fond of lessening the Civil List, and lose their Salaries and Pensions. Then if we deduct 700000 pound *per annum*, upon that account there will be 2300000 pound *per annum* for the use of the War, if the People pay the utmost penny they are able; so that the Question will not be as in the last War, how we shall carry it on against *France* at large, but how 2300000 pound shall be dispos[44]ed of to the greatest advantage; which I presume every one will believe ought to be in a good Fleet.

This leads me to consider what will be the best, if not the only way of managing a new War in case of the King of *Spain*'s death, and a new Rupture with *France;*[243] and I will suppose the Nation to be as perfectly free from all incumbrances as before the War. Most men at this time of day, I believe, will agree with me that 'tis not our business to throw Squibs[244] in *Flanders*, send out vast Sums of Mony to have our Men play

242. See above, p. 32, n. 77.
243. As would happen in 1701; see above, p. 160, n. 18.
244. Explosive devices used in warfare (*OED*, s.v. "squib," 2a).

at bopeep[245] with the *French*, and at best to have their brains beat out against stone Walls: but if a War is necessary there, 'tis our Interest to let the *Dutch* and *Germans* manage it, which is proper for their Situation, and let our Province be to undertake the Sea; yet if we have not wit and honesty enough to make such a bargain with them, but that we bring our selves again to a necessity of maintaining Armies there, we may hire Men from *Germany*[246] for half the price we can raise them here, and they will be sooner ready than they can be transported from hence, that Country being full of Men, all Soldiers inured to Fatigue, and serving for much less pay than we give our own: besides, we shall carry on the War at the expence of others blood,[247] and save our own People, which are the strength and riches of all Governments;[248] we shall save the charge of providing for the Officers when the War is don, and not meet with such difficulties in disbanding them.

There are som Gentlemen that have started a new method of making War with *France*, and tell us it will be necessary to send Forces to *Spain*[249] to hinder the *French* from possessing that Country; and therfore we must keep them up here to be ready for that service: which by the way is acknowledging the Horse ought to be disbanded, since I presume they don't design to send them to *Spain*. But to give this a full Answer, I believe it is every ones opinion that there ought to be a strong Fleet kept up at *Cales*,[250] or in the *Mediterranean*, superior to the *French;* and then 'twill

245. Defined by Johnson as "the act of looking out and then drawing back as if frighted, or with the purpose to fright some other."

246. At this time the northern states of Europe were a notorious source of mercenaries; see above, p. 253, n. 58.

247. This is also the practice of More's Utopians: "They hold their own people dear, and value one another so highly that they would not willingly exchange one of themselves for an enemy's prince. . . . So they hire mercenary soldiers from everywhere. . . ." (More, *Utopia*, p. 88).

248. A view associated particularly with Sir William Petty (1623–87), natural philosopher and Irish administrator. It is expressed with particular force and clarity in his *An Essay Concerning the Multiplication of Mankind* (1698).

249. Spain had recently been a theater of conflict following the unsuccessful uprising of the Catalans in 1690 (Boyer, *William III*, 2:233; Jones, *History of Europe*, p. 498). It would be so again during the War of the Spanish Succession (Burnet, *History*, 2:475ff; cf. John Oldmixon, *Iberia Liberata* [1706]).

250. I.e., Porto (known in Roman times as Portus Cale).

be easier and cheaper to bring the Emperor's Forces by the way of *Final*[251] to *Spain*, than to send Men from hence: and they are more likely to be acceptable there, being of the same Religion, and Subjects to the House of *Austria;* whereas [45] 'tis to be feared our Men would be in as much danger from that bigotted Nation as from the *French:* besides, the King of *Portugal* is arming for his own defence, and a sum of Mony well disposed there, will enable him to raise double the Forces upon the spot as can be sent from hence with the same charge.

But for once I will admit it necessary we should send Forces both to *Flanders* and *Spain;* yet 'tis no consequence that we must keep up a Standing Army in *England* till that time coms. We may remember *Charles* the 2d rais'd between 20 and 30000 Men to fight against *France* in less than forty days;[252] and the Regiments this King raised the first year of his Reign were compleated in a very short time: for my own part I am of opinion, that a new Army may be raised, before Ships and Provisions will be ready for their transportation, at least if the management is no better than 'twas once upon a time; and perhaps it may happen that the King of *Spain* will not die in the summer time, and then we shall have the winter before us. We may add to this, that the King of *France* has disbanded a great many men, that his Country now lies open in a great many places; that the *Germans* and *Dutch* keep great numbers of Men in constant pay; and in all probability there will be a Peace with the *Turks:*[253] That *Portugal* and the *Italian* Princes must enter into the Confederacy in their own defence; and that the *French* will lie under an equal necessity to raise Forces with a much less Country than in the former War, to oppose such a mighty Union of Princes, who will attack him[254] upon the first attempt he makes upon *Spain*.

And after all, what's the mighty Advantage we propose by keeping this Force? Why forsooth, having a small number of Men more (for the Officers will always be ready, and now a great part of the private Soldiers are to be rais'd in case of a new War) ready six Weeks sooner to attack *France*.

251. I.e., Funchal, the capital of the Madeira Islands.

252. In 1678; see Coke, *Detection*, p. 525.

253. Peace with Turkey would be concluded on 26 January 1699 (Boyer, *William III*, 3:367).

254. I.e., Louis XIV.

And I durst almost appeal to these Gentlemen themselves, whether so small a Balance against *France* is equivalent to the hazard of our Liberties, destruction of our Constitution, and the constant Expence of keeping them up, to expect when the King of *Spain* will be pleased to die.

If these Gentlemen are really afraid of a new War, and don't use it as a Bugbear[255] to fright us out of our Liberties, and to gain [46] their little party-Ends, the way to bring the People into it heartily, is to shew them that all their Actions tend to the public Advantage, to lessen the National Expences, to manage the Revenue with the greatest frugality, to postpone part of their own Salaries, and not grow rich while their Country grows poor, to give their hearty Assistance for appropriating the *Irish* Lands gain'd by the Peoples Blood and Sweat to the public Service, as was promis'd by his Majesty, and not to shew an unhappy Wit in punishing som Men, and excusing others for the same fault, and spend three Months in Intrigues how to keep up a Standing Army to the dread of the greatest part of the Nation: for let them fancy what they please, the People will never consent to the raising a new Army till they are satisfied they shall be rid of them when the War is don; and there is no way of convincing them of that, but the disbanding these with willingness. When we see this don, we shall believe they are in earnest, and the People will join unanimously in a new War; otherwise there will always be a considerable part of the Nation (whatever personal Honor they have for his Majesty, or fears of *France*) that will lie upon the Wheels[256] with all their weight, and do them more harm than their Army will do them good.

To conclude, we have a wise and virtuous Prince, who has always indeavor'd to please his People by taking those Men into his Councils which they have recommended to him by their own Choice; and when their Interest has declin'd, he has gratified the Nation by turning them out. I would therfore give this seasonable advice to those who were once call'd Whigs,[257] that the way to preserve their Interest with his Majesty is to keep it with the People; that their old Friends will not desert them till they desert their Country, which when they do, they will be left to their

255. See above, p. 36, n. 88.
256. I.e., resist the operations of government; an idiom not recorded in *OED*.
257. See above, p. 347, n. 223.

own proper Merits: and tho I am not much given to believing Prophecys, yet I dare be a Prophet for once, and foretel that then they will meet with the fate of King *Phys.* and King *Ush.*[258] in the Rehearsal, *Their new Masters will turn them off, and no Body else will take them.*

THE END.

258. A reference to Buckingham's burlesque play *The Rehearsal* (1672), in which a Physician and an Usher ludicrously make themselves kings for fear of being punished by their masters. The quotation (slightly inaccurate) corresponds to II.iv.22–24 (Buckingham, *Plays*, 1:416).

Daniel Defoe

*A Brief Reply to the History
of Standing Armies in England*

1698

A BRIEF
REPLY
TO THE
HISTORY
OF
Standing Armies
IN *ENGLAND*.

With some Account of the Authors.

LONDON:
Printed in the Year 1698.

The Preface

In all Ages of the World, and under the Best of Governments, there were always some Persons to be found, who either for Envy at the Prosperity of some; Ambition, Popular Vanity, or Private Ends, took Occasion to appear as Male-contents, and set themselves to Expose and Censure the Actions of Their Governors: History is so full of Instances of this Nature, that 'twould be an affront to the Gentlemen I am dealing with, to suppose them ignorant of 'em.

In Our Age, where Nick-Names are so much in fashion, we have call'd them Murmurers, Grumbletonians[1] *and the like, of whom one of our Poets has said not improperly.*

And should King *Jesus* Reign, they'd Murmur too.[2]

'Twould not ha' been foreign to the Purpose, as an Answer to the History of Standing Armies, *to have Entertain'd the World with a* History of these Dissenters to Government, the Murmurers of the World; who always look with sowre Faces upon the Magistrates, and cry out of so much as the little Fingers of their Superiors. *But we have not room for it here; nor to descend too far into the General Character of them; but 'tis necessary to observe, that these sort of People have one inseparable* Adjunct, *as an Essential and Chief Prop both of their Nature and Design; They always Cry Wo, Wo, and fright themselves and the World with sad Tidings. Religion, or Liberty, or*

1. See above, p. 78, n. 15.
2. Defoe here slightly misquotes himself. In *The True-Born Englishman* (1700), pt. 2, p. 40, the line reads: *"And did King Jesus reign, they'd murmur too."*

both, are infallibly the Ensigns of their Order. *And I wonder we have not Ribbands in their Hats, with* No Popery, No Slavery, *or* No Standing Armies, No Lords of the Treasury, *&c.*

If the Bottom of this Case was to be Examined, and the Authors dealt with in their own way, Preferment always lists them on the t'other side: And tho' I do not say these Gentlemen who write so strenuously for Liberty, would do so; yet they have told us plainly who did, Viz. The Lord Strafford, *and* Noy,[3] *and I could name them some more.* King Charles the First, *say they,* began the Custom of making an Opposition to himself in the House of Commons, the Road to Preferment; *and how came it about?* Truly, because he found they were Mercenary, and made a Noise that their Mouths might be stopp'd; this has been too much a Method since, no doubt.

> For Parliament-Men to rail at the Court,
> And get a Preferment immediately for't.[4]

But how comes it to pass, because private Ends lie so generally at the bottom of such Clamour, that we never found them proof against the Offer?

And here I could give innumerable Instances of great Ones, on the other hand, who as soon as ever the Court-Favour has fail'd them, and they found themselves not Rewarded according to their Merit, turn'd Popular, Champions for the Peoples Liberties, and Railers at the Court. I do not say, I mean by

3. For Strafford, see above, p. 249, n. 52. William Noy, or Noye (1577–1634), lawyer and politician. Noy's early career as an MP for a variety of Cornish constituencies saw him adopt the stance of an opponent of the Stuart regime, being particularly conspicuous in resistance to the forced loan of 1626 (see above, p. 277, n. 39), in his support of the petition of right, and in the attempt to deny Charles I the right to levy tonnage and poundage (see above, p. 121, n. 15). On being made Attorney General in 1631, Noy showed his flexibility by turning his hand to the king's so-called "fiscal feudalism": that is to say, the attempt to exploit ancient Crown rights (principally forest fines, monopolies, and ship money) for financial benefit. For this loyal and professional service to Charles I, Noy was condemned by the Long Parliament in 1640.

4. A slight misquotation from "A Dialogue between the Two Horses," sometimes attributed to Andrew Marvell, where the couplet reads (with greater metrical smoothness than in Defoe's version): "That Parliament men should rail at the Court, / And get good preferment Imediately for't" (Marvell, *Poems and Letters,* 1:193, ll. 73–74).

this, the Lords S—— D—— *Mr.* H—— *Mr.* H——[5] *or any body else in particular; but whoever the Coat fits, let them wear it.*[6]

This Evil Spirit of Discontent is now at Work under the best Reign, and the mildest Government that ever England *knew; particularly so, in suffering the Affairs of the Government to be thus disputed in Print, by, not an Author or Single Person, but a whole Club of Mistaken Politicians, who in any Reign but this would have been us'd as they deserv'd.*

Had such a Cabal of the best Men in the Nation attempted the like in Queen Elizabeth's *Reign, who we must all acknowledge was a true* English *Queen, and Govern'd the Nation with a Matchless Prudence, they would have been very severely handled; but full Liberty is given them now to say almost any thing; and truly they take the Extent of it, even to Indecency and Ill Manners. For they Treat the King himself with Jeers and Banter, and make Ridiculous Encomiums on him, to expose His Majesty to very Scurrilous Reflections.*

This is so mean a Way of Writing, that I shall not descend to Returns in kind, but shall use them like Gentlemen, whether they behave themselves so or no, and leave that to themselves.

---

5. *Lord S*——: Charles Talbot (1660–1718), Duke of Shrewsbury; politician; disaffected from William III by 1690, and in treasonable contact with the Jacobite court in exile. *Lord D*——: Thomas Osborne (1632–1712), first Duke of Leeds; Earl of Danby and Marquess of Carmarthen; active in the overtures made to William of Orange by English aristocrats in 1688 but already reproaching William for not sufficiently rewarding his supporters only five days after his coronation; by the late 1690s an oppositional figure, and one of those who challenged William's retention of his Dutch Guards. *Mr. H*——: Robert Harley (1661–1724), first Earl of Oxford and Mortimer; a supporter of William of Orange in 1688; by 1695 the acknowledged leader of opposition to the measures of the court; with Paul Foley one of the leaders of the New Country Party (above, p. xii). *Mr. H*——: possibly Simon Harcourt (1661?–1727), first Viscount Harcourt; an associate of Harley's and active in the opposition to William III in the 1690s.

6. See above, p. 5, n. 2.

A Brief Reply
to the
History of Standing Armies

The Outcry against an Army in *England* is carried on with so high a hand, that nothing can be said to it with any hope of Effect on the Complainants. They go on with their own Arguments, never thinking any thing that is or can be said to them, worth while to take notice of: For it seems to be more their Design to render the Government suspected, than to argue fairly whether it be really true or not, That an Army must be our ruine.

I have considered their former Books according to their Desire, and to which they refer in this, and the several Answers to them; some of which seem to me to carry a great Weight with them; but to them are of so small a Consequence, that they do not think them worth a notice.

They have now given the World what they call a *History of Standing Armies*, in which they have been [2] guilty of some Mistakes, some Omissions, and some Contradictions; and tho' the Historical part might very well have been omitted, as being nothing at all to the purpose; yet 'tis very proper to tell them,

First, 'Tis a Mistake that the *Spaniards* did any thing to purpose in the Seventeen Provinces[7] with 9000 Men, which they call a *Standing Army;* and if they please to review *Strada* and *Bentivoglio*,[8] their own Author,

---

7. I.e., the Low Countries in the Eighty Years' War (1568–1648), the war of Dutch independence from Spain which led to the formation of the United Provinces of the Netherlands, or the Dutch Republic.

8. See above, p. 266, n. 12.

they will find that the Duke *D'Alva*[9] and *Don Lewis de Requescens*[10] had very great Armies at the Battle near *Groningen*,[11] against Count *Lodowick* of *Nassau*,[12] and at the Sieges of *Harlem* and *Mons;*[13] the Duke *D'Alva* brought Fourteen thousand Men with him at first; raised Twenty-four thousand more at another time against the Siege of *Mons;* and when the Count *D'Egmont*[14] presented the Petition against the Foreign Forces, they alledg'd the *Spaniards* had Thirty thousand Men in Pay, besides the Troops of the Country.

As to other Armies, I wonder the Authors did not instance the small Forces with which the *Spaniards* conquer'd the Mighty Empires of *Mexico* and *Peru;* in all which Work, I never yet read that they had above 800 Horse and 5750 Foot.[15]

Armies, as well as every thing else, are great or small in proportion; and 4000 Archers in *Cheshire* rais'd by *Richard* the Second,[16] though they only made way to their Master's Ruin, were really a more formidable Force than Twenty thousand men in Arms can be now.

9. See above, p. 248, n. 49.

10. Luis de Requesens y Zúñiga (1528–76), successor to the duque de Alba as Spanish governor of the Netherlands from 1573 until 1576.

11. An engagement at Heiligerlee, east of Groningen, on 23 May 1568, at which the Dutch rebels under Lodewijk van Nassau (see below, n. 12) defeated Spanish troops.

12. Lodewijk van Nassau (1538–74), military and political leader in the initial stages of the revolt of the Netherlands against Spanish rule, under the overall command of his elder brother, William the Silent (1533–84), Prince of Orange.

13. Haarlem, in the Low Countries, held out from 11 December 1572 to 13 July 1573 when the defenders were forced by hunger to capitulate to the besieging Spanish army. Mons was besieged from 23 June to 19 September 1572.

14. Lamoraal, graaf van Egmond (1522–68), soldier and politician; early leader of the resistance to the policies of Philip II of Spain in his government of the Netherlands; a victim of the repressive regime of the duque de Alba (1567–73), who had Egmond beheaded for treason. The petition to which Defoe refers was presented to Philip II by Egmond and William the Silent in 1564.

15. Defoe's figures seem on the high side (but may include native auxiliaries). Hernán Cortés (1485–1547) invaded Mexico in 1519 with approximately 500 men and 13 horses. Francisco Pizarro (1471?–1541) led his first expedition for the conquest of Peru in 1524 with 80 men and 40 horses. The second expedition in 1526 comprised 160 men, and the final, successful, expedition in 1530 comprised 180 men and 27 horses.

16. See above, p. 125, n. 22.

[3] The Authors (for I am inform'd their Name is *Legion*)[17] have carri'd on their History to Queen *Mary*, and there break off, and tell us, the Standing Forces were then 1200 men, in Queen *Elizabeth*'s Reign 3500; where, by the way, 'tis to be noted, they grant, that it has all along been allowed to have a Standing Force in *England* for above 140 Years past; for we are not now arguing the Quantity, but the Thing, *A Standing Army:* And they have often in former Papers asserted, That any Standing Forces are destructive of our Constitution, and inconsistent with the *English* Liberty; and yet our Constitution consisted very well in Queen *Elizabeth*'s time.—Nor have these Gentlemen given their Quotations faithfully; for they have been told, and are not ignorant, That, First, whereas Queen *Mary* had but 1200 men, she shamefully lost *Calais* to the *French*,[18] for want of Strength to relieve it. Indeed if she had rais'd the Militia, they might ha' kept the *French* from coming on to take *Dover*, but if she had had 10000 men in Pay, *Calais*, which had been ours for some Ages before,[19] had been ours still; and if it had, the Loss of *Dunkirk*[20] had not been so much to our disadvantage. Then, as to Queen *Elizabeth*, they omit that she always had a very good Army in the *Low-Countries*, which to her was a Nursery of Soldiers: And in the time of her apprehension of an Invasion, I would ask how many she transported hither for her own Defence; for the Armies she prepar'd, at *Tilbury* Camp 44000, and 20000 at *Plimouth*, were not all Militia, but Soldiers disciplin'd and train'd in the Wars in *Ireland* and *Holland*.

[4] What the Authors say Queen *Elizabeth* did, and with what Glory she reign'd, and how she left us when she died, is all true, and much more; and what her Revenue was, and what Taxes she had, for ought we know may be so: But I hope these Gentlemen will excuse me for saying they very much misrepresent the Case, when they would tell us what Revenues she

---

17. Mark 5:9 and Luke 8:30. Defoe would return to these biblical texts in 1701 when on 14 May he intervened in the Kentish Petition by presenting the then Speaker of the House of Commons, Robert Harley, with a document titled "Legion's Memorial" in which the right of the electorate to mandate their representatives is asserted. The document was signed "Our Name is Legion, and we are many."

18. In 1558, to the duc de Guise.

19. After its capture by Edward III in 1346.

20. Finally recovered by the French in 1662.

had; as if those Revenues perform'd all the Great Things she did: They ought to have told us also what Taxes she had, and how she took from the *Spaniard* above 60 Millions of Pieces of Eight at several times, at the *West Indies*, at *Cadiz*, and at Sea; which together with what Subsidies, Customs of Towns, and Interests the *Dutch* paid her, were Infinite: And with this she did all those great things, and with this she always kept an Army on foot, and left them so after the Peace; by the same token that King *James* let 3000 of them starve and desert for want of Subsistence, on the *Dutch* refusing to pay the Garisons of the *Brill*, *Ramekins*, and *Flushing*.[21]

I shall not enter into the History of King *James* the First, King *Charles* the First, or his Sons; the Historical part does not argue either way in this Case, as I understand the Point: The Question before us is not so much what has been, or has not been, but what is now needful to be done; and I wish these Gentlemen would admit a calm Argument; in which Case I offer to prove, First, That 'tis absolutely necessary to have some Standing Force; and then, That with Consent of Parliament 'tis not Illegal.

[5] I remember one Reply[22] to the former Argument entred into the Historical part of the matter, and undertook to prove, That every Government in *England* had for many Years maintain'd some Standing Force; and 'tis too true to be denied.

Then they descend to examine the Reign of King *James* the First, and of K. *Charles* the First; and tho' they grant they had no Armies, yet they reckon up all the Tyrannies and Oppressions they were guilty of; how they Enslav'd the Nation, Buffoon'd[23] the Parliament, Oppress'd the Subjects, Levied Taxes; but all without a Standing Army: Nay, when King *Charles* the First affronted the *House of Commons*, he was fain, as these Authors themselves say, to Rifle the Taverns, Gaming-houses, and

---

21. The so-called cautionary towns; see above, p. 270, n. 21.

22. Defoe here characteristically refers to one of his own earlier contributions to the controversy, *An Argument Shewing that a Standing Army with Consent of Parliament Is Not Inconsistent with a Free Government* (1698), in which he asserted that "the Kingdom has never been without some Standing Troops of Souldiers entertain'd in pay, and always either kept at Home or employ'd Abroad" (above, p. 233).

23. To ridicule or burlesque (*OED*, s.v. "buffoon," 1).

Brothel-houses, to pick out 3 or 400 Men; which if true, tho' I do not see it deserves any credit; yet 'tis plain he could have no Army, no, not so much as any Guards. Now if all this can be done by a King without an Army, why then the having an Army can do no more; the Mischief does not lie in an Army, but in the Tyrant.

The Authors conclude of King *Charles* the First *having No Army to support him, his Tyranny was precarious, and at last his ruin.* And may we not say so of his Son,[24] who had a great Army, and as Mercenary as any *English* Army ever was? And yet tho' he had an Army to support him, *his Tyranny was precarious, and at last his ruin:* So that *Tyranny* is a Weed that never throve in *England;* it always poison'd the Planter; and an Army, or no Army, it is all one.

[6] This is only toucht at, to let the World know, that these Gentlemen have not been faithful Historians; for that they have not fairly stated the Case, but left out such things as are really true, because against their purpose; which is not a fair way of Arguing.

But if the Case must be debated, I think 'tis very proper to reduce it to Two Heads:

First, Whether a Standing Army, in time of Peace, may not be Lawful?

Secondly, Whether it be not Expedient?

As to the first Question, it has really been prov'd in a small Discourse formerly published,[25] entituled, *An Argument,* shewing that a Standing Army is not inconsistent, *&c.* which these Gentlemen never thought fit to Answer, and now do tacitly acknowledge to be true, but say 'tis nevertheless dangerous: However, if it may be Legal then, it cannot be true that 'tis destructive of our Liberty and Constitution; for that can never be destructive of our Constitution which can be Legal; That were to make a thing Lawful and Unlawful at the same time.

A Standing Army, with Consent of Parliament, is a Legal Army; and if the Legislative Power erect an Army, 'tis as much a Qualification to

24. I.e., James II.
25. And written by Defoe himself; see above, pp. 225-54.

the Army, as a Charter is to a Corporation; for what else do these Gentlemen call an Establishment? that cannot be Illegal [7] which is done by Parliament. The Titles of a *Bankrupt House of Lords*, a *Pensioner House of Commons*,[26] a *flattering Clergy*, and a *prostituted Ministry*, are virulent Phrases, and savour both of Passion and Ill Manners. We have them not now, nor am I convinc'd we ever had, nor hope we ever shall.

And yet if they were so, they are the Parliament of *England;* and what they do, is the Act of the whole Kingdom, and cannot be Illegal.

I shall not spend time to prove what the Authors own, and cannot deny. I therefore lay down the first Head as proved before, and granted by our Adversaries;

That a Standing Army in time of Peace with Consent of Parliament, is not inconsistent with a Free Government, and is a Legal Army.

The Second main Argument is, Whether it be necessary? for all things that are lawful, are not expedient. Whether there be so much need of an Army, as that we should run the hazards that we are told we shall be expos'd to, from them.

That we have very great Reason to be always in a Posture fit to maintain the Peace purchased now with so much Blood and Treasure, I believe no Body will dispute. Whether with or without an Army, I don't yet debate. That an Army was the procuring Cause of this Peace, I hope it will be allow'd me; and that had we not appear'd in a very powerful Figure, the Terms had not [8] been so good, and *Lewis* the 14*th* would not have parted with so many Vast Countries, Impregnable Fortifications, and Sovereign Titles; our Army in Conjunction with our Allies have under God's Providence obtain'd this. Now, whether it be proper to let go this Lyon upon Parole, and tying the *French* King by his Honour only, which he has not formerly valued at much in such Cases; Disband our Forces, and rely upon the League? This is the direct Question.

If the King of *France* were so much to be depended upon, the *Spaniard* and the *Emperor* need not have strain'd so hard for the strong Towns of *Brisac, Friburg, Philipsburgh, Mons, Aeth, Luxemburgh*, and *Charleroy*, which are very chargeable to keep, and no real Profit to them; and the King of

26. See above, p. 40, n. 99.

France would readily have given up *Franche-Compte, Burgundy*, and vast Territories of Land instead of them, with large Revenues and Advantages; but these are given as Pledges of the Peace, and are maintain'd by the Confederates at a vast Charge, that they might have a sufficient Strength to oblige the *French* King to perform the Stipulation of the League.

Now I do not know what vast Securities these Gentlemen may flatter themselves with; but to me it seems one of the most ridiculous things in the World to be wholly Disarm'd at such a time, when all the Nations in the World have Forces in Pay.

I am willing to give the Gentlemen of the Club all the Latitude in Argument they can desire, and therefore I'll grant that the *French* King has surrendred all the [9] Towns and Countries he was to surrender, though he really has not. That King *James* is neither in Power nor Person at all formidable, nor indeed worth mentioning in the Case. That the King of *Spain* is not Dead, nor like to be so.[27] That these are not, nor ever were Arguments for a Standing Force, at least not singly considered.

But notwithstanding all this, I cannot but say that some competent Standing Force is absolutely necessary to preserve that Peace which has cost the Nation so dear; and it would seem a most unaccountable Weakness to run the hazard of it, and expose us to the uncertainty of it: We say, *Temptation makes a Thief*.[28] There is nothing in the World will be so likely to make the Peace precarious, and allure the *French* to break it, as to find us Naked and Defenceless.

If it be true, that an Army may be dangerous at Home, 'tis as true, that having no Army must be fatal Abroad: The danger of an Army is uncertain, and may be none; the damage of the contrary is infallible. 'Tis not saying we have formerly Conquer'd *France*, and therefore ought not to be

27. Carlos II would die on 1 November 1700.
28. Defoe perhaps has in mind here Agur's (sometimes Agar's) prayer (Proverbs 30:7–9): "Two things have I required of thee; / Deny me them not before I die: / Remove me far from vanity and lies: / Give me neither poverty nor riches; / Feed me with food convenient for me: / Lest I be full, and deny thee, and say, Who is the LORD? / Or lest I be poor, and steal, / And take the name of my God in vain." Defoe will later allude to this passage of the Bible in his novels: e.g., Defoe, *Robinson Crusoe*, p. 4, and Defoe, *Moll Flanders*, p. 160.

so frighted with Apprehensions of it now all the *French* Fools they say are Dead. *France* now, without Reflection upon *England*, is much too strong a Match for any single Nation in *Europe*, and the only means to keep her within bounds, is by Confederacies, and *Leagues Offensive;* how these can be maintain'd without *Quota's* of Forces ready to unite, is a Mystery too dark for my Understanding. Indeed the King may say to his Confederates, "Truly my Subjects [10] won't trust me with any Soldiers, and therefore I must pay my proportion in Money." But other Countries may refuse to keep up Forces as well as we, and so a League would be to small purpose indeed. These things have been offer'd before now, and in better Terms, and the Gentlemen with whom we argue have thought fit to forget to speak to them.

But now we are Banter'd about a Fleet and a Militia, and these are the Equivalents with which all the pretences of a Standing Army are to be Answer'd. Indeed a Fleet well ordered is a good thing; and a Militia well regulated, *That Black Swan, that unheard-of thing*, if ever it could be had would be a good thing too. But pray, Gentlemen, give some people leave to understand things in the World as well as you: Suppose this Fleet and this Militia to be all that you can pretend, what would this be to a War in *Flanders?* 'Tis the carrying the War into *Flanders*, that is our great Interest; the Barrier of Strong Towns there is our best Security against *France* in the World: Now suppose the *French* King should with 80000 men fall into those Countries like a Tempest, as he did in 1672,[29] without declaring War, would our Militia go over with the King to help our Confederates? Or could our Fleet relieve *Charleroy?*[30] Would raising an Army, though it could be done in forty days, as you say King *Charles* did,[31] be quick enough? 'Tis strange these things are not worth while to consider: Why does the *French* King keep up an Army? 'Tis not for fear, but to increase his Glory; and for that very reason it would be preposterous for us to be naked.

[11] *England* has always gone hand in hand with the Times; and Arm'd or not Arm'd, as her Neighbours did, and must always do so: in the Days

29. See above, p. 161, n. 20.
30. An inland town 30 miles due south of Brussels.
31. See above, p. 355.

when we kept no Forces at home, our Neighbours kept none abroad, and then there was no need of it, we were as well provided as they; but now they are all strong in Men, and shall we be naked! that is certainly to be exposed?

"'Tis Argued, an Army may soon be raised; King *Charles* the Second raised an Army in Forty Days, and the present King very speedily." I would but desire these Gentlemen to Examine, how it fared with both those Armies? I saw them both[32] and they were composed of as jolly, brave, young Fellows as ever were seen; but being raw, and not us'd to hardship, the first Army lay, and rotted in *Flanders*,[33] with Agues and Fluxes, the very first Campaign; and the last did the like at *Dundalk;*[34] and so 'twill always fare with any Army of *English* Men, 'till they have been abroad, and inur'd to the Service. I appeal to any Man, who knows the Nature of our Men; they are the worst raw Men in the World, and the best when once got over it.

But to return to the Point: If 'tis necessary to preserve our Peace, and maintain the Leagues and Confederacies, which are the Bands and Barrs of it; if 'tis necessary to be always ready to prevent an Affront of an Enemy? if 'tis necessary to support the Reputation of our *English* Power? 'tis necessary then to be, not only in a posture to Defend our selves at home, but to Defend our Confederates abroad, and to assist them in [12] any sudden Insult from the Enemy; and this can be done neither by a Fleet, nor a Militia.

But to come further: We have been Invaded in *England*, notwithstanding our Fleet; and that many times. *Henry* the Seventh Landed with an Army in spight of *Richard* the Third and his Fleet.[35] The Duke of

32. As he was born in 1660, it would have been entirely possible for Defoe to have seen the forces raised by Charles II in 1678, although this possibility has not been commented on by his recent biographers.

33. After the cessation of hostilities in the Low Countries in July 1678, Charles left most of his forces in the Netherlands to protect them from Parliament's demands that he disband the army. On the subject of the uselessness of auxiliaries (as these English troops were), see Machiavelli, *Discourses*, bk. 2, chap. 20.

34. See below, p. 379, n. 49.

35. Henry Tudor landed at Mill Bay, in Milford Sound, on 7 August 1485 with fewer than 1,000 men. The decisive encounter with Richard III and his forces occurred at Bosworth Field, near Leicester, on 22 August.

Monmouth Landed in the *West*, tho' King *James* had a very good Fleet: And had not King *James*'s standing Army, tho' that was but Two Thousand Men, there routed them; I appeal to all Men to judge, what could the Militia have done to him?[36] Now I'le suppose the Duke of *Monmouth* had been a *French* Man, or any thing, he had time to Land and Invade us, and unlade his Arms, and might have sent his Ships away again, and never have been hindred by our Fleet; and had he been but 5000 Regular Men, he had beat King *James* out of his Kingdom. Again, his Men were raw, a meer Militia, and you see what came of it, they were Defeated by a quarter of their Number, tho' I must say, they were better than any of our Militia too, by much.[37]

Again, the *Prince* of *Orange* Landed his whole Army quickly, notwithstanding a Fleet, and had leisure enough to have sent away all his Ships again: So that 'tis a mistake, to say we cannot be Invaded if we have a Fleet, for we have been Invaded tho' we have had a good Fleet; and Demonstration is beyond Argument.[38] And I would undertake, without Vanity, to Invade *England*, from any part, beyond Sea, without any fear [13] of the Fleet, unless you will have a Fleet able to block up your Neighbours Ports; and when you hear of any Ships fitting out any where, send and forbid them, as Queen *Elizabeth* did to *Henry* the 4th of *France*.[39]

Now if I could come safe on Shore, notwithstanding the Fleet, then, if you have no Army to oppose me with, but your Country Militia, I would but ask any understanding Soldier, how many Men he would require to Conquer the whole Nation? Truly, not a great many; for, I dare say, 40000 of the best Militia we have, back'd with no disciplin'd Troops, would not Fight 8000 old Soldiers: The Instance of the *Iniskilling* Men[40] in *Ireland* will not bear here; for, on the one hand, they were Men made desperate by the ruin of their Families and Estates, and exasperated to

36. See above, p. 28, n. 68.
37. Defoe himself had fought with Monmouth's forces at Sedgemoor, so was an eyewitness to this; see above, p. 100, n. 91.
38. See above, p. 34, n. 84.
39. For the background to relations between Elizabeth I and Henri IV, see J. B. Black, *The Reign of Elizabeth 1558–1603*, vol. 8 of *The Oxford History of England*, 2nd ed. (Oxford: Clarendon Press, 1959), pp. 415–16.
40. See above, p. 93, n. 64, and p. 323, n. 178.

the highest degree, and had no recourse for their Lives but to their Arms; and on the other hand, the *Irish* were the most despicable scandalous Fellows the World ever saw; Fellows that shut their Eyes when they shot off their Musquets, and *tied Strings about their right Hands to know them from their left:* These are wretched Instances, and only prove what we knew before, that the Militia are always brave Soldiers when they have to do with Children or Fools; but what could our Militia have done to the P. of O.[41] old *Veteran* Troops, had they been willing to have opposed him; truly just as much as King *James* did, *run away.*

The Story of making them useful has been much talk'd of, and a Book was printed to that purpose;[42] it were a good Project, if practica[14]ble, but I think the Attempt will never be made by any wise Man, because no such will go upon Impossibilities.

War is no longer an Accident, but a Trade, and they that will be any thing in it, must serve a long Apprenticeship to it: Human Wit and Industry has rais'd it to such a Perfection; and it is grown such a piece of Mannage, that it requires People to make it their whole Employment; the War is now like the Gospel, Men must be set apart for it; the Gentlemen of the Club may say what they please, and talk fine things at home of the natural Courage of the *English*, but I must tell them, Courage is now grown less a Qualification of a Soldier than formerly; not but that 'tis necessary too, but Mannagement is the principle Art of War. An Instance of this may be had no farther off than *Ireland;* what a pitiful piece of Work the *Irish* made of a War all Men know: now 'tis plain the *Irish* do not want Courage, for the very same Men, when sent abroad,[43] well

41. I.e., the Prince of Orange, later William III.

42. By John Toland; above, pp. 173–224.

43. Ireland at this time was a plentiful source of mercenaries and exported its surplus young males as "wild geese" to the armies of mainland Europe (Connolly, *Religion*, p. 238). English policy since the early seventeenth century had been to encourage Irish swordsmen to serve abroad as mercenaries, because (for one reason or another) few of them returned. Military emigration from Ireland had been further accelerated by the Williamite settlement, which had excluded most of the population from the political nation and declared them "unfit to render military service." Consequently after 1690 Irish soldiers were "as numerous in the French royal army as the Swiss" (Manning, *Apprenticeship*, pp. 233, 399, vii; see also pp. 63–66, 316–17).

Train'd, and put under exact Discipline, how have they behav'd them-selvs in *Piemont* and *Hungary*,[44] they are allow'd to be as good Troops as any in the Armies.

And if the state of Things alter, we must alter our Posture too, and what then comes of the *History of Standing Armies?* Tho' there had never been any in the World, they may be necessary now, and so absolutely necessary, as that we cannot be safe without them.

We must now examine a little the Danger of a Standing Army at home; in which it will ap[15]pear, whether the Gentlemen of the Club are in the right, when they turn all the Stream of the Government into one Chan-nel, as if they all drove but one Wheel, and as if the whole Design of the King and his Ministers were to obtain the despotick Power, and to Gov-ern by an Army.

They do indeed Caress the King sometimes with large Encomiums; but on the other hand, they speak it as directly as English can express, "They intimate to us, that he design'd the Government by an Army, even before he came over; and therefore in his Declaration omitted to promise the Disbanding it." I wish these Gentlemen would leave out their Rail-lery, as a thing that never helps an Argument,——as Mr. *Dryden* says.[45]

——*For Disputants, when Reasons fail,*
Have one sure Refuge left, and that's to rail.

However, we shall not treat them in the same manner. I cannot think all those Artifices of the Court, (for a Standing Army) are true, and some of them are plain Forgeries. "*To tell us the Parliament thought*, they might have mannaged their part of the War by Sea. That the word *Authority of Parliament* was urg'd to that Article of the Declaration of Right, about Standing Armies, by such as design'd so early to play the Game of a Stand-ing Army: That the Kingdom of *Ireland* was neglected, and *London*

44. A reference to, respectively, campaigns fought in Savoy during the War of the League of Augsburg (1688–97) and the campaigns fought in Hungary by Eu-gene of Savoy between 1683 and 1686 which drove back Turkish forces following the raising of the siege of Vienna in 1683.

45. A slight misquotation of the opening couplet to the epilogue to *All for Love* (1678), which reads: "Poets, like Disputants, when Reasons fail, / Have one sure Refuge left; and that's to rail."

Derry not Reliev'd; that a pretence for a greater Army might be fram'd."[46] These are horrid suggestions, [16] and savour only of ill Nature; and it may be very easy, had I leisure to examine, to prove to those Gentlemen, that the Parliament had as great a Sense of the necessity of Force to reduce *Ireland*, as the King had, and were as forward to grant Supplies for it. When the King told the House, that 'twas not advisable to attempt it without 20000 Men.[47] If these Gentlemen had ask'd who advised his Majesty to say so, I could ha' told them, Duke *Schomberge*[48] himself did it; a Man who was much a Soldier, and as honest as ever Commanded an Army; a General of the greatest Experience of any of his Age, who no Man could despise without our Reproach to his Judgment; a Man us'd to Conquering of Kingdoms and Armies; and yet he thought it very unsafe to Fight with that Army at *Dundalk*.[49] And we were beholding to his

---

46. All insinuations made by Trenchard in the *Short History of Standing Armies;* see above, pp. 321–23.

47. See above, p. 321, n. 171.

48. See above, p. 322-23, n. 174.

49. Burnet's account of Schomberg's conduct corroborates that of Defoe:

All this while, an Army was preparing in *England,* to be sent over for the Reduction of *Ireland,* commanded by *Schomberg,* who was made a Duke in *England,* and to whom the Parliament gave 100,000 Pounds for the services he had done. The Levies were carried on in *England* with great zeal: And the Bodies were quickly full. But, tho' both Officers and Soldiers shewed much courage and affection to the service; yet they were raw, without experience, and without skill. *Schomberg* had a quick and happy passage; with about 10,000 men. He landed at *Belfast,* and brought the Forces that lay in *Ulster* together. His Army, when strongest, was not above 14,000 men; and he had not above 2000 Horse. He marched to *Dundalk;* and there posted himself. King *James* came to *Ardee,* within five or six miles of him, being above thrice his number. *Schomberg* had not the Supplies from *England,* that had been promised him: Much treachery or ravenousness appeared in many, who were employed. And he finding his numbers so unequal to the *Irish,* resolved to lie on the defensive. He lay there six weeks in a very rainy Season. His men, for want of due care and good management, contracted such Diseases, that he lost almost the one half of his Army. Some blamed him for not putting things more to hazard: It was said, that he measured the *Irish* by their Numbers, and not by their want of Sense and Courage. Such complaints were sent of this to the King, that he wrote twice to him, pressing him to put somewhat to the venture: But he saw the Enemy was well posted, and well provided: And he knew they had several good Officers among them. If he had pushed matters,

Conduct for the saving the whole Nation by that Caution, tho' Thousands lost their Lives by it, and some foolishly reflected on him for want of Courage; which 'twas thought, cost him his Life at the *Boyne*.[50] King *James* had 50000 Men in *Ireland*, furnished with every thing necessary but a General; and can any body say, that to attempt reducing them with less than 20000, was a pretence to get an Army.

This is straining a Text, a Trade, (without reflection) which our Adversaries are very ready at; but which is more useful for them, in their *Socinian* Principles,[51] than in their Politicks.

By this, I must beg leave to tell the Gentlemen, it most plainly appears, that they drive at Villify[17]ing the present Establishment, rather than at the Liberty they talk so much of.

---

and had met with a misfortune, his whole Army, and consequently all *Ireland*, would have been lost: For he could not have made a regular Retreat. The sure game was to preserve his Army: And that would save *Ulster*, and keep matters entire for another year. This was censured by some; But better judges thought, the managing this Campaign as he did, was one of the greatest parts of his Life. (Burnet, *History*, 2:19–20: cf. Boyer, *William III*, 2:132–39)

Later assessments have been less charitable, and have found that Schomberg's addiction to elaborate planning was ill adapted to the circumstances of the Irish campaign (*ODNB*).

50. Schomberg, reportedly mortified by William's criticism of his conduct of the Irish campaign and by the coldness William showed toward him after he had arrived in Ireland in June 1690, was impelled to expunge the imputation of faintheartedness by recklessly exposing his life during the Battle of the Boyne.

51. Socinianism is a Christian religious movement and doctrine characterized by antitrinitarianism, rationalism, and denial of the divinity of Jesus (*OED*, s.v. "Socinian"). It is named after two Italian antitrinitarian theologians of the early sixteenth century: Fausto Sozzini (1539–1604) and his uncle Lelio Sozzini (1525–62). Socinian writings had been introduced into England in the seventeenth century: see Burnet, *History*, 2:211–14. For commentary, see most recently Sarah Mortimer, *Reason and Religion in the English Revolution: The Challenge of Socinianism* (Cambridge: Cambridge University Press, 2010). Defoe, although a Dissenter, was a staunch trinitarian (for commentary, see Katherine Clark, *Daniel Defoe: The Whole Frame of Nature, Time, and Providence* [Basingstoke: Palgrave Macmillan, 2007]). The imputation of heterodoxy to the "Gentlemen of the Club," as Defoe calls them—principally Moyle and Trenchard, but also perhaps Toland, and behind him Shaftesbury—is shrewd. Moyle occasionally tried his hand at anticlerical writing (for example, in his critique of the supposed miracle of the "Thundering Legion"), and Trenchard has the reputation of an "aggressive anti-clerical polemicist who denied the Trinity" (*ODNB*).

The next absurdity I find, is *Page* 23. Where, tho' they do not affirm, because like cunning Disputants, they won't hamper themselves in Argument, yet they plainly intimate, that all the omissions of our Fleet were design'd to produce this Argument from it, that a Fleet is no Security to us. As if his Majesty, or his Ministers, should Order our Fleet to do nothing Considerable, and spend Six or Seven Years, and as many Millions of Mony, only to be able to say to the Parliament, *that a Fleet is no Security to us.* This is such a thing, that I cannot pass over, without desiring these Gentlemen to Examine a little, whether his Majesty has not, on the contrary, more improv'd our Fleet and Shipping, than any King before him ever did? Whether he has not built more Ships, and by his own Fancy, peculiar in that way, better Ships than any of his Predecessors? Whether the Docks, the Yards, the Stores, the Saylors, and the Ships, are not in the best Condition that ever *England* knew? Whether the King has not in all his Speeches to the Parliament, and in all the state of the Navy laid before them, put forward, to his utmost, the greatness of the Navy? Whether the Decoration of the Navy and Stores, are not regulated by him, to a degree never before put in practice; and whether, now the war is over, he has not taken care to have the greatest Fleet in the World, and in the best posture for Action?[52] And is all this to let us know that a Fleet is no Security to us? I blush [18] for these Gentlemen, when I think they should thus fly in the Faces of their own Arguments; and abuse the Care his Majesty has taken for that Security, which they ought to look on, with as much satisfaction, as our Enemies do with Concern.

Besides, I do not remember that ever the King, or any of his Ministers, offered to lessen the value of a good Fleet in any of their Speeches, or Discourses; if so, to what end have they been so careful of it, and why have we a Registring Act to secure Men for it, and a Royal Foundation at *Greenwich* Hospital[53] to incourage them? why so many Bounties given to the Sea-men, and such vast Stores laid in to increase and continue them?

52. A very topical passage. In April 1699 the House of Commons would urge William to take the navy in hand on grounds of mismanagement by the Earl of Orford (Boyer, *William III*, 3:375–77).

53. Another topical reference. The project of building a royal hospital for seamen had been begun by Queen Mary in 1692, and her chosen architect was Sir

But must we not distinguish things? Our Defence is of two sorts, and so must be our Strength. Our Fleet is an undeniable defence and security for us; and we will grant, to oblige them, whether so or no, that both the Fleet and our Militia, which they are so fond of, are as great a Security at home as they can desire; but 'tis plain, and they cannot pretend to deny it, they are neither of them any thing to *Flanders;* which all the World will own must be the Scene of a War when ever it begins.[54] To say we may assist with Mony, is to say nothing; for Men may be wanting as much as Mony; and are so too, and have been so this War at an unusual rate.

[19] These Arguments might be inlarg'd, even to a Twelve-penny Book,[55] like the Author's, if the Printer desir'd it; but short as they are, they cannot be rationally confuted.

"The Gentlemen who argue thus against Force, have taken upon them to lay down a Method, how to assist *Spain*, in case of a War, by bringing Soldiers from *Final*";[56] not letting us know, if we did not enquire, that those Forces must Sail by *Thoulon*, and that we must have a great Fleet in the *Straights*[57] for that Service, or they will be prevented; nor not enquiring which way those Troops shall come at *Final*, while the Duke of *Savoy* possesses *Montferrat*, and all the higher part of *Italy* for the *French*: If they could argue no better than they can guide a War, if their Logic was not better than their Geography, they would make poor work of their Argument.

But because they seem to understand such things, I would fain ask these Gentlemen, if a War should break out now in the Empire, between the Papists and the Protestants, which a Man, without the Spirit of Prophesie, may say is very likely; pray which way would these Gentlemen have the King aid the Protestants in the *Palatinate*, what Service could our

---

Christopher Wren (1632–1723). Work had commenced in 1696 but was not completed until several years after Wren's death.

54. Although the initial phases of the War of the Spanish Succession took place in Germany (notably at the Battle of Blenheim in 1704), the crucial engagements of Ramillies (1706) and Oudenarde (1708) which drove the French out of the Low Countries occurred in Flanders.

55. In the 1690s the price of a moderately cheap pamphlet.

56. See above, p. 355, n. 251.

57. I.e. the Straits of Gibraltar.

Fleet and Militia do in this Case. Why, say our Gentlemen, *we may aid them with Mony*. So did King *James* the First, after a most wretched manner, tho' his own Daughter was to lose her Patrimony by it;[58] and the Protestant Interest in *Germany*, which now is in more hazard than ever it was since *Gustavus Adolphus*[59] his time, must be supported by the Leagues and Confederacies, which [20] our King must make, and our Forces uphold, or 'tis a great question whether it will be supported at all.

England is to be considered in several Capacities, though these Gentlemen seem to confine themselves to *England;* within it self *England* is, at this time, the Head of two Leagues, both which are essentially necessary to the preservation of our Welfare: One a League of Property, and the other of Religion. One a League against *French* Slavery, and the other a League against *German* Popery; and we can maintain neither of these without some Strength. I could tell these Gentlemen, That while they would disarm us to protect our Liberties, they strike a fatal Stroke at our Religion, which, I confess, I ought not to expect they should value, because I know their Principles to be both Irreligious and Blasphemous.[60]

After all that has been said, 'twere not amiss to examine what this Army is we speak of, and how to be maintain'd; for these Gentlemen argue all along upon a great Army, enough to subject a Kingdom; and to raise it up to a magnitude, they have gone into *Ireland* and *Scotland*, and rak'd into the Settlement of those Kingdoms to muster up a great Army; though after all, their Calculations are wrong, almost a third part. In short, they have reckon'd up small and great to make up the number. To which it is convenient to reply.

[21] *First*, What Forces are maintain'd in *Scotland* and *Ireland*, is nothing to the purpose; for both the Parliaments of those Kingdoms have concurr'd; and found it necessary, though these Gentlemen think otherwise.

58. See above, p. 272, n. 27.

59. Gustav Adolf (1594–1632), king of Sweden; innovative tactician and great military leader of Protestant forces in the Thirty Years' War (1618–48). These were campaigns to which Defoe would return over twenty years later when composing part 1 of his *Memoirs of a Cavalier* (1720), a novel which also engages, albeit obliquely, with the question of standing armies.

60. See above, p. 380, n. 51.

Secondly, If the King does see it proper to have some Forces ready on such Occasions as we have discours'd, but, to ease us of our Jealousies and Fears, keeps them in other Kingdoms, and with consent of those Kingdoms; is not the *English* Nation so much the more oblig'd to him for his tenderness of their Safety and Satisfaction?

Thirdly, Why do not the Gentlemen as well argue against his having the Stad-holdership of *Holland*, by virtue of which he can, when ever he pleases, command over Ten or Twenty Thousand Men from thence, to enslave us when there is no War abroad. For it seems the Distance of the Army is no safety to us.

To go on, we have the War at an end, the King has dismiss'd the foreign Troops, disbanded Ten Regiments at home, besides Horse and Dragoons; most of the Scots abroad, sent Twelve Regiments to *Ireland*, and broke them there, and reduced the Army to so small a degree, as that much cannot be fear'd from them, nor fewer can hardly consist with our Safety; and yet these are the Grievances we are to be so terrify'd at, that nothing but Slavery must be the consequence.

Neither has any attempt been made to make this Army perpetual, nor has any number been prescrib'd. But such an Army, so proportioned, so qualified, and such a regulation as the Parlia[22]ment, shall see needful, may be legal, must be necessary, and cannot be dangerous: And to the King and Parliament we may with Satisfaction refer it. The Parliament will consent to no Force, but such as they shall judge safe and necessary; and the King will insist on no other Army than the Parliament consents to; and while they agree to it, why should we be concern'd. For while the King allows the disposal of the Army to the Vote of the Parliament, by which they may be either continued or dismissed, no future danger can appear; unless a Parliament shall part with that Power, which in this Reign is not likely to be desir'd of them.

The Conclusion

I cannot pass over this Matter without a short Reflection upon the Persons and Designs of the Authors of this, and the like Pamphlets against the Government, and to enter a little into the History of their Practices for some years past.

His Majesty has found the influence of their more secret Actions,[61] during the War, in their Delaying and Disappointing of Funds and Supplies, which, two Years together, prolong'd the War, and had like to have been fatal to the [23] Army in *Flanders*, who went without Pay longer than any Army in the World (but themselves) would have done; and let his Majesty know, that they would not only Fight for him, but Starve for him, if there was occasion; and which his Majesty took great notice of in his Speeches at the opening of the next Parliament.

After this, they set up for Male-Contents, and always went about Town, complaining of mis-management, ill Officers, State Ministers, and the like: Angry that they were not preferr'd, and envying all that were; crying out, we must have Peace, and we should be ruin'd by the War; magnifying the Power of the *French*, which now they Undervalue so much; and saying, we should be subdued by the Power of *France*, if we did not save our selves by a Peace; and the like.

---

61. Defoe here locates the authors of the anti–standing army pamphlets more broadly within the Whiggish opposition to the administration of William III. Burnet remarked that in 1698–99 "a great alienation discovered itself in many from the King and his Government" (Burnet, *History*, 2:221; for Burnet's broader analysis, which chimes in certain respects with that of Defoe, see pp. 219–21).

At last, the King, contrary to their Expectations, and false Prophesies, brought the *French* to Terms safe and honourable; and a Peace has been obtain'd as good as was not only expected, but desired.

This was no sooner done, but they strike at the Root; and now for fear of his hurting us, we must disarm the King, and leave him no more Weapons than should be trusted to a Child, or a Mad Man: And in order to secure us from a Tyrant, the whole Nation must be disarm'd, our Confederates deserted, and all the Leagues and Treaties (made for mutual Defence and Security) be broken, and the King left unable to perform the Postulata's[62] of his own part. In or[24]der to this, they appear in Print; and setting up as Champions of the Peoples Liberty, form'd themselves into a Club, and appear openly both in Print, and publick Discourses; and being all of them maintainers of the most infamous Heresie of *Socinus,*[63] they bid defiance to the Son of God on one hand, and to the King and Government on the other.

And that their Blasphemy might go hand in hand with their Politicks, they Publish'd two *Socinian* Books, and two Books against the Army, almost together.[64]

Much about the same time, from the same people, came out into the World, two Volumes of *Ludlow*'s *Memoires;*[65] in all which, the Conduct of the Parliament against the King is exceedingly magnified; the Government of a single Person opposed covertly, under the Person of *O. C.* but

---

62. Things required to be done (*OED*, s.v. "postulatum," 3).

63. See above, p. 380, n. 51.

64. The later 1690s were a period of furious Socinian controversy in England (on which consult Sarah Mortimer, *Reason and Religion in the English Revolution: The Challenge of Socinianism* [Cambridge: Cambridge University Press, 2010]). These years saw the publication of a large number of Socinian tracts, many of them printed and distributed at the expense of the Whig philanthropist Thomas Firmin (1632–97), including a number by Stephen Nye (1647/8–1719). However, it is likely that Defoe is referring to John Locke, *The Reasonableness of Christianity* (1695), and John Toland, *Christianity Not Mysterious* (1696), both of which were attacked for alleged Socinianism. The books against the army are of course the works on that side of the standing army question reprinted above.

65. See above, p. 267, n. 14.

in general, of any single Person whatever; and all the Common-Wealth-Principles advanced and defended.

And having much Work of this sort to do, and being under some Fears of a restraint, from an Act for Regulating the Press,[66] they endeavoured to ward off that Blow by publishing a Book for the Liberty of the Press, which they mannaged with such Artifice, that the Bill was not past, and so their Fears vanisht.

This was a Victory they knew how to make use of, and it was immediately followed by a publication of Coll. *Sidney's* Maxims of Government,[67] writ against *Filmer;* for which the Author dyed [25] a Martyr, and of which one of the Publishers had the impudence to say[68] it was the best Book, the Bible excepted, that ever came abroad in the World.

And now from the same Forge is hammer'd out the *History of the Standing Armies,* in which all the Artifice in the World is made use of, to set things in a false light, to raise the Cry of Tyranny and Despotick Government, which has been so long abdicated; to decry state Ministers, ridicule our Settlement, banter the King, and terrifie the People.

And that it might have its due force, to sow Dissention and Disagreement between the King and his People, both these attacks made against the Army were tim'd to appear just at the opening of the Parliament, and so industriously handed about, that they have been seen in the remotest Countries of *England* before they were published in *London.*[69]

---

66. In 1662 a Licensing Act regulating and controlling the press was passed for two years, and later extended to 1679. It lapsed between 1679 and 1685, and then was revived until 1694. At this point Parliament refused to renew it (albeit on grounds of its ineffectiveness, not because of any favoring of liberty of expression; see the introduction, pp. xxvi–xxvii). Bills to restrain the press were introduced in the following years but failed to obtain approval.

67. Algernon Sidney's *Discourses Concerning Government,* the dangerous text for which he had been executed on 7 December 1683, was first published in 1698, edited by John Toland.

68. Untraced.

69. A fascinating glimpse of the distribution of these pamphlets, about which otherwise little seems to be known. See Schwoerer, "Chronology."

'Tis hoped these Circumstances will a little open the Eyes of the World, and teach us to mark such as sow Divisions among us, and not to meddle with those who are given to Change.

But to leave the matter to the Parliament, who are proper Judges of the Fact, and have always been very careful both of our Liberty and our Safety.

FINIS.

Anonymous

The Case of a Standing Army
Fairly and Impartially Stated

1698

THE
CASE
Of a Standing
ARMY
Fairly and Impartially
STATED.

IN

ANSWER
To the late History of
STANDING ARMIES

IN

ENGLAND:
And other Pamphlets writ on that Subject.

LONDON: Printed in the Year, 1698.

The Preface

I *cannot but with Grief behold, how active some persons have been of late, in contriving ways to divide us into Parties and Factions. 'Tis wonderful to imagine how many Arts and Stratagems they daily make use of to promote their* Ill Designs. *In the War time they were continually bellowing,* the *French* wou'd be too hard for us, and spin out the War, till we were ruin'd by the expence of it; *and that, talk what we wou'd,* it was impossible we shou'd ever bring our Potent Enemy to terms of Agreement, either safe or Honourable. *This was their Trick they us'd then, to compass the Nation's Ruin, by discouraging the People from assisting with their Purses, the endeavours of his Majesty; but God be thanked, the Wisdom of our Parliaments, and the Love the People bore his Majesty, caus'd us chearfully to carry on the War, to the wonder of our Enemies both at home and abroad, and Confusion of all their dev'lish Designs.*

And now, that we have bravely gain'd an Honourable Peace; they as Industriously wrack their wicked Inventions, to find means to rob us of the benefits we might hope from it, and render it ineffectual, by setting us in Flames at home, and embroiling us into Fatal Fewds, and Discontents; that if possible our Foreign Enemies may be oblig'd to them for what they were never able to do themselves, and be forc'd for once to own, English *Wits have been sharper than* French *Swords. To this end they shift Sails,*[1] *and tell us, the* French *are weak and Impotent, and unable to attempt any thing against us, that consequently a* Standing Army *is unnecessary, and a needless expence; and least the People shou'd not regard that, they fright them with Dangers, and Chimerical*

---

1. Change direction or tack.

Bugbears.[2] *And seeing these Men's designs have, in both these changes, evidently endeavour'd the Interest of our Foreign Enemies; It is not at all absurd to imagine they have had the handling of a few* Lewidores,[3] *and then we need no longer wonder at their Actions; for that Mettal carries a great weight with it; and has a way of perswading, which their corrupted Consciences is no wise able to resist; Nay least we shou'd believe they cou'd, this Author has given us two Instances to the contrary; in hopes perhaps of reviving here the Trade of Bribery, which to their unspeakable Grief has been Dead so Long.*

This I believe, will afford us the true cause of their complaining of the split-ting and Multiplying of Places, as he calls it; for indeed if any sober man con-siders it, he can't but think it more safe; and that the Trust is likelier to be manag'd with more Integrity in the hands of many, than one; for they are as a Guard or Watch upon one another: If there be but one honest man in Five, Seven, *or* Nine, *his example will oblige the rest to be so too, least they are found fault with; whereas there is not that obligation on a single Person; But if there is not an honest man to be found in* Five, Seven, *or* Nine; *we are in a hopeless state, and our Affairs in a desperate Condition.*

If these Gentlemen were scatter'd among those places, one among the Five, *another among the* Seven, *another among the* Nine, &c. *then I suppose, 'twou'd be full as well, as if the Commissions were entrusted with single Persons; (them-selves excepted) and the places wou'd be well mannag'd to be sure, tho' there were* Ninety Nine *joyn'd with them; so that 'tis plain their Quarrel do's not lye against the Splitting of Offices; but they are angry that none of the splinters fell to their share: They think they have as much capacity, and therefore as good pretensions to preferment as any one. This is the ground of their Quarrels, and true reason of all their Complaints, and as we deal with peevish froward Children, the readiest way to quiet them is to give them something to* Play *with.*

In the following Pages I have endeavour'd to shew the Necessity *of a* Standing Force, *not as they do, by what was formerly in Use; but by considering the Present Circumstances of things, which is the only true way of obtaining*

2. See above, p. 36, n. 88.

3. Louis d'or, a gold coin issued in the reign of Louis XIII and thereafter until the reign of Louis XVI. In 1717 its legal value in England was 17s. The broad im-putation is of French bribery.

the right; for 'tis not what our Ancestors did formerly, but what we ought to do now.

Our Ancestors acted according to the state of their Affairs, and I dare affirm, if they were living now, they wou'd alter their Measures, to the present occasions, and make no scruple of varying their Counsels as they saw necessity requir'd.

Such a Method of acting is a sure sign of Wisdom, and seldom fails of success; whereas never to alter, tho' there's Necessity for it, shews Positiveness in the highest degree; proves incureable folly, and ever ends in unpitied Misery.

These Gentlemen, wise in their own Conceits, are always instructing others; they have not patience to let the Wisdom of the Nation act as they shall think fit; but by an impudent boldness they pretend to Model the Government, and regulate the Affairs of the Nation in a Club Room, over a heap of Sot's Weed,[4] with as much assurance as if they were all Privy Counsellors, and are as Dogmatical and Positive in what they advance, as if they had chous'd[5] the Pope of his Infallibility.[6]

They might have been so Civil as to have stay'd, to see what His Majesty's thoughts were, and what the Parliament will do in the business; since all good Men are assur'd, that His Majesty will never intend, nor the Parliament ever consent, to any thing, but what will be evidently for the Glory, Honour, *and* Safety *of these Nations.*

4. I.e., tobacco.
5. Duped, tricked, or swindled (*OED*, s.v. "chouse").
6. Reference is rarely made during the period of the early and medieval church to the doctrine that the pope cannot err in matters of faith or morals. As a doctrine it was not defined until the First Vatican Council (1869–70).

The Case of a Standing Army
Freely and Impartially Stated, &c.

'Tis not at all strange to see the best things Evil spoken of. The Wisest Counsels and most Regular Conduct have often been severely Censur'd even by those who have largely shar'd their good Effects. There have been some in all Ages, who have had such a predominant and unhappy mixture of Ill-nature in their Constitutions, that they have taken a pleasure to [2] be always out of Humour, ever complaining and murmuring, never pleas'd with either good or bad Fortune; and since the whole delight of such wretches consists in a constant exercise of their Spleen, [7] they take care never to want this dev'lish diversion, by continually employing themselves in finding faults in others; not putting themselves to the trouble of distinguishing between *Good,* and *Ill,* unless it be to bestow their bitterest Reproaches where they find the greatest Excellencies, because most directly opposite to their own Imperfections.

That this is the case of most of our *Malecontents* I believe we may be pretty sure; for it can easily be shewn, that the very *same* Persons have been *noted Grumbletonians*[8] in the Luxurious and Effeminate Reign of

7. Violent ill-nature and ill-humor; irritability and peevishness (*OED*, s.v. "spleen," 6a); a grudge or ill-will (7b); resentment (8b).

8. See above, p. 78, n. 15.

Charles the II. the Arbitrary and Tyrannical Reign of the late King *James*, and still keep up their snarling Humours even in the Mild and Easie one of his present Majesty King *William*: So that 'tis plain the fault lies only in their own *corrupted Blood* and *vicious Tempers*.

That such People shou'd have any regard, or that any one shou'd be drawn in to mind or value, much less to cry up, their wicked Insinuations and mischeivous Complaints, which have no other source than the too great abundance of their Spleen; and their own settled ill dispositions, which no Art can correct or cure, is a very surprizing and sad Accident, and ought to be dreaded by every good person; for in the end the Consequences may prove very fatal and prejudicial.

[3] Amongst these sort of Men none have made a greater Noise or seem'd to have more plausible pretences, than those Persons who have employ'd their Pens in terrifying the People with the danger of a Standing Army. *Liberty* is their Cry, a Glorious Topick indeed when it is not abus'd; but it has ever been made the Stalking-Horse [9] to all Designs, and dress'd up in as various shapes as the Witt and Cunning of Designing Persons found necessary and convenient to their Ends and Purposes; 'tis an Argument very specious and plausible, never failing to dazle the Eyes of the Unthinking Vulgar, who run away with the word, and consider no farther than the bare out-side of things.

Whether or no there lies any ill Designs, at the bottom of the present clamour against a Standing Army, I know not; but I am afraid of what might follow if these Gentlemens Notions were embrac'd, and their desires satisfied, I cannot but think we shou'd be in very ill Circumstances if we were left Unguarded, and without Forces sufficient to secure us from the Insults of our Enemies; but I hope their ill counsels will never prevail to reduce us to so lamentable a condition, as to be more beholden to the Generosity or Imprudence of an Enemy, than to our own Strength and Wisdom.

Nay I dare engage, that these same Gentlemen, who are now so very hot for the Disbanding the Army, shou'd the Army be Disbanded, wou'd

9. A person or object exploited to disguise the true purpose of a stratagem or undertaking; an expedient for making an attack (*OED*, s.v. "stalking-horse," 2a, 2b).

be so far from being better satisfied, or cur'd of the [4] spleenetick Humours they are overrun with, that they wou'd then make the *Want* of an Army the Grounds and Occasions of new Complaints; they wou'd then with open Mouths, and a full Cry, and with something more reason on their side, roar out, that we were neither safe nor secure, but left naked and defenceless to a Potent and Inveterate Enemy, who might, (if he pleas'd) make an easie Conquest of us, and quickly be Master both of our Lives and Estates; This wou'd then be the Outcry, and we shou'd be Impos'd on with the continual Alarms of an Invasion from abroad, by the very *same* Persons, who now endeavour to frighten us with the Loss of our Freedom and Liberties by an Army at home; the grumbling Humor wou'd still find something to feed on, and preserve it self alive in spite of either Cure or Poison.

But to begin with our Author of the *History of Standing Armies in England*; Page first he says, *If any Man doubts*[10] *whether a standing Army is Slavery, Popery, Mahometism, Paganism, Atheism, or any thing which they please.* How *Sir,* A *Standing Army* to be so many several things or what you please, this is strange indeed, and if this is all, we need not fear; for to be every thing or what you please, is to be nothing at all. I admire this Gentleman shou'd stumble on so odd a beginning; but to go on, *let him read first, the story of* Matho *and* Spendius *on* Carthage; *Secondly, the Histories of* Strada *and* Bentivoglio;[11] *where he will find what work Nine Thousand* Spaniards *made in the* 17 *Provinces, tho'* [5] *the Country was full of fortified Towns, possess'd by the Low-Country Lords, and they had assistance from* Germany, England *and* France. I think this one Paragraph is a direct Confutation of the whole Book; for if Nine Thousand *Spaniards* well Disciplin'd, made such havock in the 17 Provinces, tho' the Country was full of fortified Towns, and in the Possession of the Low-Country Lords, assisted too by *Germany, England* and *France;* I think we, (who can't boast of many strong fortified Towns, nor can't reasonably expect any quick Assistance from Abroad,) shou'd think of keeping up a Force able and sufficient to protect us in case of Necessity, and not of leaving our selves

10. See above, p. 265.
11. See above, pp. 265–66.

Open and Unguarded; this is so very obvious to the meanest degree of Sense, that I wonder how these Gentlemen or any one else can have a thought to the contrary.

But he goes on confuting his own Notions; for he confesses *that we have always had an Establish'd Force among us,* if so, then I think the dispute may be brought into a narrow Compass; for the question will not be, *if a Standing Force here is Legal;* for that's granted, but the question will be, *what Forces are Necessary to be kept in Pay at this time;* which may be immediately resolv'd, by considering what an Army is rais'd and kept in Pay for; and it is either to *Invade* and *Offend* our Enemies, or to be a *Security* and *Defence* to our selves, when we have reason to fear an Annoyance or Invasion from Abroad; and I suppose all *Englishmen* will see the occasion of a *Standing Force,* and a pretty large one too; for if [6] we have not an *Army sufficient for our Security and Preservation, we had as good have none;* so that all the pains this Gentleman has been at in computing the Forces now in Pay, on purpose to instill Fears and Jealousies in the hearts of his Majesty's good Subjects, is to no manner of purpose, unless it be to give us the greater reason to rejoyce in our Security, and to thank God that we are so well provided for our Defence. 'Tis true indeed we have just had a Peace; which gives these Gentlemen occasion to say, that we have nothing to fear, and consequently no Use for an Army, but if we consider how apt a certain Prince[12] is to disturb and Invade his Neighbours, and how able he is at this time to do it; how often also he has found pretences to break the most Solemn Leagues, we shou'd quickly be convinc'd of the contrary, and find very good Grounds to fear an attempt upon us if we are not able to prevent it. In Page 3 he highly extolls the Merits of Queen *Elizabeth,* and deservedly too, he tells us, She assisted *the Dutch,* whereby She trained up her Subjects in the Art of War, *That She wou'd never permit them nor* France *to build any great Ships; kept the Keys of the* Maes *and* Scheld *in her own hands; and died with an uncontrol'd Dominion of the Seas, and Arbitress of Christendom; all this She did with a Revenue not exceeding* 300000 *l.* per Annum, *and had but inconsiderable Taxes from her People.*[13]

12. I.e., Louis XIV.
13. See above, p. 269.

To dispute with these Men, we must set things in a right Light. 'Tis plain, they built upon false suppositions, which few People observe, being dazled [7] with the plausibleness of their Arguments, and blinded with their pretended concern for their Country; but to argue truly upon the matter, and to state the Case aright, we must consider the Alterations, and Revolutions, that have happen'd in *Europe*, within these hundred Years. *France* is now arriv'd to a vast Height, 'tis now no more that *France* which we could Invade and almost Conquer at our pleasure. We may indeed forbid them building great Ships, but I fancy they wou'd hardly mind us. Ships they have to compose a strong and mighty Fleet, with Seamen able and experienc'd to Man them, great Armies at Land in constant Pay; this is a State far differing from what they were formerly; therefore we go a wrong way to work, when we *suppose them in the same condition they were in a hundred Years ago,* and build *Maxims for present use on those suppositions;* for 'tis evident they are encreas'd to an incredible pitch in extent of their Country, Riches, and multitudes of the Inhabitants; that this is no groundless supposition, is very clear, by their being able to cope with a Confederacy of the most Potent Princes of *Europe* for ten Years together: As the Author of the account of *Denmark*[14] says in his Preface, *we have lately bought the experience of this truth too dear not to be now sensible of it.* 'Tis not very long ago since nothing was more generally believ'd (even by Men of the best Sense) than that the Power of England was so unquestionably establish'd at Sea, that no Force cou'd possibly shake it; that the English Valour and Manner of Fighting was so far beyond all others, that nothing was more desirable than a War with France. Shou'd any [8] one have been so regardless of his reputation at that time to have represented the French an overmatch for the United Forces of England and Holland; or have said, that we shou'd live to see our selves insulted on our own Coasts, and our Trade endanger'd by them, that we shou'd be in apprehensions of an Invasion and a French Conquest, such a venturesome Man must have expected to have pass'd for a very Traveller, or at best, for an illnatur'd and unthinking Person, who little consider'd what the resistless Force of an English Arm was; but our late Experience has reclaim'd us from these Mistakes: Our Fathers and Grand-Fathers

14. Robert Molesworth. For the quotation, see Molesworth, *Denmark*, p. 12.

told us indeed these things, when they were true, *when our Yeomanry and Commonalty were every day Exercis'd in drawing* the Long Bow, *and handling* the Brown Bill, *with other Weapons* then in use, *wherein we excell'd all the World.*

To set this still in a clearer Light, 'twill not be amiss if we consider the State of *England* in respect of what it was formerly; and I believe we may, without much thought, affirm that our Monarchy was at its highest pitch in the Reign of our glorious Queen *Elizabeth,* the remissness and carelessness of some of the late Reigns have soften'd our Spirits, and brought a Luxury unknown to our Fore-Fathers in vogue among us, whereby we are degenerated from that old hardiness and Fortitude, our Ancestors were so famous for. This being the true State of the Case without partiality on either side; these Gentlemens Notions will naturally fall to pieces; and I hope that true Englishmen will no longer suffer themselves to be impos'd on by [9] a jingle of Words, that have only an empty sound to recommend them; 'tis time I think to look about us, and consider seriously on the matter, before we part with those Forces that have so bravely fought for us Abroad, and are still so willing and able to defend us at Home: but before I part with this Gentleman on this head, I can't but take notice of the sly Insinuation he makes of Queen *Elizabeth's* doing all those great things with only 300000 *l. per Annum,* and some inconsiderable Taxes besides; his design is that People shou'd immediately make reflections on the Taxes that have been rais'd to Maintain this War; but if this Gentleman had that Ingenuity he pretends to, he wou'd hinder such Reflections, by letting us know that such a Summ was more than 3 times as much in our Days, and that by her Privateers[15] She took several Millions from the *Spaniards,* besides the Customs and Interest were paid her by the *Dutch,* with these She did all those great things: that She had but an Army between 1400 and 2000 Men in time of Peace is evidently false; for there were a greater Number than that requisite to the Garrisoning of the Cautionary Towns in her hands in *Flanders;*[16] but I think 'tis needless to follow him in his Historical Account of things, for they are very little, to his purpose, or indeed to any purpose at all.

15. A point also made by Defoe, above, p. 370.
16. See above, p. 270, n. 21.

In Page 19 he tells us, *That his present Majesty was invited over, and landed at* Torbay, *publishing a Declaration, which set forth all the Oppressions of the late Reign,* (but the keeping up a Standing Army) *declar'd for a free Parliament, in which things* [10] *were to be so settled, that there shou'd be no danger of falling again into Slavery; and promis'd to send back all his foreign Forces as soon as this was done.*[17]

Sure these Gentlemen imagine they may say any thing; they are great Instances of the Mildness of the present Government, when they are not brought to an Account, for taking such Liberties both in their Speeches and Writings, to Insinuate whatever they think may be prejudicial to those above them; for to tell us that a *Standing Army* is certain Slavery, and to Insinuate that his present Majesty intended from the very first to maintain a *Standing Army,* is as plain as they can speak, to asperse His Majesty with what they daily experience to be false: such Liberties are too bold, and that they are not call'd to Account for them, is plain demonstration of the Idleness and Vanity of their Fears.

Here again he lays the blame of *Ireland*'s not being timely succour'd on the Government, when we all know how earnest His Majesty was for the Relief of those distressed People; tho' he tell us, that *Ireland* was neglected to be relieved, for a pretence for the raising a greater Army; I wou'd have these Gentlemen take care how they provoke Mercy.

In Page 21, he tells us, *the King acquainted the Parliament the* 8th *of* March, *when speaking of the deplorable Condition of* Ireland, *that he thought it not adviseable to undertake the reducing of it, with less than* 20000 *Horse and Foot. This was a bitter Pill to the Parliament, who thought they might have managed their* [11] *share of the War with* France *by a Fleet at Sea, but there was no Remedy, a greater Army must be rais'd, or* Ireland *lost.*[18] This Gentleman writes fast I suppose, and seldom minds his Sense. Did the Parliament think of Conquering *Ireland* by a Fleet? He wou'd have had them landed their Seamen, and left their Ships a prey to the *French.* We'll forgive him one blunder however, if he'll take care what he writes hereafter: but I admire how this Gentleman makes the Conquest of *Ireland* and a War with *France* the same thing; for I take them to be

17. See above, p. 318.
18. See above, pp. 321–22.

distinct: *Ireland* is our own Country, and when we fought for that, we fought for what was immediately our own, we were not at War with *France,* or any Foreign Prince, we were reducing a People, who were in actual Rebellion to the Crown of *England*, but we'll not quarrel about Terms; tho' by the way, the miseries and hardships our Fellow Subjects of *Ireland* felt, shou'd make us terribly afraid of giving any Neighbouring Prince the least hopes of succeeding in any Attempt upon us; for 'tis an undeniable Maxim, *that opportunity makes the Thief,*[19] and by *Disbanding* our Troops, we may possibly give some grounds for hopes of Success to a Prince naturally Aspiring and Ambitious, and very apt to fancy himself capable of doing more than he is able; but to return, I wou'd ask this Gentleman how he came to be so sure *that the Parliament thought to have managed their share of this War by a Fleet at Sea,* which he so positively asserts. We are all sure that the Parliaments of *England* were of another mind in former Days, or they wou'd never have contributed so largely and liberally towards an Invasion of *France* as they often did, Nay, in all our [12] Histories, I never found they ever parted with their Money more heartily, than when it was for a War with that Country, and yet they never so much as dream't of their carrying on a War, only by a Fleet at Sea, but quite the contrary; for we all of us know, that our Kings very frequently Transported great Armies over into *Flanders, Normandy,* or some part of *France,* thinking it more adviseable to Seat the War in an Enemies Country rather than their own. To give some Instances,

William the Conqueror enter'd *France* with a great Army. *William Rufus* Invaded *Normandy,* so did *Henry* the V. and *Richard* the I. *Henry* the III. twice Transported great Armies over to *France. Edward* the I. twice Invaded *France.* There were no less than five several Armies Transported over to *France* in the Reign of *Edward* the II. *Henry* the V. had continually an Army in *France.* Many more Instances might be given of the like nature, but these are enough to let us see, that in former times our Parliaments thought it no diminution to their Wisdom to carry on their Warrs in Foreign Parts by Land-Forces; tho' in those Days they were confessedly stronger at Sea than any of their Neighbours; and amongst all our Princes

19. Another echo of Defoe; see above, p. 373 and n. 28.

we find none more belov'd, and extoll'd, than those Martial Monarchs, who Transported and Headed their *English* Armies in Foreign Parts. Besides, whoever do's but consider how liberally and largely our late Parliaments have contributed towards the Expence of a ten Years War,[20] and what a happy Agreement and Union there has been all along betwixt the King and [13] them, I say, whoever considers this, can by no means believe he speaks truth, when he tells us, *that the Parliament thought they might have manag'd their share of the War with* France *by a Fleet at Sea, and that they thought the raising a Land Force a bitter Pill.*[21]

I think this Gentleman should be requir'd to give a more publick account of this Assertion. To make us believe the King out-witted the Parliament, and that the Parliament themselves acted disagreeably to their own opinions, this is a New contrivance, and may in time produce very evil Consequences. But I hope Men of Sense will take care how they are cajol'd by such horrid Insinuations.

Well, now he comes to his dear beloved Militia, and tells us what wonders were done in *Ireland* by the *Iniskilling-Men*, and those of *Londonderry;*[22] but pray let us stop a little to consider the matter, and not suffer this Pamphleteer to run away with Noise and Nonsense. The *Iniskilling-Men* were People made desperate by the Ruins of their Estates and Fortunes, almost weary of their Lives by the Cruelties and Hardships they suffer'd from the *Irish Papists,* having the cries of their Wives and Children, (labouring under the greatest Miseries) ever in their Ears, and the deplorable condition of their *Native Country* before their Eyes; beside they were not a *Militia,* as our Author falsely boasts, but were for the most part Gentlemen and others that fled from the Barbarities of the *Irish Papists* from all parts of *Ireland,* and gather'd in a Body for their security at *Iniskilling,* and great Numbers of them Officers and private Soldiers [14] of the Army, whom *Tyrconnel* had Disbanded because Protestants, Men that had been in Pay and Discipline a great part of the Reign of King *Charles* the II. So that 'tis a mistake to say they were a *Militia;* farther, if it be consider'd whom they fought with, there's none

20. I.e., the War of the League of Augsburg (1689–97).
21. See above, p. 321.
22. See above, p. 93, n. 64, p. 319, n. 165, and p. 323, n. 178.

will wonder at what they did, they encountred poor senseless wretches that knew not their Right hands from their Left;[23] and always look behind them when they draw their Swords. And if these are the Wonders they boast of, they had as good be silent, and say nothing of the matter.

In the next Page he says, *at last by our great Armies and Fleets, and the constant Expence of maintaining them, we were too hard for the OEconomy, Skill, and Policy of France, and notwithstanding all our difficulties, brought them to terms both Safe and Honourable.*[24] Did we so *Sir,* then I think we have very little reason to complain, and if our *Fleet and Armies* procur'd us this Peace, They only can preserve it; by parting with *either* we make it precarious, and to depend meerly on the *Generosity* of an Enemy, who is not us'd to be firmer to his Word than his Interest; several true sensible *Englishmen* are of the opinion, that the longer we maintain a *Standing Armed Force,* we shall be the longer from having Occasion to make use of them; but that on the contrary, the sooner we *Disband* them, the sooner we shall be put to the trouble and charge of raising New; For 'tis certainly true, that that Nation which is most *able* to wage War, will be the unlikeliest to be put to the trouble of it.

[15] But here he says, *I shall omit giving any account of the Conduct of our Fleet during this War, how few Advantages we reap'd by it, and how many occasions was lost of Destroying the* French; *only thus much I will Observe, that tho' a great part of it may be attributed to the Negligence, Ignorance, or Treachery of Inferior Officers, yet it cou'd not universally happen* (the Gentleman is positive in what he says) *and unpunish'd too, notwithstanding the Clamours of the Merchants, and repeated complaints in Parliament, unless the Cause had laid deeper.*[25] Now this Gentleman shou'd take care to be well inform'd, before he so positively Asserts things of this Nature; he may be call'd on to give an Account of his knowledge in the Affairs he pretends to be so well acquainted with, and it may go very hard with him if he can't prove what he Affirms, and produce Grounds for his malicious Insinuations; but if he is inform'd of the Nature of Affairs, and so well knows the miscarriages that have befell us, where the Source and Original

23. Another echo of Defoe; see above, p. 377.
24. See above, p. 325.
25. See above, p. 325.

of them lay, their secret Springs and Movements; he ought, especially since he pretends to be such a *Patriot*, to have pointed out the Persons, discover'd the Authors, and openly accus'd them to the World; for *God* be thanked, none need be silent now in a just Cause, none need be afraid or backward to reveal the Truth; we are unacquainted with *Threats* and *Closettings*[26] so frequent in the *late Reigns*, and are neither Brib'd nor terrified out of the Truth; if they are only his own private Suggestions, and Chimera's rais'd and fomented by his own ill Humors, he ought to have forbore them, particularly at this time of Day, when they may embroil the King and Parliament into Heats and Jealousies of [16] each other, which might create greater hardships to the Nation, than the whole ten Years War, and might prove more fatal in the end.

However, to satisfie these murmuring Gentlemen in this point, we may give very good reasons that our Affairs at Sea were not manag'd to more advantage, and also that they are not capable of being better manag'd without our having a *Land Force* at home; for the *French King* found his Account lay in *Pyrating* on our Merchants, where something was to be had, rather than in Fighting our Fleets, where, besides the Uncertainty of Victory, nothing but dry Blows[27] were to be gain'd; whereas, by taking our Trading Vessels, he not only impoverish'd us, but at the same time enrich'd himself, which was a double advantage; and to hinder this Misfortune there was no way but one, that was the dividing our Fleet, as he did his, into several small Squadrons, and send them Cruising, and Coasting about in all places where our Merchants had any business; but then the Remedy wou'd have been worse than the Disease; for we shou'd have left ourselves *Open* and *Unguarded*, at a time when our King was out of the Nation, and all our Forces in *Flanders*; and I believe the *French* wou'd scarce have let slip the opportunity of Invading us, and hardly fail'd of making their Advantage of such an Over-sight. This I think is enough to convince these *Purblind Politicians* of the *Necessity* of a *Standing Army*; for if a War shou'd break out again, having a *Land Force* to secure us, our Fleet may divide themselves, and either block our Enemies

26. See above, p. 97, n. 81.

27. Blows that do not draw blood (*OED*, s.v. "dry," 12), but perhaps also with the meaning of fruitless or unavailing (*OED*, s.v. "dry," 15).

in their own Ports, or attend and Convoy [17] our Merchants in all places of Danger, so hinder our Enemies from Enriching themselves by our Losses; Whereas, if we are without a *Land Force* sufficient to Protect us, our *Naval Forces* cou'd take little care of our Merchants (whereby they wou'd every where, become an easie Prey to the Enemies Privateers) for they must keep together in a Body at home, to be able to secure us from Invasions, least our Enemies shou'd come upon us; so while we were Protecting our Trade, we might lose the Kingdom.

Now he comes to his Computations, which as I said, signifie nothing to the purpose, unless it be to make us rejoyce that we are in so good a Condition to resist our *Enemies Abroad*, for I know of none we have at home; if he knows of any, let him speak out, which I suppose is more than he is willing to do: 'Tis generally observ'd of such as make the greatest Noise and Stir, that they are always the readiest to pull in their Horns, and cry they know nothing of the matter. Besides when he was computing, 'twou'd have been but a little more trouble to have inform'd us the Number of the *French Forces*, and what Troops the *Dutch* and other Nations have in Pay, this wou'd have been very convenient, we might have known the *Strength* of our *Neighbours* as well as our selves, and then perhaps thought it might be prudent to keep it up in some tolerable degree of equality with theirs; this I am persuaded would be the natural result of our reflecting on their great Strength.

If indeed this Gentleman, or any of his Adherents, cou'd actually engage our *Neighbours* to *Disband their Forces*, we shou'd no longer dispute this point with him, [18] but I suppose this is more than he will promise; therefore since all around us are in Arms, and entertain *vast Numbers of Armed Troops* in constant Pay, 'twou'd be a fatal blot in our Politicks to part with ours; for, *since the Practice is grown so general, No King or Prince, tho' endowed with never so peaceable a Spirit, and never so desirous of being at ease, dares lead the Dance and disarm, for fear of his Armed Neighbours, whose Necessities or Ambition make them wait only for an opportunity to fall upon him that is worst provided to make resistance.* So that while our *Neighbours* keep up their *Standing Forces*, 'tis evident we must do so, unless we will submit our selves to be Insulted by them.

Farther, when this Gentleman tells us the greatness of our *Standing Forces* now, and that in former Days they were very inconsiderable, he only lets us know just as much as will serve his own turn and no more, for there's a vast alteration[28] crept into the very Constitution of our Government within these hundred and fifty Years; formerly the Nobility and Gentry held their Possessions and Lands from the Crown by *Knight's Service*, and so were always bound to attend on their Kings in his Wars with certain Numbers of Armed Men, according to the Tenure and Extent of their several Lordships or Lands, and they had their *Villains*[29] or *Vassals*, who, by a like Tenure from them, were oblig'd to wait on their respective Lords or Landlords, when requir'd for the Service of their King and Country, and that they might not be Undisciplin'd when they were call'd for, every Parish was to take care that all Boys shou'd at set times Exercise the Arms then in Use, as Shooting in Bows, handling the Battle Ax, and such like; so that by this Method there was no occasion for any great [19] *Standing Force*, for the People were Soldiers themselves, and might be rais'd on any sudden Occasion, by the Kings giving Notice to the Nobility and Gentry of his want of their Service, and by their immediate Summoning their *Vassals* for the Attendance they were bound to pay. 'Twill be immediately reply'd why may it not be so now,[30] by this means we might rid our selves of the fears of a *Standing Army*, and yet be able to defend our selves, or Annoy our Enemy. To this I answer, I shou'd be very glad if some such Method cou'd be taken now, and a *Militia* formed capable of managing their share of War, and supporting our Credit and Reputation Abroad in the World, without our being put to the Uneasiness and Expence of a *Standing Force*, for I am not so rash as to affirm a *Standing Army* to be at all a *Benefit* or *Advantage* to the Nation, if it might be dispens'd with on good Terms, no, rather quite the contrary, I think

28. The author alludes to the discontinuing of feudal tenures, a factor in the transition from the medieval to the modern world which had also attracted the attention of Andrew Fletcher (see above, pp. 152–54).

29. In the feudal system, a serf or peasant farmer entirely subject to a lord (*OED*, s.v. "villein," 1a).

30. This is effectively the argument of Toland's *The Militia Reform'd* (1698) (above, pp. 173–224).

the only Reason, that can be giving for the keeping a *Standing Force* in Pay, is *Necessity:* But I hardly think a *Militia* can be form'd to serve our occasions now. For,

First, by the cunning and contrivance of Humane reach and Invention, and the charge of Times and Accidents, War now is become a Trade,[31] it consists not so much in strength of Body, or a real Courage, as in Slight and Witt; to be able to fortifie Camps and Towns, to draw your Enemy into Ambuscades, or drill[32] him along into disadvantageous Places, to be able to draw him to Battle, or secure your self from being forc'd to one, these are now the best Martial Qualifications, and these are things must be learnt by *Use* and *Practice*, none can be perfect in them but by *Experience*, there must be an *Apprenticeship* serv'd for the learning them. [20] This I think is sufficient, to make us believe that a *Militia* can very hardly be so regulated, as to prove useful at this time of Day.

2dly, Supposing a *Militia* might be brought to good Discipline and Order, yet 'twou'd be a very great while before such a thing cou'd be done, and wou'd these inconsiderate Gentlemen have us leave our selves *Naked* and *Open* all the time, this wou'd be an Imprudence that our Enemies perhaps wou'd be glad to find us guilty of, since I believe they only wou'd be the gainers by it.

3dly, Tho' our *Militia* was serviceable, yet we shou'd find very few of them forward to go over to any Foreign Parts, where it might be convenient and necessary for us to employ our Forces, for they wou'd be Men that were settled and fixt by Wives and Families at home, whereas our *Standing Forces* (the Private Soldiers) are most of them Men that have no fixt Habitations are not ty'd at home by Wives and Families, but taken either young before they had settled themselves, or mostly from among those that were Vagabonds, and Wanderers, that had no business, and were rather a Burthen than Benefit to their Country, but by being put into the Army are now become useful and beneficial to it; whereas if they are Disbanded, what can be expected from such people, who are not fixt at home by the tye of Families or Interest, but to go abroad, and enter

---

31. A direct quotation from Defoe; see above, p. 377.
32. Draw or entice (*OED*, s.v. "drill," 4).

into any Service that will be so kind as to entertain them; and who can blame them, since they know no other way of Livelihood; the Consequence of which thing alone might fright us from what these Gentlemen wou'd have us immediately do, and make us very cautious how we part from that Force, which have done [21] us so much good even when they were but learning their Trade, which at our Cost and Expenses they have learnt so well as to be Masters of; but by Disbanding them, and turning them abroad, we give our Neighbours the opportunity of reaping the Profit and Advantage.

But this Gentleman tells us *we need not send Forces into Foreign Parts, we need only have a strong Fleet at Sea, and that wou'd be security enough:* But I think the Practice of all our Kings and Parliaments, as I have already Instanc'd, may be enough to confute one part of this Assertion; for I take it, our Fore Fathers were as wise and knowing in what concern'd their Interest, as any of us now can pretend to; and if we look back into former Stories we shall find enough to convince us of the folly of trusting too much to the other part; by seeing what has happen'd, we shall quickly find that a Fleet will not secure us from Invasions. To give some Instances to these Positive[33] Gentlemen, How often did the *Danes*[34] land great Numbers of Armed Forces, in almost every part of this Island? continually alarming the poor People, ruining and making horrible devastations wherever they came; exercising all manner of Barbaraties on the poor unprovided *English*, putting whole Towns, Men, Women and Children to the Sword; till at last they Lorded it over the whole Island; and perhaps there are a People in the World, wou'd not be much civiller on an occasion, which God forbid they shou'd ever have; and which while we have a good Army, we need not fear; but to give some more Instances. *William* the Conqueror landed with an Army here, so did his Son *Robert*,

33. Opinionated or dogmatic (*OED*, s.v. "positive," 3).

34. Viking raids on Britain began on a small scale in the late 700s. Plundering expeditions were made during the following decades in Northumbria, East Anglia, Kent, and Wessex until in 865 a large Danish army landed in England intent on conquest. After defeat at the Battle of Ashdown (871), a portion of this army settled in Northumbria. Following another defeat at the hands of Alfred the Great in 878, the Danes settled in East Anglia. Northumbria was not re-integrated into England until the death of Erik Bloodax in 954.

Duke of *Normandy*, in the Reign of *William Rufus*, and in the Reign of *Henry* the First.[35] The [22] Empress *Maud* landed an Army in the Reign of King *Stephen*, so did *Henry* II. The *French* Invaded the Land in the Reign of *Henry* III. Queen *Isabel* landed with an Army at *Orwel*, in *Sussex*, in the Reign of *Edward* the Second. *Henry* the Seventh landed with an Army, tho' *Richard* the Third took all possible care to hinder him.[36] And whenever there have been heats and discontents in this Kingdom, the *French* have ever assisted one or another party to keep up the Contention; tho' our Princes by their Fleets have always endeavour'd to hinder it. These are enough to convince every lover of his Country, of the falsity of these Gentlemen's, saying that a Fleet only is able to protect us.

Perhaps they will object against what has been said, and say, That in those days we were weak at Sea, but that now we are grown much stronger. So is our Neighbours too, as we very well know by experience; I scarce think any of these angry Gentlemen will venture to affirm, that we are at this time, the most potent at Sea, or that none of our Neighbours dare to look us in the face on that Element; whereas in former days, tho' we were but mean at Sea, in comparison of what we are now; yet our Neighbours were much meaner, we were formerly confessedly the most powerful in Shipping, and enjoyed an absolute and uncontroul'd dominion on the Seas; and if in those days, when we bore so great a sway on the Ocean, and all the Nations around us so little, a Fleet cou'd not hinder Armies from landing in *England;* I can't think how it shou'd do it now, when our Neighbours are as strong in Shipping,[37] and as Powerful at Sea as our Selves. This I think is a plain case, an Argument so clear, that I wonder how any sensible persons can overlook it. And if we may be Invaded, tho' [23] we have a good Fleet, as 'tis plain we may, we shou'd be careful how we parted with a Land Force; which wou'd then be our only safety, and can be no Injury at all to us, as long as his Majesty is so clearly in the Interest of his People.

---

35. William I invaded in 1066; Robert Duke of Normandy invaded first in 1088, and then again in 1101.

36. Maud (or Matilda) invaded in 1139; Henry invaded in 1153.

37. Concerns over England's naval strength were common in the later seventeenth century after humiliations at the hands of the Dutch (see above, p. 294, n. 86).

All this great Clamour and Noise against a *Standing Army*, can have no other meaning than this, That they dare not trust his Majesty, or rely on his Integrity; these are hard things, and a very ungrateful way of dealing with a Prince, who has all his Life-time hazarded his Person for the relief and succour of the Distressed; who cou'd never be wrought upon, either by bribes or menaces, to be unjust to his word,[38] even in the smallest particle; a Prince whose single Reputation caused a strict band and Union[39] amongst Princes of the most disagreeing Interests, Humours, and Religions. That this Prince shou'd be mistrusted by a People of the *same Religion*, is a thing wonderful and surprizing; and will hardly be credited in after Ages, especially when they shall know that he *rescued these same People from the Jaws of Slavery and Popery;*[40] and sav'd them just sinking into the Pit of Destruction; but this is more than these Gentlemen dare openly own; therefore they complain against the *Court,* and the *Government;* concealing their base Reflections and ill manner'd Insinuations, under double and ambiguous meanings; but the skreen is too thin and transparent; 'tis easily seen through, and their thoughts as readily apprehended as if they had writ them at length.

But to go on with this Gentleman, and come to his *Crisis*, Page 42, where he says, *several Accidents*[41] *concur to make the Disbanding of an Army practicable which may not happen again.* To be even with him, and give [24] him a *Rowland* for his *Oliver;*[42] several Accidents concur to oblige us to keep up a *Standing Army* here, which never did happen, nor never may again: There's a King beyond Sea,[43] who maintains pretensions to the Crown, with a Prince whom he owns to be his Lawful Son and Heir;[44] so young that he may live according to an indifferent Computation these

38. An echo of William's own bitter complaint (see above, p. 331, n. 196).

39. For the League of Augsburg, founded in 1686, see above, p. 9, n. 13. The members of the League, the purpose of which was to resist the expansionist policies of Louis XIV, were, at various times: Austria, Bavaria, Brandenburg, the Dutch Republic, England, the Holy Roman Empire, Ireland, the Palatinate of the Rhine, Portugal, Savoy, Saxony, Scotland, Spain, and Sweden.

40. I.e., the reign of James II.

41. See above, p. 351.

42. I.e., tit for tat, or to give as good as one gets (*OED*, s.v. "Roland").

43. I.e., James II.

44. I.e., the Old Pretender; see above, p. 314, n. 145.

40 Years or more, and tho' they may seem quiet and dormant for a time, yet 'tis hardly to be expected they will let slip any opportunity, they may think favourable to the regaining their pretended Rights; 'tis to be consider'd also, that they are of a Religion which no Oaths can bind or secure,[45] when their Church will be a gainer by the Breach of them; add to this, that this Nation has been always the bar and hindrance to all the ambitious designs and Projects of that Communion, and this has created an incurable hatred in them towards us, which they never fail to let us know upon all occasions; so that we have all the reason in the World to look about us, especially, considering there are such Multitudes against us, and so few to assist us; tis true we have just made a Peace,[46] after a chargeable and Expensive War; but as 'twas the *Number and Valour of our Troops* that forc't it from an Ambitious and inveterate Enemy; so nothing but the *same* can preserve it to us; for we are all pretty confident, that he whom we have had to deal with,[47] has not been tender in breaking the most solemn Leagues, when either his Interest or Ambition has thought it convenient.

Besides we see he has not deliver'd *Brisack*[48] to the Emperour, which he ought to have done, but finds pretences to delay it till Spring, and we know not whether he'l do it then or no, unless he finds he shall be forc't to it. Add to these, the great Number of *Jacobites* we have at home, [25] who are a People restless and uneasie; ready to Plot and execute any base and Villainous designs: Add also, that the King of *Spain* lies a dying,[49] and the King of *France* has *great Armies* ready to enter into that Country; at so favourable a Juncture, to support the right he pretends to that Crown; I say, all these things truly consider'd, *Here's a concurrence of Circumstances that never happen'd at once till now, nor perhaps never may again, that call upon us, and oblige us to keep up our Standing Forces at this Time.*

45. I.e., Roman Catholicism (because of the fundamental loyalty of Roman Catholics to the Pope).
46. By the Treaty of Ryswick; see above, p. 9, n. 13.
47. I.e., Louis XIV.
48. Now spelled Breisach; a town on the Rhine some thirty miles south of Strasbourg. It had been conquered by France and heavily fortified by Vauban, but was ceded to the Emperor under the terms of the Treaty of Ryswick (1697).
49. See above, p. 326, n. 184.

I think I have said enough to convince any reasonable Persons of the Necessity of an Army at this time; which is all need be done, to answer this *Historian;* for if there is a necessity of an Army, 'tis certain it shou'd be one that may be sufficient and able to cope with any force our Enemies may bring against us; or else we had as good have none at all. In former times when our Neighbours had but *five* or *ten thousand* Men in Arms there was no occasion for our having a greater Number; but if they encrease to a Hundred thousand or more, we must also be in some tolerable degree equal with them, or be contented to be Insulted or Invaded by those that are stronger; this is so very plain and clear, I shall argue it no farther, but shew the danger of trusting to a *Militia*, when they are attack'd by regular and disciplin'd Troops and so conclude,

And the *Want* of a sufficient Number of Standing and Disciplin'd Troops may be learnt from the *Dutch*, who were almost brought to the brink of ruin, in the Year 1672,[50] when the *French*, who seldom fail to make their advantages of the over-sights and Neglects of their Neighbours; Invaded them with mighty Armies, which [26] like a Torrent over-run Three large Provinces, taking above Forty strong Towns in almost as many days. Whoever reads Sir *William Temple*'s Observations, will find that Great Man makes out the *want of regular Standing Forces*, one of the chief reasons of their Misfortunes, which had like to have been the utter Ruin of their Commonwealth; he says, *it was their too great parsimony in disbanding the best of their Foreign Officers and Troops, after the Peace of* Munster; he tells us, *those Ministers who had the Directions of Affairs, bent their Chief application to the Strength and Order of their Fleet, and totally Neglected their Land Army;* so that those few Souldiers they had were without Discipline.[51] These were the Reasons made the *French* King suppose their Conquest Easie, and invited him to invade them, and upon Tryal he found he was not mistaken, for they were not able to resist him; tho' 'tis Observable that for Twenty Years before, they had been regulating their *Militia*, and endeavouring to make it serviceable, but 'twas so far from being so, that they suffer'd the *French* to become Masters of their

50. See above, p. 103–4, n. 99, p. 161, n. 20, and p. 235, n. 16.
51. Temple, *Works*, 1:73. For Sir William Temple (1628–99), see above, p. 295, n. 89. In his *Observations* Temple reflected thoughtfully on the cause of the modern

strong *Fortified Towns* almost as soon as they approach'd them, this is so lively and near an Example and so well fitted for our Instruction, that methinks we shou'd take warning by it, without desiring to make the Experiment our selves.

Faelix quem faciunt aliena pericula Cautum.[52]

How often has *Poland*, (a Country these Gentlemen are pleas'd to produce as an Instance of supporting themselves by a *Militia*) been ravag'd and insulted by the *Sweeds*, *Muscovites*, and *Tartars*, and suffer'd all the Extremities of Fire and Sword *for the want of Standing and Regular Troops*.[53]

[27] Now I think I have sufficiently shew'd the weakness of these Gentlemen's Arguments, and the *absolute Necessity* for our keeping up a *Land Force*, not by *false Computations* of things, but by a true consideration

---

need for standing armies, as opposed to the militias which had previously been satisfactory:

> A Battel or two, fairly fought, decided a War; and a War ended the Quarrel of an Age, and either lost or gain'd the Cause or Country contended for: 'Till the change of Times and Accidents brought it to a new Decision; 'till the Virtues and Vices of Princes made them stronger or weaker, either in the Love and Obedience of their People, or in such Orders and Customs as render'd their Subjects more or less Warlike or Effeminate. Standing-Forces, or Guards in constant Pay, were no where us'd by lawful Princes in their Native or Hereditary Countries, but only by Conquerors in subdued Provinces, or Usurpers at home; and were a Defence only against Subjects, not against Enemies. These Orders seem first to have been changed in *Europe* by the Two States of *Venice* and *Holland:* Both of them small in Territories at Land, and those extended in Frontier upon powerful Neighbours; both of them weak in number of Native Subjects; and those less warlike at Land, by turning so much to Traffick, and to Sea: But both of them mighty in Riches and Trade; which made them endeavour to balance their Neighbours Strength in Native Subjects, by Foreign Stipendiary Bands; and to defend their Frontiers by the Arts of Fortification, and Strength of Places, which might draw out a War into length by Sieges, when they durst not venture it upon a Battel; and so make it many times determine by force of Mony, rather than of Arms. This forced those Princes, who frontier'd upon these States, to the same Provisions; . . . (Temple, *Works*, 1:70)

52. "Happy the man made wise by the perils of others"; untraced, and apparently not a phrase in classical Latin literature.

53. Poland had suffered from two decades of war and occupation in the mid-seventeenth century.

of the present Circumstances of Affairs, which is the only means to find the right of this Matter; So that I hope no true *Englishman*, who desires the good of his Country, will be for the *Disbanding the Forces* till either our Neighbours have done the same, or that our *Militia* be so well regulated, that they may be able to Cope with any *Disciplin'd Troops* whatsoever.

For supposing, on our *Immediate Disbanding our Forces* any of our Neighbours shou'd think it the Critical time to attempt an Invasion of *England*, before our *Militia* was ready to receive them, and this is none of the unlikeliest Suppositions, I wou'd ask these Gentlemen, if we shou'd not have some Reasons for apprehending of danger, when we have only the Success of a Fleet to depend on, several Accidents might happen to render it unserviceable to us, as our being kept in Port by contrary Winds, or our not being in a readiness enough to hinder them, these are no very Improbable things, we have had the knowledge of their Possibility by Experience, and I say, imagining it happen'd that we were Invaded, I desire to know what resistance our *Militia* cou'd make against 20 *or* 30 *Thousand Regular Troops* well Disciplin'd and inur'd the War; we shou'd then *wish* for our *Forces* when they were not to be had, nay perhaps when a considerable Number of them were listed in the Enemies Service, having been so ungratefully us'd here as to be turn'd loose to Want and Misery, after having spent their Youth and Blood in our Service; and what Nation wou'd pitty us? Wou'd not all the [28] World cry out we deservedly fell Martyrs of our Folly? that we cou'd blame none but our selves, for that our selves only were the Authors of our Destruction.

After all that can be said on both sides, and to suppose even all the Idle Chimeras these *Grumbletonians*[54] wou'd fright us with, the whole matter absolutely depends on our choosing one of these two things, viz. *either to trust King* William *or King* Lewis.

FINIS.

---

54. See above, p. 78, n. 15.

Anonymous

The Case of Disbanding the Army at Present,
Briefly and Impartially Consider'd

1698

THE
CASE
OF
Disbanding the ARMY
AT PRESENT,
Briefly and Impartially Consider'd.

Published by John Nutt, near Stationer's Hall, 1698.

The Case of Disbanding
the Army at Present,
Briefly and Impartially Consider'd

I shall reduce my Thoughts about this Matter within as small a compass as may be, and therefore shall not trouble the Reader with Historical Quotations either out of Ancient or Modern Authors, as altogether foreign to the Pur[2]pose, unless they are prov'd to agree with the present Conjuncture of Affairs in every Particular; and so far it may be own'd, *that Men in the same Circumstances will do the same Things;* for 'tis a plain Case, that in taking true Measures for the Safety of any Government, Men must Examine the present State of Affairs both within and without it, and things that may happen hereafter; and always to provide against the most evident and likely Dangers.

I shall take it for granted, that an Army in time of Peace is consistent with our Constitution if the Safety of the Realm require it, and that it be with the Consent of the Parliament; And therefore if it be made appear, that the present Government, which (under God) is the best Security we have for our Religion, Liberty, and Property, is in evident Danger without an Army, and that in the present State of Affairs our Liberties and Properties cannot be infring'd nor molested by one, this I hope will set this great Case in a true Light.

First, That the present Government is in evident Danger without a competent Number of Land Forces for its Defence. The Posture of *England* at present is this, in relation to Safety, that [3] there are Princes abroad that pretend a Right[1] to wear its Imperial Crown, who are Protected and Supported by the most Powerful Monarch in *Christendom*,[2] who is able enough still, notwithstanding his late Restitutions, to do what he pleases with the Empire, *Spain*, and *Holland*, unless *England* joins with them for the Common Liberty, in which its own is certainly involv'd. It is very well known, that this Powerful Monarch pretends in the behalf of the Princes that are descended from him a Right to the Crown of *Spain*,[3] and all the Dominions thereunto belonging, upon the Death of the present King, which is a fair Step to Universal Monarchy:[4] And it is as plain, that if this Monarch can once secure *England*, then he

1. I.e., James II and his son, the Old Pretender.
2. I.e., Louis XIV.
3. See above, p. 160, n. 18.

4. The issue of universal monarchy in early modern Europe was tied to the rivalry between the Hapsburg and Bourbon dynasties for supremacy in Europe. The pretension was first and most tellingly associated with Charles V; subsequently it was ascribed to the Spanish monarchy of Phillip II and his successors, and finally to Louis XIV of France. As an ideal it was capable of favourable construction, the most remarkable apologia being that written on behalf of the Spanish monarchy by the Neapolitan Campanella. But generally universal monarchy was an accusation rather than an ideal, a term of condemnation, branding the alleged aspirant as an over-ambitious warmonger, bent on territorial aggrandisement by conquest. (John Robertson, "Universal Monarchy and the Liberties of Europe: David Hume's Critique of an English Whig Doctrine," in *Political Discourse in Early Modern Britain*, ed. N. Phillipson and Q. Skinner [Cambridge: Cambridge University Press, 1993], p. 356; see also Franz Bosbach, *Monarchia Universalis. Ein politischer Leitbegriff der frühen Neuzeit* [Göttingen: Vandenhoeck & Ruprecht, 1988])

For commentary on the concept almost exactly contemporary with the present text, see Charles Davenant, "An Essay Upon Universal Monarchy," in *Essays* (1701), pp. 233–88; Jones, *Secret History*, pp. 2, 12; and Jones, *History of Europe*, introduction. Slightly later, see Montesquieu, *Réflexions sur la monarchie universelle en Europe* (1734). In 1714 Toland would maintain that the Protestant succession of the House of Hanover was crucial to the withstanding of French pretensions to universal monarchy (Toland, *Restoring*, p. iii).

will be able to make good his Pretensions in spight of the rest of the Allies, and *Portugal* too if it joins with them. This demonstrates, that it is absolutely his Interest to have *England* at his Devotion,[5] which he can hardly expect from the present Government: And if the Case be so, then the Question is, Whether it is Safe and Advisable to lay our selves open to a Neighbour so Powerful both by Sea and Land, whose Interest it is to subdue us, who wants no Pretence for it, and who has seldom fail'd to prosecute his Interest when a [4] fair Opportunity has offer'd for it? But they say, that a good Fleet, and a well Train'd Militia, is sufficient to put us out of Danger. As to the first, it must be own'd, that the Honour, Glory, and Safety of the Nation does chiefly depend upon our Fleet; but it is fit to consider at the same time, that the French King can put out all his Fleet whenever he pleases, and that he can pursue his Designs with more Secrecy and Expedition than the Constitution of this Government can admit: But the King of *England* cannot put out a Fleet without the help of his Parliament, which must meet together, and settle Funds for the setting out of the Fleet, without which the King cannot have a sufficient Credit. The Case being so, it cannot otherwise be, (or it is but too probable that it will be so) that the *French* King in time of Peace will put out his whole Fleet sooner than we can put out ours, even though His Majesty should immediately call a Parliament, and desire Supplies for a Fleet every time the *French* work in their Docks at *Brest*, *Rochefort*, and *Dunkirk*, as if they design'd to set out their Fleet: Or the Parliament must of course allow the King every year a Fund for the setting out a Fleet, as in time of War: And [5] besides, though we could be ready as soon as they, yet it is fit to consider, whether if they should Arm in these three Places at once, and the *Hogue*, we can, (considering the accidents of Weather) hinder their Landing upon us from every one, or any one of these Places.

This seems to demonstrate, that it is very necessary to have another Defence ready in case the first should fail, which (as it appears from what has been said) may very well be: This Defence therefore must be a Land Force. That the Militia is not at present a competent Defence, is own'd

5. At his command or disposal (*OED*, s.v. "devotion," 6a).

by those who propose Methods to render it serviceable. I would not be thought to undervalue Militia's, no doubt they could render Service, especially the Foot, being interlin'd[6] with Regular Troops, or they may be put into the less expos'd Garrisons, to draw out from thence the Regular Troops to reinforce an Army: But as for Horse, the Horse must be Train'd as well as the Man, or else the Bravest Men in the World can render no Service upon Horses that are not Train'd. But if the Militia can be render'd serviceable for our Defence against the Invasions of Disciplin'd Troops, as those very Persons that would Disband the Army must own that it is not at present, it is fit to consider, that [6] a Militia under such Regulations as are proper to make it Serviceable, will then enter into the very Constitutions of the Kingdom, that it will be a very great and perpetual Expence upon the Subject, and that it must vest as great a Military Power in the King, as if he had an Army at his Command, or else it cannot be thought to make it Serviceable. This is the very Case of *Sweden;*[7] *Puffendorf* tells us, that the King of *Sweden* pays no other Forces out of his Coffers but the Life-Guard and the Foot-Guards, I mean in *Sweden;* the rest is the Militia of the Country, maintain'd by Tenures from the Crown (which is the very Original of Militia's) and kept in constant Duty and Discipline: But pray, has this Militia preserv'd the Rights and Properties of the People? Is not the King of *Sweden* as

---

6. An arrangement of alternating ranks of militia and regular troops (*OED*, s.v. "interline," 6a).

7. Sweden was at the forefront of English minds in the late 1690s because the fifteen-year-old Charles XII (see below, p. 526, n. 50) had succeeded his father Charles XI in 1697, and because of the recent publication of a translation of the Abbé Vertot's *The History of the Revolutions in Sweden, Occasioned by the Change of Religion, and Alteration of the Government in that Kingdom* (1696); see also Sir William Temple, *Miscellanea* (1680), pp. 12–16. Samuel Pufendorf (1632–94), political philosopher, historian, and courtier. The reference is to Pufendorf's *An Introduction to the History of the Principal Kingdoms and States of Europe* (1682; English translation, 1697): "This present King [Charles XI] has put their Forces both Horse and Foot in a better Condition than ever they were before, which are maintained in *Sweden*, with a small charge to the Crown, the Foot being maintained by the Boors [Swedish peasants or yeomen], but the Horsemen have for the most part some Farms in their possession belonging to the Crown, the Revenues of which are their pay. But the King's Guards are paid out of his Treasury" (p. 513).

Absolute a Monarch as any in Christendom?[8] And on the contrary we find a Country in the World not far off, call'd *Holland*, where they maintain all the Liberty that can be imagin'd in a Common-wealth, with an Army and the King at the Head of it, without any such thing as Militia in its Constitution. But an Army, being requir'd only during the present State of Affairs in Christendom, which (as Experience tells us) have never continued long in the same Posture, cannot enter into the Con[7]stitution of the Monarchy, nor can it be made a Precedent any longer than the Posture of Affairs is the same as 'tis now; It is a better Defence than a Militia, and infinitely Cheaper, and less Vexatious and Troublesome to the Subject; neither can a competent Number of Land-Forces for our Defence, I may venture to say a good Army, attempt in the least, during the present juncture of Affairs, to invade the Rights and Properties of the People of *England*, (the second Thing to be proved) which is the common Bugbear[9] to put People out of conceit with what seems so necessary at present for their safety; and when the State of Affairs alters, it will consequently be as easie then to Disband them as it is now, and certainly much more proper.

The Author or Authors of the History of Standing Armies, have already prov'd to our Hands, that no Kings of *England* either with or without Armies, have hitherto made any steps towards Tyranny and Arbitrary Power, but it has prov'd Fatal to them; and if this has been the success of their Attempts when they have had no jealousie of Competitors supported by Formidable Neighbours, it must be much more impossible for any King of *England* that comes in upon the present Settlement [8]

---

8. The nature of the Swedish monarchy in the late seventeenth century goes back to the political reforms instigated by the great Swedish king Gustav Vasa (1496?–1560), who confiscated the property of the Catholic church and established an absolute monarchy in Sweden in which the Crown (now hereditary rather than elective) owned approximately 60 percent of the land. "He [Gustav Vasa] ow'd his Crown meerly to his own Valor, and Reign'd with as absolute a Power as if the Crown had been his Birth-right. He made what Alterations he pleas'd in Religion, the Laws, and the Property of his Subjects, and yet dy'd ador'd by the People, and admir'd by the Nobility" (Vertot, *Sweden*, p. 109). In recent years these innovations had been developed by Charles XI (1655–97), who had further expanded the power of the Crown at the expense of the higher and lower nobility.

9. See above, p. 36, n. 88.

to set up for Tyranny and Arbitrary Power: And he cannot make any Steps towards it, as Affairs are now, without bringing evident Ruine upon himself; because the Competitors (being supported by the most powerful Prince in Christendom, whose Interest it is to have *England* at his Devotion) will take the Advantage of that great ferment in the Nation, which such an Attempt must produce, to assert their Claim. This is but too good a collateral Security for our Rights and Properties under the Present settlement; and when it shall please God to put Affairs upon another Foot, and that we shall have no occasion for these Fears and Apprehensions, then let the Army be Disbanded, no True Englishman can plead for it; but whilst Affairs continue in the state they are in at present, it is a plain Case that our Liberty and Property can be in no Danger, but will rather be preserv'd by an Army ready for our Defence.

Those that have writ against an Army during the present Peace, are pleased to Compliment His Majesty out of what seems so necessary for his and our Safety: They say, That indeed they are under no Apprehensions of such Attempts upon the Liberties of the People, during his Reign, and so far they are in the Right; but they are afraid of [9] what may come hereafter, when the having an Army at present may serve as a Precedent for succeeding Monarchs. To which it may be answer'd, First, That it cannot serve as a Precedent to succeeding Kings, unless the State of Affairs be the same as it is now; if they have not the same Occasion for their Defence, and that of *England*, they cannot draw our having an Army at present into a Precedent. Secondly, I answer, That whenever that unhappy Hour shall come which will deprive us of our King, (whom GOD long preserve to Reign over us) our present Constitution will then run the greatest Risk, if Affairs remain in the same Posture as they are in now; it will be the most favorable conjuncture for Competitors to the Crown, and their too powerful Protectors, to enter upon us: And therefore, since His Majesty's Life is such an Obstacle to them, is it not very much to Expose His Majesty's Person, and with it the Present Government, to have no Army on Foot in this Conjuncture? It is likewise very fit to consider, That in such a Case, besides the Danger on that Hand, we have Neighbours that need not Cross the Seas to come upon us, and who may be tempted to make us a Visit on the other.

[10] I may add as a collateral Argument, That those who have writ against the Army with so much Virulency and Malice, (for none have writ with Temper) have sufficiently discover'd their ill Inclinations towards Monarchy and the Church of *England*,[10] but more openly and expresly towards the Latter; which plainly shews, That their designs against both can hardly be compassed whilst there is an Army on foot for the Defence of the Present Government; and therefore 'tis to be hop'd, that those who are Well-wishers to the Church and to the State, will take care not to be drawn into the Snare, under the plausible Pretext of Providing for the Liberty of the People, which, 'tis very Evident, cannot be invaded by an Army, during the present Conjuncture.

FINIS.

---

10. An echo of the suspicions of Defoe (above, p. 380). On the religious opinions of Moyle and Trenchard, see above, p. 380, n. 51, and p. 386, n. 64.

Anonymous

Reasons Against a
Standing Army

1717

REASONS
Against a
Standing Army.

LONDON,
Printed, and Sold by J. Morphew, near Stationers-Hall;
and the Booksellers of London and Westminster. 1717.
(Price One Shilling.)

The Preface

The Reduction or keeping up of the Army being publickly talk'd of in most Companies, and not without much Heat and Concern; 'tis thought proper to give the Publick the Reasons against its Continuance, drawn not only from the greatest Authorities, but the Experience of all Ages and Countries, especially our own, that Gentlemen may make themselves Masters of so important a Question, before it comes to be debated in the House.

And tho 'tis not propos'd in the following Tract, to what Standard the Forces should be reduc'd; yet there is no doubt but those, who have always appear'd Patriots of British Liberty, will so confine its Number, that our Posterity may not be endanger'd thereby, even in the latest Ages to come.

Reasons against a Standing Army

The first Footsteps I find of a Standing Army in *England* since the *Romans* left the Island, were in *Richard* the Second's Time,[1] who rais'd Four Thousand Archers in *Cheshire*, and suffer'd them to plunder, live upon free Quarter, beat, wound, ravish and kill where-ever they went; and afterwards he call'd a Parliament, encompass'd them with his Archers, forc'd them to give up the whole Power of Parliaments, and make it Treason to endeavour to repeal any of the Arbitrary Constitutions then made: But being afterwards obliged to go to *Ireland* to suppress a Rebellion there, the People took Advantage of it, and dethron'd him.

The Nation had such a Specimen in this Reign of a Standing Army, that I don't find any King from his Time to that of *Charles* [2] the First, who attempted to keep up any Forces in Time of Peace, except the Yeomen of the Guard, who were constituted by *Henry* the Seventh. And tho there were several Armies rais'd in that Time for *French, Scotch, Irish*, and other foreign and domestick Wars; yet they were constantly Disbanded as soon as the Occasion was over. And in all the Wars of *York* and *Lancaster*, whatever Party prevail'd, we don't find they ever attempted to keep up a Standing Army. Such was the Vertue of those Times, that they would rather run the Hazard of forfeiting their Heads and Estates to the Rage of the opposite Party, than certainly enslave their Country, though they themselves were to be the Tyrants.

Nor would they suffer our Kings to keep up an Army in *Ireland*, tho there were frequent Rebellions there, and by that Means their Subjection

1. See above, p. 125, n. 22.

very precarious; as well knowing they would soon be in *England* if call'd for. In the first three Hundred Years that the *English* had Possession of that Country, there were no Armies there but in the Times of War. The first Force that was establish'd, was in the 14th of *Edward* the Fourth, when one Hundred and twenty Archers on Horseback, Forty Horsemen, and Forty Pages, were establish'd by Parliament there; which six Years after were reduced to Eighty Archers and Twenty Spearmen on Horseback. Afterwards, in *Henry* the Eighth's Time, in the Year 1535, the Army in *Ireland* was three Hundred; and in 1543, they were increased to three Hundred and eighty [3] Horse, and sixteen Hundred Foot, which was the Establishment then. I speak this of Times of Peace; for when the *Irish* were in Rebellion, which was very frequent, the Armies were much more considerable. In Queen *Mary*'s Days the Standing Forces were about twelve Hundred. In most of Queen *Elizabeth*'s Time the *Irish* were in open Rebellion: but when they were all suppress'd, the Army establish'd was between fifteen Hundred and two Thousand; about which Number they continu'd till the Army rais'd by *Strafford*,[2] in the 15th of *Charles* the First.

Our thrice happy Situation defends us from the Necessity of a Standing Army, which the Indiscretion of some of our Neighbouring Nations have permitted, to the Destruction of their *Liberty*. Besides, lying open to continual Invasion, they can never enjoy Quiet and Security, nor take a sound Sleep, but *Hercules* like with Clubs in their Hands.[3] So that the *Halcyon* Days[4] which we for the most part enjoy, must be solely attributed to our Tutelar God *Neptune*, who with a Guard of winged Coursers so strongly intrenches us, that we may be said to be *media insuperabiles unda*,[5] and not unfitly compar'd to the Earth, which stands fix'd and immovable, and never to be shaken, but by an internal Convulsion. And yet we have much talk of a Standing Army which is to be in Time of Peace, but no Body can tell us what they are to do: We know their usual Commission is to kill and slay, but where now is the Enemy? Many talk of this

2. See above, p. 249, n. 52.
3. See above, p. 9, n. 14.
4. See above, p. 9, n. 15.
5. "Unconquerable amidst the waves"; see above, p. 10, n. 16.

with as much Certainty, as if [4] they were already establish'd, and are pleas'd to affirm it necessary to have a vast Body of Forces continu'd on Foot. Whereas the first Project we find for a Standing Army, in the Year 1629,[6] required only three Thousand Foot in constant Pay, which were to bridle the Impertinence of Parliaments, and to over-run the Nation, to make Edicts to be Laws, to force upon the People vast Numbers of Excises; and, in short, to overturn the whole Frame of this noble *British* Government. Whoever has a mind to peruse that dangerous Scheme, in *Rushworth's Appendix*, Page 12. and what he says of it in his History, will see enough.[7]

I marvel whose Advocates those Men are, who talk so warmly of this Matter; for I am satisfy'd none of those brave *Britons*, who have fought honourably for their Country, ever meant, when the Service was over, to be a Charge, Burden and Terror at Home; nor to disfranchise us of two of our Native Liberties, Freedom from Martial Law, and Billeting of Soldiers; and thereby directly to take away from themselves, as well as from their Fellow-Subjects, one half of the Benefit of the *Petition of Right*,[8] and in consequence the other half too, the Freedom of their Persons and Estates. Neither can it be supposed a gratifying of His Majesty to establish greater Forces than have been usual in former Reigns, in Times of Peace. His Majesty has shewed and expressed so much Tenderness and Concern for the Liberties and Ease of his Subjects, and even [5] when the Necessity of the State seem'd to require it, was so very cautious in the Use of that Power invested in him by the Parliament, with respect to the raising of Forces for the Defence of the Kingdom and the suppressing of the late Rebellion,[9] that every Body admir'd his wonderful

6. See above, p. 118, n. 5.

7. See Rushworth, *Collections*, appendix, pp. 12–17.

8. The enduring significance of this document for later Whigs is made clear by Roger Coke: "But good Laws often arise from corrupt Times and bad Manners: for *Magna Charta* did arise from the Usurpations of K. *John*, and *Henry* III. above the Laws and Liberties of this Nation; so did the *Petition of Right* the *Magna Charta* of this Age, from the Usurpations of this King [Charles I]" (Coke, *Detection*, p. 206). For the text of the Petition of Right, see Appendix A, below, pp. 577–80.

9. The Jacobite invasion of 1715.

Resolution, in trusting his Royal Life and Crown to so inconsiderable a Number of Troops, in the most dangerous Juncture which threaten'd both. How then can it be imagin'd that His Majesty inclines to continue a Burthen upon his Subjects, which he was so loath to impose when the greatest Exigences of State call'd for it? But there are some Gentlemen who a few Years since were the pretended Patriots of their Country, who had nothing in their Mouths but the sacred Name of *Liberty*, who in the late Reigns could hardly afford the Monarchs the Prerogative that was due to them, and which was absolutely necessary to put in Motion this Machine of our Government, and to make the Springs and Wheels of it act naturally and perform their Function; I say, these Gentlemen that in some former Reigns could not with Patience hear of the King's ordinary Guards, can now discourse familiarly of Thirty Thousand Men to be maintain'd in Time of Peace.[10] But let them not deceive themselves, for supposing they vainly think to make their Court this way, yet they would quickly find themselves out-flatter'd by the Party they fear,[11] who have been long the Darlings of Arbitrary Power, and whose Principles as well as Practices teach them to be Enemies to all the legal [6] Rights and just Liberties of their Native Country; and so these wretched Bunglers would be made use of only to bring together the Materials of Tyranny, and then must give Place to more expert Architects to finish the Building.

And tho we are secure from any Attempts of this kind during the Reign of a Prince, who preserves us from a Captivity that would be equal to what *Moses* redeem'd the People of *Israel* from; a Prince whose Life is so necessary to the Preservation of *Europe*, that both Protestant and Popish Princes have forgot their ancient Maxims, and laid aside their innate Animosities, and made it their common Interest to chuse him their Arbitrator:[12] A Prince in whom we know no Vice, but what has been esteem'd a Virtue in others, *viz.* his undeserv'd Clemency to his

10. An allusion to the transformation of the Whigs from a party of revolution to a party of administration; see above, p. 347, n. 223.

11. I.e., the Tories.

12. A reference to the greatest diplomatic success of the reign of George I, the conclusion in 1717 of the Triple Alliance between Britain, France, and the Dutch Republic, and perhaps also to the influential role that George, as elector of Hanover, had begun to play since 1715 in the Second Northern War (1700–1721).

Enemies.[13] I say, was this most excellent Prince to be immortal, we ought in common Prudence to abandon all Thoughts of Self-preservation, and wholly to rely on his Care and Conduct. Or had we as certain a Prospect of the Nation's being perpetually bless'd with Monarchs, that shall inherit his Royal Virtues as well as Kingdoms, as we have in the next immediate Heir, his Royal Highness the Prince of *Wales*,[14] there were no great Occasion or Necessity of appearing anxious for the future Welfare of our Country, more than for the present. But since no Vertue nor Pitch of Glory, will exempt these Princes from paying the common Debt to Nature; and Death hath a Scythe which cuts off the most noble Lives; we [7] ought not to entrust any Power with them which we don't think proper to be continu'd to their Successors. And doubtless his Majesty will not regret this, or any thing else that can reasonably be requir'd, in order to compleat that Deliverance, and Happiness of his People, so far advanc'd by his wonderful Conduct. For to set us within View of the promis'd Land,[15] with a *ne plus ultra*,[16] is the greatest of all human

13. Most immediately, a topical reference to the treatment of the Jacobite lords who had been captured after the failure of the rebellion of 1715, and whose trial and treatment had raised a constitutional problem. The Act of Settlement had stated that "no pardon under the Great Seal of England be pleadable to an Impeachment by the Commons in Parliament," but it had said nothing about the king's right to pardon an impeached person after he had been sentenced. However, it was widely held that the king could not pardon in such circumstances, and the Commons in resolving to impeach the Scottish lords had accepted the assurance of the solicitor-general that if the Scottish peers were convicted they could not be pardoned by the king. Nevertheless, friends of the Scottish earls at court and in the Lords pressed the king to grant a pardon. In the end, two of the Scottish lords were executed in 1716 and three were reprieved, to be pardoned eventually not by royal clemency but by act of Parliament. Nevertheless, a reputation for vindictiveness clung thereafter to George I, particularly among those liable to spasms of Jacobite sentiment, such as Swift, who in October 1722 would write sarcastically to Robert Cope: "It is a wonderful thing to see the Tories provoking his present majesty, whose clemency, mercy, and forgiving temper, have been so signal, so extraordinary, so more than humane during the whole course of his reign" (Swift, *Correspondence*, 2:432).

14. The future George II, with whom his father had spectacularly fallen out in April 1717.

15. Deuteronomy 34:1–4; see above, p. 15, n. 31.

16. See above, p. 15, n. 32.

Infelicities, and such I shall always take our Case to be, whilst a Standing Army must be kept up to prey upon our Entrails, and which must in the Hands of an ill Prince (which we have had the Misfortune frequently to meet with) infallibly destroy our Constitution.

And this is so evident and important a Truth, that no Legislator ever founded a free Government, but avoided this *Charibdis*,[17] as a Rock against which his Commonwealth must certainly be shipwrack'd, as the *Israelites, Athenians, Corinthians, Achaians, Lacedemonians, Thebans, Samnites* and *Romans;* none of which Nations, whilst they kept their Liberty, were ever known to maintain any Soldier in constant Pay within their Cities, or ever suffer'd any of their Subjects to make War their Profession; well knowing that the Sword and Soveraignty always march Hand in Hand; and therefore they train'd their own Citizens, and Territories about them, perpetually in Arms, and their whole Commonwealths by this Means became so many form'd Militia's: A general Exercise of the best of their People in the use of Arms, was the only Bulwark of [8] their Liberties; this was reckon'd the surest Way to preserve them both at Home and Abroad, the People being secur'd thereby as well against the Domestick Affronts of any of their own Citizens, as against the Foreign Invasions of ambitious and unruly Neighbours. Their Arms were never lodg'd in the Hands of any who had not an Interest in preserving the publick Peace, who fought *pro aris & focis*,[18] and thought themselves sufficiently paid by repelling Invaders, that they might with Freedom return to their own Affairs. In those Days there was no Difference between the Citizen, the Soldier, and the Husbandman; for all promiscuously took Arms when the publick Safety requir'd it, and afterwards laid 'em down with more Alacrity than they took them up: So that we find among the *Romans*, the best and bravest of their Generals came from the Plough, contentedly returning when the Work was over, and never demanding their Triumphs, till they had laid down their Commands, and reduc'd themselves to the State of private Men.[19] Nor do we find this famous Commonwealth ever permitted a Deposition of their Arms in any other

17. See above, p. 81, n. 24.
18. See above, p. 16, n. 34.
19. A virtue most evident in Cincinnatus; see above, p. 17, n. 36.

Hands, till their Empire increasing, necessity constrain'd them to erect a constant Stipendiary Soldiery abroad in foreign Parts, either for the holding or winning of Provinces. Then Luxury increasing with Dominion, the strict Rule and Discipline of Freedom soon abated, and Forces were kept up at home, which soon prov'd of such dangerous Consequence, that the People were forc'd to make a Law to employ them at a convenient [9] Distance; which was that if any General march'd over the River *Rubicon*, he should be declared a publick Enemy. And in the Passage of that River this following Inscription was erected; *Imperator sive Miles, sive Tyrannus armatus quisquis sistito; vexillum armaque deponito, nec citra hunc amnem trajicito.* And this made Caesar, when he had presum'd to pass this River, to think of nothing but the pressing on to the total Oppression of that glorious Empire.[20]

Nor, as I said before, did any Nation deviate from these Rules but they lost their Liberty; and of this Kind there are infinite Examples, out of which I shall give a few in several Ages, which are most known, and occur to every ones Reading.

The first Example I shall give is of *Pisistratus*,[21] who artfully prevailing with the *Athenians* to allow him Fifty Guards for the Defence of his Person, he so improv'd that Number, that he seiz'd upon the Castle and Government, destroy'd the Commonwealth, and made himself Tyrant of *Athens*.

The *Corinthians* being in Apprehension of their Enemies, made a Decree for Four Hundred Men to be kept to defend their City, and gave *Tymophanes* the Command over them, who overturn'd their Government, cut off all the principal Citizens, and proclaim'd himself King of *Corinth*.[22]

[10] *Agathocles* being Captain General of the *Syracusians*, got such Interest in the Army, that he cut all the Senators to Pieces, and the richest of the People, and made himself their King.[23]

20. See above, pp. 17–18, nn. 38, 39, and 40.
21. See above, p. 18, n. 41.
22. See above, p. 19, n. 42.
23. See above, p. 19, n. 43.

The *Romans* for fear of the *Teutones* and *Cimbri*,[24] who like vast Inundations threaten'd their Empire, chose *Marius* their General; and contrary to the Constitution of their Government, continu'd him Five Years in his Command, which gave him such Opportunity to insinuate, and gain an Interest in their Army, that he oppress'd their Liberty: And to this were owing all the Miseries, Massacres and Ruins which that City suffer'd under him and *Sylla*, who made the best Blood in the World run like Water in the Streets of *Rome*, and turn'd the whole City into a Shambles of the Nobility, Gentry and People. The same Thing enabl'd *Caesar* totally to overthrow that famous Commonwealth; for the Prolongation of his Commission in *Gaul*, gave him an Opportunity to debauch his Army, and then upon a pretended Disgust he march'd to *Rome*, drove out the Senators, seiz'd the Treasury, fought their Forces, and made himself perpetual Dictator.[25]

Olivarotto di Fermo desir'd Leave of his Fellow Citizens, that he might be admitted into their Town with a Hundred Horse of his Companions; which being granted, he put to the Sword all their principal Citizens, and proclaimed himself their Prince.[26]

[11] *Francis Sforza* being General of the *Milanese*, usurp'd upon them, and made himself Duke of *Milan*.[27]

After *Christiern* the Second King of *Denmark* had conquer'd *Sweden*, he invited all the Senators and Nobility to a magnificent Entertainment, where after he had treated them highly for two Days, he most barbarously butchered them. None escaped this Massacre but the brave *Gustavus Ericson*, who was then a Prisoner; but he afterward escaping thro' a Thousand Difficulties, by his good Fortune, Courage and Conduct, drove the *Danes* out of *Sweden*, and restor'd the *Swedes* to their ancient Kingdom. Nothing then was thought too great for their generous Deliverer, every Mouth was full of his Praises, and by the universal Voice of

24. Germanic tribes which had invaded Gaul and Italy and inflicted defeats on Roman armies. For Marius, see above, p. 19, n. 44, p. 86, n. 40, and p. 161, n. 21. Marius defeated the Teutones and Cimbri in 102 and 101 B.C. at the Battles of Aquae Sextiae and Vercellae. Cf. Machiavelli, *Discourses*, bk. 2, chap. 8.

25. See above, p. 19, nn. 44 and 45.

26. See above, p. 20, n. 46.

27. See above, p. 20, n. 47.

the People, he was chosen their King; and to consummate the last Testimony of their Gratitude, they trusted him with an Army: But they soon found their Mistake, for it cost them their Liberty; and having granted that *unum magnum*, it was too late to dispute any thing else, his Successors having been pleas'd to take all the rest, and now they remain the miserable Examples of too credulous Generosity.[28]

The Story of *Denmark* is so very well known, and so well related by an excellent Author that it would be Impertinence in me to repeat it; only this I will observe, that if the King had not had an Army at his Command, the Nobles had never delivered up their Government.[29]

[12] Our Countryman *Oliver Cromwel* turned out the Parliament under which he serv'd; and this he effected by the Assistance of an Army.[30]

The last Instance I shall give is of a *French* Colony, as I remember in the *West-Indies*, who having War with the Neighbouring *Indians*, and being tired in their March with the Extremity of Heat, made their Slaves carry their Arms; who taking that Opportunity, fell upon them and cut them to Pieces, a just Punishment for their Folly.[31] And this will always be the Fate of those that trust their Arms out of their Hands; for 'tis a ridiculous Imagination to conceive Men will be Servants, when they can be Masters. And as Mr. *Harrington* judiciously observes, whatever Nation suffers their Servants to carry their Arms, their Servants will make them hold their Trenchers.[32]

Some People object, that the Republicks of *Venice* and *Holland* are Instances to disprove my Assertion, who both keep great Armies, and yet have not lost their Liberty.

I answer, that neither keep any Standing Forces within the Seats of their Government, that is, within the City of *Venice*, or the great Towns of the *United Provinces;* but they defend these by their own Burghers, and quarter their Mercenaries in their conquer'd Countries, *viz.* the *Venetians* in *Greece* and the Continent of *Italy*, and the *Dutch* in *Flanders*. And

28. See above, p. 21, nn. 48 and 49.
29. See above, p. 21, n. 50.
30. See above, p. 22, n. 51.
31. Untraced; see above, p. 22, n. 52
32. See above, p. 23, n. 53.

the Situation of these States [13] makes their Armies, so posted, not dangerous to them; for the *Venetians* cannot be attack'd without a Fleet, nor the *Dutch* be ever conquer'd by their own Forces, their Country being so full of strong Towns, fortify'd both by Art and Nature, and defended by their own Citizens, that it would be a fruitless Attempt for their own Armies to invade them; for if they should march against any of their Cities, 'tis but shutting up their Gates, and the Design is spoil'd.

I would not here be mistaken, as if I advanced any Argument against the Quartering of Guards in and about the City of *London;* for these being appointed for the Defence and Guard of the King and Royal Family, are obliged to be posted in all such Places where-ever the Court resides. Neither do I object against the maintaining of a competent Number of Troops, such as have been allowed our former Kings to be kept in Pay in Times of Peace. But that an Army of Thirty Thousand Men[33] should now in a profound Peace be kept standing, is what no honest Man or

---

33. The number is broadly correct, but it needs to be contextualized in order justly to be assessed:

> The army, unemployed for a quarter of a century, except to suppress riots or for the relatively small operations of 1715 and 1719, was neither popular nor efficient. The old seventeenth-century fear of a standing army as a menace to civil liberties was as deep-seated as ever. . . . At the death of Anne, apart from the three regiments still in Flanders, the strength of the army at home had been reduced to less than 8,000, while even the Irish establishment, paid for by Ireland, was only about 5,000 strong. Under the menace of Jacobitism the British army was perforce raised to 36,000 in 1716, but in the succeeding years it was steadily reduced so that by 1718 it totalled 16,300 and in 1721, 12,400. During Walpole's ministry, between 1722 and 1738 it stood normally at between 16,000 and 17,700, with slight increases in 1726–8 and 1734 owing to continental unrest. During the war-period 1739–48 the numbers rose from 35,900 to a maximum of 74,000 in 1745, then dropped to a uniform 18,857 until 1754, after which the Seven Years war brought them up to a maximum of 67,776. . . . The result was that in times of foreign invasion or even civil strife England was in the humiliating position of having to borrow regiments from the Irish establishment, normally kept at 12,000 strong, or hire troops from the Dutch, Hanover, or the Landgrave of Hesse-Cassel to defend her own soil. (Basil Williams, *The Whig Supremacy 1714–1760*, vol. II of *The Oxford History of England*, 2nd ed., rev. C. H. Stuart [Oxford: Clarendon Press, 1962], pp. 213–14; see also Charles Dalton, *George I's Army, 1714–27*, 2 vols. (London: Eyre and Spottiswoode, Ltd., [1910–12])

Lover of his Country will venture to affirm. And, to return to the last Objection, tho we should admit, that an Army might be consistent with Freedom in a Commonwealth, yet it is otherwise in a free Monarchy; for in the former 'tis wholly in the Disposal of the People, who nominate, appoint, discard and punish the Generals and Officers as they think fit, and 'tis certain Death to make any Attempt upon their Liberties; whereas in the latter, the King is [14] perpetual General,[34] may model the Army as he pleases, and it will be call'd High-Treason to oppose him.

And tho some Princes, as the Family of the *Medices*,[35] *Lewis* the Eleventh[36] and others, laid the Foundation of their Tyrannies, without the immediate Assistance of an Army, yet they all found an Army necessary to establish them; or otherwise a little Experience in the People of the Change of their Condition, would have made them disgorge in a Day that ill-gotten Power they had been acquiring for an Age.

This Subject is so self-evident, that I am almost asham'd to prove it; for if we look through the World, we shall find in no Country, Liberty and an Army stand together; so that to know whether a People are Free or Slaves, it is necessary only to ask, Whether there is an Army kept amongst them? And the Solution of that Preliminary Question resolves the Doubt; as we see in *China, India, Tartary, Persia, Ethiopia, Turkey, Morocco, Muscovy, Austria, France, Portugal, Denmark, Sweden, Tuscany,* and all the little Principalities of *Italy* and some of *Germany,* where the People live in the most abandon'd Slavery: And in Countries, where no Armies are kept within the Seat of their Government, the People are Free, as *Poland, Biscay, Switzerland,* the *Grizons,*[37] *Venice, Holland, Genoa, Geneva, Ragusa, Algiers, Tunis, Hamborough,*[38] *Lubeck,* all the Free Towns in *Germany* and *Great-Britain.* This Truth is so obvious, [15] that the most bare-fac'd Advocates for an Army do not directly deny it, but qualify the Matter by telling us, that a Number not exceeding twenty or thirty

34. The phrase "perpetual general" does not form part of the title of the British monarch, although the monarch is ex officio head of all the British armed forces.

35. See above, p. 24, n. 54.

36. See above, p. 24, n. 54.

37. See above, p. 24, n. 55.

38. I.e., Hamburg. See above, p. 24, n. 56.

Thousand are a handful to so populous a Nation as this. Now I think that Number may bring as certain Ruin upon us, as if they were as many Millions, and I will give my Reasons for it.

It's the Misfortune of all Countries, that they sometimes lie under an unhappy Necessity to defend themselves by Arms against the Ambition of their Governours, and to fight for what's their own; for if a Prince will rule us with a Rod of Iron, and invade our Laws and Liberties, and neither be prevail'd upon by our Miseries, Supplications, or Tears, we have no Power upon Earth to appeal to, and therefore must patiently submit to our Bondage, or stand upon our own Defence; which if we are enabled to do, we shall never be put upon it, but our Swords may grow rusty in our Hands; for that Nation is surest to live in Peace, that is most capable of making War; and a Man that hath a Sword by his side, shall have least occasion to make use of it. Now, I say, if a King hath thirty Thousand Men beforehand with his Subjects, the People can make no Effort to defend their Liberties, without the Assistance of a foreign Power, which is a Remedy most commonly as bad as the Disease; and if we have not a Power within our selves to defend our Laws, we are no Government.

[16] For *England* being a small Country, few strong Towns in it, and those in the King's Hands, the Nobility disarm'd by the Destruction of Tenures,[39] and the Militia not to be rais'd but by the King's Command, there can be no Force levied in any Part of *England,* but must be destroy'd in its Infancy by a few Regiments: for what will Twenty or Thirty Thousand naked unarm'd Men signify against as many Troops of mercenary Soldiers?[40] What if they should come into the Field, and say, You must chuse these and these Men your Representatives, Where is your Choice? What if they should say, Parliaments are seditious and factious Assemblies, and therefore ought to be abolish'd; What is become of your Freedom? If they should encompass the Parliament House, and threaten if they do not surrender up their Government, they will put them to the Sword; What

---

39. I.e., the abandonment of feudalism; see above, p. 25, n. 58, p. 244, n. 39, and p. 409, n. 28.

40. A clear instance of the classic conflation, on the part of those opposed to standing armies, of professional troops with mercenaries. See above, p. 153 and n. 5.

is become of your Constitution? These Things may be under a Tyranni-cal Prince, and have been done in several Parts of the World. What is it that causeth the Tyranny of the *Turks* at this Day,[41] but Servants in Arms? What is it that preserv'd the glorious Commonwealth of *Rome*, but Swords in the Hands of its Citizens?

I will add here, that most of the Nations I instanc'd before, were enslav'd by small Armies: *Oliver Cromwel* left behind him but Twenty Seven Thousand Men;[42] and the Duke of *Monmouth*, who was the Dar-ling of the People, was suppress'd with Two Thousand;[43] nay, *Caesar* seiz'd *Rome* it self with Five [17] Thousand, and fought the Battle of *Pharsalia*, where the Fate of the World was decided, with Twenty Two Thousand:[44] And most of the Revolutions of the *Roman* and *Ottoman* Empires since were caus'd by the *Pretorian* Bands, and the Court *Jane-zaries;*[45] the former of which never exceeded Eight, nor the latter Twelve Thousand Men. And if no greater Numbers could make such Distur-bances in those vast Empires, what will double or triple the Force do with us? And they themselves confess it, when they argue for an Army; for they tell us, we may be surpriz'd with Ten or Fifteen Thousand Men from *France*, and having no regular Force to oppose them, they will over-run the Kingdom. Now, if so small a Force can oppose the King, the Militia, with the United Power of the Nobility, Gentry and Commons, what would an equal Power do against the People, when supported by the Royal Authority and a never failing Interest that will attend it, except when it acts for the publick Good?

We are told, this Army is not design'd to be made a part of our Con-stitution, but to be kept only for a little Time, till the Circumstances of *Europe*, and of this Nation in particular, will better permit us to be without them. But I would know of these Gentlemen, when they think that Time will be, if it is not now? We are at present not only at Peace

41. See above, p. 28, n. 71, and p. 282, n. 51.
42. Recent estimates for the armed force of the Protectorate allow 6,000 men to England, but no fewer than 40,000 men to Scotland and Ireland (*ODNB*).
43. See above, p. 28, n. 68, and p. 39, n. 98.
44. See above, p. 28, n. 69.
45. See above, p. 28, nn. 70 and 71.

with all our Neighbours, but are also ty'd in the firmest Alliance with *France*,[46] formerly our most formidable Enemy; shall we have less to fear from the Pre[18]tender to the Crown[47] and his Friends at any Time hereafter, than at this present Time? Or are we apprehensive, lest *France* will keep Treaties with us no longer than is consistent with her own Interest? Or that she will be more capable of offending us just after the late tedious and consumptive War,[48] than many Years hereafter when she has had a Breathing Time to repair the Calamities she has suffer'd by it? No: we can never disband our Army with so much Safety as at this Time; and this is well known by those Advocates for them, who are satisfy'd that a Continuation of them now, is an Establishment of them for ever: For whilst the Circumstances of *Europe* stand in the present Posture, the Argument will be equal to continue them; if the State of *Europe* should alter to the Advantage of *France*, the Reason will grow stronger, and we shall be told, we must increase our Number. But if there should be such a Turn of Affairs in the World, that we were no longer in Apprehension of the *French* Power, they may be kept up without our Assistance; nay, the very Discontents they may create, shall be made an Argument for the continuing of them. But if they should be kept from oppressing the People, in a little Time they would grow habitual to us, and almost become a Part of our Constitution, and by degrees we shall be brought to believe them not only not dangerous, but necessary: for every Body sees, but few understand: And those few will never be able to persuade the Multitude that there is any Danger in those Men they have liv'd [19] quietly with for some Years, especially when the disbanding them will (as they will be made believe) cost them more Money out of their own Pockets than to maintain a Militia.

But we are told, that we need be in no Apprehension of Slavery, whilst we keep the Power of the Purse in our own Hands: which is very true; but they do not tell us, that he has the Power of raising Money, to whom no one dares refuse it.

46. See above, p. 440, n. 12.
47. I.e., the Old Pretender; see above, p. 30, n. 73, and p. 314, n. 145.
48. I.e., the War of the Spanish Succession (1702–13); see above, p. 160, n. 18, and p. 326, n. 184.

Arma dat tenenti
Omnia dat qui justa negat.[49]

For 'tis as certain that an Army will raise Money, as that Money will raise an Army; but if this Course should be thought too desperate, 'tis only shutting up the *Exchequer*,[50] and disobliging a few Tally-Jobbers[51] (who have bought them for Fifty *per Cent*. Discount) and there will be near Three Millions a Year ready cut and dry'd for them: And whoever doubts whether such a Method as this is practicable, let him look back to the Reign of *Charles* the Second.

But when all other Arguments fail, they call to their Assistance the old Tyrant Necessity, and tell us the Power of *France* is so great, and Treaties are of so little Force with that perfidious Nation, that let the Consequence of an Army be what it will, we cannot be without one; and if we must be Slaves, we had better be so to a Protestant [20] Prince than a Popish one, and the worst of all Popish ones, one under the Direction of *France*. Now I am of Opinion, that the putting an Epithet upon Tyranny is false Heraldry;[52] for Protestant and Popish are both alike; and if I must be a Slave, it is very indifferent to me who is my Master; and therefore I shall never consent to be rul'd by an Army, which is the worst that the most barbarous Conquest can impose upon me; which notwithstanding we have little Reason to fear, whilst we keep the Seas well guarded.

It is certain there is no Country so situated for Naval Power as *Great-Britain*. The Sea is our Element, our Seamen have as much hardy Bravery, and our Ships are as numerous, and built of as good Materials as any in the World: Such a Force well apply'd and manag'd, is able to give Laws to the Universe; and if we keep a competent Part of it well arm'd in Times of Peace, it is the most ridiculous thing in Nature, to believe any Prince will have thoughts of invading us, unless he proposes to be superior to us in Naval Power: For the Preparations necessary for such an Undertaking

---

49. See above, p. 32, n. 76.
50. I.e., ceasing temporarily to service the public debt; see above, p. 32, n. 77.
51. See above, p. 32, n. 78.
52. See above, p. 33, n. 81.

will alarm all *Europe*, give both to us and our Confederates time to arm, and put our selves in a Posture of Defence. And whoever considers, that the Prince of *Orange* with Six Hundred Ships brought but Fourteen Thousand Men,[53] and the mighty *Spanish Armado* (then the Terror of the World) imbark'd but Eighteen Thousand,[54] will be assur'd, that [21] no Invasion can be so sudden upon us, but we shall have time to get ready our whole Fleet, bring some Forces from *Ireland*, and prepare our own Militia if there shall be occasion for it; especially in Times of Peace, when we shall have the Liberty of all the Ports of *France*, and shall or may have Intelligence from every one of them.

But they tell us such a Wind may happen as may be favourable to our Enemy, and keep us within our Ports; which, I say, as *France* lies to *England*, is almost impossible: For if we lie about *Falmouth*, or the *Land's-End*, no Fleet from *Brest* or the Ocean can escape us without a Miracle; and if the Design be to invade us from any Port in the Channel, a very few Ships (which may safely lye at Anchor) will certainly prevent it. Nor is it to be conceiv'd, that the *French* will be at a vast Expence for the Contingency of such a critical Wind, or will send an Army into a Country where their Retreat is certainly cut off, when the failing of any part of their Design will bring a new War upon them.

And here I must confess, that the Misapplication of our Naval Force (which is our known Strength) for these several Years past, is the strongest, as it is the most usual Argument against me; which unriddles a Mystery I did not understand before, tho I never was so foolish as to believe all the Errors of that Kind were the Effects of Chance or Ignorance, or that losing so many Opportunities of de[22]stroying the *French* Fleet had not some extraordinary, tho occult Cause; and yet notwithstanding the restless Attempts of our Enemies and the paltry Politicks and even Treachery of some preceeding Ministries, this Fleet triumphantly defended us, so that our Enemies in many Years War could not get an Opportunity of invading our Country.

53. See above, p. 34, n. 82.
54. See above, p. 34, n. 83.

It is objected, that the Officers of our Fleet may be corrupted, or that a Storm may arise, which may destroy it all at once, and therefore we ought to have two Strings to our Bow. By which I perceive all their Fears lye one Way, and that they doe not care, if they precipitate us into inevitable Ruin at home, to prevent a distant Possibility of it from *France*. But I think this Phantom too may be laid by a well-trained Militia, and then all their Bugbears[55] will vanish. This Word can be no sooner out, but there's a Volly of Small Shot let fly at me: What! must we trust our Safety to an undisciplin'd Mob, who never dream'd of fighting when they undertook the Service; who are not inur'd to the Fatigue of a Camp, or ever saw the Face of an Enemy?[56] And then they magnify mercenary Troops; as if there was an intrinsick Vertue in a red Coat, or that a Raggamuffin from Robbing a Henroosts,[57] in two Campaigns, could be cudgell'd into a Hero. Tho I must confess the Conduct of the Advocates for a Standing Army industriously Enervating this Force, does in some Measure justify their Objections: For [23] the detestable Policies of the Reigns of King *Charles* the Second and his immediate Successor, were with the utmost Art and Application to disarm the People, and make the Militia useless, to countenance a Standing Army in order to bring in Popery and Slavery; and if any Methods were propos'd to make it more serviceable, the Court would never suffer them to be debated; and such Officers as were more zealous in Exercising their Companies than others, were reprimanded, as designing to raise a Rebellion. This Conduct was exactly imitated in the latter Part of Queen *Anne*'s Reign,[58] when the Militia of *England* was neglected and discountenanc'd, and that of *Scotland* attempted to be reduc'd to the Standard in *England*, by which Means that Force would

55. See above, p. 36, n. 88.
56. See above, p. 36, n. 89.
57. At the time a common expression used to mock petty military exploits; see, e.g., William Freke, *Select essays tending to the universal reformation of learning concluded with The art of war, or, A summary of the martial precepts necessary for an officer* (1693), p. 277; "Nor is't a little imprudence for a General to divide himself to Destruction in besieging little Henroosts before a Royal Army."
58. The implication is that the Tory administration of Harley and Bolingbroke was secretly negotiating a Stuart restoration.

have been rendered entirely useless in that Part of the Kingdom, the first Scene where the Enemy was to act the designed bloody Tragedy; and when the Army itself was daily more and more reform'd and modell'd to their Purpose of bringing in the *Pretender.*

And now it seems some Men in this Reign are taking the Advantage of this trayterous Neglect and infamous Politicks of those we just now mention'd. But why may not a Militia be made useful? Why may not the Nobility, Gentry, and Freeholders of *England* be trusted with the Defence of their own Lives, Estates, and Liberties, without having Guardians and Keepers assign'd them? And why may they not defend these with as much Vigour and Courage as Mercenaries who have nothing to lose, nor any other Tye to engage [24] their Fidelity, than the inconsiderable Sixpence a Day, which they may have from the Conqueror?

Why may not a competent Number of Firelocks be kept in every Parish for the young Men to exercise with on Holy-days, and Rewards offer'd to the most expert, to stir up their Emulation?

Why may not a Third Part of the Militia be kept by Turns in constant Exercise?

Why may not a Man be listed in the Militia, till he be discharged by his Master, as well as in the Army, till he be discharged by his Captain? And why may not the same Horse be always sent forth, unless it can be made appear, he is dead or maim'd?

Why may not the private Soldiers of the Army, when they are dispers'd in the several Parts of the Kingdom, be sent to the Militia? And why may not the inferior Officers of the Army in some Proportion command them?

I say, these and other like Things may be done, and some of them are done in our own Plantations, and the Islands of *Jersy* and *Guernsey;* as also in *Poland, Switzerland,* and the Country of the *Grisons,*[59] which are Nations much less considerable than *England,* have as formidable Neighbours, no Seas nor Fleet to defend them, nothing but a Militia [25] to depend upon, and yet no one dares attack them. And we have seen as great Performances done formerly by the Apprentices of *London,* and in

59. See above, p. 24, n. 55.

the War by the *Vaudois* in *Savoy*, the *Miquelets* in *Catalonia*, and the Militia in *Ireland*,[60] as can be parallel'd in History. And so it would be with us, if the Court would give their hearty Assistance in promoting this Design; if the King would appear in Person at the Head of them, and give Rewards and Honours to such as deserve them, we should quickly see the young Nobility and Gentry appear magnificently in Arms and Equipage, shew a generous Emulation in outvying one another in Military Exercises, and place a noble Ambition in making themselves serviceable to their Country; as anciently the *Achaians* and *Thebans* from the most contemptible Nations in *Greece*, by the Conduct of *Pelopidas*, *Epaminondas*, and *Philopemen*,[61] came to have the best disciplin'd Troops, and most excellent Soldiers in the World.

They object, that such a Militia as this is a Standing Army, and will be as dangerous, and much more chargeable. I answer,

That there can be no Danger from an Army, where the Nobility and Gentry of *England* are the Commanders, and the Body of it made up of the Free-holders, their Sons and Servants; unless we can conceive that the Nobility and Gentry will join in an unnatural Design to make void their own Titles to their Estates and Liberties; and if [26] they could entertain so ridiculous a Proposition, they would never be obey'd by the Soldiers, who will have a respect to those that send them forth and pay them, and to whom they must return again when their Time is expir'd. For if I send a Man, I will as surely chuse one who will fight for me, as a mercenary Officer will chuse one that shall fight for me: And the Governments of King *Charles* the Second, and King *James* before-mentioned, are Witnesses to the Truth of this, who debauched the Militia more than ever I hope to see it again, and yet durst never rely upon them to assist their Arbitrary Designs; as we may remember at the Duke of *Monmouth*'s Invasion, their Officers durst not bring them near his Army for fear of a Revolt.[62] Nay, the Pensioner Parliament[63] themselves turn'd short upon

60. See above, pp. 37–38, nn. 92–96.
61. See above, p. 39, n. 97.
62. See above, p. 39, n. 98.
63. See above, p. 40, n. 99.

the Court, when they expected to give them the finishing Stroke to our Ruin.

To the last Part of the Objection, That this Militia will be more charge-able than an Army; I answer, That since (as I suppose) no Man proposes wholly to lay them aside, if we add the extraordinary Expence of Main-taining twenty Thousand Men to the ordinary Charge of the Militia, it is much more than sufficient to make the latter useful. But if this Objec-tion were true, it ought not to enter into Competition with the Preserva-tion of our Laws and Liberties; for it is better to give a third Part of my Estate, if it were necessary, than to have all taken from me.

[27] And tho it should be granted, that a Militia is not as serviceable as an Army kept in constant Discipline, yet I believe these Gentlemen themselves will confess, that sixty Thousand of them train'd as before, are as good as twenty Thousand of their standing Troops, which is the Question; for 'tis impossible to have them both useful at the same Time, they being as incompatible as broad and clipt Money,[64] never current together; and therefore the Kingdom must depend wholly upon a Mili-tia, or else it will not depend upon them at all.

And this by the Way may silence that Objection, that we must keep our Army till the Militia be disciplin'd; for that will never be done whilst the Court has an Army; and the same Objection will be made seven Years hence as now; so that even a small Army can be of no use to us, but to make our Fleet neglected, to hinder the Militia from being train'd, and enslave us at Home; for they are too few to defend us against an In-vasion, and too many for the People to oppose.

I dare speak with the greater Assurance upon this Subject, having the Authority of as great Men as the World hath produced for my Justifica-tion. *Machiavel* spends several Chapters to prove that no Prince or State ought to suffer any of their Subjects to make War their Profession, and that no Nation can be secure with any other Forces than a settled Mili-tia.[65] My Lord *Bacon* in several [28] Places bears his Testimony against a Standing Army, and particularly he tells us, that a mercenary Army is

64. See above, p. 41, n. 100.
65. See above, p. 42, n. 101.

fittest to invade a Country, but a Militia to defend it; because the first have Estates to get, and the latter to protect.[66] Mr. *Harrington* has founded his whole *Oceana* upon a train'd Militia;[67] and I have read a *French* Book call'd a History of the Politicks of *France*, which says, *Enfin si on veut ruiner les Anglois il suffit de les obliger a tenir des Troupes sur pied.*[68]

Nay, I believe no Author ever treated of a Free Government, that did not express his Abhorrence of an Army; for (as my Lord *Bacon* says) whoever does use them, tho he may spread his Feathers for a Time, he will mew them soon after;[69] and raise them with what Design you please, yet, like the *West-Indian* Dogs in *Boccaline*,[70] in a little time they will certainly turn Sheep-biters.

Perhaps it will be said, that the Artillery of the World is changed since some of those wrote, and War is become more a Mystery, and therefore more Experience is necessary to make good Soldiers. But wherein does this Mystery consist? Not in exercising a Company, and obeying a few Words of Command; these are Mysteries that the dullest Noddle will comprehend in a few Weeks. Nay, I have heard that the Modern Exercise is much shorter and easier than the Ancient. But the great Improvements in War, are in regular Encampments, Fortification, Gunnery, skilful Engineering, &c. [29] These are Arts not to be learn'd without much Labour and Experience, and are as much gain'd in the Closet as in the Field; and, I suppose, no Man will say, that the keeping Standing Forces is necessary to make a good Engineer.

As to actual Experience in War, that is not essential either to a Standing Army or Militia, as such; but the former may be without it, and the latter gain it according as they have Opportunities of Action. 'Tis true at present the Army hath been train'd up in long Wars, and hath gain'd great Knowledge: But these Men will not be lost when they are disbanded, they will be still in the Kingdom; and if the Parliament does give them a Gratuity suitable to the Service they have done their

66. See above, p. 42, n. 102.
67. See above, p. 42, n. 103.
68. See above, p. 42, n. 104.
69. See above, p. 42, n. 102.
70. See above, p. 43, n. 106.

Country, they will be ready to resume their Arms whenever Occasion offers.

I conclude this Subject of the Militia with this Observation, that a Standing Army in Peace will grow more effeminate by living dissolutely in Quarters, than a Militia that for the most Part will be exercised with hard Labour; So that upon the whole Matter, a Standing Army in Peace will be worse than a Militia; and in War a Militia will soon become a disciplin'd Army.

But I desire to know of these Gentlemen, how comes an Army necessary to our Preservation now, and never since the Conquest before in Times of Peace? Did ever [30] the prevailing Party in the Wars of *York* and *Lancaster* (as I observ'd before) attempt to keep up a Standing Army to support themselves?[71] No: they had more Sense than to sacrifice their own Liberty, and more Honour than to enslave their Country, the more easily to carry on their own Faction. Were not the *Spaniards* as powerful, as good Soldiers, and as much our Enemies as the *French* lately were? Was not *Flanders* as near us as *France*? And the Popish Interest in Queen *Elizabeth*'s Time as strong as the Jacobite is now? And yet that most excellent Princess never dream'd of a Standing Army; but thought her surest Empire was to reign in the Hearts of her Subjects, which the following Story sufficiently testifies. When the Duke of *Alanson*[72] came over to *England*, and for some time had admir'd the Riches of the City, the Conduct of her Government, and the Magnificence of her Court; he ask'd her amidst so much Splendor, Where were her Guards? Which Question she resolv'd a few Days after, when she took him in her Coach through the City, and pointing to the People (who receiv'd her in Crowds, with repeated Acclamations) *These*, said she, *my Lord, are my Guards; these have their Hands, their Hearts, and their Purses always ready at my Command*: And these were Guards indeed, who defended her through a long and successful Reign of Forty Four Years, against all the Machinations of *Rome*, the Power of *Spain*, a disputed Title, and the perpetual

71. See above, p. 44, n. 108.
72. See above, p. 44, n. 109.

Conspiracies of her own Popish Subjects; a Security the *Roman* Emperors could not [31] boast of with their *Pretorian* Bands,[73] and their *Eastern* and *Western* Armies.

Were not the *French* as powerful in *Charles* the Second and King *James*'s Time, as they are now, after the long and destructive Wars wherein they have been since engag'd? And yet we then thought a much less Army than is now contended for, a most insupportable Grievance; insomuch that in *Charles* the Second's Reign, the Grand-Jury presented them, and the Pensioner-Parliament voted them to be a Nuisance; sent Sir *J. Williamson* to the *Tower*, for saying, *The King might keep Guards for the Defence of his Person*, and addressed to have them disbanded.[74] And now, which is strange to think, some Gentlemen would make their Court, by doing what the worst of Parliaments could not think of without Horror and Confusion.

They say, the King of *France* was in League with our late Kings,[75] so *France* is with us; and they would have broke it then, if they had thought it safe, and for their Interest as much as now. But they add, we have more disaffected Persons to join with them; which I must deny, for I believe his present Majesty hath deservedly as much Interest as any of his Predecessors; and if during the later Part of the late Reign,[76] when the Interest of the *Pretender* was so much advanc'd by the Ministry itself,[77] and the Friends to his Majesty's Succession affronted and discourag'd; if during the late formidable Rebellion,[78] which was rais'd to dethrone and murder his Maje[32]sty and the whole Royal Family, and to overturn the present Religion, Laws and Liberties of which he is the Defender and Protector; I say, if at such dangerous Times he had so many Friends, there can be no doubt but in Times of Peace, when the People reap the Fruits of that Conduct he hath shewn in their Defence, he will be the most beloved and glorious Prince that ever fill'd the *English* Throne.

73. See above, p. 28, n. 70.
74. See above, pp. 45–46, nn. 111–13.
75. See above, p. 46, n. 114.
76. I.e., the final years of Queen Anne, who reigned from 1702 to 1714.
77. See above, p. 453, n. 58.
78. I.e., the Jacobite rebellion of 1715.

I will assert farther, That the most likely Way of bringing in the *Pretender*, is Maintaining a Standing Army to keep him out.

For the King's Safety stands upon a Rock, whilst it depends upon the solid Foundation of the Affections of his People, which is never to be shaken till 'tis as evident as the Sun is in the Firmament, that there is a new form'd Design to overthrow our Laws and Liberties, which I think we have no Reason to fear, when I reflect on the wise Provisions his Majesty has made against any future Attempts of that Kind: But if we keep a Standing Army, all depends upon the uncertain and capricious Humours of the Soldiery, which in all Ages have produc'd more and violent sudden Revolutions, than ever have been known in any unarm'd Governments: For there is such a Chain of Dependence amongst them, that if Two or Three of the Chief Officers should be disobliged, or have Intrigues with Jacobite Mistresses; or if a King of *France* could once again buy his Pensioners into the Court or Army, or offer a better Market to some [33] that are in already, we shall have another Rehearsal Revolution,[79] and the People be only idle Spectators of their own Ruin.

And whosoever considers the Composition of an Army, and doubts this, let him look back to the *Roman* Empire, where he will find out of Twenty Six Emperors, Sixteen depos'd and murdered by their own Armies.[80] Nay half the History of the World is made up of Examples of this Kind: But we need not go any farther than our own Country, where we have twice kept Armies in Time of Peace, and both Times they turn'd out their own Masters. The first under *Cromwel*, expell'd that Parliament under which they had fought too successfully for many Years; afterwards under General *Monk*, they destroy'd the Government they before set up, and restored King *Charles* the Second; and he afterwards disbanded them, lest they should have conspired to exclude him again. The other Instance is fresh in every One's Memory, how King *James's* Army joyn'd with the Prince of *Orange*, afterwards our Rightful and Lawful King.[81]

79. See above, p. 47, n. 116.
80. See above, p. 47, n. 117.
81. See above, p. 48, nn. 118–20.

And what could have been expected otherwise from Men, who call themselves *Soldiers of Fortune?* Who having no other Profession or Subsistance to depend upon, are forc'd to stir up the Ambition of Princes, and engage them in perpetual Quarrels, that they may share of the Spoils they make? Such Men, like some Sort of Ravenous Fish, fare best in a Storm; and therefore we may reasonably [34] suppose they will be better pleas'd with a tyrannical Government, such as was that of the late King *James*, than the mild and gracious Administration of his present Majesty, who is come to preserve us from a greater Oppression; and he has done it, and triumphs in it, in Spite of his Enemies.

But farther, there is a Crisis in all Affairs, which when once lost can never be retriev'd. Several Accidents concur to make the Disbanding the Army practicable now, which may not happen again: We have a loyal and uncorrupted Parliament, and we have a good Prince, whose Inclinations as well as Circumstances will oblige him to comply with the reasonable Desires of his People. But let us not flatter ourselves, this will be always so; for if the Army should be continu'd, they may in time be accounted Part of the Prerogative,[82] and then it will be thought as great a Violation to attempt the Disbanding them, as of the Guards in King *Charles* the Second's Time; it will be interpreted a Design to dethrone the King, and be made an Argument for the keeping them up.

But there are other Reasons yet: The Publick Necessities call upon us to contract our Charge, that we may be the sooner out of Debt, and in a Condition to make a new War if there is a Necessity for it: And 'tis not the keeping great Armies on Foot that will enable us to do so, but putting ourselves in a Capacity to pay them. We should put ourselves into such Circumstances, that our [35] Enemies may dread a new Quarrel, which can be no otherways done, but by lessening our Expences, and paying off the publick Engagements as fast as we are able. For Money is the Sinews of War; but the Sinews once weakened, the Body is in a tottering Condition. A Standing Army must be fed, and when once without Pay, must live upon free Quarter; for there is no Reason that Men rais'd for the Service of their Country, should starve in it.

82. See above, p. 13, n. 24.

In this Discourse, I purposely omit speaking of the lesser Inconveniences attending a Standing Army, such as frequent Quarrels, Murders and Robberies; the Destruction of all the Game in the Country, the Quartering upon publick, and sometimes private Houses; the influencing Elections of Parliament[83] by an artificial Distribution of Quarters; the rendring so many Men useless to Labour, and almost Propagation, together with a much greater Destruction of them, by taking them from a laborious Way of living to a loose idle Life; and besides this, the Insolence and Debaucheries that are committed in all the Towns they come in, to the Ruin of Multitudes of Women, Dishonour of their Families, and ill Example to others; and a numerous Train of Mischiefs besides, almost endless to enumerate. These are trivial as well as particular Grievances, in Respect of those I have treated about, which strike at the Heart's Blood of our Constitution; and therefore I think these not considerable enough to bear a Part in a Discourse of this [36] Nature: Besides, these often procure their own Remedy, working Miracles, and making some Men see that were born blind, and impregnable against all the Artillery of Reason; for Experience is only the Mistress of Fools: A wise Man will know a Pike will bite when he sees his Teeth, which another will not make Discovery of but by the Loss of a Finger.

I shall now endeavour to confirm the Arguments I have brought, by considering of a Standing Army, without minding who is for it, or who is against it in this Age, and only shewing what are like to be the Consequences of it in future Reigns. And I have Reason to do thus, because if the Parliament give the best King a Standing Army, the worst King shall hereafter claim and have it. What I shall say on this Head, I hope will be of the greater Weight, because taken from our own History.

We have many Instances where Parliaments in a kind Fit, by one sudden Grant, have entail'd a World of lasting Misery upon the Nation. I will mention but One: The Kingdom was newly delivered from a bitter Tyrant, I mean King *John*, and had likewise got rid of their perfidious Deliverer the Dauphine of *France;* who after the *English* had accepted him for their King, had secretly vow'd their Extirpation, which the

83. See above, p. 49, n. 122.

Viscount of *Melun*, a *Frenchman*, being at the Point of Death, disclos'd.
They were moreover bless'd with a Young Prince, of whom they con-
cei[37]ved mighty Hopes, in the Hands of a very wise and honest Council.[84] This was Life from the Dead, and a true Revolution. In the Transport
of all this Happiness, about the Seventh Year of this new King, *Henry*
the Third, the Parliament granted him the Wardship of their Heirs.
Knighton, Pag. 2430 records it thus: *Magnates Angliae concesserunt Regi
Henrico Wardas Haeredum & Terrarum suarum, quod fuit initium multorum
malorum in Anglia.* He says this Grant was the Beginning of many Mischiefs in *England*.[85] In the Year 1222, these Mischiefs had their Rise and
Beginning; but where they ended no old Chronicle could ever tell, for
after this intolerable Bondage had continu'd above Four Hundred Years,
the Nation at last ransom'd themselves in our Time by giving the Excise.[86] It is a Grief to all After-ages, to find a Parliament so miserably
overseen;[87] for they both mistook their Man, and the hopeful Prince
prov'd as bad as if the very Soul of his Father *John*[88] had pass'd into him,
which is the common Character given him by all the ancient Historians:
And then they utterly mistook the Nature of the Grant, and did not foresee what a Misery and Vassalage it might prove to their Posterity. I appeal
to all the ancient Nobility and Gentry, who know any thing of the Affairs
of their own Families, whether it was so or not: And yet these were honest
and brave Men, who would rather have died than have been the Authors
of so much Mischief; but they were led by false Appearances, that by

84. See above, p. 119, nn. 8–9.

85. See above, p. 120, n. 10.

86. See above, p. 120, n. 11.

87. A moment of very complicated usage, combining the senses of "dominated"
(*OED*, s.v. "oversee," 2b), "bewitched" (4), and "duped" (7).

88. John (1167–1216), king of England, Lord of Ireland, Duke of Normandy and
of Aquitaine, Count of Anjou; reigned 1199–1216; a king whose reputation has
been exceptionally volatile and influenced by deeper historiographical tides. Con-
troversial in his own day, John was partially redeemed by the historiography of the
Reformation, which depicted him as a predecessor of Henry VIII in his struggle
with the papacy. However, the cult of Magna Carta in the seventeenth century
depressed John's reputation. More recently, historians have acknowledged John's
personal wickedness while at the same time drawing attention to his political
astuteness.

having the King Guardian of their Children, they could not [38] be wrong'd; they would have the best Education at Court, stand fair for future Preferment, and that a happier Provision for their Posterity could not be made: Neither could it; for the very Learning which this Instructive Passage has given to their late Posterity, countervails all the Mischiefs that are past.

But the Advocates for a Standing Army tell us, That tho the Wards, by being annex'd to the Crown, and so becoming a Prerogative, could not be parted with, which was the Cause of the long Continuance of that Mischief, after it was known and felt to be so; yet all this is cur'd by making the Act temporary, and settling a Standing Army only for a certain Number of Years, or they know not how.

I answer, that succeeding Princes, if they find an Army, will keep it, and will not trouble themselves whether the Law be temporary or perpetual. A plain Instance we have of this in the Customs; for tho Tunnage and Poundage,[89] and the other Impositions, are a Subsidy and free Gift, and the King's Answer to the Bill thanks the Subjects for their good Wills; and tho Parliaments have always us'd such Cautions and Limitations in those Grants as might prevent any Claim, and heretofore limited them to a short Time, as for a Year or two; and if they were continu'd longer, they have directed a certain space of Cessation or Intermission, that so the Right of the Subject might be the more evi[39]dent; at other Times, they have been granted upon occasion of War for a certain Number of Years, with *Proviso*,[90] that if the War were ended in the mean Time, then the Grant should cease, and of course they have been sequester'd into the Hands of some Subjects for the guarding of the Seas. Notwithstanding all this, tho the Parliament so carefully guarded their Grants, yet King *Charles* the First took the Subsidy, without any Grant at all, for Sixteen Years together; tho several Parliaments in the mean Time forbad the Payment of it, and voted all those to be publick Enemies that did not refuse it.[91] The like did his Son, the late King *James*, till his Parliament

89. See above, p. 121, n. 15.

90. A clause in a legal or formal document, making some condition, stipulation, exception, or limitation (*OED*, s.v. "proviso," B, a).

91. See above, p. 122, n. 16.

gave it him: And in his first Speech to them he demanded it as his own, by the Name of *my Revenue*;[92] and why then shall not another Prince come and say the same, *Give me my Army*, if he ever have a Parliament to ask? To limit a Prince with Laws, where there is an Army, is to bind *Sampson* with his Locks on.[93]

Having made appear that an Army now will be an Army always, I come in the next Place to shew what the Consequences of it will be, both by the Experience of former Ages, and by the Nature of the Thing.

In all Ages and Parts of the World, a Standing Army has been the never failing Instrument of enslaving a Nation; which *Richard* the Second[94] (*Walsing.* p. 354) compassing to do here in *England*, accordingly us'd the Means. For the Safety of his Per[40]son he assembled together (*multos Malefactores*)[95] a great Number of profligate Persons out of the County of *Chester*, who should keep Watch and Ward[96] continually about him in their Turns. These consisted of Four Thousand Archers, who committed such Outrages amongst the People, over-aw'd the Parliament, and aided him in his tyrannical Proceedings in such a manner, as could not be believ'd, if it were not witness'd by a whole Parliament, and his own Confession.

In short, tho many of those *Cheshire* Men plunder'd and liv'd upon free Quarter, beat, wounded, kill'd and ravish'd where-ever they came; yet because they enabled him to execute all his cruel and arbitrary Designs in Parliament, he countenanc'd them in all their Crimes, as confiding in them, and trusting in their Defence of him against all the Realm beside; for which Cause all the Lieges of his Realm had great matter of Commotion and Indignation.

This Parliament was in the Twenty First of his Reign, and in it the Frame of the *English* Government was quite destroy'd. I need not shew in what Particulars, for that is done already by *Bacon*,[97] and many other

92. See above, p. 122, n. 17.
93. See above, p. 123, n. 18.
94. See above, p. 123, n. 19.
95. "Many criminals."
96. Performing the duty of a watchman or sentinel, esp. as a feudal obligation (*OED*, s.v. "watch," 7a, "watch and ward").
97. See above, p. 125, n. 23.

Lawyers: But in short, the King was made absolute, and the whole Power of Parliament, which might remedy Things afterwards, was given up; for it was made Treason for any Man to endeavour to repeal any of the arbitrary Constitutions that were then made.

[41] I am even asham'd, when I observe some former Princes so zealous for oppressing and wronging a Nation, and so bent upon it; to reflect how cold and remiss many Subjects have been in all Times, and how unconcern'd to preserve their indispensable Rights, which are the very Being both of themselves and their Posterity. To see King *John* ready to pawn his Soul, and offer *Miramolim* the Emperor of *Morocco* to turn Turk, and make his Kingdom Tributary to him, only to get his Assistance to enslave this Nation;[98] and Subjects to take no care of their *English* Liberties; which certainly are prov'd to be worth keeping, by the Eagerness of bad Princes to take them away.

But to return to our *Cheshire*-Men, and to the Parliament which they had in Charge, *Sagittariis innumerabilibus vallato*, wall'd about with an infinite Number of Archers. The Parliament was hereby so over-aw'd, that in what they did they were *magis timore Regis ducti quam mentium ratione*, led more for fear of the King than their Consciences; their Souls were not their own.[99] And besides the standing Awe and Terror which this Guard was to both Houses, during their Session, there happen'd a Passage at last, which put them all into a very great Fright: It is thus set down by *Stow*,[100] p. 316. "And then License being had to depart, a great Stir was made, as is us'd, whereupon the King's Archers, in Number Four Thousand, compass'd the Parliament-House (thinking there had been in the House some Broil by [42] fighting) with their Bows bent, their Arrows knotch'd, and drawing ready to shoot, to the Terror of all that were there; but the King herewith coming, pacify'd them."

These Men did the King such acceptable Service, that he could do no less than make some Return to his Implements, which he did in honouring *Cheshire* for their Sakes. In this Session of Parliament he made it a Principality, and himself Prince of *Chester*. And so, as *Bacon* says, *Counties go*

98. See above, p. 126, n. 24.
99. See above, p. 126, nn. 25 and 26.
100. See above, p. 126, n. 27.

up, and Kingdoms go down.[101] This had never risen again, but by a happy Revolution,[102] which follow'd in less than Two Years. So much for the *Cheshire*-Men.

But what signify the Proceedings of this villanous Crew to an Army, who are all of them Men of Honour, and perhaps in Parliament Time shall be order'd a Hundred Miles off? These cannot wall in, surround, begirt and beset a Parliament, nor consequently hinder it from being a free Parliament. That I deny, for, I hope, such an Army may differ in Judgment, and can petition a Parliament at that Distance; and we very well know that their Desires have always been Commands. The Petition of an Army is like that of the *Cornish*-Men in *Henry* the Seventh's Time, it is always a strong Petition.[103]

Nay, an Army can never fail in this humble Way to over-rule a Parliament. If they are in being, they influence; and in *Caesar*'s easy [43] Way[104] they conquer by looking on. The very Reputation of a Force to back them, will make all Court Proposals speak big, tho ever so contrary to the Interest of the Nation: For there is no debating nor disputing against Legions. It will tempt them to do many Things they durst not otherways think of: What is much out of our Reach, is rarely the Object of our Thoughts; But the Facility of Execution is generally the first Motive to an Attempt. Now 'tis abundantly the Interest of Court Flatterers to live under a corrupt Reign: Then Bribes and Confiscations fill their Coffers. No Man's Wife or Daughter is free from their Lust, or Estate from their Avarice. They extort Presents from the Nobility, Goods from the Tradesmen, and Labour from the Poor. In short, all is their own. And 'tis to be fear'd, these Gentlemen (unless they have more Vertue than usually falls to their Share) will put Princes upon such Councils as promote their own Advantage. They will tell them, how mean it is to be aw'd by a few Country Gentlemen, when all the Kings of Europe besides are *got out of Pupilage*, as *Lewis* the Eleventh call'd it.[105] They will fill their Heads with

101. See above, p. 127, n. 29.
102. The deposition of Richard II by the future Henry IV in the autumn of 1399.
103. See above, p. 128, n. 34.
104. See above, p. 129, n. 35.
105. See above, p. 129, n. 36.

a Thousand trifling Jealousies of Monsters, Commonwealths, and such like Bugbears:[106] And it hath been difficult even for the wisest of Princes to free themselves from this sort of Cattel.[107] Nothing but the Fear of Punishment, and the being made a Sacrifice to the Peoples just Revenge, can make such Men honest. But if they have an Army to protect them, under a tyrannical Prince, all [44] these Considerations will be laid aside, and all Arguments will be answer'd in a Word, *The King has an Army*, which will cut off all Reply. *The King has an Army* will be a confuting Answer to every Thing, but a better Army, which Thanks be to God and the late King *William* we once found at the happy Revolution.[108] But as we are not to live upon Miracles,[109] so we are not to tempt Dangers.

I have stay'd the longer upon this Point, in shewing how inconsistent an Army (under a bad Prince I always mean) is with the Freedom of Parliaments, because they being the Keepers of our *British* Liberties can ill perform that Office when they have parted with their Power into other Hands. They are the last Resort of the Subject for the Redress of their Grievances. But how shall they relieve others from the Oppression and Insolences of the Soldiery, when perhaps they shall be subject to the like themselves? The Projectors are aware of this terrible Inconvenience, and therefore they have this Expedient, That it shall be the King's Army, but the Parliament shall have the Paying of them; whereby they shall in all future Times be as much the Parliament's humble Servants, as the Parliament their proper Masters.

Much at one[110] I believe. For the long Parliament had not such a King and Parliament Army as this, but an Army that was all their own, their Creatures, rais'd, listed, commission'd, and paid wholly by themselves, and [45] not in Partnership, and that had manfully fought all their Battles: And yet, upon the first Distaste they were pleased to take, they distress'd their own Masters, and with a high Hand forc'd them to banish

106. See above, p. 36, n. 88.
107. See above, p. 130, n. 38.
108. I.e., 1688.
109. Proverbial, although apparently not a biblical saying. At this time, it was capable of a sardonic or satirical application: see, e.g., Anonymous, *A Satyr Upon Old Maids* (1713), p. 5.
110. See above, p. 131, n. 42.

Eleven of their principal Members, *Denzil Holles*, Sir *Philip Stapylton*, *Glyn* and such other great Men. Sir *Philip Stapylton* dy'd in his Banishment. At another Time they would not suffer near a Hundred Members to enter into the House, whom they thought not well affected to the Business then in Hand: And at the same Time evilly intreated and imprisoned about Forty Members:[111] This they call'd Purging the House. After they had thus handled them at several Times, in Conclusion, the Officers came and reprimanded the House, bid them take away their Fool's Bauble, the Mace, violently pull'd the Speaker out of the Chair, drove out the Members, and lock'd up the Doors, and so good Night to the Parliament.[112] The Wisdom of that Parliament was said to be very great by their own Party, but it was Nonsense for them to think, that an Army does not know its own Strength. For, without dear bought Experience, any Body may know before Hand, what will be the natural Consequences of a Standing Army, in the Case above suppos'd of a bad Prince, which may possibly happen in some future Ages, tho indeed we have a long and glorious Prospect[113] of a better Fate to these Kingdoms. It will be the Conquest of the Nation in the silentest shortest and surest Way. They will be able to dispose of Mens Lives and Estates at Will and Pleasure: and what [46] can a foreign Conqueror do more? If after this the Subjects live and possess any thing, it will be because they let them; and how long that shall be, no Body knows.

Nay in many Respects an authoriz'd Standing Army may prove far worse than a foreign Invasion, and a Conquest from Abroad: For there we have a Chance for it, but this would be a Conquest in cold Blood, which might not be resisted. And thus we should lose the inseparable Rights of the Conquer'd, which is to rescue and deliver themselves, and to throw off the Yoke[114] as soon as they can.

111. See above, pp. 131–33, nn. 43–46.

112. See above, pp. 133–34, nn. 47–48.

113. George I had two children by his wife, Sophia Dorothea of Celle (1666–1726): the future George II (1683–1760) and Sophia Dorothea, born in 1687, who would become the queen of Frederick William I of Prussia. George I's marriage had been dissolved in 1694.

114. See above, p. 75, n. 10.

It would likewise be a great Aggravation of their Misery to be enslav'd at their own Cost and Charges: Besides the bitter Resentments of Unkindness and Breach of Trust, if it be done by those who ought to protect us, and provide better for us, at least should not leave us in a worse Condition than they found us. But above all, if we contribute to this Thraldom by our Folly, Flattery and little self-seeking: If the Destruction of our Posterity be of ourselves, that Reflection hereafter, when we come to foresee the bad Consequences that are yet hid from the Advocates for a Standing Army, will have a Sting in it; and it will not then be enough to say, who would have thought it.

Now in being overpower'd and conquer'd by a foreign Enemy, we contract none of [47] this Guilt, and suffer it as a bare Calamity. But there is no great fear of that (as we formerly insinuated) for the Duke *de Rohan* is our Guarantee, that we cannot be conquer'd from Abroad, who in a spightful Description of *England* says, It is a great Animal that can be destroy'd by nothing but it self.[115] Every Body must die when their Time is come, and Empires as well as private Men must submit to Time and Fate; Governments have their Infancy, their Meridian, and their Decay. But the Destruction of ours is more to be apprehended from our selves than from a foreign Enemy.

That unless we have an Army to lye Lieger,[116] we are liable to be overrun by a foreign Enemy e'er we are aware, is a Thought that could not possibly escape our Fore-fathers, yet we cannot learn that ever they put it in Practice, which is a great sign they did not like it. No, we are well assur'd, that they would not have suffer'd a Standing Army to defend the Nation, if they would have done it *gratis*. They would rather have mistrusted it would double the Invasion, and make it as big again as it was. I do not speak this by Guess, but have it from the wise Sir *Robert Cotton*, who being consulted 3 *Caroli*, in a difficult State of Affairs, amongst other Things, gave this Advice at the Council-Table: *Rushworth*, p. 469. "There must be, to withstand a foreign Invasion, a Proportion of Sea and Land Forces; and it is to be consider'd, that [48] no March by Land can be of

115. See above, p. 135, n. 50.
116. See above, p. 135, n. 51.

that speed to make Head against the landing of an Enemy. Then it follows, that there is no such Prevention, as to be Master of the Sea.

"For Land Forces, if it were for an offensive War, the Men of less Livelihood were best spar'd; and we us'd formerly to make such Wars *Purgamenta Reipublicae*, if we made no farther Purchase by it. But for the Safety of the Commonwealth, the Wisdom of all Times did never intrust the publick Cause to any other than to such as had a Portion in the publick Adventure. And that we saw in Eighty Eight, when the Care of the Queen and of the Council did make the Body of that large Army no other than the Train'd Bands."[117]

In the same Advice to the King, he lets him know how the People resented his keeping up an Army in the Winter, tho we were then in War with *France* and *Spain*. The Words are these:

"And the dangerous Distastes to the People are not a little improv'd by the unexampled Course, as they conceive, of retaining an Inland Army in Winter Season, when former Times of general Fear, as in Eighty Eight, produc'd none such; and makes them in their distracted Fears conjecture idly, it was rais'd wholly to subject their Fortunes to the Will of Power [49] rather than of Law, and to make good some farther Breach upon their Liberties and Freedoms at Home, rather than defend us from any Force Abroad." And he tells the King, the Consequences of these Jealousies are worthy a prudent and preventing Care.[118]

But what signify the Proceedings of former Ages to us? says these Men, *the World is strangely alter'd, and the Power of* France *is become so formidable, that it can never be oppos'd in the* Elizabeth *Way.* They still keep up a great Army, and how shall we defend our selves against them (if they think fit to break Treaties with us, and assist the Pretender to invade us) without an Army of Twenty or Thirty Thousand disciplin'd Troops?

I think I have already sufficiently shew'd the Difficulty, if not Impossibility of a foreign Invasion, whilst we are superior at Sea; the great Improbability the *French* should engage in such a Design, and much greater they should succeed in it. But that we may for ever lay this Goblin,[119] we

117. See above, p. 136, n. 55.
118. See above, p. 136, n. 56.
119. See above, p. 137, n. 58.

will admit our Fleets to be kidnapp'd by an unlucky Wind, whilst the *French* land Twenty Thousand Men in our Country. Tho in Gratitude for this Concession, I hope my Adversaries will grant that their Fleet cannot get back again without our meeting with them, (since the same Wind that carries them Home will carry us out) or if they will not be so good natur'd as to allow this, I will undertake for them (for we live in an Undertaking Age)[120] [50] that they will agree we shall intercept their Supplies. Then the Case is thus, that Twenty Thousand Men, of which few can be Horse, are landed in *England* without any Human possibility of being supply'd from Abroad.

I say, this Army shall never march Twenty Miles into the Country, for they cannot put themselves in a marching Posture in less than a Fortnight or three Weeks; and by that Time we may have a Hundred Thousand Militia drawn down upon them, whereof Ten Thousand shall be Horse, and as many Dragoons as we please: And if this Militia does nothing else but drive the Country, cut off their Foragers and Straglers, possess themselves of the Defilees,[121] and intercept Provisions, their Army must be destroy'd in a small Time. Neither will Domestick Enemies, the Favourers of the Pretender, be able in the mean Time to give us much Disturbance; for by the prudent Care the present Government has already taken, and 'tis hop'd will take for the future, these Malecontents can never be in a Condition to make any Head, or contribute the least Assistance to a foreign Enemy.

Of this kind I could give many Instances out of History; but because ancient ones, they say, will not fit our Purpose, I will give you a late one out of *Ireland*.

First, I think it will be readily agreed, that there are Ten Men in *England* for one in *Ireland*.

[51] *Secondly*, That King *William* had more *English* and *Scotch* to join with him in *Ireland*, than there are Malecontents in *England*.

---

120. A fascinating and ambivalent moment of usage which crystallizes the veiled satire of this pamphlet, since "to undertake" at this time can mean both (negatively) to entrap or deceive (*OED*, s.v. "undertake," I, 1a) and (positively) to take upon oneself or take in hand (*OED*, s.v. "undertake," I, 4a).

121. See above, p. 137, n. 59.

Thirdly, That our Militia have as much Courage as the *Irish:* And yet, tho we had Eight Thousand Horse, and above Thirty Thousand Foot in *Ireland*, and a great part of the Country in our Possession, we were more than Four Years in conquering the rest, and almost a Miracle we did it then. And I believe no Man will deny, if we could not have supply'd our Army from *England*, but they had all there perish'd; such is the Advantage of fighting upon one's own Dunghill.

And to shew what Treatment the *French* would be like to meet with in *England*, I will put you in Mind of the *Purbeck* Invasion,[122] which was so private, that it was seen only by an old Man and a Boy: And yet tho the Country thought the Government against them, we had above Forty Thousand Voluntiers in Arms in two or three Days time, who came thither on their own accord to give them the Meeting; and if they had been there, I doubt not would have given a good Account of them. Our Court, when it was over, shew'd their Dislike of it, and question'd the Sheriff of *Dorsetshire* about it. And tho we have forgot it, yet I believe the *French* will remember *Purbeck;* for it shewed the true Spirit and Genius of the *English* Nation.

[52] But the Policy of *France* having now assum'd a quite different Face since the Death of *Lewis* their late King,[123] whose aspiring Temper gave so much Uneasiness to all *Europe*, all Arguments and Pretences for a Standing Army, that are drawn from any Views of a Breach with that Kingdom, are entirely cut off by this one Consideration.

Indeed, most of the Reasons these Gentlemen advance to enforce their Design, (and which without this additional Confutation, we have already sufficiently repell'd) as they were chiefly made use of by the same Set of Men, in the Reign of the late King *William*, when the Nation with one Voice as it were[124] declar'd for the disbanding of the Army after the Peace; so the Circumstances of those Times added a great deal of Weight to the same, and the Dispute on both Sides was then manag'd with so much

---

122. See above, p. 138, n. 61.

123. Louis XIV died on 1 September 1715.

124. That is to say, in the first flaring-up of the standing armies debate in the years 1697 and 1698. The nation, however, was far from speaking with one voice on that occasion.

strength of Argument, as well as Wit and Art, that it was not an easy Matter for the best Judgment to decide the Case justly, so as neither the Safety of the Nation, or the Liberties and Ease of the People from heavy Taxes might suffer by it.

And yet, notwithstanding all the seeming ballancing Difficulties that were then obvious from the reducing the Forces, the Wisdom of the King and his Parliament thought fit to over-rule the Matter, and to give their Determination on the other Side. So that allowing the Projectors Arguments[125] to carry with them the same Force and Energy now [53] that the same had then, yet they ought in good Manners to yield up the Cause, because after the most obstinate, nice, and subtile Controversy and Debate by the wisest Heads of the Nation, the most impartial Decision of a Parliament has given their Authority against them.

But will any Man pretend to affirm, that an Argument relating to the Policy of a Commonwealth, is at all Times supported with equal Reason and Necessity? What Absurdities and Contradictions must needs be the Consequences of such a ridiculous Assertion?

It may be averr'd with the like Parity of Reason, that our Monarchs ought always to keep Garrisons in most of the Cities, Towns and Castles of *England*, because *William* the Conqueror found it absolutely necessary to do so, for the securing of his new-gain'd Kingdom. No: there is nothing within the Compass of State Policy that is not as changeable as the Weather and the Seasons of the Year, and those Alterations are as necessary to the Preservation of the Political Oeconomy, as these are to the Body Natural: And there is nothing unalterable in the Nature of a Government, but that which is its very Essence, [54] the Fundamental Laws of its Constitution, which can't be chang'd or remov'd without the Overthrow and Destruction of the whole Building.

Now as to the particular Point in Debate. We are to consider the *French* Affairs and Circumstances in a quite different Light, at present, from the Appearances these had in the Reign last mentioned.

It is true, King *William* did not a little contribute by his heroic Courage and Conduct, to humble the Pride of that common Enemy of *Europe*,

125. See above, p. 136, n. 57.

who aim'd at no less than an universal Conquest; but the victorious confederate Army in the last War,[126] had brought him[127] even to the Brink of Ruin, and would certainly have disabled that State from even a possibility of raising its Head, or of giving any Annoyance to his Neighbours, had not our Ministry of the late Reign[128] been too easily circumvented and brib'd by *French* Policy and *French* Gold, to make a most inglorious and dishonourable Peace[129] with that Nation.

However, the dismal Effects of the late War sat so heavy upon them, that these were a Clog and Hindrance to all [55] that King's ambitious Projects and Designs, who was content to hold what he had preserved from a raging, unfortunate and destructive War, without running the Hazard of any future Attempts.

But besides the miserable State of that Kingdom, occasion'd by the War, we are presented with an entire new Prospect of their Affairs since that King's Death;[130] and they have their Hands too full at Home, to be meddling with their Neighbours. Every Body knows what domestick Heats and Quarrels they have among themselves at present, by which they are brewing a great deal of Mischief to the whole Kingdom, and which must necessarily determine in the Destruction of one of the Parties. The Affair of the Succession to the Crown of *France*,[131] about which great Part of that Kingdom is already divided against the other, may produce as much Noise, Wars and Bloodshed as did lately that of *Spain:* And *Great-Britain* being likely to have a considerable Share, some Time or other, in deciding the former as well as it had in the latter, which was the Ground of the late War, it is the Interest of both Kingdoms to carry

126. I.e., the War of the Spanish Succession (1702–13).

127. I.e., Louis XIV.

128. The Harley–St. John administration of the last years of Queen Anne, which was suspected of negotiating with the Old Pretender for a restoration of the Stuart dynasty; see above, p. 453, n. 58, and p. 459, n. 76.

129. The Treaty of Utrecht (1713).

130. See above, p. 473, n. 123.

131. Because Louis XV was only five years old when he ascended the throne of France in 1715, until he attained his legal majority in 1723 France was governed by a regent, Phillippe II, duc d'Orléans (1674–1723), the nephew of Louis XIV and the premier prince of the blood royal.

fair[132] with us. But it being stipulated as one of [56] the grand Conditions and Articles of the Peace that *Philip*[133] should renounce his Pretensions to the *French* Crown, and he having accordingly solemnly done so, it is evident whom we are to side with, if the Matter should come to be disputed. And this is the Foundation of the tripartite Alliance,[134] Offensive and Defensive, lately concluded between *Great-Britain*, *France*, and *Holland*, which makes so great a Noise in the World, and by which we seem to be infallibly quieted and secured from all Fears of any Disturbance from Abroad.

But these Gentlemen, when all their other Arguments are refuted, betake themselves to their last Refuge, which they are persuaded can never fail them, and that is the Discontents and Disaffection of the Pretender's Party, who only wait a fresh Opportunity by raising a new Rebellion to restore their King, and revenge their late bad Successes.

I can assure these Gentlemen, that tho I argue against a Standing Army, and tho the Jacobites may perhaps be of the same Opinion, yet I am no Friend to the Pretender, but believe my self as firmly attach'd to the Protestant Suc[57]cession, and the Interest of the present Government, and am as great an Admirer of His Majesty's Conduct and Personal Vertues, as any of them all. But nevertheless, I hope no Man will discover himself so void of good Sense, as to imagine that it is Treason to entertain any Notion in common with that Party. And notwithstanding they may vainly apprehend, that some Advantage will accrue to their Interest by disbanding the Army, this does not in the least incline me to the Opinion of the other side; for I think I have already plainly shewn how little Foundation there is for such Fears from domestick Enemies by former Experiences, which that I may not be obliged to repeat, I shall turn my Readers back to the 31st and 32d Pages of this Discourse.[135]

Besides, I do not doubt but even these Malecontents will make greater use of the Army, (supposing it impossible to draw them off to their Side)

132. Behave well (*OED*, s.v. "carry," 33c).
133. I.e., Philip V of Spain, previously Philippe, duc d'Anjou (1683–1746); grandson of Louis XIV.
134. See above, p. 440, n. 12.
135. In this edition, pp. 459–460.

by representing in ill Colours their Behaviour in those Parts where they are placed, in hopes to gain Numbers to their Disaffection. And this is the more certain, if we consider that their first Manifesto's were full of the Grievances of an Army, even before any Army was in being: [58] Such a prevailing Address did they think this Argument to the Resentments of *Englishmen.* Nor do we find they have been more silent upon this Subject, since the Rebellion[136] has been suppress'd. What Noise have we heard of the Riot at *Oxford?*[137] And of the other little Disorders of the Soldiery, in the several Parts of the Kingdom? And this has not been without its Effect; for many, who were good Subjects to his Majesty, have talk'd warmly on this Head, being jealous of their Liberties, who otherwise would not have waver'd in their Respect to the present Government. How far therefore the Favourers of the Pretender may carry their Success, by insisting on the farther Effects of an Army, established by Law, who certainly cannot commit fewer Outrages, is not difficult to imagine: Whereas this Obstacle being remov'd, many will grow good Subjects for want of this Cause of Complaint, and others, hopeless of Success, will grow supine, and the whole Body of the Disaffected insensibly disappear.

In short, the whole Management of this Project of a Standing Army is ridiculous; but the fatal Consequences of it require deeper Thought. For when we have fool'd out our selves into the [59] Bondage of a Standing Army, how shall we ever get out of it again? Not as the Nation freed themselves from the Court of Wards.[138] We cannot buy it off, for two very good Reasons: No Money will be taken for it; and we shall have nothing

136. I.e., the Jacobite rebellion of 1715.

137. On 29 May 1715 a mob had partially demolished a Presbyterian meeting-house in Oxford, and serious rioting had again broken out on the occasion of the Prince of Wales's birthday on 20 October 1716. Such was the government's concern about disaffection in Oxford that a full regiment of foot had been quartered there since late 1715. For context and commentary, see *History of Oxford*, 5:99–111. On 27 November 1715 John Russell wrote: "You cannot be ignorant of the deplorable condition of the University of Oxford. . . . Rebellion is avowedly own'd & encouraged. . . . Some Tutors read Lectures to their Pupils on Hereditary Right, &c. And there are several Houses in which there's not so much as One (what they please to call a) Whig" (Christ Church MS Arch. W. Epis. 15).

138. See above, p. 120, n. 10.

to give which is not theirs already, in the Case we mentioned above. Our Estates, Lives and Liberties will be all at their Command. They will have the Keys of our Money and the Titles to our Lands in their Power.

This Mischief and Misery the Projectors for a Standing Army, it seems, do not foresee, or if they do, they are inexcusable. But under a gracious King and a wise Parliament, I hope we shall never see it.

The Prince of *Orange*'s Declaration[139] is directly against a Standing Army, *as a Means to assist all Arbitrary Designs, and thereby enslave the Nation;* directly against all wicked Attempts of Conquest, and all despotick Government, 'tis full of Liberty and Property in every Part. And His present Majesty, who is endowed with the same generous and heroick Temper, has, as we have above hinted, given undeniable Proof of the same gracious Inclinations; we may reasonably [60] suppose that the wisest of Kings, in conjunction with the best of Parliaments, will, in this important Affair, discover the same Sentiments with our glorious Deliverer,[140] to whom we principally owe our present Happiness. That Declaration was so highly valu'd, and so wholly rely'd upon by the Parliament then, that it is incorporated into our Laws, as the only Redress of our past Grievances and Oppressions, and the best Foundation of our future Happiness: And with entire Confidence that His Majesty King *William* would continue to act in pursuance of that Declaration, the Parliament resolv'd that he should be, and be declared King; so that it is to be accounted the *Pacta Conventa*[141] of the Government.

Here I know the Projectors will say, that the Army condemned by the Declaration, was the late King *James*'s Army, kept up in Time of Peace without Consent of Parliament; whereas this Standing Army is to be kept up with their Consent.

True it was so, and therefore, it was a Riot[142] and unlawful Assembly every Hour it stood; and having no Law for it, it might have been presented or [61] indicted; to no Purpose indeed: But as an Invasion upon the Subject, it might be resisted and pull'd down as a Nuisance, whenever

---

139. See Appendix C, below, p. 622.

140. I.e., William III.

141. See above, p. 140, n. 64.

142. Here used in a technical legal sense to denote a violent disturbance of the peace by a crowd (*OED*, s.v. "riot," 4a).

the Nation found themselves able. But suppose this Army had been made Part of the Constitution, and had obtain'd an Act of Parliament for it, what then had become of us? They were Aids and Instruments of Arbitrary Government before, but then they had been legal Instruments, and had enslav'd us by Authority. In short, we could not have reliev'd our selves from them, nor any one else in our behalf, because our own Act and Deed would have always been good against us.

What I have said here against Standing Armies, I would be understood of such as are the Instruments of Tyranny, and their Country's Ruin, and therefore I need make no Apology to our own, which next unto God, have by their Bravery and Conduct preserv'd our Liberties and the Protestant Religion thro *Europe*, and have so lately delivered these Nations[143] from the unnatural Designs and Attempts of their Fellow-Subjects to dethrone His present most gracious Majesty, who is the Guardian of our Laws and Privileges, and of the said Protestant Faith, and to introduce [62] Idolatry and Arbitrary Power. For if in future Reigns any Designs should be levell'd against our Laws, we may be assur'd these Men would be discarded, and others promoted in their Rooms, who are fit for such Arbitrary Purposes.

Nor do I think it reasonable that our Army should be ruin'd by that Tranquility and Peace, which by their Courage and Fidelity they have procur'd for their Country; and I doubt not but the Generosity and Gratitude of the Parliament will give them a Donative equal to their Commissions, which will amount to no extraordinary Sum, at least it will be an easy Composition for the Charge of keeping them.

But if there are any Gentlemen amongst them, who think we can no otherwise express our Gratitude, but by signing and sealing our Posterity's Ruin, I hope we shall disappoint their Expectations, and not give the World occasion to tell so foolish a Story of us. They know very well, an Army has nothing in it so charming that could induce the Nation to raise one, but upon some pressing Necessity, and not to keep them up perpetually; nor can the [63] Service perform'd be ever so great, as not to be requited under such a Return.

143. In suppressing the Jacobite rebellion of 1715.

To conclude: The Honour and Safety of the Nation is the commendable Design; and so far as any Side is for that, it is certainly in the Right,
since all Countries must have some Force to defend them against foreign
Invasions and domestick Tumults; for as it was their own Good and Security which occasion'd Men first to quit the State of Nature,[144] and to
associate themselves into Governments; so the Raising and Regulation

144. A reference to a central and disputed element in seventeenth-century English political philosophy. In *Leviathan* (1651), pt. 1, chap. 13, Hobbes had equated
the state of nature with a state of war, and in pt. 2, chap. 17, he had argued that
society and the restraints upon natural liberty which accompany it (laws, punishment, government) had arisen because of man's desire to escape from the much
more onerous inconveniences of the state of nature:

> The finall Cause, End, or Designe of men, (who naturally love Liberty, and
> Dominion over others,) in the introduction of that restraint upon them-
> selves, (in which wee see them live in Commonwealths,) is the foresight of
> their own preservation, and of a more contented life thereby; that is to say,
> of getting themselves out from that miserable condition of Warre, which is
> necessarily consequent (as hath been shewn) to the naturall Passions of men,
> when there is no visible Power to keep them in awe, and tye them by fear of
> punishment to the performance of their Covenants. (Hobbes, *Leviathan*,
> p. 117)

In his *Second Treatise of Government* (1689–90), however, Locke had drawn the relationship between the state of nature and political society differently. Like
Hobbes, Locke saw the latter as being in some sense opposed to or a substitute for
the former: "Where-ever therefore any number of Men are so united into one Society, as to quit every one his Executive Power of the Law of Nature, and to resign
it to the publick, there and there only is a *Political, or Civil Society*. And this is
done where-ever any number of Men, in the state of Nature, enter into Society to
make one People, one Body Politick under one Supreme Government, or else
when any one joyns himself to, and incorporates with any Government already
made" (Locke, *Treatises*, § 89, p. 325). But Locke characterized the state of nature
in terms calculated to contrast sharply with the definition of Hobbes:

> But though this [the state of nature] be a *State of Liberty*, yet it is *not a State
> of Licence*, though Man in that State have an uncontroleable Liberty, to dis-
> pose of his Person or Possessions, yet he has not Liberty to destroy himself,
> or so much as any Creature in his Possession, but where some nobler use,
> than its bare Preservation calls for it. The *State of Nature* has a Law of Na-
> ture to govern it, which obliges every one: And Reason, which is that Law,
> teaches all Mankind, who will but consult it, that being all equal and inde-
> pendent, no one ought to harm another in his Life, Health, Liberty, or Pos-
> sessions. (Locke, *Treatises*, § 6, pp. 270–71)

of their Forces must be directed and accommodated to the same Ends. An Island is best situated for Preservation, as having need of little other Force either to infest foreign Coasts, or to protect its own, besides a numerous Fleet, which it need never want. But if it be likewise a Government for Increase,[145] such as ours, its Situation naturally leading to Trade and planting of Colonies; and if it has the noble Ambition of holding the Balance steddy between other Governments, of succouring the Distress'd, and grudging Liberty to none, then it must be always provided with a considerable Land Force. Of this there is no Dispute. Then the only Question is, Whe[64]ther it be safest to trust Arms continually in the Hands of idle and needy Persons; or only, when there is occasion for it, in the Hands of sober and industrious Freemen. That the latter can never be dangerous to our Liberty and Property at Home, and will be infinitely more effectual against an Enemy attacking, or invaded by us, I think I have sufficiently proved both by Reason and Experience. But that the former may hereafter prove of the worst Consequence, is a Truth equally undeniable, I am satisfied every impartial Judgment, that weighs seriously what has been here said on that Head, will readily grant.

FINIS.

145. See above, p. 184, n. 13.

Anonymous

The Necessity of a Plot

1720?

The Necessity of a Plot:
Or, Reasons for a Standing Army.
By a Friend to K. G.[1]

In a Time of profound Tranquillity, whilst a great and wise Prince adorns the Throne, it may seem an Error in Politicks for the Government to alarm the Minds of Men with the Apprehensions of a Plot, or the Necessity of a Standing Army. And this may appear yet more impolitick, if that Prince happen to be free from any domestick Fewds; and if, in the full possession of the Hearts of his People, he be at the same Time assisted by Ministers of consummate Wisdom and unquestionable Integrity. Men of Speculation may, perhaps, think it most adviseable for a Prince, so happily circumstantiated, to govern by the Affections of his Subjects, and to avoid even the Shew of Constraint, especially if his Subjects should have some odd Fancies of their own Independency; or be inveterate Admirers of the Name of Liberty.

But with all the Respect due to Persons of such crude and unfashionable Notions, I would offer it to the Consideration of the candid Reader whether Force and Power, that is a Standing Army, well appointed, and wholly at the Disposal of their Superior, be he never so good Natur'd in himself, or never so great a Promoter of Moderation in others; as likewise whether the Apprehension of some dangerous Plot, design'd against either the Life of the Prince, or the Liberties of the Subject, be not absolutely necessary at this Juncture; in order to establish a Standing Army, and to dissipate all [2] Objections that may possibly be started against it, by Men of either shallow Judgments or evil Intentions.

1. The keynote for the very broad irony that follows.

Not to wander into remote Considerations concerning Danger, which, as some of the Learned apprehend, is like the Distemper of sore Eyes,[2] to be caught by looking at, that is, by fixing our Thoughts too intensely upon the Object; and not to create to our selves chimerical Enemies, who have no existence but in our own pregnant Imaginations, there are certainly very substantial Arguments, why the Nation should be always under the mild Administration of a Standing Army; and why, at this particular Season, a Plot is expedient, in order to secure to us and our Posterity that Invaluable Blessing.

I presume it will easily be granted me, that an Invasion from some Quarter or other, either from North or South, East, or, it may be, West, may happen at some Time or other: And therefore it wou'd seem but of a piece with the other Instances of our provident Administration, to be armed against what may or may not happen. I wou'd fain ask any clamorous Champion for the adverse Cause, what, in all humane Probability, might have become of us, if this second Spanish Armada[3] had been turn'd against us, instead of Sardinia, and we had been in such a destitute Condition, as to be unprovided of Thirty Thousand brave Britains in Red to preserve us? Is it not a clear Point, that any, or all the Princes and States in Europe, suppose the Pope, the King of Sweden, the Turk, or even the Republick of San Marino,[4] may take it into their Heads, that we live plentifully in England, have Bread and Beef, and good Cheer in Abundance, and that it is worth their While to abandon their sterile Territories to come and fatten in this rich Soil? and then, Is it not as clear that we should always have our Swords ready drawn to repel the insolent Intruder?

Neither are Suppositions of this Kind to be looked upon as Wild or Foreign. It is one of the wisest Sayings [3] of any of our modern Litterati,

---

2. "Sore eyes are got by looking on sore eyes" (*Ovid De Arte Amandi* [1701], p. 104: "Dum spectant laesos oculi, laeduntur"; Ovid, *Remedia Amoris*, l. 615).

3. See above, p. 34, n. 83.

4. A minuscule state slightly set back from the eastern coast of Italy, covering only 61 square kilometers. Founded in A.D. 301, it is the oldest republic in Europe.

which a* noble Lord[5] hath chosen for his Motto, (Tuta Time[6]). This, well translated, may teach us, That "when we are most Safe, we are most in Danger"; That "there is and can be nothing secure in this transitory World"; That "all sublunary Things are liable to Change"; and that, "That which doth not happen to Day may, through the Instability of human Affairs, arrive to Morrow."

Matchiavel, in his Prince, adviseth all Men to treat their Friends, as if they were one Day to become their Enemies:[7] and Lipsius upon Tacitus observeth somewhere, That a Prince, in the Times of the fullest Peace, should be armed, as if in the Midst of a flaming War: And the Reason he gives for this, is, That Princes (he only spoke of the Princes of his Time) are the least to be trusted, of any Sort of Persons with whom you deal: Because (as he refines according to his Manner) they have one general Salvo, viz. Reasons of State,[8] for all the Breaches of Faith, Vows, Ties of Honour and of Gratitude; and, in general, for all sorts of Injuries, which they can possibly commit.[9]

* Lord C———nd.

5. Untraced.

6. "Be fearful when you feel yourself safe."

7. Although this maxim is very much in the vein of what Machiavelli says in *The Prince* about friends and enemies, he does not express the thought in so many words. Cf., however, one of the notable sayings gathered at the end of his *Life of Castruccio Castracani*: "Having put to death a citizen of Lucca who had been a cause of his greatness, and being told that he had done wrong in killing one of his old friends, he answered that they were deceiving themselves, because he had put to death a new enemy" (*Machiavelli: The Chief Works*, trans. Allan Gilbert, 3 vols. [Durham, N.C.: Duke University Press, 1965], 2:558).

8. A translation of the Italian *ragioni di stato*, meaning political considerations, usually of an amoral or Machiavellian complexion, and often involving the renunciation of natural ties of blood or gratitude: see, e.g., Jones, *Secret History*, p. 5. For a helpful discussion, see Malcolm, *Reason of State*, esp. pp. 92–123.

9. Justus Lipsius (in Flemish, Joest Lips; 1547–1606), Flemish humanist, classical scholar, and moral and political theorist. His edition of Tacitus appeared in 1574, and there is a detectable Tacitean quality to Lipsius's own political theory, published as *Politicorum libri sex* (1589). The sentiment that, if you wish for peace, you should prepare for war ("Si vis pacem, para bellum"), can be traced back to the third book of Vegetius's *Epitoma rei militaris* ("Igitur qui desiderat pacem praeparet bellum"; III.prol. 8); however, Vegetius himself was merely echoing a maxim of Roman prudence which we can find already in Sallust (*Oratio ad Caesarem*, VI.ii) and Cicero (*De Officiis*, I.xxiii.80). Lipsius's versions of the insight tend to be more

But let all the Admirers of such sententious Politicians know, that there is now a living Exception to their Rule: A great and glorious Prince, who hath never swerved from his royal Word in the least Tittle; never pretended Necessities of State; nay, never will pretend any Thing like it, (for in his Time we can answer for Futurity) to do a hard, unjust, or cruel Thing.[10]

But yet to do Justice to all People, and more especially to the renown'd Lipsius, I must own, that for the Generality of Princes, there is no Faith among them; nor are any Alliances with them much to be depended upon. And altho' I shall not venture to say, what a great Minister of State did the last Sessions, in the House of Commons, "That we have not one good Ally in the World,"[11] yet it may not, perhaps be unbecoming to offer it to the Consideration of the World, Whether all the Princes with whom we are in Alliance, be not Men; [4] and which is more, Princes, that is, Friends, who have always their own Interest first in view? and, Whether we ought so far to rely on their Friendship in assisting us in the Times of Danger, as to leave our selves Defenceless?

It is very readily granted that the Regent[12] is our fast Friend and Ally; and that he hath courted the Friendship of K. G. at a most astonishing Rate. But his Enemies give out, that he is not always in the same Humour: And, indeed, even here he hath at several Times undergone great Revolutions, in our Opinions. I have heard him at a great Minister's Table

---

diffuse than the form it takes in his classical sources: "Neither are armes to be directed to any other end (if thou desire that they be iust) but to peace and defence. *Let warre be undertaken, that nothing but quietnesse may be sought thereby. Wise men make warre, that they may haue peace, and endure labour under hope of rest*"; "Cicero *saith*, if we desire to enioy peace, we must make warre, if we forbeare to take armes, we shall neuer enioy peace. For peace is best established through warre" (*Sixe Bookes of Politickes or Ciuil Doctrine* [1594], pp. 133 and 181). Cf. also Machiavelli's judgment that "in time of peace [a well-ordered kingdom] does not suspend arrangements for war" (*Discourses*, bk. 1, chap. 21) and Algernon Sidney's apothegm that "those only can be safe who are strong; and . . . no people was ever well defended, but those who fought for themselves" (Sidney, *Discourses*, p. 205).

10. See above, p. 441, n. 13.
11. Untraced.
12. See above, p. 475, n. 131.

toasted one Day, as the best Protestant in Europe; and damn'd the next Day as the veriest ——[13]

But not to search too far into his Character, which I dare say, is as Faultless as that of most Princes, we do not know what his own Necessities may compel him to, and how far he may be under the influence of Reasons of State.

The King of Spain,[14] tho' he keeps in a civil Sort of Friendship with us; yet, for many good Reasons, may be no well-wisher to us at the Bottom; unless he should have Christianity enough to forgive us our Intentions to dethrone him;[15] and unless he should be so little mindful of future Prospects, as not to regard how nearly related he is to the Crown of England,[16] by that imaginary Right Line, whereof some People seem so wildly fond. Not that I have any Doubt, that he can have a Thought of putting in his Claim, even tho' our present royal Family were out of the Way (which God avert): For he shou'd consider, that there are even in that Case, two or three that must come in, before his Title could be set up; but one doth not know what strange Thoughts may be suggested by ambitious Courtiers. Neither is it easy to comprehend what his Ambassador, the M—— of M——[17] (whom all People allow to be a great Politician) means by his Balls and Assemblees, unless it be, that he hath some strange Things in his Head.

[5] I should not say any Thing of the Emperor,[18] were it not that he is a most zealous Papist, and that it is a stated Rule with all of that Profession, that no Faith is to be kept with Hereticks; and it is to be

13. Possibly "atheist."

14. Philip V (1683–1746), king of Spain from 1700.

15. In the War of the Spanish Succession (1702–13); see above, p. 326, n. 184.

16. The "imaginary Right Line" which associated the throne of England with a Spanish claimant had been mischievously argued for by the Jesuit historian and polemicist Robert Persons (1546–1610), whose *Conference about the Next Succession to the Crowne* (Antwerp, 1595) had promoted the claims of the Infanta to the English throne on the death of Elizabeth.

17. Isidoro Casado y Rosales, Marqués de Monteleón, Spanish ambassador to the Court of St. James in 1712–13, 1714–18, and 1724.

18. Charles VI (1685–1740), Holy Roman Emperor from 1711; archduke of Austria and king of Hungary.

apprehended, that the Emperor may look upon K. G. to be a Heretick, because his Majesty is not only a Protestant, but the best Protestant in the World; and consequently, in the Sense of the Papists, the greatest Heretick.

It cannot be deny'd but there is a strict Confederacy between his Majesty and the High and Mighty States;[19] as many late Incidents and extraordinary Steps in Government, may sufficiently evince: And truly I do look upon them to be, in some respects (not to derogate from others) the best Ally which his Majesty hath; tho', not to run too far that Way neither, they may perhaps, in other respects be our national Rival, which is a different Word for national Enemies. It is the Nature of Rivals to do one another all the Mischief they can: And all the World, at least a great Part of it, knows, and some Part of it hath felt, that the Dutch are not only Jealous of us, in Point of Trade; but, that they have treated us accordingly: Tho' perhaps it may not be so proper to revive the Memory of their past Behaviour, relating either to Amboyna;[20] or their presuming to Dispute with us the Empire of the Ocean. But this we must say, that since their Interests and Ambition clash with ours in the two tender Points of Money and Honour, who knows whether there may not some little Grudges remain thereupon, which might blaze forth upon a seasonable Opportunity? There is one Way, and but One, that I can recollect, of securing them to us, that is by giving them a Compensation in those main Articles, or by wholly sacrificing the Interest of England to that of Holland: But it is to be fear'd, his Majesty, zealous for the Reputation and Trade of Great Britain, will never submit to that, in which Case, the old Jealousies, and consequently the old Dangers, must still subsist.

Your great Man, Monsieur Pettecum,[21] it is true, affirms, over and over, That the Czar of Muscovy is up[6]on no Account whatever, to be apprehended[22] by England: He says, That the Dominions of his Czarish Majesty are at such a Distance; his Fleet so unprovided of all Necessaries, that if he had a Mind to distress us, he could not do it. But with all

---

19. I.e., the United Provinces of the Netherlands.
20. See above, p. 269, n. 20.
21. The resident minister in London of the Duke of Holstein.
22. I.e., feared.

the Submission imaginable to that little great Man,[23] I am of a different Opinion; at least, I think his Reasons require some Examination. For altho' the Dominions of Muscovy be, in Appearance, vastly remote from us, yet they are contiguous to Sweden, and Sweden is contiguous to Norway, and Norway is not above Forty-eight Hours Sail from Scotland, and Scotland is not above Eight Days March from London: By which accumulative Argument, it is evident that Russia and London are too near Neighbours; And allowing only some little Difference of Time, we may as well be invaded from Petersburgh, as Mardyke.[24]

We every Day hear of Naval Preparations made by the King of Sicily;[25] upon what Design is not known: But he being next in Succession of the Pretender's Line, as it is pretended, and being one of the refin'd Politicks,[26] who knows what he may attempt?

The King of Prussia is the King's Son-in-law,[27] and consequently being so near a-kin to him, there must be (altho' there be some Exceptions to the contrary, as in the Case of King William and King James) a great deal of paternal and filial Love and Affection between them. But yet, all That will not secure us without an Army: For as I have before hinted, there are Reasons of State, and perhaps other Reasons (not so proper, or rather, not so needful to be insisted upon) which may make it necessary for People to be upon the Watch; tho' still without any Mistrust on either Side.

We may talk as much as we please, That the King of Denmark[28] is ours entirely. If so, how can it be accounted for, that he will go on to demolish Wismar,[29] in spight of all King George's Remonstrances to the

23. I.e., Pettecum (and not Peter the Great, who was over two meters tall).

24. I.e., St. Petersburgh (which had been constructed by Peter the Great between 1703 and 1712 and made the capital of Russia). Mardyke is a port adjacent to Dunkirk, on the northern coast of France.

25. Victor Amadeus II (1666–1732), Duke of Savoy; given the title of king of Sicily by the Treaty of Utrecht (1713).

26. I.e., politicians.

27. Frederick William I (1688–1740), king of Prussia from 1713; in 1706 he had married Sophia Dorothea, the daughter of the future George I.

28. Frederick IV (1671–1730), king of Denmark and Norway from 1699.

29. *Wismar*, a Hanse-Town, is seated at the bottom of a Bay of the *Baltick* Sea, 12 Miles from *Swerin* to the N. *Henry de Mecklenburg* about the Year 1266. establish'd the same manner of Government here as was at *Lubeck*

contrary? For a little Prince, of his Figure, to persist such a Design, not only without King George's consent, [7] but expresly against it, seems to me very extrordinary; and, in my poor Opinion, shews, that he is therein buoy'd up by some powerful Prince in Masquerade.

But above all, and the most to be apprehended is, the King of Sweden,[30] the Terror of Mankind, the Scourge of the North. A Person, who with less than twenty Men, attacked more than 20000 Janizaries.[31] We have provok'd him: I do not say how wisely: Or at least the Letters publish'd, as if found in Gyllenbourg's Closet,[32] shew, he hath had some wicked Imaginations against us. What are we not to dread from one of his Resentments and his Intrepidity?

I am sensible that here is some room for a Cavil against my Argumentation; because it may be urged, that we have nothing in nature to fear from the King of Sweden's Practices. His Majesty was most graciously pleas'd last Sessions of Parliament to find out an effectual Cure for all Dangers from that Quarter: His Message to the Commons by Mr. Stanhope,[33] then Secretary of State, on the third of April was, That

---

by which it quickly grew rich, and the Haven being convenient, it was made the Harbour of the Men of War belonging to the *Hanseatick* Society, and the Town very strongly fortified. This City was granted to the *Sweed* by the Treaty of *Munster*, and was taken from him by the *Dane* in 1675. By the last Treaty of Peace between these two Princes, it was agreed to be deliver'd to the *Sweed* upon payment of certain Sums of Money, which it seems are not yet paid, for the Town still remains in the Hands of the King of *Denmark*. (Anonymous, *The Compleat Geographer* [1709], p. 222).

On the Hanseatic states, see Sidney, *Discourses*, p. 207.

30. Charles XII; see below, p. 526, n. 50, and p. 527, n. 55.

31. A hyperbolic version of Charles's exploits at the Battle of Bender in February 1713, which had passed into popular culture in the following years: "His Conscience is of a make very tender / That allows him to fight for the *Turk* and *Pretender*, / You ne'er saw the like, but only at *Bender*, / When he headed a poor ragged Crew: / Where tho' we allow, his Stars were but Cross, / And *Turkish* Civility wanted a Gloss / Yet had he been shot, there had been no great Loss, / Of this troublesom *Hero in Blue*" (Anonymous, *The Hero in Blue* [1717], p. 1; see also John Smith, *Poems Upon Several Occasions* [1713], p. 271).

32. See below, p. 501, n. 57.

33. James Stanhope (1673–1721), first Earl Stanhope; army officer, diplomat, and politician.

"His Majesty being desirous above all things not only to secure his Kingdoms against the present Danger with which they are threatned by Sweden, but likewise to prevent the like Apprehensions for the future, thinks it necessary that Measures should be early concerted, &c. Then, He hopes his Commons will enable Him to make good such Engagements, as may ease his People of all future Charge and Apprehensions." The Sum demanded, in order to enable his Majesty to do this, was 250,000 l. that Sum was given; and it is so far from being a Question, whether the Money were employed to answer the said Ends, that we can never enough admire the great Wisdom of his Majesty, in finding out so cheap and expedite a Method of ending a War without striking a Blow; and of securing to latest Posterity such a Peace, as no vicissitude or revolution of times or things can deprive us of. All this may, I own, be urged, as likewise that it may probably be criminal in any one to say, we have any thing to fear from Sweden, since his Ma[8]jesty hath passed his Royal Word, which never yet hath fallen in the least Article, That he would "enter into such Engagements as should ease us from all future Charge or Apprehensions on that account."

This is the force of the Objection, which I have heard more than a thousand times started by little People, who talk at random and know nothing of the Arcana[34] of Government. It is most certain, the King did promise he would secure us from the Dangers, present and future, threatened by Sweden. But I leave it to the Judgment of every dispassionate Reader, whether the Word, Sweden, implied the King thereof; I think not: I am sure, the King of Sweden was not therein mention'd, and the Reason of that Omission is evident: For it is as impossible to answer for him or his Motions, as for those of a Comet, which may drop into our Vortex, the Lord knows when. So that if the King of Sweden, he, who as I said before, fell upon 20000 Janizaries, with only a few of his own Servants, should take a Fancy to come here, it is obvious we should yet want 19,000 Britains at least, allowing 19 Englishmen to answer 20 Janizaries. This appears to me a fair Computation: And whether I have not given full Satisfaction in this whole Point, I must leave to be decided by others.

34. I.e., secrets.

Thus, from a fair and impartial Examination of the State of Great Britain, with regard to most, or all of the foreign Princes and States, from whom we are to Hope or Fear, I think it will appear, that there is no Sort of Reason in the World that we should lull our selves into so happy, or to speak more justly, unhappy a Security, as to be without a Standing Army.

But to look within our selves; and weigh the State of our Affairs at home, the Reasons for a Standing Force are yet stronger, if that be possible.

Altho' His Majesty King George, who like another Titus,[35] might well deserve to be stiled, The Delight of Mankind; be received, where-ever he goes, with loud Acclamations, Feasts, Balls, nay Bacchanals,[36] yet some [9] Gentlemen of the House of C——s[37] have said, That there is a great disaffection in the Country to His Majesty's Person and Government: A Language which I do not altogether approve of, nor do I think it strictly true. For tho' the English be naturally so unpolite, as not to affect the German Language, Modes, Habits, Customs, Ministers, or Ladies; and tho' many Lyes may be scatter'd about, yet what hath all this to do with His Majesty's Person or Government? upon what Grounds, by what Laws, could Men of their great Understanding; form so illegal and unjust a Declaration? And yet I cannot but think they knew why they spoke it. Perhaps they drew their Inference from some Indecencies committed by the Vulgar; and if they had only dwelt upon that, they had done right: The Vulgar are a rude, bold, merry, sawcy Pack, and it is very true they should be restrain'd: So that I agree with what these Ministers of State in the End propos'd from their Speech, tho' not in the Expression. For whatever others may say, I am wholly of Opinion, that a standing Army is requisite to suppress all Badges of Rebellion; such as Roses, Horns, Lawrel, or Turnips,[38] which so justly offend the Eyes of our discerning Magistracy.

35. Titus Vespasianus Augustus (39–81), Roman emperor from 79; referred to by Suetonius as the "darling of the human race"; "amor ac deliciae generis humani" ("Divus Titus," I).

36. See above, p. 292, n. 80.

37. I.e., Commons.

38. The first three of these are all Jacobite emblems. Turnips might be taken as a disaffected allusion to the agricultural associations of the House of Hanover: see Nicholas Amhurst, *Poems on Several Occasions* (1720), p. v, and the Jacobite ballad

Again: I take it to be a great Advantage to the Publick, to increase the Debts of the Nation. Philip de Comines gives it as a Reason, why the Londoners were eager for the Restoration of Edward IV. because he had run much in their Debt, and they could never hope to be paid, till he were restor'd.[39] And a great Prelate, who came over at the Revolution, gave this solid and wholesome Advice to King William, to plunge the Nation into such a Debt, as should be impossible to be paid, in Case any alteration in the State should happen:[40] Which Counsel His Majesty (of Glorious Memory) took care to follow. Thus our Government was confirm'd by our Taxes; and our Freedom most happily founded upon our Necessities.

And to do Justice to our Prince of late, so much wiser than their Predecessors, that sort of Policy hath [10] been so well understood, that whereas before the Revolution the Government did not owe one Shilling, it now owes 50,000,000 l. Sterl. And whereas in April, 1697. the Income of the Crown, with all Duties, &c. was but 2,120,149l. 11s. 3d. it is now yearly near 7,000,000 l. and yet we are still running more and more in Debt, to the great Emolument of the Publick. And is it not notorious, that an Army, with all usual appointments, contributes extreamly to the Article of Exigence, and of course, to this great Branch of the Safety of the Kingdom?

Besides, I do not conceive where our Youth of Spirit could be so well Educated as in a Military School; the laudable Accomplishments of a fine Gentleman are there so suddenly acquired, that a Fellow, who but

---

"The Hanover Turnip." Troops stationed in Oxford had been pelted with turnip tops by a Jacobite mob during the riot on the Prince of Wales's birthday on 20 October 1716 (see above, p. 477, n. 137, and *The Several Papers . . . Relating to the Riots at Oxford* [1717], pp. 16–17).

39. "There were three Things especially which contributed to this kind Reception into *London*; . . . The next was the great Debts which he [Edward IV] ow'd in the Town, which oblig'd all the Tradesmen that depended upon his Restoration, to appear for him" (*The Memoirs of Philip de Comines*, trans. Thomas Uvedale, 2 vols. [1712], 1:268).

40. Gilbert Burnet (1643–1715), bishop of Salisbury and historian. On the political stability arising from the financial revolution of the 1690s, see P. G. M. Dickson, *The Financial Revolution in England: A Study in the Development of Public Credit, 1688–1756* (London: Macmillan, 1967; corrected ed., Aldershot: Gregg Revivals, 1993); and above, p. 352, n. 241.

just throws off a private Person's Livery to wear that of the King's, com-
mences immediately a most accomplish'd Beau; he can Swear with as
good a Grace, talk as rationally against Jesus Christ, the Church and
Parsons, as if he had serv'd an Apprenticeship at the Grecian.[41]

Neither is it unworthy our Observation, that the Army supplies the
House of Commons with many worthy Members; who might have been
wholly lost to the Publick, or employ'd in some lower Sphere of Life, had
they not been thrown into the World by Fortune and the Chance of War,
perhaps at a Fire-side, or in Hyde-park.

It is to be allowed indeed, that some of the Officers of the Army are
Men of honourable Birth and paternal Estates, and behave themselves
accordingly in the House and elsewhere, but I speak of some worthy Members, who owe their Rise wholly to the Army; and who, perhaps might
still have been clattering their Oaken Plants[42] in the Lobby, if thro' the
Army they had not made their Way to the House. Happy hath been the
State of Great-Britain, that these Officer's Regiments quarter'd at the
Boroughs where they were Elected![43] and happier will it be when, instead
of a Writ for an Election, there will need no more for the Return, but to
send down a Regiment of Dragoons!

[11] Is it not likewise a great Honour to us, that a Standing Army will
very near reduce us to the State of our Fellow-subjects in Hannover?[44]
where we hear of no complaints against the Government: Where the
Army is Part of the Constitution, and the People all hope to have their
Share therein: Where the Men go to War according as they are hired

41. A coffeehouse in Devereux Court, off Essex Street in London, kept by
George Constantine ("*Constantine* the *Grecian*, / Who fourteen years was th'onely
man / That made *Coffee* for th'great *Bashaw*, / Although the man he never saw":
Anonymous, *The Character of a Coffee-House* [1665], p. 2). It was frequented by
scientists, lawyers, and scholars, and served as a meeting place for John Trenchard,
Walter Moyle, Andrew Fletcher, John Toland, and other opponents of standing
armies (Schwoerer, *Armies*, pp. 167, 177; Ellis, *Coffee-House*, pp. 108, 150, 189; Robbins, *Commonwealthman*, p. 6; Downie, *Harley*, p. 36). The Grecian was also one
of the coffeehouses frequented by Mr. Spectator (*The Spectator*, no. 1, [1 March 1711]).
It was reputed to have an "Old Whig" flavor (Downie, *Harley*, p. 22).

42. I.e., heavy cudgels; cf. *The Spectator*, no. 335 (25 March 1712).

43. See above, p. 49, n. 122.

44. Where George I was an absolute monarch.

out,[45] and the Women manure the Ground and bring in the Harvest. In short, where the King was so universally admired, that they could not part with him, even for a short Term, without Floods of Tears from all the People; and where they will still keep the young Prince[46] to comfort them, and exemplify in him the bright Pattern of his Royal Grandfather.

There are moreover imminent Dangers from the North; to prevent which, we should be powerfully armed. The Ghost of Mackintosh[47] hath been seen frequently of late in the Highlands, by our Newsmonger. Rob Roy[48] travels about there, as if he were sole Lord of those black Realms. And tho' I have the greatest Idea of the Lord Lovat,[49] and think him capable of almost every Thing, from his Principles and Dexterity, yet he, with all his Interest, will not be able to keep those Parts in quiet, unless he be seconded by a Standing Army of at least 30,000 Men. It is an old Observation, That you should take Things early, nip Dangers in the Bud; and therefore, since from such small Seeds of Rebellion in those Parts, great Matters may arise, you ought to prepare your self

45. See above, p. 253, n. 58.

46. I.e., Frederick Lewis (1707–51), son of the future George II and father of the future George III. During the absences of George I, Frederick acted as the ceremonial head of the Hanoverian court.

47. William Mackintosh of Borlum (ca. 1657–1743), Jacobite army officer. Captured after the failure of the Jacobite rebellion of 1715, Borlum was held in Newgate prison. While exercising in the prison yard on 4 May 1716, the day before his trial for high treason, Borlum charged the turnkeys and led a daring breakout. Although some prisoners were recaptured, by September Borlum and his brother had escaped to Paris. Borlum returned to Scotland in May 1719 and met with the Earl Marischal and others at Loch Long. He commanded the forces to the right of William, Earl of Seaforth, at the Battle of Glenshiel. In the aftermath he again escaped to France but returned to Scotland in 1722 and 1724 before he was finally captured by government troops in November 1727. He was sent a state prisoner to Edinburgh Castle, where he remained for the rest of his life.

48. Robert MacGregor (1671–1734), outlaw and folk hero. Although Rob acted at least in part as a Hanoverian agent during the Jacobite rebellion of 1715, in June 1716 his name appeared on the list of Scottish Jacobites attainted for high treason. In 1717 at the time of the publication of this pamphlet, Rob was eluding capture in the highlands and conducting a guerrilla war against the Hanoverian Duke of Montrose. He is the eponymous hero of Sir Walter Scott's *Rob Roy* (1817).

49. Simon Fraser (1667/8–1747), eleventh Lord Lovat; Jacobite conspirator, army officer, and outlaw.

accordingly, and look upon what such a Thing may possibly come to, as if it really had happened: Were I fit to advise, our Army should be every Day drawn out in Battle array, as if Mackintosh and Rob Roy were at the Gates of St. James's.

But this I do not altogether insist upon; I only just give the Hint, leaving the Execution or Improvement of it to others, better versed in the Niceties of Politicks.

Against all these Reasons which I have advanced for a Standing Army, and many more, which might offer, if [12] the Thing were not almost Self-evident, the Factious, I suppose, will cry out, as they usually do, with great Noise; they will perhaps say, that a Standing Army in Time of Peace, entirely overturns the old English Constitution:⁵⁰ That the only Idea Men have of the Slavery of a Nation, is, that it is subject to a Military Power; that his Majesty came to deliver us from Bondage; but that if we are to groan under this insupportable Load, we had as good, almost, not have been deliver'd; that the Officers, especially the Subalterns, generally every where throughout the Country, commit the greatest Insolencies at this Time; That, under the Sanction or Pretence of the Act about quartering of Soldiers, there are no Sort of Oppressions and Outrages, which are not daily justified; and, That the Murmurings of the People, harassed with Taxes, and insulted by their pretended Deliverers, are endless and inexpressible.

Such are the trifling Objections, which are started against our Scheme: And, for my Part I do not much wonder at it. When Men are out of Humour, they never cease to find Fault. But yet I do not think that such a prudent Ministry and so wise a King as we are bless'd with, will wholly neglect these Complaints; tho' certainly there be nothing in them, yet I should not oppose some Project to stop their Mouths, if it were for no other Reason, than that we might have it to say, the People of England, at last, contentedly submit to a Standing Army.

In order to effect this, I have heard it propos'd, that a Reduction, as it is called, of some few private Men in each Troop or Company should be made; but that the Regiment or Corps shou'd still remain: Hereby the

50. See above, p. 125, n. 23.

Sound of Disbanding will run through the Kingdom, the People will be pleas'd; and yet the Power of the Army will be as great as ever, and the Expence not much less. If, for Instance, you reduce the 37,000 Men which are in Pay in Great Britain and Ireland to 32,000 or 30,000, the Power of that Body will not be lessen'd, nor the Savings be above 150,000 l. it may be less.

[13] I thought it a good Observation, which a Gentleman made t'other Day in a Coffee-house, that a Reduction of the Army, as it is called, is like pruning a Tree; it strengthens the Body, and makes it take Root the deeper. The Notion is perfectly right; so that the Army would not be less formidable after such a Reduction, and yet the Quieting of the Minds of the Multitude might be thereby attained.

This Project certainly hath a Shew of great Reason, and may have its Weight in the World: But there is another Stroke, which I take to be much more effective which shall stop all Mouths, reconcile all Parties, endear the Soldiers to us, and rivet upon us and ours for ever, or as long as our Governours please, a triumphant Standing Army. The Thing I mean is a Plot, which if it be but handsomely introduced, shall expose every Man, who dares to mutter against the Army, to the Infamy of being reputed an Enemy to his King and Country.

To observe the several Gradations of a Plot is a Matter of great Curiosity, as well as Use. At first, by the Knowers of Secrets, it should be whisperd at Court: The first Glimmerings should be faint and uncertain: A Composition of half Words, significant Gestures, and references to Time, and few Days. This naturally engageth the Inquisitive and Newsmongers, which spreads the Secret, as all Secrets are spread, thro' the Town and Country. I think the late Lord Sunderland[51] called all Secrets, Spouts. A Multitude of Drops of Rain fall gently from the Tiles into the Spouts, and thence the whole is poured into the Streets and Common Sewers.

When the Secret is thus half divulg'd, in some little Time, the Conjectures of every one are added to the first imperfect Accounts: The World is at a Gaze: The Populace, always susceptible of Terrors, gape for

51. Robert Spencer (1641–1702), second Earl of Sunderland; politician.

the Discovery, and in the mean Time see Armies in the Clouds: And then after this regular Preparation, the chief Person comes forth in Publick, tells some terrible Story of horrid Designs, bloody Massacres, dangerous Confederacies, or barbarous Assassinations, that, thro' the Providence of God, have been detected.

[14] As far as my small Observation hath reached, this is the natural Progress of a Plot: And the good Effects are not to be described. In the Hurry and Amazement we are ready to swallow any Thing for Truth: The grossest Impositions upon the Understandings of Mankind are embraced as Oracles, and immediate Assistance sent from Heaven for our preservation.

Thus the Managers in 41[52] usher'd in all their Extravagancies, with some previous Whispers or Accounts of horrid Conspiracies against the Government; and by that single Artifice chiefly carried every Thing they had a mind to. It is true indeed, the Precedent is none of the Best; yet a wise Prince may extract Good out of Evil; and besides he will have this Argument on his Side, that if a Plot can thus actuate and inspire Men in flagitious Attempts, how much more Vigour will it have on them in the Prosecution of glorious Ends?

The memorable Plot at the Time of the Revolution, concerning the Irish Army,[53] did more Wonders than the then Prince of Orange, with his

---

52. I.e., 1641, at the outset of the Civil War.

53. In the spurious *A Third Declaration* (1688), which purported to be an official communication by William of Orange, Hugh Speke (see below, p. 501, n. 56) had stirred up anti-Catholic hysteria in December 1688 by warning the English people that

> great Numbers of armed Papists have of late resorted to *London* and *Westminster*, and parts adjacent, where they remain, as we have reason to suspect, not so much for their own Security, as out of a wicked and barbarous Design to make some desperate Attempt upon the said Cities, and their Inhabitants by Fire, or a sudden Massacre, or both; or else to be more ready to joyn themselves to a Body of French Troops, designed, if it be possible, to land in *England*, procured of the French King, by the Interest and Power of the Jesuits in Pursuance of the Engagements, his most Christian Majesty, with one of his Neighbouring Princes of the same Communion, has entered into for the utter Extirpation of the Protestant Religion out of Europe. (p. 6)

9000 Dutch Forces[54] could have brought about. It had such an Influence, that even after it was known, that there was no Irish Army near us, nor a Throat to be cut, yet so thoroughly did the first Impressions of Dread possess the Hearts of Man, Woman, and Child, that they thought they liv'd but by the Protection of that tutelar Angel.

For my Part I have such a Veneration for the Author of that pious Fraud, that I can never forgive the late Duke Schomberg,[55] who had the Honour of it. For it may incontestably appear from the Works of the famous Capt. Speke,[56] that he alone was the original Parent of it, whilst another reap'd the Glory, and which is worse, the Profit. But this may lead us into the moral Reflection, how Fortune and not Merit governs the World.

In all Ages, Plots have been in great Repute with wise Men; and as to the Effect, it is of no Sort of Consequence, in popular Governments, whether they be ill or well grounded: For the pretended Plot will always serve the present Turn, as well as the real One: [15] The same Way that Credit will carry a Man, for some Time, through the World, as well as if he had a substantial Fund: And it is his Fault if in that Season he do not establish himself for the future.

So to come to the Point in question, if a Plot can but secure to us the Blessing of a Standing Army for one Year more, in the Time of Peace, would it not be to think ill of our Government, to suppose in that Time, they would not settle Matters so, as for the future to need no such Artifices?

Did not the Swedish Plot, last Spring,[57] conduct the Designs of the Court smoothly through both Houses? and may not something of the same

---

54. For the size of William's forces in 1688, see above, p. 346, n. 219.

55. See above, p. 322, n. 174.

56. Hugh Speke (1656–ca. 1724), Whig agitator. In late 1688 Speke had been active in fanning the flames of antipapist hysteria in London, spreading stories about French and Irish troops ready to invade and massacre Protestants (see above, p. 500, n. 53). Speke's memoirs of 1688, first published in 1707 as *Some Memoirs of the most Remarkable Passages and Transactions on the Late Happy Revolution*, had recently been republished in 1715 as *The Secret History of the Happy Revolution in 1688*.

57. In 1716 the politician and Jacobite agent Charles Caesar (1673–1741) had negotiated with the Swedish ambassador, Count Karl Gyllenborg, for Swedish

Nature have the same Effect this Year? Of That, there never was offer'd the least Proof, but a few Letters,[58] which are yet Children of Darkness,[59] their Authority having never been sufficiently clear'd up. Yet lame and imperfect as this Plot was, it had Weight enough to keep up the Army for a Twelve-month, to countenance several Hardships, and to occasion a Prohibition of all Commerce with a Kingdom, without whose Trade we can scarce subsist.[60]

The only Difference between a Plot that is well grounded, and One that is otherwise, is, That the Former strikes at the worst Sort of Men, but the Latter affects the Best.

For this Reason, as well as some others, I hope it cannot be imagined, that I would hereby insinuate, that the Ministry have the least Design of putting any Plot upon the World, but such as is founded upon a solid Truth. Altho', if I were to speak my Mind, I wish we were to have a Plot of some Kind or other; and if Reason of State did so require it, I cannot see the least Cause why the Ministry should hesitate upon it, thro' Tenderness of Conscience, or Passion for Truth. I am clear in my own Judgment in the Point, that if the Exigencies of the Government did need a Plot, it is Just in itself, and Laudable in the Eye of the World, to find one out, some way or other, altho' perhaps Proofs [16] there might be none; and I should look upon it as a general Calamity, if any Person concern'd should defeat the good Ends, propos'd hereby, out of Scruples of Conscience.

---

military assistance in a Jacobite coup d'état. Both Caesar and Gyllenborg were arrested and imprisoned. See Anonymous, *Letters Which Passed Between Count Gyllenborg, the Barons Gortz, Spar, and Others, Relating to the Design of Raising a Rebellion . . . To be Supported by a Force from Sweden* (1717).

58. An understatement. In 1716 Edward Willes (1694–1773), the clergyman and cryptanalyst, had intercepted pro-Jacobite messages between Georg Heinrich von Görtz, a Swedish diplomat, and Count Karl Gyllenborg, his ambassador in London. Willes cracked the code and translated 300 pages of cipher. In January 1717, despite protesting that he enjoyed diplomatic immunity, Gyllenborg was arrested for conspiracy.

59. 1 Thessalonians 5:5.

60. Britain's trade with Sweden at this time consisted largely of iron ore and timber for shipping. In 1716 Parliament had passed an act allowing George I to prohibit or restrain commerce with Sweden.

There is one Circumstance which gives me and others great Hopes that some important Matters are to be brought to Light. A Gentleman, who hath been as deep as any one, in all Plots, against the Government, and the Illustrious House, both in the late and present Reign; and who, at present, is under the heaviest Censure of the Law, is preparing, as we are inform'd, to return to his native Soil:[61] His late Intimacies may dispose him to see his former Errors: His demands from Nature oblige him to an Expence, to which his Fortune is by no means equal: His Abilities are very great; so we have all the reason in the World to hope, both from his Power and Inclinations, that a Plot may be form'd for the Salutary Uses already specified, and which may crown the great Services he hath hitherto rendred to the Government.

As to my Self I am prepared, by the Blessing of God, whenever any such thing begins to appear, to give into it with all my Faculties; and not to examine too nicely into the grounds or probability; the thing is good in it self, and should be received with an implicite Faith: Such a saving Faith I declare to all the World I have, and am resolv'd to preserve: And let all those who will not profit by my Example, and the plain Dictates of right Reason, answer it to God and their Country, that neither Religion nor the publick Welfare could induce them to believe as the Government would have them.

FINIS.

61. Possibly an allusion to the notoriously duplicitous Simon Fraser; see above, p. 497, n. 49.

"Cato" [Thomas Gordon]

A Discourse of Standing Armies

1722

1. "Even victory was bound to be a most bitter experience, fraught as it must be with destruction for the vanquished, and slavery for the vanquishers" (Cicero, *Ad Familiares*, VI.xxi.1 [Letter 246]).

A

DISCOURSE

OF

Standing Armies;

SHEWING

The Folly, Uselesness, and Danger of STANDING ARMIES

IN

GREAT BRITAIN.

By *CATO.*

Ipsa victoria futura esset acerbissima, quae aut interitum allatura esset, si victus esses, aut si vicisses, servitutem.[1]

Cicer. Epist. ad Toranium. Lib. vi.

LONDON:

Printed for T. WARNER, at the Black Boy in Pater-noster Row. 1722.

Price Six Pence

A Discourse of *Standing Armies*, &c.

When, in King *William's* Reign,[2] the Question was in Debate, Whether *England* should be rul'd by Standing Armies? the Argument commonly us'd by some who had the Presumption to call themselves Whigs,[3] and own'd in the *Ballancing Letter*, suppos'd to be written by one who gave the Word to all the rest,[4] was, That all Governments must have their Periods one Time or other, and when that Time came, all Endeavours to preserve Liberty were fruitless; and shrewd Hints were given in that Letter, that *England* was reduced [4] to such a Condition; that our Corruptions were so great, and the Dissatisfaction of the People was so general, that the publick Safety could not be preserved, but by encreasing the Power of the Crown: And this Argument was us'd by those shameless Men, who had caus'd all that Corruption, and all that Dissatisfaction.

But that Gentleman and his Followers were soon taught to speak other Language: They were remov'd from the Capacity of perplexing publick

2. I.e., 1697–98.

3. Gordon presents the transformation of a group of Whigs from a party of revolution to a party of administration as an apostasy; see above, p. xii, n. 9. Charles Hornby expressed the suspicions of many: "After the Peace [the Treaty of Ryswick, September 1697] was concluded, the Whigg Ministry apprehending they should be laid by, enter'd into a Compact with King *William*, that if he would keep them and their Friends in the Ministry, they would use their utmost Interest in the House of Commons to procure him a standing Army; which they struggled very hard for" (Charles Hornby, *A Third Part of the Caveat against the Whiggs*, 2nd ed. [1712], p. 96).

4. I.e., John Somers, *A Letter, Ballancing the Necessity of Keeping a Land-Force in Times of Peace: with the Dangers that May Follow On It* (1697); above, pp. 51–67.

Affairs any more:[5] The Nation shew'd a Spirit that would not submit to Slavery, and their unhappy and betray'd Master, from being the most popular Prince who ever sat upon the *English* Throne, became, through the Treachery of his Servants, suspected by many of his best Subjects, and was render'd unable, by their Jealousies, to defend himself and them; and so considerable a Faction was form'd against his Administration, that no good Man can reflect without Concern and Horror, on the Difficulties which that Great and Good King was reduced to grapple with, during the Remainder of his troublesome Reign.

I have lately met with some Creatures and Tools of Power, who speak the same Language now: They tell us, that Mat[5]ters are come to that Pass, that we must either receive the Pretender,[6] or keep him out with Bribes and Standing Armies: That the Nation is so corrupt, that there is no governing it by any other Means: And, in short, that we must submit to this great Evil, to prevent a greater; as if any Mischief could be more terrible than the highest and most terrible of all Mischiefs, universal Corruption, and a military Government. It is indeed impossible for the Subtilty of Traitors, the Malice of Devils, or for the Cunning and Cruelty of our most implacable Enemies, to suggest stronger Motives for the undermining and Overthrow of our excellent Establishment, which is built upon the Destruction of Tyranny, and can stand upon no other Bottom. It is Madness in Extremity, to hope that a Government founded upon Liberty, and the free Choice of the Assertors of it, can be supported by other Principles; and whoever would maintain it by contrary ones, intends to blow it up, let him alledge what he will. This gives me every Day new Reasons to believe what I have long suspected; for, if ever a Question should arise, Whether a Nation shall submit to certain Ruin, or struggle for a Remedy? these Gentlemen well know which Side [6] they will chuse, and certainly intend that which they must chuse.

I am willing to think, that these impotent Babblers speak not the Sense of their Superiors, but would make servile Court to them from Topicks which they abhor. Their Superiors must know, that it is Raving

5. A reference to the removal of the Junto Whigs from office in 1699, following the general election of 1698.
6. I.e., the Old Pretender; see above, p. 30, n. 73.

and Phrenzy to affirm, that a free People can be long govern'd by impotent Terrors; that Millions will not consent to be ruin'd by the Corruptions of a few; or that those few will join in their Ruine any longer than the Corruption lasts: That every Day new and greater Demands will rise upon the Corruptors; that no Revenue, how great soever, will feed the Voraciousness of the Corrupted; and that every Disappointment will make them turn upon the Oppressors of their Country, and fall into its true Interest and their own: That there is no Way in Nature to preserve a Revolution in Government, but by making the People easy under it, and shewing them their Interest in it; and that Corruption, Bribery, and Terrors, will make no lasting Friends, but infinite and implacable Enemies; and that the best Security of a Prince amongst a free People, is the Affections of his People, which he can always gain by making their Interest his own, and by shewing that all [7] his Views tend to their Good. They will then, as they love themselves, love him, and defend him who defends them. Upon this faithful Basis, his Safety will be better established, than upon the ambitious and variable Leaders of a few Legions, who may be corrupted, disoblig'd, or surpriz'd, and often have been so; and hence great Revolutions have been brought about, and great Nations undone, only by the Revolt of single Regiments.

Shew a Nation their Interest, and they will certainly fall into it: A whole People can have no Ambition but to be govern'd justly; and when they are so, the Intrigues and Dissatisfactions of Particulars will fall upon their own Heads. What has any of our former Courts ever got by Corruption, but to disaffect the People, and weaken themselves? Let us now think of other Methods, if it is only for the Sake of the Experiment. The Ways of Corruption have been tried long enough in past Administrations: Let us try in this what publick Honesty will do; and not condemn it, before we have fully prov'd it, and found it ineffectual; and it will be Time enough to try other Methods, when this fails.

That we must either receive the Pretender, or keep up great Armies to keep [8] him out, is frightful and unnatural Language to *English* Ears: It is an odd Way of dealing with us, that of offering us, or forcing upon us, an Alternative, where the Side which they would recommend, is full as formidable as the Side from which they would terrify us. If we are to be govern'd by Armies, it is all one to us, whether they be Protestant or Popish Armies; the Distinction is ridiculous, like that between a good and a bad Tyranny:[7] We see, in Effect, that it is the Power and Arms of a Country, that forms and directs the Religion of a Country; and I have before shewn,[8] that true Religion cannot subsist, where true Liberty does not. It was chiefly, if not wholly King *James*'s usurp'd Power, and his many Forces, and not his being a Papist, that render'd him dreadful to his People. Military Governments are all alike; nor does the Liberty and Property of the Subject fare a bit the better or the worse, for the Faith and Opinion of the Soldiery. Nor does an Arbitrary Protestant Prince use his People better than an Arbitrary Popish Prince; and we have seen both Sorts of them[9] changing the Religion of their Country, according to their Lust.

[9] They are therefore stupid Politicians, who would derive Advantages from a Distinction which is manifestly without a Difference: It is like, however, that they may improve in their Subtilties, and come, in time, to distinguish between corrupt Corruption, and uncorrupt Corruption, between a good ill Administration, and an ill good Administration, between oppressive Oppression, and unoppressive Oppression, and between *French* Dragooning[10] and *English* Dragooning; for there is scarce any other new Pitch of Nonsense and Contradiction left to such Men in their Reasonings upon Publick Affairs, and in the Part they act in them.

Of a Piece with the rest, is the stupid Cunning of some Sort of Statesmen, and practis'd by most Foreign Courts, to blame the poor People for

7. A point made several times earlier in the controversy, and traceable to a remark of the Whig pamphleteer Samuel Johnson; see above, p. 33, n. 81.

8. Between November 1720 and December 1723 Trenchard and Gordon would collaborate in a periodical entitled *Cato's Letters: Or, Essays on Liberty, Civil and Religious, And Other Important Subjects*, and it is to these essays that Gordon alludes. Two of the essays, no. 94 (15 September 1722) and no. 95 (22 September 1722), are on the subject of standing armies, and they have been conflated to produce this pamphlet.

9. The tart observation that there is no effectual difference between a Protestant and a Roman Catholic military despotism is by 1722 a topos among writers against standing armies; see above, p. 33, n. 81.

10. See above, p. 89, n. 51.

the Misery they bring upon them. They say they are extremely corrupt, and so keep them starving and enslav'd by Way of Protection. They corrupt them by all manner of Ways and Inventions, and then reproach them for being corrupt. A whole Nation cannot be bribed, and if its Representatives are, it is not the Fault, but the Misfortune of the Nation: And if the Corrupt save themselves by corrupting others; the People who suffer by the [10] Corruptions of both, are to be pittied, and not abus'd. Nothing can be more shameless and provoking, than to bring a Nation by execrable Frauds and Extortions, against its daily Protestations and Remonstrances, into a miserable pass, and then father all those Villanies upon the People who would have gladly hang'd the Authors of them. At *Rome*, the whole People could be entertain'd, feasted, and bribed; but it is not so elsewhere, where the People are too numerous, and too far spread, to be debauch'd, cajol'd, and purchas'd; and if any of their Leaders are, it is without the People's Consent.

There is scarce such a Thing under the Sun as a corrupt People, where the Government is uncorrupt: It is that, and that alone, which makes them so; and to calumniate them for what they do not seek, but suffer by, is as great Impudence as it would be, to knock a Man down, and then rail at him for hurting himself. In what Instances do the People of any Country in the World throw away their Money by Millions, unless by trusting it to those who do so? Where do the People send great Fleets, at a great Charge, to be frozen up in one Climate, or to be eaten out by Worms in another, unless for their Trade and [11] Advantage? Where do the People enter into mad Wars against their Interest, or, after victorious ones, make Peace, without stipulating for one new Advantage for themselves; but, on the contrary, pay the Enemy for having beaten them? Where do the People plant Colonies or purchase Provinces, at a vast Expence, without reaping, or expecting to reap, one Farthing from them, and yet still defend them at a further Expence? Where do the People make distracted Bargains, to get imaginary Millions, and after having lost by such Bargains almost all the real Millions they had, yet give more Millions to get rid of them? What wise or dutiful People consents to be without the Influence of the Presence of their Prince, and of his Vertues, or of those of his Family, who are to come after him? No—these Things are never done by any People; but, wherever they are done, they are done without their Consent; and yet all these Things have been done in former Ages, and in neighbouring Kingdoms.

For such guilty and corrupt Men, therefore, to charge the People with Corruption, whom either they have corrupted, or cannot corrupt, and, having brought great Misery upon them, to threaten them with more; is, in effect, to tell them plainly, "Gentlemen, we [12] have us'd you very ill, for which you who are innocent of it, are to blame; we therefore find it necessary, for your Good, to use you no better or rather worse: And if you will not accept of this our Kindness, which, however, we will force upon you, if we can, we will give you up into the terrible Hands of raw Head and bloody Bones,[11] who, being your Enemy, may do you as much Mischief as we who are your Friends, have done you." I appeal to common Sense, Whether this be not the Sum of such Threats and Reasonings in their native Colours.

The Partizans of *Oliver Cromwell*, when he was meditating Tyranny over the Three Nations, gave out, that it was the only Expedient to ballance Factions, and to keep out *Charles Stuart*; and so they did worse Things to keep him out, than he could have done if they had let him in. And, after that King's Restoration, when there was an Attempt made to make him absolute, by enabling him to raise Money without Parliament; an Attempt which every Courtier, except Lord *Clarendon*,[12] came into; it was alledg'd to be the only Expedient to keep the Nation from falling back into a Commonwealth; as if any Commonwealth upon Earth, was not better than [13] any Absolute Monarchy. His Courtiers foresaw, that by their mad and extravagant Measures, they should make the Nation mad, and were willing to save themselves by the final Destruction of the Nation; they therefore employ'd their Creatures to whisper abroad stupid

11. A bugbear or bogeyman, typically imagined as having a head in the form of a skull, or one whose flesh has been stripped of its skin, invoked to frighten children (*OED*, s.v. "raw-head").

12. For Clarendon, see above, p. 301, n. 104. Gordon's judgment is puzzling, as in the crisis of 1667 which precipitated his disgrace and exile Clarendon had been urging Charles toward a more autocratic style of government by encouraging him to dissolve Parliament and to use his prerogative powers to raise money by means of a forced loan.

and villanous Reasons why People should be content to be finally undone, lest something not near so bad, should befall them.

Those who have, by abusing a Nation, forfeited its Affections, will never be for trusting a People, who, they know, do justly detest them; but having procur'd their Aversion and Enmity, will be for fortifying themselves against it by all proper Ways; and the Ways of Corruption, Depredation, and Force, being the only proper ones, they will not fail to be practis'd; and those who practise them, when they can no longer deny them, will be finding Reasons to justify them; and, because they dare not avow the true Reasons, they must find such false ones as are most likely to amuse and terrify: And hence so much Nonsense and Improbability utter'd in that Reign, and sometimes since, to vindicate guilty Men, and vilify an innocent People, who were so extravagantly fond of that Prince, that their Liberties were al[14]most gone, before they would believe them in Danger.

It is as certain, that King *James* II. wanted no Army to help him to preserve the Constitution, nor to reconcile the People to their own Interest: But, as he intended to invade and destroy both, nothing but Corruption and a Standing Army, could enable him to do it; and, thank God, even his Army fail'd him, when he brought in *Irish* Troops[13] to help them. This therefore was his true Design; but his Pretences were very different: He pleaded the Necessity of his Affairs, nay, of publick Affairs, and of keeping up a good Standing Force to preserve his Kingdoms forsooth from Insults at home and from abroad. This was the Bait; but his People, who had no longer any Faith in him, and to whom the Hook appear'd threatening and bare, would not believe him, nor swallow it; and if they were jealous of him, restless under him, and ready to rise against him, he gave them sufficient Cause. He was under no Hardship nor Necessity but what he created to himself, nor did his People withdraw their Affections from him, till he had withdrawn his Right to those Affections. Those who have us'd you ill, will never forgive you; and it is no new Thing wantonly to make an Enemy, and then to calumniate and destroy him for being so.

13. See above, p. 314, n. 147.

[15] When People, through continual ill Usage, grow weary of their present ill Condition, they will be so far from being frighten'd with a Change, that they will wish for one; and instead of terrifying them, by threatning them with one, you do but please them, even in Instances where they have no Reason to be pleas'd. Make them happy, and they will dread any Change; but while they are ill us'd, they will not fear the worst. The Authors of publick Misery and Plunder, may seek their only Safety in general Desolation; but, to the People, nothing can be worse than Ruin, from what Hand soever it comes: A Protestant Musket kills as sure as a Popish one; and an Oppressor is an Oppressor, to whatever Church he belongs: The Sword and the Gun are of every Church, and so are the Instruments of Oppression. The late Directors were all stanch Protestants; and *Cromwell* had a violent Aversion to Popery.[14]

We are, doubtless, under great Necessities in our present Circumstances; but to increase them, in order to cure them, would be a preposterous Remedy, worthy only of them who brought them upon us; and who, if they had common Shame in them, would conceal, as far as they could, under Silence, the heavy Evils, which, tho' they lie upon every [16] Man's Shoulders, yet lie only at the Doors of a few. The Plea of Necessity, if it can be taken, will justify any Mischief, and the worst Mischiefs. Private Necessity makes Men Thieves and Robbers; but publick Necessity requires that Robbers of all Sizes should be hang'd. Publick Necessity therefore, and the Necessity of such pedant Politicians, are different and opposite Things. There is no Doubt, but Men guilty of great Crimes, would be glad of an enormous Power to protect them in the greatest; and then tell us there is a Necessity for it. Those against whom Justice is arm'd, will ever talk thus, and ever think it necessary to disarm her. But whatever sincere Services they may mean to themselves by it, they can mean none to his Majesty, who would be undone with his Subjects, by such treacherous and ruinous Services: And therefore it is fit that Mankind should know, and they themselves should know, that his Majesty can and will be defended against them and their Pretender, without Standing Armies, which wou'd make him formidable only to his People, and

14. See above, p. 512, n. 7, and p. 33, n. 81.

contemptible to his Foes, who take justly the Measure of his Power from his Credit with his Subjects.

But I shall consider what present Occasion there is of keeping up more Troops [17] than the usual Guards and Garrisons, and shall a little further animadvert upon the Arts and frivolous Pretences made Use of, in former Reigns, to reduce this Government to the Condition and Model of the pretended *jure Divino*–Monarchies,[15] where Millions must be miserable and undone, to make one and a few of his Creatures lawless, rampant, and unsafe.

It is certain, that Liberty is never so much in danger, as upon a Deliverance from Slavery. The remaining Dread of the Mischiefs escaped, generally drives, or decoys Men into the same or greater; for then the Passions and Expectations of some, run high; and the Fears of others make them submit to any Misfortunes to avoid an Evil that is over; and both Sorts concur in giving to a Deliverer all that they are delivered from: In the Transports of a Restoration, or Victory, or upon a Plot discover'd, or a Rebellion quell'd, nothing is thought too much for the Benefactor, nor any Power too great to be left to his Discretion, tho' there can never be less Reason for giving it to him than at those Times; because, for the most part, the Danger is past, his Enemies are defeated and intimidated, and consequently that is a proper Juncture for the People to settle themselves, and secure their Liberties, since no one is likely to disturb them in doing so.

However, I confess, that Custom, from Time immemorial, is against me, and the [18] same Custom has made most of Mankind Slaves: *Agathocles*[16] saved the *Syracusans*, and afterwards destroy'd them. *Pisistratus*[17] pretending to be wounded for protecting the People, prevail'd with them to allow him a Guard for the Defence of his Person, and by the Help of that Guard usurp'd the Sovereignty: *Caesar* and *Marius*[18] deliver'd the Commons of *Rome* from the Tyranny of the Nobles, and

15. See above, p. 7, n. 10.
16. See above, p. 19, n. 43.
17. See above, p. 18, n. 41.
18. See above, pp. 19–20, nn. 44 and 45.

made themselves Masters of both Commons and Nobles: *Sylla*[19] deliver'd the Senate from the Insolence of the People, and did them more Mischief than the Rabble could have done in a Thousand Years: *Gustavus Ericson*[20] delivered the *Swedes* from the Oppression of the *Danes*, and made large Steps towards enslaving them himself: The *Antwerpians* call'd in the Duke of *Allençon*, to defend them against the *Spaniards;* but he was no sooner got, as he thought, in full Possession of their Town, but he fell upon them himself with the Forces which he brought for their Defence. But the Townsmen happen'd to be too many for him, and drove these their new Protectors home again: Which Disappointment, and just Disgrace, broke that good Duke's Heart.[21] *Oliver Cromwell* headed an Army which pretended to fight for Liberty, and by that Army became a bloody Tyrant;[22] as I once saw a Hawk very generously rescue a Turtle Dove from the Persecution of two Crows, and then eat him up himself.[23]

[19] Almost all Men desire Power, and few lose any Opportunity to get it, and all who are like to suffer under it, ought to be strictly upon their Guard in such Conjunctures as are most likely to encrease, and make it uncontroulable. There are but two Ways in Nature to enslave a People, and continue that Slavery over them; the first is Superstition, and the last is Force: By the one, we are perswaded that it is our Duty to be undone; and the other undoes us whether we will or no. I take it, that we are pretty much out of Danger of the first, at present; and, I think, we cannot be too much upon our guard against the other; for, tho' we have nothing to fear from the best Prince in the World, yet we have every thing to fear from those who would give him a Power inconsistent with Liberty, and with a Constitution which has lasted almost a Thousand Years[24] without such a Power, which will never be ask'd with an Intention to make no Use of it.

19. See above, p. 19, n. 44.

20. See above, p. 21, n. 49.

21. For Alençon, see above, p. 44, n. 109.

22. See above, p. 22, n. 51.

23. A version of the Aesopian fable of the hawks and pigeons (*Aesop Naturaliz'd* [1711], p. 14).

24. Gordon invokes the ancient constitution; see above, p. 13, n. 21.

The Nation was so mad, upon the Restoration of King *Charles* II. that they gave to him all that he ask'd, and more than he ask'd: They complemented him with a vast Revenue for Life, and almost with our Liberties and Religion too; and if unforeseen Accidents had not happen'd to prevent it, without doubt we had lost both; and if his Successor[25] could have had a little Patience, and had used no Rogues but his old Rogues, he might have accomplished the Business, and Popery and [20] Arbitrary Power[26] had been *Jure Divino*[27] at this Day; but he made too much haste to be at the End of his Journey; and his Priests were in too much haste to be on Horseback too, and so the Beast grew skittish, and overthrew them both.

Then a new Set of Deliverers[28] arose, who had saved us from King *James*'s Army, and would have given us a bigger in the Room of it, and some of them Foreigners;[29] and told us that the King longed for them, and it was a Pity that so good a Prince should lose his Longing, and

25. I.e., James II.

26. A phrase with great resonance in the political struggles of the reign of Charles II. In 1677 Andrew Marvell had published *An Account of the Growth of Popery and Arbitrary Government in England*. That there was a natural affinity between Roman Catholicism and arbitrary government was a commonplace of Whiggism.

27. See above, p. 7, n. 10.

28. I.e., William III and his followers.

29. An allusion to William's Dutch bodyguards. On 16 December 1698 Parliament had voted to reduce the land forces garrisoned in England to 7,000, and had further specified that these forces must be "*Natural born Subjects of* England" (Boyer, *William III*, 3:370), a measure which clearly required William to send his personal regiment of Dutch guards back to the United Provinces.

> This great Reform [the reduction of the land forces to the level of 7,000] cost the King many a heavy and melancholy Thought; But what touch'd his Majesty to the very Quick, was the Necessity he was under of sending away his *Dutch* Guards; A Regiment who had faithfully attended his Person from his Cradle; follow'd his Fortunes every where, and to whom, besides innumerable other signal Services, he ow'd his Victory at the famous Battle of the *Boyne*. With these his Majesty had the utmost, and indeed, the justest Regret to part: . . . The *Dutch* Guards were soon after Ship'd off for *Holland*, which occasion'd some Murmurings among the Well-affected, who thought it a Hardship upon his Majesty, to have them forc'd away from him. (Boyer, *William III*, 3:373, 375; see also Burnet, *History*, 2:219)

miscarry; but he did lose it, and miscarried no otherwise than by losing a great Part of the Confidence which many of his best Subjects before had in his Moderation; which Loss, made the Remainder of his Reign uneasy to him, and to every good Man who saw it: I remember, all Men then declared against a Standing Army,[30] and the Courtiers amongst the rest, who were only for a *Land-Force*, to be kept up no longer than till the King of *France* disbanded his, and till the Kingdom was setled, and the People better satisfy'd with the Administration; and then there was nothing left to do, in order to perpetuate them, but to take care that the People should never be satisfy'd: An Art often practis'd with an amazing Success.

The Reasons then given for keeping up an Army were, the great Number of Jacobites, the Disaffection of the Clergy and Univer[21]sities,[31] the Power and Enmity of *France*, and the Necessity of preserving so excellent a Body of Troops to maintain the Treaty of Partition,[32] which they had newly and wisely made: But notwithstanding the Army was disbanded; no Plot, Conspiracy, or Rebellion, happen'd by their disbanding: The Partition Treaty was broke; a new Army was rais'd, which won Ten times as many Victories as the former, and *Europe*, at last, is settled upon a much

---

30. An exaggeration, although it is clear that resistance to the maintenance of a land force was substantial and well-managed.

31. After 1689 the existence of the "non-jurors" (i.e., those who, although they might acknowledge William III to be king de facto, could not bring themselves to recognize him as king de jure, and therefore could not take the new oath of allegiance) was a constant reminder of widespread compromised loyalty to the new regime among the clergy. Oxford and to a lesser degree Cambridge were both suspected of nurturing Jacobitism:

> It will take but little Labour to prove, why a Stream is muddy and foul that flows from a corrupt and degenerate Fountain. Can any one bring a clean Thing from an unclean? *No not one!* What wonder will it be, that the inferior Clergy are debauch'd in Morals, disloyal in Politicks, heretical in Principles, prophane in Conversation, when we shall trace them back to their Erudition, and find that they were bred up in all these at the Colleges, where they were placed to be finish'd with Learning and good Morals, and where they suck in Vice instead of Virtue, profligate Manners instead of Piety. (Anonymous, *Reasons for Visiting the Universities* [1717], p. 15)

32. See above, p. 160, n. 18, and p. 349, n. 228.

better Foot than it would have been by the Partition Treaty. The Emperor is as strong as he ought to be. The *Dutch* have a good Barrier. Another Power is rais'd in *Europe* to keep the Ballance even, which neither can nor will be formidable to us without our own Fault; *France* is undone, and the Regent must be our Friend, and have Dependance upon our Protection; so that some few of these Reasons are to do now, what altogether could not do then, tho' we are not the tenth Part so well able to maintain them as we were then.

I should be glad to know in what Situation of our Affairs it can be safe, to reduce our Troops to the usual Guards and Garrisons, if it cannot be done now: There is no Power in *Europe* considerable enough to threaten us, who can have any Motives to do so, if we pursue the old Maxims and natural Interest of *Great Britain;* which is, *To meddle no farther with Foreign Squabbles,* [22] *than to keep the Ballance even between* France *and* Spain: And this is less necessary too for us to do now, than formerly; because the Emperor and *Holland* are able to do it, and must and will do it without us, or at least with but little of our Assistance; but if we unnecessarily engage against the Interests of either, we must thank ourselves, if they endeavour to prevent the Effects of it, by finding us Work at Home.

When the Army was disbanded in King *William's* Reign, a Prince was in Being[33] who was personally known to many of his former Subjects, and had obliged great Numbers of them; who was supported by one of the most powerful Monarchs in the World,[34] that had won numerous Victories, and had almost always defeated his Enemies, and who still preserved his Power and his Animosity: His pretended Son[35] was then an Infant, and for any Thing that then appear'd, might have proved an active and a dangerous Enemy, and it was to be fear'd, that his Tutors might have educated him a half Protestant, or at least have taught him to have disguis'd his true Religion: At that Time, the Revolution, and Revolution-Principles, were in their Infancy; and most of the Bishops and dignify'd Clergy, as well as many others in Employment, owed their Preferments

33. I.e., the exiled James II.
34. I.e., Louis XIV.
35. I.e., the Old Pretender; see above, p. 30, n. 73.

and Principles to the abdicated Family, and the Reverse of this, is our Case now.

[23] *France* has been torn to pieces by numerous Defeats, its People and Manufactures destroy'd by War, Famine, the Plague, and their *Missisippi* Company;[36] and they are so divided at Home, that they will find enough to do to save themselves without troubling their Neighbours, and especially a Neighbour from whom the governing Powers there, hope for Protection.[37] The Prince who pretended to the Thrones of these Kingdoms is dead,[38] and he who calls himself his Heir[39] is a bigotted Papist; and has given but little Cause to fear any Thing from his Abilities or his Prowess. The Principles of Liberty are now well understood, and few People in this Age, are Romantick[40] enough to venture their Lives and Estates for the personal Interests of one they know nothing of, or nothing to his Advantage; and we ought to take Care that they shall not find

36. A reference to the innovative—and ultimately disastrous—expedients of John Law (1671–1729), a Scottish gambler, murderer, and absconder who briefly exerted a powerful influence over French financial policy. Law had proposed a scheme for a royal bank to Louis XIV and his finance minister, Nicolas Desmarets, which had come close to acceptance shortly before the king's death in September 1715. During the regency of Philippe d'Orléans, Law's influence at court increased, and at Law's prompting a general bank was established in May 1716. This was followed on 21 August 1717 by the Company of the West (Compagnie d'Occident), which had exclusive rights to exploit the French colony in Louisiana (hence the title Mississippi Company). On 4 December 1718 the General Bank (Banque Générale) was renamed a royal bank (*banque royale*). Gradually, from August to October 1719, the Banque Royale came to assume control of the entire revenue-raising system of the French crown, for both direct and indirect taxes. The Mississippi System eventuated in a giant holding company controlling almost the entire revenue-raising system of the French state, the national debt, the overseas companies, the mint, and the note-issuing bank. It collapsed on 17 July 1720. Adam Smith would call the Mississippi Company "the most extravagant project both of banking and stock-jobbing that, perhaps, the world ever saw" and would identify its root in the conceit of "multiplying paper money to almost any extent" (Smith, *Wealth of Nations*, p. 317).

37. After defeat in the War of the Spanish Succession, when France had narrowly escaped invasion, and after the death of Louis XIV in 1715, France had sought to avoid large-scale conflict in Europe.

38. I.e., James II, who had died on 5 September 1701.

39. An allusion to the alleged supposititious nature of the Old Pretender; see above, p. 314, n. 145.

40. Quixotic; impractical and fanciful (*OED*, s.v. "romantic," 3a, 3b).

their own Interest in doing it; and, I conceive, nothing is necessary to effect this, but to resolve upon it. Almost all the dignified Clergy, and all the Civil and Military Officers in the Kingdom, owe their Preferments to the Revolution, and are as loyal to his Majesty as he himself can wish. A very great Part of the Property of the Kingdom stands upon the same Bottom with the Revolution. Every Day's Experience, shews us how devoted the Nobility are to gratify their King's just Desires and Inclinations, and nothing can be more certain, than that [24] the present House of Commons, are most dutifully and affectionately inclin'd to the true Interest of the Crown, and to the Principles to which his Majesty owes it. And besides all this Security, a new Conspiracy has been discovered and defeated;[41] which gives full Occasion and Opportunity to prevent any such Attempts for the future; which can never be done, but by punishing the present Conspirators, and giving no Provocation to new ones; in both which, I hope, we shall have the hearty Concurrence of those who have the Honour to be employ'd by his Majesty; by which they will shew, that they are as zealous to prevent the Necessity of Standing Armies, as I doubt not but the Parliament will be.

I presume, no Man will be audacious enough to propose, that we should make a Standing Army Part of our Constitution; and, if not, When can we reduce them to a competent Number better than at this Time? Shall we wait till *France* has recover'd its present Difficulties; till its King is grown to full Age and Ripeness of Judgment;[42] till he has dissipated all Factions and Discontents at Home, and is fallen into the natural Interests of his Kingdom, or perhaps aspires to Empire again? Or shall we wait till the Emperor, and King of *Spain*, have divided the Bear's Skin,[43] and possibly become good Friends, as their Predecessors have been for

---

41. A very topical reference to the Atterbury conspiracy. In November 1721 Francis Atterbury (1663–1732), bishop of Rochester and an inveterate Stuart sympathizer, had agreed to proposals presented by the Pretender's agents for an armed landing in England. The plot was betrayed to the administration of Sir Robert Walpole, and on 24 August 1722 Atterbury had been arrested.

42. See above, p. 475, n. 131.

43. I.e., the partitioning of Prussia; cf. Anonymous [Chesterfield?], *A Farther Vindication of the Case of the Hanover Troops* (1743), p. 80, n. *. "Dividing the bearskin" is a phrase encountered elsewhere in anti-Jacobite writing of this period: see, e.g., Anonymous, *Secret Memoirs of Barleduc* (Dublin, 1716), p. 23.

the greatest Part of [25] Two Centuries, and perhaps cement that Friendship, by uniting for the common Interests of their Religion? Or till Madam *Sobiesky*'s Heir[44] is of Age, who may have Wit enough to think, that the Popish Religion is dearly bought at the Price of Three Kingdoms? Or are we never to Disband, till *Europe* is settled according to some modern Schemes? Or till there are no Malecontents in *England*, and no People out of Employments who desire to be in them.

'Tis certain, that all Parts of *Europe* which are enslaved, have been enslaved by Armies, and 'tis absolutely impossible, that any Nation which keeps them amongst themselves, can long preserve their Liberties; nor can any Nation perfectly lose their Liberties, who are without such Guests: And yet, though all Men see this, and at Times confess it, yet all have join'd, in their Turns, to bring this heavy Evil upon themselves and their Country. *Charles* the Second[45] formed his Guards into a little Army, and his Successor encreased them to three or four Times their Number;[46] and without doubt these Kingdoms had been enslaved, if known Events had not prevented it. We had no sooner escaped these Dangers, but King *William*'s Ministry form'd Designs for an Army again, and neglected *Ireland* (which might have been reduced by a Message) till the Enemy was so strong, [26] that a great Army was necessary to recover it;[47] and when all was done abroad, that an Army was wanted for, they thought it convenient to find some Employment for them at Home. However, the Nation happened not to be of their Mind, and disbanded the greatest Part of them, without finding any of these Dangers they were threatned with from their Disbanding. A new Army was raised again, when it became

44. On 2 September 1719 the Old Pretender had married Maria Clementina Sobieska, the youngest daughter of Prince James and Hedwig Elizabeth of Neuberg. On 31 December 1720 they had a son, Charles Edward Stuart (the Young Pretender), who was raised as a Roman Catholic. The phrase "Madam *Sobiesky*'s Heir" is a deliberately offensive reminder of the alleged illegitimacy of the Old Pretender.

45. See above, p. 31, n. 74, and below, p. 543, n. 13.

46. I.e., James II. At its peak in October 1688, the nominal strength of James's army had been increased to some 40,000 men. But that figure included noncombatants (such as officers' servants) and large numbers of low-grade, probably useless, new levies. See John Childs, *The Army, James II, and the Glorious Revolution* (Manchester: Manchester University Press, 1980).

47. See above, pp. 321–22, nn. 171–73, and p. 324, n. 179.

necessary, and disbanded again, when there was no more Need of them; and his present Majesty came peaceably to his Crowns, by the Laws alone, notwithstanding all the Endeavours to keep him out, by long Measures concerted to that Purpose.

It could not be expected from the Nature of human Affairs, that those who had formed a Design for restoring the Pretender, had taken such large Steps towards it, and were sure to be supported in it by so powerful an Assistance as *France* was then capable of giving, should immediately lose Sight of so agreeable a Prospect of Wealth and Power, as they had before enjoyed in Imagination; yet it seems very plain to me, that all the Disturbance which afterwards happen'd, might have been prevented by a few timely Remedies; and when at last it was defeated with a vast Charge and Hazard, we had the Means in our Hands of rooting out all Seeds of Faction and future Rebellions, without doing any thing to [27] provoke them; and 'tis certain, his Majesty was ready to do every thing on his Part to that Purpose, which others over and over promised us; and what they have done, besides obliging the Nation with a Septennial Parliament,[48] encreasing the publick Debts a great many Millions, and by the *South-Sea* Project[49] paying them off, I leave to themselves to declare.

However, I confess, an Army at last became necessary, and an Army was raised time enough to beat all who opposed it: Some of them have been knock'd on the Head, many carried in Triumph, some hang'd, and

48. In 1716 Parliament had passed the Septennial Act, which replaced the Triennial Act of 1694 and increased the maximum period between general elections from three years to seven. This measure was naturally unpopular with commonwealth Whigs such as Thomas Gordon, for whom frequency of elections was a cardinal political principle and a safeguard against corruption.

49. The South Sea Company had been founded in 1711 as a trading and finance company. In 1719 its directors offered to take over a large portion of the national debt previously managed by the Bank of England. The Whig administration endorsed this takeover, and in return the company made gifts of its new stock to influential Whig politicians. By 1720 investing in the South Sea Company had become a mania; South Sea stock was at 120 in January and rose to 1,000 by August. But in September the price of the stock fell sharply. Many were ruined, and Parliament demanded an inquiry, thus raising the possibility that members of the government and the royal family would be implicated in financial scandal. In 1720 Gordon had written a series of severe and inflammatory essays on the subject of the South Sea Company (*Cato's Letters*, nos. 1–12 [5 November 1720–14 January 1721]).

others confiscated, as they well deserved; and, I presume, the Nation would scarce have been in the Humour to have kept up an Army to fight their Guests, if a terrible Invasion had not threatened us from *Sweden*, which however was at last frightened into a Fleet of Colliers, or naval Stores, indeed I have forgot which.[50] This Danger being over, another succeeded, and had like to have stole upon us from *Cales*,[51] notwithstanding all the Intelligence we could possibly get from *Gibraltar*, which lyes just by it; and this shews, by the way, the little Use of that Place: But we have miraculously escaped that Danger too; the greatest Part of their Fleet was dispersed in a Storm, and our Troops have actually defeated in the *Highlands*[52] some Hundreds of the Enemy, before many People would believe they [28] were there. Since this, we have been in great Fear of the Czar;[53] and last Year, one Reason given by many for continuing the Army was, to preserve us against the Plague.[54]

50. In 1717–18 there were persistent rumors that Charles XII of Sweden (1682–1718), stung by Hanoverian incursions into his territory, would commit his forces in support of a Jacobite invasion: see, e.g., Anonymous, *An Account of the Swedish and Jacobite Plot* (1717); Nicholas Amhurst, *Protestant Popery: Or, The Convocation. A Poem* (1718), p. 31; Susanna Centlivre, *An Epistle to the King of Sweden from a Lady of Great Britain* (1717); Daniel Defoe, *What If the Swedes Should Come?* (1717); Anonymous, *The Gottenburgh Frolick: Or, the Swedish Invasion Burlesq'd* (1717); Charles Lambe, *Stedfastness to the Protestant Religion and to the King, Recommended upon the Alarm of an Invasion from Sweden* (1717); and Anonymous, *A Short View of the Conduct of the King of Sweden* (1717). For earlier rumors of a Swedish invasion, see above, p. 501–2, nn. 57 and 58.

51. I.e., Porto (known in Roman times as Portus Cale).

52. A reference to the Jacobite invasion of 1719, assisted by Spain, which was halted at the Battle of Glenshiel on 10 June.

53. I.e., Peter the Great (1672–1725). This was another complication in British foreign policy arising from the continental possessions of the House of Hanover. In the winter of 1716–17 a Russian army had been quartered in the Duchy of Mecklenburg, adjacent to the Duchies of Bremen and Verden, which Hanover had seized from Sweden. When Britain and Sweden signed a treaty in 1719 ceding Bremen and Verden to Hanover, this meant that the long-standing Russian hostility toward Sweden expressed in the Second Northern War (1700–1721) was now in part also directed toward Hanover and Great Britain. The presence of a British squadron in the Baltic at this time was also viewed by Russia as a provocation (*The Annals of King George, Year the Fifth* [1720], pp. 37–38).

54. A mocking reference to the fact that the barracks constructed as a consequence of the Quarantine Act of 1721 were feared to be intended for a standing army. See the introduction, p. xxxii.

But now the King of *Sweden* is dead,[55] the Czar is gone a Sophi-hunting,[56] the Plague is ceased,[57] and the King of *Spain*'s best Troops have taken up their Quarters in *Italy*,[58] where if I guess right, they will have Employment enough, and what are we to keep up the Army now to do, unless to keep out the Small Pox? Oh! But there is a better Reason than that, namely, a Plot is discovered,[59] and we can't find out yet all who are concerned in it, but we have pretty good Assurance, that all the Jacobites are for the Pretender, and therefore we ought to keep in Readiness a great Number of Troops (who are to sleep on Horseback, or lye in their Jack-Boots) which may be sufficient to beat them all together, if they had a Twelvemonth's Time given them to beat up for Volunteers, to buy Horses and Arms, to form themselves into Regiments, and exercise them, lest, instead of lurking in Corners, and prating in Taverns, and at Cock-Matches,[60] they should surprize Ten or Twelve Thousand armed Men in their Quarters: I dare appeal to any unprejudiced Person, whether this is not the Sum of some Mens Reasonings upon this Subject?

But I desire to know of these sagacious Gentlemen, in what Respect shall we be in [29] a worse State of Defence than we are now, if the Army was reduced to the same Number as in King *William*'s Time, and in the latter End of the Queen's Reign,[61] and that it consisted of the same

55. Charles XII of Sweden had died on 30 November 1718, at an early stage of his invasion of Norway, when he was shot through the head at the siege of Fredrik-shald. Rumors quickly spread that Charles had been killed by one of his own soldiers.

56. I.e., directed his attention toward Turkey, after the Peace of Nystad (10 September 1721) had concluded the Second Northern War and so for the time being resolved tensions on Russia's western border.

57. An epidemic of plague had raged through the city and surrounding area of Marseilles in 1720, and there had been an outbreak of fever and ague in Dublin in the spring of that year.

58. The Treaties of Maastricht and Utrecht (1713) had stripped Spain of her Italian territories (Milan, Sardinia, Sicily, and Naples). Thus an objective of Spanish foreign policy until 1748 and the conclusion of the War of the Austrian Succession was the recovery of these Italian possessions, and pursuit of this objective had brought her into conflict with Austria, which was now the great power on the Italian peninsula. The Spanish had suffered a naval defeat off Sicily in 1718 at the Battle of Cape Passero.

59. See above, p. 523, n. 41.

60. I.e., a cockfighting match.

61. I.e., Queen Anne, who had died in 1714.

Proportion of Horse and Foot, that every Regiment had its compleat Number of Troops and Companies, and every Troop and Company had its Complement of private Men? 'Tis certain, upon any sudden Exigency, his Majesty would have as many Men at command as he has now, and, I presume, more common Soldiers, who are most difficultly to be got upon such Occasions; for Officers will never be wanting, and all that are now regimented will be in Half-pay, and ready at Call to beat up[62] and raise new Regiments, as fast as the others could be filled up, and they may change any of the old Men into them, which reduces it to the same Thing: By this we shall save the Charge of double or treble Officering our Troops, and the Terror of keeping up the Corps of Thirty or Forty Thousand Men, though they are called only Thirteen or Fourteen; and sure it is high Time to save all which can be saved, and, by removing all Causes of Jealousy, to unite all, who are for the Cause of Liberty, and zealous for the present Establishment, in order to oppose effectually those who would destroy it.

I will suppose, for once, what I will not grant, that those call'd Whiggs are the only [30] Men amongst us who are heartily attached to his Majesty's Interest; for I believe the greatest Part of the Tories, and the Clergy too, would tremble at the Thought of Popery and Arbitrary Power;[63] which must come in with the Pretender: But taking it to be otherwise, 'tis certain that the Body of the Whigs, and indeed I may say almost all except the Possessors and Candidates for Employments or Pensions, have as terrible Apprehensions of a Standing Army, as the Tories themselves;[64]

---

62. I.e., to raise recruits.

63. See above, p. 519, n. 26.

64. Boyer had commented on the curious coincidence of Whig and Tory opposition to a standing army:

> The Country Party and the Republicans [i.e., the Tories and the commonwealth Whigs], who upon this occasion, spoke the same Language, tho' diametrically opposite in their Views, both in this Debate *viva voce*, and in Print, represented the Danger of keeping a Standing Army, Urging, "That it is absolutely destructive to the Constitution of the *English* Monarchy; That no Legislator ever founded a free Government, but avoided this, as a Rock against which his Common Wealth must certainly be Shipwrack'd." (Boyer, *William III*, 3:290–91)

and dare any Man lay his Hand upon his Heart and say, that his Majesty will find greater Security in a few Thousand more Men already regimented, than in the Steady Affections of so many Hundred Thousands who will be always ready to be regimented: When the People are easy and satisfy'd, the whole Kingdom is his Army; and King *James* found what Dependance there was upon his Troops, when his People deserted him.[65] Would not any wise and honest Minister desire, during his Administration, that the Publick Affairs should run glibly,[66] and find the hearty Concurrence of the States of the Kingdom, rather than to carry their Measures by perpetual Struggles and Entrigues, to waste the Civil List by constant and needless Pensions and Gratuities, be always asking for new Supplies, and rend'ring themselves, and all who assist them, odious to their Country-Men?

[31] In short, there can be but two Ways in Nature to govern a Nation, one is by their own Consent, and the other by Force: One gains their Hearts, and the other holds their Hands: The first is always chosen by those who design to govern the People for the People's Interest, and the other by those who design to oppress them for their own; for whoever desires only to protect them, will covet no useless Power to injure them: There is no fear of a People's acting against their own Interest, when they know what it is, and when, through ill Conduct or unfortunate Accidents, they become dissatisfied with their present Condition, the only effectual Way to avoid the threatning Evil, is to remove their Grievances.

When *Charles* Duke of *Burgundy*, with most of the Princes of *France*, at the Head of an Hundred Thousand Men, took up Arms against *Lewis* the Eleventh, that Prince sent an Embassy to *Sforza* Duke of *Milan*, desiring that he would lend him some of his Veteran Troops; and the Duke returned him for Answer, That he could not be content to have them cut to Pieces, (as they would assuredly have been) but told him at the same time, That he would send him some Advice which would be worth Ten times as many Troops as he had; namely, that he should give Satisfaction to the

---

65. See above, p. 48, n. 120.
66. Smoothly, without impediment (*OED*, s.v. "glibly," 1).

Princes, and then they would disperse of [32] Course; and the King improv'd so well upon the Advice, that he diverted the Storm, by giving but little Satisfaction to the Princes, and none at all to those who follow'd them:[67] The Body of the People in all Counties are so desirous to live in quiet, that a few good Words, and a little good Usage from their Governors, will at any Time pacifie them, and make them very often turn upon those Benefactors, who by their Pains, Expence, and Hazard, have obtained those Advantages for them; and indeed, when they are not outrageously oppress'd and starved, are almost as ready to part with their Liberties, as others are to ask for them.

By what I have before said, I would not be understood, to declare absolutely against continuing our present Forces, or increasing them, if the Importance of the Occasion requires either; and the Evils threaten'd, are not yet dissipated: But I could wish that, if such an Occasion appears, those who think them at this Time necessary, would declare effectually, and in the fullest Manner, that they design to keep them no longer than during the present Emergency; and that, when it is over, they will be as ready to break them, as I believe the Nation will be to give them, when just Reasons offer themselves for doing so.

67. Gordon refers to the League of the Public Weal of 1465, an alliance of malcontent princes opposed to the monarchy of Louis XI.

A List of the Present Standing Forces

Foot Guards.

		Number of Men	Abroad and where
D. of *Marlborough*, 1st Reg.	*England*	1529	
Earl *Cadogan*, 2d Regim.	*England*	982	
Earl of *Dunmore*, 3d Regim.	*England*	982	
Total		3493	
Earl *Orkney*	*Ireland*		
Col. *Kirk*	*Britain*	445	
Lieutenant-Gen. *Wills*	*England*	445	
Coll. *Cadogan*	*England*	445	
Major-Gen. *Pierce*			*Gibraltar*
Brigadier *Dormer*	*Ireland*		
Col. *O'Hara*	*Ireland*		
Col. *Pocock*	*Ireland*		
Col. *James Otway*			*Port Mahone*
Brigad. *Groves*	*England*	445	
Col. *Mountague*	*England*	445	
Brigad. *Stanwix*	*England*	445	
Col. *Cotton*			*Gibraltar*
Col. *Clayton*	*Britain*	445	
Col. *Henry Harrison*	*Britain*	445	
Col. *Cholmly*	*Britain*	445	
Major-Gen. *Wightman*	*Ireland*		
Col. *Crosby*			*Port Mahone*
Col. *George Groves*	*Ireland*		
Col. *Egerton*			*Gibraltar*
Lieutenant-Gen. *Macartney*	*England*	445	
Col. *Handaside*	*Ireland*		
Major-Gen. *Sabine*	*England*	445	
Total		4895	
Col. *Howard*	*Ireland*		
Col. *Middleton*	*Ireland*		
Col. *Anstruther*	*Ireland*		
Major-Gen. *Whetham*	*Ireland*		
Col. *Barril*	*Ireland*		
Lord *Mark Kerr*	*Ireland*		
Brigad. *Bisset*			*Port Mahone*

(Continued)

FOOT GUARDS. *(cont.)*

		Number of Men	Abroad and where
Lord *John Kerr*	*Ireland*		
Brigad. *Bon*	*Ireland*		
Col. *Hawly*	*Ireland*		
Col. *Chudleigh*	*Ireland*		
Col. *Charles Otway*			*Port Mahone*
Col. *Lanoe*	*Ireland*		
Lord *Hinchingbrook*	*Ireland*		
Col. *Lucas*			*West-Indies*
Brigad. *Ferrars*	*Ireland*		
Col. *Philips*			*America*
	In all 40 Regiments.		

HORSE GUARDS.

		Number of Men
Duke of *Montague*, 1st Troop	*England*	181
Marq. of *Hartford*, 2d Ditto	*England*	181
Lord *Newburgh*, 3d Ditto	*England*	181
Lord *Forrester*, 4th Ditto	*England*	181
Col. *Fane*, 1st Troop of Gren.	*England*	176
Col. *Berkeley*, 2d Ditto	*England*	177
Total of Horse Guards		**1077**
Marquess of *Winchester*	*England*	310
Lord *Cobham*	*England*	292
Lord *Londonderry*	*England*	196
Major-Gen. *Wade*	*England*	196
Major-Gen. *Wynn*	*Ireland*	
Lord *Seannon*	*Ireland*	
Brigadier *Napier*	*Ireland*	
Col. Legoniers	*Ireland*	
In *England* Total of Horse		2071

DRAGOONS.

		Number of Men	Abroad and where
Sir *Charles Hotham*	*England*	207	
Col. *Campbel*	*England*	207	
Lord *Carpenter*	*England*	207	
Major-Gen. *Evans*	*Britain*	207	
Col. *Sidney*	*Ireland*		
Earl of *Stairs*	*Britain*	207	
Col. *Kerr*	*Britain*	207	
Brigadier *Bowles*	*Ireland*		
Brigadier *Crofts*	*Ireland*		
Brigadier *Gore*	*England*	207	
Brigadier *Honywood*	*England*	207	
Col. *Bowles*	*Ireland*		
Brigadier *Munden*	*Ireland*		
Col. *Neville*	*Ireland*		
In *England* Total of Dragoons		1656	
Horse and Dragoons		3727	

ENGLISH AND *BRITISH* ESTABLISHMENTS AT PRESENT.

Foot-Guards,	3493.
Foot in *England* and *Britain*, II Regiments,	4895.
Horse-Guards, and light Horse,	2071.
Dragoons in *England* and *Britain*, 8 Regiments;	1656.
	12115.

IRISH ESTABLISHMENT.

Foot, 20 Regiments, is two Batallions,	9303.
Horse four Regiments,	770.
Dragoons eight Regiments,	1333.
	11412.

FINIS.

"C. S."

[Charles Sackville, second Duke of Dorset]

A Treatise Concerning the Militia

1752

1. And I prophesy either that there now is, or that there will arise, a great prince, who will correct this disorderly and vicious military spirit, and who will arrange and order it in the old manner. If only that time were now! what triumphs and victories would I see? O God, bring this about, and especially restore our military spirit back to its original Roman form. When our discoveries are allied to the care, discipline, and regularity of the old ways, what power or army could withstand it? (Justus Lipsius, *De Militia Romana* [Antwerp, 1596], bk. 1, dialogue 1, p. 2; cf. Machiavelli, *Discourses*, bk. 3, chap. 36, and *The Art of War*, bk. 1 [Machiavelli, *Chief Works*, 2:580])

Sackville has abbreviated and de-Christianized Lipsius's original text, which reads as follows:

& meo animo ac vaticinio, aut iam est aut erit Princeps aliquis magnus, qui prauam & laxam hanc militiam corrigat, & ad veterem illam ordinet atque adstringat. O si ille dies! quas laureas & victorias videam? quam longe lateque sparsa Christiana signa? Injice hanc mentem Deus, & ad priscam illam ac Romanam maxime militiam flecte. Cum cuius Dilectu, Disciplina, Ordine, si nostra haec nouitia arma iungantur, quae vis aut acies resistat? (contractions expanded).

For Lipsius, see above, p. 487, n. 9.

A

TREATISE

Concerning the

MILITIA,

IN

FOUR SECTIONS.

I. Of the MILITIA in general.

II. Of the *Roman* MILITIA.

III. The proper Plan of a MILITIA, for this Country.

IV. Observations upon this Plan.

By *C. S.*

Meo animo ac vaticinio, aut jam est aut erit Princeps magnus, qui pravam & laxam hanc Militiam corrigat, & ad veterem illam ordinet atque adstringat. O si ille dies! quas laureas & victorias videam? Injice hanc mentem Deus, & ad priscam illam ac Romanam maximè militiam flecte: Cum cujus dilectu, disciplinâ, ordine si nostra haec novitia jungantur, quae vis aut acies resistat?[1]

LIPSIUS.

LONDON:

Printed for J. MILLAN, near Whitehall.

M.D.CC.LII.

To the Readers

The several Schemes that have been proposed for restoring the MILITIA; *the many Debates in Parliament about it; the principal Objection to it, (which is the want of a practicable Scheme;) and the Experience of former Ages, in this Country, both before and after the illustrious Reign of* ELIZABETH; *are all Arguments to shew, both the Sense the People have of the Military State of their Country, and how necessary it is to restore the* Militia.

[vi] *The following Scheme is not merely speculative; or, as the phrase now is,* well enough upon Paper, but impossible to execute: *For the Execution is much more easy than the modern manner of Recruiting; and instead of being attended with Difficulties, will remove them. In this Scheme, Provision is made for continuing the* Crown Army; *and increasing it, at any time, to any number of Men.*

But the Advantages of this Plan, *will be best known by reading it; and I do not chuse to give myself, or my Reader, the trouble of telling him in the Porch, all he is to see when he enters my House.*

Here is no Favour to Parties *of any Name or Distinction. It is entirely calculated for the Honour and Security of the present* FAMILY *on the Throne;[2] for the perpetuating Peace at Home, and making us re*[vii]*spected Abroad; and for restoring Virtue, Regularity, and the execution of good Government in this Country.*

I shall only add here, that the Passage from Lipsius, *in the Title-Page, suited my purpose, as well as it had done that of the learned Author: For when I wrote these Papers, I had the Honour to attend upon the Person of the best and*

---

2. I.e., the House of Hanover.

539

most truly PATRIOT PRINCE,[3] *that, I believe, ever adorned, or blest any Country in the World; and whose Loss*[4] *I had, next to His own* FAMILY, *the greatest Reason to lament, of any other Person in his Service. But I lament it more for the Sake of my* Country, *than for myself. I know He intended many excellent Regulations for the Happiness of* ENGLAND; *and did me the honour to approve of this Scheme for a* Militia, *in many Conversations I have* [viii] *had with Him upon it. And at His Request, (which was always a Command to me,) I committed it to writing, but too late for His Inspection.*

I now make it public, that the present Generation may know, the thoughts of their favourite PRINCE, *upon this favourite Subject: And if they reject it, that Posterity may justify, or condemn their Choice; and neglect, or adopt it. I only wish, if this* Plan *is not pursued, that there may never come a time, in which we may want that* SECURITY *This promises Us.*

3. See above, p. 497, n. 46. For the particular resonances of the word "patriot" in the eighteenth century, see above, p. 347, n. 223. In the 1730s the term "patriot" would be especially associated with the opposition to Sir Robert Walpole, which had coalesced around the person of Frederick, Prince of Wales, and his alternative court at Leicester House. Bolingbroke's *The Idea of a Patriot King* (1738) was composed as a manifesto for this group.

4. Frederick, Prince of Wales, had died suddenly after a short illness on 20 March 1751.

A Treatise, &c.

Of the Militia *in general*

The Subject of these Sections has been the Subject of Debate in every Session of Parliament, from the Restoration to this time; and of so many Pamphlets and Papers, that it should seem to be exhausted. And unless a Writer sets out with a Promise of advancing something New, upon this Old Subject, it will be very dif[2]ficult for him to procure Readers. *Bis coctum crambe venenum.*[5] Nor is it sure that even Novelty will excite Attention. No such extraordinary Regard was paid to a late *"Plan of establishing and disciplining a National Militia, in* Great Britain, Ireland, *and* America," (tho' it was new), as to induce any Man to attempt the Revival of a lost Power, that has been successively oppos'd, and ridicul'd,[6] ever since the Reign of Queen *Elizabeth:* Or to *write down* the POWER that has grown up in its room; and which, instead of lessening by *Opposition,* gains ground every Year, and will, it is to be fear'd, soon become too *formidable* for any Man to oppose; if it will, in time, give leave for any OPPOSITION at all. It is true, the Existence of a STANDING ARMY is annual, and depends upon the Will of *Parliament;* but is it not very possible, that this Renewal may in future Times become a meer Matter of *Form?* Or may it not be renewed, from time to time, till it grows big enough TO PROVIDE FOR IT SELF; and forsakes the [3] Nurse that has fostered it, with so much Care, for so many Years? We know there once was an Army of

---

5. "Warmed-over cabbage is nauseating": proverbial (but see Juvenal, VII.154).
6. For ridicule of the militia, see above, p. 36, n. 89, and p. 306, n. 121.

MERCENARIES in this Country, under the Name of the *Parliament's Army*, who were but Executioners indeed to the Parliament, when they cut off the King's Head:[7] But having so done, they deposed their Masters; raised one *Protector;*[8] obliged another to abdicate;[9] and having raised up, and pulled down so many different sorts of Government; they at last restored the Monarchy in the same Royal Family they had kept in Exile so long. *Arabia, Persia, Rome* in her old Age, and *Egypt*, afford too many fatal Instances, of the bad Effects of *mercenary Troops*, not to excuse the Jealousies and Concern of *a free and loyal People* for their own LIBERTIES, and the Security of their PRINCES. But I will not attempt to frighten the Reader, by enumerating all the possible Evils of *Mercenaries;* or give him an Abstract of the History of *standing Armies* in this Country, which is so well done by Mr. *Trenchard*.[10]

[4] Perhaps the Advocates for a *Militia*, have urged their Objections too home, against the *Standing Forces* in this Country. Permitted by *Parliament*, and under the Command of our SOVEREIGN, we may flatter ourselves, that they will never be prostituted to the Purposes of *Egyptian Mamalukes*, or *Turkish Jamizaries*.[11] That no General will ever start up like CAESAR among the *Romans*, or like OLIVER in *England*, to make the Army dependent on himself; and then establish a *Military*, instead of a *Civil Government*. How vain these Apprehensions may be, I know not; but it is now commonly said, that *we cannot be governed without an Army*. But, I say, GOD FORBID, THAT WE SHOULD EVER BE GOVERNED BY SOLDIERS! We may be told, that they depend upon the *People* for their Pay, and will never fight against their Pay-masters; (which would be true, perhaps, if they were paid in the Name of the *People*, by a PAY-MASTER of the *People;* whereas the Fact is otherwise: And I submit to [5] Consideration the Force of those Expressions so familiarly used, the KING's BREAD, the KING's SERVICE.) I hope they will never fight against their

---

7. A reference to the execution of Charles I in 1649.
8. I.e., Oliver Cromwell.
9. I.e., Richard Cromwell, who ruled briefly as Lord Protector following the death of his father from 3 September 1658 until his resignation on 25 May 1659.
10. In his *Short History of Standing Armies*, above, pp. 255–357.
11. See above, p. 265, n. 11, and p. 28, n. 71.

Pay-masters: But if the *People* should refuse to continue them in Pay, no Man alive can believe, that they will quietly disband themselves; especially if incited by any Authority, which *They* may think superior, to continue in Arms. And what should then hinder them from exacting the Continuance of their PAY? Nothing, I am sure, but their own Condescension and Goodness: For how can the *People*, without Arms or Discipline, resist any Body of regular Forces? And thus, at length, the old Dispute about *Resistance* and *Non-Resistance*, (upon which the glorious REVOLUTION was justified) is become as ridiculous as the modern *Militia!* So true it is, (as some Gentleman have, in Defence of a *standing Army*, advanced) that *England* is no more what she anciently was; and can no longer boast the Existence of a MILITIA, TO SUBDUE FRANCE, AND AWE THE WORLD: But then it is as true, that [6] no *standing Army*, supported by this Country, at the most modest Rate of our present most frugal *Disbursements*, can perform such great Atchievements. The Expence of G——t[12] is already so burthensome, that almost every Man dreads a *National Bankruptcy*; and then, I suppose, a *standing Army* will be found very necessary, to teach Men Patience and Resignation. If the military Man is provoked, by this manner of treating the Subject of a *standing Army*, (which must be owned to be a Matter of the most serious Nature) he will soon unbend his Brow, if you propose to his Consideration, the present State of our NATIONAL MILITIA. If you are too serious, in your Animadversions on the One; he will be as ludicrous, in his Description of the Other: And I, for my part, wish I may be able to reconcile you both.

I believe no Man in the Opposition, is so sanguine in his Hopes, as to think we shall ever entirely get rid of a *standing Army*. It was attempted, but in vain, soon after the Restoration. (The Army [7] which restored King *Charles*, indeed, was disbanded: Not out of any Aversion to *standing Armies*, but to that particular Army, which had proved so fatal to the King-ship: But *Venner* the Enthusiast's Insurrection,[13] soon furnished the

12. I.e., government.
13. Thomas Venner (1608/9–61), Fifth Monarchist. On 6 January 1661 Venner had attempted an insurrection against the restored monarchy of Charles II. After a few days of fighting in the city of London the uprising was suppressed, and

Court with a Pretence, to raise and establish a Body of Guards, which was the Root of the present STANDING ARMY.) The Suppression of a standing Army was again endeavoured, with as little Success, a few Years after the *Revolution;* and is now grown too familiar to be turned off: And, to confess the Truth, our *Militia* is too contemptible, in its present State, to supply its Place. But the *Militia* may be restored, and the *standing Army* not entirely disbanded; and then there can be no reasonable Objection to either. The *Crown Army* may be readily augmented to any Number of Men, by Draughts from the County Regiments of *Militia;* and a much more formidable Army sent upon the Continent; (if it were possible that we could have a justifiable Call, in our present exhausted State,[14] to wage War [8] upon the Continent,) than ever yet made its Appearance there from this Country: And our Fellow-Subjects at home be much more secure, from *Invasions* or *Insurrections*, than when left to the Protection of all the *standing Forces* ever allowed by Parliament. For then, every Man being enabled to defend his Property; all the Coasts of *Britain* will be covered with Soldiers; who fight not for Pay but for *Property;* for their *Families;* for their *Religion*, and *Liberties*. And if the Enemy should land, he must fight every Inch of Ground, and still find People in Arms against him wherever he goes; and upon every vanquished Spot recovered, ready to fight him over again.

But can this be done by an Army of 16 or 20000 Men? Can they defend this Island, without marching to more Places than one at the same time; and is that possible? What more can they do, than protract a *lingering Rebellion*, if the Enemy is nimble enough to get often out of their way? And should the King's Army be defeated!—I leave the Consequences of [9] such a *Defeat*, to the Mind and Heart, of every Man who loves his Country and his KING.

When *England* was threatned with the *Spanish* Invasion, in the Time of Queen *Elizabeth;*[15] when the Youth of *England* were trained up in the

---

Venner himself was executed on 19 January. Although a fiasco, the uprising had important consequences in that the following month Charles II created the Royal Guards (Schwoerer, *Armies*, pp. 79–81).

14. After the conclusion of the War of the Austrian Succession by the Treaty of Aix-la-Chapelle in October 1748.

15. In 1588; see above, p. 34, n. 83.

Use of Arms, they all took the Field in defence of their much-loved Sovereign; and She, (that incomparable QUEEN) had more to apprehend, from the Neglect of cultivating Lands, than from the Armies of *Spain:* For it was with great Difficulty, that any of her Subjects could be prevailed upon to return to their Farms. The Spirit of Loyalty, in the People of *England*, was not less for his present MAJESTY, during the late Rebellion;[16] when the Want of Vigilance, and Providence in his Ministers, rendered that Loyalty at once so conspicuous, and so reasonably serviceable.—But they are now a People undisciplined, and without Arms.—Nothing could be more evident to all Men, at that time, than the Want of a NATIONAL MILITIA.

[10] The People of this Island would soon be brought to the Use of Arms: They are naturally brave, and all their Sports are of a martial kind. And I do not think, the restoring a *Militia* upon the following Plan, could give any just cause of Suspicion, or Jealousy to the *Crown*, or *Crown Army*. For it will be as much under the Command of the Sovereign, as is the *standing Army* at present; no Regiment will be at Liberty to leave its County; and unless every Man in the Kingdom agrees upon a Revolt, it will be impossible. And that Any, in the Succession of this *Royal Family* will ever be forsaken, by the Nobility, and all the People of *England*, is un-imaginable.

An *Invasion*, as I observed before, will be impossible. There can be no Insurrections, nor Incursions, that will not be immediately stopt; and it seems to be the only Way to get rid of SMUGGLERS and *Highwaymen.*— Such an Increase of Power to the King, and Kingdom; such a perpetual Guard to the SUCCESSION *of our Princes*, and the Freedom of their Sub[11] jects; such a public Security against all Enemies, from an Army to a single Ruffian, will, (it is hoped,) meet with no Opposition, from any but Those, who would wish to see the present FAMILY indefensible, and without an Army.—*Party* is, or ought to be, out of the Question; and all Men, except the *Jacobites*, should unite in obtaining a Power for the Nation, that will make it rise again in Grandeur and Respect, to the Height it was at in the Reign of Queen *Elizabeth.*

16. The Jacobite Rebellion of 1745.

I cannot suppose, there will be any Jealousy between the *Militia* and the *Crown Army*, as the Latter will be perpetually recruited out of the Former; and so both be united together as one body of Men. And from the Regard I have to the *Officers* of the present Army, (many of whom are of great Rank and Fortune) I am unwilling to imagine, that they can be against such a *Plan;* which will for ever extinguish all the prejudice of the *People* to an *Army.*

SECT. II.
Of the ROMAN MILITIA.

It is often said, and it is true; (and, when it is not used for an Evasion, or Excuse, it is right,) That however plausible, or fine, *Schemes* upon Paper may appear to be; if they are not practicable, tho' they may entertain the Fancy, they can be of no service to Society.

The Example of former Ages; the Experience of other Men, recorded in History, (like Precedents in courts of Judicature) will have more power to persuade and influence, than all the most subtle Arguments that ever were contrived by the most ingenious Men.

Experiments are of as great Use in political, as they are in philosophical Matters; and no more Credit is due to a *political Scheme*, that is not supported by Facts; than to a System of Nature, formed from the Suppositions and Guesses of [13] a Man, who finds it much easier to tell you how he would have contrived Things, than to explain them as they are.

In favour of a *Militia* there is no want of Examples; almost every free State affords an instance of a NATIONAL MILITIA: For Freedom cannot be maintained without Power; and Men who are not in a Capacity to defend their *Liberties*, will certainly lose them; for when Power is not retained in their Service, it will never fail to be employed against Them.

The Battles of *Agincourt*, *Poictiers*, and *Cressy*, [17] abroad, and the several Wars at home, are proofs of the martial Powers of our old *Militia*. The irreproachable military Character of the *Swiss*, is an unanswerable argument for the bravery, utility, and honour, of a *national Militia*. And the

17. All notable English victories over the French; see above, p. 297, n. 93.

Glory of the *Roman* Arms, that subdued the World; not to a state of Slavery, but to the influence of *Roman* Laws, the participation of *Roman* Liberty, and the protection of the invincible ROMAN MILITIA; is too great to admit of any doubt, whether such an Example should be fol[14]lowed by a People, *who pretend to an equal share of Liberty*, and of no less ardour for military Exploits; and whose Boast it is, to have a form of Government that approaches nearer to the *Roman* Government, than any other in the World.[18]

The *Roman* Government was formed upon a MILITARY PLAN. Their first King was feigned to be the Son of *Mars*,[19] the God of War; and the People were admitted to a share in the Government, by the free choice of *Senators*. Men in Arms will enslave others, but not themselves. When they conquer for their General, they will plunder for themselves: They will hold the Lands of a conquered People, by the same Tenure that they at first acquired them, the Sword: And will sooner change their Commander, than lose their Possessions. In some of our antient *Councils;* (which are supposed to have given rise to the present COUNCILS of Parliament,) when *Laws* were proposed, the People were present; and gave their Votes, or Assent, by striking their [15] Swords or Lances upon their Shields.[20]—Whilst the *Roman* Army consisted of none but *Romans;* and of such *Romans* as were Men of Property and Worth, *Rome* must have continued Mistress of the World. But when Numbers only were consider'd;

---

18. In book 6 of his history Polybius had memorably praised the Roman constitution as a blend of the three simple political forms: democracy, aristocracy, and monarchy. In bk. 11, chap. 6 of the *Esprit des Lois* (1748) Montesquieu had reapplied this formula to the British constitution (*Oeuvres complètes*, pp. 586–90). A similar point had recently been made by Edward Spelman, in his *A Fragment out of the Sixth Book of Polybius* (1743): "*The great Advantages flowing from the happy Temper, and equal Mixture of the three Orders, for which he* [Polybius] *so justly celebrates the Roman Government, are all to be found in our own; with this Circumstance in our Favour, that our Situation, as an Island, forbids us either to fear, or aim at Conquests; by the gaining, as well as the suffering of which, that political Harmony is in Danger of being destroyed:* . . ." (sig. a 2ʳ).

19. In Roman mythology the founder and first king of Rome, Romulus, was the son of the Vestal virgin Rhea Silvia and Mars, the god of war.

20. See above, p. 224, n. 68.

when the Interest of a *Marius* or a *Caesar*,[21] who had bought the Army by augmenting their Wages, became more the concern of a *Roman Army*, than the Interest of *Rome* herself; when a *Roman* Army, (if *Caesar*'s Army may be called *Roman*) could be found, that would oppose the *Senate* and their *Fellow-Citizens;* whatever Actions, under particular Commanders, might be done abroad; *Tyranny* would be exercised at home: The General would be the King; the Army would elect, and depose him; and but few Kings would be permitted to die a natural Death: The Army must be kept in perpetual employ; and in time the Mistress of the World, be no more the Mistress of Herself.

That this was the State of the Army, at first, in the Decline of that vast Empire; [16] and then in the entire Ruin of it, is evident from every Writer: But whether that State did not rise, (as it fell,) from Banditti; from Men that had lost every Virtue but Ferocity, has been matter of doubt. *St. Evremont* represents the Origin of that great People in a very mean Light;[22] and Abbé *Vertot* begins his Account of the *Roman* Republic thus.—*Un Prince d'une naissance incertaine, nourri par une femme prosti-tuée, elevé par des bergers, et depuis devenu chef de Brigans, jetta les premiers*

21. See above, pp. 19–20, nn. 44 and 45.

22. Charles de Marguetel de Saint Denis de Saint-Évremond (1614–1703), soldier, essayist, and minor poet. In 1661 Saint-Évremond had fled to London, having fallen foul of Colbert, Louis XIV's new *surintendant des finances*. Apart from five years in Holland (1665–70), Saint-Évremond spent the rest of his life in England. It was during his period of residence in Holland that he published his only substantial historical work, *Réflexions sur les divers génies du peuple romain dans les divers temps de la République* (1665–70). In the opening chapters of this book Saint-Évremond deplored the primitivism of the early Romans:

> The *Genius* of this People was as rustical as it was wild; Dictators were sometimes taken from the Plough, to which they return'd again after their Expedition was over, not so much out of a preference of an innocent and undisturbed Condition, as because they had been accustomed to an unpolite and unsociable sort of Life. As for that Frugality which is so extreamly boasted of, it was not a retrenchment of Superfluities, or a voluntary Abstinence from Things agreeable, but a gross use of what they enjoyed. 'Tis true, they were not ambitious after Riches, because they did not understand them; they were content with a little, because they conceived no more; those Pleasures too they omitted, of which they had no idea. Notwithstanding, these old *Romans* have been taken for the most considerable Persons in the World; . . . (*The Works of M. de St. Evremont*, 2 vols. [1700], 1:11–12)

fondemens de la Capitale du Monde. Il y admit pour habitans Grecs. &c. la plûpart Pastres et Bandits.[23] But if this Author had attended more to *Polybius*,[24] he would have had a more thorough Knowledge of the *Roman Senate;* and if he had followed *Dionysius*,[25] in his account of the Origin of *Rome*, he had given his Readers a more favourable Impression of the Men, who first laid the Foundations of the *Roman* City, and the *Roman* Government. Modern Writers of the *Roman* History, have made too little use of the *Greek* Authors; which is the more sur[17]prizing, as the *Greeks* professedly wrote for the Use of Foreigners; and mention many Circumstances, omitted by the *Latin* Authors; and have been translated, with some Diligence, into *French:* Tho' I hope a Countryman of our own[26] will soon do more justice to *Dionysius*, who is by much the best Writer upon the *Roman* Antiquities. He was well provided with Materials; he was diligent, accurate, and faithful in his Relations; an able Critic upon other Authors, and very correct in his own Writings: Tho' it must be confest, that he has shewn more the fine Writer, than the scrupulous Historian, in the several Speeches he has made for his *Roman* Orators: But then it must also be acknowledged, that his Reader will be better informed of the true State of the Times, and the Circumstances of Action upon which the Speech is planned, than from all other Writings, Records, or Monuments now remaining in the World.—I could not speak of *Dionysius*, without giving this Character of him; for as I have always been an admirer of the severe [18] Virtue, and amazing Grandeur of old *Rome;* so I have found the best Account of them in his

23. René Aubert de Vertot d'Auberf (1655–1735), historian. "A Prince of uncertain Birth, nursed by a Prostitute, brought up by Shepherds, and afterwards the Leader of a Gang of Robbers, laid the first Foundations of the Capital of the World . . . and admitted for it's [*sic*] Inhabitants all sorts of Men, and from all Parts, *Greeks, Latins, Albans* and *Tuscans*, most of them Shepherds and Robbers; . . ." (Abbé Vertot, *The History of the Revolutions that Happened in the Government of the Roman Republic*, trans. John Ozell, 2 vols. [1720], 1:3).

24. I.e., to bk. 6 of Polybius's history; see above, p. 547, n. 18.

25. Dionysius of Halicarnassus (fl. ca. 25 B.C.), author of an early history of Rome intended as an introduction to Polybius.

26. Edward Spelman (d. 1767), writer and translator. Spelman's translation of *The Roman Antiquities of Dionysius Halicarnassensis* would be published in four volumes in 1758.

Writings.[27]—"This CITY was no sooner built, (says that Author) than it produced a thousand Virtues in the Men, who, for Worship of the Gods, for Acts of Justice, for the constant Practice of the greatest Temperance through Life, and for Deeds of martial Strife; no City, whether *Greek* or Barbarian, ever produced more excellent Men."

And towards the End of his first Book: "It is not a late Flow of prosperous Events, that has been the Mistress to teach them the advantage of Friendship, and the knowledge of every useful Art: Nor is it since that Time only, in which they first entertained a passion for MARINE AFFAIRS, and overthrew the States of *Macedon* and *Carthage*; but in all times, ever since They were a People, they have lived after the *Grecian* manner; and are not more curious or careful now, than they have [19] always been, of every Thing that is excellent.

"I can prove this by a thousand Circumstances; by many evident Tokens; and by the Testimony of Men who deserve to be believed: But I refer them to another Treatise."

Is it possible, that a parcel of *Banditti* could have established so perfect a Form of Government, modelled upon the finest parts of the *Grecian Plans;* contrived to promote Order, and Virtue; to prevent Irregularity, and Poverty, and Vice; to secure Liberty to Themselves, and communicate it to the World; and excite to every brave and patriot Action?—No: There is too much of Wisdom, of Virtue, and Valour in the Enterprize and Actions of ROMULUS and his Companions, ever to suffer me to think of them as a Band of Robbers, or outlaw'd Men of Violence; unacquainted with, and uninfluenced by, the best of social Laws. For of all *Politics,* (says *Dionysius*) suited to all the Circumstances of Peace or War; [20] this of *Rome*, (I maintain) *to have been the most perfect.*[28]

Romulus was not King, till he had the Voice of the People; and their choice had been confirmed by Religious Rites. He was rather the *first* MAGISTRATE in the service of the State, than the MASTER of it; not a *Tyrant*, but a *Father to the People:* And he chose rather to serve with Men, who were free, than to command those who were Slaves; to share the

27. Dionysius of Halicarnassus, I.v.3 and I.xc.1–2.
28. Dionysius of Halicarnassus, I. iii. 5.

Government with the People, than to be absolute. In order to this, he divided the People into three *Tribes*, and each *Tribe* into ten *Curiae;* (each *Curia* consisting of a hundred Men.) He then directed each *Tribe* to chuse three Men, each *Curia* three; but the King to chuse no more than one, to form a *Senate* of a hundred Men, who, from their Age, their Family, their Fortunes, and a noble Concern for the Success of their infant State, were called the ROMAN FATHERS.

Besides this, there was another distribution of the *Romans,* into *Patricians,* [21] and *Plebeians.* Such as had no Experience or Knowledge of political Affairs; and, for want of Riches, could not be at Leisure to attend upon such Employments, were excused from serving in the Magistracy; at the same Time that they served the State in as useful, tho' a more humble Capacity, in Tillage, and Pasture. These industrious Men of Labour were under the Protection of the PATRICIANS, whom they acknowledged as their Patrons; and to whom they ever after became *Clients* for advice, as well as Suitors for justice; which, in the virtuous Ages of the Republic, they were never denied.

Besides, the Excellency of the Form of Government, there were three remarkable and concurring Causes, of the amazing and immediate Progress of the *Roman* Grandeur. One was *the Reception of Strangers; Rome* being an Asylum, to all who suffered in other Cities. Another Cause was, *the manner of obtaining Wives for their Young Men,* by surprizing the Women, who came from the neighbouring Cities and Country to a public Shew, [22] (a Measure that was become necessary; these People having refused to give their Daughters in Marriage to the *Romans:*) But when the young Women were surprized and taken, they were not violated; but kept till the next Day, and then made *Roman* Wives. The Third Cause of the extended Greatness of the *Roman* Empire was, *their Lenity to conquered Nations.* One proof of the Virtues of the first Inhabitants of *Rome,* is the great Increase of their Numbers. At first they did not exceed 3000 Foot, and 300 Horse; but in 37 Years, (and so long reigned *Romulus*) they were increased to 46000 Foot, and 3000 Horse. And such was the Harmony, arising from the Manners introduced and established by *Romulus;* that, for 120 Years, no blood of Citizens was spilt, no Murders were committed, tho' there had been many and great Controversies between the Magistrates and People. And tho' *Divorces* were allowed by Law, there was no Instance of any One for 520 Years, (says *Dionysius;*) and the Man who first took advantage of the [23] Law, and divorced his Wife, tho' a Man of Family, (not only justified, but in a manner compelled to it by the *Censors*) was hated by the People.

If some part of what is said, in this Section, seems little to the purpose of a *Militia;* I must tell my Reader, that if I admit the Charge, I shall still think it was to my purpose, to vindicate the Character of a People, who, in several Respects, my Country-men resemble; who are, in most Things, worthy their Imitation; and whose MILITIA and MILITARY HONOURS, I propose, as the greatest and best Example that can be followed.

The *Roman* manner of making Levies, is described, by *Polybius,*[29] to have been as follows.—At the beginning of the Year, when the new Consuls made their appearance, they appointed the military *Tribunes;* taking fourteen from those *Equites*[30] who had served five Years in the Army; and ten from the Foot who had served ten Campaigns. For, in all, the Horse were to serve ten, and the Foot twenty [24] Campaigns, by the time they were forty-six Years of Age. They took up Arms when they were about seventeen Years old; and if they had served twenty Campaigns, in thirty Years, they could not be obliged to serve again; they were then *Emeriti:* And if they were desired to serve as *Evocati;*[31] they were greatly respected, and not employed in the laborious or severer Duties of a *Soldier,* but kept as a Guard for the principal Standard. Such was the treatment of *Old Soldiers* in the *Roman* Army. But if they had not served twenty Campaigns, in the time they were forty six Years of Age, they might be compelled to serve till they were fifty, but not after that age.

Among the *Athenians*, the Youth did not enter the Service till eighteen Years of Age. For the two first Years they served for Guard and Garrison at home; and their Service ended when they were forty Years old.

---

29. Polybius, VI.19.

30. I.e., cavalrymen, or knights; see below, pp. 554–55.

31. Literally, those who have been called forth; the term of distinction applied to those soldiers in the Roman army who had served out their time but who had nevertheless been called upon to serve as veterans on account of their prowess.

Polybius, in his Account of the *Roman Military*, excludes such as had no Property, from serving in the Army: I ex[25]cept, (says He) those who are not rated at 40 *Drachmae*. Under this rate were the *Proletarii* and *Capiticensi*,[32] who never served unless in extreme Exigency: For Property is the safest pledge of Love and Duty to our Country.

They who were not admitted into the *Land Service*, were received into the *Marine*, and manned the *Roman* Fleet. It was a great and mutual Advantage, to both the State and the Army, that no Man could be admitted into any civil Employment, who had not served ten complete Years in the Army.

The manner of the *Roman Levies* was this: The *Consuls* proclaimed the Day, on which all the *Romans*, of military Age, were obliged to appear. This was annual. The appointed Day being come, the military People from all parts arrived in *Rome;* and thronging to the *Capitol*, the Junior *Tribunes* (who because taken from the *Horse*, when they had served five Years, were therefore called *Junior;* with respect to those taken from the *Foot*, where they were obliged to serve ten [26] Campaigns, before they could be chosen *Tribunes*) divided themselves into four Parts, according to their usual Division of their Forces into four *Legions;* in such order, (to prevent Jealousies) as the People or Commanders should determine. The

32. Those of the Roman commons who were humblest and of smallest means, and who reported no more than fifteen hundred asses at the census, were called *proletarii*, but those who were rated as having no property at all, or next to none, were termed *capite censi*, or "counted by head." And the lowest rating of the *capite censi* was three hundred and seventy-five asses. But since property and money were regarded as a hostage and pledge of loyalty to the State, and since there was in them a kind of guarantee and assurance of patriotism, neither the *proletarii* nor the *capite censi* were enrolled as soldiers except in some time of extraordinary disorder, because they had little or no property and money. However, the class of *proletarii* was somewhat more honourable in fact and in name than that of the *capite censi;* for in times of danger to the State, when there was a scarcity of men of military age, they were enrolled for hasty service, and arms were furnished them at public expense. And they were called, not *capite censi*, but by a more auspicious name derived from their duty and function of producing offspring, for although they could not greatly aid the State with what small property they had, yet they added to the population of their country by their power of begetting children. (Aulus Gellius, *Noctes Atticae*, XVI.10)

first four were assigned to the first *Legion;* the three next to the second; the other four to the third; and the three last to the fourth Legion. The two first of the senior *Tribunes* to the first Legion; the next three to the second; the two following to the third; and the three last to the fourth *Legion.* The Distribution of the *Tribunes* ended, in such manner, that each Legion might have an equal Number of equal Commanders. The *Tribunes* of each Legion taking their Seats at a proper distance from each other, (to prevent Confusion) the *Tribes* were called out by Lot; and then, (according to *Lipsius,*[33] in his Commentary upon *Polybius*) each *Tribe* divided into *Centuries;* and from each *Century,* the Soldiers according to their Rank and *Census,* were called forth by Name [27] from the Rolls or Tables, which gave an account of their Age and Property.

Out of this *Century* were four young Men chosen, as much alike as could be found. These being produced, the *Tribunes* of the first Legion chose one; of the second another; of the next a third; and, of the last, the fourth Man. Then four more being in like manner drawn out, the choice of the first Man was made by the *Tribunes* of the second; and of the last Man, by the *Tribunes* of the first Legion. After this, four others being drawn out, the *Tribunes* of the third Legion chose the first Man, and the Tribunes of the second Legion the last Man. And in this equal manner of Rotation they proceeded, that the choice of Men, of each Legion, might be equal: Tho' there are Instances of *Tribunes* having taken their Men by Lot, instead of chusing them in the manner described by *Polybius.*

After this particular Description of Levies for the *Foot* Service, I shall be very short in my account of the *Roman Cavalry,*

[28] *Romulus* had 300 Horse at the beginning; 3000 at the end of his Reign. But when the *Census* was established, all who were estimated as worth 400 *Sestertia,* were admitted into the Order of *Equites;* and if there was no Objection to their Character, they were presented with a Ring, and a Horse; and served in the Cavalry. Once in five Years, (that is, every *Lustrum,*) there was a *Census* and *Recensio,* or review of every Man's

33. See Justus Lipsius, *De Militia Romana* (Antwerp, 1596), bk. 1, dialogue 3, pp. 18–28. Cf. Machiavelli, *The Art of War,* bk. 1 (Machiavelli, *Chief Works,* 2:589–90).

Fortune and Circumstances; and, each Year, a *Probatio*, or Enquiry into the Behaviour of the *Equites*, and the Condition of their Horses and Arms. But nothing could exceed the Magnificence of that public review of the *Cavalry*, in the *Forum*, which was called *Transvectio;* when all were cloathed in Purple and Gold, and crowned with *Olive;* a glorious Sight, (says *Dionysius*)[34] and worthy the Majesty of so great a City! Nor would it be a less glorious Sight, to see the Youth of this Nation make the like Majestic Appearance. As no inconsiderable part of the *Roman* art of War is [29] retained in the Modern Service, and therefore known; and what is dropt, has been rendered useless by the Alterations in warlike Instruments; I shall not think I leave this pleasing subject of a *Roman* Militia too soon; if, I close my short account of it, with observing, that if a *Roman* Soldier was punished, it was oftner with Disgrace than with Death; that *Rewards* out-numbered *Punishments;* and that he was more likely to be influenced by Those, than aw'd by These.[35]

Besides the Triumphs, *Beneficiarii*, and the Rewards of several sorts of Crowns; there were *Vexillae* or Banners, the *Hasta Pura*, the *Phalerae Torques*, and *Armillae*. [36] And he that is a Stranger to the Effect of public Favours, to distinguish Merit, is a Stranger to the human Heart and

34. Dionysius of Halicarnassus, IV.xxii.1.

35. Gibbon would form a less charitable view of Roman military discipline: "The centurions were authorized to chastise with blows, the generals had a right to punish with death; and it was an inflexible maxim of Roman discipline, that a good soldier should dread his officers far more than the enemy. From such laudable arts did the valour of the Imperial troops receive a degree of firmness and docility, unattainable by the impetuous and irregular passions of barbarians" (Gibbon, *Decline and Fall*, 1:40).

36. All either Roman military insignia or rewards for valor. On the Roman triumph, see above, p. 17, n. 37. The *beneficiarii* were elite soldiers exempted from menial duties on account of their valor, although the term may also refer to grants of land made to military veterans:

In the Romane empire lands were giuen vnto souldiors of good desert for them to take the profit of during their liues, in reward of their good seruice and valour, which were called *Beneficia*, and they which had them, *Beneficiarij*, or as wee tearme them, Benefices, and Beneficed men. *Alexander Seuerus* graunted vnto such souldiors heires that they might enjoy those lands and commendams, vpon condition also, that they themselues should serue as had their fathers, otherwise not. *Constantine* also the great gaue vnto his

Passions, tho' of how little value in itself the token of the Favour is. A
Leaf may serve as well as a Crown, and with equal Honour; till, by
misapplication of the Favour to unworthy Men, it is prostituted, and
therefore sinks beneath the acceptance of a brave and honest Man: [30]
In which case, whether it be a Kingdom, or a Commission, it is all one.
Let the *Militia* of *Rome*, and the brave Actions of the *Roman* Soldiery, be
opposed to Him who shall speak of a *Militia* with contempt. Arms and
War are not objects of Laughter: But if by great Abuse and Neglect, a
National Militia, tho' once the Terror of the World, should ever become the Ridicule of Those who ought to serve in it; let it be the concern
of every other Man to restore it to its antient Glory: And how this may
be done, with allowance for a Crown Army, without much detriment
to the Gentlemen who now serve in that Army; and for the mutual Security of the King, and the People, against all Invasions, Civil Wars, or
Foreign Insults, shall be shewn in the next Section.

SECT. III.

The proper Plan of a Militia *for this Country, proposed.*

After all that has been said, of Militia in general, and of the *Roman
Militia* in particular: Or if we survey the Conduct and Example of Any,
or of all the great and free Nations, that have ever existed within the
Memory of Time; it will not, (I persuade myself,) be denied, that the
only Persons proper to be intrusted with Arms, for the defence of the *Liberties*, for the conservation of the *Government*, and for extending the
Glory of a brave and free People; are the Men Who have Property[37] as

---

captaines that had well deserued of him, certaine lands for them to liue
vpon during the tearme of their life. (Knolles, *Turkes*, p. 598)

See also Harrington, *Oceana*, pp. 44–45, 57, and Neville, *Plato Redivivus*, p. 110.
On the various sorts of crown, see below, p. 567, n. 43. The *hasta pura* (a spear un-
stained with blood) was awarded to a soldier who had wounded an enemy in single
combat. The *phalerae* were medals worn on the breast. The *torques* were honorific
neck chains or collars. The *armillae* were honorific bracelets. For commentary, see
Polybius, VI.xxxix.

37. The prejudice that the possession of property was necessary for the shaping
of the virtuous civic personality is a cardinal element in the early modern

well as Liberty to secure; and who are connected with the Government, by chusing a Body of Men for their Representatives, without whose CONSENT no Laws can be made. This was once the great prerogative of *Romans*, in their purest Age; [32] and now is, (and may it ever continue to be!) the priviledge of *Britons*.

I shall therefore propose, in the first place, That every Man in *Great Britain*, at a certain Age; and possessed of, or connected with a certain degree of Property, shall be of the *Militia;* those only excepted, whose Professions, or different Occupations in the various Services of the State, ought to exempt them from any Military Service; and those whose Quality, or considerable Property demands their being excused from, at least, personal Service. These therefore excepted, it is proposed, that every Man in *Great Britain*, from seventeen to forty-six Years of Age, having forty Shillings a Year in Land, or under fifty Pounds a Year; or who is worth forty Pounds in personal Estate, and under 600 *l.* and his Son or Sons, being of the proper Age; and all those not having forty Shillings a Year, or forty Pounds in Money or Goods, who have *Votes* for Members to serve in Parliament, and their Sons, of the proper Age, to be of the FOOT. And Persons [33] having an Estate of fifty Pounds a Year in Land, and under 300 *l.* a Year; or who are worth 600 *l.* in personal Estate, and under 3600 *l.* (and their Sons,) to be of the HORSE. And He who has 300 *l.* a Year in Land, and under 500 *l.* or has 3600 *l.* in personal Estate, and under 6000 *l.* may have it in his choice to serve personally in the *Horse;* or furnish a Man for the *Foot* Service, at his own proper Expence. But every one who has in possession 500 *l.* a Year, and upwards; or a personal Estate of 6000 *l.* and upwards; shall be obliged, at his own Expence, to furnish a Man, and Horse, for the *Horse* Service. Those proposed to be excepted from personal Service, out of this general Rule, are as follow:

---

republicanism associated with Machiavelli; for commentary, see J. G. A. Pocock, *The Machiavellian Moment: Florentine Political Thought and the Atlantic Republican Tradition* (Princeton: Princeton University Press, 1975). It had been introduced into seventeenth-century English political thought primarily by Harrington (Harrington, *Oceana*, pp. 8–42). The dissemination and broader ramifications of the prejudice in eighteenth-century England are discussed by John Barrell, in his *English Literature in History 1730–80: An Equal, Wide Survey* (London: Hutchinson, 1983).

Peers and their Sons; Privy Councellors; Members of the House of Commons and their Sons; Knights of all degrees; Justices of the Peace who *act;* all the Clergy; the Gentlemen of the Law; Practitioners in Physic; all Persons employed in the Service of the ROYAL FAMILY, or the Go[34]vernment; and all such as by their Religion, (being Papists) render themselves incapable of serving.[38] All Civil-Magistrates, Parish-Officers, Sailors, Sea-faring Men, Fishermen, and Watermen.

Having described the Persons who are to compose this GENERAL MILITIA; the next thing that offers itself is, the Necessity of a REGISTER, by which the number of our fighting Men, (qualified as above) may appear: And this I shall propose to be effected in the following Manner.

That the *Constables* of every Parish be appointed to make *Returns,* every Year, to the Head Constables in every Hundred; and to the *Mayors* and other Head Officers in every City and Borough; of all the Men in their several Parishes, under such Circumstances of Age, and Fortune, as before mentioned. These *Returns* to be transmitted by the Head Constables, Mayors, and other Head Officers to the Sessions, there to be allow'd; and from the Sessions to the *Lord Lieutenant,* and *Custos Rotulorum,*[39] by his Officer, the [35] Clerk of the Peace. By this means the number of fighting Men, in every Parish in *Great Britain,* will, every Year, appear upon Record.

The Manner I shall propose, of training these Men shall be, that the *Church-Wardens* of every Parish, be obliged to call out all the fighting Men of their respective Parishes to EXERCISE, the first Sunday of every Month, before or after Divine Service; and the Church-Wardens to have the keeping of all the ARMS belonging to their respective Parishes; and to deliver the same out to the Men on the Days appointed for their Exercise; after which they shall be re-delivered to them, or their Officers; and

38. Because as Roman Catholics they were unable to comply with the provisions of the Test Act (1673), which made the receiving of holy communion according to the rites of the Church of England a necessary precondition for holding public office.

39. The principal justice of the peace in a county (so called because he had safekeeping of the rolls, or records of the public sessions).

proper Allowance made for Workmen to keep their *Arms* in order. But above all, severe Penalties ought to be laid on all Church-Wardens, as well as on all Parishioners, who should, (without a lawful Excuse, to be attested by the Minister; and, if required, sworn before one of his Majesty's Justices of the Peace,) ABSENT themselves from these monthly Exercises. Those of [36] the *Horse* should be oblig'd to find, at their own Expence, a Horse, Saddle, Bridle, and Boots; their Arms to be furnish'd by the Parish, in the same manner as has been directed for the *Foot*. Besides this monthly Exercise of the Parishes, there should be, at least, one GENERAL MUSTER of every County in a Year; at any place in each respective County, as shall be judged most proper and convenient by the Lord Lieutenant: And as this *general Muster* will be found by the following *Plan*, to be of the greatest Consequence; the Penalties for *Absence* should be much higher, than those inflicted for Absence from the Parish monthly Exercises.

The GENERAL MILITIA establish'd, I come to the most useful Part of this Scheme, which is, to propose the manner of forming a select or standing MILITIA, by *County Regiments*, (Horse and Foot) to be chosen out of the general *Militia*. And,

First, To proportion, as near as possible, to the Property of each respective [37] County, the number of Men they are each to maintain for their standing *Militia;* I shall propose, that one Man in ten be chosen by Lot or Ballot out of the general *Militia* of every County; to be oblig'd to serve in the standing *Militia* of every said County; by which means, (I think) every County will maintain an equal number of Men, in Proportion to its Extent and Property; because, as all the *Militia* is compos'd of Men of some Property, the number of such Men will be equal to the Property and Extent of each respective County.

Secondly, That these Men, so chosen, be formed into two REGIMENTS in every County; one of *Light-Horse*, and one of *Foot*, which are to be divided into Companies and Troops; so that, altho' every County in *Great Britain* will have two Regiments, yet the Regiments of the larger and richer Counties, will be compos'd of a greater number of Troops and Companies; and, of course, have a greater number of Men to maintain, than the lesser and poorer Counties.

[38] *Thirdly*, That this proportion of Men, to each County, be fix'd at the first Establishment of the standing *Militia*, never to be alter'd; for it would be endless to be adding or diminishing every Year, according to the number of fighting Men, who should happen to be upon every annual *Register*.

Fourthly, That these County Regiments have an Uniform, and be paid by the County.

Fifthly, That the time of their Service be two Years; to be reckoned from the time of their being chosen out of the general *Militia;* at the Expiration of which, each Man may demand his Discharge; and upon his return home, to the Parish from whence he was chosen, be exempted from all *Militia* Duty, for one whole Year; except he chuses to attend as a *Voluntier*. And as this two Years Service, (besides Deaths and other Accidents) will naturally cause great Vacancies; the manner of recruiting them should be as plain and easy as possible; which, (I think,) is answer'd in every [39] respect, when I propose the *County Regiments* to be recruited out of the general Militia, assembled together at the annual County *Muster;* or whenever else the *Lord Lieutenant* thinks proper to appoint a *general Muster:* Which, perhaps, will be sometimes found necessary, more than once a Year; especially in time of War, threaten'd Invasion, or actual Rebellion.

Sixthly, The method of chusing Those, who are to serve in the *County Regiments*, should be by Lot; much in the same Manner as was proposed above, at the first establishing these *Regiments:* Only, instead of every tenth Man, it should be the exact number, (more or less) than every tenth; which the Regiments, at that time, should happen to want; and these to be drawn, by Lot or Ballot, out of the whole number of the *Militia*, present at the general Muster. But in order to make this Military Service as little burdensome to the People, as possible; I shall here propose, that if any Man, whose [40] Trade or Calling depends on his personal Attendance, and whose Family depends on his Trade, should chance to draw the Lot for entering into the Service of the *County Regiments*, he shall have it in his Option to substitute another in his Stead; provided the Person so substituted, be equally qualified as to Height, Age, &c. with himself.

Seventhly, The head Quarters of the *County Regiments,* to be, in or near, the County Town of each County.

Eighthly, Neither the *general Militia,* nor the *County Regiments,* or any part of them, so as to make a Body of armed Men, to march out of their respective Counties UPON ANY PRETEXT, OR BY ANY COMMAND WHAT-SOEVER; upon pain of being declared ENEMIES to their Country, and guilty of HIGH TREASON.

Ninthly, A reasonable Standard, for Height, should be fixed, under which no Man should be admitted into the County Regiments, notwith-standing he draws a Lot for such admission: And, in this [41] case, the Lot drawn by a Person not of the standard Height, should be thrown in again to the common Heap.

Tenthly, The *Lord Lieutenant* of each County, to have the Command of the whole *Militia,* (under the KING, which is always to be understood) within the County: And to be *Colonel* of each Regiment of Horse and Foot, without Pay; and to appoint the Officers of each, who are to be paid by the County.

Eleventhly, If any *Lord Lieutenant* attempt to persuade, or presume to command, the whole, or any part of the GENERAL MILITIA; or of the County Regiments, so as to make a body of armed Men, to march out of the County; He shall be guilty of HIGH TREASON.

N. B. All *Cities,* which are *Counties* in themselves, are, by these Pro-posals, to be under the same Regulations in regard to their *Militia,* as the Counties; the chief Magistrate of each City having the same Power and Command, over the *Militia,* as the *Lord Lieutenant* of a County.

[42] But the great METROPOLIS, the Cities of *London* and *Westminster,* having a *Militia,* which they may at any time render useful, are left in the full Power of improving and commanding it. And I flatter myself with the hopes, of seeing the *Magistrates* of these Corporations exerting them-selves, in restoring the Credit of their antient *Militia;*[40] that, in cases of sudden Emergency, they may make use of their own natural Strength, and constitutional Enforcement of *Obedience* to the LAWS; and begin,

---

40. For the former prowess of the London trained bands, see above, p. 37, n. 92.

early, to set the great Example to every other City in the Kingdom, of instructing a warlike Generation of Men (once more) in the *Use* of ARMS; in defence of Themselves, their Liberty, Religion, Government, and Laws.

This new Species of MILITIA, by *County Regiments* being established, BRITAIN will boast a *standing Army*, which, so far from endangering the LIBERTIES of the People, will be their greatest Security; and instead of raising Jealousies and Fears, in *Britons*, will restore their antient GLORY, and once more *awe* the *World*.

[43] If this Encomium is thought too great, I hope I shall be allowed, (at least) to declare, that I think it is the only safe, useful, and glorious *Militia*, (or, if you please, STANDING ARMY, for such in reality it is,) which a free People can have, a good Prince desire, or a mixt Government endure. Not that I think a *Crown Army*, (for by that Name I must beg leave to call, what is at present distinguished by the Name of a *standing Army*) inconsistent with such a *Militia;* for it will be the Root, (whenever occasion calls upon our PRINCES to lead forth their Armies) immediately to draw to itself, from the *County Regiments*, and *general Militia*, Numbers equal to any service for which they may be required. In what manner these *Draughts* are to be made; how the *Crown Army* is to be formed and recruited, out of the County Regiments, I shall shew, after I have observed, that the *Crown Army* should never consist of more, (in time of Peace) than the Guards, the foreign Garrisons, and [44] the necessary Regiments for the *Plantations*,[41] and *Ireland*.

And, *First*, For recruiting the Regiments of the *Crown Army*. This I shall propose to be by LOT, once a Year in time of *Peace;* and, in time of *War*, as often as shall be judged necessary, in manner following:

The Names of all the *Counties* in *Great Britain*, and all the *Cities*, (being Counties in themselves) should be writ each upon a slip of Paper, to be rolled up, and put into an *Urn* or *Vase*. In like manner, the *Names* of all the marching Regiments of Horse, Dragoons, and Foot, to be distinguished by the Names of their respective Colonels; the four Troops of Horse Guards, by the Names of their Commanders; and the three Regiments of Foot Guards, to be distinguished by their Battalions: All These

---

41. I.e., the colonies (in this case, presumably the American colonies).

should be writ (severally) upon slips of Paper, to be rolled up, and put into a different *Urn* or *Vase*; in order to be drawn out against the Names of the Counties; in the same manner as [45] the *Numbers* are drawn out of one Wheel, against the Prizes and Blanks in the other, in our State Lotteries. The number of Rolls of Paper, in each *Vase*, ought to be the same; the deficiency of number, in the *Vase* where the Names of the Regiments are put, should be made up by *Blanks*. When the Rolls of Paper are thus disposed of, in their respective *Vases*, the two Persons, appointed for that purpose, should proceed to draw the *Lots;* beginning with him who is to draw from the *Vase* where the Names of the Counties are; and having taken one out, he is to read aloud the *Name* of the County he finds writ upon the Paper He has drawn; then the Person at the opposite *Vase* draws a *Ticket* in like manner from thence. If it prove a *Blank*, he declares it such; if not, he is to read aloud the Name of the Regiment, Troop, or Battalion, he finds written upon the *Ticket*. And in this manner they are to proceed, till all the *Tickets* or Rolls of Paper are drawn out of each *Vase*.

[46] During the course of this *Lottery*, (as I may, I think, not very improperly call it) a Clerk should be ready, to take down in writing, the Names of the *Counties* as they are drawn; with the Names of the *Regiments*, *Troops*, or *Battalions*, opposite to them, as *they* happen to be drawn: By which Method, you will be able to see, at one Glance, from what particular County every respective Regiment, Troop, or Battalion in the *Crown Army* is to be recruited. When the *Lottery* is over, and the Clerk has prepared his Paper, by writing the Names of the Counties and Regiments, in the manner before mentioned; the Paper so prepared, should immediately be given to the *Secretary at War*, who, I think, ought always to be present at these *Ballotings*; as well as One of the *Representatives* of each County or City; in order to prevent any Injustice or Unfairness, which may possibly happen upon these occasions, either to the *Army*, or the *Counties:* And He, the Secretary at War, should as soon as possible inform every *Lord Lieutenant*, and every chief [47] *Magistrate*, whose County or City is allotted to recruit any Regiment, Troop, or Battalion. Upon receiving this notice, (from the Secretary at War) every such *Lord Lieutenant*, or chief *Magistrate*, should send Orders to the Officers of their respective Regiments, to be in readiness with their Men, to receive the

recruiting Officers from the Regiment of the *Crown Army*, appointed to take recruits from that particular County or City, according to the destination of the *Lots*: And the Day appointed by the *Lord Lieutenant*, or chief *Magistrate*, for the recruiting Officers to repair to the County Town or City, in order to recruit their several *Corps*, should be within three Days, (at most) of the annual Muster of the GENERAL MILITIA for that County or City; in order that the Deficiencies, (occasioned by these *Draughts*, to be taken out of the *County Regiments*) may be immediately made up from the general *Militia:* For it is a necessary and unalterable part of this Scheme, always [48] to keep the select *Militia*, or *County Regiments*, compleat.

The manner of Draughting the Men, out of the *County Regiments*, for the Service of the CROWN, should be the same as from the *general Militia* to the County Regiments, *viz.* by *Lot* or *Ballot*. The Men so chosen, to enter immediately into the Service and Pay of the CROWN; to leave their *Arms* with the Regiment they are taken from; to receive one *Guinea* for enlisting Money, from the recruiting Officer; and to engage for three Years, if in time of *Peace;* if in time of *War*, for seven Years certain, or till disbanded. At their return Home, after having fulfilled their Engagements, every Man, producing a *Certificate* from his proper *Officer*, of having served his full time, (and every Man shall have a RIGHT to demand of his *Officer*, at the Expiration of the three, or the seven Years, or at the time of his being disbanded, such a *Certificate*) shall be exempted two whole Years from all *Militia* duty; if he has performed the [49] three Years Service only: But if his Service has been in time of War, or for seven Years, then he shall be released from all Military Duty whatever, during the remainder of his Life; except He should chuse to act as a *Voluntier*, upon any occasion, or in case of Invasions or Insurrections.

The method of raising *New Regiments*, or increasing the *Crown Army*, which I am next to speak of, (and which, according to this *Plan*, can only be in case of a foreign War design'd, a Rebellion breaking out, or an Invasion threatened,) I shall propose to be by *Lottery*, the same, as to the manner of drawing, as was before proposed for recruiting the *Crown Army;* only upon this occasion, where entire New Regiments are to be raised, the Names of two *Counties* or *Cities*, should be writ upon each TICKET, or slip of Paper; in order to be drawn out against a single

Regiment: And the reason of this, to me, seems plain; because, tho' a single County or City, may be very sufficient to recruit a *Regiment;* I hardly [50] think One alone, (without draining the *Militia* too much,) would be able to raise an entire New Regiment. The *Lords Lieutenants,* and *Chief Magistrates,* when, upon this occasion, they have received the proper Notice from the *Secretary at War;* must not wait, (if at any distance of Time,) for the annual Muster of the *Militia;* but must order, as soon as possible, an EXTRAORDINARY *General Muster* of the *Militia;* and, three Days before that General Muster, must be the Time appointed for the Officers of the new intended Regiments, to repair to the several County Towns and Cities, in order to raise their New *Regiments.*

Tho' this our great METROPOLIS, the Cities of *London* and *Westminster,* were excepted out of the *Scheme,* (so far as related to the manner of their raising, disciplining, and governing their respective *Militia;*) yet it was never intended, that they should be debarred from the great Honour of defending, with their Arms, their KING and COUNTRY, (when properly called upon,) by entering into [51] the *Crown Army;* and from taking an equal share in this Service, with the rest of their Countrymen, in proportion to their great Property and Numbers.

The Proportion I propose therefore, for *London,* should be, as to four Counties; and for *Westminster,* as to two. For example, in the *Lottery* for recruiting, the Name of the City of *London* should be wrote four times, upon four separate TICKETS or Lots; that of the City of *Westminster* twice, upon different Papers; in the *Lottery* for raising New Regiments, *London* to be wrote twice, and *Westminster* once.

AN ADDITION

To the Plan, *for a* MILITIA, *concerning* MILITARY REWARDS *and* PUNISHMENTS.

Military *Rewards* and *Punishments* have been thought necessary in every Army, in every Country; for which reason, I shall beg leave to say something concerning Them in this place: And *First,* as to *Punishments;* which, I am afraid, have [52] been more severe in the *Armies* of this free Nation, (tho' our Discipline has generally been the worst,) than in the *Armies* of any other Country in the World, under the most arbitrary

Government. But as what regards the *Punishments* of the *Crown Army*, will annually come under the Eye of the *Parliament*, in the MUTINY BILL; I shall propose nothing here, in regard to Them; contenting myself with hoping, that the *Parliament*, (if this PLAN should take place, by which means, the greatest Part of the *Crown Army* would be composed of *Freeholders*, and Men of some Property) will not think fitting to extend Military *Punishments* to Life or Limb, in time of Peace; upon such an Army, so composed. But as to the *County Regiments*, it is absolutely necessary, that the *Punishments* there should be never any Other than *Disgrace*, or *Pecuniary* MULCTS:[42] The proportion of which, according to the Crime, to be judged by their own *Courts Martial;* and confirmed, or disapproved, by the *Lord Lieutenant*, or *Chief Magistrate*.

[53] Coming now to speak of REWARDS, for Military Virtue, I am afraid We shall find, that our *Rewards*, of this kind, have fallen as far short of all other Nations, as our *Punishments* have exceeded Them in Severity. But notwithstanding the great Neglect we have been guilty of, in not giving suitable *Rewards* to Military Merit; and notwithstanding the great Courage of our People, and the great Success which has attended the *British* Arms, upon almost all Occasions, without these *Rewards:* Yet I can't help thinking, that *that* COURAGE, (great as it is,) would have been more exerted; *that* Success would have been more certain, had the active Spirit of *Britons* been kept awake, by a Prospect of some GRATUITY, to be given by their grateful Country, at the end of their Toils and Dangers; and their native Courage been properly rouzed, by a laudable Emulation of attaining some *Marks of Distinction* for superiour Military VIRTUE. We see what surprizing Effects these Things had upon the *Greek* and *Roman* Courage: Why then, may [54] we not expect, from the same Cause, the same Effect; especially when we consider, that *British* Courage is naturally equal to That of those IMMORTAL PEOPLE?

The Necessity of Something of this kind, being taken for granted, I shall venture to propose, that every *Foot Soldier*, in the *Crown Army*, at the Expiration of his seven Years Service, (provided that whole Space has been in time of War) should be intitled to an ANNUITY of ten Pounds,

42. I.e., fines.

per annum, during his own Life; if only part of the time, of such Service, has been employed in War, then in proportion less than ten Pounds, *per annum*, according to the number of Years he has served during a War. The *Sergeant* and *Corporals* of the *Foot*, as well as the *Horse* and *Dragoons*, with their non-commissioned Officers, *more*, in proportion, according to their Pay.

But as *Rewards* amongst us, have been chiefly *Pecuniary;* as MONEY has thereby acquired such an Ascendancy, as to be held superiour to all other Considerations; and as HONOUR, which ought to be the [55] highest Inducement, has been degraded in proportion; I would add to this some *Marks of Distinction*, to Those who shall particularly distinguish Themselves, by any Action of personal Bravery. A RIBBON, perhaps, of a particular Colour, with a Silver, or Silver-gilt MEDAL hanging to it, to be worn at a Button-hole, like some of the inferior Orders of Knighthood abroad, (with a Right of Precedency annex'd,) might have as good an Effect upon our Soldiers, as a *Sprig* of LAUREL, or a *Civic* or *Mural* CROWN,[43] had upon the antient Conquerors of the World; who, I firmly believe, owed that Title to nothing more, than to the Emulation raised among Them, for possessing These (trifling as they may seem to be in Themselves) MARKS *of Distinction*, for personal Courage [56].

SECT. IV.

OBSERVATIONS *upon the foregoing* PLAN.

[*The only Persons proper to be intrusted with Arms*, &c. Page 556.] This Assertion cannot be better illustrated, than by the Words of the incomparable *Sidney*[44] upon Government, Chap. ii. §. 21. "No State can be said to stand

---

43. A victorious Roman general who had been granted a triumph was permitted to wear a crown of laurel during the procession. A civic crown was a crown or garland of oak leaves and acorns given in ancient Rome as a mark of distinction to a person who saved the life of a fellow citizen in war (*OED*, s.v. "civic," 1b(a): "civic crown"; see, e.g., Lucan, *Pharsalia*, I.358). A mural crown was a garland or wreath conferred as a mark of honor by the ancient Romans on the first soldier to scale the walls of a besieged town (*OED*, s.v. "mural," 1b: "mural crown"); see, e.g., Polybius, VI.xxxix.

44. Algernon Sidney (1623–83), political writer. Sidney, *Discourses*, p. 198.

upon a steady Foundation, except Those whose strength is in their own Soldiery, and the body of their own People. Such as serve for Wages only, often betray their Masters in Distress; and always want the Courage, and Industry, which is found in those who fight for their own Interests, and are to have a Part in the Victory."

The same Author proves the Necessity of a WELL DISCIPLINED MILITIA in this Island, from the Dangers we are naturally exposed to: No *Crown Army* can, at one and the same time, defend the whole [57] Coast of *Britain*; or engage an Enemy in the North; and protect us from an *Invasion* in the West. There is no Security for Prince, or People, but in a GENERAL MILITIA. Our inextricable Fears, in the late REBELLION,[45] were a Proof of this; as was, in the Reign of *Charles* the Second, the Terror that the City of *London* was possessed with, when a few *Dutch* Ships came to *Chatham*:[46] which plainly shews, that no number of Men, (tho' naturally valiant,) are able to defend Themselves; unless they be well armed, disciplined, and conducted. Their Multitude brings Confusion: Their Wealth (when it is likely to be made a Prey,) increases the Fears of the Owners; and They, who, if they were brought into good Order, might conquer a great part of the World, (being destitute of it) dare not think of defending Themselves. Nothing can better illustrate the Difference between this State of our Country, in the Reign of *Charles* the Second; and when possessed of a well regulated *Militia*, in the Reign of Queen *Elizabeth*; or shew [58] the Preference due to such a MILITIA, than the following Account[47] of the Behaviour of our Countrymen, in the Year 1588, when threatened with an INVASION from *Spain*.

"The maritime Counties from *Cornwall*, all along the South-side of *England*, to *Kent*; and from *Kent* Eastward, by *Essex*, *Suffolk*, and *Norfolk*, to *Lincolnshire*, were so furnished, (both of Themselves, and with resort of aid from their next Shires,) that there was no place to be doubted, for landing of any foreign Forces, but there were, within eight and forty Hours, to come to the place above 20,000 fighting Men on Horseback, and on Foot; with Field Ordnance, Victuals, Pioneers, and Carriages; and all those governed by the principal NOBLEMEN of the Counties; and

45. See above, p. 545, n. 16.
46. See above, p. 294, n. 86.
47. A quotation from William Cecil, *The State of England in 1588* (1746), p. 7ff.

reduced under Captains of Knowledge. And to make the *Bands* strong and constant, Choice was made of the principal KNIGHTS of all Counties, to bring their *Tenants* to the Field, being Men of Strength, and landed, and of Wealth; whereby all the Forces so compounded, [59] were of a resolute Disposition to stick to their LORDS and CHIEFTAINS, and the Chieftains to trust to their own TENANTS.

It was avowed for Truth, that one GENTLEMAN in *Kent*, had a Band of 150 *Footmen*, worth 150,000 *l*. besides their Lands. Such Men would fight stoutly, before they would have lost their Goods. There were Numbers of the SHIPS of the Subjects of *London*, and other Port Towns and Cities, that voluntarily were armed, able to make a full NAVY of themselves; and all at the proper Cost of the Burgesses, for certain Months; with Men, Victuals, and Munition, which did join the *Queen's* Navy all that Summer. The *Queen* had also an Army of about 40,000 *Footmen*, and 6000 *Horsemen*, under the Lord Chamberlain HUNSDON; made ready from the inland Parts of the Realm, to be about Her own Person, without disarming the Maritime Counties; so as many marched out of sundry Counties towards Her, at the very time that she was in the Camp. Some came to the Suburbs, and Towns near [60] *London*, whom she remanded to their Counties, because their Harvest was at hand; and Many of them would not be countermanded; but still approached onward at their own Charges, (as They said,) to see her Person; and to fight with Them that boasted, to conquer the Realm. All the *Noblemen* in the Kingdom, from East and West, from North and South, (excepting only such great LORDS as had special Governments in Counties, that might not lawfully be absent from their Charge; and some Few who were not able to make Forces according to their Desire,) came to the QUEEN, bringing with Them according to their Degrees, and to the uttermost of their Powers, goodly Bands of *Horsemen;* maintaining them in Pay, and at their own Charge all the time, until the *Navy* of *Spain* was certainly known to be passed beyond *Scotland*.†

[*From seventeen to forty-six Years of Age, to be of the Militia*, Page 557.] This was the time of Service, in the *Roman Infan*[61]*try*. The *Roman* Youth were obliged to serve twenty Years. If that Service was performed by the time they were thirty-seven Years of Age, they might take up their

---

† *See a Letter from a Priest at* London, *to the* Spanish *Ambassador at* Paris.

Discharge; but, till they had served that number of Years, they were continued in the Army, but could not be compelled, after they were fifty Years of Age: And to prevent the *Roman* Youth from arriving too soon to Military Honours; *Gracchus*[48] provided, by Law, that no Person should be admitted into the Army, under seventeen Years of Age.

[*Every Man—possessed of—a certain degree of Property, shall be of the Militia*, Page 557.] The proportioning of *Service* to *Property* is not only the most equitable Rule, for determining the due Measure, or Degree, of each Man's Service; but is the greatest Security to the Whole: To the SOVEREIGN who mildly governs us; to the LAWS that protect us; and to the Continuance of Peace, to the undisturbed State of Property and Persons. He that desires most Advantage, from the Protection of a GOOD GOVERNMENT, should pay most towards the Support of it; or, [62] in other words, all *Duties*, whether personal or pecuniary, should be in proportion to the Property they are designed to protect; and no Man will be found so faithful, or resolute in defending the Property of Another, as in fighting for his Own. But Men of Property may safely be trusted with *Arms;* for they will not disturb the Peace of their own Possessions; nor ever rise against a Government, that shall protect their LIBERTIES and FORTUNES.

[*All such—incapable of serving*, Pag. 558.] PAPISTS, by their Religion, acknowledging themselves to be the SLAVES, (I should rather say, than the *Servants,*) of a *foreign* Power, ought not to be admitted to serve; but should be obliged to pay, (as at present,) towards the *Militia*, for the Protection they receive. All disaffected Persons, who refuse the legal OATHS of *Supremacy* and *Abjuration*,[49] should be obliged to pay, but not permitted to SERVE. All Peace-Officers, Clergymen, Physicians, Gentlemen of the Law; and Such, as by their Profession, cannot be absent from the Place [63] of their Residence, without a Detriment to Society; or have the

---

48. Gaius Sempronius Gracchus (d. 121 B.C.), Roman politician and reformer. The law to which Sackville refers was passed during Gracchus's first period of office as tribune, in 123 B.C. Sackville is probably drawing on the lives of Gracchus and his brother, Tiberius Sempronius Gracchus, written by Plutarch.

49. The practice of imposing state oaths was a consequence of the Glorious Revolution of 1688, when it was conceived as a way of addressing the problems of allegiance which had newly arisen. The oath of supremacy required a renunciation

Misfortune to be maimed or weak; all Such should certainly be excused personal Duty.

[*The Necessity of a Register*, Page 558.] This is too evident, to require any Arguments or Reasoning in Support of it. No Man can be ignorant, of the Advantage it must be to every State, to know, not only the number of Men fit to bear Arms; but the Places of their Residence, where they may be found; and drawn forth to Service immediately, as the Service may demand. And as to the establishing a *Register* of Men, (if the manner offered in the *Plan* should be objected to, as new, and therefore difficult,) I should propose to follow, upon this Occasion, a REGULATION, which is, (as I apprehend) no new One; for I am informed, that a list of Persons born, baptized, and buried, is every Year delivered in, from every Parish, in every Diocese, to the *Bishop;* or some inferior Church-Officer; who may order Duplicates, one for the *Diocesan*, and the other for the [64] *Lord Lieutenant* of the County, (to be sent him by the *Bishop*;) or the *Lord Lieutenant* may have his own Officer attend Visitations; and receive the Account of the State of each Parish in every Diocese; with the addition, of one *Article* more than these *Registers* contain at present; that is, the number of fighting Men, or Men from seventeen to forty-six Years of Age.

[*To exercise the first Sunday of every Month*, Page 558.] Every Man will by this Regulation, be obliged to attend upon the Duty, he owes to his GOD, as well as to his *King*, and his *Country*. No Army is ever hurt by *Religion*; and as is well known, that the best and bravest have been the most religious.

[*One general Muster of every County*, Pag. 559.] It may here, (perhaps,) be objected; That the March, from the Extremes, to the Center of large

---

of the power or jurisdiction of any foreigner (principally the Pope). The oath of abjuration required the disavowal of any loyalty toward the House of Stuart. For the texts of the oaths, see e.g., Jones, *History of Europe*, p. 359; for commentary, see J. C. D. Clark, *Samuel Johnson: Literature, religion and English cultural politics from the Restoration to Romanticism* (Cambridge: Cambridge University Press, 1994), pp. 93–99. For Marvell's tart comments on the perverse outcomes of the requirement to take oaths, see Marvell, *Prose Works*, 2:281–83. Cf. also Toland, *Restoring*, pp. 9, 11–12, 29; Joseph Addison, *The Freeholder*, no. 6 (9 January 1716); and *Whole Kingdoms*, p. 11.

Counties, would be too fatiguing; would take up too much time; and be too expensive. To remove this Objection, therefore, I shall propose, that the GENERAL MUSTERS be made in the [65] *Hundreds*, instead of the *Counties;* for it will not make the least Difference in this *Plan*, provided there be general *annual Musters;* whether those Musters be made in the *Hundreds*, or the *Counties*. And indeed, (now I recollect,) this was the Method of our *Saxon* Ancestors, in the annual Musters of their Militia. "They mustered[50] their Arms once every Year, both in Towns and Hundreds; and such whose Bodies were unfit for Service, were to find sufficient Men for Service, in their Stead."†

[*The Regiments be paid by the County*, Pag. 560.] This Expence to the County will be sufficiently repaid, (I should think) by the Service of these *Regiments*, who, by being properly posted in any part of the County, as the *Lord Lieutenant* shall see necessary, will protect Trade and Travellers; add to this, the Ease that the Kingdom in general would feel, and of course every County in particular, in being delivered from the Burthen of supporting a numerous [66] STANDING ARMY in time of Peace. But if all these Reasons should be thought insufficient; if the Safety of our Persons, the free Enjoyment of our Properties; the Security we shall live in, both from foreign and domestic Enemies, should be yet thought too dearly purchased, by the Expence the Counties must be at, to maintain their respective Regiments; and some new FUND must be thought of for paying them: Can any thing more rational, seasonable, or politic be thought of, than to ease the Country at once of the POOR's RATES, now grown so oppressive on one Hand, and such a shelter for Idleness on the other? This is the only Country in *Europe*, where there is such a TAX; and the PERNICIOUS EFFECTS of it are seen and acknowledged by every Body. I am, for my own Part, persuaded, that no other *Scheme*, but this of the *County Regiments*, will subdue the numerous Bands of SMUGGLERS and of HIGHWAYMEN, who infest our Roads. Monthly *Executions* have been tried too long, and were complained of many Years since, by *Chancellor* [67] *More*, in his UTOPIA, as insufficient for the End they were designed

---

† *Bacon* upon Government.

50. Nathaniel Bacon, *An Historical and Political Discourse of the Laws and Government of England* (1689), p. 40.

to obtain.[51] It is horrible to think of the devastation of our Species, by Executions of the *Law*, in this Way; and by that more fatal Incendiary, DISTILLED SPIRITS, a powerful Ally to Acts of Villainy, and the Gallows; and the Debility of Those among the common People, who are as Yet unhanged. I have wondered, how such grave, serious; and, (I believe) religious Beings, as our * * * * * *[52] are, could continue to order so many human Sacrifices, (for I can give these monthly Executions no better Appellation) without representing the Cruelties of Them; and obtaining, from the Legislature, some more effectual means to prevent EXECUTIONS, as well as ROBBERIES. It seems to me extremely evident, that if the public Roads are not patroled by the MILITIA, they will for ever continue to be infested by *Highwaymen*. But if the *County Regiments* are established, and proper MANUFACTURES set up, instead of *Alms-Houses*, and other Encouragements for *Beggary;* I should [68] think it would be very easy, (by means of these COUNTY REGIMENTS and the REGISTER,) to give an account of every Man in the Kingdom; to prevent almost every Act of Villainy; to cure Idleness, and relieve Distress, by obliging Such to work, as are able to work; and by turning our Charities into Hospitals, for the Maintenance of *deserted Children;* and of Such as are disabled by Age, or loss of Limbs, or of Senses.

FINIS.

---

51. More, *Utopia*, p. 15. In the text it is in fact Raphael Hythlodaeus who makes this point, not More himself.
52. I.e., judges.

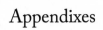

Appendixes

The Petition of Right (1628)

The Petition exhibited to his Majesty by the Lords Spiritual and Temporal, and Commons, in this present Parliament assembled, concerning divers Rights and Liberties of the Subjects, with the King's Majesty's royal answer thereunto in full Parliament.

To the King's Most Excellent Majesty,
Humbly show unto our Sovereign Lord the King, the Lords Spiritual and Temporal, and Commons in Parliament assembled, that whereas it is declared and enacted by a statute made in the time of the reign of King Edward I, commonly called Statutum de Tallagio non Concedendo, that no tallage or aid shall be laid or levied by the king or his heirs in this realm, without the good will and assent of the archbishops, bishops, earls, barons, knights, burgesses, and other the freemen of the commonalty of this realm; and by authority of parliament holden in the five-and-twentieth year of the reign of King Edward III, it is declared and enacted, that from thenceforth no person should be compelled to make any loans to the king against his will, because such loans were against reason and the franchise of the land; and by other laws of this realm it is provided, that none should be charged by any charge or imposition called a benevolence, nor by such like charge; by which statutes before mentioned, and other the good laws and statutes of this realm, your subjects have inherited this freedom, that they should not be compelled to contribute to any tax, tallage, aid, or other like charge not set by common consent, in parliament.

II. Yet nevertheless of late divers commissions directed to sundry commissioners in several counties, with instructions, have issued; by means whereof your people have been in divers places assembled, and required to lend certain sums of money unto your Majesty, and many of them, upon their refusal so to do, have had an oath administered unto them not warrantable by the laws or statutes of this realm, and have been constrained to become bound and make appearance and give utterance before your Privy Council and in other places, and others of them have been therfore imprisoned, confined, and sundry other ways molested and disquieted; and divers other charges have been laid and levied upon your people in several counties by lord lieutenants, deputy lieutenants, commissioners for musters, justices of peace and others, by command or direction from your Majesty, or your Privy Council, against the laws and free custom of the realm.

III. And whereas also by the statute called "The Great Charter of the Liberties of England," it is declared and enacted, that no freeman may be taken or imprisoned or be disseized of his freehold or liberties, or his free customs, or be outlawed or exiled, or in any manner destroyed, but by the lawful judgment of his peers, or by the law of the land.

IV. And in the eight-and-twentieth year of the reign of King Edward III, it was declared and enacted by authority of parliament, that no man, of what estate or condition that he be, should be put out of his land or tenements, nor taken, nor imprisoned, nor disinherited nor put to death without being brought to answer by due process of law.

V. Nevertheless, against the tenor of the said statutes, and other the good laws and statutes of your realm to that end provided, divers of your subjects have of late been imprisoned without any cause showed; and when for their deliverance they were brought before your justices by your Majesty's writs of habeas corpus, there to undergo and receive as the court should order, and their keepers commanded to certify the causes of their detainer, no cause was certified, but that they were detained by your Majesty's special command, signified by the lords of your Privy Council, and yet were returned back to several prisons, without being charged with anything to which they might make answer according to the law.

VI. And whereas of late great companies of soldiers and mariners have been dispersed into divers counties of the realm, and the inhabitants against their wills have been compelled to receive them into their houses, and there to suffer them to sojourn against the laws and customs of this realm, and to the great grievance and vexation of the people.

VII. And whereas also by authority of parliament, in the five-and-twentieth year of the reign of King Edward III, it is declared and enacted, that no man shall be forejudged of life or limb against the form of the Great Charter and the law of the land; and by the said Great Charter and other the laws and statutes of this your realm, no man ought to be adjudged to death but by the laws established in this your realm, either by the customs of the same realm, or by acts of parliament: and whereas no offender of what kind soever is exempted from the proceedings to be used, and punishments to be inflicted by the laws and statutes of this your realm; nevertheless of late time divers commissions under your Majesty's great seal have issued forth, by which certain persons have been assigned and appointed commissioners with power and authority to proceed within the land, according to the justice of martial law, against such soldiers or mariners, or other dissolute persons joining with them, as should commit any murder, robbery, felony, mutiny, or other outrage or misdemeanor whatsoever, and by such summary course and order as is agreeable to martial law, and is used in armies in time of war, to proceed to the trial and condemnation of such offenders, and them to cause to be executed and put to death according to the law martial.

VIII. By pretext whereof some of your Majesty's subjects have been by some of the said commissioners put to death, when and where, if by the laws and statutes of the land they had deserved death, by the same laws and statutes also they might, and by no other ought to have been judged and executed.

IX. And also sundry grievous offenders, by color thereof claiming an exemption, have escaped the punishments due to them by the laws and statutes of this your realm, by reason that divers of your officers and ministers of justice have unjustly refused or forborne to proceed against such offenders according to the same laws and statutes, upon pretense that the said offenders were punishable only by martial law, and by authority of such commissions as aforesaid; which commissions, and all other of like nature, are wholly and directly contrary to the said laws and statutes of this your realm.

X. They do therefore humbly pray your most excellent Majesty, that no man hereafter be compelled to make or yield any gift, loan, benevolence, tax, or such like charge, without common consent by act of parliament; and that none be called to make answer, or take such oath, or to give attendance, or be confined, or otherwise molested or disquieted concerning the same or for refusal thereof; and that no freeman, in any such manner as is before mentioned, be imprisoned or detained; and that your Majesty would be pleased to remove the said soldiers and mariners, and that your people may not be so burdened in time to come; and that the aforesaid commissions, for proceeding by martial law, may be revoked and annulled; and that hereafter no commissions of like nature may issue forth to any person or persons whatsoever to be executed as aforesaid, lest by color of them any of your Majesty's subjects be destroyed or put to death contrary to the laws and franchise of the land.

XI. All which they most humbly pray of your most excellent Majesty as their rights and liberties, according to the laws and statutes of this realm; and that your Majesty would also vouchsafe to declare, that the awards, doings, and proceedings, to the prejudice of your people in any of the premises, shall not be drawn hereafter into consequence or example; and that your Majesty would be also graciously pleased, for the further comfort and safety of your people, to declare your royal will and pleasure, that in the things aforesaid all your officers and ministers shall serve you according to the laws and statutes of this realm, as they tender the honor of your Majesty, and the prosperity of this kingdom.

The Grand Remonstrance (1641)

The Grand Remonstrance, with the Petition accompanying it.
[Presented to the King, December 1, 1641]
The Petition of the House of Commons, which accompanied the Remonstrance of the state of the kingdom, when it was presented to His Majesty at Hampton Court, December 1, 1641.

Most Gracious Sovereign,
Your Majesty's most humble and faithful subjects the Commons in this present Parliament assembled, do with much thankfulness and joy acknowledge the great mercy and favour of God, in giving your Majesty a safe and peaceable return out of Scotland into your kingdom of England, where the pressing dangers and distempers of the State have caused us with much earnestness to desire the comfort of your gracious presence, and likewise the unity and justice of your royal authority, to give more life and power to the dutiful and loyal counsels and endeavours of your Parliament, for the prevention of that eminent ruin and destruction wherein your kingdoms of England and Scotland are threatened. The duty which we owe to your Majesty and our country, cannot but make us very sensible and apprehensive, that the multiplicity, sharpness and malignity of those evils under which we have now many years suffered, are fomented and cherished by a corrupt and ill-affected party, who amongst other their mischievous devices for the alteration of religion and government, have sought by many false scandals and imputations, cunningly insinuated and dispersed amongst the people, to blemish and disgrace

our proceedings in this Parliament, and to get themselves a party and faction amongst your subjects, for the better strengthening themselves in their wicked courses, and hindering those provisions and remedies which might, by the wisdom of your Majesty and counsel of your Parliament, be opposed against them.

For preventing whereof, and the better information of your Majesty, your Peers and all other your loyal subjects, we have been necessitated to make a declaration of the state of the kingdom, both before and since the assembly of this Parliament, unto this time, which we do humbly present to your Majesty, without the least intention to lay any blemish upon your royal person, but only to represent how your royal authority and trust have been abused, to the great prejudice and danger of your Majesty, and of all your good subjects.

And because we have reason to believe that those malignant parties, whose proceedings evidently appear to be mainly for the advantage and increase of Popery, is composed, set up, and acted by the subtile practice of the Jesuits and other engineers and factors for Rome, and to the great danger of this kingdom, and most grievous affliction of your loyal subjects, have so far prevailed as to corrupt divers of your Bishops and others in prime places of the Church, and also to bring divers of these instruments to be of your Privy Council, and other employments of trust and nearness about your Majesty, the Prince, and the rest of your royal children.

And by this means have had such an operation in your counsel and the most important affairs and proceedings of your government, that a most dangerous division and chargeable preparation for war betwixt your kingdoms of England and Scotland, the increase of jealousies betwixt your Majesty and your most obedient subjects, the violent distraction and interruption of this Parliament, the insurrection of the Papists in your kingdom of Ireland, and bloody massacre of your people, have been not only endeavoured and attempted, but in a great measure compassed and effected.

For preventing the final accomplishment whereof, your poor subjects are enforced to engage their persons and estates to the maintaining of a very expensive and dangerous war, notwithstanding they have already since the beginning of this Parliament undergone the charge of £150,000 sterling, or thereabouts, for the necessary support and supply of your Majesty in these present and perilous designs. And because all our most faithful endeavours and engagements will be ineffectual for the peace, safety and preservation of your Majesty and your people, if some present, real and effectual course be not taken for suppressing this wicked and malignant party:—

We, your most humble and obedient subjects, do with all faithfulness and humility beseech your Majesty,—

1. That you will be graciously pleased to concur with the humble desires of your people in a parliamentary way, for the preserving the peace and safety of the kingdom from the malicious designs of the Popish party:—

For depriving the Bishops of their votes in Parliament, and abridging their immoderate power usurped over the Clergy, and other your good subjects, which they have perniciously abused to the hazard of religion, and great prejudice and oppression to the laws of the kingdom, and just liberty of your people—

For the taking away such oppressions in religion, Church government and discipline, as have been brought in and fomented by them:—

For uniting all such your loyal subjects together as join in the same fundamental truths against the Papists, by removing some oppressive and unnecessary ceremonies by which divers weak consciences have been scrupled, and seem to be divided from the rest, and for the due execution of those good laws which have been made for securing the liberty of your subjects.

2. That your Majesty will likewise be pleased to remove from your council all such as persist to favour and promote any of those pressures and corruptions wherewith your people have been grieved; and that for the future your Majesty will vouchsafe to employ such persons in your great and public affairs, and to take such to be near you in places of trust, as your Parliament may have cause to confide in; that in your princely goodness to your people you will reject and refuse all mediation and solicitation to the contrary, how powerful and near soever.

3. That you will be pleased to forbear to alienate any of the forfeited and escheated lands in Ireland which shall accrue to your Crown by reason

of this rebellion, that out of them the Crown may be the better supported, and some satisfaction made to your subjects of this kingdom for the great expenses they are like to undergo [in] this war.

Which humble desires of ours being graciously fulfilled by your Majesty, we will, by the blessing and favour of God, most cheerfully undergo the hazard and expenses of this war, and apply ourselves to such other courses and counsels as may support your real estate with honour and plenty at home, with power and reputation abroad, and by our loyal affections, obedience and service, lay a sure and lasting foundation of the greatness and prosperity of your Majesty, and your royal posterity in future times.

The Grand Remonstrance

The Commons in this present Parliament assembled, having with much earnestness and faithfulness of affection and zeal to the public good of this kingdom, and His Majesty's honour and service, for the space of twelve months wrestled with great dangers and fears, the pressing miseries and calamities, the various distempers and disorders which had not only assaulted, but even overwhelmed and extinguished the liberty, peace and prosperity of this kingdom, the comfort and hopes of all His Majesty's good subjects, and exceedingly weakened and undermined the foundation and strength of his own royal throne, do yet find an abounding malignity and opposition in those parties and factions who have been the cause of those evils, and do still labour to cast aspersions upon that which hath been done, and to raise many difficulties for the hindrance of that which remains yet undone, and to foment jealousies between the King and Parliament, that so they may deprive him and his people of the fruit of his own gracious intentions, and their humble desires of procuring the public peace, safety and happiness of this realm.

For the preventing of those miserable effects which such malicious endeavours may produce, we have thought good to declare the root and the growth of these mischievous designs: the maturity and ripeness to which they have attained before the beginning of the Parliament: the effectual means which have been used for the extirpation of those dangerous evils, and the progress which hath therein been made by His

Majesty's goodness and the wisdom of the Parliament: the ways of obstruction and opposition by which that progress hath been interrupted: the courses to be taken for the removing those obstacles, and for the accomplishing of our most dutiful and faithful intentions and endeavours of restoring and establishing the ancient honour, greatness and security of this Crown and nation.

The root of all this mischief we find to be a malignant and pernicious design of subverting the fundamental laws and principles of government, upon which the religion and justice of this kingdom are firmly established. The actors and promoters hereof have been:

1. The Jesuited Papists, who hate the laws, as the obstacles of that change and subversion of religion which they so much long for.

2. The Bishops, and the corrupt part of the Clergy, who cherish formality and superstition as the natural effects and more probable supports of their own ecclesiastical tyranny and usurpation.

3. Such Councillors and Courtiers as for private ends have engaged themselves to further the interests of some foreign princes or states to the prejudice of His Majesty and the State at home.

The common principles by which they moulded and governed all their particular counsels and actions were these:

First, to maintain continual differences and discontents between the King and the people, upon questions of prerogative and liberty, that so they might have the advantage of siding with him, and under the notions of men addicted to his service, gain to themselves and their parties the places of greatest trust and power in the kingdom.

A second, to suppress the purity and power of religion and such persons as were best affected to it, as being contrary to their own ends, and the greatest impediment to that change which they thought to introduce.

A third, to conjoin those parties of the kingdom which were most propitious to their own ends, and to divide those who were most opposite, which consisted in many particular observations.

To cherish the Arminian part in those points wherein they agree with the Papists, to multiply and enlarge the difference between the common Protestants and those whom they call Puritans, to introduce and countenance such opinions and ceremonies as are fittest for accommodation with

Popery, to increase and maintain ignorance, looseness and profaneness in the people; that of those three parties, Papists, Arminians and Libertines, they might compose a body fit to act such counsels and resolutions as were most conducible to their own ends.

A fourth, to disaffect the King to Parliaments by slander and false imputations, and by putting him upon other ways of supply, which in show and appearance were fuller of advantage than the ordinary course of subsidies, though in truth they brought more loss than gain both to the King and people, and have caused the great distractions under which we both suffer.

As in all compounded bodies the operations are qualified according to the predominant element, so in this mixed party, the Jesuited counsels, being most active and prevailing, may easily be discovered to have had the greatest sway in all their determinations, and if they be not prevented, are likely to devour the rest, or to turn them into their own nature.

In the beginning of His Majesty's reign the party began to revive and flourish again, having been somewhat damped by the breach with Spain in the last year of King James, and by His Majesty's marriage with France; the interests and counsels of that State being not so contrary to the good of religion and the prosperity of this kingdom as those of Spain; and the Papists of England, having been ever more addicted to Spain than France, yet they still retained a purpose and resolution to weaken the Protestant parties in all parts, and even in France, whereby to make way for the change of religion which they intended at home.

1. The first effect and evidence of their recovery and strength was the dissolution of the Parliament at Oxford, after there had been given two subsidies to His Majesty, and before they received relief in any one grievance many other more miserable effects followed.

2. The loss of the Rochel fleet, by the help of our shipping, set forth and delivered over to the French in opposition to the advice of Parliament, which left that town without defence by sea, and made way, not only to the loss of that important place, but likewise to the loss of all the strength and security of the Protestant religion in France.

3. The diverting of His Majesty's course of wars from the West Indies, which was the most facile and hopeful way for this kingdom to prevail

against the Spaniard, to an expenseful and successless attempt upon Cadiz, which was so ordered as if it had rather been intended to make us weary of war than to prosper in it.

4. The precipitate breach with France, by taking their ships to a great value without making recompense to the English, whose goods were thereupon imbarred and confiscated in that kingdom.

5. The peace with Spain without consent of Parliament, contrary to the promise of King James to both Houses, whereby the Palatine's cause was deserted and left to chargeable and hopeless treaties, which for the most part were managed by those who might justly be suspected to be no friends to that cause.

6. The charging of the kingdom with billeted soldiers in all parts of it, and the concomitant design of German horse, that the land might either submit with fear or be enforced with rigour to such arbitrary contributions as should be required of them.

7. The dissolving of the Parliament in the second year of His Majesty's reign, after a declaration of their intent to grant five subsidies.

8. The exacting of the like proportion of five subsidies, after the Parliament dissolved, by commission of loan, and divers gentlemen and others imprisoned for not yielding to pay that loan, whereby many of them contracted such sicknesses as cost them their lives.

9. Great sums of money required and raised by privy seals.

10. An unjust and pernicious attempt to extort great payments from the subject by way of excise, and a commission issued under the seal to that purpose.

11. The Petition of Right, which was granted in full Parliament, blasted, with an illegal declaration to make it destructive to itself, to the power of Parliament, to the liberty of the subject, and to that purpose printed with it, and the Petition made of no use but to show the bold and presumptuous injustice of such ministers as durst break the laws and suppress the liberties of the kingdom, after they had been so solemnly and evidently declared.

12. Another Parliament dissolved 4 Car., the privilege of Parliament broken, by imprisoning divers members of the House, detaining them close prisoners for many months together, without the liberty of using

books, pen, ink or paper; denying them all the comforts of life, all means of preservation of health, not permitting their wives to come unto them even in the time of their sickness.

13. And for the completing of that cruelty, after years spent in such miserable durance, depriving them of the necessary means of spiritual consolation, not suffering them to go abroad to enjoy God's ordinances in God's House, or God's ministers to come to them to minister comfort to them in their private chambers.

14. And to keep them still in this oppressed condition, not admitting them to be bailed according to law, yet vexing them with informations in inferior courts, sentencing and fining some of them for matters done in Parliament; and extorting the payments of those fines from them, enforcing others to put in security of good behaviour before they could be released.

15. The imprisonment of the rest, which refused to be bound, still continued, which might have been perpetual if necessity had not the last year brought another Parliament to relieve them, of whom one died by the cruelty and harshness of his imprisonment, which would admit of no relaxation, notwithstanding the imminent danger of his life did sufficiently appear by the declaration of his physician, and his release, or at least his refreshment, was sought by many humble petitions, and his blood still cries either for vengeance or repentance of those Ministers of State, who have at once obstructed the course both of His Majesty's justice and mercy.

16. Upon the dissolution of both these Parliaments, untrue and scandalous declarations were published to asperse their proceedings, and some of their members unjustly; to make them odious, and colour the violence which was used against them; proclamations set out to the same purpose; and to the great dejecting of the hearts of the people, forbidding them even to speak of Parliaments.

17. After the breach of the Parliament in the fourth of His Majesty, injustice, oppression and violence broke in upon us without any restraint or moderation, and yet the first project was the great sums exacted through the whole kingdom for default of knighthood, which seemed to have some colour and shadow of a law, yet if it be rightly examined by

that obsolete law which was pretended for it, it will be found to be against all the rules of justice, both in respect of the persons charged, the proportion of the fines demanded, and the absurd and unreasonable manner of their proceedings.

18. Tonnage and Poundage hath been received without colour or pretence of law; many other heavy impositions continued against law, and some so unreasonable that the sum of the charge exceeds the value of the goods.

19. The Book of Rates lately enhanced to a high proportion, and such merchants that would not submit to their illegal and unreasonable payments, were vexed and oppressed above measure; and the ordinary course of justice, the common birthright of the subject of England, wholly obstructed unto them.

20. And although all this was taken upon pretence of guarding the seas, yet a new unheard-of tax of ship-money was devised, and upon the same pretence, by both which there was charged upon the subject near £700,000 some years, and yet the merchants have been left so naked to the violence of the Turkish pirates, that many great ships of value and thousands of His Majesty's subjects have been taken by them, and do still remain in miserable slavery.

21. The enlargements of forests, contrary to *Carta de Foresta*, and the composition thereupon.

22. The exactions of coat and conduct money and divers other military charges.

23. The taking away the arms of trained bands of divers Counties.

24. The desperate design of engrossing all the gunpowder into one hand, keeping it in the Tower of London, and setting so high a rate upon it that the poorer sort were not able to buy it, nor could any have it without licence, thereby to leave the several parts of the kingdom destitute of their necessary defence, and by selling so dear that which was sold to make an unlawful advantage of it, to the great charge and detriment of the subject.

25. The general destruction of the King's timber, especially that in the Forest of Deane, sold to Papists, which was the best store-house of this kingdom for the maintenance of our shipping.

26. The taking away of men's right, under the colour of the King's title to land, between high and low water marks.

27. The monopolies of soap, salt, wine, leather, sea-coal, and in a manner of all things of most common and necessary use.

28. The restraint of the liberties of the subjects in their habitation, trades and other interests.

29. Their vexation and oppression by purveyors, clerks of the market and saltpetre men.

30. The sale of pretended nuisances, as building in and about London.

31. Conversion of arable into pasture, continuance of pasture, under the name of depopulation, have driven many millions out of the subjects' purses, without any considerable profit to His Majesty.

32. Large quantities of common and several grounds hath been taken from the subject by colour of the Statute of Improvement, and by abuse of the Commission of Sewers, without their consent, and against it.

33. And not only private interest, but also public faith, have been broken in seizing of the money and bullion in the mint, and the whole kingdom like to be robbed at once in that abominable project of brass money.

34. Great numbers of His Majesty's subjects for refusing those unlawful charges, have been vexed with long and expensive suits, some fined and censured, others committed to long and hard imprisonments and confinements, to the loss of health in many, of life in some, and others have had their houses broken up, their goods seized, some have been restrained from their lawful callings.

35. Ships have been interrupted in their voyages, surprised at sea in a hostile manner by projectors, as by a common enemy.

36. Merchants prohibited to unlade their goods in such ports as were for their own advantage, and forced to bring them to those places which were much for the advantage of the monopolisers and projectors.

37. The Court of Star Chamber hath abounded in extravagant censures, not only for the maintenance and improvement of monopolies and their unlawful taxes, but for divers other causes where there hath been no offence, or very small; whereby His Majesty's subjects have been oppressed by grievous fines, imprisonments, stigmatisings, mutilations, whippings, pillories, gags, confinements, banishments; after so rigid a manner as hath

not only deprived men of the society of their friends, exercise of their professions, comfort of books, use of paper or ink, but even violated that near union which God hath established between men and their wives, by forced and constrained separation, whereby they have been bereaved of the comfort and conversation one of another for many years together, without hope of relief, if God had not by His overruling providence given some interruption to the prevailing power, and counsel of those who were the authors and promoters of such peremptory and heady courses.

38. Judges have been put out of their places for refusing to do against their oaths and consciences; others have been so awed that they durst not do their duties, and the better to hold a rod over them, the clause *Quam diu se bene gesserit* was left out of their patents, and a new clause *Durante bene placito* inserted.

39. Lawyers have been checked for being faithful to their clients; solicitors and attorneys have been threatened, and some punished, for following lawful suits. And by this means all the approaches to justice were interrupted and foreclosed.

40. New oaths have been forced upon the subject against law.

41. New judicatories erected without law. The Council Table have by their orders offered to bind the subjects in their freeholds, estates, suits and actions.

42. The pretended Court of the Earl Marshal was arbitrary and illegal in its being and proceedings.

43. The Chancery, Exchequer Chamber, Court of Wards, and other English Courts, have been grievous in exceeding their jurisdiction.

44. The estate of many families weakened, and some ruined by excessive fines, exacted from them for compositions of wardships.

45. All leases of above a hundred years made to draw on wardship contrary to law.

46. Undue proceedings used in the finding of offices to make the jury find for the King.

47. The Common Law Courts, seeing all men more inclined to seek justice there, where it may be fitted to their own desire, are known frequently to forsake the rules of the Common Law, and straying beyond their bounds, under pretence of equity, to do injustice.

48. Titles of honour, judicial places, serjeantships at law, and other offices have been sold for great sums of money, whereby the common justice of the kingdom hath been much endangered, not only by opening a way of employment in places of great trust, and advantage to men of weak parts, but also by giving occasion to bribery, extortion, partiality, it seldom happening that places ill-gotten are well used.

49. Commissions have been granted for examining the excess of fees, and when great exactions have been discovered, compositions have been made with delinquents, not only for the time past, but likewise for immunity and security in offending for the time to come, which under colour of remedy hath but confirmed and increased the grievance to the subject.

50. The usual course of pricking Sheriffs not observed, but many times Sheriffs made in an extraordinary way, sometimes as a punishment and charge unto them; sometimes such were pricked out as would be instruments to execute whatsoever they would have to be done.

51. The Bishops and the rest of the Clergy did triumph in the suspensions, excommunications, deprivations, and degradations of divers painful, learned and pious ministers, in the vexation and grievous oppression of great numbers of His Majesty's good subjects.

52. The High Commission grew to such excess of sharpness and severity as was not much less than the Romish Inquisition, and yet in many cases by the Archbishop's power was made much more heavy, being assisted and strengthened by authority of the Council Table.

53. The Bishops and their Courts were as eager in the country; although their jurisdiction could not reach so high in rigour and extremity of punishment, yet were they no less grievous in respect of the generality and multiplicity of vexations, which lighting upon the meaner sort of tradesmen and artificers did impoverish many thousands.

54. And so afflict and trouble others, that great numbers to avoid their miseries departed out of the kingdom, some into New England and other parts of America, others into Holland,

55. Where they have transported their manufactures of cloth, which is not only a loss by diminishing the present stock of the kingdom, but a great mischief by impairing and endangering the loss of that particular trade of clothing, which hath been a plentiful fountain of wealth and honour to this nation.

56. Those were fittest for ecclesiastical preferment, and soonest obtained it, who were most officious in promoting superstition, most virulent in railing against godliness and honesty.

57. The most public and solemn sermons before His Majesty were either to advance prerogative above law, and decry the property of the subject, or full of such kind of invectives.

58. Whereby they might make those odious who sought to maintain the religion, laws and liberties of the kingdom, and such men were sure to be weeded out of the commission of the peace, and out of all other employments of power in the government of the country.

59. Many noble personages were councillors in name, but the power and authority remained in a few of such as were most addicted to this party, whose resolutions and determinations were brought to the table for countenance and execution, and not for debate and deliberation, and no man could offer to oppose them without disgrace and hazard to himself.

60. Nay, all those that did not wholly concur and actively contribute to the furtherance of their designs, though otherwise persons of never so great honour and abilities, were so far from being employed in any place of trust and power, that they were neglected, discountenanced, and upon all occasions injured and oppressed.

61. This faction was grown to that height and entireness of power, that now they began to think of finishing their Work, which consisted of these three parts.

62. I. The government must be set free from all restraint of laws concerning our persons and estates.

63. II. There must be a conjunction between Papists and Protestants in doctrine, discipline and ceremonies; only it must not yet be called Popery.

64. III. The Puritans, under which name they include all those that desire to preserve the laws and liberties of the kingdom, and to maintain religion in the power of it, must be either rooted out of the kingdom with force, or driven out with fear.

65. For the effecting of this it was thought necessary to reduce Scotland to such Popish superstitions and innovations as might make them apt to join with England in that great change which was intended.

66. Whereupon new canons and a new liturgy were pressed upon them, and when they refused to admit of them, an army was raised to force

them to it, towards which the Clergy and the Papists were very forward in their contribution.

67. The Scots likewise raised an army for their defence.

68. And when both armies were come together, and ready for a bloody encounter, His Majesty's own gracious disposition, and the counsel of the English nobility and dutiful submission of the Scots, did so far prevail against the evil counsel of others, that a pacification was made, and His Majesty returned with peace and much honour to London.

69. The unexpected reconciliation was most acceptable to all the kingdom, except to the malignant party; whereof the Archbishop and the Earl of Strafford being heads, they and their faction began to inveigh against the peace, and to aggravate the proceedings of the states, which so incensed His Majesty, that he forthwith prepared again for war.

70. And such was their confidence, that having corrupted and distempered the whole frame and government of the kingdom, they did now hope to corrupt that which was the only means to restore all to a right frame and temper again.

71. To which end they persuaded His Majesty to call a Parliament, not to seek counsel and advice of them, but to draw countenance and supply from them, and to engage the whole kingdom in their quarrel.

72. And in the meantime continued all their unjust levies of money, resolving either to make the Parliament pliant to their will, and to establish mischief by a law, or else to break it, and with more colour to go on by violence to take what they could not obtain by consent. The ground alleged for the justification of this war was this,

73. That the undutiful demands of the Parliaments in Scotland was a sufficient reason for His Majesty to take arms against them, without hearing the reason of those demands, and thereupon a new army was prepared against them, their ships were seized in all ports both of England and Ireland, and at sea, their petitions rejected, their commissioners refused audience.

74. This whole kingdom most miserably distempered with levies of men and money, and imprisonments of those who denied to submit to those levies.

75. The Earl of Strafford passed into Ireland, caused the Parliament there to declare against the Scots, to give four subsidies towards that war,

and to engage themselves, their lives and fortunes, for the prosecution of it, and gave directions for an army of eight thousand foot and one thousand horse to be levied there, which were for the most part Papists.

76. The Parliament met upon the 13th of April, 1640. The Earl of Strafford and Archbishop of Canterbury, with their party, so prevailed with His Majesty, that the House of Commons was pressed to yield a supply for maintenance of the war with Scotland, before they had provided any relief for the great and pressing grievances of the people, which being against the fundamental privilege and proceeding of Parliament, was yet in humble respect to His Majesty, so far admitted as that they agreed to take the matter of supply into consideration, and two several days it was debated.

77. Twelve subsidies were demanded for the release of ship-money alone, a third day was appointed for conclusion, when the heads of that party began to fear the people might close with the King, in satisfying his desires of money; but that withal they were like to blast their malicious designs against Scotland, finding them very much indisposed to give any countenance to that war.

78. Thereupon they wickedly advised the King to break off the Parliament and to return to the ways of confusion, in which their own evil intentions were most likely to prosper and succeed.

79. After the Parliament ended the 5th of May, 1640, this party grew so bold as to counsel the King to supply himself out of his subjects' estates by his own power, at his own will, without their consent.

80. The very next day some members of both Houses had their studies and cabinets, yea, their pockets searched: another of them not long after was committed close prisoner for not delivering some petitions which he received by authority of that House.

81. And if harsher courses were intended (as was reported) it is very probable that the sickness of the Earl of Strafford, and the tumultuous rising in Southwark and about Lambeth were the causes that such violent intentions were not brought into execution.

82. A false and scandalous Declaration against the House of Commons was published in His Majesty's name, which yet wrought little effect with the people, but only to manifest the impudence of those who were authors of it.

83. A forced loan of money was attempted in the City of London.

84. The Lord Mayor and Aldermen in their several wards, enjoined to bring in a list of the names of such persons as they judged fit to lend, and of the sums they should lend. And such Aldermen as refused to do so were committed to prison.

85. The Archbishop and the other Bishops and Clergy continued the Convocation, and by a new commission turned it into a provincial Synod, in which, by an unheard-of presumption, they made canons that contain in them many matters contrary to the King's prerogative, to the fundamental laws and statutes of the realm, to the right of Parliaments, to the property and liberty of the subject, and matters tending to sedition and of dangerous consequence, thereby establishing their own usurpations, justifying their altar-worship, and those other superstitious innovations which they formerly introduced without warrant of law.

86. They imposed a new oath upon divers of His Majesty's subjects, both ecclesiastical and lay, for maintenance of their own tyranny, and laid a great tax on the Clergy, for supply of His Majesty, and generally they showed themselves very affectionate to the war with Scotland, which was by some of them styled *Bellum Episcopale*, and a prayer composed and enjoined to be read in all churches, calling the Scots rebels, to put the two nations in blood and make them irreconcileable.

87. All those pretended canons and constitutions were armed with the several censures of suspension, excommunication, deprivation, by which they would have thrust out all the good ministers, and most of the well-affected people of the kingdom, and left an easy passage to their own design of reconciliation with Rome.

88. The Popish party enjoyed such exemptions from penal laws as amounted to a toleration, besides many other encouragements and Court favours.

89. They had a Secretary of State, Sir Francis Windebanck, a powerful agent for speeding all their desires.

90. A Pope's Nuncio residing here, to act and govern them according to such influences as he received from Rome, and to intercede for them with the most powerful concurrence of the foreign Princes of that religion.

91. By his authority the Papists of all sorts, nobility, gentry, and clergy, were convocated after the manner of a Parliament.

92. New jurisdictions were erected of Romish Archbishops, taxes levied, another state moulded within this state, independent in government, contrary in interest and affection, secretly corrupting the ignorant or negligent professors of our religion, and closely uniting and combining themselves against such as were found in this posture, waiting for an opportunity by force to destroy those whom they could not hope to seduce.

93. For the effecting whereof they were strengthened with arms and munitions, encouraged by superstitious prayers, enjoined by the Nuncio to be weekly made for the prosperity of some great design.

94. And such power had they at Court, that secretly a commission was issued out, or intended to be issued to some great men of that profession, for the levying of soldiers, and to command and employ them according to private instructions, which we doubt were framed for the advantage of those who were the contrivers of them,

95. His Majesty's treasure was consumed, his revenue anticipated.

96. His servants and officers compelled to lend great sums of money.

97. Multitudes were called to the Council Table, who were tired with long attendances there for refusing illegal payments.

98. The prisons were filled with their commitments; many of the Sheriffs summoned into the Star Chamber, and some imprisoned for not being quick enough in levying the ship-money; the people languished under grief and fear, no visible hope being left but in desperation.

99. The nobility began to weary of their silence and patience, and sensible of the duty and trust which belongs to them: and thereupon some of the most ancient of them did petition His Majesty at such a time, when evil counsels were so strong, that they had occasion to expect more hazard to themselves, than redress of those public evils for which they interceded.

100. Whilst the kingdom was in this agitation and distemper, the Scots, restrained in their trades, impoverished by the loss of many of their ships, bereaved of all possibility of satisfying His Majesty by any naked supplication, entered with a powerful army into the kingdom, and without any hostile act or spoil in the country they passed, more than forcing a

passage over the Tyne at Newburn, near Newcastle, possessed themselves of Newcastle, and had a fair opportunity to press on further upon the King's army.

101. But duty and reverence to His Majesty, and brotherly love to the English nation, made them stay there, whereby the King had leisure to entertain better counsels.

102. Wherein God so blessed and directed him that he summoned the Great Council of Peers to meet at York upon the 24th of September, and there declared a Parliament to begin the 3rd of November then following.

103. The Scots, the first day of the Great Council, presented an humble Petition to His Majesty, whereupon the Treaty was appointed at Ripon.

104. A present cessation of arms agreed upon, and the full conclusion of all differences referred to the wisdom and care of the Parliament.

105. At our first meeting, all oppositions seemed to vanish, the mischiefs were so evident which those evil counsellors produced, that no man durst stand up to defend them: yet the work itself afforded difficulty enough.

106. The multiplied evils and corruption of fifteen years, strengthened by custom and authority, and the concurrent interest of many powerful delinquents, were now to be brought to judgment and reformation.

107. The King's household was to be provided for:—they had brought him to that want, that he could not supply his ordinary and necessary expenses without the assistance of his people.

108. Two armies were to be paid, which amounted very near to eighty thousand pounds a month.

109. The people were to be tenderly charged, having been formerly exhausted with many burdensome projects.

110. The difficulties seemed to be insuperable, which by the Divine Providence we have overcome. The contrarieties incompatible, which yet in a great measure we have reconciled.

111. Six subsidies have been granted and a Bill of poll-money, which if it be duly levied, may equal six subsidies more, in all £600,000.

112. Besides we have contracted a debt to the Scots of £220,000, yet God hath so blessed the endeavours of this Parliament, that the kingdom is a great gainer by all these charges.

113. The ship-money is abolished, which cost the kingdom about £200,000 a year.

114. The coat and conduct-money, and other military charges are taken away, which in many countries amounted to little less than the ship-money.

115. The monopolies are all suppressed, whereof some few did prejudice the subject, above £1,000,000 yearly.

116. The soap £100,000.

117. The wine £300,000.

118. The leather must needs exceed both, and salt could be no less than that.

119. Besides the inferior monopolies, which, if they could be exactly computed, would make up a great sum.

120. That which is more beneficial than all this is, that the root of these evils is taken away, which was the arbitrary power pretended to be in His Majesty of taxing the subject, or charging their estates without consent in Parliament, which is now declared to be against law by the judgment of both Houses, and likewise by an Act of Parliament.

121. Another step of great advantage is this, the living grievances, the evil counsellors and actors of these mischiefs have been so quelled.

122. By the justice done upon the Earl of Strafford, the flight of the Lord Finch and Secretary Windebanck,

123. The accusation and imprisonment of the Archbishop of Canterbury, of Judge Berkeley; and

124. The impeachment of divers other Bishops and Judges, that it is like not only to be an ease to the present times, but a preservation to the future.

125. The discontinuance of Parliaments is prevented by the Bill for a triennial Parliament, and the abrupt dissolution of this Parliament by another Bill, by which it is provided it shall not be dissolved or adjourned without the consent of both Houses.

126. Which two laws well considered may be thought more advantageous than all the former, because they secure a full operation of the present remedy, and afford a perpetual spring of remedies for the future.

127. The Star Chamber,

128. The High Commission,

129. The Courts of the President, and Council in the North were so many forges of misery, oppression and violence, and are all taken away, whereby men are more secured in their persons, liberties and estates, than they could be by any law or example for the regulation of those Courts or terror of the Judges.

130. The immoderate power of the Council Table, and the excessive abuse of that power is so ordered and restrained, that we may well hope that no such things as were frequently done by them, to the prejudice of the public liberty, will appear in future times but only in stories, to give us and our posterity more occasion to praise God for His Majesty's goodness, and the faithful endeavours of this Parliament.

131. The canons and power of canon-making are blasted by the votes of both Houses.

132. The exorbitant power of Bishops and their courts are much abated, by some provisions in the Bill against the High Commission Court, the authors of the many innovations in doctrine and ceremonies.

133. The ministers that have been scandalous in their lives, have been so terrified in just complaints and accusations, that we may well hope they will be more modest for the time to come; either inwardly convicted by the sight of their own folly, or outwardly restrained by the fear of punishment.

134. The forests are by a good law reduced to their right bounds;

135. The encroachments and oppressions of the Stannary Courts, the extortions of the clerk of the market,

136. And the compulsion of the subject to receive the Order of Knighthood against his will, paying of fines for not receiving it, and the vexatious proceedings thereupon for levying of those fines, are by other beneficial laws reformed and prevented.

137. Many excellent laws and provisions are in preparation for removing the inordinate power, vexation and usurpation of Bishops, for reforming the pride and idleness of many of the clergy, for easing the people of unnecessary ceremonies in religion, for censuring and removing unworthy and unprofitable ministers, and for maintaining godly and diligent preachers through the kingdom.

138. Other things of main importance for the good of this kingdom are in proposition, though little could hitherto be done in regard of the

many other more pressing businesses, which yet before the end of this Session we hope may receive some progress and perfection.

139. The establishing and ordering the King's revenue, that so the abuse of officers and superfluity of expenses may be cut off, and the necessary disbursements for His Majesty's honour, the defence and government of the kingdom, may be more certainly provided for.

140. The regulating of courts of justice, and abridging both the delays and charges of law-suits.

141. The settling of some good courses for preventing the exportation of gold and silver, and the inequality of exchanges between us and other nations, for the advancing of native commodities, increase of our manufactures, and well balancing of trade, whereby the stock of the kingdom may be increased, or at least kept from impairing, as through neglect hereof it hath done for many years last past.

142. Improving the herring-fishing upon our coasts, which will be of mighty use in the employment of the poor, and a plentiful nursery of mariners for enabling the kingdom in any great action.

143. The oppositions, obstructions and the difficulties wherewith we have been encountered, and which still lie in our way with some strength and much obstinacy, are these; the malignant party whom we have formerly described to be the actors and promoters of all our misery, they have taken heart again.

144. They have been able to prefer some of their own factors and agents to degrees of honour, to places of trust and employment, even during the Parliament.

145. They have endeavoured to work in His Majesty ill impressions and opinions of our proceedings, as if we had altogether done our own work, and not his; and had obtained from him many things very prejudicial to the Crown, both in respect of prerogative and profit.

146. To wipe out this slander we think good only to say thus much: that all that we have done is for His Majesty, his greatness, honour and support, when we yield to give £25,000 a month for the relief of the Northern Counties; this was given to the King, for he was bound to protect his subjects.

147. They were His Majesty's evil counsellors, and their ill instruments that were actors in those grievances which brought in the Scots.

148. And if His Majesty please to force those who were the authors of this war to make satisfaction, as he might justly and easily do, it seems very reasonable that the people might well be excused from taking upon them this burden, being altogether innocent and free from being any cause of it.

149. When we undertook the charge of the army, which cost above £50,000 a month, was not this given to the King? Was it not His Majesty's army? Were not all the commanders under contract with His Majesty, at higher rates and greater wages than ordinary?

150. And have we not taken upon us to discharge all the brotherly assistance of £300,000, which we gave the Scots? Was it not toward repair of those damages and losses which they received from the King's ships and from his ministers?

151. These three particulars amount to above £1,100,000.

152. Besides, His Majesty hath received by impositions upon merchandise at least £400,000.

153. So that His Majesty hath had out of the subjects' purse since the Parliament began, £1,500,000, and yet these men can be so impudent as to tell His Majesty that we have done nothing for him.

154. As to the second branch of this slander, we acknowledge with much thankfulness that His Majesty hath passed more good Bills to the advantage of the subjects than have been in many ages.

155. But withal we cannot forget that these venomous councils did manifest themselves in some endeavours to hinder these good acts.

156. And for both Houses of Parliament we may with truth and modesty say thus much: that we have ever been careful not to desire anything that should weaken the Crown either in just profit or useful power.

157. The triennial Parliament for the matter of it, doth not extend to so much as by law we ought to have required (there being two statutes still in force for a Parliament to be once a year), and for the manner of it, it is in the King's power that it shall never take effect, if he by a timely summons shall prevent any other way of assembling.

158. In the Bill for continuance of this present Parliament, there seems to be some restraint of the royal power in dissolving of Parliaments, not to take it out of the Crown, but to suspend the execution of it for this time and occasion only: which was so necessary for the King's own security

and the public peace, that without it we could not have undertaken any of these great charges, but must have left both the armies to disorder and confusion, and the whole kingdom to blood and rapine.

159. The Star Chamber was much more fruitful in oppression than in profit, the great fines being for the most part given away, and the rest stalled at long times.

160. The fines of the High Commission were in themselves unjust, and seldom or never came into the King's purse. These four Bills are particularly and more specially instanced.

161. In the rest there will not be found so much as a shadow of prejudice to the Crown.

162. They have sought to diminish our reputation with the people, and to bring them out of love with Parliaments.

163. The aspersions which they have attempted this way have been such as these:

164. That we have spent much time and done little, especially in those grievances which concern religion.

165. That the Parliament is a burden to the kingdom by the abundance of protections which hinder justice and trade; and by many subsidies granted much more heavy than any formerly endured.

166. To which there is a ready answer; if the time spent in this Parliament be considered in relation backward to the long growth and deep root of those grievances, which we have removed, to the powerful supports of those delinquents, which we have pursued, to the great necessities and other charges of the commonwealth for which we have provided.

167. Or if it be considered in relation forward to many advantages, which not only the present but future ages are like to reap by the good laws and other proceedings in this Parliament, we doubt not but it will be thought by all indifferent judgments, that our time hath been much better employed than in a far greater proportion of time in many former Parliaments put together; and the charges which have been laid upon the subject, and the other inconveniences which they have borne, will seem very light in respect of the benefit they have and may receive.

168. And for the matter of protections, the Parliament is so sensible of it that therein they intended to give them whatsoever ease may stand

with honour and justice, and are in a way of passing a Bill to give them satisfaction.

169. They have sought by many subtle practices to cause jealousies and divisions betwixt us and our brethren of Scotland, by slandering their proceedings and intentions towards us, and by secret endeavours to instigate and incense them and us one against another.

170. They have had such a party of Bishops and Popish lords in the House of Peers, as hath caused much opposition and delay in the prosecution of delinquents, hindered the proceedings of divers good Bills passed in the Commons' House, concerning the reformation of sundry great abuses and corruptions both in Church and State.

171. They have laboured to seduce and corrupt some of the Commons' House to draw them into conspiracies and combinations against the liberty of the Parliament.

172. And by their instruments and agents they have attempted to disaffect and discontent His Majesty's army, and to engage it for the maintenance of their wicked and traitorous designs; the keeping up of Bishops in votes and functions, and by force to compel the Parliament to order, limit and dispose their proceedings in such manner as might best concur with the intentions of this dangerous and potent faction.

173. And when one mischievous design and attempt of theirs to bring on the army against the Parliament and the City of London hath been discovered and prevented;

174. They presently undertook another of the same damnable nature, with this addition to it, to endeavour to make the Scottish army neutral, whilst the English army, which they had laboured to corrupt and envenom against us by their false and slanderous suggestions, should execute their malice to the subversion of our religion and the dissolution of our government.

175. Thus they have been continually practising to disturb the peace, and plotting the destruction even of all the King's dominions; and have employed their emissaries and agents in them, all for the promoting their devilish designs, which the vigilancy of those who were well affected hath still discovered and defeated before they were ripe for execution in England and Scotland.

176. Only in Ireland, which was farther off, they have had time and opportunity to mould and prepare their work, and had brought it to that perfection that they had possessed themselves of that whole kingdom, totally subverted the government of it, routed out religion, and destroyed all the Protestants whom the conscience of their duty to God, their King and country, would not have permitted to join with them, if by God's wonderful providence their main enterprise upon the city and castle of Dublin had not been detected and prevented upon the very eve before it should have been executed.

177. Notwithstanding they have in other parts of that kingdom broken out into open rebellion, surprising towns and castles, committed murders, rapes and other villainies, and shaken off all bonds of obedience to His Majesty and the laws of the realm.

178. And in general have kindled such a fire, as nothing but God's infinite blessing upon the wisdom and endeavours of this State will be able to quench it.

179. And certainly had not God in His great mercy unto this land discovered and confounded their former designs, we had been the prologue to this tragedy in Ireland, and had by this been made the lamentable spectacle of misery and confusion.

180. And now what hope have we but in God, when as the only means of our subsistence and power of reformation is under Him in the Parliament?

181. But what can we the Commons, without the conjunction of the House of Lords, and what conjunction can we expect there, when the Bishops and recusant lords are so numerous and prevalent that they are able to cross and interrupt our best endeavours for reformation, and by that means give advantage to this malignant party to traduce our proceedings?

182. They infuse into the people that we mean to abolish all Church government, and leave every man to his own fancy for the service and worship of God, absolving him of that obedience which he owes under God unto His Majesty, whom we know to be entrusted with the ecclesiastical law as well as with the temporal, to regulate all the members of the Church of England, by such rules of order and discipline as are

established by Parliament, which is his great council, in all affairs both in Church and State.

183. We confess our intention is, and our endeavours have been, to reduce within bounds that exorbitant power which the prelates have assumed unto themselves, so contrary both to the Word of God and to the laws of the land, to which end we passed the Bill for the removing them from their temporal power and employments, that so the better they might with meekness apply themselves to the discharge of their functions, which Bill themselves opposed, and were the principal instruments of crossing it.

184. And we do here declare that it is far from our purpose or desire to let loose the golden reins of discipline and government in the Church, to leave private persons or particular congregations to take up what form of Divine Service they please, for we hold it requisite that there should be throughout the whole realm a conformity to that order which the laws enjoin according to the Word of God. And we desire to unburden the consciences of men of needless and superstitious ceremonies, suppress innovations, and take away the monuments of idolatry.

185. And the better to effect the intended reformation, we desire there may be a general synod of the most grave, pious, learned and judicious divines of this island; assisted with some from foreign parts, professing the same religion with us, who may consider of all things necessary for the peace and good government of the Church, and represent the results of their consultations unto the Parliament, to be there allowed of and confirmed, and receive the stamp of authority, thereby to find passage and obedience throughout the kingdom.

186. They have maliciously charged us that we intend to destroy and discourage learning, whereas it is our chiefest care and desire to advance it, and to provide a competent maintenance for conscionable and preaching ministers throughout the kingdom, which will be a great encouragement to scholars, and a certain means whereby the want, meanness and ignorance, to which a great part of the clergy is now subject, will be prevented.

187. And we intended likewise to reform and purge the fountains of learning, the two Universities, that the streams flowing from thence may be clear and pure, and an honour and comfort to the whole land.

188. They have strained to blast our proceedings in Parliament, by wresting the interpretations of our orders from their genuine intention.

189. They tell the people that our meddling with the power of episcopacy hath caused sectaries and conventicles, when idolatrous and Popish ceremonies, introduced into the Church by the command of the Bishops, have not only debarred the people from thence, but expelled them from the kingdom.

190. Thus with Elijah, we are called by this malignant party the troublers of the State, and still, while we endeavour to reform their abuses, they make us the authors of those mischiefs we study to prevent.

191. For the perfecting of the work begun, and removing all future impediments, we conceive these courses will be very effectual, seeing the religion of the Papists hath such principles as do certainly tend to the destruction and extirpation of all Protestants, when they shall have opportunity to effect it.

192. It is necessary in the first place to keep them in such condition as that they may not be able to do us any hurt, and for avoiding of such connivance and favour as hath heretofore been shown unto them.

193. That His Majesty be pleased to grant a standing Commission to some choice men named in Parliament, who may take notice of their increase, their counsels and proceedings, and use all due means by execution of the laws to prevent all mischievous designs against the peace and safety of this kingdom.

194. Thus some good course be taken to discover the counterfeit and false conformity of Papists to the Church, by colour whereof persons very much disaffected to the true religion have been admitted into place of greatest authority and trust in the kingdom.

195. For the better preservation of the laws and liberties of the kingdom, that all illegal grievances and exactions be presented and punished at the sessions and assizes.

196. And that Judges and Justices be very careful to give this in charge to the grand jury, and both the Sheriff and Justices to be sworn to the due execution of the Petition of Right and other laws.

197. That His Majesty be humbly petitioned by both Houses to employ such councillors, ambassadors and other ministers, in managing his business at home and abroad as the Parliament may have cause to confide

in, without which we cannot give His Majesty such supplies for support of his own estate, nor such assistance to the Protestant party beyond the sea, as is desired.

198. It may often fall out that the Commons may have just cause to take exceptions at some men for being councillors, and yet not charge those men with crimes, for there be grounds of diffidence which lie not in proof.

199. There are others, which though they may be proved, yet are not legally criminal.

200. To be a known favourer of Papists, or to have been very forward in defending or countenancing some great offenders questioned in Parliament; or to speak contemptuously of either Houses of Parliament or Parliamentary proceedings.

201. Or such as are factors or agents for any foreign prince of another religion; such are justly suspected to get councillors' places, or any other of trust concerning public employment for money; for all these and divers others we may have great reason to be earnest with His Majesty, not to put his great affairs into such hands, though we may be unwilling to proceed against them in any legal way of charge or impeachment.

202. That all Councillors of State may be sworn to observe those laws which concern the subject in his liberty, that they may likewise take an oath not to receive or give reward or pension from any foreign prince, but such as they shall within some reasonable time discover to the Lords of His Majesty's Council.

203. And although they should wickedly forswear themselves, yet it may herein do good to make them known to be false and perjured to those who employ them, and thereby bring them into as little credit with them as with us.

204. That His Majesty may have cause to be in love with good counsel and good men, by showing him in an humble and dutiful manner how full of advantage it would be to himself, to see his own estate settled in a plentiful condition to support his honour; to see his people united in ways of duty to him, and endeavours of the public good; to see happiness, wealth, peace and safety derived to his own kingdom, and procured to his allies by the influence of his own power and government. That all

good courses may be taken to unite the two Kingdomes of England and Scotland to be mutually ayding and assisting one another for the common good of the Island, and honour of both. To take away all differences among our selves for matters indifferent in their owne nature concerning religion, and to unite our selves against the common enemies, which are the better inabled by our divisions to destroy us all, as they hope and have often endeavoured. To labour by all offices of friendship to unite the forrain Churches with us in the same cause, and to seek their liberty, safety, and prosperity, as bound thereunto both by charity to them, and by wisdome for our own good. For by this means our own strength shall be encreased, and by a mutuall concurrence to the same common end, we shall be enabled to procure the good of the whole body of the Protestant profession. If these things may be observed, we doubt not but God will crown this Parliament with such successe as shall be the beginning and foundation of more honour and happinesse to his Majesty, then ever yet was enjoyed by any of his Royall Predecessors.

FINIS.

The Declaration of William of Orange (1688)

The Declaration of his Highnes William Henry, By the Grace of
God Prince of Orange, &c.
Of the Reasons Inducing him, to appear in Armes in the Kingdome of
England, for Preserving of the Protestant Religion, and for Restoring the
Lawes and Liberties of England, Scotland and Ireland.

It is both certain and evident to all men, that the publike Peace and Happines of any State or Kingdome can not be preserved, where the Lawes,
Liberties, and Customes established, by the Lawfull authority in it, are
openly Transgressed and Annulled: More especially where the alteration
of *Religion* is endeavoured, and that a *Religion* which is contrary to Law
is endeavoured to be introduced: Upon which those who are most Immediatly Concerned in it, are Indispensably bound to endeavour to Preserve and maintain the established Lawes Liberties and Customes: and
above all the *Religion* and worship of God, that is Established among
them: And to take such an effectuall care, that the Inhabitants of the said
State or Kingdome, may neither be deprived of their *Religion*, nor of their
Civill Rights. Which is so much the more Necessary because the Greatnes
and Security both of Kings, Royall families, and of all such as are in
Authority, as well as the Happines of their Subjects and People, depend,
in a most especiall manner, upon the exact observation, and maintenance
of these their Lawes Liberties, and Customes.

Upon these grounds it is, that we cannot any longer forbear, to Declare that to our great regret, wee see that those Councellours, who have

now the chieffe credit with the King, have overturned the *Religion*, Lawes, and Liberties of those Realmes: and subjected them in all things relating to their Consciences, Liberties, and Properties, to Arbitrary Government: and that not only by secret and Indirect waies, but in an open and undisguised manner.

Those Evill Councellours for the advancing and colouring this with some plausible pretexts, did Invent and set on foot, the Kings *Dispencing power,* by vertue of which, they pretend that according to *Law,* he can *Suspend* and *Dispence* with the Execution of the *Lawes,* that have been enacted by the Authority, of the King and Parliament, for the security and happines of the Subject and so have rendered those Lawes of no effect: Tho there is nothing more certain, then that as no Lawes can be made, but by the joint concurrence of King and Parliament, so likewise lawes so enacted, which secure the Publike peace, and safety of the Nation, and the lives and liberties of every subject in it, can not be repealed or suspended but by the same authority.

For tho the King may pardon the punishment, that a Transgressour has incurred, and to which he is condemned, as in the cases of *Treason* or *Felony;* yet it cannot be with any colour of reason, Inferred from thence, that the King can entirely suspend the execution of those Lawes, relating to *Treason* or *Felony:* Unlesse it is pretended, that he is clothed with a Despotick and Arbitrary power, and that the Lives Liberties Honours and Estates of the Subjects, depend wholly on his good will and Pleasure, and are entirely subject to him; which must infallibly follow, on the Kings having a power to *suspend* the execution of the *Lawes,* and to dispence with them.

Those Evill Councellours, in order to the giving some credit to this strange and execrable Maxime, have so conducted the matter, that they have obtained a Sentence from the Judges, declaring that this *Dispencing power,* is a Right belonging to the *Crown;* as if it were in the power of the twelve Judges, to offer up the Lawes, Rights, and Liberties, of the whole Nation, to the King, to be disposed of by him Arbitrarily and at his Pleasure, and expressly contrary to Lawes enacted, for the security of the Subjects. In order to the obtaining this Judgment, those Evill Councellours did before hand, examine secretly, the Opinion of the Judges, and

procured such of them, as could not in Conscience concurre in so pernicious a Sentence, to be turned out, and others to be substituted in their
Rooms, till by the changes which were made, in the Courts of Judicature,
they at last obtained that Judgment. And they have raised some to those
Trusts, who make open Profession of the Popish Religion, tho those are
by Law Rendred Incapable of all such Employments.

It is also Manifest and Notorious, that as his Majestie was, upon his
coming to the Crown, received and acknowledged by all the subjects of
England, *Scotland*, and *Ireland*, as their *King* without the least opposition, tho he made then open profession, of the *Popish Religion*, so he
did then Promise, and Solemnly Swear, at his Coronation, that he would
maintain his subjects, in the free enjoyment of their Lawes, Rights,
and Liberties, and in particular, that he would maintain the *Church of
England as it was established by Law:* It is likewise certain, that there have
been at diverse and sundry times, severall Lawes enacted for the preservation of those Rights, and Liberties, and of the Protestant Religion: and
among other Securities, it has been enacted that all Persons whatsoever,
that are advanced to any Ecclesiasticall Dignity, or to bear Office in
either University, as likewise all others, that should be put in any Imployment, Civill or Military, should declare that they were not Papists, but
were of the Protestant Religion, and that, by their taking of the Oaths of
Allegeance, and *Supreamacy* and the *Test,* yet these Evill Councellours
have in effect annulled and abolished all those Lawes, both with relation
to Ecclesiasticall and Civill Employments.

In order to Ecclesiasticall Dignities and Offices, they have not only
without any colour of Law, but against most expresse Lawes to the contrary, set up a Commission of a certain Number of persons, to whom they
have committed the cognisance and direction of all Ecclesiasticall matters:
in the which Commission there has been and still is one of His Majesties
Ministers of State, who makes now publike profession of the Popish Religion, and who at the time of his first professing it, declared that for a
great while before, he had beleeved that to be the only true Religion. By
all this, the deplorable State to which the Protestant Religion is reduced
is apparent, since the Affairs of the Church of England, are now put
into the hands of Persons, who have accepted of a Commission that is

manifestly Illegal; and who have executed it contrary to all Law: and that now one of their chiefe Members has abjured the *Protestant Religion*, and declared himselfe a *Papist;* by which he is become Incapable of holding any Publike Imployment: The said Commissioners have hitherto given such proof of their submission to the directions given them, that there is no reason to doubt, but they will still continue to promote all such designs as will be most aggreable to them. And those Evill Councellours take care to raise none to any Ecclesiasticall dignities, but persons that have no zeal for the *Protestant Religion,* and that now hide their unconcernednes for it, under the specious pretence of *Moderation.* The said Commissioners have suspended the Bishop of *London,* only because he refused to obey an order, that was sent him to suspend a Worthy Divine, without so much as citing him before him, to make his own Defence, or observing the common formes of processe. They have turned out a President, chosen by the fellows of *Magdalen Colledge,* and afterwards all the Fellows of that Colledge, without so much as citing them before any Court that could take legall cognissance of that affair; or obtaining any Sentence against them by a Competent Judge. And the only reason that was given for turning them out, was their refusing to choose for their President, a Person that was recommended to them, by the Instigation of those Evill Councellours; tho the right of a free Election belonged undoubtedly to them. But they were turned out of their freeholds, contrary to Law, and to that expresse provision in the *Magna Charta; that no man shall lose life or goods, but by the Law of the land*. And now these Evill Councellours have put the said Colledge wholly into the hands of Papists, tho as is abovesaid, they are Incapable, of all such Employments, both by the Law of the Land, and the statutes of the Colledge. These Commissioners have also cited before them all the Chancellours and Archdeacons of England, requiring them to certifie to them the names, of all such Clergymen, as have read the Kings declaration for *Liberty of Conscience,* and of such as have not read it: without considering that the reading of it was not enjoined the Clergy by the Bishops, who are their Ordinaries. The Illegality and Incompetency of the said Court of the Ecclesiasticall Commissioners was so notoriously known, and it did so evidently appear, that it tended to the Subversion of the *Protestant Religion,* that the Most Reverend Father in God, *William* Archbishop of *Canterbury*, Primate and Metropolitan of all *England*, seeing that it was raised for no other end, but to opresse such persons as were of Eminent Vertue, Learning, and Piety, refused to sit or to concurre in it.

And tho there are many expresse Lawes against all Churches or Chappells, for the exercise of the Popish Religion, and also against all Monasteries and Convents, and more particularly against the order of the *Jesuites*, yet those Evill Councellours have procured orders for the building of severall Churches and Chappells, for the exercise of that Religion: They have also procured diverse Monasteries to be erected, and in contempt of the Law they have not only set up severall Colledges of *Jesuites*, in diverse places, for the corrupting of the youth, but have raised up one of the *Order* to be a Privy Councellour and a Minister of State. By all which they doe evidently show, that they are restrained by no rules or Law whatsoever; but that they have subjected the Honours and Estates of the subjects, and the establisht Religion to a Despotick power and to Arbitrary Government: In all which they are served and seconded by those Ecclesiastical Commissioners.

They have also followed the same methods with relation to Civill affairs: For they have procured orders to examine all Lords Lieutenants, Deputy Lieutenants, Sheriffs, Justices of Peace, and all others that were in any publike Imployment, if they would concurre with the King in the repeal of the *Test* and *Penal Lawes:* and all such, whose consciences did not suffer them to comply with their designes, were turned out; and others were put in their places, who they beleeved would be more compliant to them, in their designs of defeating the intent and Execution of those Lawes, which had been made with so much care and caution, for the Security of the *Protestant Religion.* And in many of these places they have put professed Papists, tho the Law has disabled them, and warranted the subjects not to have any regard to their Orders.

They have also invaded the Priviledges, and seised on the Charters of most of those Towns that have a right to be represented by their Burgesses in Parliament: and have procured surrenders to be made of them, by which the Magistrates in them have delivered up all their Rights, and Priviledges, to be disposed of, at the pleasure of those Evill

Councellours: who have thereupon placed new Magistrates in those Towns, such as they can most entirely confide in: and in many of them, they have put Popish Magistrates notwithstanding the Incapacities under which the Law has put them.

And whereas no Nation whatsoever can subsist without the administration of good and impartiall Justice, upon which mens Lives, Liberties, Honours and Estates doe depend; those Evill Councellours have subjected these to an Arbitrary and Despotick power: In the most important affairs they have studied to discover before hand the Opinions of the Judges; and have turned out such, as they found would not conform themselves to their intentions: and have put others in their places, of whom they were more assured, without having any regard to their abilities. And they have not stuck to raise even professed Papists to the Courts of Judicature, notwithstanding their Incapacity by Law, and that no Regard is due to any Sentences flowing from them. They have carried this so far, as to deprive such Judges, who in the common administration of Justice, shewed that they were governed by their Consciences, and not by the directions which the others gave them: By which it is apparent that they designe, to render themselves the absolute Masters of the Lives, Honours, and Estates of the subjects, of what rank or dignity soever they may be: and that without having any regard either to the equity of the cause, or to the consciences of the Judges, whom they will have to submit in all things to their own will and pleasure: hoping by such waies to Intimidate those other Judges, who are yet in Imployment, as also such others, as they shall think fit to put in the Rooms of those whom they have turned out; and to make them see what they must look for, if they should at any time act in the least contrary to their good liking: and that no failings of that kind, are pardoned, in any persons whatsoever. A great deale of blood has been shed in many places of the Kingdome, by Judges governed by those Evill Councellours, against all the rules and forms of Law; without so much as suffering the persons that were accused to plead in their own Defence.

They have also, by putting the administration of justice in the hands of Papists, brought all the matters of Civill Justice into great uncertainties: with how much exactnes and Justice soever that these Sentences may

have been given. For since the Lawes of the Land doe not only exclude
Papists from all places of Judicature, but have put them under an Incapacity, none are bound to acknowledge or to obey their Judgements, and
all Sentences given by them, are null and void of themselves: so that all
persons who have been cast in Trialls before such Popish Judges, may
justly look on their pretended Sentences, as having no more force then
the Sentences of any private and unauthorised person whatsoever. So deplorable is the case of the Subjects, who are obliged to answer to such
Judges, that must in all things stick to the rules which are set them by
those Evill Councellours, who as they raised them up to those Imployments, so can turn them out of them at pleasure; and who can never be
esteemed Lawfull Judges: so that all their Sentences are in the Construction of the Law, of no force and efficacy. They have likewise disposed of
all Military Imployments, in the same manner: For tho the Lawes have
not only excluded Papists from all such Imployments, but have in particular provided that they should be disarmed; yet they in contempt of those
Lawes, have not only armed the Papists, but have likewise raised them
up to the greatest Military Trusts, both by Sea and Land and that Strangers as well as Natives, and Irish as well as English, that so by these means
they having rendred themselves Masters both of the affairs of the
Church, of the Government of the Nation, and of the course of Justice,
and subjected them all to a Despotick and Arbitrary power, they might
be in a Capacity to maintain and execute their wicked designs by the assistance of the Army, and thereby to enslave the Nation.

The dismall effects of this subversion of the established Religion,
Lawes and Liberties in England appear more evidently to us, by what
wee see done in Ireland: Where the whole Government is put in the hands
of Papists, and where all the Protestant Inhabitants are under the daily
fears of what may be justly apprehended from the Arbitrary power which
is set up there: which has made great numbers of them leave that Kingdome and abandon their Estates in it, remembring well that cruell and
bloody Massacre which fell out in that Island in the year 1641.

Those Evill Councellours have also prevailed with the King to declare
in Scotland that he is clothed with *Absolute power,* and that all the subjects are bound *to obey him without Reserve:* upon which he has assumed

an Arbitrary power, both over the Religion and Lawes of that King-dome: from all which it is apparent, what is to be looked for in England, as soon as matters are duely prepared for it.

Those great and insufferable Oppressions, and the open Contempt of all Law, together with the apprehensions of the sad consequences that must certainly follow upon it, have put the subjects under great and just fears; and have made them look after such lawfull remedies as are al-lowed of in all Nations: yet all has been without effect. And those Evill Councellours have endeavoured to make all men apprehend the losse of their Lives, Liberties, Honours and Estates, if they should goe about to preserve themselves from this Oppression by Petitions, Representations, or other means authorised by Law. Thus did they proceed with the Arch-bishop of *Canterbury,* and the other Bishops, who having offered a most humble petition to the King, in termes full of Respect, and not exceeding the number limited by Law, in which they set forth in short the Reasons for which they could not obey that order, which by the Instigation of those Evill Councellours was sent them, requiring them to appoint their Clergy to read in their Churches the Declaration for *Liberty of Conscience;* were sent to prison and afterwards brought to a Triall, as if they had been guilty of some enormous Crime. They were not only obliged to defend themselves in that pursute, but to appear before professed Papists, who had not taken the Test and by consequence were men whose interest led them to condemne them; and the Judges that gave their opinion in their favours were thereupon turned out.

And yet it can not be pretended that any Kings, how great soever their power has been, and how Arbitrary and Despotick soever they have been in the exercise of it, have ever reckoned it a crime for their Subjects to come in all submission and respect, and in a due number, not exceeding the limits of the Law, and represent to them the reasons that made it impossible for them to obey their orders. Those Evill Councellours have also treated, a Peer of the Realme, as a criminall, only because he said that the subjects were not bound to obey the orders of a Popish Justice of Peace: tho it is evident, that they being by Law rendred incapable of all such trust, no regard is due to their orders: This being the security which the people have by the Law for their Lives, Liberties, Honours and Estates, that they are not to be subjected to the Arbitrary procedings of Papists, that are contrary to Law, put into any Employments Civill or Military.

Both Wee our selves and our Dearest and most Entirely Beloved Consort, the Princesse, have endeavoured to signify in termes full of respect to the King the just and deep Regret which all these Proceedings have given us; and in Compliance with his Majesties desires signified to us, Wee declared both by word of mouth, to his Envoy, and in writing, what our Thoughts were touching the Repealing of the *Test and Penall Lawes;* which wee did in such a manner, that wee hoped wee had proposed an Expedient, by which the Peace of those Kingdomes, and a happy aggreement among the Subjects, of all Persuasions, might have been setled: but those Evill Councellours have put such ill Constructions on these our good Intentions, that they have endeavoured to alienate the King more and more from us: as if Wee had designed to disturb the quiet and happines of the Kingdome.

The last and great Remedy for all those Evills, Is *the Calling of a Parliament,* for securing the Nation against the Evill practises of those wicked Councellours: but this could not be yet compassed, nor can it be easily brought about. For those men apprehending that a lawfull Parliament, being once assembled, they would be brought to an account for all their open violations of Law, and for their Plots and Conspiracies against the Protestant Religion, and the Lives and Liberties of the Subjects, they have endeavoured under the specious Pretence of *Liberty of Conscience;* first to sow divisions among Protestants, between those of the Church of *England* and the Dissenters: The designe being laid to engage Protestants, that are all equally concerned, to preserve themselves from Popish Oppression, into mutuall quarrellings; that so by these, some advantages might be given to them to bring about their Designes; and that both in the Election of the Members of Parliament, and afterwards in the Parliament it selfe. For they see well that if all Protestants, could enter into a mutuall Good Understanding, one with another, and concurre together in the Preserving of their Religion, it would not be possible for them to compasse their wicked ends. They have also required all Persons in the severall Counties of England, that either were in any Imployment, or were in any considerable Esteem, to declare before hand, that they would concurre in the Repeal of the *Test and Penal Lawes;* and that they would give their voices in the Elections to Parliament, only for such as would concurre in it. Such as would not thus preingage themselves were turned out of all Imployments; and others who entred into those engagements were put in their places, many of them being Papists: And contrary to the Charters and Priviledges of those Burroughs, that have a Right to send Burgesses to Parliament, they have ordered such Regulations to be made, as they thought fit and necessary, for assuring themselves of all the Members, that are to be chosen by those Corporations: and by this means they hope to avoid that Punishment which they have Deserved: tho it is apparent, that all Acts made by Popish Magistrates are null, and Void of themselves; So that no Parliament can be Lawfull, for which the Elections and Returns are made by Popish Sheriffs and Mayors of Towns; and therefore as long as the Authority and Magistracy is in such hands, it is not possible to have any Lawfull Parliament. And tho according to the Constitution of the English Government, and Immemoriall Custome, all Elections of Parliament men ought to be made with an Entire Liberty without any sort of force, or the requiring the Electors to choose such Persons as shall be named to them, and the Persons thus freely Elected, ought to give their Opinions freely, upon all Matters, that are brought before them, having the good of the Nation ever before their Eyes, and following in all things the dictates of their Conscience, yet now the People of England can not expect a Remedy from a free Parliament, Legally Called and Chosen. But they may perhaps see one Called, in which all Elections will be carried by Fraud or Force, and which will be composed of such Persons, of whom those Evill Councellours hold themselves well assured, in which all things will be carried on according to their Direction and Interest, without any regard to the Good or Happines of the Nation. Which may appear Evidently from this, that the same Persons tried the Members of the last Parliament, to gain them to Consent to the Repeal of the *Test and Penal Lawes,* and procured that Parliament to be dissolved, when they found that they could not, neither by promises nor Threatnings, Prevail with the Members to Comply with their wicked Designs.

But to Crown all, there are Great and Violent Presumptions, Inducing us to Beleeve, that those Evill Councellours, in order to the carrying on of their ill Designes, and to the Gaining to themselves the more time for the Effecting of them, for the encouraging of their Complices, and for the discouraging of all Good Subjects, have published that the *Queen* hath brought forth a *Son:* tho there have appeared both during the *Queens* pretended Bignes, and in the manner in which the Birth was managed, so many just and Visible grounds of suspition, that not only wee our selves, but all the good subjects of those Kingdomes, doe Vehemently suspect, that the pretended Prince of *Wales* was not born by the *Queen*. And it is notoriously known to all the world, that many both doubted of the Queens Bignes, and of the Birth of the Child, and yet there was not any one thing done to Satisfy them, or to put an end to their Doubts.

And since our Dearest and most Entirely Beloved Consort, the Princesse, and likewise wee Our Selves, have so great an Interest in this Matter, and such a Right, as all the world knows, to the Succession to the Crown, Since also the English did in the year 1672. when the States Generall of the *United Provinces,* were Invaded, in a most Injust warre, use their uttermost Endeavours to put an end to that Warre, and that in opposition to those who were then in the Government: and by their so doing, they run the hasard, of losing, both the favour of the Court, and their Imployments; And since the English Nation has ever testified a most particular Affection and Esteem, both to our Dearest Consort the Princesse, and to Our selves, WEE cannot excuse our selves from espousing their Interests, in a matter of such high Consequence, and from Contributing all that lies in us, for the Maintaining both of the Protestant Religion, and of the Lawes and Liberties of those Kingdomes, and for the Securing to them, the Continuall Enjoyment of all their just Rights. To the doing of which, wee are most Earnestly Solicited by a Great many Lords, both Spirituall and Temporall, and by many Gentlemen and other subjects of all Ranks.

THEREFORE it is, that wee have thought fit to goe over to England, and to Carry over with us a force, sufficient by the blessing of God, to defend us from the Violence of those Evill Councellours. AND WEE being desirous that our Intentions in this, may be Rightly Understood, have for this end prepared this *Declaration,* in which as wee have hitherto given a True Account of the Reasons Inducing us to it, So wee now think fit to DECLARE that this our Expedition, is intended for no other Designe, but to have a free and lawfull Parliament assembled, as soon as is possible: and that in order to this, all the late Charters by which the Elections of Burgesses are limited contrary to the Ancient custome, shall be considered as null and of no force: and likewise all Magistrates who have been Injustly turned out, shall forthwith resume their former Imployments, as well as all the Borroughs of England shall return again to their Antient Prescriptions and Charters: And more particularly that the Ancient Charter of the Great and famous City of London, shall again be in Force: and that the Writts for the Members of Parliament shall be addressed to the Proper Officers, according to Law and Custome. That also none be suffered to choose or to be chosen Members of Parliament, but such as are qualified by Law: And that the Members of Parliament being thus lawfully chosen they shall meet and sit in full Freedome; that so the Two Houses may concurre in the preparing of such Lawes, as they upon full and free debate, shall Judge necessary and convenient, both for the confirming and executing the Law concerning the *Test* and such other *Lawes* as are necessary for the Security and Maintenance of the Protestant Religion; as likewise for making such Lawes as may establish a good aggreement between the Church of England, and all Protestant Dissenters, as also for the covering and securing of all such, who will live Peaceably under the Government as becomes good Subjects, from all Persecution upon the account of their Religion, even *Papists* themselves not excepted; and for the doing of all other things, which the Two Houses of Parliament shall find necessary for the Peace, Honour, and Safety of the Nation, so that there may be no more danger of the Nations falling at any time hereafter, under *Arbitrary Government*. To this Parliament wee will also referre the Enquiry into the birth of the Pretended Prince of Wales, and of all things relating to it and to the Right of Succession.

And Wee for our part will concurre in every thing, that may procure the Peace and Happines of the Nation, which a Free and Lawfull Parliament shall determine; Since wee have nothing before our eyes in this our undertaking, but the Preservation of the Protestant Religion, the Covering of all men from Persecution for their Consciences, and the Securing to the whole Nation the free enjoyment of all their Lawes, Rights and Liberties, under a Just and Legall Government.

This is the designe, that wee have Proposed to our selves, in Appearing upon this occasion in Armes: In the Conduct of which, Wee will keep the Forces under our Command, under all the Strictnes of Martiall Discipline: and take a speciall Care, that the People of the Countries thro which wee must march, shall not suffer by their means: and as soon as the State of the Nation will admit of it, Wee promise that wee will send back all those Forreigne Forces, that wee have brought along with us.

Wee doe therefore hope that all People will judge rightly of us, and approve of these our Proceedings: But wee chiefly rely on the blessing of God, for the successe of this our undertaking, in which Wee place our whole and only Confidence.

Wee doe in the last place, invite and require all Persons whatsoever, All the Peers of the Realme, both Spirituall and Temporal, all Lords Lieutenants, Deputy Lieutenants, and all Gentlemen, Citisens and other Commons of all ranks, to come and assist us, in order to the Executing of this our Designe; against all such as shall Endeavour to Oppose us; that so wee may prevent all those Miseries, which must needs follow upon the Nations being kept under Arbitrary Government and Slavery: And that all the Violences and disorders, which have overturned the whole Constitution of the English Government, may be fully redressed, in a Free and Legall Parliament.

And Wee doe likewise resolve that as soon as the Nations are brought to a state of Quiet, Wee will take care that a Parliament shall be called in *Scotland*, for the restoring the Ancient Constitution of that Kingdome, and for bringing the Matters of Religion to such a Setlement, that the people may live easy and happy, and for putting an end to all the Injust Violences that have been in a course of so many years Committed there.

Wee will also study to bring the Kingdome of *Ireland* to such a state, that the Setlement there may be Religiously observed: and that the Protestant and Brittish Interest there, may be secured. And wee will endeavour by all possible means, to procure such an establishment in all the Three Kingdomes that they may all live in a happy Union and Correspondence together; and that the Protestant Religion, and the Peace, Honour, and Happines of those Nations, may be established upon Lasting Foundations.

Given under our Hand and Seal, at our Court in the Hague, the tenth day of October in the year 1688.

WILLIAM HENRY, Prince of Orange.

By his Highnesses speciall command
C: Huygens.

His Highnesses Additionall Declaration.

After wee had prepared and printed this our Declaration, wee have understood, that the subverters of the Religion and Lawes of those Kingdomes, hearing of our Preparations, to assist the People against them, have begun to retract some of the Arbitrary and Despotick powers, that they had assumed, and to vacate some of their Injust Judgments and Decrees. The sense of their Guilt, and the distrust of their force, have induced them to offer to the City of London some seeming releefe from their Great Oppressions: hoping thereby to quiet the People, and to divert them from demanding a Secure Re-establishment of their Religion and Lawes under the shelter of our Armes: They doe also give out that wee Intend to Conquer and Enslave the Nation, And therefore it is that wee have thought fit to adde a few words to our Declaration.

Wee are Confident, that no persons can have such hard thought of us, as to Imagine that wee have any other Designe in this Undertaking, then to procure a setlement of the Religion and of the Liberties and Properties of the subjects upon so sure a foundation, that there may be no danger of the Nations relapsing into the like miseries at any time hereafter. And as the forces that wee have brought along with us, are utterly disproportioned to that wicked designe of Conquering the Nation, if wee were Capable of Intending it, so the Great Numbers of the Principall Nobility and Gentry, that are men of Eminent Quality and Estates, and persons of known Integrity and Zeal both for the Religion and Government of England, many of them being also distinguished by their Constant fidelity to the Crown, who doe both accompany us in this Expedition, and have earnestly solicited us to it, will cover us from all such Malicious

Insinuations: For it is not to be imagined, that either those who have Invited us, or those that are already come to assist us, can joyne in a wicked attempt of Conquest, to make void their own lawfull Titles to their Honours, Estates and Interests: Wee are also Confident that all men see how litle weight there is to be laid, on all Promises and Engagments that can be now made: since there has been so litle regard had in time past, to the most solemne Promises. And as that Imperfect redresse that is now offered, is a plain Confession of those Violations of the Government that wee have set forth, So the Defectivenes of it is no lesse Apparent: for they lay doune nothing which they may not take up at Pleasure: and they reserve entire and not so much as mentioned, their claimes and pretences to an Arbitrary and Despotick power: which has been the root of all their Oppression, and of the totall subversion of the Government. And it is plain, that there can be no redresse nor Remedy offered but in Parliament: by a Declaration of the Rights of the Subjects that have been invaded: and not by any Pretended Acts of Grace, to which the extremity of their affairs has driven them. Therefore it is that wee have thought fit to declare, that wee will referre all to a Free Assembly of the Nation, in a Lawfull Parliament.

Given under our Hand and Seal, at our Court in the Hague, the 24. day of October in the year of our Lord 1688.

WILLIAM HENRY, PRINCE OF ORANGE.
By his Highnesses speciall Command
C: HUYGENS.

The Bill of Rights (1689)

An Act Declaring the Rights and Liberties of the Subject and Settling the Succession of the Crown

Whereas the Lords Spiritual and Temporal and Commons assembled at Westminster, lawfully, fully and freely representing all the estates of the people of this realm, did upon the thirteenth day of February in the year of our Lord one thousand six hundred eighty-eight [Old Style date] present unto their Majesties, then called and known by the names and style of William and Mary, prince and princess of Orange, being present in their proper persons, a certain declaration in writing made by the said Lords and Commons in the words following, viz.:

Whereas the late King James the Second, by the assistance of divers evil counsellors, judges and ministers employed by him, did endeavour to subvert and extirpate the Protestant religion and the laws and liberties of this kingdom;

By assuming and exercising a power of dispensing with and suspending of laws and the execution of laws without consent of Parliament;

By committing and prosecuting divers worthy prelates for humbly petitioning to be excused from concurring to the said assumed power;

By issuing and causing to be executed a commission under the great seal for erecting a court called the Court of Commissioners for Ecclesiastical Causes;

By levying money for and to the use of the Crown by pretence of prerogative for other time and in other manner than the same was granted by Parliament;

By raising and keeping a standing army within this kingdom in time of peace without consent of Parliament, and quartering soldiers contrary to law;

By causing several good subjects being Protestants to be disarmed at the same time when papists were both armed and employed contrary to law;

By violating the freedom of election of members to serve in Parliament;

By prosecutions in the Court of King's Bench for matters and causes cognizable only in Parliament, and by divers other arbitrary and illegal courses;

And whereas of late years partial corrupt and unqualified persons have been returned and served on juries in trials, and particularly divers jurors in trials for high treason which were not freeholders;

And excessive bail hath been required of persons committed in criminal cases to elude the benefit of the laws made for the liberty of the subjects;

And excessive fines have been imposed;

And illegal and cruel punishments inflicted;

And several grants and promises made of fines and forfeitures before any conviction or judgment against the persons upon whom the same were to be levied;

All which are utterly and directly contrary to the known laws and statutes and freedom of this realm;

And whereas the said late King James the Second having abdicated the government and the throne being thereby vacant, his Highness the prince of Orange (whom it hath pleased Almighty God to make the glorious instrument of delivering this kingdom from popery and arbitrary power) did (by the advice of the Lords Spiritual and Temporal and divers principal persons of the Commons) cause letters to be written to the Lords Spiritual and Temporal being Protestants, and other letters to the several counties, cities, universities, boroughs and cinque ports, for the choosing of such persons to represent them as were of right to be sent to Parliament, to meet and sit at Westminster upon the two and twentieth day of January in this year one thousand six hundred eighty and eight [Old Style date], in order to such an establishment as that their religion, laws and liberties might not again be in danger of being subverted, upon which letters elections having been accordingly made;

And thereupon the said Lords Spiritual and Temporal and Commons, pursuant to their respective letters and elections, being now assembled in a full and free representative of this nation, taking into their most serious consideration the best means for attaining the ends aforesaid, do in the first place (as their ancestors in like case have usually done) for the vindicating and asserting their ancient rights and liberties declare

That the pretended power of suspending the laws or the execution of laws by regal authority without consent of Parliament is illegal;

That the pretended power of dispensing with laws or the execution of laws by regal authority, as it hath been assumed and exercised of late, is illegal;

That the commission for erecting the late Court of Commissioners for Ecclesiastical Causes, and all other commissions and courts of like nature, are illegal and pernicious;

That levying money for or to the use of the Crown by pretence of prerogative, without grant of Parliament, for longer time, or in other manner than the same is or shall be granted, is illegal;

That it is the right of the subjects to petition the king, and all commitments and prosecutions for such petitioning are illegal;

That the raising or keeping a standing army within the kingdom in time of peace, unless it be with consent of Parliament, is against law;

That the subjects which are Protestants may have arms for their defence suitable to their conditions and as allowed by law;

That election of members of Parliament ought to be free;

That the freedom of speech and debates or proceedings in Parliament ought not to be impeached or questioned in any court or place out of Parliament;

That excessive bail ought not to be required, nor excessive fines imposed, nor cruel and unusual punishments inflicted;

That jurors ought to be duly impanelled and returned, and jurors which pass upon men in trials for high treason ought to be freeholders;

That all grants and promises of fines and forfeitures of particular persons before conviction are illegal and void;

And that for redress of all grievances, and for the amending, strengthening and preserving of the laws, Parliaments ought to be held frequently.

And they do claim, demand and insist upon all and singular the premises as their undoubted rights and liberties, and that no declarations, judgments, doings or proceedings to the prejudice of the people in any of the said premises ought in any wise to be drawn hereafter into consequence or example; to which demand of their rights they are particularly encouraged by the declaration of his Highness the prince of Orange as being the only means for obtaining a full redress and remedy therein. Having therefore an entire confidence that his said Highness the prince of Orange will perfect the deliverance so far advanced by him, and will still preserve them from the violation of their rights which they have here asserted, and from all other attempts upon their religion, rights and liberties, the said Lords Spiritual and Temporal and Commons assembled at Westminster do resolve that William and Mary, prince and princess of Orange, be and be declared king and queen of England, France and Ireland and the dominions thereunto belonging, to hold the crown and royal dignity of the said kingdoms and dominions to them, the said prince and princess, during their lives and the life of the survivor to them, and that the sole and full exercise of the regal power be only in and executed by the said prince of Orange in the names of the said prince and princess during their joint lives, and after their deceases the said crown and royal dignity of the same kingdoms and dominions to be to the heirs of the body of the said princess, and for default of such issue to the Princess Anne of Denmark and the heirs of her body, and for default of such issue to the heirs of the body of the said prince of Orange. And the Lords Spiritual and Temporal and Commons do pray the said prince and princess to accept the same accordingly.

And that the oaths hereafter mentioned be taken by all persons of whom the oaths of allegiance and supremacy might be required by law, instead of them; and that the said oaths of allegiance and supremacy be abrogated.

I, A.B., do sincerely promise and swear that I will be faithful and bear true allegiance to their Majesties King William and Queen Mary. So help me God.

I, A.B., do swear that I do from my heart abhor, detest and abjure as impious and heretical this damnable doctrine and position, that princes excommunicated or deprived by the Pope or any authority of the see of Rome may be deposed or murdered by their subjects or any other whatsoever. And I do declare that no foreign prince, person, prelate, state or potentate hath or ought to have any jurisdiction, power, superiority, preeminence or authority, ecclesiastical or spiritual, within this realm. So help me God.

Upon which their said Majesties did accept the crown and royal dignity of the kingdoms of England, France and Ireland, and the dominions thereunto belonging, according to the resolution and desire of the said Lords and Commons contained in the said declaration. And thereupon their Majesties were pleased that the said Lords Spiritual and Temporal and Commons, being the two Houses of Parliament, should continue to sit, and with their Majesties' royal concurrence make effectual provision for the settlement of the religion, laws and liberties of this kingdom, so that the same for the future might not be in danger again of being subverted, to which the said Lords Spiritual and Temporal and Commons did agree, and proceed to act accordingly. Now in pursuance of the premises the said Lords Spiritual and Temporal and Commons in Parliament assembled, for the ratifying, confirming and establishing the said declaration and the articles, clauses, matters and things therein contained by the force of law made in due form by authority of Parliament, do pray that it may be declared and enacted that all and singular the rights and liberties asserted and claimed in the said declaration are the true, ancient and indubitable rights and liberties of the people of this kingdom, and so shall be esteemed, allowed, adjudged, deemed and taken to be; and that all and every the particulars aforesaid shall be firmly and strictly holden and observed as they are expressed in the said declaration, and all officers and ministers whatsoever shall serve their Majesties and their successors according to the same in all time to come. And the said Lords Spiritual and Temporal and Commons, seriously considering how it hath pleased Almighty God in his marvellous providence and merciful goodness to this nation to provide and preserve their said Majesties' royal persons most happily to reign over us upon the throne of their ancestors, for which they render unto him from the bottom of their hearts their humblest thanks and praises, do truly, firmly, assuredly and in the sincerity of their hearts think, and do hereby recognize, acknowledge and declare, that King James the Second having abdicated the government, and their Majesties having accepted the crown and royal dignity as aforesaid, their said Majesties did become, were, are and of right ought to be by the laws of this realm our sovereign liege lord and lady, king and queen of England, France and Ireland and the dominions thereunto belonging, in and to whose princely persons the royal state, crown and dignity of the said realms with all honours, styles, titles, regalities, prerogatives, powers, jurisdictions and authorities to the same belonging and appertaining are most fully, rightfully and entirely invested and incorporated, united and annexed. And for preventing all questions and divisions in this realm by reason of any pretended titles to the crown, and for preserving a certainty in the succession thereof, in and upon which the unity, peace, tranquility and safety of this nation doth under God wholly consist and depend, the said Lords Spiritual and Temporal and Commons do beseech their Majesties that it may be enacted, established and declared, that the crown and regal government of the said kingdoms and dominions, with all and singular the premises thereunto belonging and appertaining, shall be and continue to their said Majesties and the survivor of them during their lives and the life of the survivor of them, and that the entire, perfect and full exercise of the regal power and government be only in and executed by his Majesty in the names of both their Majesties during their joint lives; and after their deceases the said crown and premises shall be and remain to the heirs of the body of her Majesty, and for default of such issue to her Royal Highness the Princess Anne of Denmark and the heirs of the body of his said Majesty; and thereunto the said Lords Spiritual and Temporal and Commons do in the name of all the people aforesaid most humbly and faithfully submit themselves, their heirs and posterities for ever, and do faithfully promise that they will stand to, maintain and defend their said Majesties, and also the limitation and succession of the crown herein specified and contained, to the utmost of their powers with their lives and estates against all persons whatsoever that shall attempt anything to the contrary. And whereas it hath been found by experience that it is inconsistent with the safety and welfare of this Protestant kingdom to be governed by a popish prince, or by any king or queen marrying a papist, the said Lords Spiritual and Temporal and Commons do further pray that it may be enacted, that all and every person and persons that is, are or shall be reconciled to or shall hold communion with the see or Church of Rome, or shall profess the popish religion, or shall marry a papist, shall be excluded and be for ever incapable to inherit, possess or enjoy the crown and government of this realm and Ireland and the dominions thereunto belonging or any part of the same, or to have, use or exercise any regal power, authority or jurisdiction within the same; and in all and every such case or cases the people of these realms shall be and are hereby absolved of their allegiance; and the said crown and government shall from time to time descend to and be enjoyed by such person or persons being Protestants as should have inherited and enjoyed the same in case the said person or persons so reconciled, holding communion or professing or marrying as aforesaid were naturally dead; and that every king and queen of this realm who at any time hereafter shall come to and succeed in the imperial crown of this kingdom shall on the first day of the meeting of the first Parliament next after his or her coming to the crown, sitting in his or her throne in the House of Peers in the presence of the Lords and Commons therein assembled, or at his or her coronation before such person or persons who shall administer the coronation oath to him or her at the time of his or her taking the said oath (which shall first happen), make, subscribe and audibly repeat the declaration mentioned in the statute made in the thirtieth year of the reign of King Charles the Second entitled, *An Act for the more effectual preserving the king's person and government by disabling papists from sitting in either House of Parliament*. But if it shall happen that such king or queen upon his or her succession to the crown of this realm shall be under the age of twelve years, then every such king or queen shall make, subscribe and audibly repeat the same declaration at his or her coronation or the first day of the meeting of the first Parliament as aforesaid which shall first happen after such king or queen shall have attained the said age of twelve years. All which their Majesties are contented and pleased shall be declared, enacted and established by authority of this present Parliament, and shall stand, remain and be the law of this realm for ever; and the same are by their said Majesties, by and with the advice and consent of the Lords Spiritual and Temporal and Commons in Parliament assembled and by the authority of the same, declared, enacted and established accordingly.

II. And be it further declared and enacted by the authority aforesaid, that from and after this present session of Parliament no dispensation by *non obstante* of or to any statute or any part thereof shall be allowed, but that the same shall be held void and of no effect, except a dispensation be allowed of in such statute, and except in such cases as shall be specially provided for by one or more bill or bills to be passed during this present session of Parliament.

III. Provided that no charter or grant or pardon granted before the three and twentieth day of October in the year of our Lord one thousand six hundred eighty-nine shall be any ways impeached or invalidated by this Act, but that the same shall be and remain of the same force and effect in law and no other than as if this Act had never been made.

Abel Boyer's Précis *of the Parliamentary Debates on Standing Armies* (1702–3)

The next day the Parliament being met, pursuant to their Prorogation, the King addrest himself to the Lords and Commons in these words: "The War which I enter'd into by the Advice of my People, is, by the Blessing of God, and their zealous and affectionate Assistance, brought to the end we all propos'd, an Honourable Peace; which I was willing to conclude, not so much to ease my self from any trouble or hazard, as to free the Kingdom from the continuing Burthen of an Expensive War. I am heartily sorry my Subjects will not at first find all that Relief from the Peace, which I could wish, and they may expect; but the Funds intended for the last Year's Service have fallen short of answering the Sums for which they were given, so that there remain considerable Deficiencies to be provided for. There is a Debt upon account of the Fleet and the Army. The Revenues of the Crown have been anticipated by my Consent, for the publick Uses, so that I am wholly destitute of Means to support the Civil List; and I can never distrust you will suffer this to turn to my Disadvantage, but will provide for me during my Life, in such a man[287]ner as may be for my Honour, and for the Honour of the Government. Our Naval Force being encreased to near double to what it was at my Accession to the Crown, the Charge of maintaining it will be proportionably augmented, and it is certainly necessary for the Interest and Reputation of *England*, to have always a great strength at Sea. The Circumstances of Affairs abroad are such, that I think my self obliged to tell you my Opinion, that for the present, *England cannot be safe without a Land-Force;* and I hope we shall not give those that mean Us ill, the opportunity of effecting that under the Notion of a Peace, which they could not bring to pass by a War. I doubt not but you, Gentlemen of the House of Commons, will take those Particulars into your Consideration, in such a manner as to provide the necessary Supplies, which I do earnestly recommend to you. My Lords and Gentlemen, That which I do most delight to think of, and am best pleased to own, is, That I have all the Proofs of my People's Affection that a Prince can desire: And I take this Occasion to give you the most solemn Assurance, That as I never had, so I never will, nor can have, any Interest separate from theirs. I esteem it one of the greatest Advantages of the Peace, that I shall now have Leisure to rectifie such Corruptions or Abuses as may have crept into any Part of the Administration during the War, and effectually to discourage Prophaneness and Immorality; and I shall imploy my Thoughts in promoting Trade, and advancing the Happiness and flourishing Estate of the Kingdom. I shall conclude with telling you, that as I have, with the hazard of every thing, rescu'd your Religion, Laws and Liberties, when they were in the extreamest Danger, so I shall place the Glory of my Reign, in preserving them entire, and leaving them so to Posterity."

Thereupon the House of Lords made an Address to his Majesty, wherein having "Congratulated his happy Return, accompanied with the Blessings [288] of a safe and honourable Peace; which, next under God, they were sensible was owing to his Courage and Conduct; they told him That after the Hazards and Labours he had so long sustain'd for the Good of *Europe*, there wanted nothing but this to compleat the Glory of his Reign; and assur'd his Majesty, that they should never be wanting in their Endeavours to assist his Majesty in maintaining that Quiet which he had so gloriously restor'd to these his Kingdoms, and in contributing all they could to the Safety of his Person, and the securing the Peace and Prosperity of his Government." His Majesty, in Return, *"assured their Lordships of his kindness,* and told them, *he hop'd this Peace would be so bless'd, that they might long enjoy it."*

His Majesty's Speech did variously affect the Commons: Some thought some Expressions in it too Magisterial: Others seem'd to be offended at his Majesty's putting them in Mind, of what he had done for the Nation: Others again distrusted the great Promises of what he would do for them, and many others began to be jealous of what he had told them, *That* England *could not be Safe without a Land Force*: As if his Majesty meant to keep a *Standing Army*, to invade their Liberties, in the Defence of which the Nation had spent so vast a Stock of Blood and Treasure. However, they did, not many days after,* present an Address to his Majesty, wherein they told him; "That they who had so frequently waited on his Majesty, with the Tender of their Assistance for carrying on the War; came now to congratulate his Majesty upon the happy Conclusion of it, in a Peace, so honourable and advantageous to the Nation, as sufficiently justified the Wisdom of the Commons, in advising, and his Majesty's Conduct in the Prosecution of it. That the Prospect of the Benefits his People would receive from the Peace, was very pleasing; that the Honour his Majesty had restor'd to *England*, of holding the Ballance of *Europe*, gave his Subjects great Content; but what his Commons were most affected and de[289]lighted with, was, That his Majesty's sacred Person would now be secure from those many and great Dangers, to which he had so often exposed it, for their sakes; nothing being so evident as that his Majesty's return in safety was a Blessing more welcome to his People than Peace, and receiv'd with greater Demonstrations of Joy. That therefore with Hearts full of Affection, Duty and Gratitude; They did assure his Majesty, in the name of all the Commons of *England*, that this House would be ever ready to assist and support his Majesty; who, by putting a Period to the War, had confirmed them in the quiet Possession of their Rights and Liberties, and so fully compleated the glorious Work of their Deliverance." To this Address his Majesty answered: *That nothing that related to the Peace pleased him so much, as the Satisfaction they had in it*; *and as they had assisted him in the War, beyond all Expression, so he did not doubt, but they would be as zealous in maintaining the Peace.*

Before we proceed, 'tis necessary to take notice that this House of Commons was compos'd of three sorts of Persons: The first were altogether in the Court Interest; not only because some of them had

* Dec. 9.

profitable Places in the Government, but also because they were all entirely satisfied, that King *William* had nothing but the Good of the Nation in Prospect; and that he would never encroach on their Liberties. The Second, Who stiled themselves the Country-Party, and most of whom the Court look'd upon as Disaffected, were such as never approved the Methods by which the Revolution was accomplish'd; who always entertain'd a Jealousie of King *William*, and therefore, upon several Occasions, endeavour'd to cross his Designs. The Third, and most dangerous, tho' fewest in Number, were those who hitherto had warmly stickled for the present Government; but who, at the same time, were secretly laying the Foundation of a Common-Wealth. 'Twas through the Encouragement of the latter, and the indefatigable Industry of some Men of desperate Fortunes [290] and Principles, that the Nation was now over run with the Works of the boldest and most learned Advocates for a Republick, such as *Hobbs, Milton, Ludlow, Harrington*, and *Algernon Sidney*; some of which Books appear'd under the Patronage of the Chief Magistrates of the City of *London*: and whose Title Pages, as it were in Defiance of Monarchy, were publickly affixed to the Gate of the Royal Palace of *Whitehall*. This short Account of the different Inclinations of the Commons being premised, let's now enter upon their Proceedings.

That Honourable Body having voted* a Supply, and order'd an Account to be laid before them of the Deficiencies of the last Year's Aids; of the Arrears of the Army and Navy, and of the Debts charged on the Revenue, They consider'd in a Grand† Committee, the State of the Nation, and what Forces should be disbanded, was the main Point in Debate. The Court Party, who were for preserving part of the Army, alledg'd, That the Nation was still unsettled, and not quite deliver'd from the Fear of King *James*; that the Friends of that Abdicated Prince were as bold and as numerous as ever; and himself still protected by the King of *France*, who having as yet, reform'd none of his Troops, was consequently as formidable as before; That if the Army was entirely disbanded, the Peace which was obtain'd at the Expence of so much Blood

* Dec.9.
† Dec. 10.

and Treasure, would be altogether precarious, and not only *England*, but all *Europe*, lie, once more, at the Mercy of that ambitious Monarch, an inveterate Enemy to King *William*, the Protestant Religion, and the Liberties of Christendom; whom the Necessity of his Affairs, not his Inclination, had reconciled. On the other hand, the Country Party and the Republicans, who upon this occasion, spoke the same Language, tho' diametrically opposite in their Views, both in this Debate *viva voce*, and in Print, represented the Danger of keeping a Standing Army, Urging, "That it is absolutely destructive to the Constitution of the *English* Monarchy; That no Legislator ever founded a free Government, but avoided this, as a Rock a[291]gainst which his Common Wealth must certainly be Shipwrack'd; That the *Israelites, Athenians, Corinthians, Achaians, Lacedemonians, Thebans, Samnites*, and *Romans*, whilst they kept their Liberty, were never known to maintain any Soldiers in constant Pay within their Cities, nor ever suffer'd any of their Subjects to make War their Profession; well knowing that the Sword and Sovereignty always march hand in hand; And therefore they train'd their own Citizens and the Territories about them perpetually in Arms, and their whole Common Wealths by this means became so many several form'd Militias; That a general Exercise of the best of their People in the Use of Arms was the only Bulwark of their Liberties; and was reckon'd the surest way to preserve them both at Home and Abroad; the People being secur'd thereby as well against the Domestick Affronts of any of their own Citizens, as against the Foreign Invasions of ambitious and unruly Neighbours. That in those Days there was no Difference between the Citizen, the Soldier, and the Husbandman, for all promiscuously took Arms when the publick Safety required it, and afterwards laid them down, with more Alacrity than they took them up; but never lodg'd them in the Hands of any who had not an Interest in preserving the publick Peace, and did not fight *pro Aris & Focis*. They added, that the *Romans* maintain'd their Freedom, till their Empire encreasing, necessity constrain'd them to erect a constant stipendiary Soldiery, either for the Holding or Winning of Provinces, which gave *Julius Caesar* an opportunity to debauch his Army, and then upon a pretended Disgust, totally to overthrow that famous Common-Wealth; That if they enquired how the *Swedes, Danes*, and *French*, and other unhappy Nations had lost that precious Jewel, Liberty, and the *English* as yet preserv'd it, they should find that their Miseries and our Happiness proceed from this, that their Necessities or Indiscretion, had permitted a Standing Army to be kept amongst them, and our Situation, rather [292] than our Prudence had hitherto defended us from it. That our Constitution depending upon a due Ballance between King, Lords and Commons, and that Ballance depending upon the mutual Occasions and Necessities they have of one another, if this Cement be once broke, there is an actual Dissolution of the Government; That this Ballance could never be preserv'd but by an Union of the natural and artificial Strength of the Kingdom, that is, by making the Militia to consist of the same Persons that have the Property; or otherwise the Government was violent and against Nature, and could not possibly continue, but the Constitution must either break the Army, or the Army would destroy the Constitution. That it is universally true, that where-ever the Militia is, there is, or will be, the Government in a short time; and therefore the Institutors of the *Gothick* Ballance (which was establish'd in all Parts of *Europe*) made the Militia to consist of the same Parts as the Government, where the King was General; the Lords, by virtue of their Castles and Honours, the great Commanders; and the Freeholders, by their Tenures, the Body of the Army; so that it was next to impossible for an Army thus constituted, to act to the Disadvantage of the Constitution. Upon this Occasion they took notice of those, who, in the late Reigns could hardly afford the King the Prerogative that was due to him, and which was absolutely necessary to put in Motion this Machine of our Government; who could not with Patience hear of the King's Ordinary Guards, and yet could now discourse familiarly of Twenty Thousand Men to be maintain'd in times of Peace; That if they thought to make their Court this way, they would quickly find themselves out-flatter'd by the Party they fear'd, who had been long the Darlings of Arbitrary Power, and whose Principles as well as Practises taught them to be Enemies to all the legal Rights, and just Liberties of their Native Country; and so they would be made use of only to bring together the Materials of Tyranny [293] and then must give place to more expert Architects to finish the Building. They insisted, that tho' they were secure from any Attempts of this kind during his present Majesty's Reign, yet, since no Virtue or Pitch of Glory would exempt that most excellent Prince from Paying the common Debt to Nature, they ought not to entrust any Power with him, which they did not think proper to be continued to his Successors. That *Oliver Cromwel* turn'd out that Parliament under which he serv'd, by the Assistance of an Army; which must be allow'd to have had as much Virtue, Sobriety, and publick Spirit, as has been known in the World amongst that sort of Men. As to the Objection, that the Republicks of *Venice* and *Holland* maintain'd great Armies, and yet had not lost their Liberty, 'twas answer'd, that neither keep any Standing Forces within the Seats of their Government, that is, within the City of *Venice*, or the great Towns of the United Provinces; but they defend these by their own Burghers, and quarter their Mercenaries in their conquer'd Countries; And tho' they should admit that an Army might be consistent with Freedom in a Common-Wealth, yet it is otherwise in a free Monarchy; for in the former, 'tis wholly in the disposal of the People, who nominate, appoint, discard and punish the Generals and Officers, as they think fit, and 'tis certain Death to make any Attempt upon their Liberties; whereas in the latter the King is perpetual General, may model the Army as he pleases, and it would be call'd High Treason to oppose him. That tho' some Princes, as *Lewis* XI. and others laid the Foundation of their Tyrannies without the immediate Assistance of an Army, yet they all found an Army necessary to establish them; or otherwise a little Experience in the People of the Change of their Condition, would have made them disgorge in a Day that ill gotten Power they had been acquiring for an Age. That if they look'd thro' the World, they should find in no Country, Liberty and an Army stand together; so that to [294] know whether People are free or Slaves, it is necessary only to ask, whether there is an Army kept amongst them? And the solution of that Preliminary Question resolves the doubt. That it is the Misfortune of all Countries, that they sometimes lie under an unhappy necessity to defend themselves by Arms against the Ambition of their Governors, and to fight for what's their own; Now if the King had Twenty thousand Men before hand, or even much less than half that Number, the People could make no Effort to defend their Liberties, without the Assistance of a Foreign Power, which is a Remedy most commonly as bad as the Disease. That if we had not a Power within our selves to defend our Laws, we were no Government; for *England* being a small Country, few strong Towns in it, and these in the King's Hands, the Nobility disarm'd by the Destruction of Tenures, and the Militia not to be rais'd but by the King's Command, there could be no Force levied in any Part of *England*, but must be destroy'd, in its Infancy, by a few disciplin'd Regiments. That if, besides this, People consider'd the great Prerogatives of the Crown, and the vast Interest the King had and might acquire by the Distribution of so many profitable Offices of the Houshold, of the Revenue, of State, of Law, of Religion and the Navy; together with the Assistance of a Powerful Party, who had been always the constant Friends to Arbitrary Power, whose only Quarrel to King *William* was, that he had knock'd off the Fetters, which they thought they had lock'd fast upon the Nation; if, said they, any one did consider this, he would be convinc'd that they had enough to guard themselves against the Power of the Court, without having an Army throw'n into the Scale against them. That they had found oftener than once, by fatal Experience, the Truth of this; for if they look'd back to the late Reigns, they should see this Nation brought to the brink of Destruction, and breathing out the last Gasp of their Liberty. That if King *Charles* I. had had five Thousand Men before hand with his People, the latter had never struck a stroke for their Liberties; or if the late [295] King *James* would have been contented with Arbitrary Power, without bringing in Popery, he would have bound the Nation Hand and Foot before this Time. That most of the Nations instanc'd in before, were enslav'd by small Armies. That *Oliver Cromwel* left behind him but 17000 Men; And the Duke of *Monmouth*, who was the Darling of the People, was suppress'd with Two thousand. Nay, *Caesar* seiz'd *Rome* it self with Five Thousand, and fought the Battle of *Pharsalia*, where the Fate of the World was decided, with 22000 Men; And that most of the Revolutions of the *Roman* and *Ottoman* Empires since, were caus'd by the Pretorian Bands, and the Court Janizaries, the former of which never exceeded eight, nor the latter Twelve thousand Men. That if no greater Numbers could make such Disturbances in those vast Empires, what would double the Force do in *England?* That those who argued for an Army confest it themselves, when they said, we might be surpriz'd with Ten or Fifteen thousand Men from *France*, and having no regular Force to oppose them, they would over-run the Kingdom; for if so small a Force could oppose the King, and the Militia, with the united Power of the Nobility, Gentry, and Commons, what would an equal Power do against the People; when supported by the Royal Authority, and a never failing Interest that would attend it, except when it acted for the publick Good? Now because the contrary side alledg'd, that this Army was not design'd to make a Part of the Constitution, but to be kept only for a little Time, till the Circumstances of *Europe* would better permit the Nation to be without them; It was demanded, when they thought that Time would be? Whether in the Life of King *James?* or after his Death? Whether the Nation should have less to fear from the Youth and Vigour of the Titular Prince of *Wales*, than now from an unhappy Man sinking under the Load of Age and Misfortunes? Or whether *France* would be more capable of offending us, just after this tedious and consumptive War, than hereafter, when she should have had a Breathing Time to repair the Calami[296]ties she had suffer'd by it? And answering their own Questions in the Negative, they Concluded, That the Army could never be Disbanded with so much Safety, as at this Time. They urg'd, that a Continuation of them now, was an Establishment of them for ever; for whilst the Circumstances of *Europe*, stood in the present Posture, the Argument would be equal to continue them; That if the State of *Europe* should alter to the Advantage of *France*, the Reason would go stronger, and we should be told we should encrease our Number; But if there should be such a Turn of Affairs in the World, that we were no longer in Apprehension of the *French* Power, they might be kept up without our Assistance; That the very Discontents they might create should be made an Argument for the continuing of them; But if they should be kept from oppressing the People, in a little Time they would grow habitual to us, and almost become a Part of our Constitution, and by degrees we should be brought to believe them, not only not dangerous, but necessary. That King *Charles* II. being conniv'd at in keeping a few Guards, (which were the first ever known to an *English*

King, besides his Pensioners and his* *Beef-Eaters*) He insensibly encreas'd
their Number, till he left a Body of Men to his Successor, great enough to
tell the Parliament, he would be no longer bound by the Laws he had
Sworn to; and under the Shelter and Protection of these, he rais'd an
Army that had put a Period to our Government, if a Complication of
Causes, (which might never happen again) had not presented the Prince
of *Orange* with a conjuncture to assert his own and the Nation's Rights.
That tho' we had so lately escap'd this Precipice, yet Habit had made
Soldiers so familiar to us, that some who pretended to be Zealous for
Liberty, spoke of it as a Hardship to his present Majesty, to refuse him as
many Men as his Predecessors; not considering, that the Raising them
then was a Violation of the Laws, and that his Government was built
upon the Destruction of theirs. As to what was said, that the Nation
needed be in no Apprehensions of Slavery, whilst they kept the Power of
the Purse in their [297] own Hands, 'twas replyed, that this was very
true, but that it was as certain, that an Army would raise Money, as that
Money would raise an Army. That if they could suppose that our Courtiers design'd nothing but the publick Good; yet they ought not to hazard
such unusual Virtue, by leading it into Temptation: But that they were
afraid this was not an Age of Miracles, especially of that sort; and that
our Heroes were made of courser Alloy, and had too much Dross mix'd
with their Constitutions, for such refin'd Principles. That whereas it was
alledg'd, that let the Consequence of an Army be what it would, the Nation could not be without one; and if they must be Slaves, they had better
be so to a Protestant Prince than a Popish, and the worst of all Popish
ones, the *F*. King; it was answer'd, that Tyranny wants no Epithet, for
Protestant and *Popish* are both alike; which however, they had little Reason to fear, whilst they kept the Seas well guarded. That there is no
Country so scituated for Naval Strength as *England*, which being well
applied, is able to give Laws to the Universe; That if they kept a competent Part of it well arm'd in Times of Peace, it was the most ridiculous
Thing in the World, to believe any Prince would have Thoughts of Invading us, unless he propos'd to be Superior to us in Naval Power; for the

---

* *So are vulgarly call'd, the Yeomen of the Guard.*

Preparations necessary for such an Undertaking, would alarm all *Europe*, give both to us and our Confederates Time to arm, and put our selves in a Posture of Defence; and whoever consider'd that the Prince of *Orange* with 600 Ships brought but 1400 Men, and the mighty *Spanish* Armada, (then the Terror of the World) Embarked but 18000, he would be assur'd, that no Invasion could be so sudden upon us, but we should have Time to get ready our whole Fleet, bring some Forces from *Scotland* and *Ireland*, and prepare our own Militia, if there should be occasion for it; Especially in Times of Peace, when we should have the Liberty of all the Ports of *France*, and should, or might, have Intelligence from every one of them. As to what was said, that such a Wind [298] might happen as might be favourable to the Enemy, and keep us within our own Ports, it was answer'd, that as *France* lies to *England*, that is almost impossible; for if we lie about *Falmouth* or the *Lands-end*, no Fleet from *Brest* can escape us, without a Miracle; And if the Design be to invade us from any Part in the Channel, a very few Ships, (which might safely lie at Anchor) would certainly prevent it; But that it was not to be conceiv'd, that that cautious Prince would be at a vast Expence for the Contingency of such a critical Wind; or would send an Army into a Country where their Retreat would certainly be cut off, when the failing in any Part of his Design would certainly bring a new War upon him, which lately cost him a third Part of his People, a great many large Countries and strong Towns, with all the Honour he had heap'd up by his former Victories, to get rid of. As to the Objection, that the Officers of the Fleet might be corrupted; or that a Storm might arise, which might destroy it all at once; They replied, That these Fears would be remov'd by a *Well-Train'd Militia;* That the Policy of the Court in the late Reigns, was with the utmost Art and Application to disarm the People, and make the Militia useless, to countenance a Standing Army, in order to bring in Popery and Slavery; and they wonder'd that those who pretended to be Patriots in this Reign, would take Advantage of the traiterous Neglect and infamous Policies of the last; That the Nobility, Gentry, and Free-holders of *England* might well be trusted with the Defence of their own Lives, Estates and Liberties, without having Guardians and Keepers assign'd them; and that they would certainly defend them, with more Courage and Vigour than Mercenaries, who have nothing to lose, nor any other Tie to engage their Fidelity, than their Pay, which they might have from the Conqueror. That in order to make the *Militia* of *England* useful, the same might be reduc'd to 60000, and a third Part of those kept by Turns in constant Exercise; That a Man might be listed in the *Militia* till he be Discharg'd [299] by his Master, as well as in the Army, till he be Discharg'd by his Captain; And the same Horse might be always sent forth, unless it could be made appear that he was Dead or Maim'd; That the private Soldiers of the Army, when they should be dispers'd in the several Parts of the Kingdom, might be sent to the *Militia*, and the inferior Officers of the Army, in some proportion, command them; and lastly, that the Laws for shooting in *Cross-Bows* might be chang'd into *Firelocks*, and a competent Number of them be kept in every Parish for the young Men to exercise with on Holy-days, and Rewards offer'd to the most expert, to stir up their Emulation. That these and other like Things might be done, and some of them were done in our own Plantations, and the Islands of *Jersey* and *Guernsey*, as also in *Poland*, *Switzerland*, and the Country of the *Grisons;* which are Nations much less considerable than *England*, have as formidable Neighbours, no Sea, nor Fleet to defend them, nothing but a *Militia* to depend upon, and yet no one dares attack them. That in the late War as great Performances had been done by the *Vaudois* in *Savoy*, the *Miquelets* in *Catalonia*, and the *Militia* in *Ireland*, as can be parallel'd in History; That so it would be in *England*, if the Court would give their hearty Assistance in promoting this Design; if the King would appear in Person at the Head of them, and give Rewards and Honour to such as should deserve them. And because it might be objected, that such a *Militia* as this is a *Standing-Army*, and would be as dangerous, and much more chargeable, it was answer'd That there can be no Danger from an Army where the Nobility and chief Gentry of *England* are the Commanders, and the Body of it made up of Free-holders, their Sons and Servants; unless it could be conceived that they would all join in an unnatural Design to make void their own Titles to their Estates and Liberties; and as for the Charge, that it ought not to enter in Competition with the Preservation of our Laws and Liberties. As to the Disaffected, who were mention'd as a Reason to keep up [300] Standing Forces, it was shrewdly replied, that no King of *England* in any Age had deservedly more Interest than the present; and if during such an expensive War, in which the Nation had consumed so much Blood and Treasure; paid such vast and unequal Taxes; lost so many Thousand Ships, and bore a shock by recoining the Money, which would have torn up another Nation from its Foundation, when most Countries would have sunk under the Misfortune, and repin'd at their Deliverance, if, said they, at that time, the King had so great and universal an Interest, there could be no doubt but in times of Peace, when the People should reap the Fruits of that Courage and Conduct he had shewn in their Defence, he would be the most belov'd and glorious Prince that ever filled the *English* Throne. Moreover, they made Use of an Argument which, at first Blush, look'd like a Paradox, to wit, that the most likely way of restoring King *James*, was maintaining a *Standing Army* to keep him out. To prove this, they said, That King *William*'s Safety stood upon a Rock, whilst it depended upon the solid Foundation of the Affections of the People, which is never to be shaken, till 'tis evident that there is a form'd Design to overthrow the Laws and Liberties of the Nation; but if they kept a Standing Army, all must depend upon the uncertain and capricious Humours of the Soldiery, which in all Ages have produc'd more violent and sudden Revolutions, than ever have been known in unarm'd Governments. That there is such a Chain of Dependance amongst Soldiers, that if two or three of the Chief Officers should be disoblig'd, or have Intrigues with *Jacobite* Mistresses, or if the King of *France* could once again buy his Pensioners into the Court or Army, or offer a better Market to those that were in already, there should be another Revolution, and the People be only idle Spectators of their Ruin; That of Twenty six *Roman* Emperors, Sixteen were deposed and murder'd by their own Armies, and without fetching Foreign Examples, that the two Ar[301]mies, that had been kept up in *England* in times of Peace, both had turn'd out their own Masters. That the first under *Cromwel* expell'd that Parliament under which they had fought successively for many Years; afterwards under General *Monk* they destroy'd the Government they had set up, and brought back King *Charles* II. who wisely disbanded them, lest they might have turn'd him out again; That the other Instance was fresh in every one's Memory, how King *James*'s Army join'd with the present King. That no more could be expected from Men of dissolute and debauch'd Principles, who call themselves *Soldiers of Fortune;* who make Murder their Profession, and enquire no further into the Justice of the Cause, than how they shall be paid; and who having no other Profession or Subsistence to depend upon, are forced to stir up the Ambition of Princes, and engage them in perpetual Quarrels, that they may share of the Spoils they make. To all these they added the lesser Inconveniencies attending a *Standing-Army,* as frequent Quarrels, Murders and Robberies; the Destruction of all the Game in the Country, the Quartering upon publick, and sometimes private Houses; the influencing Elections of Parliament by an artificial Distribution of Quarters; the rendring so many Men useless to Labour, and almost Propagation, together with a much greater Destruction of them, by taking them from a laborious way of Living, to a loose idle Life; and besides this, the Insolence of the Officers and the Debaucheries that are committed both by them, and their Soldiers in all the Towns they come in, to the Ruin of multitudes of Women, Dishonour of their Families, and ill Example to others; and a great Train of Mischiefs, almost endless to enumerate. However they concluded, that they did not think it reasonable that the Army should be ruin'd by that Peace, which by their Courage and Fidelity they had procur'd for their Country; and therefore the Parliament, out of Generosity and [302] Gratitude, ought to give them a Donative proportionable to their Commissions."

After a long Debate the Committee of the whole House came to this Resolution, *That all the Land-Forces of this Kingdom, that had been rais'd since the 29th of* September 1680. *should be paid and disbanded*; which being reported to* the House, and the Courtiers Motion, *that the said Report be recommitted*, rejected, the House agreed with the Committee in the said Resolution. Three Days after they took into Consideration the Services of the Officers and common Men, who, amidst so many Hardships, Dangers and Disappointments, in Nine successive Campaigns, had recover'd the declining Reputation of the *English* Valour, and preserv'd the Kingdom from the Assaults of the most Potent Empire that perhaps

---

* Dec. 11.

was ever erected in the World. Wherefore the House of Commons,* past a Vote, *That it be an Instruction to the Committee, who were to consider of the Supply, that they should likewise consider of a Gratuity to be given to such Officers and Soldiers of the* English *Army, who were or should be disbanded;* and, at the same time order'd Mr. *Hammond*, and Mr. *Moyle* to bring in a Bill, *to enable Soldiers who should be disbanded, to exercise their Trades in any Town or Corporation throughout the Country.* Now to provide for the Security of the Kingdom, when the Army should be disbanded, they[†] appointed several Members to prepare and bring in a Bill *to regulate the Militia and make them more useful.* And[§] resolved that *Ten Thousand Men were sufficient for a Summer and Winter Guard at Sea for the Year* 1698.

The King was very much dissatisfied with these Resolutions; not but that his Majesty was willing to ease his *English* Subjects of the Charge, and free them from the Apprehensions of a Standing Army: (for which purpose at his last coming over, he had caus'd several Regiments of Horse, Dragoons and Foot to be disbanded; others to be reduced, and sent most of the latter either to *Scotland* or *Ireland*;)[||] But his Majesty did not think it proper absolutely to comply with the Commons, as to the Licentiating all the Troops that had been raised since the [303] Year 1680 whereby he must leave himself and his Kingdoms too much expos'd.

The Commons, on the 20th of *December*, took the Supply into Consideration, and Resolv'd, *That in a just Sense and Acknowledgment of what great things his Majesty had done for these Kingdoms, the Sum of* 700000 l. per Annum, *be granted to his Majesty during his Life for the Support of the Civil* List; which Resolution was the next day approv'd, not withstanding the Opposition of some Members, who mov'd that it should be recommitted. About three Weeks after the King went to the Parliament, and gave his Royal Assent to an *Act to prevent the further Currency of any Hammer'd Silver Coin, for Recoining such as was now in Being, and for the making out new* Exchequer *Bills, where the former Bills were or should be filled up by Indorsements; An Act against corresponding with the late King*

---

* Dec. 14.
† Dec 17.
§ Dec. 18.
|| Dec. 20.

James *and his Adherents; An Act for the continuing the Imprisonment of several Conspirators; And an Act to give further time for the Administring of Oaths relating to Tallies and Orders, and for the easier dispatch of publick Business in the* Exchequer, *and in the Bank of* England. The same day the House of Commons agreed to the Resolutions which had been taken in a Grand Committee, about the Supply, to wit, "*First*, That the Sum of Three Hundred and Fifty Thousand Pound be granted to his Majesty, for Maintaining Guards and Garrisons for the Year 1698. *Secondly*, That a Supply be granted to his Majesty, which together with the Funds already settled for that purpose, should be sufficient to answer and cancel all *Exchequer* Bills, issued, or to be issued, not exceeding Two Millions Seven Hundred Thousand Pounds; and *Thirdly*, That a Supply be granted to his Majesty for the speedy Paying and Disbanding the Army." Four* days after the House regulated the Bounty that should be given to every Trooper, Foot-Soldier, and Non-Commission Officer, upon their being licentiated; voted a Supply of 250000 for that Charge, and resolved, that Provision be made, for giving Half-pay to the Commission-Officers (his Majesty's natural [304] Born Subjects) disbanded or to be disbanded, till they should be fully paid off and clear'd, and otherwise provided for. They order'd, at the same time, that a List be laid before them of such Commission Officers as were to enjoy the Benefit of the preceding Resolution, but the Court, who was unwilling to let the Commons know how few of the Regiments were actually disbanded, took Care that this List was not presented to them; and when the Commons prest the King to it, by an Address, his Majesty put them off by telling them, *He would comply with their Desire, as soon as conveniently he could*.

Boyer, *William III*, 3:286–304.

* Jan. 18.

APPENDIX F

Emendations to the Copy Texts

Entries in this list of corrections to the copy texts take the following form:

page and line number in this edition   faulty reading] corrected reading

John Trenchard and Walter Moyle, *An Argument Shewing that a Standing Army Is Inconsistent with a Free Government* (1697)
English Short Title Catalog (ESTC) R16212
CORRECTED AS FOLLOWS:

p. 15, l. 14   Sythe] Scythe

John Somers, *A Letter, Ballancing the Necessity of Keeping a Land-Force in Times of Peace: with the Dangers that May Follow On It* (1697)
ESTC R11547
CORRECTED AS FOLLOWS:

p. 60, l. 11   unbecomming] unbecoming

Daniel Defoe, *Some Reflections on a Pamphlet Lately Published* (1697)
ESTC R40379
CORRECTED AS FOLLOWS:

p. 75, l. 2   *Demolishid*] *Demolished*
p. 75, l. 15   *ought*] *aught*
p. 77, l. 7   which] with
p. 81, l. 8   thing;] thing
p. 81, l. 19   *Sammites*] *Samnites*
p. 81, l. 23   Millitary] Military

p. 82, l. 13	Amunition] Ammunition
p. 88, l. 16	course] coarse
p. 89, l. 8	no] not
p. 92, l. 12	Ataques] Attaques
p. 92, l. 20	*perdue*] *perdus*
p. 93, l. 11	to despicable] to the despicable
p. 95, l. 5	Guarrantee] Guarantee
p. 96, l. 22	Bafles] Baffles
p. 97, l. 11	*destreyed*] *destroyed*
p. 102, l. 18	Invinsible] Invincible
p. 102, l. 19	irrepairable] irreparable
p. 107, l. 10	disconted] discontented
p. 107, l. 22	Fatiegues] Fatigues
p. 108, l. 29	beit] be it
p. 109, l. 8	them] him

Walter Moyle, *The Second Part of An Argument* (1697)
ESTC R17336
CORRECTED AS FOLLOWS:

p. 122, l. 8	Seas:] ~.
p. 122, l. 12	paiment] payment
p. 127, l. 9	ys,] says,
p. 140, l. 27	Nusance] Nuisance
p. 141, l. 3	ct] Act

Andrew Fletcher, *A Discourse Concerning Militia's and Standing Armies* (1697)
ESTC R5238
CORRECTED AS FOLLOWS:

| p. 156, l. 3 | other Men,] ~. |

John Toland, *The Militia Reform'd* (1698)
ESTC R35218
CORRECTED AS FOLLOWS:

p. 183, l. 28	keep 'em] keep it
p. 193, l. 3	exemtion] exemption
p. 198, l. 10	sixty] twenty
p. 207, l. 7	is that is] that is

p. 207, l. 19   Maning] Manning
p. 211, l. 17   Eigth] Eighth

Daniel Defoe, *An Argument Shewing that a Standing Army with Consent of Parliament Is Not Inconsistent with a Free Government* (1698)
ESTC R20142
CORRECTED AS FOLLOWS:

p. 231, l. 2   Consen tof] Consent of
p. 232, l. 15   Soldery.] Soldiery,
p. 237, l. 5   Houses.] Horses.
p. 240, l. 11   Wat] War
p. 241, l. 4   the Spaniards] the Spaniards'
p. 243, l. 5   eteernal] eternal
p. 251, l. 1   Souldery] Souldiery
p. 251, l. 8   *Souldery] Souldiery*
p. 252, l. 12   Oponents] Opponents

John Trenchard, *A Short History of Standing Armies in England* (1698)
ESTC R9739
CORRECTED AS FOLLOWS:

p. 291, l. 8   weild] wield
p. 353, l. 1   haxe] have
p. 355, l. 6   *Potugal] Portugal*

Daniel Defoe, *A Brief Reply to the History of Standing Armies in England* (1698)
ESTC R233839
CORRECTED AS FOLLOWS:

p. 375, l. 1   Neighbous] Neighbours
p. 382, l. 15   leting] letting

Anonymous, *The Case of a Standing Army Fairly and Impartially Stated* (1698)
ESTC R3955
CORRECTED AS FOLLOWS:

p. 395, l. 7   *fail] fails*
p. 402, l. 14   peices] pieces
p. 403, l. 28   fiast] fast

p. 405, l. 29   *Tryconnel*] *Tyrconnel*
p. 405, l. 31   *Chales*] *Charles*
p. 406, l. 27   possitively] positively
p. 407, l. 28   slip'd] slip
p. 411, l. 2   Consequenec] Consequence
p. 411, l. 4   w6] we
p. 411, l. 15   loak] look
p. 415, l. 16   over-sites] over-sights

Anonymous, *The Case of Disbanding the Army at Present, Briefly and Impartially Consider'd* (1698)
ESTC R4007
CORRECTED AS FOLLOWS:
p. 428, l. 34   rempted] tempted

Anonymous, *Reasons Against a Standing Army* (1717)
ESTC T46346
CORRECTED AS FOLLOWS:
p. 438, l. 17   *Stafford*] *Strafford*
p. 438, l. 23   Club's] Clubs
p. 440, l. 19   Buinglers] Bunglers
p. 441, l. 10   Sythe] Scythe
p. 442, l. 14   bythis] by this
p. 451, l. 18   must a] must be a
p. 453, l. 13   Robing] Robbing
p. 458, l. 5   Malitia] Militia
p. 459, l. 9   Nusance] Nuisance
p. 459, l. 23   Rebelllon] Rebellion
p. 465, l. 17   tyranical] tyrannical
p. 469, l. 19   Thay] They
p. 469, l. 22   knows,]~.
p. 473, l. 25   whithout] without
p. 476, l. 17   attack'd] attach'd
p. 478, l. 13   resonably] reasonably
p. 478, l. 31   Nusance] Nuisance
p. 479, l. 22   Countty] Country
p. 481, l. 1   accomodated] accommodated

Anonymous, *The Necessity of a Plot* (1720?)
ESTC T39722
CORRECTED AS FOLLOWS:

p. 490, l. 23	and-Trade] and Trade
p. 492, l. 1	noc] not
p. 492, l. 2	witoout] without
p. 493, l. 3	bnt] but
p. 493, l. 9	Mony] Money
p. 493, l. 22	threatned] threatened
p. 494, l. 14	he] be
p. 494, l. 23	with these] with what these
p. 496, l. 13	owe-their] owe their
p. 496, l. 13	RIse] Rise
p. 498, l. 20	Murmerings] Murmurings
p. 498, l. 22	in inexpressible] inexpressible
p. 499, l. 24	Jestures] Gestures
p. 503, l. 6	Soul] Soil

"Cato" [Thomas Gordon], *A Discourse of Standing Armies* (1722)
ESTC T737
CORRECTED AS FOLLOWS:

p. 517, l. 26	*Syracusians*] *Syracusans*
p. 525, l. 22	on Head] on the Head

"C. S." [Charles Sackville, second Duke of Dorset], *A Treatise Concerning the Militia* (1752)
ESTC T63541
CORRECTED AS FOLLOWS:

p. 563, l. 31	*Counties:*)] *Counties:*

Index

Note: English rulers are given by name only, while nationality is indicated for rulers of other countries and empires. Battles and treaties are indexed by the distinctive part of the name (e.g., "Battle of Agincourt" is found at "Agincourt, Battle of").

This book is set in Adobe Caslon Pro, a modern adaptation by Carol Twombly of faces cut by William Caslon, London, in the 1730s. Caslon's types were based on seventeenth-century Dutch old style designs and became very popular throughout Europe and the American colonies.

Printed on paper that is acid-free and meets the requirements of the American National Standard for Permanence of Paper for Printed Library Materials, z39.48–1992. ∞

Book design by Louise OFarrell, Gainesville, Florida
Typography by Westchester Publishing Services
Danbury, Connecticut
Index by Indexing Partners, LLC, Rehoboth Beach, Delaware
Printed and bound by Sheridan Books, Chelsea, Michigan